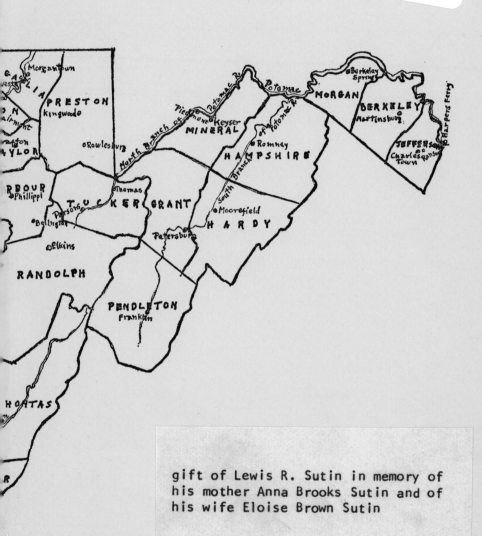

# WEST VIRGINIA JEWRY:

## ORIGINS AND HISTORY

### 1850 — 1958

*Books by Abraham I. Shinedling*

History of the Beckley Jewish Community (Beckley, W. Va.) (with Manuel Pickus) (1955)

History of the Los Alamos Jewish Center (Los Alamos, N. Mex.) (1958)

PROFESSOR JACOB R. MARCUS

(of the Hebrew Union College - Jewish Institute
of Religion, of Cincinnati, Ohio)

Formerly a resident of Farmington and Wheeling, W. Va.

(see pages 842–845)

# WEST VIRGINIA JEWRY:

## ORIGINS AND HISTORY

### 1850—1958

*By*

ABRAHAM I. SHINEDLING

Volume I

1963

PRINTED IN THE UNITED STATES OF AMERICA

PRESS OF *Maurice Jacobs*, INC.

1010 ARCH STREET, PHILADELPHIA 7, PA.

Dedicated to the Memories of

DORA MORRIS SHINEDLING

My Mother

A Native West Virginian born in Wheeling

(July 4, 1873 — January 30, 1923)


MOSES SHINEDLING

My Father

(September, 1860 — November 30, 1928)


ISIDORE JOCELYN ("JOE") SHINEDLING

My Eldest Brother

(November 22, 1893 — January 16, 1949)


JULIAN MARK SHINEDLING

My Younger Brother

(December 27, 1899 — December 4, 1957)

"The Brother of My Childhood, Youth, and Manhood"

Dedicated also to the Memory of

ELOISE BROWN SUTIN

(born in Terre Haute, Ind., on March 22, 1908;

died in Albuquerque, N. Mex., on April 2, 1959)

wife of

LEWIS R. SUTIN

(of Albuquerque, N. Mex.)

Friend, Philanthropist, and Lover of Jewish Literature

Who has, in part, generously subsidized

the publication of this volume

# TO MAURICE JACOBS

## and to MAURICE JACOBS, INC.

This work can not go to press without an expression of appreciation and gratitude to its printer, my dear friend of more than twenty years, the publisher who is without peer for his encouragement of Jewish research and publication in the United States, Dr. Maurice Jacobs, of Philadelphia. For more than five years Dr. Jacobs has worked with me, patiently and in most kindly manner; he has devoted a great deal of his time, energies, and even material means to this West Virginia Jewish history project of mine — indeed, in a spirit of genuine self-sacrifice. His staff, too, has labored on this project with remarkable efficiency and accuracy. Without Dr. Jacobs' cooperation and helpfulness, this book would not have seen the light of day. But that is nothing new, for Jewish scholars and institutions all over America, and many Christian agencies as well, have become the beneficiaries of his faith in scholarship and his unselfish and generous devotion — his dedication — to the making of good books. As the poet Horace wrote some two thousand years ago, in Rome: *Serus in caelum redeas.* As we in Judaism would say: *Ad meah shanah tichyeh*!

ABRAHAM I. SHINEDLING

*Albuquerque, New Mexico*
*August, 1963*

Dedicated also to my

Colleague and Friend

DR. BERTRAM W. KORN

Rabbi, Scholar, and Friend

Lover of Jewish Literature

and

Assiduous Laborer in the Field of American Jewish History

and to his

Reform Congregation Keneseth Israel

in Philadelphia

Who have also, in part, generously subsidized

the publication of this volume

# List of the Abbreviations Used in This Volume

A. J. C. = American Jewish Committee (of New York)

*AJYB = American Jewish Year Book*

C. C. A. R. = Central Conference of American Rabbis (of New York)

*CCAR = Central Conference of American Rabbis Yearbook*

D. G. L. = District Grand Lodge (of the B'nai B'rith)

H. U. C. = Hebrew Union College (of Cincinnati)

H. U. C. - J. I. R. = Hebrew Union College - Jewish Institute of Religion (of Cincinnati and New York)

J. C. S. = Jewish Chautauqua Society (of Cincinnati, and then of New York City)

*JE = Jewish Encyclopedia* (1900–1906)

J. I. R. = Jewish Institute of Religion (of New York City)

J. P. S. A. = Jewish Publication Society of America (of Philadelphia)

N. C. J. W. = National Council of Jewish Women (of New York City)

N. F. T. B. = National Federation of Temple Brotherhoods (of Cincinnati, and then of New York)

N. F. T. S. = National Federation of Temple Sisterhoods (of Cincinnati, and then of New York)

N. F. T. Y. = National Federation of Temple Youth (of Cincinnati, and then of New York)

*PAJHS = Publications of the American Jewish Historical Society* (of New York City)

U. A. H. C. = Union of American Hebrew Congregations (of Cincinnati, and then of New York)

U. J. A. = United Jewish Appeal

*UJE = Universal Jewish Encyclopedia* (1939–1943)

W. V. F. T. S. = West Virginia Federation of Temple Sisterhoods

# Contents

# List of Illustrations

# Preface

THE impulse towards, and the genesis of, the writing of this volume on *West Virginia Jewry: Origins and History* began early in the year 1953, at which time my rabbinical colleague, Rabbi Martin M. Weitz, the scholarly and historical-minded religious leader of Temple Beth Israel, of Atlantic City, N. J., was serving as the chairman of a special Committee of the Central Conference of American Rabbis. This special historical Committee of the C.C.A.R. had been appointed for the peculiar task of securing materials, data, and articles on the histories of the various State and city Jewish communities of the United States, for presentation at a pre-session meeting of the assembly of the C.C.A.R. at Estes Park, Colo., in June, 1953.

Martin M. Weitz, a younger colleague but even then an old friend of mine, wrote me a letter, requesting me to prepare, at not too great a length, an article on the history of the Jews and of the Jewish communities of West Virginia. He had originally asked me to do the same for the two additional States of Kentucky and Tennessee, but I managed to "beg off" of this extra "assignment," on the ground that only West Virginia was, after all, "my State," and on the additional ground that it would be far better, and much more efficacious, to ask rabbis actually living and serving in those two other States to prepare those two articles. Martin Weitz agreed with me, and released me from all obligation except that of covering the history of the Jewish communities of West Virginia, briefly. This was, of course, in connection with the forthcoming (1954–1955) countrywide celebration of the Tercentenary of the first settlement of Jews (twenty-three Jews, at New Amsterdam, now New York City, in September, 1654) in what is now the United States of America, but which was then the American colonies.

The above assignment was not so easy nor so brief as it might have appeared at first sight, since the materials, especially for the earlier period (from 1840 on, in West Virginia) were skimpy, scanty, widely separated, and difficult to obtain. There were fairly good but quite incomplete and much too short articles on the history of the Jews in West Virginia in the old *Jewish Encyclopedia* (the *JE*; 1900–1906), as well as in the newer *Universal Jewish Encyclopedia* (the *UJE*; 1939–1943), but both these articles were, of course, "up-to-date" only up to the year 1905 in the case of the *JE*, and only up to the year 1943 in the case of the *UJE*. The *JE* article on West Virginia had been written by Harry Levi, a brilliant scholar, preacher, and rabbi who served as rabbi of the Wheeling Congregation Leshem Shomayim (the Eoff Street Temple) from 1897 to 1911, when he moved to Boston, Mass. The *UJE* article on West Virginia had been written by several authors, or it was a composite piece of work, and it was carried anonymously in Volume X of the *UJE*. There were also a few sporadic and widely scattered references to West Virginia, West Virginia Jews, and West Virginia Jewries in the *American Jewish Year Book*, in the *Publications of the American Jewish Historical Society*, and in the pages of *The Occident*, of Philadelphia, and of *The Israelite* (or *American Israelite*; of Cincinnati), all of which material I utilized either then, or at a later time.

Much of the above-mentioned material I conned, tracked down, and used, upon consideration, but I added a great many data and facts of my own, especially for the period from 1947 to 1953, which I had gathered, or which I had learned, and knew, on the basis of my then six or seven years in West Virginia (1947 to 1953–1954). I was unable to use all the available material, or all the data which I had assembled, because I was limited as to my wordage.

Thus, after intermittent labors of fully a good half year, and also on the basis of new materials and data on the various Jewish congregations, communities, and organizations of West Virginia which were furnished to me by several of the very few rabbis of the State, as well as by some few of the interested Jewish leaders of some of the congregations and communities of West Virginia; as well as on the basis of my own notes, researches, observations, travels, and findings — inasmuch as, from Septem-

ber, 1947, up to 1953, I had visited many of the cities and towns
of West Virginia, including:

| | | |
|---|---|---|
| Athens | Fairmont | North Fork |
| Beckley | Huntington | Oak Hill |
| Bluefield | Keystone | Parkersburg |
| Buckhannon | Logan | Princeton |
| Charleston | Montgomery | Welch |
| Clarksburg | Mount Hope | Wheeling |
| Elkins | Mullens | Williamson |

and since I had learned to know several hundred Jewish persons
in the above communities, cities, and towns, and had lived, and
served as a rabbi, in Bluefield for three years (1947–1950),
and I had, at that time, been living in Beckley and serving as
rabbi for four years up to that time, from 1950 to 1954, I
produced the desired manuscript, retyping it in presentable and
legible form.

Accordingly, after I had finished the manuscript, I sent the
original, or first typed copy, off to Rabbi Weitz, in Atlantic
City, for use in connection with the Tercentenary. It was, I
believe, read in its rather brief entirety at the pre-Conference
session on American Jewish history at Estes Park, Colo., together
with a number of other papers or articles on the histories of the
Jewries of other States. One copy was sent to, and deposited
in the files of, the American Jewish Archives, in Cincinnati, a
part-time member of whose staff I became in June or July, of
the year 1950. The third copy, which consisted of barely more
than sixteen double-spaced typed pages, I retained in my own
possession, as the sole "fruit of my labors."

This sixteen-page article was a sort of preliminary, primitive
and nonthoroughgoing work, or piece of work, but it did form
the basis of and the incentive towards this major and very long
*West Virginia Jewry: Origins and History*, the final copy of which,
to be sent to the printer, I have just begun to type out in mid-
April, 1959, six years later after the initial "impulse" was given
me by Rabbi Martin M. Weitz. I publish the text of this early
and primitive little monograph, which I called by the title of
*The History of the Jews of West Virginia (West Virginia Jewry)*,

further on in this Preface. This I am doing so that the reader
may form an idea of the great contrast between this earlier
work — if it may be dignified by the term "work" — of smaller
scope and this volume representing later and much more
thorough work and much larger scope, consisting of its hundreds
upon hundreds of typewritten double-spaced pages.

But it need not be said that I was thoroughly dissatisfied with
the former work or monograph, and not too happy or content
with the "job" which I had performed on it. I felt that it was
*not* a good piece of work, or of research, and I determined, now
that I had plunged into the subject, to pursue the matter much
farther, and to do a much better job, at greater leisure and at a
greater expenditure of time, on the subject of the history of the
Jews in West Virginia. Another — perhaps a rather childish —
incentive, or inducement, to me to pursue the subject of West
Virginia Jewish history further, is the fact that my mother,
Dora Morris Shinedling (died at Paterson, N. J., on January 30,
1923), was born in Wheeling, W. Va., on July 4, 1873, and that
her parents, my maternal grandparents, Meyer and Rose Meyer
Morris, had lived in Wheeling from 1872 to 1875, when they
removed to Pittsburgh. My mother was their first-born child.
Meyer Morris, my maternal grandfather, who died at Paterson,
N. J., in April, 1920, had been a peddler, or an itinerant dry-
goods merchant, in and around Wheeling during those three
years of his residence there, just a few years after the end of the
Civil War.

As the result of the above resolution, and since in the interim
I had gotten deeply interested in the history of the Beckley,
W. Va., Jewish community and of Congregation Beth El, of
Beckley (previously known as the Beckley Hebrew Association),
whose rabbi I became on September 1, 1950, and whose rabbi I
remained until the very last day of July, 1956, I continued to
gather data and facts by letter, by means of personal visits and
contacts, through visits paid to colleges, universities, and other
institutions, and through contacts with friends and coreligionists — even with occasional non-Jews — by correspondence
and personally, in and on most of the above-named cities of
the State where I had visited, beginning with August, 1953,

after my return from the C.C.A.R. sessions at Estes Park, Colo., until the end of the year 1955, and even thereafter, chiefly on the history of the Jews of Beckley and of Raleigh and Fayette Counties, but also on the general history of the Jews of West Virginia, for the purpose of amplifying my rather skimpy and by-no-means complete history of the Jews of this State.

Thus, for example, as was stated in the Preface to the Beckley Jewish history referred to below, I secured from my younger colleague and friend, Rabbi Theodore S. Levy, then the generous and historical-minded rabbi of Oheb Sholom Congregation, in Huntington, W. Va., a great amount of additional material on the history of the Huntington Jewish community and congregation, especially after the year 1916. From my old friend and devoted co-worker in B'nai B'rith, Lawrence M. Brile, then of Fairmont, W. Va. (and whose departure for Brooklyn, N. Y., in February, 1958, represented a distinct loss to West Virginia Jewry), I secured some sorely needed, additional data on the history of the Jewish community of Fairmont, way up in the northern part of the State, not far from Pittsburgh. The following also, through their letters and data which were furnished to me, or their historical materials previously collected, which they generously placed at my disposal for use or for excerpting, were of incalculable value and assistance to me in the compilation, by me, of the great and nowhere otherwise obtainable wealth of material which appears in this volume:

Lee Silverstein, of Charleston
Leo Loeb, of Charleston
Rabbi Samuel Volkman, of Charleston
Isaac (Ike) Diamond, of Bluefield
Mrs. Charles (Reba B.) Cohen, of Charleston
Mrs. Charles (Helaine) Rotgin, of Charleston
Rabbi Samuel Cooper, of Charleston
Nathan Platnick, of Bluefield
Mrs. Nathan (Edna E.) Platnick, of Bluefield
Mrs. Nathan (Anna A.) Effron, of Bluefield
Isadore Cohen, of Bluefield
Rabbi Herbert J. Wilner, then of Bluefield

Mrs. Anna G. (Henry) Rodgin, of Bluefield

Richard N. Bluestein, then Assistant to the President of the Hebrew Union College, of Cincinnati

Dora Aaronsohn, later appointed Registrar of the Hebrew Union College - Jewish Institute of Religion, of Cincinnati[1]

Rabbi George B. Lieberman, formerly of Wheeling

Frank Nelson, of Princeton, W. Va.

Harry Barbakow, of Princeton, W. Va.

Dr. Alfred Jospe, of New York (formerly of Morgantown)

Rabbi Avery J. Grossfield, formerly of Fairmont

Rabbi Julius Kravetz, formerly of Bluefield

Louis Zaltzman, of Bluefield (formerly of North Fork and Keystone)

Harry Abel (late of Mount Hope, W. Va.)

Mrs. Samuel I. (Esther B.) Abrams, of Beckley

Rabbi Frank N. Sundheim, of Huntington

Rabbi William A. Rosenthall, of Wheeling

to all of whom I express my deepest gratitude, also (and especially) to my classmate and colleague, Professor Jacob R. Marcus, who is Adolph S. Ochs Professor of American Jewish History (formerly, Professor of Jewish History) at the Hebrew Union College - Jewish Institute of Religion, in Cincinnati, who is himself an "adopted" son of West Virginia, and who, although born in Connellsville, Pa., lived for some fifteen years in West Virginia — in Wheeling and in Farmington — before and after he came to the Hebrew Union College, in September, 1911, to begin his studies for the rabbinate. It was Dr. Jacob R. Marcus, who since 1950 has been my "director," my superior, and my colleague on the staff of the American Jewish Archives of the H. U. C.-J. I. R., in Cincinnati, of which he is the Director, who not only encouraged me — and helped me materially — to devote at least a part of my time and efforts, even of my spare and leisure time, to the subject of American Jewish history, of which he is the master and leading exponent in the

---

[1] In 1948, the name of the Hebrew Union College was officially changed to the Hebrew Union College - Jewish Institute of Religion.

United States, but also placed at my disposal — whenever such were not restricted — vast quantities of the material and data to be found in the American Jewish Archives on the subject of West Virginia Jewry and of some of its individual Jewish communities as they exist, or as they existed, in the State.

It is quite possible that I have made this history too replete with data, details, and names, and therefore too long, almost too thorough, too detailed, too full of facts and figures and statistics. For I have indeed presented it in very complete detailed, biographical, institutional, and chronological form, giving all facts, dates, data, names, and institutions and organizations which I was able to discover or "unearth" in the course of my five-year work, research, and correspondence. I felt, however, that this detailedness, as it were, all these details and minutiae, this huge and mighty conglomeration of facts, which I have collected and assembled, are bound to prove — perhaps — of very great importance and value in later years, since none of us knows what will be of use or of importance historically fifty or a hundred years from now, and what will prove to be valueless and insignificant. I chose a plethora over paucity, sufficiency over dearth, and I preferred a surfeit to skimpiness, and I sincerely hope that the present generation, and posterity as well, will not too greatly mind.

ABRAHAM I. SHINEDLING

*Albuquerque, N. Mex.*
April, 1959

# Introduction

PRESENTATION ON WEST VIRGINIA JEWRY
BY ABRAHAM I. SHINEDLING
(1953)

Text of the article:

"History of the Jews of West Virginia (West Virginia Jewry)" prepared by Abraham I. Shinedling in April and May, 1953, for Rabbi Martin M. Weitz and His Committee on Jewish History of the Central Conference of American Rabbis (slightly revised in January, 1954).

There were no Jewish communities in what is now the State of West Virginia until the 1840's. In 1953, the Jewish population of the State was estimated at from 1,500 to 2,500 families, with a total individual population of 6,000 to 7,000 persons. In 1950, out of a total State population of slightly more than 2,000,000, West Virginia had close to 6,000 Jews. Charleston, Huntington, and Wheeling, which were the three largest cities in the State, also had the largest Jewish populations, in that order. (Beckley, Bluefield, Clarksburg, Fairmont, Morgantown, Parkersburg, and Weirton also had smaller, but sizable and active Jewish congregations and communities in the 1940's and early 1950's.)

The first Jewish community in West Virginia was organized in Wheeling, in the 1840's [1849]. On June 20, 1863, West Virginia, which had been previously a part of Virginia, seceded from that State, in the middle of the Civil War, and became a separate State. Seven Jewish soldiers from West Virginia served in the Union Army in the Civil War; one of these was wounded. In the year 1880, the Jewish population of West Virginia was 511, out of a total population, at that time, of 230,257. In 1897, the Jewish population of the State was estimated at between 1,000 and 2,000, out of a total State population of 937,800. In 1903, out of a total general population of about 958,000, the Jews of the State were estimated to number 1,500.

In 1950, according to the *American Jewish Year Book* (Volume

52, page 21), 12 of the 13 Jewish communities of West Virginia, with estimated Jewish populations of 100 persons or over, were listed as follows:

(Logan, with its approximately 20 to 25 Jewish families at that time, was not listed, since it had fewer than 100 Jewish persons.)

| Beckley | 228 | Morgantown | 211 |
|---|---|---|---|
| Bluefield | 300 | Parkersburg | 100 |
| Charleston | 2,000 | Weirton | 300 |
| Clarksburg | 270 | Welch | 144 |
| Fairmont | 160 | Wheeling | 800 |
| Huntington | 700 | Williamson | 173 |
| | | Total | 5,386 |

These estimates may be compared with the Jewish populations of the individual Jewish communities listed below. In some cases, the figures of the *American Jewish Year Book* appear to be too low.

In addition, there were individual Jewish families, or several Jewish families, in 1953, living in the following cities and towns of West Virginia:

Grafton
Iaeger
Keystone (belonging to the Welch congregation)
Montgomery (belonging to the Charleston congregation)
Mount Hope (belonging to the Beckley congregation)
Mullens (belonging to the Welch, Bluefield, or Beckley congregations)
North Fork (belonging to the Bluefield or Welch congregations)
Oak Hill (belonging to the Beckley congregation)
Princeton (belonging to the Bluefield congregation)
Richwood
War (belonging to the Welch congregation)

At one time, up to about the 1930's, North Fork (spelled also as Northfork) and the adjoining Keystone, situated to the northwest of Bluefield between Bluefield and Welch (about twenty or more miles from Bluefield), had a sizable joint Jewish community (Conservative), consisting of about 30 to 35 families, with a frame synagogue building in Keystone. However, thereafter (after the end of the 1940's and subsequently) most of these Jewish families in the two towns removed to other communities, many of them to Bluefield, and the synagogue building in Keystone was finally sold, in 1951. In 1953, North Fork had only four or five Jewish families, and Keystone only two or three Jewish families.

In the latter part of the 19th century, in West Virginia, Jews and non-Jewish Sabbatarians, like those of some twelve other States, who observed the seventh day of the week as sacred, were allowed to work at their regular trades and occupations on Sundays, if their work did not disturb those who observed the Christian Sabbath as a day of prayer and rest.

### REFORM JEWISH CONGREGATIONS IN WEST VIRGINIA

In 1953, the following seven West Virginia Reform congregations were members of the Union of American Hebrew Congregations:

BLUEFIELD: Congregation Ahavath Sholom
CHARLESTON: Congregation B'nai Israel (the Virginia Street Temple)
HUNTINGTON: Ohev (Oheb) Sholom Congregation
LOGAN: Congregation B'nai El
PARKERSBURG: Congregation B'nai Israel
WHEELING: the Eoff Street Temple (Congregation Leshem Shomayim)
WILLIAMSON: Congregation B'nai Israel

The following four congregations, although Reform (that in Fairmont was in part of Conservative tendencies), were not affiliated with the Union of American Hebrew Congregations in 1953:

BECKLEY: Congregation Beth El (the Beckley Hebrew Association)
FAIRMONT: Beth Israel Congregation
MORGANTOWN: Congregation Tree of Life
WELCH: Congregation Emanuel

## CONSERVATIVE AND ORTHODOX JEWISH CONGREGATIONS IN WEST VIRGINIA

Six Conservative (or semi-Conservative) and Orthodox (or semi-Orthodox) Jewish congregations existed in West Virginia, in 1953, in the following five cities or communities:

CHARLESTON: B'nai Jacob Congregation (Orthodox, but partly Conservative)
CLARKSBURG: Congregation Tree of Life (Conservative, but partly Reform)
HUNTINGTON: B'nai Israel Congregation (Orthodox, but partly Conservative)
WEIRTON: Beth Israel Congregation (Orthodox, but partly Conservative)
WHEELING: the Edgington Lane Synagogue, known also by the name of The Synagogue of Israel (Conservative)

In 1953, Wheeling had another, smaller, Orthodox congregation, as well: Ohev Sholem Congregation.

## THE B'NAI B'RITH

In 1953, there were 13 B'nai B'rith (Independent Order of B'nai B'rith, or I. O. B. B.) local lodges in West Virginia, with a statewide membership of 900 Jewish men:

| | |
|---|---|
| Beckley | Morgantown |
| Bluefield | Parkersburg |
| Charleston | Weirton |
| Clarksburg | Welch (the McDowell County Lodge) |
| Fairmont | |
| Huntington | Wheeling |
| Logan | Williamson |

The West Virginia Council of the B'nai B'rith had Robert H. Levine, of Beckley, as its president, and Malcolm Pickus, also of Beckley, as its secretary, in 1953. The West Virginia Council of the B'nai B'rith formed a part of District Grand Lodge No. 3, with its headquarters in Philadelphia, and including also the three States of New Jersey, Delaware, and Pennsylvania.

## HADASSAH (THE WOMEN'S ZIONIST ORGANIZATION OF AMERICA)

There were five local chapters of the Hadassah in existence in West Virginia in 1953, as follows:

Beckley            Charleston
Bluefield          Huntington
        Wheeling

## JEWISH WELFARE FEDERATIONS

Jewish welfare federations, or federated Jewish charities, existed in the following four communities of West Virginia in 1953:

Bluefield          Huntington
Charleston         Wheeling

## NATIONAL COUNCIL OF JEWISH WOMEN

There was a section of the National Council of Jewish Women in Charleston. [This was the only one in the State, in 1953.]

## TEMPLE SISTERHOODS

In 1953, there were twelve local Sisterhoods in West Virginia, affiliated with the National Federation of Temple Sisterhoods, [and with the West Virginia State Federation of Temple Sisterhoods,] with its headquarters in New York City:

|                |              |
|----------------|--------------|
| Beckley        | Logan        |
| Bluefield      | Morgantown   |
| Charleston     | Parkersburg  |
| Clarksburg[1]  | Welch        |
| Fairmont       | Wheeling     |
| Huntington     | Williamson   |

These twelve local Sisterhoods were, in 1953, federated into the West Virginia Federation of Temple Sisterhoods, with Mrs. Edward S. (Belle) Fields, of Morgantown, as its president (1952–1953). The State Federation of Temple Sisterhoods had a total membership of close to 800 Jewish women in 1953.

## ZIONIST ORGANIZATIONS

Zionist organizations were in existence in the following five communities of West Virginia in 1953:

|            |            |
|------------|------------|
| Bluefield  | Morgantown |
| Huntington | Weirton    |
|   Wheeling |            |

## NOTED JEWS OF WEST VIRGINIA

Eminent Jews of West Virginia of the past and of the present, distinguished throughout the State for their contributions to the building of synagogues, to Jewish philanthropy, to Jewish social work, to fraternal or organizational work, to civic affairs, or to state industry and commerce, or who served in the State or national governments, included the following:

*Beckley*

A. David Abrams
Isadore R. Wein

*Bluefield*

Isadore Cohen
Sidney J. Kwass

---

[1] In late 1955, the Clarksburg Tree of Life Sisterhood resigned from the West Virginia State Federation of Temple Sisterhoods, and affiliated itself with a similar Conservative Jewish group.

Abram J. Lubliner
Nathan Platnick

*Charleston*

Harry N. Barton
Mrs. Louis J. (Eve)
    Cashdan
Mrs. Reba B. (Charles)
    Cohen
Max Frankenberger
Leo Loeb
Samuel D. Lopinsky
Daniel Mayer
Joseph Shields
Harry Weiss

*Clarksburg*

Louis Hiller

*Fairmont*

Lawrence M. Brile
Emil Hirsch
Harry N. Pollock
Simon Goodman

*Huntington*

Samuel Gideon
Budd L. Moser
Isidore B. Romer
Mrs. Esther C.
    Weinberger

*Morgantown*

Samson Finn
Harold Slaven

*Parkersburg*

Max Yunker

*Wheeling*

Jacob Fisher
Rabbi Joseph H.
    Freedman
Nathan Harrison
Morris Horkheimer
Rabbi Harry Levi
Rabbi George B.
    Lieberman
Benjamin L. Rosenbloom
R. A. Salomons [?] [Solins?]

## BRIEF HISTORIES OF THE INDIVIDUAL JEWISH COMMUNITIES OF WEST VIRGINIA

Here follow brief historical accounts of the twelve most important and the largest Jewish communities in the State of West Virginia, with all data as of 1953[1].

---

[1] Weirton and its congregation were inadvertently omitted. Later, Rabbi Nandor Marton, of Weirton, graciously supplied data on Weirton and its Jewish community which are included later on in this volume.

## BECKLEY

In 1925, Congregation Beth El (Reform; originally called the Beckley Hebrew Association) was organized in Beckley by some fifteen Jewish families. No synagogue building was erected at that time, but religious services were held by Jewish laymen at the Women's Club building (the old building). A religious school, with women of the congregation as volunteer teachers, was conducted on Sunday mornings at the Institute School, a public grade school.

In the summer of 1936, the synagogue building of Congregation Beth El was erected, at the corner of Bellevue Lane and Second Street, by a group of twenty-nine founders, including the brothers Harry Abel and Albert Abel (of Mount Hope, West Va.), Nathan Berman (who served as the first president of the congregation, from 1934 until his death in 1942), Samuel I. Abrams, Israel Fink, L. [Louis] J. Fink, S. [Sidney] Fink, Irving Goldstein, Benjamin E. Lewis, the three brothers James Pickus, Louis Pickus, and Nathan Pickus, Abe Saks, Jacob Silverberg, and Thomas Sopher (then of Mount Hope, later of Beckley).

In addition to part-time student rabbis from the Hebrew Union College, in Cincinnati, who served up to 1940, and from 1948 to 1950 (especially Richard G. Hirsch and Norman M. Kahan), the following have served as the permanent rabbis of Beth El Congregation: Maxwell Berger, Harold L. Gelfman, Jacob Soschuk, Herbert Pollans, and Abraham I. Shinedling (1950–53 [1956]).[1] In 1953, the congregation numbered 65 families, with a total of 250 persons (including several Jewish families from nearby Mount Hope and Oak Hill, in Fayette County), out of a total general population of over 20,000. Its Religious School had five teachers and 38 pupils in 1953.

The Beckley community has a local Sisterhood, a chapter of the Hadassah, and a B'nai B'rith lodge (Beckley Lodge No. 1360, in District Grand Lodge No. 3).

---

[1] The names of Rabbi Jacob G. Soschuk and Rabbi Bertrand E. Pollans were inadvertently misspelled here. *See* pages 289–290. Rabbi Soshuk's correct name was

BLUEFIELD

Bluefield, in 1953, out of a total general population of about 22,000, had 105 Jewish families, with 350 persons, including some 15 families in nearby Princeton, W. Va., who were affiliated with Congregation Ahavath Sholom (Reform). Congregation Ahavath Sholom dedicated its new synagogue building on Albemarle Street in May, 1949. Previously it had worshipped in a frame building on Scott Street, and, after this original building was sold to a church, it held its services and religious school sessions, as well as the meetings of all its organizations, in several rooms located above the Consolidated Bus terminal, in the downtown business section, between Federal and Bland Streets. Originally, Congregation Ahavath Sholom was an Orthodox congregation; later it became Conservative, and by 1945 it was Reform. It affiliated with the Union of American Hebrew Congregations on December 8, 1947.

Full-time rabbis who served Congregation Ahavath Sholom include: Alexander Alan Steinbach, Nathan A. Perilman, Julius A. Kravetz, Abraham I. Shinedling (1947–1950), Harold L. Gelfman (1950–1952), and Herbert J. Wilner (1952–1953 [1957]). For some years, it was served, intermittently, by students from the Hebrew Union College, in Cincinnati, on a part-time, biweekly basis. These student rabbis [rabbinical students] included: A. Stanley Dreyfus, Sanford E. Rosen, and Jerome W. Grollman. In 1953 its Religious School had 8 teachers and 55 pupils. The fifteen or more Jewish families or individuals of nearby Princeton, W. Va., about ten miles from Bluefield, are affiliated with Congregation Ahavath Sholom, in Bluefield, but they generally conduct their own services in a private home in Princeton for the High Holy Days each year.

In 1953, the Bluefield-Princeton Jewish community, of about 110 families combined, had local branches of the Hadassah, Sisterhood, B'nai B'rith, and the Zionist Organization, as well as the Bluefield-Princeton United Jewish Charities.

---

Jacob G. *Soshuk* (not Soschuk). Rabbi Pollans' correct name was *Bertrand* E. Pollans (not Herbert).

CHARLESTON

Congregation Bene Yeshurun was organized in 1873, as an Orthodox congregation; later it became Conservative, and finally passed out of existence. In 1953, the Charleston Jewish community had two congregations: the Virginia Street Temple (B'nai Israel Congregation; Reform), with 250 member families; and B'nai Jacob Congregation (Conservative), originally Orthodox, with about 300 families.

Congregation B'nai Israel, the Reform congregation, was organized in 1873 as the Reform B'nai Israel Hebrew Educational Society; it erected its first synagogue building two years later. Today it is known also as the Virginia Street Temple. The congregation joined the Union of American Hebrew Congregations on October 5, 1873; this year was the very year in which Rabbi Isaac Mayer Wise founded the Union of American Hebrew Congregations. It was the very first West Virginia congregation to affiliate itself with the Union. In 1953 it had a membership of 250 families.

Rabbis who served B'nai Israel Congregation included: Israel Bettan (1912–1922 [died at Cincinnati, in 1957]), Morris H. Youngerman (died at Charleston, in 1924), Maurice N. Eisendrath, Ariel L. Goldburg, Louis J. Cashdan, and Samuel Volkman (1952 —).

B'nai Jacob Congregation, the Conservative congregation of Charleston Jewry, had, in 1953, a membership of over 300 families, with Samuel Cooper as its rabbi; he was called to the leadership of B'nai Jacob Congregation in 1932. The congregation, in 1953, also had a cantor, Paul Reiss, and a Mohel, Benjamin Samuels. B'nai Jacob Congregation dedicated its new synagogue building and Temple Center, situated at the corner of Virginia and Elizabeth Streets, on April 16, 1950. The congregation conducts a four-day-a-week Hebrew School, in addition to its Religious School on Sunday morning. It also has a Hebrah Kaddisha [a Jewish religious burial society], which is an autonomous organization.

Charleston Jewry, in 1953, was estimated to number over 2,000 persons, out of a total city population of more than 80,000.

The community has a Temple Sisterhood, a Ladies' Auxiliary of B'nai Jacob Congregation, a Hadassah chapter, a B'nai B'rith Lodge, a section of the National Council of Jewish Women, and a Jewish Welfare Federation, the latter including the small number of Jewish families in nearby Dunbar and Montgomery, W. Va. Harry N. Barton, a Charleston attorney, a member of the Charleston B'nai B'rith lodge, served as president, from 1950 to 1952, of the West Virginia Council of the B'nai B'rith.

CLARKSBURG

Out of a total general city population of about 35,000, Clarksburg, in 1953, had 60 to 70 Jewish families. [This estimate was, in all likelihood, too high.] Congregation Tree of Life, still Conservative (but partly Reform) in 1953, was organized in 1918. In September, 1919, Rabbi Abraham I. Shinedling, then a senior student at the Hebrew Union College, in Cincinnati, served as High Holy Day student rabbi for the then existent Congregation Emanuel, which was later merged with the Tree of Life Congregation. The synagogue of Tree of Life Congregation was formerly a church, which was purchased in 1940 and remodeled into a synagogue. Before that, the religious services of Tree of Life Congregation were held in a local hotel salon and in other places.

Rabbi Elliot J. Einhorn served as rabbi of Tree of Life Congregation for a number of years, and he was succeeded by Rabbi Israel Goodman, about the year 1948. Rabbi Israel Goodman served until 1952, and in 1953 Solomon Poupko became the rabbi of Tree of Life Congregation.

In 1953, Clarksburg had a Temple Sisterhood (Reform) and a B'nai B'rith Lodge. [In October, 1955, the Clarksburg Temple Sisterhood withdrew from the West Virginia Federation of Temple Sisterhoods, and joined the Conservative Sisterhood organization, the congregation at the same time re-emphasizing its Conservative composition.] [Rabbi Solomon Poupko served until September, 1955, when Milton Kanter became rabbi of the Clarksburg congregation.]

FAIRMONT

Congregation Beth Israel was organized in Fairmont in 1916. In later years this congregation and another one by the name of Congregation Beth-El, which had been formed, were merged, under the former title, thus bringing both the Conservative and the Reform groups together in one organization and one synagogue, which is the present status of Fairmont Jewry, whose official organizational title is the Fairmont Jewish Community Center. A new Temple building was erected in the middle 1940's. In 1953 the Fairmont Jewish Community Center was not affiliated with the Union of American Hebrew Congregations.

Harold Friedman served from 1951 to 1953 as rabbi of the congregation. In 1953 Rabbi Joseph S. Zuckerbram was called to Congregation Beth Israel as rabbi. [He served until September 1, 1956, when Moses Morgenstern became its rabbi, the latter serving for one year.] Past rabbis of Temple Beth Israel included: Avery J. Grossfield (1936–1938), Bertram Klausner (1938–1939), Max Wiener, Selig Miller, Harold Lasker, and Louis A. Josephson.

In 1953, the Fairmont Jewish community numbered some 50 to 60 families, out of a total general population of about 30,000. [This estimate was later seen to have been too high.] The community has a local Temple Sisterhood, and a B'nai B'rith lodge. Jacob Broidy for many years was active in the work of the Fairmont Jewish congregation and community. In the 1950's Lawrence M. Brile and Harry N. Pollock were active in the community, especially in the work of the B'nai B'rith on a local and statewide level.

HUNTINGTON

In 1953, the Huntington Jewish community numbered about 1,000 persons, out of a total general population of close to 100,000 (the largest city in the State). [The estimate of 1,000 Jewish population in Huntington, in 1953, was later seen to have been considerably too high.] The Jewish community in Huntington was the second largest in the State in 1953, being surpassed only by that of Charleston. The city of Huntington has two Jewish congregations: Ohev (Oheb) Sholom Congregation (Reform); and B'nai Israel Congregation (Orthodox-Conservative).

Ohev Sholom Congregation (Reform) was organized in 1887 by a group of 20 Jewish families. (Others give the date of the founding of the congregation as 1889.) Its student rabbis, all from the Hebrew Union College, of Cincinnati, in the 1910's and up to the year 1920 [1919], included the following: a man named Rosenbloom; [I have since wondered whether this was an error, or a misrecollection, for Adolph (or Adolf) Rosenberg, who was ordained by the Hebrew Union College in June, 1913; or for David Rosenbaum, who was ordained by the same theological seminary in June, 1909, and who therefore could have served the Huntington congregation as student rabbi from 1908 to 1909, perhaps;] Jacob B. Pollak (1912–1913); Isadore Isaacson (1913–1914); Samuel S. Mayerberg (1916–1917); S. Felix Mendelsohn (1917–1918); and Abraham Feinstein (1918–1919). In 1920 [1919], Abraham Feinstein became its first permanent rabbi, serving from that year until 1932. Permanent or resident rabbis of Ohev Sholom Congregation who succeeded Rabbi Abraham Feinstein, up to the year 1953, have included: Samuel D. Soskin, Ralph H. Blumenthal (1939–1941), Lawrence A. Block (1941–1948), Eugene E. Hibshman (1948–1952), and Theodore S. Levy, who came to Huntington in 1952 [and who served as the rabbi of the congregation until 1959]. In 1953, Ohev Sholom Congregation had more than 175 family members. Congregation Ohev Sholom joined the Union of American Hebrew Congregations on May 31, 1935.

B'nai Israel Congregation (Conservative-Orthodox) was organized in 1910. In 1953, it had over 100 families, and its rabbi was Jacob M. Danziger, who has been serving the congregation since 1934. Previous rabbis of B'nai Israel Congregation included: Samuel Mandel, Meyer Goldman, and Hyman Sharfman. B'nai Israel Congregation conducts a four-day-a-week Hebrew School which serves the entire Jewish community.

In 1953, the Huntington Jewish community had a local Temple Sisterhood, a Ladies' Auxiliary of the Conservative congregation, a B'nai B'rith Lodge (with its own building and headquarters), a chapter of the Hadassah, a Jewish Welfare Federation, and a branch of the Zionist Organization of America.

## LOGAN

In 1953, Logan had about 30 to 35 Jewish families, out of a total general population of about 7,000. [This estimate of the number of Jewish families of Logan for the year 1953 was later seen to have been too high.] It has no permanent rabbi, being served by part-time students rabbis from the Hebrew Union College, in Cincinnati. Congregation B'nai El (Reform) built and dedicated its Temple building in 1950. The congregation affiliated with the Union of American Hebrew Congregations on October 26, 1926.

Students rabbis of the Logan Congregation B'nai El up to 1953 have included: Martin I. Hinchin, Sidney Akselrad, C. Melvyn Helfgott, Earl A. Grollman, Malcolm I. Cohen, Wolfgang Hamburger, and Stanley Kaplan.

In 1953, the Logan Jewish community had a B'nai B'rith Lodge and a Temple Sisterhood.

## MORGANTOWN

The beginnings of the Jewish community in Morgantown go back to before the turn of the 20th century, when only four Jewish families were settled in the city. Congregation Tree of Life was not organized until about 1920; it is moderately Conservative and partly Reform. By 1953 it had not affiliated with the Union of American Hebrew Congregations. [Its affiliation with the Union of American Hebrew Congregations took place in March, 1957.]

The first permanent rabbi to serve Congregation Tree of Life was Alfred Jospe, who came to the city in 1939. Part-time rabbis who had served in Morgantown from other cities, chiefly for the West Virginia University Hillel Foundation, before the coming of Rabbi Alfred Jospe, included Samuel H. Baron, Henry A. Kagan, Avery J. Grossfield, and Meyer Miller. Alfred

Jospe was followed by full-time rabbis, who devoted part of their time to the Hillel Foundation, and part to the Tree of Life Congregation and to its Religious School. These included, up to the year 1953: David Herson, Justin Hofmann, Norman Samson, Edwin Schoffmann, Morrison D. Bial, and Morris M. Rose, who came to Morgantown from Brooklyn, N. Y., in 1951. [Rabbi Morris M. Rose left Morgantown to go back to the New York City area in August, 1956.] A new synagogue was built by the congregation in 1949–1950, at 242 South High Street.

In 1953, out of a general city population of about 20,000, the Jewish population was estimated at about 100 families. [This estimate was later seen to have been much too high.] The community had, also, a B'nai B'rith Lodge, a Temple Sisterhood, and a branch of the Zionist Organization. From 1951 to 1953, Mrs. Edward S. (Belle) Fields, of Morgantown, served as the president of the West Virginia Federation of Temple Sisterhoods; in the latter year she was elected to the National Executive Board of the National Federation of Temple Sisterhoods.

Morgantown is the seat of West Virginia University, with about eighty students of the Jewish faith from West Virginia and from other States (1953), and with several Jewish members of the faculty. The Hillel Foundation at the University was organized in 1927, and it has its own building, rebuilt and refitted out from a previous structure. Mention has been made previously in this article of a number of part-time Hillel Foundation directors at the University, the earlier ones from other cities who visited Morgantown and the University occasionally, for several days each month, and the later ones (from 1939 on), rabbis of Congregation Tree of Life, serving also the Hillel Foundation on a part-time basis.

The Hillel Foundation at Morgantown is in part supported by the thirteen local West Virginia lodges of the B'nai B'rith, and in part by District Grand Lodge No. 3 of the B'nai B'rith and by the National Hillel Commission. Many of the B'nai B'rith lodges in West Virginia contribute a per capita amount for the maintenance of the Hillel Foundation building in Morgantown, and for the reduction of the mortgage on the building. Max Levine, of the Morgantown congregation, was for years (also from 1953 on) very active in assisting in the work of the Hillel Foundation.

Mrs. Samson (Lillian) Finn has served for a number of years as a teacher and as the superintendent of the Tree of Life Congregation Religious School, and she and Mrs. Belle Fields have been active locally and statewide in Sisterhood work.

## PARKERSBURG

Out of a total general population of over 40,000, Parkersburg had fifty Jewish families in 1953. Its congregation, B'nai Israel, located on Twentieth Street, is Reform, and has never had a full-time rabbi, being served on a biweekly basis by part-time student rabbis from the Hebrew Union College, in Cincinnati. These students have included the following (up to 1953): Jerome W. Grollman, Eugene B. Borowitz, Herbert M. Yarrish, Irwin M. Blank, Louis J. Sigel, Jerome B. Cohen, Richard S. Stern-berger, and Henry Cohen.

The congregation erected its own (its first) new Temple building at 1703 Twentieth Street in 1949; it was consecrated that same year. [Previously, the activities of the congregation were conducted in rented rooms or halls in the business section of the city.] The congregation affiliated with the Union of American Hebrew Congregations on April 3, 1939.

The Parkersburg community has also a local Sisterhood, and a B'nai B'rith Lodge. It is very active in the work of, and in contributions to, the United Jewish Appeal.

## WELCH

Welch, in 1953, had only about fifteen Jewish families, and a Temple building, but its religious community and its Temple, Congregation Emanuel, include also ten or more additional Jewish families from the nearby towns of Iaeger, Keystone, Kimball, North Fork, and War, all in McDowell County. The general population of Welch, in 1953, was about 7,000. The community has never had a full-time rabbi, being served ever since its incipiency by either the rabbi of the Bluefield congregation, or by part-time student rabbis from the Hebrew Union College, in Cincinnati.

From 1950 to 1953, its part-time student rabbi was Jakob J. Petuchowski [and he served the congregation also as a graduate rabbi from 1953 to 1955]. [Rabbi Jakob J. Petuchowski served Congregation Emanuel, in Welch, until 1955, when he became a member of the Faculty of the Hebrew Union College-Jewish Institute of Religion, in Cincinnati.] Previous student rabbis who served Congregation Emanuel in the period from 1943 to 1953 included: Alton Winters, Leonard H. Devine, Steven S. Schwarzschild, Mordecai [Max] Podet, Rav A. Soloff, and Jerome B. Cohen.

The Jewish community of Welch and of McDowell County has also a B'nai B'rith Lodge (the McDowell County Lodge) and a Temple Sisterhood; in the latter organization, Mrs. Anna H. (Isidore) Katzen and Mrs. Hazel (Morton) Rosensweig have been extremely active, the former also on a statewide Sisterhood basis.

Congregation Emanuel affiliated with the Union of American Hebrew Congregations on June 22, 1950.

WHEELING

In 1953, Wheeling had slightly more than 1,000 Jews. [This figure was later revised downward to total about 800 Jews.] It is the second largest Jewish community and the third largest city in West Virginia, the total general population of Wheeling being about 72,000. Wheeling was the first Jewish community to be organized in the State of West Virginia.

On April 20, 1849, when it was still a part of Virginia, a group of nine Jews of Wheeling incorporated the Jewish Cemetery Association in the city; among these were Marx Graf, Alexander Heyman, Meyer Heyman, Isaac Horkheimer, Seligman Oppenheimer, and Simon Stein. The first religious Minyan ever to be held in the city was conducted at that time. In May, 1849, Congregation Leshem Shomayim (Congregation For the Sake of Heaven; now generally called the Eoff Street Temple, and often spelled as L'shem Shomayim as well) was founded;

its first rabbi was Myer (Meyer) Mannheim. Originally Orthodox, the congregation became moderately Reform about the year 1870. In 1892, the new Eoff Street Temple building, at 1214 Eoff Street, was dedicated. The congregation joined the Union of American Hebrew Congregations on May 8, 1874, being the second in the entire State to do so, and being preceded therein only by B'nai Israel Congregation (the Virginia Street Temple), of Charleston.

In 1953, the Eoff Street Temple had about 100 Jewish families as members, after a schism in the congregation over the issue of Zionism which led to the withdrawal of some fifty families from the congregation in the middle-1940's. Rabbis who served the Eoff Street Temple from its very beginnings up to the year 1953, many of whom gained national or international fame after they left the congregation and went to serve as rabbis in other cities, included: Harry Levi (later of Boston), Abram Brill (later of Shreveport, La.), Abba Hillel Silver (later of Cleveland), Morris S. Lazaron (later of Baltimore), Louis A. Mischkind, Louis D. Gross, Hyman A. Iola, Abraham L. Feinberg (later of Toronto), Charles E. Shulman (later of Glencoe, Ill., and of the Riverdale Temple, in New York City), George B. Lieberman (later of Canton, Ohio), Charles B. Lesser, Mordecai M. Thurman, Baruch Braunstein, Moshay P. Mann, M. Nathaniel Bension, and Joseph H. Freedman; the last-mentioned came to the Wheeling congregation as rabbi in 1950. [Joseph H. Freedman served until the summer of 1957, when he went to Denver to become rabbi of the newly organized Congregation Micah.]

The Ladies' Hebrew Benevolent Society, organized in 1865, subsequently became the Temple Sisterhood.

In 1926, the originally Orthodox but later Conservative Synagogue of Israel was organized, called also by the name of the Edgington Lane Synagogue. In 1953, this congregation had a membership of over 150 families, including some members in the neighboring Ohio towns of Bellaire, Bridgeport, Martin's Ferry, St. Clairsville, and Shadyside, who were members of the Synagogue of Israel Congregation and sent their children, for instruction, to its Hebrew School, conducted four days a week. Rabbi Joseph Wagner became the rabbi of the congregation in 1941, and was still serving in this capacity in 1953. [Later, he was succeeded by Rabbi Solomon Shoulson.] Previous rabbis of the Synagogue of Israel included: Bernard Cohen, Louis Fischer, Lewis Goldberg, Bertram Klein, Nathan Levinson, and Gershon Tolotchko. In 1953 the Synagogue of Israel was reported to be in part at least Conservative.

The Wheeling Jewish community has a third congregation, smaller in size, called Ohev Sholem Congregation. It is an Orthodox congregation, and it is sometimes considered as the second Orthodox congregation of Wheeling.

In 1953, the Wheeling Jewish community had a B'nai B'rith Lodge, a Temple Sisterhood, a chapter of Hadassah, a branch of the Zionist Organization of America, and a Jewish Federated Charities.

## WILLIAMSON

Out of a general city population of about 10,000, the Jewish community of Williamson had between 55 and 60 Jewish families in 1953. [It was later ascertained that this figure was much too highly estimated. A more accurate figure for the Jewish population of Williamson would be about 25 to 30 families.] It had a Temple building and congregation, B'nai Israel (Reform), but it has never had a permanent rabbi, being served by part-time student rabbis from the Hebrew Union College, in Cincinnati. From 1943 to 1953 the following such student rabbis served Congregation B'nai Israel on a biweekly basis: [H.] Bruce Ehrmann, Murray Blackman, Jerome W. Grollman, Bernard Martin, Minard Klein, and Alexander M. Schindler.

In 1953, the Williamson Jewish community had a B'nai B'rith Lodge, and a Temple Sisterhood.

Congregation B'nai Israel became affiliated with the Union of American Hebrew Congregations on May 28, 1922.

## SOURCES FOR THE HISTORY OF WEST VIRGINIA JEWRY

On May 1, 1956, I addressed the following mimeographed letter to some 230 or more fellow Jews and Jewesses residing in all but one of the cities, towns, and communities of West Virginia, whose names I list further on, many of whom I knew from my previous congregation in Bluefield, from visits to Sisterhood State Conventions, from visits to B'nai B'rith local lodge meetings and State Council meetings in some of the cities of West Virginia, from visits to several communities in the interests of the United Jewish Appeal, the Joint Defense Appeal, Sisterhood State Conventions or regional conventions or local Sisterhood installation ceremonies, or visits to several of the communities of West Virginia in the interests of the Jewish Chautauqua Society. This was at a time when I already knew that late in July, 1956, I was definitely going to leave Beckley and West Virginia for good, and move to Albuquerque, New Mexico, where I was to retire for all time from the active congregational rabbinate. Also, in order to secure a complete mailing list, I consulted lists of officers of the B'nai B'rith lodges and the local Sisterhoods of the State, and, in addition, some of the names on my list were those of Christian ministers whom I had met in the course of my visits to college campuses and church camps when I went out, in the interests of the Jewish Chautauqua Society, on brief speaking tours or visits in towns and cities in the neighborhood of Beckley and Charleston, and other parts of West Virginia. Included on my list were also several names of non-Jewish lay people whom I had also met, or had correspondence with, in the pursuit of this work.

The sole exception — mentioned above — was my own community of Beckley, West Virginia, with which I was, of course, extremely familiar after my close to six years of service with the congregation there, and from whose members and congregational records I, as well as Manuel Pickus, a young member of the Beckley congregation, had derived a wealth of material and personal information, on the basis of which we wrote our *History of the Beckley Jewish Community* (Beckley, 1955). The questionnaire which I sent out to these two hundred thirty and more fellow West Virginian coreligionists and compatriots read as follows — and, incidentally, several copies of this novel and interesting letter, or questionnaire, were requested of me by the American Jewish Archives, of Cincinnati, for possible future use, as a model, for other Jewish communities of all the States of the United States which in the future might seek to gather historical materials for preservation in the files of the American Jewish Archives and also for possible eventual publication —:

Rabbi Abraham I. Shinedling
219 Crawford Street
Beckley, West Virginia

May 1, 1956

Dear — :

I am writing this letter to you because I need your help, and I do hope that you will grant it to me, at least in part. Please do not regard this as a *mimeographed letter*, but as a *personal letter*, which I hope that you will answer. Please give it your attention as soon as possible. I regret that I shall not be able to send you a "follow-up" letter on this subject, so please act on it as soon as you can. Therefore, if you do *not* answer, the information which I am requesting you to supply may be lost forever.

*I am seeking information about the Jewish communities and congregations of West Virginia.* About three years ago, in the early part of the year 1953, in connection with the Tercentenary of the first Jewish settlement in what is now the United States of America [1654–1954], by request of the Tercentenary Committee of the Central Conference of American Rabbis, I prepared a short article on the *History of West Virginia Jewry*. In this essay I included as much information as I could possibly gather and secure at that time on such West Virginia Jewish communities and congregations as: Beckley, Bluefield, Charleston, Clarksburg, Fairmont, Huntington, Logan, Morgantown, Parkersburg, Welch, Wheeling, and Williamson. (Princeton was included in the item on Bluefield.) [Weirton was inadvertently omitted.]

Some of the rabbis and congregational members in some of these cities were most helpful in providing me with data and information. Now I am planning to amplify, revise, and bring up-to-date, and publish in book form, the above sketch on the history of the Jewries of West Virginia, and for this purpose *I need additional material and data, especially from 1950 through April, 1956.*

In addition to the larger communities listed above, I need also material on the following smaller Jewish groups and communities, both organized and unorganized, as follows:

| | |
|---|---|
| Charles Town | Kimball |
| Elkins | Martinsburg |
| Grafton | Montgomery |
| Harpers Ferry | North Fork |
| Iaeger | Princeton |
| Keystone | Richwood |

War

With reference to the *larger* communities, I would be grateful for more information (especially from the year 1950 to the present) on the following:

| | |
|---|---|
| Bluefield (including Princeton) | Morgantown |
| Clarksburg | Parkersburg |
| Fairmont | Weirton |
| Huntington (especially after 1916) | Welch |
| Logan | Wheeling |

Williamson

If you have copies of community or organizational records, or pictures of your community centers, buildings, and leading Jewish men and women, please send them to me, and I shall try to include them in the volume.

I especially need *the following items*, and I shall be grateful to you for supplying me with whatever you can:

*Congregations and Communities*: the dates of the founding of the congregation or community; the exact names; the present officers; the charter members' names; the present members (1956); the past presidents and other past officers, and the years when they served. Some data about the original founders. Aims and purposes. If possible, a copy of the constitution of the congregation.

*Sisterhoods or Ladies' Auxiliaries:* the exact name; when founded; the charter members; the present officers; the past officers, and their dates of service; a list of the present members (as of 1956); aims and purposes. If possible, I should like you to send me a copy of the constitution. Achievements and goals.

*B'nai B'rith Lodges*: the exact name of the lodge; when it was founded; the charter members; its constitution; the present members; the present officers; the past officers, and their dates of service. All possible data, from consultation of the records. Also, B'nai B'rith women's auxiliary groups.

*Hadassah Chapters*: the same data.

*Zionist Organizations and Groups*: the same data.

*National Council of Jewish Women Sections*: the same data.

*Biographical data* about any of the above-listed Jewish personalities, charter members, officers, etc.

*Jews in public service, civic service,* academic positions, service clubs, public office, throughout the State; prominent coreligionists.

(In all the above cases, *please give the full names,* and *not just the initials* or *the last names.*)

[Over a year later, in July, 1957, I sent out additional letters to all the above-mentioned communities or congregations in West Virginia, requesting data on Jews in the armed forces of the United States, in the two World Wars, in the Civil War, in the Spanish-American War, and on Jews in military service generally in West Virginia. I requested data as follows: the name of the person; the city from which he came; his rank in the service; his branch of service; his years of service; honors, awards, and citations for distinguished service; casualties or wounds in service; other data or details.]

Note, please, in the above, that I am very eager to secure data about Jews prominent in public affairs throughout the State, in the past or present: Jews who have held public office in the various communities of West Virginia, Jews in civic work, Jewish men and women prominent in women's clubs, in politics, in civic, social, and philanthropic work, Jews who were and are business leaders, leaders in the United Jewish Appeal and in the Jewish community chest or Jewish welfare fund work, etc.

*Data about Our Jewish Religious Schools, Hebrew Schools, and the like,* in all parts of the State: When were they founded? By whom? Their curricula? The names of their officers? The names of the members of their present teaching staff and student body? The names of their past teachers and students — lists. Also, data about any Jewish day schools.

*Data about the United Jewish Appeal Drives, Jewish Welfare Fund Drives,* Jewish Community Chests, and the like, including statistics as to the amount raised, and in what years. The names of present and past officers. When were these organizations founded? Charter members?

*Jewish Cemeteries*: Data about the Jewish cemetery or cemeteries in your congregation and community or city. When were they founded? The names of their charter members? The names of their present and past officers? The history of the Jewish cemetery in your community?

For both congregations *with* organized institutions, as well as for smaller towns and communities *without* organizations, where handfuls or smaller numbers of individual Jews live, please send information, wherever possible, and as much as is available, on the following matters:

the names of early Jewish settlers in the communities; the dates when they arrived; from what cities or towns they came; the businesses, occupations, or professions in which they engaged; the beginnings of the congregations or communities; data about the biographies of these early and later settlers in your community; *copies* of congregational or Sisterhood records, of B'nai B'rith records, or of data taken from these congregational, Sisterhood, B'nai B'rith, Hadassah, Zionist Organization, or National Council of Jewish Women records, and from the records of Temple Brotherhoods, Jewish Welfare or Community Chest organizations, ladies' auxiliaries of congregations, and the like.

I can use every possible bit of information or of data which can be collected and sent in on the above communities or groups. If these are not gathered *now*, they may *never* be able to be collected.

*I need your help in this project!* I am writing this *personal form letter* also to other persons in your community, wherever possible. Perhaps you can get in touch with these coreligionists and work together with them on this matter.

Needless to say, I shall insert in the *Preface* to this volume on the history of West Virginia Jewry a list of the names of all those who have helped me and provided me with information and assistance along the above lines.

I shall be most grateful to you for replying as soon as you can. Please do not delay too long! You do not have to do *the entire job* yourself, but please *do what you can*. Send in as many facts and data about your community and people as you can, and about the organizations in your community. I regret that I do not have either the time or the means to visit your city and community personally, in order to gather all the above data, as I should, but I am doing the next best thing, and the next most efficacious thing, in thus communicating with my coreligionists throughout the State of West Virginia, many of whom I have met personally, many of whom I know, and with many of whom I have worked together in the cause of Judaism and Jewry in West Virginia.

As you can see, I have obviously had to have this letter mimeographed, since it would have been an impossible task for me to type out, by myself, the more than 200 copies of this letter which I am sending out to our coreligionists in the various cities and towns of West Virginia. [I had more than 300 copies of this questionnaire prepared, and sent out 230 or more in the original, first batch. Later, as the result of extra "leads" and suggestions, and of additional lists of names furnished to me by some of those on the first list, I was able to send out practically all the rest, amounting to some 85 additional, with the result that only six copies of the questionnaire remained in my hands as of July, 1957.]

However, I have signed each letter *personally*, and I have written the salutation to each letter *personally*, and thus, as I have stated above, I would beg you to regard this as being *a personal letter to you*. I am sure that it deserves your *personal attention*, and therefore *please do what you can* to help out in this work.

Cordially and sincerely yours, and in the interests of Judaism and of American Jewish history,

(Signed)

(RABBI) ABRAHAM I. SHINEDLING
219 Crawford Street,
Beckley, West Virginia.

The original list of the names of persons to whom I sent out the above questionnaire should be of interest, as representative of the most noteworthy Jewish personages (and in a few cases, non-Jewish personages) most active in congregations, Sisterhoods, B'nai B'rith lodges, and other Jewish organizations, living in the various cities, towns, villages, and other communities of the State of West Virginia. This list, given below alphabetically by cities and towns, and alphabetically within the list of persons of the individual cities and towns, etc., numbered some 230 persons.

Those names which are marked with an asterisk (*) are those of persons who were kind enough to reply and to furnish me with some valuable and indispensable data. However, 123 of the 230 or more Jewish men and women whose names are listed below either never replied, or replied most abruptly and negatively and hastily, or wrote that they had nothing to send in to me or to report; or they promised to send me data later, or soon, which data or bits of information never were forthcoming, and never reached me: "never did arrive," although in such cases I *did* "follow up" and wrote hopeful letters of anticipation after the receipt by me of such initially encouraging replies.

About 110 persons were gracious, generous, and cooperative enough to reply, sooner or later, and to send in much of the valuable and otherwise unobtainable data contained in this volume. To all these persons, as marked with an asterisk below, in the list, I express herewith my extreme gratitude and my grateful thanks and appreciation. For without their assistance, their time and effort, and, in some cases, their generous expenditure of their own funds, this volume either would never have been able to be written, or would be infinitely thinner and poorer than it is now in its present, completed form.

### LIST OF CORRESPONDENTS WRITTEN TO ORIGINALLY FOR DATA FOR THE VOLUME ON THE HISTORY OF WEST VIRGINIA JEWRY

May 1, 1956

Alphabetically arranged by cities and towns, and then alphabetically arranged by persons.

*Bethany*

*Dr. Perry E. Gresham

*Bluefield*

*Isadore Cohen
*Mrs. Nathan (Anna A.) Effron
Fred Gilbert
William P. Gottlieb
*Frank Klauber
*Sidney J. Kwass
Ben Lazer
*Nathan Platnick
*Mrs. Nathan (Edna E.) Platnick

Philip Platnick
*Mrs. Philip (Fannie) Platnick
*Dr. Joseph I. (J. I.) Rodgin
*Mrs. Henry (Anna G.) Rodgin
Sidney Rosenthal
Mrs. Sidney (Helen B.) Rosenthal
Samuel Shaman
Joseph Tomchin
Mrs. Joseph (Ethel) Tomchin
*Rabbi Herbert J. Wilner

*Buckhannon*

Max Schindler

*Cass*

*Adolph E. Cooper
(of Marlinton)

*Charleston*

Mrs. David Badner
Harry N. Barton
Mrs. Joe Bekenstein
Mrs. Lake Brown
Edward T. Buff
*Mrs. Charles (Reba B.)
Cohen
*Rabbi Samuel Cooper
David Freed
Mrs. Morton Hess
Sydney M. Kleeman
Robert H. Levine
Samuel D. Lopinsky
Mrs. Newton Margolis
*Mrs. Charles (Helaine)
Rotgin
Samuel Rudin
Reverend Benjamin
Samuels
Mrs. Anne Seletz
*Mrs. Ben (Lena) Shore
*Lee Silverstein
*Rabbi Samuel Volkman
Mrs. Norma Webster

*Clarksburg*

Walter H. Adler
*Mrs. William (Martha)
Caplan

*Aaron Cohen
*Mrs. Aaron Cohen
Bernard Gottlieb
Rabbi Milton Kantor
Mrs. M. Lerner
Mrs. A. J. Rosenshine
Stanley Samuel
Mrs. Harry Tannenbaum
Mrs. Robert Weiner

*Dunbar*

Irving Ross

*Elkins*

*Dr. David K. Allen
*Alex Goldberg

*Fairmont*

Mrs. Marvin Abrams
Mrs. B. Bressler
*Lawrence M. Brile
Mrs. Harry Goldin
*Rabbi Louis A.
Josephson
Mrs. Joseph Levine
*Otis H. Milam, Jr.
*Rabbi Moses Morgenstern
*Harry N. Pollock
Morris Silverman
*Carl Susskind
*Rabbi Theodore Wiener
*Rabbi Joseph S.
Zuckerbram

*Farmington*

*Isaac Marcus
*Professor Jacob R. Marcus

*Glenville*

*Miss Bessie B. Bell
*Dr. Harry B. Heflin
Isadore Nachman
Max Nachman

*Grafton*

*Harry Friedman

*Harpers Ferry*

*Mrs. Bessie (Abram)
Kaplon

*Huntington*

Mrs. David Baker
*Rabbi Lawrence A. Block
*Rabbi Ralph H.
Blumenthal
Eph [Ephraim] Broh
Mrs. Eph [Ephraim] Broh
*Jerome Cantor
*Mrs. Arlonine Case
*Louis Cohen
*Rabbi Jacob M.
Danziger
*Rabbi Abraham Feinstein
*Herman Fetter
Raymond Hepner
*Rabbi Eugene E.
Hibshman
Dr. Harold Kagan
*Rabbi Theodore S. Levy
Mrs. Walter Lewis
Mrs. Ralph (Gazella)
Masinter
*Budd L. Moser

Mrs. I. [Isaac] N.
Schoenfeld
Mrs. H. Schradski
Mrs. Arthur Weisberg

*Institute*

*Dr. Frederick Lehner
*Dr. William J. L. Wallace

*Keystone*

*Louis Zaltzman

*Lewisburg*

Louis Schuchat

*Logan*

Rudolph R. Eiland
Mrs. J. T. Fish
Ben Harris
Mrs. B. L. Miller
Mrs. Jack Moss
Mrs. Sam Weiner
Nathan Zimskind

*Marlinton*

*Adolph E. Cooper
*Mrs. Fannie (Paul R.)
Overholt
*Summers H. Sharp
*Reverend Donald Taylor

*Martinsburg*

*Sol [Solomon] Cohen
*William Berkman
*Mrs. Harry C. Fine

*Montgomery*

Mrs. Emmanuel Appelstein
*David E. Borstein
*Palmer L. Hall
*Isidore Margolis
*Mrs. Aaron (Dora) Meyer
*Mrs. Ben (Lena) Shore
*Dr. Roscoe M. Vining

*Morgantown*

*Mrs. Belle (Edward S.)
  Fields
Mrs. Max Fields
*Mrs. Samson (Lillian)
  Finn
Mrs. Laura (E.) Goldsmith
Mrs. Meyer Handmaker
*Rabbi Alfred Jospe
*Max Levine
Mrs. Godfrey Millstone
Miss Naomi Rose
*Rabbi Morris M. Rose
*Harold D. Slaven
Howard R. Weiss
*Mrs. Howard R. (Zelda
  S.) Weiss

*Mount Hope*

Albert Abel
*Benjamin Lewis
Alfred Lovitz, Sr.

*Mullens*

Paul Markowitz
Selig Markowitz
*Mrs. George (Lillian D.)
  Taxey

*North Fork*

*Isadore Cohen
*Louis Zaltzman

*Oak Hill*

Hugo Bornheim
*Ben H. Wender
*Max H. Wender
*Morris S. Wender

*Osage*

*Max Levine
*Harold D. Slaven

*Parkersburg*

*Mrs. Sidney A. (Milda
  G.) Ardman
Max Berin
Harry Chaitin
Mrs. Harry (Jean) Chaitin
Mrs. Louis Cremer
Mrs. Martin Cremer
Meyer Falk
Joseph Freed
Herbert Gottlieb
Mrs. Henry Hersh
*Mrs. Ben C. Kart
*Leo Levey
*David Reich
Mrs. Allen Staub
*Walter Wertheim
Sherman Wine
Edwin Yunker
Mrs. Edwin (Dorothy)
  Yunker
*Max Yunker

*Philippi*

  *Reverend Joseph B.
    Dryfield

*Princeton*

  *Harry Barbakow
  *Yankee Barbakow
  Oscar Baum
  Boris Borinsky
  *Frank Nelson

*Red Star*

  *Ben H. Wender
  *Max H. Wender
  *Morris S. Wender, Jr.

*Richwood*

  *Jerome L. Breckstein

*Ronceverte*

  *William B. Blake, Jr.
  *Mrs. Paul R. (Fannie)
    Overholt
  *Summers H. Sharp

*War*

  *Mrs. Milton (Sarah)
    Gottlieb

*Webster Springs*

  *Sam Rubenstein

*Weirton*

  Dr. Meyer Bogarad
  Hyman Orlansky

*Rabbi Nandor Marton
Dr. David Thompson

*Welch*

  Mrs. Julian (Gertrude)
    Budnick
  Herman Diamond
  *Isaac Diamond
  Hershel Fleck
  Sidney Friedman
  Milton Gottlieb
  *Mrs. Isadore (Anna H.)
    Katzen
  *Rabbi Leonard Kravitz
  *Rabbi Jakob J.
    Petuchowski
  Morton Rosensweig
  Mrs. Morton (Hazel)
    Rosensweig
  Mrs. Ellis Roston

*Weston*

  *Harry Gassoff
  *Mrs. Morton S. (Eleanor)
    Weinberg

*Wheeling*

  *Rabbi M. Nathaniel
    Bension
  Mrs. S. Crone
  *Rabbi Joseph H. Freedman
  *Mrs. Lillian B. Getzler (my
    older maternal aunt)
  Julius Harr
  Mrs. Julius Harr
  Nathan Harrison

*Mrs. Frank (Anna E.) Ivry
  (my younger maternal
  aunt)
*Rabbi Morris S. Lazaron
*Rabbi George B.
  Lieberman
 Mrs. Seymour Michael
 Mrs. Simon Penn
 Mrs. Kermit A. Rosenberg
 Mrs. Catherine Rudner
*Rabbi Solomon Shoulson
*Rabbi Charles E. Shulman
*Mrs. Charles J. (Janis)
  Stein

*White Sulphur Springs*

*Richard M. Bock

*Williamson*

 Charles Albert
 Irving Albert
 Mrs. Irving (May)
  Albert
 Janet Bank
 Robert Blinder
 Mrs. Frank Bodenger
 Sam Friedberg
 Mrs. Sam Friedberg
 Mrs. W. M. Goodman
 Mrs. Harry Klayman
 Mrs. Clarence Lovitch
 Alex H. Preiser
 Mrs. William H. (Betty)
  Rosen
 Mrs. Simon Shein

The above questionnaire, in the course of the following few months — and despite the tens upon tens of persons who never bothered to reply to it — resulted in a veritable spate of letters, postal cards, data, and material on many of the Jewish communities, congregations, and organizations of West Virginia, a response which was extremely gratifying in spite of the large number of persons who never replied, and to this day have never replied, despite a friendly follow-up letter or postal card or two, which I sent to them, in a spirit of modestly amiable and encouraging inquiry and of additional request for assistance. I also sent out to all the student rabbis (rabbinical students) from the Hebrew Union College, in Cincinnati, whose names I could secure, and who had served the smaller congregations in West Virginia in the past, or were then serving them at that present time, similar requests for data and information on themselves and on their congregation or congregations and community or communities in various parts of West Virginia — Beckley, Bluefield, Logan, Parkersburg, Williamson, and Welch — which they served as student rabbis of a part-time nature, or were

even then serving, either at the present time or in previous
years — and I was literally astonished and delighted at and by
the remarkably fine cooperation and the cheerful and friendly
answers which I received from 90% of them, and at and by
the fine letters of reminiscence and information which these
young men, all of them "rabbis in Israel" now, sent to me,
including:

Nathan Bark                             Stanley Kaplan
Irwin M. Blank                          Robert L. Lehman
Jerome B. Cohen                         Bernard Martin
   (now deceased)        Jakob J. Petuchowski
H. Bruce Ehrmann                        Mordecai (Max) Podet
Wolfgang Hamburger                      Sanford E. Rosen
C. Melvyn Helfgott                      Alexander M. Schindler
Jerome W. Grollman                      Steven S. Schwarzschild
Earl A. Grollman                        Louis J. Sigel
Isaac Jerusalmi[1]                      Alton Winters
         Herbert M. Yarrish

Very few of my colleagues failed to reply to me. The names
of all of them are recorded with great pleasure in this volume.
   I hereby pay tribute also to the following, who were "towers
of strength" to me in my research endeavors, and who aided
me, with encouragement, sympathy, and with data, to collect
the material which I needed: (Some of them have already been
mentioned, and their names marked with an asterisk, above.)

Harry Barbakow (of Princeton, W. Va.)
Jerome L. Breckstein (of Richwood, W. Va.)
Lawrence M. Brile (of Fairmont, W. Va.)
Jerome Cantor (of Huntington, W. Va.)
Mrs. William (Martha) Caplan (of Clarksburg, W. Va.)
Isadore Cohen (of Bluefield, W. Va.)
Mrs. Reba B. (Charles) Cohen (of Charleston, W. Va.)
Adolph E. Cooper (of Marlinton, W. Va.)

---

[1] A native of Turkey, who later returned to Turkey, and is now doing advanced
studying in Paris.

Rabbi Samuel Cooper (of Charleston, W. Va.)

Mrs. Nathan (Anna A.) Effron (of Bluefield, W. Va.)

Rabbi Abraham Feinstein (of Chattanooga, Tenn.)

Herman Fetter (of Huntington, W. Va.)

Rabbi Joseph H. Freedman (then of Wheeling, W. Va.)

Harry Friedman (of Grafton, W. Va.)

Harry Gassoff (of Weston, W. Va.)

Rabbi Avery J. Grossfield (formerly of Fairmont, W. Va.)

Rabbi Louis A. Josephson (formerly of Fairmont, W. Va.)

Rabbi Alfred Jospe (of the Hillel Foundations, of New York, formerly of Morgantown, W. Va.)

Mrs. Bessie (Abram) Kaplon (of Washington, D. C.)

Mrs. Anna H. (Isadore) Katzen (of Welch, W. Va.)

Rabbi Theodore S. Levy (of Huntington, W. Va.)

Isidore Margolis (of Montgomery, W. Va.)

Mrs. Aaron (Dora) Meyer (of Montgomery, W. Va.)

Frank Nelson (of Princeton, W. Va.)

Nathan Platnick (of Bluefield, W. Va.)

Mrs. Nathan (Edna E.) Platnick (of Bluefield, W. Va.)

Mrs. Philip (Fannie) Platnick (of Bluefield, W. Va.)

Harry N. Pollock (of Fairmont, W. Va.)

David Reich (of Parkersburg, W. Va.)

Mrs. Henry (Anna G.) Rodgin (of Bluefield, W. Va.)

Rabbi William A. Rosenthall (of Wheeling, W. Va.)

Mrs. Charles (Helaine) Rotgin (of Charleston, W. Va.)

Ruby Rubenstein (of Thomas, W. Va.)

Sam Rubenstein (of Webster Springs, W. Va.)

Mrs. Sara S. Schuchat (of Baltimore, Md.; formerly of Marlinton, W. Va.)

Mrs. Ben Shore (of Montgomery, W. Va.)

Rabbi Solomon Shoulson (of Wheeling, W. Va.)

Lee Silverstein (of Charleston, W. Va.)

Harold D. Slaven (of Morgantown, W. Va.)

Rabbi Frank N. Sundheim (of Huntington, W. Va.)

Rabbi Samuel Volkman (of Charleston, W. Va.)

Mrs. Morton S. (Eleanor K.) Weinberg (of Weston, W. Va.)

Rabbi Theodore Wiener (of Cincinnati, Ohio)

Rabbi Herbert J. Wilner (of Bluefield, W. Va., at that time)

Max Yunker (of Parkersburg, W. Va.)
Louis Zaltzman (of Bluefield, W. Va.)

There were many others, the names of all of whom will be found listed by cities, and by alphabetical arrangement, in the following section of this Preface, under the heading Sources for the History of West Virginia Jewry: Personal Sources. The wonder is, not that so many persons failed to reply to me — although that hurt and disappointed me considerably, and I would be less than human if I did not admit this — but that so many of my former coreligionists of West Virginia took the time, and went to the effort, and the trouble (and, in some cases, to the expense), of writing to me, of gathering material for me, and of sending this material on to me, and, in some — indeed, in a number of cases — following up their initial efforts on my behalf with supplementary material from their communities which greatly enhanced still more my knowledge of the history of the several Jewries of West Virginia. To all of them, there-fore — to these finer coreligionists of mine from West Virginia — both rabbis and student rabbis, and lay people — I extend and I record my most heartfelt and my most grateful thanks.


## ADDITIONAL QUESTS FOR DATA

I also sent letters to mayors, secretaries of Chambers of Commerce, and various other public officials, as well as to Jewish residents, of smaller towns, cities, villages, and hamlets of West Virginia, whose names later came to my attention, and whom I wished to ask for data about such localities as were not yet on my list, and about which I desired to have some information, of either a Jewish or a general nature, for inclusion in this volume, especially as regards places in which I had some reason to suspect that there had been Jewish residents in the past. These later series of letters were all personal ones, in-dividually typed, addressed, and signed by me; they were not mimeographed, like the first batch of letters which I sent out. Almost every week, in the course of my research, or as I perused and studied the letters, data, and material sent to me, I came across the names of Jewish residents of West Virginia, of the past or of the present, whose names I had never heard of before; and I also came across the names of towns, hamlets, cities, villages, and even smaller, unincorporated places, in which I had not previously, even remotely, suspected or heard that Jews were living, or had lived, in the present or in the past. There follow — I included them for the historic interest that they may possess, or possibly because they may serve as models for future use along these lines — samples of the texts of the letters of these four or five subsequent types which I addressed to those whose names and habitats were thus later brought, or came, to my attention. Many valuable and otherwise unobtainable data, and the names of many Jews of West Virginia, both of the past and of the present, were thus sent to me, and were assembled by me, as the result of the good response made to such later letters sent out by me.

I

420 Solano Drive N.E.,
Albuquerque, New Mexico.
March 19, 1957.

Dear Sir:

I am at the present time engaged in the compiling of data and material in connection with a forthcoming volume on the *History of West Virginia Jewry*, which I hope to publish by the end of the year 1959.

In this connection, I am addressing this letter to you, seeking information and data about Jewish residents, businessmen, merchants, and professional Jewish men and women, who used to live in (*exempli gratia*) Hurricane, West Virginia, if any; or who still live in Hurricane at the present time.

Were there ever any Jewish families or residents living in Hurricane, and are there any there at the present time?

Could you possibly inform me as to their names, if there were or are any such?

When, and from what cities or towns, did they come to Hurricane?

What were the businesses, or the occupations or professions, in which they were, or still are, engaged?

When they left Hurricane (in the case of those Jewish persons who no longer live in your city or town)?

To what cities or towns they went when they left Hurricane?

Can you possibly send me some data on Jewish professional men and women who lived in Hurricane in the past, or who may still be living there at the present time: doctors, judges, lawyers, public officials, or civic-minded persons, teachers, dentists?

Can you furnish me with any information or data about Jewish religious life, organized or unorganized, in Hurricane in the past or at the present time, or about Jewish communal life?

Or did the Jews of Hurricane, if there were any, go to nearby, larger, cities or towns — and which? — for religious, communal, and social purposes?

Also, since I desire to include a few data about each town and city comprehended in my volume from the *general* point of view, for the sake of general interest and in order to present to the reader a complete picture of each city and town in the volume, could you please send me the following information about Hurricane, itself, from the *general* point of view:

Its present population?

The county in which it is located?

How far is it from the nearest large city or town of West Virginia, and in which direction?

When was it founded?

Can you give me a little bit of its early history, and the names of some of its early founders and settlers? (Above and beyond the few data which I have managed to find in *Webster's Geographical Dictionary*, in *The Columbia Encyclopedia*, and in *Rand-McNally's World Atlas*, which I have, of course, already consulted).

Has it been incorporated, and when, or is it still unincorporated?

Is it a village, or a town?

What are its principal industries?

What does it produce?

Does it have any special features, or any special points of interest? Are there any other facts of importance about its history, features, and population?

Also, what is its present population?

I shall, of course, be most grateful to you for any data or information which you may be able to send to me along the above-suggested lines; or for referring this letter to some person or persons who may be able to reply to me, giving me the above-requested and needed data.

Sincerely yours — and I would greatly appreciate an early reply from you, even if your reply is totally negative as far as information of a Jewish nature may be concerned, or may contain very skimpy data —

(Signed)

ABRAHAM I. SHINEDLING

II

420 Solano Drive N.E.,
Albuquerque, New Mexico.
January 4, 1957.

Dear Sirs:

I am writing you in connection with my forthcoming volume on the *History of West Virginia Jewry*, to inquire if you can supply me with any information about possible Jewish past and/or present residents in (*exempli gratia*) Horton, West Virginia. I regret that I have to address you in this impersonal manner, not knowing your name.

I have come across a notation in the *American Jewish Year Book* to the effect that in the year 1900–1901 high holy day services were conducted by the Jews who were then living in Horton. Could you please send me the names of any Jews of record who resided in Horton in the past, or who may be residing there at the present time; and could you please send me some information about their businesses, where they came from, when they left Horton, and anything else that may be known about them? Also, if there are any Jewish residents in Horton now?

Also, since Horton is not listed in *Webster's Geographical Dictionary*, could you please tell me something about it:

In what county is it located?
Near what city, and in what part of the State?
What is its present general population?
What is its principal industry?
Does the town or locality have any special features?
Some data about its history and settlement?
The type of the town: city, town, village, incorporated, unincorporated, etc.?
Are there any other features of interest about Horton from the historical or the general point of view?

There may be nothing at all about Jewish residents and families in Horton in past or present, but I should nonetheless be grateful to you for even a negative reply from you to this effect.

Sincerely yours,

(Signed)

ABRAHAM I. SHINEDLING

To the Editors,
Horton, West Va., Newspaper
      or to the
Mayor, City Council, or Chamber
    of Commerce, of Horton, West Va.


III

July, 1957.<br>
615 Aliso Drive S.E.,<br>
Albuquerque, New Mexico.

Mr. Harry Friedman,
59 West Main Street,
Grafton, West Virginia.

Dear Mr. Friedman:

My good friend, the Reverend Joseph B. Dryfield, of Philippi, West Virginia, suggested to me that I might write to you for data on the Jewish population or residents of Grafton, West Virginia, in connection with the issuing of my forthcoming volume on the history of the Jewish communities and the Jewry of West Virginia. I should like to ascertain some information not only about you and your family, for inclusion in this volume, which I hope to be able to publish by the end of the year 1958 or early in the year 1959, but also about other Jewish families who lived or who may now live in Grafton, in past and present, as follows:

    The names of those Jewish families who live there now, including yourself?

    Where these residents came from, from what cities, and in what years? (Of course, all the above and below information *if* it is ascertainable by you.)

    The businesses in which they were engaged?

    Were there, or are there, any professional Jewish persons among them, such as lawyers, doctors, dentists, or teachers? What were their names, if so?

When those Jewish families who left Grafton for other cities or towns left your city, and where they went?

Were there ever any Jews in public office in Grafton, and, if there were, can you give me their names, their offices, and when they served?

Were there ever any noted civic workers among the Jews of Grafton, and, if so, please give me their names, their activities, etc., and some data on their biographies.

Was there ever an organized Jewish congregation in Grafton? Did you ever hold Minyan or High Holy Day services in Grafton? Who conducted such services? Did you ever have a synagogue building? Any details about all these things in Grafton, if any?

Or did the Grafton Jews go to Clarksburg or to Morgantown for the High Holy Day services?

Was there any Jewish organization or organized group of any kind in Grafton at any time, and could you tell me something about its purposes, history, officers, membership, accomplishments, etc., *if* there was?

Any other facts about the Jewish residents, religious school if any, etc., in Grafton, that you may remember, or which you may be able to ascertain?

I shall be most grateful to you for any and all information with regard to Grafton and its Jews that you may be able to send me, and I shall be awaiting a reply from you with great pleasure and anticipation. My only regret is that I do not have the time or the means to make a personal visit to Grafton, as the subject deserves, in order to gather all this valuable material.

I shall, of course, my dear Mr. Friedman, include your name in the printed volume, in the Preface, as a contributor and source of information, if you reply, as I indeed sincerely hope you will.

Sincerely and cordially yours,

(Signed

ABRAHAM I. SHINEDLING.

IV

The following letter, each personally typed and signed by me, was sent out to all the former student rabbis of the West Virginia congregations which had student rabbis in past or present, in accordance with a large list furnished to me by

Richard Bluestein, then the registrar of the Hebrew Union College-Jewish Institute of Religion, in Cincinnati, and by his then secretary, Miss Dora Aaronsohn, herself later the registrar of the College. (All these men are now serving as fully ordained rabbis, having been ordained by the Hebrew Union College-Jewish Institute of Religion, with the exception of one who had died in the interim, and of one who, at the time that this material was being assembled by me, was serving as a soldier in the Turkish Army, but who is now (1959) doing graduate study at The Sorbonne, in Paris, as well as serving as assistant rabbi of a Reform congregation in that city.)

> 420 Solano Drive N.E.,
> Albuquerque, N. Mex.
> January 10, 1957.

Dear Friend and Colleague:

From 19— to 19— you served as the student rabbi of Congregation ————— —————, in the city of —————, West Virginia, according to information furnished to me by the registrar of the Hebrew Union College - Jewish Institute of Religion, in Cincinnati, and it is for this reason that I am writing to you, seeking information about that congregation during the year or years of your service there as student rabbi, and about yourself and your activities there as student rabbi.

I would be very grateful to you for sending me, at your earliest convenience, any or all of the following data about the congregation at —————, West Virginia:

Is the year (or years) of your student rabbinate there correct?

Biographical data about yourself: When were you ordained, and where? To what position did you go after leaving your biweekly position as student rabbi in —————? What is your present position?

Can you tell me some data about the congregation in —————, West Va., during your year or years of service there? The name of the congregation; the name of its president; the names of other officers of the congregation; data about the Sisterhood officers and membership; special historical events in the life of the congregation; the names of congregational and Sisterhood officers and membership; data about the Religious School, its teachers and pupils, during your year or years of service; information about the local B'nai B'rith

Lodge, section of the National Council of Jewish Women, the Hadassah chapter, the United Jewish Appeal drives or the United Jewish Fund or the Jewish Welfare Fund drives or campaigns; any other data of importance about your ministry there. Data about Bar Mitzvahs and about Confirmation classes.

It will be a great pleasure to hear from you, at your convenience.

Cordially and fraternally yours,

(Signed)

ABRAHAM I. SHINEDLING

## V

I sent out similar, personal, individual letters also to all the rabbis and the former rabbis of congregations in West Virginia, most of whom I knew personally from past years or from my student days at the Hebrew Union College, in Cincinnati, or from conventions of the Central Conference of American Rabbis. These rabbis and former rabbis included such famous and capable men as:

M. Nathaniel Bension (of Wheeling)
Israel Bettan (formerly of Charleston)
Lawrence A. Block (of Huntington)
Ralph H. Blumenthal (of Huntington)
Louis J. Cashdan (of Charleston)
Maurice N. Eisendrath (of Charleston)
Abraham Feinstein (of Huntington)
Joseph H. Freedman (of Wheeling)
Abraham L. Feinberg (of Wheeling)
Ariel L. Goldburg (of Charleston)
Avery J. Grossfield (of Fairmont)
Eugene E. Hibshman (of Huntington)
Alfred Jospe (of Morgantown)
Bertram Klausner (of Fairmont)
Julius Kravetz (of Bluefield)
Morris S. Lazaron (of Wheeling)

Charles B. Lesser (of Wheeling)
Theodore S. Levy (of Huntington)
George B. Lieberman (of Wheeling)
Moshay P. Mann (of Wheeling)
Jakob J. Petuchowski (of Welch)
Morris M. Rose (of Morgantown)
Charles E. Shulman (of Wheeling)
Abba Hillel Silver (of Wheeling)
Samuel Volkman (of Charleston)
Herbert J. Wilner (of Bluefield)

And there were also a number of other former rabbis of
West Virginia congregations throughout the State to whom I
addressed the same letter of inquiry. A few of these — hardly
more than four or five in all — failed to reply to this and to
succeeding letters of mine; they were, as may be seen, in the
small minority. Seemingly, most of my colleagues then in West
Virginia, or formerly serving as rabbis in State congregations,
both student rabbis as well as full-time rabbis in those days,
were interested in my projected work, set a high value on
Jewish history, and were extremely sympathetic towards my
attempt to collect, publish, and safekeep historical data, and
for this reason they provided me with very valuable and nowhere
else obtainable historical data and information.

# VI

Finally — and this was as recently as in the month of July,
1957 — I wrote special letters to all the congregations or groups
or larger communities, and to the rabbis of these congregations
or communities, some fifteen in all, throughout the State, seeking
information about Jewish men and women in War service, in
any of, and all, the wars of the United States in the past or
present; and about the contributions of Jews of West Virginia
to American military service of all kinds, from the very beginning
of the history of the State. These letters, too, were all personally
typed and signed by me. They read as follows:

615 Aliso Drive S.E.,
Albuquerque, New Mexico.
July 10, 1957.

Dear Rabbi (or Colleague) — :
(or: Dear Mr. —— )

In addition to the valuable information which you and other persons of your community were kind enough to send to me in the past, in connection with my forthcoming volume on the *History of West Virginia Jewry*, I am writing to you again, hoping not to incur your displeasure, for the purpose of seeking material and data on Jews of your congregation and community in War service, in World War II, in World War I, and in earlier wars; in fact, any data and all data about Jewish men and women from your city and congregation and community who served at any time in the Armed Forces of the United States.

I shall be most grateful to you for sending me this additional information, which I plan to include in a special general section on West Virginia Jews in the Military Service of the United States, as well as under the section dealing with your community.

I need, specifically, the following information:

The names of all Jewish men and women from your city and
congregation who served in any branch of the Armed Forces
of our country.
The city from which they came
Their rank in the Armed Forces
Their years of service
The exact name of the war or wars in which they served
Their branch of service
The honors, medals, awards, and commendations which they
received
Casualties: wounds, deaths, deaths in service
Any further details and data about their biographies

Anticipating the pleasure of hearing from you again, and with kindest regards and thanks, I remain,

Sincerely and cordially yours,

(Signed)     ABRAHAM I. SHINEDLING

Unfortunately, not all those to whom I wrote this final letter answered, but from the replies which I did receive I gathered a certain amount of data which I otherwise would never have been able to find. And on the basis of this additional material, I was able to correct, or to point out, the probable errors contained in some of the previously published material on the subject.

SOURCES FOR THE HISTORY OF WEST VIRGINIA JEWRY
LITERARY AND PERSONAL

1. *Literary Sources*

American Jewish Archives, Cincinnati, Ohio
(through Dr. Jacob R. Marcus, Miss Sarah Grossman, and
Miss Jeanette Weiss)

*American Jewish Year Books* (Volumes 1 to 59, for the years
1899–1900 to 1958; published by the Jewish Publication
Society of America, of Philadelphia)

*American Jews in World War II*, Volume II, compiled by the
Bureau of War Records of the National Jewish Welfare
Board, under the direction of Dr. Louis I. Dublin and Dr.
Samuel C. Kohs (the Dial Press)

*Bluefield Sunset-News* and *Bluefield Daily Telegraph* (of Bluefield,
W. Va.)

*Central Conference of American Rabbis Yearbooks*, Volume I to
LXIX (1890–1959) [*CCAR*]

*Columbia Encyclopedia*

*Encyclopaedia Britannica*

Hebrew Union College-Jewish Institute of Religion, Cincinnati
(through Miss Dora Aaronsohn and Richard N. Bluestein)

Hillel Foundations of the B'nai B'rith, New York
(through Dr. Alfred Jospe)

*History of the Beckley Jewish Community* (1955), by Abraham I.
Shinedling and Manuel Pickus

Jewish Chautauqua Society, of New York
(through Sylvan Lebow and Mrs. Ruth Kranz Simonson)

*Jewish Encyclopedia*

Jewish Publication Society of America, of Philadelphia
(through Lesser Zussman)

*McDowell County History: A Pictorial History of McDowell County,* *West Virginia* (1959), compiled and edited by Mrs. Samuel Solins and Mrs. Paul W. Jones. (This little volume contains data also for the nearby McDowell County smaller communities, cities, and congregations of North Fork (Clark), Keystone, Kimball, War, and Iaeger; Mrs. Samuel Solins herself wrote several of the chapters in the book.)

National Federation of Temple Sisterhoods, of New York
(through Miss Miriam Wolfe)

National Federation of Temple Youth, of New York

*Raleigh Register* (of Beckley, W. Va.)

*Rand-McNally World Guide* (1953)
(the section on West Virginia, pages 573–574)

*Rand-McNally's Unabridged World Atlas*

*Universal Jewish Encyclopedia*

*Webster's Geographical Dictionary*

West Virginia State Council of the B'nai B'rith
(through Aaron Cohen, of Clarksburg; and Jerome Cantor, of Huntington)

West Virginia State Federation of Temple Sisterhoods
(through Mrs. Sidney A. [Milda G.] Ardman, of Parkersburg; Mrs. Charles [Reba B.] Cohen, of Charleston; and Mrs. Charles [Helaine] Rotgin, of Charleston; and Mrs. Charles J. [Janis] Stein, of Wheeling)

*Who's Who in World Jewry* (1955)


2. *Personal Sources*

*Alderson*

William B. Blake, Jr. (of Ronceverte, W. Va.)

*Athens*

Dr. David Kirby (of Concord College, Athens, W. Va.)
L. C. Thornton (of Athens, W. Va.)

*Beckley*

Harry Abel (of Mount Hope, W. Va.) (deceased)
A. David Abrams (of Beckley)
Mrs. Esther (Samuel I.) Abrams (of Beckley)
Jack Binderman, Sr. (of Beckley)
Louis J. Fink (of Baltimore; then of Beckley)
Irving Goldstein (of Beckley)
Mrs. Irving (Edna B.) Goldstein (of Beckley)
Mrs. Anne K. (M. Edward) Harvit (of Beckley)
Rabbi Richard G. Hirsch (of Chicago)
Mrs. Zena Y. (Samuel) Hochman (of Beckley)
Rabbi Abraham A. Kertes (of Beckley)
Mrs. Violet G. (Charles H.) Levine (of Charleston; then
    of Beckley)
Benjamin E. Lewis (of Beckley)
James Pickus (of Beckley)
Nathan Pickus (of Beckley)
Mrs. Abe (Gussie B.) Saks (of Beckley)
Mrs. Ruth W. (Bernard L.) Saks (of Beckley)
Harry Seidman (of Beckley)
Jacob Silverberg (of Beckley)
Mrs. Faye R. (Bernard E.) Silverman (of Beckley)
Isadore R. Wein (of Beckley)
Max H. Wender (of Beckley)
Rabbi Josef Zeitin (of San Francisco, Calif.; formerly of
    Beckley)

*Belington*

Dr. Jacob Lazarus (of Baltimore, Md.)

*Benwood*

Mrs. Mary B. Flading (of Benwood, W. Va.)
Morris H. Lando (of Bellaire, Ohio)

*Bethany*

Dr. Perry Epler Gresham (of Bethany College, Bethany,
    W. Va.)

*Bluefield*

Isadore Cohen (of Bluefield)
Isaac Diamond (of Bluefield)
Mrs. Nathan (Anna A.) Effron (of Bluefield)
Rabbi Jerome W. Grollman (of St. Louis)
Rabbi Avery J. Grossfield (of Wantagh, L. I., N. Y.)
Frank Klauber (of Bluefield)
Rabbi Julius Kravetz (of New York)
Sidney J. Kwass (of Bluefield)
Mrs. Edna E. (Nathan) Platnick (of Bluefield)
Mrs. Fannie (Philip) Platnick (of Bluefield)
Nathan Platnick (of Bluefield)
Mrs. Anna G. (Henry) Rodgin (of Bluefield)
Rabbi Sanford E. Rosen (of San Mateo, Calif.)
Rabbi Alexander Alan Steinbach (of Brooklyn, N. Y.)
Rabbi Herbert J. Wilner (of Levittown, Pa.)
Louis Zaltzman (of Bluefield)
Dr. James Zambus (of Bluefield College, Bluefield, Va.)

*Bramwell*

Mrs. Anna A. (Nathan) Effron (of Bluefield)
Miss Edith Jameson (of Bramwell, W. Va.)

*Buckhannon*

R. R. Colinder (of Buckhannon, W. Va.)
Theodore Cooperman (of New York; then a student at West
    Virginia Wesleyan College, in Buckhannon, W. Va.)

*Cameron*

Miss Helen Ray (of Cameron, W. Va.)

*Cass*

Adolph E. Cooper (of Marlinton, W. Va.)

*Charleston*

Rabbi Louis J. Cashdan (of Kansas City, Mo.)
Mrs. Reba B. (Charles) Cohen (of Charleston)

Rabbi Samuel Cooper (of Charleston)
Mrs. Dora B. (Leo) Loeb (of Charleston)
Leo Loeb (of Charleston)
Mrs. Jay L. Margolis (of Charleston)
Mrs. Helaine (Charles) Rotgin (of Charleston)
Jacob Rubin (of Charleston and Beckley)
Lee Silverstein (of Charleston)
Rabbi Samuel Volkman (of Charleston)

## Clarksburg

Mrs. William (Martha) Caplan (of Clarksburg, W. Va.)
Aaron Cohen (of Clarksburg)
Mrs. Aaron Cohen (of Clarksburg)

## Davis

Ruby Rubenstein (of Thomas, W. Va.)

## Dunbar

Dr. Frederick Lehner (of Institute, W. Va.)

## East Rainelle

Charles Lynch (of East Rainelle, W. Va.)

## Elkins

David K. Allen (of Davis and Elkins College, Elkins, W. Va.)
Alex Goldberg (of Elkins)
Mrs. Sara Schwartz Schuchat (of Baltimore, Md.)

## Fairmont

Lawrence M. Brile (of Brooklyn, N. Y.; then of Fairmont)
Max M. Fields (of Fairmont, W. Va.)
Rabbi Avery J. Grossfield (of Wantagh, L. I., N. Y.)
Rabbi Louis A. Josephson (of Houston, Tex.)
Rabbi Bertram Klausner (of St. Louis)

Otis H. Milam, Jr. (of Fairmont State College, Fairmont)
Rabbi Moses Morgenstern (then of Fairmont)
Harry N. Pollock (of Fairmont)
Carl Susskind (of Fairmont)
Rabbi Theodore Wiener (of Cincinnati, Ohio)
Rabbi Joseph S. Zuckerbram (then of Fairmont)

*Farmington*

Isaac Marcus (of Pittsburgh, Pa.)
Dr. Jacob R. Marcus (of Cincinnati, Ohio)

*Fayetteville (and Fayette County)*

Harry Abel (of Mount Hope, W. Va.) (deceased)
Mrs. Esther B. (Samuel I.) Abrams (of Beckley, W. Va.)
J. H. Allen (of Fayetteville, W. Va.)

*Follansbee*

Dr. Morris Grossman (of Steubenville, Ohio)
Abraham Pinsky (of Follansbee, W. Va.)

*Glenville*

Miss Bessie B. Bell (of Glenville State College, Glenville,
   W. Va.)
Harry B. Heflin (of Glenville State College, Glenville)

*Grafton (and Court House District, Taylor County)*

W. Merle Bailey (of Grafton, W. Va.)
C. S. Elbert (of Grafton)
Harry Friedman (of Grafton)
Mrs. Sara Schwartz Schuchat (of Baltimore, Md.)

*Harpers Ferry*

Edna Bennett (of Pittsburgh, Pa.)
Murray A. Bennett (of Midland, Tex.)
Mrs. Bessie (Abram) Kaplon

*Huntington*

Rabbi Lawrence A. Block (of Santa Monica, Calif.)
Chaplain (Rabbi) Ralph H. Blumenthal
Jerome Cantor (of Huntington)
Mrs. Arlonine Case (of Huntington)
Louis Cohen (of Huntington)
Rabbi Jacob M. Danziger (of Huntington)
Rabbi Abraham Feinstein (of Chattanooga, Tenn.)
Herman Fetter (of Huntington)
Rabbi Eugene E. Hibshman (of Sioux Falls, S. Dak.)
Mrs. Julia (Eugene E.) Hibshman (of Sioux Falls, S. Dak.)
Rabbi Theodore S. Levy (then of Huntington)
Dr. Julius Lieberman (of Marshall College, Huntington, W. Va.)
Budd L. Moser (of Huntington)
Stewart H. Smith (of Marshall College, Huntington, W. Va.)
Rabbi Frank N. Sundheim (of Huntington)

*Hurricane*

Luther K. Rumbaugh (of Hurricane, W. Va.)

*Iaeger*

Mrs. Milton (Sarah) Gottlieb (then of War, W. Va.)

*Institute*

Harrison H. Ferrell (of West Virginia State College, Institute, W. Va.)
Dr. Frederick Lehner (of West Virginia State College, Institute, W. Va.)
William J. L. Wallace (of West Virginia State College, Institute, W. Va.)

*Kenova*

Rabbi Theodore S. Levy (then of Huntington, W. Va.)
Katherine Martin (of Kenova, W. Va.)

*Keyser*

Jacob Shear (of Keyser, W. Va.)

*Keystone*

Rabbi Julius Kravetz (of New York City; formerly of
    Bluefield, W. Va.)
Rabbi Alton Winters (of Bridgeport, Conn.)
Louis Zaltzman (of Bluefield, W. Va.)

*Kingwood*

John A. Crogan (of Kingwood, W. Va.)

*Lewisburg*

W. S. Coleman, Jr. (of Lewisburg, W. Va.)
Mrs. Sara Schwartz Schuchat (of Baltimore, Md.)

*Logan*

Rabbi Earl A. Grollman (of Belmont, Mass.)
Rabbi Wolfgang Hamburger (of Lincoln, Nebr.)
Rabbi C. Melvyn Helfgott (of Charlotte, N. C.)
Rabbi Martin I. Hinchin (of Albany, Ga.)
Rabbi Isaac Jerusalmi (of Istanbul, Turkey; and Paris,
    France)
Rabbi Stanley Kaplan (of Duluth, Minn.)
Rabbi Alexander M. Schindler (of Worcester, Mass.)
Mrs. Sam Weiner (of Logan, W. Va.)

*Marlinton*

Adolph E. Cooper (of Marlinton, W. Va.)
Mrs. Paul R. (Fannie G.) Overholt (of Buckeye, W. Va.)
Mrs. Sara Schwartz Schuchat (of Baltimore, Md.)
Judge Summers H. Sharp (of Marlinton, W. Va.)
Reverend Don.[ald] C. Taylor (of Huntington, W. Va.)

*Martinsburg*

William Berkman (of Martinsburg, W. Va.)
Dr. Jacob Bronitsky (of Albuquerque, N. Mex.; formerly
    of Martinsburg)

Sol [Solomon] Cohen (of Martinsburg, W. Va.)
Mrs. Harry C. Fine (of Martinsburg, W. Va.)

*Matewan*

Ben Aaron (of Dallas, Tex.; formerly of Matewan, W. Va.)

*Milton*

Robert Lee Holley (of Milton, W. Va.)

*Minden*

W. R. Bennett (of Oak Hill, W. Va.)

*Monongah*

Mrs. Rose Pickus Bilotta (Mrs. John J. Bilotta) (of Monongah, W. Va.)
Mrs. Fannye (Ben) Kaminsky (Kamons) (of Coral Gables, Fla.; formerly of Monongah, W. Va.)
Nathan Pickus (of Beckley, W. Va.; formerly of Monongah)
Mrs. John H. (Virginia) Rogers (of Monongah)

*Montgomery*

David E. Borstein (of Montgomery, W. Va.)
Palmer L. Hall (of the West Virginia Institute of Technology, Montgomery, W. Va.)
Isidore Margolis (of Montgomery, W. Va.)
Mrs. Dora (Aaron) Meyer (of Montgomery)
Lee Silverstein (of Charleston, W. Va.)
Mrs. Lena (Ben) Shore (of Charleston, W. Va.; formerly of Montgomery)
Dr. Roscoe M. Vining (of the West Virginia Institute of Technology, Montgomery, W. Va.)

*Morgantown*

Mrs. Belle (Edward S.) Fields (of Morgantown, W. Va.)
Mrs. Samson (Lillian) Finn (of Morgantown)
Rabbi Avery J. Grossfield (of Wantagh, L. I., N. Y.)

Rabbi Alfred Jospe (of the B'nai B'rith Hillel Foundations,
New York City)
Max Levine (of Morgantown)
Rabbi Morris M. Rose (formerly of Morgantown)
Harold D. Slaven (of Morgantown)
Mrs. Howard R. (Zelda S.) Weiss (of Morgantown)

*Mount Hope*

Harry Abel (of Mount Hope, W. Va.; deceased)
Mrs. Samuel I. (Esther B.) Abrams (of Beckley, W. Va.)

*North Fork*

Isadore Cohen (of Bluefield, W. Va.)
Rabbi Julius Kravetz (of New York City; formerly of
Bluefield)
Rabbi Alton Winters (of Bridgeport, Conn.)
Louis Zaltzman (of Bluefield)

*Oak Hill*

Harry Abel (of Mount Hope, W. Va.; deceased)
Mrs. Samuel I. (Esther B.) Abrams (of Beckley, W. Va.)
Max H. Wender (of Beckley, W. Va.)
Morris S. Wender (of Oak Hill, W. Va.)

*Parkersburg*

Mrs. Sidney A. (Milda G.) Ardman (of Parkersburg,
W. Va.)
Rabbi Irwin M. Blank (of Englewood, N. J.)
Rabbi Eugene Borowitz (of Port Washington, N. Y.)
Rabbi Henry Cohen (of Champaign, Ill.)
Rabbi Jerome B. Cohen (of Closter, N. J.; deceased)
Rabbi Jerome W. Grollman (of St. Louis, Mo.)
Mrs. Ben C. Kart (of Parkersburg)
Rabbi Robert L. Lehman (of New York City)
Leo Levey (of Parkersburg)
David Reich (of Parkersburg)
Rabbi Lester W. Roubey (of Reading, Pa.)

Rabbi Louis J. Sigel (of Malden, Mass.)
Rabbi Richard S. Sternberger (of Baltimore, Md.)
Walter Wertheim (of Vienna, W. Va.)
Rabbi Herbert M. Yarrish (of Haddonfield, N. J.)
Max Yunker (of Parkersburg)

### Parsons

Ruby Rubenstein (of Thomas, W. Va.)

### Pennsboro

J. Carl Rinehart (of Pennsboro, W. Va.)

### Philippi

Reverend Joseph B. Dryfield (then of Philippi, W. Va.)

### Piedmont

Miss Anna Abramson (of Baltimore, Md.) (formerly of
   Piedmont, W. Va.)
David Abramson (of Baltimore, Md.) (formerly of Pied-
   mont, W. Va.)
Edna Bennett (of Pittsburgh, Pa.)
Roy A. Mulledy (of Piedmont)

### Point Pleasant

Rabbi Eugene E. Hibshman (of Sioux Falls, S. Dak.)
Rabbi Theodore S. Levy (then of Huntington, W. Va.)
John M. Sayre (of Point Pleasant, W. Va.)
Max Yunker (of Parkersburg, W. Va.)

### Princeton

Harry Barbakow (of Princeton, W. Va.)
Frank Nelson (of Princeton)
Rabbi Herbert J. Wilner (of Levittown, Pa.; formerly of
   Bluefield, W. Va.)

*Red Star*

> Harry Abel (of Mount Hope, W. Va.; deceased)
> Mrs. Samuel I. (Esther B.) Abrams (of Beckley)
> Ben H. Wender (of Beckley)
> Max H. Wender (of Beckley)
> Morris S. Wender (of Oak Hill, W. Va.)

*Richwood*

> Jerome L. Breckstein (of Richwood, W. Va.)

*Romney*

> Edna Bennett (of Pittsburgh, Pa.)
> Murray A. Bennett (of Midland, Tex.)
> David Shear (of Romney, W. Va.)

*Ronceverte*

> William B. Blake, Jr. (of Ronceverte, W. Va.)
> W. A. Boone (of Ronceverte)
> Mrs. Paul R. (Fannie G.) Overholt (of Buckeye, W. Va.;
>     formerly of Ronceverte)
> Judge Summers H. Sharp (of Marlinton, W. Va.)

*Scarbro*

> Harry Abel (of Mount Hope, W. Va.; deceased)
> Mrs. Samuel I. (Esther B.) Abrams (of Beckley, W. Va.)
> Max H. Wender (of Beckley)

*Sewell*

> Harry Abel (of Mount Hope, W. Va.; deceased)
> Mrs. Nell M. Bannister (of Thurmond, W. Va.)

*Shepherdstown*

> Dr. Leon Swell (of Shepherdstown, W. Va.)

*Shinnston*

Allen L. Gerrard (of Shinnston, W. Va.)

*Spencer*

Peggy Lee Nitz (of Spencer, W. Va.)

*Sutton*

Albert K. Walker (of Sutton, W. Va.)

*Thomas*

Ruby Rubenstein (of Thomas, W. Va.)

*Thurmond*

Harry Abel (of Mount Hope, W. Va.; deceased)
Mrs. Samuel I. (Esther B.) Abrams (of Beckley, W. Va.)
Mrs. Nell M. Bannister (of Thurmond, W. Va.)

*War*

Mrs. Milton (Sarah) Gottlieb (then of War, W. Va.)

*Webster Springs*

Sam Rubenstein (of Webster Springs, W. Va.)

*Weirton*

Rabbi Nandor Marton (of Weirton, W. Va.)

*Welch*

Rabbi Stanley F. Chyet (of Cincinnati)
Rabbi Jerome B. Cohen (of Closter, N. J.; deceased)
Rabbi Leonard H. Devine (of Elmira, N. Y.)
Rabbi Jerome W. Grollman (of St. Louis, Mo.)
Mrs. Isadore (Anna H.) Katzen (of Welch, W. Va.)
Rabbi Julius Kravetz (of New York City) (formerly of
    Bluefield, W. Va.)
Rabbi Leonard S. Kravitz (of the Hebrew Union College-
    Jewish Institute of Religion, Cincinnati, Ohio)

Rabbi Jakob J. Petuchowski (of the Hebrew Union College-
   Jewish Institute of Religion, Cincinnati)
Rabbi Mordecai [Max] Podet (of Salt Lake City, Utah)
Rabbi Steven S. Schwarzschild (of Lynn, Mass.)
Samuel Solins (of Welch, W. Va.)
Mrs. Lillian D. (George) Taxey (of Welch, W. Va.)
Rabbi Alton Winters (of Bridgeport, Conn.)

## Wellsburg

Abraham Pinsky (of Follansbee, W. Va.)
Sanford Watzman (of Wellsburg, W. Va.)

## Weston

Harry Gassoff (of Weston, W. Va.)
Mrs. Morton S. (Eleanor K.) Weinberg (of Weston, W. Va.)
Mrs. Sara Schwartz Schuchat (of Baltimore, Md.)

## West Union

L. G. Pigott (of West Union, W. Va.)

## Wheeling

Rabbi M. Nathaniel Bension (of Philadelphia, Pa.)
Rabbi Joseph H. Freedman (of Denver, Colo.)
Rabbi Henri E. Front (of Redondo Beach, Calif.)
Mrs. Lillian B. Getzler (of White Plains, N. Y.; Mrs.
   Lillian B. Getzler is my older maternal aunt)
Mrs. Frank (Anna E.) Ivry (of New York; Mrs. Frank
   Ivry is my younger maternal aunt)
Rabbi Morris S. Lazaron (of New York City)
Bertha G. Lazarus (of Wheeling, W. Va.)
Rabbi George B. Lieberman (of Rockville Center, L. I.,
   N. Y.)
Rabbi Moshay P. Mann (of Brunswick, Ga.)
Isaac Marcus (of Pittsburgh, Pa.)
Professor Jacob R. Marcus (of the Hebrew Union College-
   Jewish Institute of Religion, Cincinnati, Ohio)
Rabbi William A. Rosenthall (of Wheeling)

Rabbi Solomon Shoulson (of Wheeling)
Rabbi Charles E. Shulman (of Riverdale, N. Y.)
Charles L. Sonneborn (of Wheeling)
Mrs. Charles J. (Janis) Stein (of Wheeling)

*White Sulphur Springs*

Richard M. Bock (of Baltimore, Md.)
Mrs. Edna De Groot (of White Sulphur Springs, W. Va.)

*Williamson*

Rabbi Nathan Bark (of Philadelphia, Pa.)
Rabbi H. Bruce Ehrmann (of Brockton, Mass.)
Rabbi Jerome W. Grollman (of St. Louis, Mo.)
Rabbi Minard Klein (of Hollywood, Fla.)
Rabbi Bernard Martin (of Chicago, Ill.)
Mrs. William H. (Betty) Rosen (of Williamson, W. Va.)
Rabbi Alexander M. Schindler (of Worcester, Mass.)
Rabbi Steven S. Schwarzschild (of Lynn, Mass.)

In the case of many congregations or organizations of the
State, I have preferred to use, totally and almost verbatim, or
in large part, and in some cases practically intact, their own
histories, pamphlets, compilations, or letters, since I felt that I
could not possibly improve, at long range, upon the close-range
and short-range articles, pamphlets, or presentations which they
were kind enough either to write for me, at my request, or to
send to me, after they had been previously written for special
occasions, jubilees, anniversaries, or celebrations. This was especially the case with such presentations as that of the Clarksburg
congregation, sent to me, with considerable amplifications, by
Mrs. Martha (William) Caplan, of that city; the presentation
of the Clarksburg chapter of Hadassah, compiled, written, and
sent to me by Mrs. Aaron Cohen, of Clarksburg; the history of
the Parkersburg congregation, sent to me, with footnotes and
additions, by Max Yunker and his son-in-law, Walter Wertheim;
Rabbi Nandor Marton's history — all-too-brief — of the Weir-

ton Jewish community and congregation; Lawrence M. Brile's fine presentation of the history of the Fairmont Jewish Temple Center; the pamphlets and articles of Leo Loeb, Lee Silverstein, and Rabbi Samuel Volkman on the history of B'nai Israel Congregation (the Virginia Street Temple), in Charleston; the pamphlet on the history of B'nai Jacob Congregation, also in Charleston; the presentation, in the form of letters and a compilation, by Ruby Rubenstein, of Thomas, on the story of the Jewry of that West Virginia town; and a number of other presentations, special articles, items, and compilations (especially on the Wheeling Jewish community) which I was fortunate enough to receive, for use in this work, from my extremely generous and helpful coadjutants and correspondents in many parts of the State.

Wherever it has been possible, I have included statistics and data also for the years 1958 to 1960, because of a delay in the preparation of this volume.

# WEST VIRGINIA JEWRY:

## ORIGINS AND HISTORY

### 1850 — 1958

# I

# General Data on the State
# of West Virginia

WEST Virginia, one of the east central states (or, as it is sometimes reckoned, one of the South Atlantic States) of the United States, is the fortieth in size among the forty-eight States of the American Union. (With the admission of Alaska and Hawaii, in 1958 and 1959, respectively, as the forty-ninth and fiftieth States, West Virginia is now the forty-first of the States in size, as of July, 1959.) West Virginia has an area of 24,181 (later, corrected figures: 24,282.45) square miles, of which about 150 square miles consist of water area or surface. It was admitted to the Union on June 20, 1863, being the thirty-fifth State thus admitted into the American Union, in the middle of the Civil War.

West Virginia is nicknamed "The Panhandle State," since it has two panhandles, both an eastern one, The Eastern Panhandle, between Maryland and Virginia, and jutting into Maryland and into Virginia, on the east; and a northern panhandle, The Northern Panhandle, extending far into Ohio and into Pennsylvania, on the north. The State has another nickname: "The Mountain State." Its official motto is the Latin phrase *Montani Semper Liberi*, "Mountaineers [Are] Always Free." West Virginia has a total of fifty-five counties. The first settlement in what is now West Virginia was made in what is now the city of Wheeling, in the year 1769, by the English.

The population of the State of West Virginia from 1870 to 1950, the latter the date of the last Federal Census, has been as follows:

1870:   442,014
1890:   762,794
1910: 1,221,119
1940: 1,901,974

1

1949: 1,941,000 (estimated)
1950: 2,005,552 (United States Census of 1950)[1]
1956: 1,983,000 (estimate as of July 1, 1956)
1957: 1,976,000 (estimate as of July 1, 1957)

In 1940, its population of 1,901,974 made it the twenty-fifth State in rank of population. From 1950 to 1957, inclusive, the State suffered a progressive decline in population from the figure of 2,005,552 given in the United States Census for the year 1950, to 1,976,000, the population which the State was estimated to have on July 1, 1957.

According to unofficial figures, the number of employed coal miners in West Virginia declined from 125,000 in the year 1948–1949 to 68,000 in the year 1958–1959, mainly as a result of the mechanization of the coal mines. This induced many merchants and other residents of the State to leave the State for other States and for other cities during this ten-year period, and some of the Jewish communities throughout the State suffered losses from this cause, especially in the years from 1952 on. Reports current in 1959 indicated that a large number of the former coal miners of West Virginia and of the contiguous section of Eastern Kentucky were faced by the problem of leaving the State or of retraining themselves for other industries.

In 1950, a total of 698,324 of the inhabitants of West Virginia, or 34.8% of the total population, were urban. In that same year, 6.2% of the population of the State (113,735) were Negroes. The program of desegregation begun in the State shortly after the 1954 Supreme Court decision requiring the desegregation and integration of White and Negro children in the public (the elementary and high) schools of the State was carried on with very little friction in the years 1956 and 1957, except that in three counties with a large Negro population, and in Osage, W. Va., there was some friction and disorder.

In the entire State, in 1950, the Jews numbered close to 6,000, out of a slightly greater than 2,000,000 general population in the State. In 1950, 91.6% of the population were native white,

---

[1] According to the preliminary figures of the 1960 United States Census, the general population of West Virginia in 1960 was 1,849,142, a decline of 7.8% from the figure of 2,005,552 for 1950.

and 2.2% of the population were foreign-born white (33,640). In 1945, West Virginia had had an estimated Jewish population of 5,500. The estimated figure of 6,000 for the Jewish population in 1950 may not be exact, for no totally exact figures exist for the Jewish population of West Virginia, as indicated by the round number 6,000.

West Virginia is a very mountainous State, and in the 19th century it was primarily an agricultural region. It is very probable that this agricultural characteristic of the State did not prove very attractive to Jews who were moving westward in the early part of the 19th century. As a result, it was not until the fifth decade of the 19th century that small Jewish communities, or settlements, began to be formed in the territory which later came to form the present State of West Virginia.

West Virginia, although lacking in natural lakes, has many hundreds of mineral springs, the chief of these being White Sulphur Springs and Berkeley Springs.

The climate of West Virginia has been called humid continental. The summers are hot, except on such high plateaus as Bluefield and Beckley; the winters are cold. There is much snow in the entire State, and even more in the mountainous regions. The average annual rainfall is 45 inches.

The State is chiefly hilly. Its average altitude is 1,500 feet above sea level, in which respect it is the highest-lying State of any of the States east of the Mississippi River. Its highest point is Spruce Knob, 4,860 feet above sea level.

Most of the State is located in the Allegheny Mountains plateau. The Eastern Panhandle is a part of the Appalachian Mountains Ridge and valley country. Many smaller plateaus dot the State, and there are many ridges, narrow valleys, gorges, rapids, and falls.

Three rivers of West Virginia carry a great deal of barge and general river traffic: the Kanawha, the Monongahela, and the Ohio rivers. All these rivers eventually empty into, or form, the Ohio River, which flows into the Mississippi River.

The motto of West Virginia, mentioned above, was adopted at the time the State entered the Union, on June 20, 1863, as a separate State from Virginia, in the course of the Civil War. The words *Montani Semper Liberi* (Latin for "Mountaineers [Are]"

Always Free") were intended to express the fixed opposition of the inhabitants of the mountainous State to the institution and practice of Negro slavery.

Until the outbreak of the Civil War (April, 1861, to April, 1865), what is now the fifty-five counties of West Virginia formed eleven of the counties of southwestern Virginia. On May 23, 1861, these eleven southwestern counties of Virginia voted against the ordinance of secession from the American Union adopted by the State of Virginia. A government loyal to the Union was organized at Wheeling on June 11 to 25, 1861. About two years later, with the backing of the Federal (the Union) government, West Virginia was admitted under that name to the Union on June 20, 1863, a date which is celebrated annually throughout the State.

Wheeling served as the State capital from 1863 to 1870, and again from 1875 to 1885. Charleston served as the State capital from 1870 to 1875, and in 1885 it became the permanent capital of the State.

In 1950, 18.1% of the employed men in West Virginia were engaged in agriculture; 26.6% in mining (principally coal); 4.8% in construction; 18.3% in manufacturing; and 19.4% in transportation, trade, and the various mercantile branches. In the period from 1953 to 1956, there was — as already indicated above — a general decline in bituminous coal mining throughout the State, with the result that the State suffered a decline in population, and a decline in mining employment, with many miners seeking employment in other States.

Of great interest in connection with the economic condition, even plight, of West Virginia in 1959–1960, and during the preceding decade, is the article, "The Strange Case of West Virginia," by Roul Tunley, which appeared in the *Saturday Evening Post* for February 6, 1960 (pages 19–21, 64–66). From this article, written by Roul Tunley after a long tour throughout the State, the following data of interest on West Virginia have been excerpted:

In the last ten years (1949–1959) mechanization of the [coal] mines, carried out with the approval of both the [coal] operators and the union [United Mine Workers], has toppled the working force from

117,000 to less than 40,000 men, although West Virginia is still the nation's biggest producer of soft coal.

Large-scale agriculture . . . is impossible except in the Eastern Panhandle and the Greenbrier Valley . . . . In the present era of large-scale farming, West Virginia's average farm income (small-scale farming, since the many hills prevent much large-scale farming) recently hit a national low of $897. The national average was $2,269.

[Beckley refers to itself as] the smokeless coal capital of the world.

In the past, West Virginians have been famous for their inquiry and their ingenuity. It was a West Virginian, James Rumsey, who had a steamboat operating on the Potomac River at Shepherdstown twenty years before Robert Fulton's. It was another, Andrew S. Rowan, who carried the "message to Garcia," and another, William L. Wilson, who originated the rural-free-delivery postal system. It was Henry Gassaway Davis, a West Virginian by adoption, who first worked out a plan for running railway trains at night, and still another, Archibald W. Campbell, of Wheeling, who laid the groundwork for West Virginia's independence and persuaded [Abraham] Lincoln to recognize it as a separate state [in June, 1863].

The magazine *Time*, in its issue of March 28, 1960 (Volume LXXV, No. 13, page 23), contained the following brief bleak picture of the economy of West Virginia at the present time:

Most voters [of West Virginia] are . . . deeply concerned over economic matters. The state has never really recovered from the Depression, ranks as one of the least privileged members of the Union. Each year upward of 10,000 West Virginians migrate to other states in search of a better [economic] life; 70,000 men are unemployed, and the relief rolls are so distended that only authentic 'unemployables' are eligible for public assistance. The chronically depressed coal mines have cut their payrolls from 125,000 men to 50,000 in little more than a decade. The welfare statism of the New Deal [of Franklin D. Roosevelt and the national Democratic Party from March, 1933, to 1945] still carries a lot of magic in the mountain glens.

Of factual and historic interest is an article entitled "West Virginia: Battleground for Democrats," written by Harrison E. Salisbury for the *New York Times*, with the subheading of "The State is a Contrast of a Rising Economy and Depression," and dated April 29, 1960. A picture of "An unemployed coal miner's family [and house] in Blakely, W. Va. [The] Mine has been closed since 1952" accompanies the article, which is printed on pages 1 and 14 of the issue of Monday, May 2, 1960, of the

*New York Times*, from which the following excerpts have been made, dealing with the economic situation of West Virginia in 1960:

. . . the economic and social problems that beset West Virginia . . . . West Virginia was preoccupied and troubled by technological and human problems centering on the coal industry . . . . the mountain men, the miners, the business people whose lives are bound up in the fate of this State . . . their attention was riveted [not on the forthcoming election primaries but] on the ills that have invaded their beautiful valleys.

West Virginia's economic problems are a central factor in the Democratic Presidential primary on May 10 [1960], which pits Senator John F. Kennedy against Senator Hubert H. Humphrey. Both have appealed to the unemployed miners, the distressed areas and the large segment of the state's population affected by the spreading unemployment in the coal mines . . . . the aid given to West Virginia under the New Deal of President Franklin D. Roosevelt . . . and proposes plans similar to the rural rehabilitation, work projects and other measures that helped to ease West Virginia's difficulties in the Nineteen Thirties.

The visitor sees few signs of problems in Charleston, Huntington, Parkersburg and the bustling cities of the Ohio and Kanawha Valleys. For the paradox of West Virginia is that booming prosperity and desolate poverty exist almost side by side. Nowhere in the United States has there been more rapid growth of giant chemical and metallurgical complexes. Few states can rival West Virginia's aggregates for boiling, distilling and transforming molecules of hydrocarbons and transmuting them into miracles of synthesis — textiles, fibers, fuels, sprays, jellies, powders and all the chemical wonders common in contemporary commerce. West Virginia is studded with the bluebook names of American industry — Union Carbide and Carbon, du Pont, Owen-Illinois Glass, International Nickel, American Viscose, Monsanto, Interwoven Stocking, Sylvania Electric and dozens of others. Many have come to West Virginia in recent years — Kaiser, for instance, with a $200,000,000 installation on the Ohio River at Ravenswood. Others are steadily expanding. Union Carbide, for example, has added a 2,200-man technical science unit to its 10,000-man industrial plant at Charleston. Old businesses thrive, too. Charleston is still the axe capital of the world, . . . and Richwood is still known as the world's clothespin manufacturing center.

Agriculture is not important in the state. West Virginia is famous for its "perpendicular" farming. The 1958 farm output was valued at $8,300,000,000 [$8,300,000?] compared with $5,500,000,000

[$5,500,000?] in 1947. But, even so, West Virginia is fiftieth among the states in farm production.

West Virginia was settled predominantly by White Protestant immigrants, many of them originally from Virginia, a colony from which Roman Catholics were legally barred until the mid-seventeen hundreds. This Protestant tradition survives in West Virginia today. To a much greater extent than most states, West Virginia's racial stock is the same White Protestant population that originally settled the state.

Today there are in effect two West Virginias. There is the West Virginia of Charleston, with its average family income of more than $6,000 — one of the highest in the east. And there is the West Virginia of Campbell's Fork, a half-abandoned coal camp, where of ninety-one persons still living in paintless houses only five or six have jobs. There is the West Virginia of the handsome state university of Morgantown, with its multimillion dollar new medical school. And there is the West Virginia of Kelly's Creek, where men . . . have not worked since the mine closed in 1952 . . . . The second West Virginia [is that] of technological unemployment in the coal fields that casts a painful shadow over the prosperous, growing West Virginia of the big cities and their rapidly expanding industrial base.

Coal has been — and is — West Virginia's fortune. For nearly thirty years West Virginia has led the nation in coal production. Enough [soft coal] remains — 110,000,000,000 tons — to maintain production at the present rate for 800 years. Despite competition from oil and gas, West Virginia's coal production remains high. It averaged 140,000,000 tons a year for a decade — down from a record total of 174,000,000 tons. But in 1958 the figure dropped to 115,245,000 tons. This year [1960] 40,000 men will extract approximately the same amount of coal that required 117,000 men ten years ago. This is the nub of West Virginia's suffering amid a nation that has never been so prosperous. Since [the end of] World War II 40,000 persons have left the state. In unemployment no state ranks higher than West Virginia. How automation has taken jobs from mines is seen most spectacularly in Kanawha County, where a 50 per cent drop in mine employment has meant a production loss of only 1.5 per cent. The steady increase in coal wages achieved by John L. Lewis's United Mine Workers has hastened mine automation. Union miners draw $25 a day or more — if they work.

In twenty West Virginia counties 15 per cent or more of the population receive surplus food [United States Government relief]. In Mingo [County; Williamson] the rate is 41 per cent, with 19,000 recipients. In McDowell [County; Welch] it is 32 per cent, with 31,981, and in Fayette [County; Mount Hope and Oak Hill] it is 26 per cent, with 21,800 persons . . . . The most energetic and most resourceful [men of

West Virginia, who were unemployed in the coal mines] have long since gone to Akron, Detroit, Chicago or Florida . . . . State resources are limited. In per capita income West Virginia ranks forty-second.

In a dark hour of the Revolutionary War George Washington said: "Leave me but a banner to plant upon the mountains of West Augusta and I will gather around me the men who will lift our bleeding country from the dust and set her free."

The West Augusta of which he spoke was West Virginia. Today the state to an extraordinary degree is populated by the direct descendants of the men of whom Washington spoke. The current [1960] [Federal] census will show West Virginia's population dropping below the 2,000,000 mark. The State will undoubtedly lose a member [one of its six] in the House of Representatives . . . .[1]

In this volume, the following cities and towns of the State are presented, those names marked with an asterisk (*) being the larger centers of Jewish population, with Jewish congregations and other Jewish organizations and institutions. Wherever it has been possible to obtain such data, the general history and data of the cities and towns and of the smaller localities are given in this history, as well as the Jewish history and data. Where towns and other places are mentioned, having no Jewish population in past or present, or both, such statement is given in the relevant section. In some cases, due to the unavoidable delays involved in the compilation, revision, and printing of this volume, it has been possible to include a few data as of the year 1958–1959. In many cases, the data and facts available and obtainable about a particular community, town, or locality are extremely sparse and insufficient, and represent sporadic notes or materials collected in the course of this period of research, extending from 1953 to 1958.

The complete list of all the cities, towns, and smaller localities of West Virginia discussed and treated in this volume follows, in two separate lists:

---

[1] In early June, 1961, the Federal Government named, among the first 114 areas throughout the United States which are eligible for special Federal aid under the new program designed to bring relief to regions of heavy and persistent unemployment, the following 14 distressed areas of the State: Beckley, Bluefield, Charleston, Clarksburg, Fairmont, Huntington-Ashland [Ky.], Logan, Morgantown, New Martinsville, Oak Hill-Montgomery, Point Pleasant-Gallipolis [Ohio], Ronceverte-White Sulphur Springs, Welch, and Wheeling.

## List A. The Larger and Better-Known Cities, Towns, and Localities of West Virginia

Alderson
Anawalt
Athens
Barboursville
Bath District (Hancock)
  ( =Berkeley Springs)
*Beckley
Belington
Benwood
Berkeley Springs (Bath)
Bethany
*Bluefield
Bramwell
Bridgeport
Buckhannon
Cameron
Cass
Cedar Grove
Ceredo
*Charleston
  (In 1959, including South
  Charleston, Charleston
  had the largest Jewish
  community in the State,
  and it is the second larg-
  est city in West Virginia.)
Charles Town
Chester
*Clarksburg
Clendenin
Court House District,
  Taylor County
Davis
Davy

Dunbar
East Rainelle
Elkins
*Fairmont
Farmington
Fayetteville
Follansbee
Franklin
Gary
Gassaway
Glendale
Glen Jean
Glenville
Grafton
Grantsville
Harpers Ferry
Harrisville
Hinton
Horton
*Huntington
  (In 1959, Huntington,
  the largest city in West
  Virginia, had the second
  largest Jewish population
  in the State.)
Hurricane
Institute
Kenova
Kermit
Keyser
Keystone
Kimball
Kingwood
Lewisburg

*Logan
Lumberport
Madison
Man
Mannington
Marlinton
Marmet
*Martinsburg
Matewan
Matoaka
Maybeury
Milton
Minden
Monongah
Montgomery
Moorefield
*Morgantown
Moundsville
Mount Hope
Mullens
New Cumberland
Newell
New Martinsville
Nitro
North Fork
Nutter Fort
Oak Hill
Osage
Paden City
*Parkersburg
   (including South
   Parkersburg)
Parsons
Pennsboro
Petersburg
Philippi
Piedmont
Pineville

Point Pleasant
*Princeton
Rainelle
Ranson
Ravenswood
Red Star
Richwood
Ridgeley
Ripley
Rivesville
Romney
Ronceverte
Rowlesburg
St. Albans
Saint Marys
Salem
Scarbro
Sewell
Shepherdstown
Shinnston
Sistersville
Smithers
Sophia
Spencer
Summersville
Sutton
Terra Alta
*Thomas
Thurmond
Vienna
War
Wayne
Webster Springs
*Weirton
*Welch
Wellsburg
West Liberty
Weston

Westover

West Union

*Wheeling

(Wheeling, the third largest city in West Virginia, also had, in

1959, the third largest Jewish community in the State.)

White Sulphur Springs

*Williamson

Williamstown

## B. The Little-Known Villages, Towns, and Localities of West Virginia

Information about the history and residence of Jewish persons in the following ninety or more towns, hamlets, villages, and localities of West Virginia was sought by me, chiefly in vain, and the conclusion has been arrived at that these ninety, approximately, localities and places do not, at the present time (1959), have any Jewish residents, and that — except where specifically stated — they never did have any Jewish residents or families. Very little in the way of data could be obtained about these places, although some of them are listed in the 1950 United States Census reports, or in the *Rand McNally World Atlas*, or in the *Columbia Encyclopedia* and the *Encyclopaedia Britannica*, or in *Webster's Geographical Dictionary*, as well as in other source and reference books, encyclopedias, and atlases which I consulted. Many of these eighty-nine or ninety towns, villages, places, and localities, many of them unincorporated, are situated in the following counties: Raleigh, Kanawha, Fayette, Logan, Mingo, and McDowell, in western and southern West Virginia, i. e., in the great bituminous coal mining regions of the State. They are located near large cities, such as Beckley, Bluefield, Oak Hill, Welch, Charleston, Logan, and Williamson; so that these Jewish settlers and potential residents who came to the State in past decades preferred to live in the larger and smaller nearby metropolises, and "bypassed" or passed up these much smaller towns, villages, and other localities in their environment. Others of these smaller places are located near Fairmont, Wheeling, Morgantown, and Clarksburg, in the northern part of the State.

The few general data available about these places are to be found at the very end of this volume. In a number of cases, in the list below, two or more little places are considered as one and taken together, as indicated.

Accoville-Braeholm
Addison (Webster Springs)
Algonia-Elkridge
Alpoca-Bud
Amherstdale-Robinette
Anmoore
Ansted
Bartley
Beaver (Glen Hedrick)
Berwind
Boomer-Harewood
Bradshaw
Cannelton-Carbondale
Caretta
Carswell
Chapmanville
Chattaroy
Chelyan-Cabin Creek
    Junction
Chesapeake
Clay
Coal Fork
Coalwood
Cora-Mount Gay
Crab Orchard
Crawley
Cross Creek
Crumpler
Cucumber-Newhall
Delbarton
Despard
East View
Eccles

Eckman
Elbert
Elkhorn
Ethel
Falls View (Fallsview)-
    Charlton Heights
Filbert
Gauley Bridge
Glen Hedrick; *see* Beaver
Glen Rogers
Grant Town
Granville (Mona)
Handley
Henlawson
Hetzel
Holden-Beebe
Hopewell
Hugheston-Loudon
Iaeger
Jenkinjones
Kayford-Acme
Kingston
Kistler
Kopperston
Lilly Grove
Lorado
Lundale-Craneco
Mabscott
MacArthur
McComas
McMechen
Maitland-Superior
Mallory

Marytown
Maude
Mona; *see* Granville
Monaville-Rassmore
Mount Clare
Oceana
Omar-Barnabas
Page-Kincaid
Pageton
Powellton
Raleigh
Red Jacket
Seth
Spelter

Sprague
Squire
Star City
Stonewood
Stotesbury-McAlpin
Thorpe
Verdunville (Verdun)-
    Mudfork
Vivian-Bottom Creek-
    Tidewater
Ward
West Logan
Wharton
Widen

HISTORY OF THE STATE OF WEST VIRGINIA

(A MORE DETAILED PRESENTATION)

Until June 20, 1863, what is now the State of West Virginia was a part of Virginia. The first exploration of the territory which now forms West Virginia was made in the year 1671. A short time later, a number of Frenchmen made permanent settlements near the mouth of the Ohio River. In 1716, a party of men under the leadership of Alexander Spotswood, who was then the governor of Virginia, claimed the territory for King George I of England; these men had crossed over the Blue Ridge Mountains into the Valley of Virginia.

It is well within the realm of likelihood that the first permanent settlers in what is now West Virginia were German, Scotch-Irish, and Welsh pioneers coming from Pennsylvania and Maryland, perhaps beginning as early as the year 1719. It is a West Virginia tradition that a man by the name of Morgan Morgan, a Welshman, made the first permanent settlement, and was the first permanent settler, in what is now the State of West Virginia, in the present Berkeley County, in the year 1731, on Mill Creek, near Bunker Hill. The Colonial period of the history of what is now the State of West Virginia was characterized by a continual contest between the English and the French for the possession of the Ohio Valley, from 1671 on, when Abraham Wood (after whom Wood County was later named) sent an expedition out from what is today Petersburg, Va. Many settlers came into the present West Virginia at the end of the French and Indian War (1763).

It is quite probable that fur traders were among the first explorers of the State. In 1762, the first two towns of what is the present State of West Virginia were founded by Virginians, in the Eastern Panhandle; these towns were Romney and Shepherdstown.

In its earliest history, the State of West Virginia, or, rather, what was later to become the State of West Virginia, like the neighboring States of Ohio, Indiana, and Kentucky, was explored and in part developed and settled by a number of Jewish pioneers of Pennsylvania, of German Jewish origin, who helped to establish these States that were west of Pennsylvania. These early explorers of these States, including West Virginia, not only themselves had a pecuniary interest in the enterprises, which were carried on in those States, but in addition they themselves were explorers and pioneers, who left a number of traces of their settlement in what was then the great wilderness (*Publications of the American Jewish Historical Society* [= *PAJHS*], No. 22 [1914], p. xxii).

The brothers Barnard and Michael Gratz, who were "merchants in Philadelphia" from 1754 on, are credited with having both written and received a number of letters, in the two decades from 1754 to 1774, as well as having their own business papers, which "supply the connection for the data of history in the beginnings of the present states of West Virginia, Ohio, Indiana, Kentucky, Illinois, and Missouri" (*PAJHS*, No. 23 [1915], page 1). Also, Michael Gratz, of Philadelphia, a merchant, joined with a man named Willing [evidently, his first name has now been lost] and with Colonel Dorsey Pentecost in planning a new colony which is now West Virginia and northeastern Kentucky (*ibid.*, page 11).

From the year 1783 on, at the close of the Revolutionary War and thereafter, immigration into the region again increased. Many more settlers came into the lands through which the Greenbrier and the Monongahela Rivers flowed. The region which now forms the State of West Virginia was preponderatingly in favor of the adoption of the Constitution of the United States (1787). According to the first census taken in the United States, that of the year 1790, the region now forming West Virginia possessed a population numbering 55,873 persons. Growth and prosperity were achieved in the region with the opening of the Mississippi River, the appearance of steamboats on the Ohio and the Mississippi Rivers, and the completion of the new National Road from Cumberland, Md., to Wheeling, in 1818. What is now West Virginia was, economically, very closely connected with the Ohio Valley, and its inhabitants were, traditionally, opposed [politically] to the Tidewater and Piedmont sections of Virginia.

Among the inhabitants, at that time, of what is now West Virginia, a great deal of ill-suppressed resentment developed against the continued political domination of the Tidewater sections of Virginia, the less democratic part of the State, with its center in the capital city, Richmond. It was felt by these more democratic inhabitants of the then Virginia that the Constitution of the State was antiquated, and that it ought to be revised considerably. Also, the settlers in what is now West Virginia had a number of leaders who were devoted to the ideals of equality, liberty, and justice, and they were heartily in favor of making an adjustment to a new economic order. The chief grievance was concerned with the question of Negro slavery. The inhabitants of transmontane Virginia (that portion of Virginia situated west of the Appalachian and the Allegheny Mountains — what is now West Virginia), who had very few Negro slaves in their territory, felt that they were being discriminated against with reference to matters involving both representation and taxation, especially since, under the State laws of Virginia, slaves could be taxed, and were taxed, at a lower rate than the rate of taxation for cattle; and yet the numbers of the slaves were considered in the apportionment of representatives to the State Assembly.

The constitutional conventions held in Virginia in 1829 to 1830 and again in 1850 to 1851, at Richmond, were ineffectual in that they did not lead to any permanent checking of the grievances of the West Virginians. The new Virginia Constitution of the year 1830 did not in the least end or mend (as a frequent phrase put it) these grievances. However, another new charter, which was adopted in 1851, led to the reaching of a compromise whereby representation in the Lower House of the State Assembly was based solely on White population, not on the combined White and Negro population, and universal White manhood suffrage was granted. But no relief was achieved in the matter of the [political] domination of the State Senate by the Tidewater counties of eastern Virginia, and the situation entailing heavy taxation was not improved.

The unsuccessful raid by John Brown and his handful of fanatical Abolitionist followers on the United States Arsenal at

Harpers Ferry, Virginia (now West Virginia), in 1859, united most of the inhabitants of the Southern States with regard to the by that time intensified conflict and issue over slavery, with the exception of those residents in the western part of the then State of Virginia. When, on April 17, 1861, the Virginia Legislature, a few days after the attack by Confederate or Southern forces on Fort Sumter, in Charleston, S. C. (April 12–13, 1861), passed an ordinance of secession, or a resolution affirming the secession of Virginia from the Union, it was approved on May 21, 1861, but it met with the strong and overwhelming opposition and total disapproval of the eleven northwestern counties of Virginia which now form the fifty-five counties of West Virginia.

The secession of Virginia from the Federal Union into the Confederacy, and the incidence of the Civil War (the War Between the States), now furnished the inhabitants of these eleven northwestern counties of what was then Virginia with the cause and the occasion for the realization of the separatist sentiments (to separate themselves from the rest of Virginia) of the western frontiersmen of Virginia. These sentiments, incidentally, were not in the least new in 1861, nor did they first come into expression in that year, but rather their roots and origins went back as far as the years 1776 (the unsuccessful and proposed but not accepted or adopted new Vandalia colony of the year 1776) and 1783 (the separate new state of West-sylvania proposed, but not realized, in 1783). At a meeting held in Wheeling, far up in the Northern Panhandle, on June 11, 1861, just three weeks after Virginia had ratified secession from the American Union, delegates who represented the greatest majority of the inhabitants of the eleven northwestern counties of Virginia nullified both the Virginia secession ordinance of April 17, 1861, and also the approval thereof passed on May 21, 1861, and they proclaimed that the offices of the State government at Richmond had been vacated. They consequently formed what is known as "the restored government of Virginia," electing as their governor (on June 19, 1861) Francis H. Pierpont.

Events then moved slowly, but inexorably, to the final climax of the separation. On October 24, 1861, in a popular referendum held in the eleven northwestern "separatist" counties, the creation of a new and separate state from these eleven northwestern counties of West Virginia was enthusiastically approved. A second convention held at Wheeling in November, 1861, undertook the work of drafting a constitution for the proposed new State. In April, 1862, this State Constitution was approved at a third convention. Some eight months later, on December 31, 1862, West Virginia was admitted conditionally into the Union. The conditions were subsequently complied with, by means, in part, of an amendment to the State Constitution which provided for the gradual abolition of Negro slavery. The logical and appropriate name of West Virginia was given to the new State at that time. This was just one day before President Abraham Lincoln's Emancipation Proclamation went into effect, which, issued on September 23, 1862, freed, as of January 1, 1863, all Negro slaves living in areas which were still in rebellion against the United States (the Union).

On April 20, 1863, President Lincoln issued (as a war measure, as he himself termed it) the proclamation of admission of the new separate State of West Virginia into the Union, declaring that it would be effective in sixty days from that date, with State and county officers to be elected in the interim. As a result, the new State of West Virginia became an official (the thirty-fifth) State admitted into the Union, on June 20, 1863. This date is still celebrated as a statewide legal holiday throughout the entire State of West Virginia. The first governor of the new State was Arthur I. Boreman. It was with the full consent of provisional governor Francis H. Pierpont and of his "restored government of Virginia" that the new State was formed in 1863, and in this manner, through the consent of the Pierpont government, there were fulfilled the technical provisions of the Federal Constitution, which provide that "no new States shall be formed or erected within the jurisdiction of any other State . . . without the consent of the Legislatures of the States concerned as well as of the Congress of the United States . . . ." After that the Pierpont government withdrew to Alexandria, Va.

During the remaining twenty-two months of the Civil War (from June 20, 1863, to Robert E. Lee's surrender to Ulysses S. Grant at Appomattox Court House, Virginia, on April 9, 1865), and even for some time before this official separation, the Confederate Government and the Confederate Army made desperate attempts to win back the territory of the western part of the former Virginia to the Confederate cause, and to hold on to this very strategic and border territory. Union troops from Ohio, headed by General George B. McClellan at first, and later under the command of General William S. Rosecrans, defeated the Confederate forces and army parts at Philippi (at the famous Philippi covered bridge) on June 3, 1861. The Confederate troops were defeated also at Rich Mountain, by McClellan, on July 11, 1861; at Corrick's Ford, on July 13, 1861, by McClellan; and in several other battles or engagements, in July and September, of the year 1861, especially at Carnifex Ferry, on September 10, 1861. Also, a large Confederate force under the leadership of the eminent General Robert E. Lee failed to recapture the territory for the Confederacy, suffering a severe defeat at Cheat Mountain, on September 12 and 13, 1861, and Lee proved unable to make up for this severe defeat.

Thereafter no sustained efforts were made by the Confederates to recover the territory, although sporadic fighting continued until practically the end of the War, in April, 1865, with frequent marauding raids and counterraids. The above-mentioned four battles or engagements, unfavorable to the Confederate Army, are believed to have been an undoubted cause which prevented the Confederate forces from invading the North under General "Stonewall" (Thomas Jonathan) Jackson. The control of the West Virginia region by the Union armies was further extended in November, 1862, when General Rosecrans, of the Union Army, gained a signal victory at Gauley Bridge, about forty miles from (almost due north of) Beckley, thus extending Union control into the lower Kanawha River valley. Thereafter the major operations of the Civil War (beginning with late 1862) were shifted to the east and to the west.

It is of interest that during the Civil War a number of skirmishes involving small numbers of troops on both sides were fought in the neighborhood of Beckley. Two men who were destined, in later years, to become Presidents of the United States, but who were then serving in the Union Army, saw

service in West Virginia near Beckley, and experienced the
hospitality of the people of Beckley, when they were stationed
in the township with an Ohio company. These two men were
Rutherford B. Hayes and William McKinley. On the Confederate side, General Alfred Beckley (born at Washington, D. C.,
in 1802; died at Beckley, in 1888), who had previously been the
founder and "father" of the city of Beckley and of Raleigh
County, West Virginia, in the year 1850, served for a short
time as a [brigadier] general in the Confederate Army (1861–
1862), under the Confederate General Henry A. Wise. Alfred
Beckley was captured by Union troops in 1862, and about one
year later he was released under parole, and saw no further
service during the rest of the Civil War. He returned to Beckley,
and devoted many years of his life to public service, serving not
only as the first clerk of the Circuit Court of Raleigh County,
but also as the county superintendent of schools. He gave over
a large part of the remaining years of his life (1865–1888) to
building up and settling the region around Beckley and Raleigh
and Fayette Counties.

Slavery was abolished in West Virginia in 1865. Naturally,
some of the inhabitants of West Virginia remained loyal to the
old Virginia (the Old Dominion). Seven years later, in the year
1872, the new State established the right of Negroes to vote and
to hold public office in the State. Also, in the year after the close
of the Civil War, in 1866, West Virginia passed a constitutional
amendment, while the State was under the control of the
Republican Party, disfranchising all those who had aided the
Confederacy. However, when the Democrats came back into
political power in the State, the act was annulled, in 1871, by
means of the Flick Amendment.

The Reconstruction period saw feuds, partisan rivalries, and
the bitterest intolerance. The transitional period in the history
of West Virginia lasted for about twenty years, from about
1880 to about 1900, and saw the shift from Democratic to
Republican control of the State in the year 1897.

West Virginia adopted the new State Constitution in 1872.
Numerous amendments to it were adopted (twenty-three such
amendments, up to the middle of the 20th century), but sub-
stantially this is the Constitution under which the State of West

Virginia still (1958) operates. In 1902 a State registration law was passed; this law was amended several times thereafter.

Wheeling and Charleston were the only capitals which the State ever had. Wheeling served as the capital from 1863 to 1870; Charleston from 1870 to 1875; Wheeling again from 1875 to 1885; and from 1885 on, Charleston has continuously served as the permanent capital of the State, as the result of an election which took place in 1877.

Important reforms were sponsored in 1904 by William M. O. Dawson, chiefly in the financial field and with reference to the State tax burden. In 1958, West Virginia had a 2% State sales tax, but no State income tax.[1]

West Virginia was, and still is, one of the great coal States of the American Union, leading the country in the production of bituminous coal. More than half of its fifty-five counties are engaged in the production of bituminous coal. Nevertheless, according to the 1950 figures, 65.2% of the total population of the State was rural. (In 1940, over 70% of the total State population was rural.) The State has tremendous mineral resources and, as a result, late in the 19th century, it began a great industrial expansion, with immigration from the Northern States and from Maryland, and with a change to dependency on the profits of industry and on the yield from the wages of the laborers, away from the previously prevailing autarchic economy of the local communities. Most of the State's miners continued to live, and still are living (despite a great reduction in their numbers in the past decade from 1948 to 1958, as reported above), in the local rural communities. Logan, Beckley, Bluefield, and Williamson (and, on a smaller scale, also Welch) continue as the great centers and communities of the coal industry of the State. Charleston, Wheeling, Huntington, and Weirton are the great centers and cities of general industry in West Virginia.

West Virginia University, in Morgantown, is a land-grant, state-supported coeducational university. It was opened in 1867, and was chartered in that year and in the following year. Other

[1] In 1961, the West Virginia Legislature adopted a State income tax law, setting the rate at 6% of the amount of the Federal income tax paid. At the same time, the West Virginia sales tax was increased to 3%.

State colleges or universities in West Virginia are Concord College, at Athens; Bluefield State College, at Bluefield; the West Virginia Institute of Technology, at Montgomery; and the West Virginia State College, at Institute, near Charleston. A complete list of the colleges of West Virginia and its universities is presented further below.

## THE WEST VIRGINIA RESOURCES

West Virginia has three great economic resources: industry; mining and mineral resources; and agriculture.

*Agriculture*: Livestock and livestock products supply from 65 to 70% of the farming or agricultural production of the State. Farming and farm products provide the rest. The mountains and hills are generally better for livestock grazing than for agriculture or farming. West Virginia is noted for its animal husbandry, especially in its bluegrass areas. The best farming is carried on in the Eastern Panhandle, in the Allegheny Plateau next to the Ohio Valley, and in the Ohio River Valley.

The chief farm products of West Virginia are: corn, hay, apples, potatoes, peaches, wheat, oats, and fruits of other kinds. Martinsburg, in the Eastern Panhandle, is the chief fruit and wheat shipping center of the State. Huntington, in the western part of the State, on the Ohio River, and also a large railroad city, is the center of a very important tobacco growing and shipping region.

*Mineral Resources*: West Virginia produces more bituminous, or soft, coal, as indicated above, than any other State in the United States. The motto of the Consolidated Bus Company, one of the largest (and West Virginia-owned and operated) bus companies in the State, is "Serving West Virginia's Billion-Dollar Coal Industry." More than two-thirds of the area of the State contain underground deposits of soft coal, and there are also oil and natural gas in large quantities in most parts of the State, with these three fields — coal, natural gas, and oil — extending from the Northern Panhandle near the Ohio and Pennsylvania borders and running south across the State to the Virginia line.

The Northern Panhandle region has many clay deposits, as do also other parts of the State in smaller amounts, and as a result the production of pottery is a big industry in several parts of the State. There are large salt deposits in the Northern Panhandle.

*Industry*: West Virginia has become a leading State for the manufacture of steel and iron, as a result of its large supply of coal, and through the importation of iron ore from the two States of Michigan and Minnesota. The centers of this steel and iron industry are Wheeling and Weirton, in the Northern Panhandle. The principal metal products of the State include hardware, tools and implements, mining equipment, construction machinery, and railroad equipment. Many steel mills are located along the Ohio River, from Wheeling and Weirton to Benwood. Products made of iron and steel are produced also in such large cities and industrial centers as Charleston, Clarksburg, Huntington, Morgantown, and Parkersburg.

Glass products in large quantities are made in several regions of West Virginia, by virtue of the presence in the State of large deposits of silica sand, and the abundance of cheap natural gas. The major producing cities of glass products are Charleston, Clarksburg, Fairmont, and Moundsville.

A great deal of the oil produced in the State is shipped off to other States, but along the Ohio River, in the northern portion of the State, there are oil refineries.

In the Charleston region, which is the center of the Kanawha River valley, the chemical industry has developed around the salt brines which are to be found there. The chief chemical products of the region and of the State are bromine, chlorine, salt, sodium compounds, ammonia, synthetic fibers, and explosives.

## THE WEST VIRGINIA LEGISLATURE

The Legislature of West Virginia consists of two houses, the Senate, with 32 members, called senators; and the House of Delegates, with 100 members, called delegates. The State has sixteen senatorial districts, with two state senators chosen from each district. Four-year terms are in operation for senators. The delegates to the House of Delegates are apportioned among the fifty-five counties of the State on the basis of population, but each county by law has [at least] one delegate. Delegates to the House of Delegates serve two-year terms.

*The Judicial System*

The judicial system of West Virginia comprises a supreme court of appeals (with five justices), circuit courts (twenty-four in number, with twenty-five judges), and inferior courts, consisting of domestic courts. (These inferior courts number twelve.) Justices of the peace are elected by the magisterial districts of the fifty-five counties, and these magistrates or justices of the peace have jurisdiction just in petty matters.

From the Federal point of view, West Virginia has six Congressional districts, that is, it has six Representatives in Congress in Washington, D. C., and, of course, two United States Senators at Washington. West Virginia forms a part of the Fourth Circuit of the United States Circuit Court of Appeals; and it also comprises two Federal districts (the Northern and the Southern districts).

THE EDUCATIONAL INSTITUTIONS OF WEST VIRGINIA:
COLLEGES AND UNIVERSITIES

(INSTITUTIONS OF HIGHER LEARNING IN WEST VIRGINIA)

Alderson-Broaddus College (at Philippi)
Bethany College (in Bethany, W. Va.)
Bluefield College (in Bluefield; a Junior College)
Bluefield State College (Bluefield State Teachers' College) (in Bluefield)
Concord College (in Athens)
Davis and Elkins College (in Elkins)
Fairmont State College (in Fairmont)
Glenville State College (in Glenville)

Marshall College (in Huntington)
Morris Harvey College (in Charleston)
Potomac State College of West Virginia (in Keyser)
Salem College (in Salem, W. Va.)
Shepherd State College (in Shepherdstown)
Storer College (in Harpers Ferry)
West Liberty State College (in West Liberty, W. Va.)
West Virginia Institute of Technology (in Montgomery)
West Virginia State College (in Institute, W. Va.)
West Virginia University (in Morgantown)
West Virginia Wesleyan College (in Buckhannon)

Some of the above institutions of higher learning are denominational, e. g., Bethany College, Bluefield College, Davis and Elkins College, and West Virginia Wesleyan College.

# II

# Notes on the Early History of the Jews in West Virginia

THE following presentation is not intended to be a complete history of the Jews in West Virginia, but only a sporadic and staccato, rapid-fire account of Jewish population, congregations, religious schools, statistics, and Jewish welfare funds or federations in West Virginia in the one hundred or more years of its history. For the data and the statistics presented below, I am greatly indebted, in part, to the volumes of the *American Jewish Year Book* (hereinafter referred to, often, as *AJYB*), from which a great deal of the material has been collected and culled; and to the occasional reports of the Jewish Statistical Bureau (Dr. Harry S. Linfield, director), of New York; as well as to other reports found in the volumes of the *AJYB*; also to the annual list of the membership of the Jewish Publication Society of America (J. P. S. A.) printed in the annual volumes of the *AJYB* up to the year 1943. Other sources for my collected data are listed in this chapter.

For the complete histories and more complete data and presentations on and of the Jewish population, congregations, religious schools, cemeteries, welfare organizations, and other institutions of the State, *see* under the names of the individual cities and towns, further on in this volume.

1849

The first Jewish community in the State of West Virginia was that of Wheeling, which developed in the year 1849. It is, however, quite probable that Minyan services ("quorums" of at least ten Jewish men, for religious services) were held in Wheeling even before the year 1849.

*AJYB* (1902–1903 [5663 A.M. (Anno Mundi)], in an article

entitled, "A Sketch of the History of the Jews in the United States," states (page 68): "The [Jewish] communities in Virginia, West Virginia, North Carolina, Kentucky, and Ohio, as all those in the West, were of much later growth [later than the period up to the year 1790], no congregations being formed in them until post-Revolutionary times."

## 1865

About 500 Jews were resident in all of West Virginia in the period immediately following upon the conclusion of the Civil War, in April, 1865. In the Civil War, so far as can now be ascertained, eight Jews from West Virginia served in the Union Army, and none in the Confederate Army. These eight included Samuel Gideon, later of Huntington, W. Va., who served as a lieutenant in the Illinois Infantry; Captain Daniel Mayer, of Charleston, who served in the Fifth [West Virginia] Infantry; and Lesseman Straus, of Parkersburg.

According to the *Publications of the American Jewish Historical Society* [*PAJHS*], there were seven [eight?] Jewish soldiers serving in the Civil War, on the Union Side, one of whom was wounded. There were no other casualties (*PAJHS*, Volume III [1895], page 39).

Again, from the *PAJHS*, Volume III (1895), page 35:

Daniel Mayer, of Charleston
Captain and Dr. [Doctor] from West Virginia

One of these seven Jewish soldiers from West Virginia in the Civil War was Captain Daniel Mayer, of the 5th West Virginia Infantry, who "received the following complimentary communication":

State of West Virginia, Adjutant General's Office,
Wheeling, May 30, 1866.

Doctor Daniel Mayer, Charleston, West Va.

Sir: I am directed by his Excellency, the Governor, to present to you the enclosed medal, in accordance with a joint resolution of the Legislature of the State of West Virginia, adopted February 1, 1866, as a slight testimonial of the high appreciation by the State of your devotion, patriotism and services in suppressing the late rebellion.

Very respectfully, your obedient servant,

J. H. Duval, Adjutant General.

## 1873

It is of unusual interest that in 1873 an attempt was made to persuade Rabbi Isaac Mayer Wise, the rabbi of Bnai Jeshurun Congregation (the Plum Street Temple), in Cincinnati, who was then seriously considering the establishment of a Jewish theological seminary in the United States, to locate the proposed rabbinical seminary (which was later to become the Hebrew Union College, established at Cincinnati in 1875) in West Virginia, and, specifically, in the city of Charleston. A site consisting of some ten acres, with the possibility of securing additional land if later needed, was offered to Dr. Isaac M. Wise and to others of his associates in the project, but the matter came to naught. This attempt was made by J. D. Walker, of Charleston, who served as a delegate from the Charleston Bnai Israel Congregation to the first convention of the Union of American Hebrew Congregations, which met at Cincinnati in 1873. Cincinnati had an older Jewish history, which went back to before the year 1825, and a much larger Jewish population at the time.

In connection with this offer, the late Professor Samuel S. Cohon, in an article on the history of the Hebrew Union College, wrote as follows, in *PAJHS* (Volume 40 [September, 1950], page 23):

"An enthusiast from Charleston, West Virginia, offered the Union [of American Hebrew Congregations] a ten acre plot of ground for a [Jewish theological] college [in July, 1873], and a physician from the same city donated one hundred acres of timber and mineral land in Boone County, West Virginia."

[Boone County, West Virginia, is south of, and adjacent to, Kanawha County, in which Charleston is situated. Evidently, the offer was not accepted by the officials of the Union of American Hebrew Congregations, especially since Charleston at that time had no more than a handful of Jewish residents ("10 Jewish families and 15 young [single] men"), and Cincinnati was then the Western metropolis of American Jewry, with something like five to eight thousand Jewish residents, and it was the center of Reform Judaism, and also the largest Jewish community in Ohio at that time.]

## 1877

The Jewish population of West Virginia in 1877 was 511, according to *AJYB* (1927–1928). The number of Jews living in the State every ten years or every other ten years from 1877 on was given there as follows:

### West Virginia

| Year | Number of Jews living in the State |
|------|:----------------------------------:|
| 1877 | 511 |
| 1897 | 6,000 |
|  | [This figure of 6,000 was a very poor estimate, and much too high.] |
| 1907 | 1,500 |
| 1917 | 5,129 |
| 1927 | 7,471 |

## 1880

Statistics of the Jews of the United States, compiled under the authority of the Board of Delegates of American Israelites of the Union of American Hebrew Congregations (U. A. H. C.), Philadelphia, September 1, 1880:

## Congregations and Religious Schools in the State of West Virginia in 1880:

| Congregation or Society | Year Organized | Number of Members or Seat Holders | Value of Real Estate | Value of Other Property |
|---|---|---|---|---|
| *Charleston* Bnai Israel | 1873 | 16 | $2,000 | |
| *Charles Town* | | | | |
| *Fairmont* | | | | |
| *Grafton* | | | | |
| *Martinsburg* | | | | |
| *Parkersburg* | | | | |
| *Piedmont* | | | | |
| *Wheeling* 1. Congregation Leshem Shomayim | 1864 | 42 | | $500 |
| 2. Hebrew Ladies' Benevolent Society | 1864 | 41 | assists poor widows and orphans | $700 |
| 3. Montefiore Literary Society | 1875 | 20 | | |

## *Estimated Jewish Population*
### (September 1, 1880)

| *City* | *Jewish Population* |
|---|---|
| Charleston | 92 |
| Charles Town | 7 |
| Fairmont | 3 |
| Grafton | 6 |
| Martinsburg | 8 |
| Parkersburg | 77 |
| Piedmont | 18 |
| Wheeling | 300 |

*Number of Children Attending Religious
School, and Number of Teachers*
(September 1, 1880)

| City | Children | Teachers |
|------|----------|----------|
| Charleston | 14 | 1 |
| Charles Town | | |
| Fairmont | | |
| Grafton | | |
| Martinsburg | | |
| Parkersburg | | |
| Piedmont | | |
| Wheeling | 40 | 1 |

In September, 1880, according to the figures compiled by the Union of American Hebrew Congregations, on the statistics of the Jews, the entire Jewish population of the United States at that time (1880) was 230,257; the Jewish population of West Virginia was then only 511 persons.

## 1897

The Jewish population of the United States, in 1897, was 937,800, a great increase as the result of the Russian pogroms and the migrations of Russian Jews to the United States in the early 1880's.

The Jewish population of West Virginia, in 1897, was estimated as 6,000 (*PAJHS*, No. 6 [1897], page 149). [This figure is now believed to have been much too high. It is possible that in 1897 the Jews of West Virginia numbered hardly more than 1,000, or even less. In 1907, their number was estimated at only about 1,500. (*PAJHS*, No. 6 [1897], page 145.]

## 1898

As far as can be learned, the only West Virginia Jews who served in the United States Army during the Spanish-American

41278

War (1898–1899) were Benjamin Graff, Joseph Harburger, and Joseph Keller, Jr. All three were in Company L of the First West Virginia Volunteer Infantry. It is not known from what cities in West Virginia Joseph Harburger and Benjamin Graff came. Maurice Rauch also served in the Spanish-American War, in Company L of the First West Virginia Volunteer Infantry. Maurice Rauch and Joseph Keller, Jr., were residents of Parkersburg. (*See also* page 135.)

## 1899

In 1899, according to the estimates in the *AJYB*, there were 1,043,800 Jews in the United States. West Virginia was listed as having a total of 1,500 Jews. (This was merely a conjecture, and not an accurate figure.) In the preceding volume of the *AJYB* (Volume 1, for 1899–1900, or 5660 A.M.), David Sulzberger had estimated the Jewish population of West Virginia at 6,000 (page 284), but this round-number figure of 6,000 Jews was excessively high, and represented an extremely bad, if not wild, guess on his part, for which there was not the slightest warrant in statistics. In the *AJYB* for 1900–1901 (Volume 2, for 5661 A.M.), this previous grotesque figure of 6,000 was sensibly reduced to 1,500 Jews in the State (page 624).

## 1899–1900

(*AJYB*, 1899–1900, Volume 1, Year 5660 A.M.)

West Virginia is mentioned in the very first volume of the *AJYB*, that for the year 1899–1900 (5660 A.M.), on page 269, where the following three Jewish congregations — which were then the only Jewish congregations extant in the State — are given as follows, in a "Directory of Local Organizations":

*Charleston*

> [K. K. (Kahal Kadosh, i. e., "Holy Congregation," or "Congregation")] Bene Israel, south side of Virginia [Street], between Broad and Brooks. Services, Saturday, 9 a.m. Religious School: Sunday, 9.30 a.m.
> [Bene Israel is a misspelling for B'nai Israel.]

*Huntington*

> [Congregation] Ohav Sholam
> [Ohav Sholam is a misspelling for Oheb Shalom Congregation, whose name was spelled also as Ohev Sholom.]

*Wheeling*

> [Congregation] Leshem Shomayim, 12th and Eoff Streets. Founded November 12, 1849. Rabbi, Harry Levi.
> Officers: President, Samuel Kraft; Vice-President, Joseph Emsheimer.
> Other Trustees: Henry Baer, Bernard Horkheimer, Lewis Horkheimer, Ralph Kline, Lee Baer. Board meeting monthly. Members, 107. Services: Friday, 8 p.m.; Saturday, 10.30 a.m. Religious School: Saturday, 9.30 a.m.; Sunday, 9.30 a.m. Pupils, 75.

Auxiliary Societies: Ladies' Hebrew Benevolent Society, Sabbath School Teachers' Class, Eoff Street Temple Jewish Literature Class, Eoff Street Temple Bible Class, Eoff Street Temple Post-Confirmation Class, Eoff Street Temple Alumni Association.

1901–1902

*Statistical Summary by States (1901–2)*
(*AJYB*, 1901–1902, 5662 A.M., Volume 3):

In the [entire] State of West Virginia, in 1900–1901, there were 4 cities with 1 or more Jewish institutions.

Of these, 3 cities each had a regularly organized congregation, 1 holding Sabbath and holiday services, and 2 holding Friday evening and holiday services. One place holds just holiday services.

Three congregations in West Virginia report a membership of 168 [families], and 2 report a total joint income of $1,700 (annual).

One congregation, that in Wheeling, was affiliated with the Union of American Hebrew Congregations (U. A. H. C.), having joined the U.A.H.C. on May 8, 1874.[1]

---

[1] This would appear to be an error in the *AJYB*, since, according to the *U. A. H. C. Year Book*, December, 1955, the Charleston B'nai Israel Congregation, or the

Two congregations reported that they had Jewish cemeteries, and two stated that they had congregational schools with a total of 101 pupils. One of these schools was affiliated with the Hebrew Sabbath School Union of America.

In 1900–1901 there were 4 Jewish charitable societies in West Virginia, two of them possessing an annual income of $261.80.

There were three clubs [social clubs] in the State, one of them having an income of $1,400 annually. [Note the large amount of the annual income of the purely "social" club — of one of them — as compared with the very small annual income — from donations and dues, no doubt — of two of the charitable organizations of the state.]

There were two places in West Virginia which, although having no Jewish institutions at all, held High Holy Day services in that year (September, 1900).

The Jewish population of the State of West Virginia was estimated, in 1900–1901, as 1,500 persons.

## 1903–1904

In a list of "Biographical Sketches of Rabbis and Cantors Officiating in the United States," found in the *AJYB* (5664 A.M. [1903–1904, Volume 5]), only two names are given: Rabbi Harry Levi is mentioned as from Wheeling, in West Virginia; and Leon Volmer, as from Charleston, W. Va. The texts of these two items, found on page 73, read as follows:

LEVI, HARRY. Rabbi (since 1897) of Congregation Leshem Shamayim, Wheeling, W. Va. Born August 7, 1875, at Cincinnati, Ohio. Son of Isaac Levi and Belle Engelstein. Educated at [the] public schools of Cincinnati, Ohio; [the] University of Cincinnati; and [the] Hebrew Union College (Rabbi, 1897). Publications: "A History of Congregation Leshem Shamayim"; "Jewish Characters in English Fiction." Address: Eoff Street Temple, Wheeling, W. Va. [Harry Levi died in 1944.]

---

Virginia Street Temple, had joined the U. A. H. C. even before the Wheeling congregation, on October 5, 1873, thus being the first Reform congregation of West Virginia to join the U. A. H. C.

VOLMER, LEON. Rabbi of the Hebrew Educational Society Bene Jeshurun, Charleston, W. Va.[1] Born June 28, 1879, at Little Rock, Ark. Son of Louis Volmer and Henrietta Bott. Educated at the public schools of Little Rock; high school, Cincinnati, Ohio; University of Cincinnati (B.A.); and [the] Hebrew Union College (B.H.L. and Rabbi). Address: Charleston, W. Va.

[The item in the *AJYB* failed to state that it was in 1901 that Leon Volmer was ordained by the Hebrew Union College. According to the best information available from the Hebrew Union College, Leon Volmer died at Canton, Ohio, in 1934, in all probability. He lived in Canton, Ohio, where he was not an officiating rabbi, and his name appears in the Hebrew Union College Catalogue among the living alumni in 1933–1934. However, in the very next Catalogue, that for the year 1934–1935, he is listed among the deceased alumni of the College.]

## 1904

It is of interest that in the *PAJHS* (No. 12 [1904], page 172), in connection with his "Notes on Sunday Laws," Albert M. Friedenberg mentioned, for West Virginia, the following item: West Virginia (Warth's *Code of West Virginia*, 4th edition, Charleston, [W. Va.], 1900, chapter 149, section 17).

## 1905–1906

In 1905 and 1906, Samuel C. Bloch, of Wheeling, was the only member from West Virginia of the American Jewish Historical Society (A. J. H. S.).

---

[1] The name Bene Jeshurun for the Charleston, W. Va., congregation, was undoubtedly a misreading, or an error in printing, for B'nai Israel, the later name of the Hebrew Educational Society, of Charleston, W. Va. The Charleston congregation was never known as Bene Jeshurun Congregation.

1906–1907
(*AJYB*, 1906–1907 [5667 A.M.])

Contributions by eight West Virginia Jewish communities, or by individual Jews of the State, were made to the Fund Collected for the Relief of the Sufferers by the Russian Outrages of October to November, 1905, as follows:

|            |            |
|------------|------------|
| Alderson   | Martinsburg |
| Bluefield  | Morgantown |
| Charleston | Ronceverte |
| Grafton    | Wheeling   |

1907–1908

In 1907–1908, the entire Jewish population of West Virginia still totalled only about 1,500 (an estimate), with the four largest centers of Jewish population in the State listed as follows:

| Charleston:  | 190 Jews | Parkersburg: | 50 Jews  |
|--------------|----------|--------------|----------|
| Huntington:  | 100 Jews | Wheeling:    | 550 Jews |

Other, smaller, numbers of Jewish residents were to be found in that year, among other places, also in Bluefield and in Keystone.

According to the *AJYB*, 5668 A.M. (1907–1908, Volume 9, pages 424–425), the following cities of West Virginia were listed as having congregations or other Jewish organizations, in the *Directory of Jewish Local Organizations in the United States*:

|            |            |
|------------|------------|
| Bluefield  | Keystone   |
| Charleston | Parkersburg |
| Huntington | Wheeling   |

(For the details, from this point on, *see* the sections dealing with the individual cities and towns of West Virginia.)

In the year 1907–1908 [5668 A.M.], also, only the following three West Virginia congregations were members of the Union of American Hebrew Congregations (U. A. H. C.):

*Charleston*: The Hebrew Educational Society [later, B'nai Israel Congregation — The Virginia Street Temple]. Joined the U. A. H. C. on October 5, 1873.

*Huntington*: Oheb Shalom [Sholem] Congregation. [Later, the congregation changed the spelling of its name, officially, to Oheb Sholom Congregation. Later, also, the Huntington Oheb Sholem Congregation withdrew from the U. A. H. C., but rejoined it a number of years later, on May 31, 1935.]

*Wheeling*: Leshem Shomayim Congregation (joined the U. A.-H. C. on May 8, 1874).

1907

Congregational and Jewish Religious School statistics for West Virginia for the three consecutive ten-year periods of 1907, 1917, and 1927 have been collected, as follows, from the pages of the *AJYB*:

*Schools*:

In *1907*, 6 congregations in West Virginia reported 3 schools.

In *1917*, 6 congregations reported 5 schools.

In *1927*, 23 [?] congregations reported 6 Sabbath schools, 1 weekday school, and 2 weekday and Sabbath schools, or a total of 9 schools.

*Teachers*

In *1907*, 3 congregations in West Virginia reported a total of 13 religious school teachers.

In *1917*, 5 congregations reported a total of 17 teachers.

In *1927*, 6 Sabbath schools reported a total of 37 teachers; 1 weekday school reported 1 teacher; and another weekday school reported having 1 teacher. Two Sabbath schools reported 9 teachers; and 1 weekday school reported 3 teachers.

*Pupils*

In *1907*,  there were 125 pupils in the Jewish congregational schools of West Virginia.

In *1917*,  there were 122 pupils (a rather startling *decline*
of 3 pupils).

In *1927*,  there was a total of 331 pupils in congregations
maintaining only Sabbath schools. There
were 80 pupils, in 1927, in congregations
which maintained both Sabbath Schools and
weekday schools (55 pupils plus 12 pupils
for the two schools, respectively), and thus
in 1927 there were 411 pupils (331 plus 80)
in the Sabbath schools of the State, and 67
in the weekday school, a grand total of 478
Jewish pupils in the Jewish schools of West
Virginia in 1927.

*Value of the Synagogue Buildings*

|  | *1907* | *1917* | *1927* |
|---|---|---|---|
| Number of Congregations with Buildings | 3 | 3 | 7 |
| Value of These Buildings | $75,000 | $73,000 | 6 congregations with buildings valued at $454,000 |

*Debts on Synagogue Buildings*

|  | *1907* | *1917* | *1927* |
|---|---|---|---|
| Number of Congregations | 2 | 1 | 4 |
| Amount of the Debt | $ 4,721 | $ 2,000 | $122,500 |

1908–1909

(*AJYB*, 1908–1909 [5669 A.M.], pages 167–169, 188)

In an article in the above-listed *AJYB*, entitled "Sunday Laws of the United States and Leading Judicial Decisions Having Special Reference to the Jews," written by Albert M. Friedenberg, of the New York Bar, there is the following paragraph:

*West Virginia.* — A fine is imposed upon any person laboring at any trade or calling, or allowing others to so labor, on Sunday. Household duties and the works of necessity or charity excepted.

This provision does not apply to the running of railroad trains or steamboats on Sunday, nor to such persons as conscientiously believe the seventh day of the week ought to be observed as the Sabbath, provided that such persons refrain from secular business and labor on that day. [Sections 4367 and 4368, Code of 1906.]

1910–1911

In 1910–1911, West Virginia had three constituent congregations which were members of the U. A. H. C.:

Charleston: The Hebrew Education Society [later B'nai Israel
     Congregation, or the Virginia Street Temple]
Huntington: Oheb Shalom Congregation
Wheeling: Congregation Leshem Shomayim

1912–1913

(*AJYB*, 1912–1913 [5673 A.M.], page 77)

In 1911–1912, in an article on "Agricultural Activities of the Jews in America," written by Leonard G. Robinson, then general manager of the Jewish Agricultural and Industrial Aid Society, of New York City, the following figures on agriculture among the Jews in West Virginia are given:

Jewish families [farming families], 1
persons estimated, 5
farms, 1
acreage estimated, 104
value of land estimated, $2,735
value of equipment estimated, $521

[i. e., only 1 recorded Jewish family in that year, in West
Virginia, was a farming family, with 1 Jewish farmer]

*(AJYB*, 1913–1914 [5674 A.M.], page 392]

In 1912–1913, West Virginia was recorded as having the
same three congregations which were affiliated members of the
U. A. H. C.:

Charleston: The Hebrew Educational Society
Huntington: Oheb Shalom Congregation
Wheeling: Congregation Leshem Shomayim

1914–1915
*(AJYB*, 1914–1915 [5675 A.M.], page 309)

In 1914, *four* Jewish congregations in West Virginia were
listed as being affiliated with the U. A.H.C., as follows:

Charleston: The Hebrew Educational Society
Clarksburg: Temple Emanuel
Huntington: Oheb Shalom Congregation
Wheeling: Congregation Leshem Shomayim

[However, the Clarksburg Congregation Emanuel did not
survive very long; in the 1920's its members merged with the
newer Tree of Life Congregation (Etz Hayim Congregation).
From 1914 on, apparently, the Emanuel Congregation, while
never having the services of a full-time rabbi, engaged a Hebrew
Union College student for the High Holy Days each year, from
the time of its organizing until its merger with the Tree of Life
Congregation. Two Hebrew Union College students who thus

served Emanuel Congregation for the High Holy Days from
1915 to 1920 were Max Kaufman and Abraham I. Shinedling.]

## 1915–1916
### (*AJYB*, 1915–1916 [5676 A.M.], Volume 17)

In a list of the cities of the United States with more than 1,000
Jewish inhabitants, Charleston alone is listed, in the above-
mentioned source, as having 3,000 [more than 1,000] Jews in
that year. Charleston in 1905 had 142 Jews, and in 1917 it had
190 Jews. The figure of 3,000 Jews for Charleston, W. Va., in
1915–1916 was, apparently, incorrect and excessively high, for
in 1943 Charleston is recorded in the *Universal Jewish Encyclopedia*
[*UJE*] as having only slightly more than 1,500 Jewish population (in the article "West Virginia," in Volume X). A more
proper figure for the Jewish population of Charleston for the
year 1915–1916 would be slightly less than 1,000.

## 1917–1918

In 1917, the three largest centers of Jewish population in
West Virginia were as follows:

> Charleston:   1,000 Jews (estimated
> Huntington:    310 Jews
> Wheeling:     1,000 Jews (estimated)

In 1917, in cities of West Virginia having a general population
of between 1,000 and 20,000, the following figures of Jewish
population are presented in the *American Jewish Year Book*:

### *Jewish Population of West Virginia (1917)*

| | | | | | |
|---|---|---|---|---|---|
| Bluefield | 152 | Elkins | 12 | Kimball | 45 |
| Bramwell | 5 | Fairmont | 95 | Morgantown | 120 |
| Clarksburg | 245 | Gary | 6 | Parkersburg | 400 |

[The figure for Clarksburg is in all likelihood a bit too high.
The figure of 400 Jews for Parkersburg in 1917 is incorrect, and

excessively high. It is doubtful whether the Jewish community of Parkersburg in 1917 numbered more than 100 persons in all. As will be seen from the lists given later on in this volume, in 1937 the city of Parkersburg is recorded as having only 125 Jews, and the Parkersburg community is one which has seen a constant, although small and slow, rise in its Jewish population, not a decline at any time.]

[Omitted from the above list is the city of Beckley, presumably owing to the fact that as early as the year 1917 it had no organized Jewish congregation, and therefore sent in no report, or was asked for none. In 1917, as nearly as could be ascertained, Beckley had a Jewish population of some 10 families, or about 35 individuals, and, in addition, there were some half a dozen Jewish families living in nearby Fayette County. In 1921, there were 10 or 12 Jewish families in Beckley, and three single men, a total of about 40 Jewish individuals, as well as half a dozen or more Jewish families in contiguous Fayette County.]

In 1917–1918, out of a total Jewish population in the United States of 3,390,572 (forming 3.2% of the total general population), the Jews of West Virginia numbered 5,129.

In the following year, also, i. e., in the year 1918, at a time when the general population of the United States was reckoned at 103,000,000, and the general population of West Virginia was estimated to be 1,439,165, the same Jewish population of the State was given, i. e., 5,129. This figure of 5,129 Jews in West Virginia in 1917–1918 represents a great increase, of 3,617 Jews, over the estimated 1,500 [an inaccurate, round-number figure] Jewish population of West Virginia for 1907 (as given in the *AJYB*).

In 1917, in addition to the above-mentioned cities, 92 small towns in West Virginia had a total Jewish population of 2,819. Charleston, with an estimated 1,000 Jews; Wheeling, with an estimated 1,000 also; and Huntington, with 310 Jews; and the other 92 towns, with 2,819 Jewish population, thus made up the grand total of 5,129 for the Jewish population of the State in 1917. These estimated figures are presented by Dr. Harry S. Linfield, of the Jewish Statistical Bureau, of New York, in the *AJYB*.

## 1917–1918

In 1917–1918 (5678 A.M.), four rabbis were serving congregations in West Virginia, as recorded in the *AJYB* for 1917–1918 (pp. 367–395), in a "List of Rabbis and Instructors in Jewish Colleges in the United States," for the year 1916–1917:

*Charleston:* Virginia Street Temple, or Congregation B'nai Israel: Israel Bettan.

[Nachman Heller, listed in 1917–1918 as the rabbi of Congregation Adereth El in New York City, also served as a rabbi in Charleston, W. Va. (Orthodox), in 1916–1917.]

Congregation B'nai Jacob: David Stern, of 416 State Street.

*Huntington*: [S.] Felix Mendelsohn, of Oheb Shalom Congregation.

[S. Felix Mendelsohn (or Samuel Felix Mendelsohn; his name is erroneously spelled with the double *s* as Mendelssohn) was, in that year, a senior student at the Hebrew Union College, and served the Huntington congregation as the bi-weekly, part-time student rabbi.]

*Wheeling*: Congregation Ohev Sholom, at 1433 South Street: M. Nathanson, of 98 15th Street, Wheeling, rabbi.

[In 1918–1919, Louis A. Mischkind, a graduate of the Hebrew Union College, of Cincinnati, of the Class of June, 1918, served the Wheeling Congregation Leshem Shomayim as rabbi. Before him, in the two-year period 1915 to 1917, Abba Hillel Silver served as the rabbi of Congregation Leshem Shomayim, in Wheeling. In 1917–1918, Louis D. Gross served as rabbi of the Wheeling Reform congregation Leshem Shomayim (*CCAR Yearbook*, Volume XXVII, 1917, page 402), and his name was apparently omitted, through inadvertence, from the above list. Thus, actually, in the year 1916–1917, six rabbis, and not four, were serving congregations in West Virginia, the names of two of them having been omitted through error.]

1917–1919

*The First World War*

A number of West Virginia Jews served in the United States
Army in the First World War, from 1917 to 1918, or from 1917
to 1919. Details are given further on in this chapter, under the
subheading of West Virginia Jews in Military Service. These
Jewish servicemen of the First World War included:

Herbert W. Emsheimer, of Wheeling, a lieutenant
Irving Goldstein, of Beckley
Benson Lubin, of Huntington, a 2nd lieutenant
Jacob R. Marcus, of Farmington, a 2nd lieutenant
Hubert May, of Charleston, a lieutenant
James Pickus, of Beckley, a private
Philip E. Schaffer, of Charleston, a lieutenant
William Schaffer, of Charleston, a lieutenant
Irvin Schwabe, of Charleston, a lieutenant
Jesse Speyer, of Wheeling, a lieutenant

1917–1919

According to the *AJYB* for 5679 A.M. (1918–1919, Volume
20), the following was the Jewish population of the several
larger cities of West Virginia in 1917–1919:

*Charleston*: 1,000 Jews (out of a total general population of
22,996)

*Huntington*: 310 Jews (out of a total general population of
between 20,000 and 50,000)

*Weirton*: 69 Jews (in 1917) (out of a total general population of
less than 1,000)

*Wheeling*: 1,000 Jews (estimated) (out of a total general population of 43,972)

Strangely enough, the "town" of Caso, W. Va., is also
listed as having 10 Jews in 1917, out of a total general

population of less than 1,000 persons. It is difficult to identify this locality of Caso, W. Va., today. It is, in all probability, an error in printing for Cass, W. Va., in Pocahontas County, located in east central West Virginia, not far from the Virginia border and southeast of Webster Springs.

## 1919–1920

### (*AJYB*, 1919–1920 [5680 A.M.], page 332)

Of the 13 congregations in the State in 1919–1920, with only seven reporting, only 1 of them held daily religious services, and 2 held services only on the Sabbath and on holidays. One congregation held religious services only on the festivals. Of these 13 congregations, 5 held services only in Hebrew, 1 in Hebrew and English, and 1 in English only. For these facts and data, only 7 out of the 13 congregations in West Virginia in that year furnished information.

### (*AJYB*, 1919–1920 [5680 A.M.], page 333)

#### MEMBERSHIP AND RELIGIOUS SCHOOLS OF CONGREGATIONS

There were 13 congregations in the State in 1919–1920, of which 5 reported, with a total membership of 346. [The other 8 congregations in the State, to which requests or questionnaires were sent for information and data, did not even deign to reply.]

8 religious schools reported, with 37 classes and 401 pupils.

### (*AJYB*, 1919–1920 [5680 A.M.], page 334)

In West Virginia, in 1919–1920, in addition to congregations, there were 3 charitable organizations, 3 educational organizations, and 3 cemeteries (with cemetery organizations) in the State.

Louis Horkheimer, of Wheeling, assisted the editors of the *American Jewish Year Book* in compiling its Directory of Jewish

Local Organizations in the United States, published in the
*AJYB* for 1919–1920 [5680 A.M.] (pp. 330–583).


1920

In 1920, West Virginia had an estimated Jewish population
of 5,440, out of a total general State population of 1,463,701.
At this time the entire Jewish population of the United States
was given as 3,604,580 (1920), and the total general population
of the United States was given as 104,709,619.

The two largest centers of Jewish population in the State in
1920 were:

*Charleston,* with an estimated 1,000 Jews, out of a total general
population of 39,608, according to the United States Census
for 1920. Other estimates of the Jewish population of
Charleston in 1920 range as high as 1,900.

*Wheeling,* with 1,000 Jews (estimated), out of a total general
population of 56,208. Wheeling was then the largest city
in the State. In the thirty years following, both Huntington
and Charleston outstripped Wheeling in general and Jewish
population.

In 1920, the Jewish population of West Virginia was
only .4% (four-tenths of 1 per cent) of the total general
population of the State.

Other cities in West Virginia at that time (1920) had
the following estimated Jewish populations:

| | |
|---|---|
| Beckley: 50 | Huntington: 310 |
| Bluefield: 152 | Kimball: no estimate |
| Charles Town: 26 | Martinsburg: no estimate |
| Clarksburg: 245 | Morgantown: 120 |
| Fairmont: 95 (in 1919–1920) | Parkersburg: no estimate |

No figures of Jewish population are given, for 1920, for the
following eleven cities and towns of West Virginia, which later
came to have reportable Jewish populations, and which at that
time had unknown Jewish populations:

| | |
|---|---|
| Kimball | Thomas |
| Keystone | Weirton |
| Logan | Welch |
| North Fork | Weston |
| Parkersburg | Williamson |
| Princeton | |

## 1919–1922

Local Jewish organizations existing in West Virginia in the three-year period from 1919 to 1922 are listed in the *AJYB* for 1919 to 1921 (Volumes 21 to 23) as follows: (For the details, see the sections dealing with the individual cities.) The Jewish population, estimated or definitely known, is also listed for some of these cities at the same time:

*Bluefield*: Congregation Ahabath Sholom [correct spelling: Ahavath Sholom]
   Jewish population, 152

*Charleston*: B'nai Israel Hebrew Educational Society (the Virginia Street Temple) [Reform]
   B'nai Jacob Congregation [Orthodox]
   Young Men's Hebrew Association
   Young Women's Hebrew Association
   Spring Hill Cemetery
   Jewish population: 1,000 (estimated)
   Charleston-Kanawha Jewish Federated Charities

*Charles Town*: Congregation B'nai Jacob [presumably in Charleston; listed in Charles Town by error]
   Jewish population: 26

*Clarksburg*: Temple Emanu-El [Emanuel]
   [The] Hebrew Congregation of Clarksburg
   Jewish population: 245

*Fairmont*: Congregation Beth Israel
   B'nai B'rith Religious School
   Jewish population: 95

*Huntington*: Congregation Bene [Bnai] Israel [Orthodox]
    Congregation Oheb Sholom [Reform]
    Temple Sewing Society
    Temple Juniors
    Community Center
    Temple Benevolent Sewing Society
    Cemetery Association
    Jewish population: 310

*Kimball*: Congregation Beth Jacob

*Martinsburg*: Beth Jacob Congregation

*Morgantown*: Morgantown Congregation [later known as the
    Tree of Life Congregation]
    Jewish population: 120

*Parkersburg*: Congregation B'nai Israel

*Wheeling*: Congregation Leshem Shomayim [Reform] [The Eoff
    Street Temple]
    Congregation Ohav Sholem [Orthodox]
    Young Men's Hebrew Association
    Ladies' Hebrew Benevolent Society, Temple Leshem
    Shomayim
    United Hebrew Charities of Wheeling
    Mount Wood Cemetery
    Jewish population, 1,000 (estimated)


1922–1923

Four West Virginia Jews are mentioned briefly in a list entitled, "Jews of Prominence in the United States," compiled by I. George Dobsevage, and published in the *AJYB* for 1922–1923 [5683 A.M.] (pp. 109–218). These four were:

> Aaron Arkin, of Morgantown
> Bertram Frankenberger, of Charleston
> Samuel Frankenberger, of Charleston
> Benjamin L. Rosenbloom, of Wheeling

## 1927

In 1927, in a list (given in the *AJYB*) of independent Jewish communities in the United States, and in a list of the congregations, those in West Virginia were listed as follows:

| Name of the Principal Community | Number of Congregations Reported | Number of Jews |
|---|---|---|
| Bluefield | 1 | 220 |
| Charleston | 2 | 1,200[1] |
| Clarksburg | 2 | 235 |
| Fairmont | 1 | 140 |
| Huntington | 2 | 1,125[2] |
| Keystone | 1 | 37 |
| Kimball | 1 | 42 |
| Logan | 1 | 116 |
| Martinsburg | 1 | 304[3] |
| Morgantown | 2 | 250 |
| North Fork | 1 | 74 |
| Parkersburg | 1 | 98 |
| Princeton | 1 | 41[4] |
| Welch | 1 | 81 |
| Weston | 1 | 95 |
| Wheeling | 3 | 750 |
| Williamson | 1 | 128 |

According to the *AJYB* for 1928–1929 (5689 A.M., page 201), dealing with the year 1927 (or the year 1927–1928), West Virginia had a total of 17 Jewish congregations, with 5,059

---

[1] Out of a total general population of 51,236 in 1927.

[2] Out of a total general population of 65,100. Huntington had seemingly supplanted Wheeling as the largest city in the State.

[3] This figure of 304 Jews in Martinsburg is obviously and ridiculously much too high. A more likely population figure for Martinsburg, in 1927, would be about 20 to 25 Jewish families, with between 90 to 100 persons, but this is obviously mere guesswork.

[4] In 1927, the Princeton Jews had not yet affiliated with the Bluefield Congregation Ahavath Sholom.

members (individuals, not families, and obviously including also
the Jewish women and children).

8 congregations reported current expenditures of $51,781.

9 of these 17 congregations reported current annual expenditures of $66,981, presumably including some of
those mentioned among the 8 below.

1 congregation reported $12,500 in current annual ex-
penditures.

Thus a total of 9 congregations reported current annual
expenditures of $63,781.

6 of these 17 congregations reported the value of their
synagogue buildings in that year as $454,000.

Charitable expenditures reported as benevolences in 1927:
3 congregations in West Virginia reported expenditures
of $3,200.

Thus, including charitable expenditures, the total amount
of money expended by 9 congregations in West Virginia
for current expenditures for 1927 amounted to $66,981.

Places in West Virginia having 10 Jews or less in 1927 were:

| | |
|---|---|
| Berkeley Springs | Matewan |
| Bramwell | Piedmont |
| Buckhannon | Richwood |
| Franklin | Sistersville |

Each of these communities had several Jews, but not more
than ten, in 1927.

1927 figures for Jewish communal organizations in West
Virginia indicate the following (*AJYB*, 1929–1930 [5690 A.M.],
page 106):

| | Number of Congregations in the State | Number of Jews in the State |
|---|---|---|
| *1907* | 6 | 1,500 |
| *1917* | 6 | 5,129 |
| *1927* | 23 | 7,471 |

Thus, in 1907, the entire State of West Virginia had 6 congregations and some 1,500 Jews.

In 1917, there were 6 congregations and 5,129 Jews in the State. In that same year, despite the increase in the Jewish population from 1,500 to 5,129, there were still only 6 Jewish congregations in the entire State, that is, only 6 were reported. It is possible that other congregations existed, but were not reported, or were not yet reported.

In 1927, there were 17 principal Jewish communities and 23 congregations, and a total of 7,471 Jews in the State.

Of the Jewish population of 7,471 living in West Virginia in 1927, the Jews living in places having congregations (i. e., Jews residing in the 17 principal Jewish communities of the State) totalled 4,936. Jews who were living, in 1927, in places in West Virginia not having congregations (Jews in the dependent communities) totalled 2,535. Thus, 33.93%, or just slightly over one-third, of the Jews living in West Virginia in 1927 lived in places without Jewish congregations.

These same above figures were repeated in the *AJYB* for 1929–1930 (5690 A.M.), page 124.

According to the 1927–1928 *AJYB* report, places in West Virginia reported Jewish populations as follows, or figures were estimated for them, in some cases rather wildly and erroneously, as may be seen from the several notes following these figures:

| | |
|---|---|
| Bath District (Hancock), Morgan County 36 | Elkins 25 |
| Beckley 51 | Fairmont 140 |
| Bluefield 220 | Grafton 26 |
| Charleston 1,200 | Huntington 1,125[1] |
| Charles Town 32 | Keyser 20 |
| Chester Town 16 | Keystone 37 |
| Clarksburg 235 | Kimball 42 |
| | Logan 116[2] |

---

[1] The figure for Huntington is too high. Cf. the figure of 810 Jews for Huntington under the year 1937 below, which is more reasonable than the alleged 1,125 Jewish population for that city in 1927.

[2] The figure for Logan is also too high. Cf. under the year 1937, below, where the Jewish population of Logan is given as about 80.

Marlinton 11                          Parkersburg 392[3]
Martinsburg 304[1]                    Princeton 41
Montgomery 47                         Thomas 37
Morgantown 250[2]                     Wellsburg 12
Moundsville 33                        Weston 95[4]
Mount Hope 18                         Wheeling 750
New Martinsville 15                   Williamson 128
North Fork 74

No figure for Weirton is given for 1927–1928. Many of the figures are more or less inaccurate, and are the result of mere guesswork, or of exaggerated reporting.

In the *AJYB* for 1927–1928 (5688 A.M., Volume 29), for the first time, the name of a West Virginia Jewish welfare federation occurs. This was the Associated Jewish Charities of Wheeling, with Herbert O. Baer as its director, and with 500 members, and a total annual income of $5,000. [The number of members given, 500 (page 214), would appear to be excessively high, and incorrect, and possibly a typographical error for 50 or for 150.] In Volume 39 of the *AJYB*, page 721, for 5698 A.M.

---

[1] The figure of 304 Jewish population for Martinsburg in 1927–1928 is still excessively high and, undoubtedly, grossly incorrect. In all probability, a figure of between 60 and 75, or possibly between 90 to 100 persons, as stated above, would be more accurate — it is merely an estimate — for the Jewish population of Martinsburg in 1927. In 1937, the Jewish community of Martinsburg reported a Jewish population of 120.

[2] The figure of 250 Jews for Morgantown in 1927 is also excessively high. In all likelihood, 100 Jews, or a few more, would be a more accurate figure. Even in 1937, ten years later, Morgantown reported a Jewish population of only 132.

[3] As previously stated for a preceding year, the figure of 392 for the Jewish population of Parkersburg, for the year 1927, is excessively high, and totally incorrect. One wonders where such reports as those for Martinsburg, Morgantown, and Parkersburg could have originated, and on what they were based. The correct figure for the Jewish population of Parkersburg in 1927 would be much closer to 100. The figure of 392 was later changed to 98 in the *AJYB*, and in 1937 the population of the Parkersburg Jewish community was reported as 125, the latter an eminently correct figure.

[4] The figure of 95 for the Jewish population of Weston in 1927 is apparently much too high. A more accurate figure for Weston for 1927 would be about 25 Jews. In 1937, the Jewish population of Weston was much more soberly reported as 31.

(1937–1938), it is stated that the address of the (not Associated but) Federated Jewish Charities, of Wheeling, was 16th and Main Streets; that Herbert O. Baer was still its director; that it was founded in the year 1925; that it was not incorporated; that it was affiliated with the community chest; and that it was primarily a family welfare agency, with expenditures, in 1936, of $2,000. [Hence the figure for 1927–1928 of an annual expenditure or income of $5,000 is also probably excessive.] At its first mention by name in the *AJYB* for 1927–1928, Volume 28 [5688 A.M.], pages 214 and 217, its address is given in that year as 12th and Chapline Streets, no doubt the business office then of its secretary or director. At that time it was the only Jewish federated charity organization or Jewish welfare federation in the entire State of West Virginia. Later, other such Jewish charitable federations, all of them still in existence in 1959, were organized in the three cities of Bluefield, Charleston, and Huntington.

## 1928–1929

The Jewish population of West Virginia in the year 1928–1929 was still given as 7,471, out of an estimated total general State population of 1,696,000 (according to the *AJYB* for the year 5689 A.M., 1928–1929, Volume 30). [Obviously, no attempt was made, that year, to secure newer figures for the State.] In 1927, the estimated Jewish population of the entire United States was 4,228,029. In 1927, 203 places in West Virginia reported having Jews, to the total number of 5,517. Eight places in West Virginia, in that year, having from 2,500 to 5,000 population, reported 217 Jews out of a total general population of 49,646. Six places with 5,000 to 10,000 general population reported having 335 Jews out of a total general population of 40,052. Six places of from 10,000 to 25,000 general population reported having 1,344 Jews out of a total general population of 88,494. Jews in urban places of 25,000 population and over in West Virginia in 1927–1928 were reported to number 3,310 out of a total general population of 222,066 for cities of 25,000 to 100,000 population, or 1.49% of the urban population of the

State. [There were only three cities in this highest population category in that year: Charleston, Huntington, and Wheeling.]

## 1929–1930

With eight congregations reporting, $63,781 per annum was the sum total of the current expenses of the Jewish congregations of West Virginia, and also an additional annual amount of $3,200 was raised and expended in the State for and as benevolence (*AJYB*, 1929–1930 [5690 A.M.], page 207).

## 1930

In the 1930 *AJYB*, the Jewish population of the State was still given as 7,471 (no new figures were involved), out of a total general (increased) State population of 1,729,205. Charleston, Huntington, and Wheeling were still the three cities in the State with the largest Jewish populations, in that order. In 1930, these three cities had Jewish populations (in each case, merely an estimate) as follows:

Charleston: 1,200 (out of a total general population of 51,236)
Huntington: 1,200 (out of a total general population of 75,575)
Wheeling: less than 1,000

The above figures for the Jewish population are the same as those for 1927, no new estimates having been made, and no new figures having been gathered, in the three years from 1927 to 1930. The figures for both Huntington and Wheeling were, presumably, much too high. In 1937, Huntington was credited with only about 800 Jews, so that the 1930 figure of 1,200 would appear to be four or five hundred too high. The Jewish population of Wheeling, in 1930, was perhaps not much more than 800 to 900, or even less than 900. In 1930–1931, Charleston had a Jewish population of 1,250 Jews, out of a total general population of 60,411.

## 1936

In 1936, the United States census of religious bodies reported the following facts about Jews and Jewry in West Virginia, on the basis of questionnaires sent out by its director, Dr. Harry S. Linfield, of New York City:

22 Jewish congregations were in the State [in 16 principal Jewish communities].

20 of these congregations were in urban centers, and only 2 were in rural sections of the State.

The membership of individual Jews [presumably including wives, children, and unmarried persons] in these 22 congregations totalled 5,391.

15 of the Jewish congregations had religious schools.

537 children were in attendance at these 15 religious schools, the largest ones being in Charleston, Huntington, and Wheeling.

Wheeling had 3 Jewish congregations in 1936–1937, and Charleston and Huntington each had 2 Jewish congregations.

[A survey made previously, in and for the year 1900, had yielded a total of only 3 Jewish congregations in West Virginia, with 168 members. A later survey, or estimate, made in 1927, and cited above, indicated a total of 17 Jewish congregations, with 5,059 individual Jews.]

## 1937

In 1937, the two largest Jewish communities in West Virginia were:

*Charleston*: 2,540 Jews, out of a total general population of 67,914 (1940 United States Census, later).

[The Charleston Jewish populational figure is, in all probability, almost 1,000 too high. Elsewhere, the Jewish population of Charleston in 1937 is stated to be about 1,500.]

*Wheeling*: 1,150 Jews, out of a total general city population of 61,099 (United States Census of 1940, later).

[Huntington is not included in this report, which embraced only cities having 1,000 or more Jewish population. In 1937, Huntington presumably had between 800 to 850 Jews.]

In the *AJYB* for the year 5698 A.M. (Volume 39, 1937–1938), the only Jewish community having a federated Jewish charitable organization in the entire State of West Virginia is listed (on page 721) as Wheeling, which is credited (no doubt erroneously, as too low a figure; cf. above, where its Jewish population is given as 1,150 in 1937, which is too high) with the possession of 750 Jews. For the year 1937–1938, two Jewish charitable organizations in Wheeling are listed, as follows:

*Federated Jewish Charities*

> 16th and Main Streets
> H.[erbert] O. Baer, director
> Established in 1925   Not incorporated
> Affiliated with the Community Chest of the city
> Primarily a family welfare agency
> $2,000 expenditures in 1936

*Jewish Central Committee*

> A member of the Council of Jewish Federations and Welfare
>    Funds
> Sig.[mund] J. Front, chairman
> Ralph L. Miller, secretary
> Conducts a campaign for non-local causes

In 1937, the Jewish population of the various cities and towns in West Virginia was reported as follows:

| *City or Place* | *Number of Jews* |
| --- | --- |
| Bath District (Hancock), Morgan County | 36 |
| Beckley | 65[1] |
| Bluefield | 210 |

---

[1] In all probability, this figure of 65 for Beckley is quite a bit too low, unless nearby Sophia, Mount Hope, and Oak Hill are not included. In all likelihood, in 1937 Beckley had about 100 Jews, two years after the forming of the congregation there, in 1934–1935, with 29 charter [family] members (several of them from Oak Hill and from Mount Hope).

| City or Place | Number of Jews |
|---|---|
| Buckhannon | 15 |
| Butler District, Hancock County (Weirton) | 150 |
| Charleston | 1,500 |
| Charles Town | 20 |
| Chester | 25 |
| Clarksburg | 300[1] |
| Court House District (Taylor County) | 41 |
| Dunbar | 16 |
| Fairmont | 235[2] |
| Grafton | 38 |
| Huntington | 810 |
| Keyser | 20 |
| Keystone | 75 |
| Kimball | 18 |
| Logan | 83 |
| Martinsburg | 120[3] |
| Montgomery | 56 |
| Morgantown | 132 |
| Moundsville | 16 |
| Mount Hope | 18 |
| New Martinsville | 15 |
| North Fork | 58 |
| Parkersburg | 125 |
| Princeton | 40 |
| Thomas | 37 |
| War | 12 |

[1] The figure of 300 Jewish population for Clarksburg in 1937 is perhaps quite a bit too high. As will be seen in statistical lists of the Jewish population of West Virginia cities further on in this volume, Clarksburg, ten years later, in 1947, was reported to have only 269 Jews; in 1951, 270 Jews; and in 1956, 280 Jews.

[2] The figure of 235 Jewish population for Fairmont in 1937 is also, seemingly, quite a bit too high. Later lists give the Jewish population of Fairmont thus: in 1947, 160 Jews; in 1951, also 160; and in 1956, 200 Jews.

[3] The figure of 120 Jews for Martinsburg would appear to have been much too high. I would much prefer to estimate the Jewish population of Martinsburg, in 1937, at between 75 to 80, perhaps with 20 to 25 Jewish families.

| City or Place | Number of Jews |
|---|---|
| (Weirton; *see* Butler District, Hancock County) | |
| Welch | 70 |
| Wellsburg | 35 |
| Weston | 31 |
| Wheeling | 1,150 |
| Williamson | 135 |
| Total | 5,607 |

In addition to the larger cities, towns, and places listed above, the following localities in West Virginia each had ten or fewer Jews in the year 1937:

Berkeley Springs
Bramwell
Cass District (Osage),
    Monongalia County
Cedar Grove
Clendenin
East Bank (near
    Charleston)
Elkins
Kermit
Logan District (Holden),
    Logan County

Man Town
Marlinton
Monongah
New Cumberland
Salem
Shinnston
Sistersville
Triadelphia District
    (Becco), Logan County

## 1939–1940

In 1937, according to figures prepared for the *AJYB* by Dr. Harry S. Linfield, director of the Jewish Statistical Bureau (New York), West Virginia had a total Jewish population of 7,980, out of a total general population of 1,860,000 (*AJYB*, 5700 A.M., 1939–1940, Volume 41). The Jewish population of the State was thus 0.43% of the total general population.

In the year 1939, there were 5 Jewish federations and welfare funds or affiliated organizations in West Virginia; 1 of these was in Charleston, 1 in Huntington, and 3 in Wheeling, as follows:

*Charleston*: The Federated Jewish Charity Fund
Frank Baer and Harry Silverstein, co-chairmen

*Huntington*: The United Jewish Fund, organized in 1938
Samuel Samson was its executive chairman in 1939–1940.

*Wheeling*: The Jewish Central Committee, organized in 1933
Ernest S. Horkheimer was its president in 1939–1940.
Ralph L. Miller was its secretary in 1939–1940.

The Federated Jewish Charities
The Coordinating Committee for German Refugees
Sigmund S. Front was its chairman in 1939–1940.
William Combs was its secretary in 1939–1940.

## 1940

In 1940, the Jews of West Virginia numbered only 7,213 out of a total general population of 1,901,974 (1940 United States Census), according to revised figures. The figure of 7,213 Jews in the State is as of 1937. Thus they formed, at that time, 0.39% of the total population of the State, and they represented 0.15% of the total Jewish population of the United States.

In 1940, there were reported to be in West Virginia 16 principal Jewish communities, with 22 congregations.

## 1940–1941

(From the *AJYB*, 5701 A.M. [1940–1941], Volume 42)

Dr. Harry S. Linfield, director of the Jewish Statistical Bureau (the Statistical Bureau of the Synagogue Council of America), presented the following statistics and figures for the State of West Virginia for the year 1937:

United States, total population in 1937: 129,257,000
Jewish population of the United States in 1937: 4,770,647
Jewish population of West Virginia in 1937: 7,213
   (out of the total general State population of 1,865,000)
Jewish population of West Virginia: 0.39% of the total general
      State population

Principal Jewish Communities of West Virginia, Number of Congregations, and Number of Jews, by the Name of the Community, in 1937:

(For the Jewish population of Beckley, Clarksburg, Fairmont, and Martinsburg, in the list below, cf. the notes to these cities in the preceding population statistics.)

| Principal Community | Number of Congregations Reported | Number of Jews |
|---|---|---|
| Beckley | 1 | 65 |
| Bluefield | 1 | 210 |
| Butler District (Hancock County) (Weirton) | 1 | 350[1] |
| Charleston | 2 | 1,500 |
| Clarksburg | 2 | 300 |
| Fairmont | 2 | 235 |
| Huntington | 2 | 810 |
| Keystone | 1 | 75 |
| Logan | 1 | 83 |
| Martinsburg | 1 | 120 |
| Morgantown | 1 | 132 |
| Parkersburg | 1 | 125 |
| (Weirton; *see* Butler District) | | |
| Welch | 1 | 70 |
| Weston | 1 | 31 |
| Wheeling | 3 | 1,150 |
| Williamson | 1 | 135 |
| Total | 16 | 5,321 |

[1] The figure for Weirton, for 1937, would appear to be much too high.

## 1941–1942

Jewish Federations and Welfare Funds in Existence in West Virginia in 1941–1942

The Jewish Federations and Welfare Funds in the State, in 1941–1942, numbered 4, as follows:

*Bluefield*: The Bluefield-Princeton Jewish Charities
Organized in 1939, and including the whole of Mercer County
Max Matz, president; Rabbi Julius Kravetz, secretary

*Charleston*: Federated Jewish Charities, including Montgomery, W. Va.
Organized in 1937
Alvin J. Lindenberg, president; Mrs. A. M. Rosenblatt, secretary

*Huntington*: Federated Jewish Charities
Organized in 1939
D. [Dez] C. Schonthal, president; Aaron C. Cohen, secretary

*Wheeling*: Jewish Community Council (including Moundsville, W. Va.)
Organized in 1933
John Wiseman, president; Sam Crone, secretary

## 1945–1946

In 1945–1946, there were 6 permanent (resident, full-time) rabbis in West Virginia, and 4 student rabbis from the Hebrew Union College, in Cincinnati.

The permanent rabbis of the State included:

Lawrence A. Block, of Huntington
Louis J. Cashdan, of Charleston
David Herson, of Morgantown
Charles B. Lesser, of Wheeling
Jacob Soshuk, of Beckley

The student rabbis (rabbinical students) were in Bluefield, Logan, Parkersburg, and Williamson, all of them from the Hebrew Union College, in Cincinnati.

## 1946–1947

There were still four Jewish welfare federations in the State in 1946–1947, as follows:

*Bluefield*:     Bluefield-Princeton Charities
              Organized in 1939

*Charleston*:  Federated Jewish Charities (including Dunbar and
                   Montgomery)
              Organized in 1937
              Samuel D. Lopinsky, president

*Huntington*:  Federated Jewish Charities
              Organized in 1939
              M. D. Friedman, president

*Wheeling*:    Jewish Community Council and Federated Jewish
                   Charities
              Organized in 1933

## 1948

In 1948, Charleston was the only city in the State with an estimated Jewish population of 1,000 or more. (These figures are taken from the *AJYB*, Volume 51 [5709 A.M.], 1950.) The total general population of Charleston in that year was 67,914 (United States Census of 1940), and the Jewish population of Charleston was estimated, in 1948, at 2,000. Elsewhere in this same volume the Jewish population of Charleston was stated to be 1,200, but it seems unquestionable that this latter figure is too low, and that 2,000 is much more accurate, especially since only a year or two thereafter Charleston was reported to have 2,200 Jews.

Huntington, in 1948, had an estimated Jewish population of about 700, instead of the rather high figure of 810 given for 1937.

Wheeling, by 1948, had fallen in Jewish population (presumably through emigration from the city) from over 1,000 to about 800. (This, unless it be assumed that the previous figures of 1,000 and of 1,150 for its Jewish population were exaggerated, or a bit too high.) Even in 1956, the Jewish population of Wheeling was still reported as 800.

1948–1949
(*AJYB*, 1948–1949, Volume 50 [5609 A.M.])

COMMUNITIES OF WEST VIRGINIA IN 1948 WITH
100 OR MORE JEWISH POPULATION

| Name of the Community | Estimated Jewish Population 1948 | Estimated Jewish Population 1937 |
|---|---|---|
| Beckley | 142 | 65 |
| Bluefield (including Princeton) | 300 | 210 |
| Charleston | 2,000 | 1,500 |
| Clarksburg | 269 | 300 |
| Fairmont | 160 | 235 |
| Huntington | 700 | 810 |
| Morgantown | 211 | 132 |
| Parkersburg | 100 | 125 |
| Weirton | 300 | (no figures) |
| Welch | 104 | 70 |
| Wheeling | 800 | 1,150 |
| Williamson | 173 | 135 |

(In 1950, according to the United States Census, the State had a total general population of 2,005,552.)

DISTRIBUTION OF ENROLLMENT IN WEST VIRGINIA BY
TYPES OF INSTITUTIONS, BY AREAS, AND BY STATES

(From the *AJYB*, Volume 50, 1948–1949)

## *WEST VIRGINIA*

| Universities in West Virginia Total Number of Students | Jewish Students | Colleges Total Number Students | Jewish Students |
|---|---|---|---|
| 6,598 | 152 | 10,268 | 135 |

Many of these Jewish students were from out of the State.

| Junior Colleges in West Virginia Total Number of Students | Jewish Students |
|---|---|
| 904 | 8 |

| Teachers' Colleges Total Number of Students | Jewish Students |
|---|---|
| 3,688 | 6 |

1950

(From the *AJYB*, 1951, Volume 52)

CITIES IN WEST VIRGINIA WITH 100 OR MORE JEWISH
POPULATION IN THE YEAR 1950 (1950 ESTIMATES)

| Name of the City | Jewish Population |
|---|---|
| Beckley | 228 |
| (including Mount Hope and Oak Hill, in nearby Fayette County) | |
| Bluefield | 300 |
| (including Princeton) | |
| Charleston | 2,200 |
| Clarksburg | 270 |
| Fairmont | 160 |

| Name of the City | Jewish Population |
|---|---|
| Huntington | 700 |
| Morgantown | 211 |
| Parkersburg | 100[1] |
| Weirton | 300 |
| Welch | 144 |
| Wheeling | 800 |
| Williamson | 173 |

1954 and 1954–1955

(From the *AJYB*, 1954, Volume 55)

COMMUNITIES IN WEST VIRGINIA WITH JEWISH
POPULATIONS OF 100 OR MORE, ESTIMATED,
1954 AND 1954–1955:

| City | Jewish Population |
|---|---|
| Beckley (including Mount Hope and Oak Hill) | 228 |
| Bluefield (including Princeton) | 300 |
| Charleston | 2,200 |
| Clarksburg | 225 (1956 estimate: 300; another estimate for 1954–1955: 280) |
| Fairmont | 200 |
| Huntington | 700 (1946 estimate: 750; another estimate for 1954–1955: 750) |
| Logan | 25 families |
| Morgantown | 211 (another estimate for 1954–1955: 150) |

---

[1] Much too low. The figure for Parkersburg's Jewish population, in 1950, should be between 175 and 200.

| City | Jewish Population |
|------|-------------------|
| Parkersburg | 100 |

(again, much too low. More accurately, about 225)

| | |
|------|-------------------|
| Weirton | 300 |

(1956 estimate: 350)

| | |
|------|-------------------|
| Welch | 144 |

(including Kimball, War,
   and other nearby towns)

| | |
|------|-------------------|
| Wheeling | 800 |
| Williamson | 180 |
| Total in 1954: | 5,632 |

Other cities, towns, localities, or communities in West Virginia with some Jewish population in 1954 were: (The exact figures are not known.)

| | | |
|---|---|---|
| Charles Town | Martinsburg | Richwood |
| Dunbar | Montgomery | Romney |
| Elkins | Moundsville | Thomas |
| Harpers Ferry | Mount Hope | War |
| Institute | Mullens | Webster Springs |
| Keyser | North Fork | Wellsburg |
| Keystone | Oak Hill | Weston |
| Kimball | Piedmont | |

## 1955

According to the *77th-80th Annual Reports* of the Union of American Hebrew Congregations, issued in December, 1955, the following nine Reform Jewish congregations in West Virginia were members of the U. A. H. C.:

| City | Congregation | Joined the U. A. H. C. | Contributing Members |
|------|--------------|------------------------|----------------------|
| Bluefield | Ahavath Sholom | December 8, 1947 | 85 |
| Charleston | B'nai Israel (The Virginia Street Temple) | October 5, 1873 | 260 |

| City | Congregation | Joined the U. A. H. C. | Contributing Members |
|------|-------------|----------------------|---------------------|
| Huntington | Oheb Sholom (better spelled as Ohev Sholom) | May 31, 1935 | 150 |
| Logan | B'nai El | October 26, 1926 | 25 |
| Martinsburg | Beth Jacob | April 18, 1953 | 15 |
| Parkersburg | B'nai Israel | April 3, 1939 | 45 |
| Welch | Emanuel | June 22, 1950 | 19 |
| Wheeling | L'Shem Shomayim (The Eoff Street Temple) | May 8, 1874 | 100 |
| Williamson | B'nai Israel | May 28, 1922 | 39 |

Three Reform congregations of larger size in the State: Beth El Congregation in Beckley, The Fairmont Jewish Community Center in Fairmont, and the Tree of Life Congregation in Morgantown, were not affiliated with the U. A. H. C. in December, 1955, at the time of the publication of the above report. The Morgantown Tree of Life Congregation joined the U. A. H. C. in March, 1957, with about 40 members.

## 1956

In 1956, the Jewish population of the State of West Virginia was estimated at 6,000, out of a total State population of 1,947,000. The Jews of West Virginia thus constituted an estimated 0.31% of the total State population.

The *AJYB* for 1956 reported that there were only 3 Jewish welfare funds or federations in the entire State. This report was in error in one respect, for actually, in all the years from 1940 or earlier up to the present, there have been four such Jewish welfare federations or welfare organizations in existence in West Virginia, the fourth, the Bluefield-Princeton Jewish Charities, with its headquarters in Bluefield, having been in existence, and most active, throughout this entire period, into the year 1958–1959.

The other 3 were as follows:

*Charleston*:  The Federated Jewish Charities of Charleston (including Dunbar and Montgomery, W. Va.) Organized in 1937

Headquarters, 804 Quarrier Street
Lester J. Mann, president in 1956
Charles Cohen, executive secretary in 1956

*Huntington*:  The Federated Jewish Charities
Organized in 1939
M. D. Friedman, president in 1956
E. Henry Broh, secretary-treasurer in 1956

*Wheeling*:  The Jewish Community Council
(including Moundsville, W. Va.)
Organized in 1933
John Wiseman, president in 1956
Isadore Rubinstein, treasurer in 1956

## 1960 (1959–1960)

According to the *AJYB* for 1960 (Volume 61, page 395), West Virginia in that year (1959–1960) had the same following three (actually, there were four, including the Bluefield-Princeton United Jewish Charities, whose name was again, inexplicably, omitted from the list of Jewish Welfare Federations and Welfare Funds in West Virginia in the latest volume of the *AJYB*, by error, inadvertence, or carelessness) Jewish welfare federations or welfare funds:

*Charleston*: Federated Jewish Charities of Charleston, Inc. (including Dunbar and Montgomery, W. Va.) (1937); 804 Quarrier Street, Rooms 407–8); President, Ivor F. Boiarsky; Executive Secretary, Charles Cohen.

*Huntington*: Federated Jewish Charities (1939); President, Jack Cuttler; Secretary-Treasurer, E. Henry Broh.

*Wheeling*: Jewish Community Council of Wheeling (including Moundsville) (1933); Treasurer, Isadore Rubinstein, 30 Poplar Avenue.

According to the *AJYB*, Volume 58 (1957), pages 81–82, the following twelve communities of West Virginia each had an estimated Jewish population of 100 or more in 1956:

| Community | Jewish Population |
| --- | --- |
| Beckley | 228[1] |
| Bluefield-Princeton | 300 |
| Charleston | 2,000[2] |
| Clarksburg | 280 |
| Fairmont | 200 |
| Huntington | 750 |
| Morgantown | 150 |
| Parkersburg | 100[3] |
| Weirton | 350 |
| Welch (including the contiguous area of McDowell County, such as Kimball, War, and most of the Jewish families remaining in Keystone and North Fork) | 144 |
| Wheeling | 800 |
| Williamson | 180[4] |

---

[1] The figure for Beckley was merely repeated from previous issues of the *AJYB*, without any attempt to secure revised figures. It is considerably too high for the year 1957. It should be reduced to about 175 for 1957, including the three or four Jewish families in Mount Hope and in Oak Hill, in nearby Fayette County. From 1952 to 1956, the Beckley Jewish population suffered a severe decline, as the result of deaths and of the moving away of Jewish families from the city, and their resettlement in other cities, and because of the unfavorable economic conditions, largely as a result of the sharp decline or depression in the coal mining industry, and in the production of coal, a decline which was still continuing in 1958. Furthermore, according to reports which came to me from Beckley in 1956 to 1959, at least half a dozen additional Jewish families had left the city, or were planning to, in those three later years.

[2] The figure for Charleston should, in all probability, be a bit higher, possibly 2,200 to 2,300.

[3] The figure of 100 Jews in Parkersburg in 1956 is, in all probability, as indicated above once or twice, quite a bit too low. The Parkersburg Jewish community appears to have increased, in size, slowly but steadily, since 1950; hence, a more accurate figure for the Jewish population of Parkersburg for 1957–1958 would be about 175 to 200 persons.

[4] The figure of 180 for the Jewish population of Williamson in 1956 is, undoubtedly, too high. From 1955 on, and even before that, Williamson, too, suffered a decline in its Jewish population. A more accurate figure for Williamson, for the year 1956–1957, would perhaps be about 125 to 140 Jewish persons.

For the year 1956, there was an estimated Jewish population, in West Virginia, of 5,950, out of a total general State population of 1,984,000, or 0.30% of the total population of the State (three-tenths of 1%).

No Jewish periodicals of any kind were being published by the Jews in any community of West Virginia in 1956–1957.

## 1957–1958

### Membership of West Virginia Jews in the American Jewish Historical Society

Mrs. Charles Lando, of Wheeling
Ohev Sholom Religious School, of Huntington
Mrs. Sam Rudner, of Wheeling
Mrs. Alex Wishnew, of Wheeling

### U. A. H. C. Congregations in 1958

The following ten West Virginia congregations were members of the Union of American Hebrew Congregations in 1958; given also are a notation as to the name of the U. A. H. C. Regions (regional organizations) with which they are affiliated, their membership, and the names of their presidents and rabbis:

| City | Name of the Congregation | Region | President | Rabbi | Members |
|------|--------------------------|--------|-----------|-------|---------|
| Bluefield | Congregation Ahavath Sholom | Ohio-Valley | Nathan Platnick | Amos Schauss | 82 |
| Charleston | B'nai Israel Congregation | Ohio-Valley | Sydney M. Kleeman | Samuel Volkman | 239 |
| Huntington | Congregation Ohev Sholom | Ohio-Valley | S. Samson, Jr. | Theodore S. Levy | 109 |
| Logan | Congregation B'nai El | Ohio-Valley | Rudolph R. Eiland | — | 17 |
| Martinsburg | Beth Jacob Congregation | Ohio-Valley | Gene Diamond | — | 15 |
| Morgantown | Tree of Life Congregation | Ohio-Valley | Edward S. Fields[1] | Robert A. Kaufman[2] | 36 |
| Parkersburg | Temple B'nai Israel | Ohio-Valley | Henry Greenberg | — | 45 |
| Welch | Emanuel Congregation | Ohio-Valley | Morton Rosenzweig | — | 7 |

[1] Edward S. Fields moved away from Morgantown in 1958, before his term as president of the congregation in Morgantown had expired, and settled in Phoenix, Arizona.

[2] Rabbi Robert Kaufman left Morgantown before September, 1958, to go to Rochester, Minnesota.

| City | Name of the Congregation | Region | President | Rabbi | Members |
|------|--------------------------|--------|-----------|-------|---------|
| Wheeling | Woodsdale Temple (Congregation Leshem Shomayim) | Ohio-Valley | Sidney Good, Jr. | Saul Rubin[1] | 94 |
| Williamson | Temple B'nai Israel | Ohio-Valley | Philip Beinhorn | — | 39 |

In September, 1959, the Beckley Congregation Beth El affiliated with the U. A. H. C.

The above figures indicate a loss in membership by many of these congregations from December, 1955, to early 1958, due to deaths of members of congregations and the failure of other Jewish families to come into West Virginia to replace them, and due to removals of Jewish families from the State, and their resettlement in Arizona, California, Florida, Maryland, New Mexico, New York, and other States, a process which began about the year 1951 or 1952, and is still continuing. Thus, in the period from 1955 to 1958, as indicated by the above congregational membership records of the U. A. H. C., the membership of the

| Congregation | declined from | to | in the period from 1955 to 1958: |
|--------------|---------------|-----|----------------------------------|
| Charleston | 260 | 239 | |
| Huntington | 150 | 109 | |
| Logan | 25 | 17 | |
| Welch | 19 | 7 | |
| Wheeling | 100 | 94 | |

In addition, unofficially, but by estimate and local statements, the number of families, or of congregational members, in other cities suffered a decline as follows:

| | | |
|--------|-----|-----|
| Bluefield | 110 | 82 |
| Beckley | 65 | 50 |

The Parkersburg congregation, apparently, gained in Jewish population, from 1950 to 1958, by some 10 or 12 Jewish families or members.

---

[1] According to a later report, Saul Rubin left Wheeling, after one year, at the beginning of the 1958–1959 religious year, and was no longer serving as rabbi in Wheeling as of September 1, 1958. His place as rabbi of the congregation in Wheeling was taken by Rabbi William A. Rosenthall.

### THE UNION OF AMERICAN HEBREW CONGREGATIONS
### IN WEST VIRGINIA

In the years from September, 1903, on, when he was the
Director of Circuit Work [later this title was changed to Field
Secretary] of the U. A. H. C., Rabbi George Zepin, then a
recent [1900] graduate of the Hebrew Union College, aided in
the organization of congregations in West Virginia, among other
States, paying numerous visits to communities in the State.

In addition to the above lists of West Virginia congregations
which have been members of the Union of American Hebrew
Congregations from 1873 to the present, the following items of
interest are concerned with the U. A. H. C. in West Virginia:

Former members of the U. A. H. C. Board of Trustees [pre-
viously known as the Executive Board] from West Virginia were
Sydney M. Kleeman, of Charleston; and Paul Friedberg, of
Williamson.

In 1958, Rabbi Samuel Volkman, of Charleston, was serving
as the director of the Ohio Valley Council of the U. A. H. C.,
a region which includes all of Indiana except Hammond;
Kentucky; Ohio; Nashville, Tenn.; and West Virginia. Dr. Leon
Saks, of Cincinnati, was president of the Ohio Valley Council
in that year.

### PRESENTATION ON THE WEST VIRGINIA JEWISH COMMUNITIES
### BY RABBI MICHAEL AARONSOHN (1926)

From September, 1923 (shortly after his ordination by the
Hebrew Union College, of Cincinnati), to September, 1931,
Rabbi Michael Aaronsohn, a native of Baltimore, but then of
Cincinnati, served as the National Field Representative of the
Union of American Hebrew Congregations, which was then
located in Cincinnati, but later (*ca.* 1950) transferred its headquarters to New York City. In the autumn of the year 1926,
accompanied by his sister, Miss Dora Aaronsohn (now Registrar
of the H. U. C. - J. I. R., in Cincinnati), he toured West Virginia
in the interests of the U. A. H. C.; and in the spring of 1931,
accompanied by his wife, Mrs. Rachel Z. Aaronsohn, under the

PLATE I

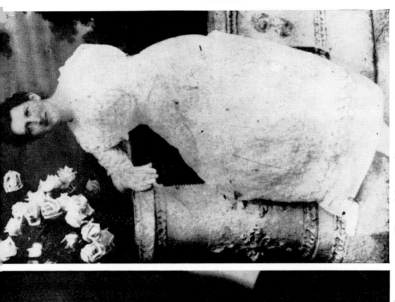

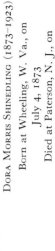

Moses Shinedling (1860–1928)
Born at Shkud, Kovno Province, Lithuania,
in September, 1860
Died at Paterson, N. J., on
November 30, 1928

Julian Mark Shinedling (1899–1957)
Born in New York City, on
December 27, 1899
Died at Paterson, N. J., on
December 4, 1957

Dora Morris Shinedling (1873–1923)
Born at Wheeling, W. Va., on
July 4, 1873
Died at Paterson, N. J., on
January 30, 1923

Isidore Jocelyn Shinedling (1893–1949)
Born at Chicago, Ill., on November 22, 1893 Died at Phoenix, Ariz., on January 16, 1949
(no picture of Isidore Jocelyn Shinedling is extant)

PLATE II

Temple Beth El, Beckley, West Virginia
Erected in 1935–1936

(see page 266)

auspices of the U. A. H. C. once more, he visited a number of the Jewish communities "in the mountains and valleys of West Virginia," as Rabbi Aaronsohn himself expressed it in a letter to me written at Cincinnati, on March 7, 1961. One of a series of five articles in which he recorded his impressions of persons and places whom and which he visited in the United States and Canada on these organizing tours, entitled "Coal, Cotton, and Congregations," treats of most of the West Virginia Jewish communities — all too briefly and sketchily — Bluefield, Beckley, and Weirton are not included in his account — and from this highly poetical, dramatic, and lively, and historically valuable article I present the following excerpts dealing with West Virginia — "the Coal . . . and Congregations" of the above title; his account of the Jewish communities of the Southern States, not presented here, represents the "Cotton . . . and Congregations" of the title of his article.

Michael Aaronsohn's picture of Jewish life in the smaller and larger (Huntington, Charleston, and Wheeling) communities of West Virginia in 1926, more than three decades ago, hopeful and cheerful in tone and nature, is a much brighter and much more optimistic one than that predicted for the "coal communities of West Virginia" in the latest letter sent to me from Cincinnati, on March 3, 1961, by Dr. Jakob J. Petuchowski, a member of the faculty of the H. U. C. - J. I. R., there. Dr. Petuchowski was formerly the student, and then the graduate, part-time rabbi of the Welch, W. Va., Congregation Emanuel, from about 1949 to 1955. He wrote as follows, with reference to this West Virginia Jewish history and to the Jewish communities of the coal sections of West Virginia:

I am afraid that your book, *West Virginia Jewry: Origins and History — 1850–1958*, will be more than a mere history. It will also be the obituary and the *matzebhah* [tombstone] of Jewish life in the West Virginia coalfields. Such, at any rate, is my understanding based on the occasional reports which I receive from the ever-dwindling *kehillah kedoshah* [Jewish congregation] of Welch. Twenty-five years from now, the Jewish historian may have to rely solely on your book for any information about the flourishing Jewish life which used to exist in West Virginia.

There follow the excerpts from Rabbi Michael Aaronsohn's article, "Coal, Cotton, and Congregations," which deal with West Virginia:

As I review the events now past, I imagine that the people of this country may be segmented into three divisions: metropolitan, pioneer, and barbarian. New York City has these three types; so has Logan, W. Va. A Sunday School teacher at Northfork, W. Va., questions the divine character of the stories in the Bible. Among the unheralded magnificence of West Virginia's majestic mountains, where the bungalows of the coal miners line the roads and where their high-powered automobiles roll over the rocky surfaces and plash through the beds of countless streams, there are Jewish congregations. In some of these congregations the members wear hats in the synagogue. In others the members import kosher meat [from larger American cities nearby]. And there are many who have been enkindled by the flame of modern Zionism.

So I asked: "What power is it that combs the great cities and selects one man for [settlement in] . . . and a seventh for Welch, W. Va.?" Once I heard a man answer: "A relative." Another told of a chance meeting in a delicatessen store in New York. Sometimes the quest for health, or it may have been the spirit of adventure, quickened him and caused him to cut the bonds which held him in the great city and to drift in[to] the lone places of West Virginia. He who once saw the sun only when the factory whistle did not belch forth its imperial call now flourishes among the mountains and the forests and the ever-lasting hills of West Virginia. But change of real estate [moving to a different place] does not make him a barbarian. When his pioneering days are ended, he is the president of the congregation, he summons a trim, American youth [from the Hebrew Union College, in Cincinnati] to deliver lectures [sermons, as the student, part-time rabbi of the congregation, every other week, in the small towns and Jewish communities of West Virginia], he subscribes to the *American Israelite* and the *New York Times*, he "runs" to New York to shop for himself, his wife, and his children, he motors to Cincinnati, Cleveland, Pittsburgh, Baltimore, Richmond, Chicago, and New York, his children are enrolled at the leading American colleges, and — presto! — he and his family and all his kin are metropolitans again.

[The reader will please bear in mind that this presentation by Rabbi Michael Aaronsohn was written in late 1926, or almost 35 years ago. Many of the conditions which he described and touched on, all too briefly, in his "sketch" have been greatly changed since his days, or no longer exist. In the 1950's many West Virginia Jews, retiring from business, especially in the smaller towns and cities, but often even in the larger cities of the State as well, did not remain in their cities, but moved to Florida, to Baltimore, to Cincinnati, to New York, or other metropolises, to spend the last years of their lives; also to California; thus "Jewishly" and otherwise rendering their former West Virginia communities poorer and a little more desolate.]

We begin in West Virginia. The train carries us along the Ohio River [the Baltimore & Ohio Railroad]. Our first stop is Wheeling.

WHEELING. Wheeling, W. Va., is a quaint place. The air is polluted with coal dust. The streets appear not well cared for. Many of the houses are ancient in style. On the outskirts of the town are high, alluring hills. The Ohio flows gently by. And the culture of Cincinnati and Pittsburgh flows gently in to this city. There is a Jewish woman in Wheeling who prescribes for a thousand and more other women a program of the master thinkers and lecturers. In Wheeling they talk of the great rabbis whom they once nurtured. [Harry Levi, Abram Brill, Morris S. Lazaron, Abba Hillel Silver, Louis D. Gross. Abraham L. Feinberg, now of Toronto, Canada, was the rabbi of the Wheeling Congregation Leshem Shomayim at the time of Rabbi Michael Aaronsohn's visit there in the fall of 1926.] Within the synagogue you will find a calm. A brooding power seems to spread a cloud of mysticism over it, heavily enveloping all things and all worshippers.

HUNTINGTON. Huntington is a sensible civic creation. The streets were laid out by experts. There is a spacious synagogue [Temple Oheb Sholom] built through the faith and the zeal of the hardy pioneers. There is a Jewish Community Center in the making. [Rabbi, in 1926, Abraham Feinstein.]

WILLIAMSON. Once, and not many years ago, Williamson, W. Va., was the camping ground of the "bad" men who came through the mountain passes of Kentucky to settle their differences in primitive fashion. Today Williamson is a flourishing mining center on the main line of the Norfolk & Western Railroad. The son of a famous feudist is the "star" on the high school football team. Our meeting was held on Sunday night in the auditorium of the principal moving picture parlor. The children are taught Hebrew in a room below. We found a [Jewish] youth, a graduate of Yale [University], whose library contains rare titles.

CHARLESTON. Charleston, W. Va., is a man's town — the Kenova [Rabbi Aaronsohn meant the Kanawha River] for a river-front and the mountains for a homestead. They have a robust congregation there for whom culture is a creed and hearty co-operation a joyous routine. There are hosts of happy children, too, in Charleston, and the mountains are their playground. The Temple [the old Virginia Street Temple of B'nai Israel Congregation] is ample and inviting. We were jubilant with praise for the Temple Center. Here our priceless children will hear the word of lore and mystery amid rationally comfortable surroundings. On Sunday night in company with Rabbi [Maurice N.] Eisendrath [then the rabbi of the Virginia Street Temple (from September, 1926, to August, 1929)], we joined a swarming group of merry folk celebrating the installation of their Orthodox leader [one of the predecessors of the present Orthodox rabbi of Charleston's B'nai Jacob Congregation, Samuel Cooper].

PARKERSBURG. Parkersburg is a small place. The Jewish meeting hall is on the third floor of a down town building. And there is a woman who remembers that Judaism ought to live. But there are fellow women and men who wonder how. A man or two in Parkersburg talked of better days.

LOGAN. Deep, deep in the valley is Logan, W. Va., encircled by mountain ranges. Some one chose her to be the city, and there is a multitude of mining camps about her. Watch your step in Logan. Formidable trucks and little cars dash in from fifty miles or so away. They tear through the two or three streets (and this is all that can be). Our host is a remnant of an imperial band of European-trained students. Our hostess is a graduate of a convent in Germany. A few years ago they lived far, far out in the wilderness that was nearby. Our host traveled muleback and horseback then. Mr. [Rudolph R.] Eiland has vivid memories of pioneer days — rich material for a ready scribe. They say that no Jew was absent from services that Friday night. The synagogue is on the top floor of a bank building. They come to worship there in Logan. The children compose the choir. The Logan community has set aside a bit of precious real estate that the Jewish congregation may build a synagogue alongside the church. Real estate is at a premium here; there is so little to be had. They are merry folk in Logan, and they talk sweetly of New York, Baltimore, and Cincinnati.

A bus may take you from Logan to Williamson in less than three hours. A train may take all day to bring you from one point to the other. The bus runs over a patch of good road, over many miles of improvised road, over mountain sides, through innumerable, seemingly endless streams, and if the rain is falling as you are riding, you will have more "thrills" than even New York can offer. You will feast on scenery gorgeous, stirring, glorious, rapturously virgin.

We did not linger this time at Williamson, but at once found seats in the day coach bound for Keystone, Northfork, and Welch. Our fellow passengers entertained us in a vivid manner. An aged Christian spoke tenderly, wondrously, of pertinent issues. He had read Josephus' *Antiquities* through more than once. He believed in the prophecies embodied in the Book of *Daniel*. He was opposed to prohibition, and did not approve of higher education for women. Across the way [aisle] an elderly woman sang songs which she had learned at church. The floor of the coach was coated inch thick with the refuse of many West Virginia cities [dust, mud, and coal dust?].

KEYSTONE. We arrived at Keystone late in the afternoon. It is a town, the outgrowth of a coal mining camp. Our meeting that afternoon was conducted in a pleasant room on the third floor of the new Knights of Pythias building. About eighty-five men, women, and children, Jews and non-Jews — from Keystone and Northfork — attended. To my surprise and delight, I met two young men from Baltimore, whom I had known years before. Coal had brought them and their families here.

WELCH. That evening we drove across the dangerous mountain roads to Welch, a neighboring town and also a fully developed mining camp. Welch has a charming little synagogue [Congregation, or Temple, Emanuel], where the men wear hats. There is a family at Welch from Cincinnati. Others have come from other large cities. A baker after working hours [Was this the late Benjamin Bernhard Matz, of Bluefield?] teaches the children Hebrew and conducts services without compensation. A bright young married woman [Anna Herzbrun (Mrs. Isadore) Katzen?] is the directing genius of the congregation. The dietary laws are observed.

Keystone, Northfork, and Welch are as well organized as any little city in Ohio, with congregation, sisterhood, and religious school.

CLARKSBURG. Clarksburg is a progressive town on the main line [of the Baltimore & Ohio Railroad] between Cincinnati and Washington. Here, for a change, the West Virginia roads excel. The people [the Reform Jews?] in Clarksburg once had a rabbi. The Orthodox insist upon separation and provide their own leader. The president of the Reform [Jewish] group served as public health doctor in West Virginia and in the mountain places of Georgia. He now has another trial, another test of his ability and patience. [In trying to foster and maintain the Reform Jewish congregation. He apparently failed, for some years after Rabbi Aaronsohn's above-described visit to Clarksburg, the Reform congregation of Clarksburg passed out of existence, and its membership and Sisterhood merged with those of the Orthodox-Conservative Tree of Life Congregation.] Recent additions to the [Reform] group in the persons of a man and his wife, who hitherto were leaders at Lexington, Ky., ought to give him the needed support and direction. Some Baltimore friends abide in Clarksburg, and accorded us a hearty welcome.

Near Clarksburg there are 5,000 souls [non-Jews] assembled in the town called Salem. On Saturday no business is conducted at Salem. It is the Sabbath day for the people of that place [Seventh-Day Baptists]. Yet no Jew lives in this city. And a few weeks ago I heard some one announce that there was only one [other?] city in the world where Saturday was [as?] scrupulously observed as the Sabbath — the city of Tel Aviv in Palestine.

Around and about Clarksburg there may be found small groups of Jews. They remember occasionally the religion of their fathers and of their childhood. Often their Christian neighbors laugh at those who will not refrain from labor on Rosh Hashanah and Yom Kippur.

Deep in the heart of West Virginia, close to the city of Clarksburg, there is a colony made up of men and women who, for the most part, once adorned the honor rolls of eminent academies. Culture is the atmosphere, comfort is unknown. I was introduced to the superintendent of the State Normal School. He is spoken of as one of the greatest, yet he looked and spoke after the manner of a farmer. Evidently, polish is not a symbol of mental aristocracy there.

FAIRMONT. In the storage room on the second floor of an "underselling store," in the city of Fairmont, each Sunday morning at eleven o'clock, a group of ten or twelve children are taught Judaism. The room contains an ark with a Sefer Torah. Mr. [Simon D.] Goodman, the proprietor, has been "rabbi" for fourteen years. He, too, is from Baltimore. The same afternoon I found a handful of other Jews who impressed me with their gentility and charm. They would be united and worship together, but there is a dispute about things Orthodox and things un-Orthodox.

MORGANTOWN. From Clarksburg and Fairmont we journeyed by automobile to Morgantown, a typical college town, the seat of the University of West Virginia. We came upon a nest of Jewish young folk, who were in no whit to be distinguished from the students whom we had met at Berkeley, California, at Ann Arbor, Michigan, and at Columbia, Missouri. A large number of the young men at West Virginia University are from New York. You will find New York boys everywhere. What brings them to these hidden places? Some of the students balked at Jewish organization. [Later, a branch of the Hillel Foundations was set up at West Virginia University; with some intervals, it has continued in operation into the present day.] They feared that separatism would mean ostracism. However, generally, the student body is in accord with the principle of religious organization and in time, doubtless, will institute a distinctive and respectable [Hillel] foundation for such particularistic activities.

West Virginia is now a fruitful memory. I wonder what might have been if New York and Cincinnati and Baltimore had not given up to West Virginia a few [persons] here and a few there. What if the sparkling coal of West Virginia had not subtly drawn a few hundreds from the monster centers of population? Even more, what if the congregation had not sprung forth to absorb, to blend, to harmonize, to unify, to give beauty, strength, dignity, power, and happiness to the pioneers that they might find within the fold the memories, the traditions, and the bonds to make them, as they were, metropolitan in dress, in speech, in thought, and in action? Of all peoples, the Jew is an intensely social individual. He could not, unless he be an exceedingly extraordinary personality, live to himself alone. He must have a social center, be it a B'nai B'rith Lodge, a Synagogue, or a Temple. And the congregation is a natural symbol and satisfaction of this universal need.

[Rabbi Michael Aaronsohn's biography is to be found in *Who's Who in World Jewry* (1955) and in *UJE*, I, 9. He was born in Baltimore, Md., on July 5, 1896, the son of Nathan and Hannah Bass Aaronsohn, and received the B.A. degree from Johns Hopkins University, in his native city, in 1920, and the same degree from the University of Cincinnati, in 1923. In June, 1923, he was ordained by the Hebrew Union College, in Cincinnati. In April, 1917, when the United States entered the First World War, he enlisted as a soldier, although as a theological student he was exempt from military service. He attained the rank of sergeant-major, and on September 29, 1918, during battle in the Allied Meuse-Argonne offensive, he was permanently blinded. Directly after his ordination, in June, 1923, he was appointed national field representative of the U. A. H. C., retiring from this post, which entailed incessant traveling and organizational, lecturing, and speaking work, in September, 1931, after which he devoted his time and energies to hospital chaplaincy work and to the writing of the story of his life, experiences, and work (autobiography), two volumes of which had already been published by 1960 (*Broken Lights*, Cincinnati, 1946; and *Red Pottage*, Cincinnati, 1956), and on the third volume of which he was working in 1960–1961, scheduled for publication in the latter year. A leader in the Henry George School of Social Science in New York for more than three decades, as well as in the Henry George Congress, he wrote a number of articles on the subject of the single tax (on undeveloped land), and wrote articles for the *American Legion Monthly*, the *B'nai B'rith Magazine* (as the *National Jewish Monthly* was then called), and other periodicals. He became one of the founders of the monthly *Jewish Braille Review* in 1931. For six years (from 1921 to 1927) he served as the National Chaplain of the Disabled American Veterans of the World War, with its headquarters in Cincinnati, and he still participates actively in the work of this association. He still serves as the chaplain of several American Legion posts in Cincinnati, and in 1960–1961, after many years of service, he was still serving as the Jewish chaplain in Veterans Administration hospitals in Cincinnati and in nearby Kentucky. He has also, for many years, been a member of the Hamilton County (Cincinnati) Council for Retarded Children.]

1959 (1959–1960)

According to the latest volume of the *American Jewish Year Book*, that for the year 1960 (Volume 61, page 8), the following 11 Jewish communities of West Virginia had estimated Jewish populations of 100 or more persons in 1959:

Beckley 230 (much too high)
Bluefield-Princeton 300
Charleston 1,625
    (undoubtedly too low)
Clarksburg 225
Fairmont 175
Huntington 925

Morgantown 130
Parkersburg 100
    (much too low)
Weirton 350
Wheeling 800
Williamson 170
    (perhaps too high)

SUBSCRIBERS TO THE JEWISH PUBLICATION SOCIETY OF
AMERICA, IN WEST VIRGINIA (1900–1901 TO 1957)

Under the sections containing the history of the various Jewish communities of West Virginia, I present, perhaps for the first time, a complete list of the names of the subscribers to the Jewish Publication Society of America (J. P. S. A.), of Philadelphia, gathered from the various issues of the *American Jewish Year Book* (*AJYB*), during the period extending from the first year of its existence, 1900–1901, through Volume 43, for the year 1941–1942, the last year in which these lists of subscribers or members were published in the *AJYB*.

In this chapter, under the State of West Virginia, I present, generally, not the names of these subscribers, or members, but general facts regarding their number in each particular year or group of years, as well as statistics regarding the various Jewish communities from which Jewish subscribers to the J. P. S. A. came. Such statistics, and lists of names, in my opinion, give valuable information as to Jewish population and conditions in the communities of the State. They also tell in what communities, and in what years, there was Jewish population; and they possibly also provide data as to the rise and decline in Jewish population in the various communities — the cities, the towns, the villages, and the smaller places — of the State.

It will be noticed that many of the localities of West Virginia which had Jewish subscribers to the J. P. S. A. in the years from 1900 to 1940, or in some of those years, are totally without Jews today (1957–1958), their Jewish populations having died out or moved away to other places. See the sections on the individual cities, towns, villages, and other localities for a complete list of the names of the J. P. S. A. subscribers from each such city, town, and locality in the State.

### 1900–1901

In 1900–1901, the J. P. S. A. had 45 members from West Virginia, located in the following 13 communities:

| | |
|---|---|
| Charleston 4 | Martinsburg 1 |
| Charles Town 2 | Morgantown 1 |
| Clarksburg 3 | Parkersburg 8 |
| Fairmont 2 | Piedmont 1 |
| Grafton 2 | Weston 2 |
| Harpers Ferry 1 | Wheeling 18 |
| Huntington 2 | |

### 1901–1902

In 1901–1902, the J. P. S. A. had a total of 37 members in West Virginia, located in 12 towns and cities of the State, representing a loss of 8 members from the previous year's total of 45 members.

### 1902–1903

In 1902–1903, the membership of the West Virginia Jews in the J. P. S. A. declined to 19 [18] individuals in 7 communities or cities.

### 1903–1904

In 1903–1904, the J. P. S. A. had only 17 members in 6 communities of the State.

## 1904–1905

In 1904–1905, there were 21 members of the J. P. S. A. from West Virginia, in the following 6 cities:

| | |
|---|---|
| Charleston 1 | Morgantown 1 |
| Charles Town 2 | Parkersburg 3 |
| Grafton 2 | Wheeling 10 |

## 1905–1906

18 members

## 1907–1908

13 members

## 1908–1909

10 members, of whom 5 were from Wheeling

## 1909–1910

In 1909–1910, the J. P. S. A. had 16 members in West Virginia, in the following 5 cities of the State:

| | |
|---|---|
| Charleston 7 | Morgantown 1 |
| Charles Town 2 | Wheeling 5 |
| Grafton 1 | |

## 1910–1911

In 1910–1911, there were 13 members of the J. P. S. A. in West Virginia, of whom five were from Charleston and four from Wheeling.

## 1912–1913 [5673 A.M.]
### (Volume 14 of the *AJYB*)

A total of only 7 cities, towns, or Jewish communities in West Virginia showed 21 members of the J. P. S. A. in the year 1912–1913, as recorded in Volume 14, as follows:

*Charleston*

Hyman Galprin
Rabbi Nachman Heller
A. [Alvin] P. Silverstein

*Charles Town*

William Kahn
M. Palmbaum & Bro.

*Elkins*

Dr. William M. Golden
A. Klein

*Grafton*

H. A. Caplan
F. Friedman
I. [Isaac] C. Klein

*Moundsville*

M. Bachenheimer

*Weston*

H. Blumberg

*Wheeling*

Ben S. Baer
I. E. Barker
Rabbi Abram Brill
Max Crone
Morris Horkheimer
David Kraus
S. M. Rice
M. [Moses] Sonneborn
C. J. Wolf

### 1911–1912

In 1911–1912, West Virginia had 15 members in the J. P. S. A., of whom 6 were from Charleston, and 6 also from Wheeling.

### 1912–1913

In 1912–1913, West Virginia had 18 [20] members of the J. P. S. A., of whom 3 were from Charleston, and 7 were from Wheeling.

### 1913–1914

In 1913–1914, the J. P. S. A. had a total of 21 members from West Virginia, of whom 3 were from Charleston, and 9 were from Wheeling.

### 1914–1915

In 1914–1915, there were 31 [25] members of the J. P. S. A. in West Virginia, of whom 3 were from Charleston, 14 from

Huntington, and 5 from Wheeling. [According to another set of figures, the J. P. S. A. had 25 members from West Virginia in 1915.]

## 1915–1916 [5676 A.M.]

In 1915–1916, there were 13 cities and towns in West Virginia which had a total of 59 [55] subscribers to the J. P. S. A., as follows:

| | | |
|---|---|---|
| Buckhannon 1 | Grafton 1 | Weston 1 |
| Bluefield 8 | Huntington 13 | Wheeling 3 |
| Charleston 12 | Kimball 4 | Williamson 1 |
| Charles Town 2 | North Fork 4 | |
| Elkins 1 | Welch 8 | |

## 1916–1917 and 1917–1918 [5677 and 5678 A.M.]

In February, 1917, the J. P. S. A. had 111 members in West Virginia, and in the following year, 1917–1918, there were 86 members, of whom 8 were from Bluefield, 30 were from Charleston, 3 from Charles Town, 13 were from Huntington, 4 were from Martinsburg, 4 from North Fork, 6 from Welch, and 4 from Wheeling. These names are herewith presented in full, as being among the highest memberships ever achieved from and in West Virginia by the J. P. S. A.

| *Bluefield* | *Charleston* |
|---|---|
| B. S. Block | Ben Baer |
| Isadore Cohen | Samuel Berman |
| Isaac Greenspon | Rabbi Israel Bettan |
| Mrs. Solomon Greenspon | D. M. Blumberg |
| Mrs. L. Kaufman | I. Blustein |
| Mrs. Henry Rodgin | Dr. J. W. Boiarsky |
| Reverend Kalman Slifkin | Judge M. Boiarsky |
| L. H. Taschman | Mrs. P. Briggs |

Charles Cohen
Max Cohen
J. Dolinsky
Simon H. Galperin
Hyman Galprin
H. Goldstein
J. I. Hark
R. Lebow
Hyman Leven
C. Loeb
Leo Loeb
Isaac Loewenstein
Philip M. May
Sam Mendelsohn
A. I. Polan
H. Polan
Mendel Pushkin
I. Rosenberg
Joseph Schwab
A. P. Silverstein
L. J. Slone
L. M. Weinberg

*Charles Town*

Mark N. Horowitz
Dr. M. Mendeloff
M. Palmbaum & Bro.

*Clarksburg*

Ben Brown

*Elkins*

Dr. William W. Golden

*Fairmont*

Simon Goodman

*Grafton*

F. Friedman

*Huntington*

Joseph Cohen
I. Davidson
M. Fetter
David Fox
Leon Gideon
H. A. Glick
S. G. Glick
Samuel Gore
Mrs. A. Kahn
Reverend Samuel Mandel
L. Polan
A. Schlossberg
D. R. [C.] Schonthal

*Kimball*

A. Forman
D. M. Klein
I. Sweig

*Martinsburg*

M. Cohen
J. Fine
George Katz
M. B. Nierenberg

*North Fork*

B. Brooks
Aaron Catzen
Mrs. S. H. Hermanson
H. Seligman

*Parkersburg*

W. A. Hersch

*Princeton*

Joseph Tomchin

*Salem*

O. Earle Karickhoff

*Scarbro*

Mrs. H. Fischer [Fisher]

*Welch*

J. Effron
S. Levinson
E. H. Lopinsky
H. Miller

J. L. Sameth
L. Talmage

*Weston*

H. Blumberg

*Wheeling*

Rabbi Morris Lazaron
Rabbi Abba Hillel Silver
M. [Moses] Sonneborn
Frank J. Yaffe

*Williamson*

Isadore Steckler

(Dr. M. Mendeloff was erroneously listed as from Charles Town. In actuality, he was a resident of Charleston.)

In the case of this historically valuable list of names, Jewish residents of the above communities, I have corrected the misspellings of several of the names to be found in the pages of the *AJYB*. Also, in the lists of subscribers to the J. P. S. A. to be found in the sections on the various cities and towns of the State, I have given the full first names, wherever possible, instead of the historically unsatisfactory initials.

On February 28, 1918, the Jewish Publication Society of America had a total of 83 members in West Virginia.

## 1918–1919 [5679 A.M.]

In 19 cities or towns of West Virginia, in the year 1918–1919, there were 77 subscribers to the J. P. S. A., as follows:

Bluefield 5                       Fairmont 1
Charleston 33                     Grafton 1
Charles Town 2                    Huntington 18
Elkins 1                          Kimball 2

| | |
|---|---|
| Martinsburg 4 | Salem 1 |
| Montgomery 1 | Scarbro 1 |
| North Fork 3 | Welch 3 |
| Parkersburg 3 | Weston 1 |
| Piedmont 3 | Wheeling 2 |
| Princeton 1 | |

The above figures represent 25 new members in the following cities and towns of West Virginia in 1918–1919:

| | |
|---|---|
| Bluefield 1 | Montgomery 1 |
| Charleston 12 | Parkersburg 2 |
| Huntington 5 | Piedmont 3 |
| Kimball 1 | |

I do not know, exactly, the ways or methods whereby such new subscribers to the Jewish Publication Society of America were secured, from time to time, or from year to year. Presumably there were a variety of methods involved: recommendations to congregational members by the various rabbis or student rabbis of the State; advertising material or letters sent out to prospective members of the J. P. S. A. from its headquarters in Philadelphia; recommendations by former or present lay members of the J. P. S. A. I always regretted it when I read that former members of the J. P. S. A. had dropped their membership, begrudging even the small amount of some $5 per year involved for minimum membership in the Jewish Publication Society of America for the support of American Jewish literature and for the subsidizing of Jewish books. Also, I always felt that I was a failure as a rabbi and as a proponent of Jewish literature and culture, and I developed an "inferiority complex" along these lines, because I was unable to induce more than two or three — or even fewer — members of my congregations in West Virginia and in previous cities to become members of, and to subscribe to, the J. P. S. A. However, I did manage to "sell" to the various members of my Bluefield and Beckley, W. Va., congregations a goodly number of Jewish Publication Society Bible translations, for use in the homes of the members as well as in the Religious School and at the Temple services. As will be commented on briefly, I was always gravely disappointed at the lack of interest in Jewish books and literature on the part of the overwhelming majority of the members of my West Virginia — and other previous — congregations, and at their reluctance and parsimoniousness in spending money for this purpose.

As of February 28, 1919, West Virginia had a total of 103 members in the Jewish Publication Society of America, at a time when the total membership of that institution in all parts of the world was 15,839.

### 1920

As of February 29, 1920, there were 103 Jews in West Virginia who were members of the J. P. S. A.

### 1921

As of February 28, 1921, there were 103 members, again, in West Virginia, of the J. P. S. A.

### 1922

As of February 28, 1922, the J. P. S. A. had a total of 155 members in West Virginia, presumably the highest membership that that organization ever had in the State.

### 1922–1923 (Volume 24)

In 1922–1923, 24 new members joined the J. P. S. A. from West Virginia in the following numbers from the below-listed cities and towns of the State:

| | |
|---|---|
| Bluefield 1 | Montgomery 4 |
| Charleston 7 | North Fork 3 |
| Huntington 4 | Parkersburg 1 |
| Keystone 2 | Wheeling 2 |

In this same year, 1922–1923, the J. P. S. A. membership in West Virginia showed a total of 24 cities and towns or communities, and 154 members, presumably the next highest total membership of all time. This complete list of membership in 1922–1923 I present below, inasmuch as Volume 23, for the year 1921–1922, failed to include in the volume a list of the names of the members.

| | |
|---|---|
| Bluefield 5 | Martinsburg 1 |
| Charleston 22 | Montgomery 1 |
| Charles Town 1 | Morgantown 8 |
| Clarksburg 24 | Moundsville 1 |
| Elkins 3 | North Fork 3 |
| Fairmont 10 | Parkersburg 5 |
| Farmington 1 | Piedmont 2 |
| Huntington 17 | Princeton 2 |
| Keyser 2 | Thomas 6 |
| Keystone 1 | Welch 3 |
| Kimball 2 | Weston 3 |
| Logan 1 | Wheeling 30 |

## Membership in the Jewish Publication Society of America (1922–1923)

(This list contains many names not otherwise found in the records of the several Jewish communities of the State. I have corrected the J. P. S. A. misspellings of names wherever I have been able to do so, through personal knowledge of the West Virginia Jews.)

*Bluefield*

Isadore Cohen
Mrs. Solomon Greenspon
J. Lowenstein
Mrs. Henry (Anna G.)
 Rodgin
Harry Stolch

*Charleston*

Ben Baer
M. Bedwinek

Mrs. P. Briggs
Simon Cohen
H. Frankenberger
Simon H. Galperin
Hyman Galperin
Mrs. M. R. Goldman
M. N. Horowitz
Rabbi M. H. Kaaplander
Leo Loeb
I. Lowenstein
Philip May

[Dr. I.] Mendeloff
J. N. Palley
H. Polan
M. Pushkin
L. J. Sclove
I. J. Shor
A. P. Silverstein
Young Men's Hebrew
  Association
J. Webb

*Charles Town*

M. Palmbaum & Bro.

*Clarksburg*

H. A. Caplan
Jacob Cohen
S. L. Edlavitch
D. B. Franz
D. M. Franz
M. Friedlander
L. Goodfriend
M. Guttman
Louis Hiller
J. Jacobs
J. Jay
Joseph Kaplan
M. M. Lampe
Benjamin Lefkowitz
J. Marks
M. Nachman (Max
  Nachman?)
S. Newman
W. Nusbaum
Louis Oliker
S. Percoff
Max Rose

Jacob Slaven
Louis Spiro
Reverend B. Trub

*Elkins*

G. Goldberg
S. Goldberg
Dr. William W. Golden

*Fairmont*

E. Deitz
I. Funt
J. Goffan
Simon Goodman
R. Hoffman
P. P. Lipson
A. Meyers
D. B. Oliker
D. M. Osgood
I. Zosloff

*Farmington*

[Rabbi] Jacob R. Marcus

*Huntington*

Samuel Biern
H. Brownstein
D. Cohen
Joseph Cohen
Rabbi Abraham Feinstein
David Fox
Samuel Gideon
S. H. Glick
Samuel Gore
L. H. Hartz
M. K. Hirschman

Mrs. I. S. Hyman
R. S. Radinsky
I. Ben Romer
S. Samson
D. C. Schonthal
I. Sweing [Sweig?]

*Keyser*

J. Leonard Baer
(later of Beckley and
Wheeling)
E. Kaplon

*Keystone*

H. Budnick

*Kimball*

Beth Jacob Congregation
A. Forman

*Logan*

Mrs. Benjamin Tobin

*Martinsburg*

George Katz

*Montgomery*

Aaron Meyer

*Morgantown*

Israel Cohen
I. A. De Lynn
Benjamin Green
C. E. Kirsch
Charles Lyon

Sam Posner
M. S. Slaven
J. P. Wolf

*Moundsville*

Samuel J. Gordon

*North Fork*

Aaron Catzen
Jack Rosen
H. Seligman

*Parkersburg*

J. Goldstein
D. H. Kahn
S. Lasky
H. Lerner
J. Stern

*Piedmont*

A. Abramson
David Abramson

*Princeton*

Boris Borinsky
Joseph Tomchin

*Thomas*

H. Baker
L. Bear
Ruby Rubenstein
Barney Schilansky
J. Schilansky
Dr. P. Schilansky

*Welch*

J. Effron
Louis Gottlieb
Dr. J. L. Sameth

*Weston*

H. Blumberg
B. Kaplan
William Malkow

*Wheeling*

B. S. Baer
C. Banov
H. H. Barach
S. Darris
S. G. Elpern
Eoff Street [Temple]
   Religious School
S. K. Frank
A. J. Friedman

H. M. Front
J. [Jacques?] Front
T. Goldinger
I. Gordon
M. Graff
F. Grossman
C. H. Jacobs
Mrs. M. Jacobs
Solomon Kirness
L. Kraft
H. S. Levine
J. Levine
J. E. Moss
L. Neistadt
A. Reichblum
Mrs. J. Robinson
Benjamin L. Rosenbloom
S. H. Sachs
Max Schafer
M. [Moses] Sonneborn
L. B. Stein
H. Sweetwine

## 1923

As of February 28, 1923 [according to a different report found in the *AJYB*], there were 107 members of the J. P. S. A. in West Virginia.

## 1924–1929

In the five-year period from 1924 to 1929, the J. P. S. A. gained 22 new members [of course, always with some members dropping out and quitting their membership every year], in 8 cities or communities of West Virginia, as follows:

| | | |
|---|---|---|
| Charleston 2 | Martinsburg 1 | North Fork 1 |
| Fairmont 2 | Montgomery 1 | Wheeling 4 |
| Huntington 5 | Morgantown 5 | Williamson 1 |

## 1925

As of February 28, 1925, there were 79 members of the J. P. S. A. in West Virginia.

As of December 31, 1925, the *AJYB* reported a further decline in the West Virginia membership in the J. P. S. A., with the reduced total of 50 [51] members in the organization.

## 1926–1927

In the year 1926–1927 (5687 A.M.), the J. P. S. A. received 7 new members from the following 6 cities or towns of the State:

| | |
|---|---|
| Charleston 1 | Keyser 1 |
| Clarksburg 1 | Logan 1 |
| Grafton 1 | Morgantown 2 |

## 1927

In 1927, West Virginia had only 35 members in the J. P. S. A.

## 1927–1928

In 1927–1928, 1 new member joined the J. P. S. A. from Romney, and 1 from Wheeling.

## 1929

As of February 29, 1929, the J. P. S. A. had a total of 100 members from among the Jews of West Virginia.

## 1930–1935

In the six-year period from 1930 to 1935, inclusive, 18 communities, cities or towns of West Virginia had a total of 59 members in the J. P. S. A., distributed as follows:

| | |
|---|---|
| Bluefield 3 | Fairmont 1 |
| Charleston 6 | Huntington 5 |
| Elkins 2 | Keyser 1 |

Kimball 1                        Osage 2
Logan 2                          Princeton 1
Martinsburg 5                    Romney 1
Montgomery 2                     Weston 1
Morgantown 8                     Wheeling 15
North Fork 2                     White Sulphur Springs 1

## 1935–1936

In 1935–1936, the membership of the J. P. S. A. had declined, in West Virginia, to a total of 27, distributed in the following 9 cities or towns of the State:

Bluefield 1                      North Fork 2
Charleston 2                     Osage 2
Elkins 1                         Wheeling 9
Martinsburg 3                    White Sulphur Springs 1
Morgantown 6

## 1936–1941

In the quinquennial period from 1936 to 1941, inclusive, 41 additional members of the J. P. S. A. from West Virginia, in 7 cities or towns, were distributed as follows:

Charleston 8                     Fairmont 3
Hollidays Cove                   Huntington 4
  (Weirton) 1                    Martinsburg 1
Clarksburg 1                     Wheeling 23

## 1941–1942

Volume 43 of the *AJYB*, for the year 1941–1942 (5702 A.M.), was the last volume in which the actual names and addresses of the members of, or the subscribers to, the Jewish Publication Society of America were published in the *American Jewish Year Book*, in alphabetical lists by states and cities and by the names of the subscribers, at the back of the volume. In that year, the West Virginia members of the J. P. S. A. numbered only 25, distributed in the following 8 cities or towns:

| | |
|---|---|
| Charleston 5 | Morgantown 1 |
| Fairmont 2 | North Fork 1 |
| Huntington 2 | Wheeling 11 |
| Martinsburg 1 | Williamson 2 |

For the sake of the historical record, and because it may be of some interest later, I present herewith the complete list of the names (and of the addresses, where given) of the members of the J. P. S. A. in the second year of its existence and in the first year in which it published annual lists of its members (1900–1901, Volume 2, 5661 A.M.), at a time when the Society had 47 West Virginia members from 13 cities, towns, or communities; as well as the list of names of subscribers printed in the last year when it published such lists, i. e., the year 1941–1942 (Volume 43, 5702 A.M.), when the Society had only 25 members, in 8 cities, towns, or communities in the State, as follows:

## 1900–1901 (5661 A.M.)

*Charleston*

Benjamin Baer
Philip Frankenberger, 415 Virginia Street
Louis Loewenstein
Lewis S. Strauss, 532 Virginia Street

*Charles Town* (spelled as Charlestown in the volume)

William Kahn
M. Palmbaum & Bro.

*Clarksburg*

D. Davidson
I. Nusbaum
M. A. Nusbaum

*Fairmont* (misspelled as Fairmount in the volume)

Louis Mansbach
Harry Nusbaum

*Grafton*

>   I. Friedman
>   C. [I. C.] Klein

*Harpers Ferry*

>   A.[bram] Kaplon

*Huntington*

>   Samuel Gideon
>   Lester Keiner

*Martinsburg*

>   Mrs. George Katz, 109 Martin [Street]

*Morgantown*

>   Milton Hirschman

*Parkersburg*

>   M. Berman, 318 9½ [Street]
>   Charles Epstein
>   S. Kahn
>   M. A. Kuder, 117 Fifth [Street]
>   Mrs. S. Rosenheim
>   Joseph Stern
>   M. S. Thanhouser
>   J. Weinberger, 1603 Spring [Street]

*Piedmont*

>   George Mansbach

*Weston*

>   Mrs. E. Klein
>   Mrs. Benjamin Lehman

*Wheeling*

>   Joseph Emsheimer, 1306 Market Street
>   David Gutman

Harburger Brothers, 100 Sixteenth Street
Hebrew Sunday School Library, care of Reverend Harry
    Levi [Eoff Street Temple]
Bernard Horkheimer
Julius Horkheimer, 716 Main Street
Louis Horkheimer, 1107 Chapline [Street]
Morris Horkheimer
Israel Isenberg
Mrs. B. Jacobs, 707 Main Street
Reverend [Rabbi] Harry Levi, 76 Fifteenth Street
Lieberman & Grosheim, 772 Twelfth Street
J. Reizenstein
S. M. Rice, 1102 Chapline [Street]
Henry Sonneborn, 1207 Market Street
M. Sonneborn
Henry Speyer
M. Steinfeld

## 1941–1942 (Volume 43, 5702 A.M.)

*Charleston*

Martin L. Braunstein, 1558 Jackson [Street]
S. H. Galperin, 628 ½ Beech Avenue
M. B. Goldman, 2020 Kanawha [Street]
Leah Buff Frankel Library, B'nai Jacob Synagogue
H. Polan, 110 Capitol Street

*Fairmont* (still misspelled as Fairmount)

L.[awrence] M. Brile, 435 Walnut Street
Rabbi Harry Lasker

*Huntington*

Rabbi R.[alph] N. [an error for H.] Blumenthal, 1214
    Eighth Street
Samuel Samson, 325 South Boulevard West

*Martinsburg*

  Allen B. Katz, 505 South Queen [Street]

*Morgantown*

  Reverend [Rabbi] Dr. A.[lfred] Jospe, 754 Willey

*North Fork*

  A.[aron] Catzen

*Wheeling*

  J. Bernhardt, 1225 Market Street
  H. L. Cooper, 11 Campbell Apartments, Edgewood
  Samuel K. Frank
  S. L. Good, Hawthorne Court
  Sidney S. Good, 1259 National Road
  Julius I. Harr, 12 Linden Avenue
  E.[rnest] S. Horkheimer, Forest Hills
  Max Horne, 1100 Main Street
  Maurice E. Kaufman, 1133 Market Street
  G. A. Levenson, Reichert Furniture Company
  H. S. Levin, 113 Washington Avenue
  Reverend Dr. [Rabbi] G.[eorge] B. Lieberman
  Samuel Posin, 136 Elm Street
  Robert Rubin, 427 North Main Street

*Williamson*

  Samuel Brown, Brown's Dress Shop
  Harry Schwachter

## 1946

West Virginia had only 18 members in the J. P. S. A. on September 1, 1946.

## 1947

The membership of West Virginia Jews in the J. P. S. A., as of August 1, 1947, was 28.

## 1948

The membership of West Virginia Jews in the J. P. S. A., as of September 1, 1948, was 49.

## 1955–1957

### WEST VIRGINIA MEMBERS OF THE J. P S. A.
#### IN 1955–1957

In 1955–1957, according to special data and figures supplied by the Jewish Publication Society of America, there were only 22 subscribers or members of the Society throughout all of West Virginia, distributed as follows in 11 cities or towns:

(The date in parentheses indicates when the individual enrolled himself in the J. P. S. A. as a member.)

*Beckley* (2 members)

Junior Congregation of Temple Beth El (1950)
Rabbi Abraham I. Shinedling (1950)

*Bluefield* (2 members)

Congregation Ahavath Sholom Religious School (1955)
Isadore Cohen (1947)

*Charleston* (4 members)

Federated Jewish Charities of Charleston (1945)
H. Polan (1945)
The Virginia Street Temple Sisterhood (1953)
Rabbi Samuel Volkman (1956)

*Ellenboro* (1 member)

Isadore Tucker

(Isadore Tucker is a former resident of Bluefield, and the brother of Sidney Tucker, of that city. In 1957, Isadore Tucker was a resident of, and in business in, Ellenboro, a town of some 500 population in Ritchie County, east of Parkersburg.)

*Fairmont* (2 members)

> Morris Kessler (1948)
> Earl P. Stevens (1956)

*Huntington* (3 members)

> J. M. Bachrach (1957)
> Samuel Samson (1956)
> Samuel Samson, Jr. (1956)

*Logan* (1 member)

> Mrs. J. T. Fish (1955)

*Morgantown* (1 member)

> The Hillel Foundation of the University of West Virginia (1942)

*Parkersburg* (1 member)

> Gershon Spivack (1954)

*Weirton* (1 member)

> Beth Israel Sunday School (1949)

*Wheeling* (4 members)

> The Jewish Community Council, care of Isadore A. Rubinstein (1955)
> H. S. Levine (1945)
> Samuel Posin (1948)
> Mrs. Alex Wishinew [Wishnew?] (1947)

The surprising fewness of the Jewish members of the Jewish Publication Society of America from West Virginia in recent years (the Jewish population of the State was about 6,000 in 1957) led Lesser Zussman, the executive secretary of the J. P. S. A., to reply to me, as follows, on August 21, 1957, in response to my letter of inquiry on the subject:

"I think that you will be disappointed to see how few members [22 members in 11 communities] there have been of the

Jewish Publication Society of America over the past three years. This is typical of the lethargic situation across the country regarding the reading of the good books published by the Society."

In an appendix to Volume XII of the old *JE* (1905), on pages iii–xxx, there was published a "List of Patrons" who, between the years 1900 and 1905, helped with the publication of this notable and important early Jewish encyclopedia, and presumably purchased sets thereof. The names of the following 15 West Virginia Jews from four cities of the State have been collected from this "List of Patrons," persons then residing in West Virginia:

*Bluefield*
Saul Greenspon
(erroneously printed as
Greensson)
N. M. Sameth

Max Rauch
[Rabbi] Leon Volmer

*Parkersburg*
M. A. Kuder

*Charleston*
H. Berkenstein [Bekenstein?]
William Kahn
Isaac Loewenstein
Leon V. May
George Palmbaum

*Wheeling*
David Gutman
Israel Isenberg
Reverend Harry Levi
S. M. Rice
M. [Moses] Sonneborn

The name of Benjamin A. Bonnheim, formerly rabbi in Wheeling, occurs as a patron of the *JE* under Las Vegas, N. Mex.

THE AMERICAN JEWISH COMMITTEE
IN WEST VIRGINIA
1908–1909

West Virginia, in 1908–1909, was a part of District No. VIII of the American Jewish Committee (with its headquarters in New York City), consisting of the four States of Indiana,

Kentucky, Ohio, and West Virginia. This Eighth District had five members on its District Committee, but in that year none of the five was from West Virginia. Later on, District No. VIII of the American Jewish Committee had a member or two from West Virginia.

## 1927

In 1927, the sum of $120 was given in contributions from West Virginia, by Jews of the State, to the American Jewish Committee, for the furtherance of its work. The American Jewish Committee had always sponsored the publication of the *American Jewish Year Book*.

## 1928

In 1928 (for the year 1928–1929), the sum of $45 was contributed by West Virginia Jews to the American Jewish Committee. (From now on referred to as the A. J. C.)

## 1929

Contributions to the A. J. C. by West Virginia Jews, in 1929, amounted to $160.

## 1930

In 1930, the Jews of West Virginia contributed to the A. J. C. the sum of $125.

## 1931–1932

In 1931–1932, Louis Horkheimer, of Wheeling, was listed in the *AJYB* (1932–1933 [5693 A.M.], page 343) [All the preceding and following data on the A. J. C. in West Virginia have been excerpted from the volumes of the *AJYB*.] as the Community Representative on the American Jewish Committee from West Virginia. He was re-elected to this position in 1933–1934, and remained a member of the American Jewish Committee, in the Community Representative Class, until 1940, when his final term expired.

## 1933–1934

David Gideon, of Huntington, was elected, in 1933–1934, to the American Jewish Committee, as a Community Representative, to fill a vacancy. He remained a member of the A. J. C., in the Community Representatives Department, until 1939, when his term expired.

## 1942–1943

In 1942–1943, Dez C. Schonthal served as a corporate member of the A. J. C. from Huntington.

## 1943–1944

In 1943–1944, Ezra Gilbert, of Bluefield, served as a member of the A. J. C., representing the Bluefield-Princeton Jewish Welfare Fund. He was noted in Mercer County as a Jewish communal and religious worker, and was the father of Hennon Gilbert.

## Jewish Immigration into West Virginia
## (1914 to 1940)

### 1914

In 1914, a total of 69 of the Jewish immigrants admitted into the United States were settled in West Virginia [with the aid of the local Jewish communities] (*AJYB*, 1915–1916 [5676 A.M.]).

### 1917

In 1917, 13 Jewish immigrants were admitted to and were settled in West Virginia, out of a total of 1,695 general immigrants who came to the United States in that year.

### 1918

In 1918, only 3 Jewish immigrants were admitted to the State, out of a total of 292 general immigrants who settled in the State in that year.

### 1918–1919

In 1918–1919, only 4 Jewish immigrants who were admitted to the United States settled in West Virginia.

### 1919–1920

Jewish immigrants who were admitted to the United States and were settled in West Virginia in 1919–1920 numbered 15.

### 1920–1921

In 1920–1921, 88 Jewish immigrants admitted to the United States settled in West Virginia.

### 1921–1922

In the year 1921–1922, 60 of the Jewish immigrants admitted into the United States settled in West Virginia.

### 1922–1923

Jewish immigrants admitted to the United States who came to, and settled in, West Virginia in 1922–1923 numbered 29.

### 1923–1924

In the year ending on June 30, 1924, a total of 64 Jews admitted into the United States settled in West Virginia.

### 1924–1925

From June, 1924, to June, 1925, 5 of the Jewish immigrants admitted to the United States settled in West Virginia.

### 1925–1926

In the year extending from July 1, 1925, to June 30, 1926, 11 of the Jewish immigrants admitted into the United States settled in West Virginia.

PLATE III

ISADORE R. WEIN
(of Beckley, West Virginia)
President of Beth El Congregation, Beckley
(1945–1946 and 1951–1959)
(see pages 270–271, 286, and 356–357)

ABRAHAM I. SHINEDLING
Rabbi of Ahavath Sholom Congregation,
Bluefield (1947–1950)
and of Beth El Congregation, Beckley
(1950–1956)
(see pages 292 and 426)

PLATE IV

The New Synagogue of Congregation Ahavath Sholom, of Bluefield, W. Va., at 632 Albemarle Street

## 1928–1929

From July 1, 1928, to June 30, 1929, 6 Jewish immigrants admitted into the United States settled in West Virginia.

## 1929–1930

In the year which ended on June 30, 1930, 6 Jewish immigrants admitted into the United States settled in West Virginia.

## 1930–1931

9 Jewish immigrants settled in West Virginia in the year ending on June 30, 1931.

## 1931–1932

In the year ending on June 30, 1932, 2 Jewish immigrants admitted into the United States settled in West Virginia.

## 1933–1934

In the year extending from July 1, 1933, to June 30, 1934, 13 Jewish immigrants admitted into the United States settled in West Virginia.

## 1934–1935

In the year which ended on June 30, 1935, 24 of the Jewish immigrants admitted into the United States settled in West Virginia.

## 1935–1936

In the year which ended on June 30, 1936, 2 Jewish immigrants admitted into the United States settled in West Virginia.

## 1936–1937

For the year which ended on June 30, 1937, 14 of the Jewish immigrants into the United States settled in West Virginia.

### 1937–1938

In the year ending on June 30, 1938, 22 of the Jewish immigrants admitted into the United States settled in West Virginia.

### 1939–1940

In the year which ended on June 30, 1940, 37 of the Jewish immigrants admitted into the United States settled in West Virginia. Thereafter, presumably, the incidence of the Second World War was a hindrance to Jewish immigrants, and I was unable to find any further statistics on this subject in the later volumes of the *AJYB*.

## THE INDUSTRIAL REMOVAL OFFICE IN WEST VIRGINIA (1910 TO 1915)

### 1910

In 1910, apparently for the first time, West Virginia had two agencies of the Industrial Removal Office, which was organized in New York City in 1900 [or 1901], and had its headquarters in New York City during the several years of its existence. These first two West Virginia agencies of the Industrial Removal Office were in Huntington and Parkersburg. In all likelihood, it was for the first time in the history of the State and of the Jewish community there that such offices or agencies were established, at Huntington and Parkersburg, two large industrial centers of the State, in that year, 1910 (*AJYB*, 1910–1911 [5671 A.M.], page 241).

The Industrial Removal Office was created as a part of the Jewish Agricultural and Industrial Aid Society, which was, in turn, a part of the Baron [Maurice] de Hirsch Fund. The goal of the Baron de Hirsch Fund was to Americanize the immigrants of the Jewish faith into the United States, and to assist them upon their arrival in the United States. The specific goal of the Industrial Removal Office was that of relieving the crowdedness of the Eastern cities, especially New York City, where almost three-fourths of the Jewish immigrants into the United States who came from Europe to the Port of New York in the last two decades of the 19th century settled or remained, not moving from that Eastern metropolis. The Industrial Removal Office succeeded in diverting at least a part of the stream of Jewish immigrants into other regions of the interior of the United States, including a small number into West Virginia, as here indicated. In the three or four larger West Virginia cities which had agencies of the Industrial Removal Office, and in which such agencies were successfully set up, its representatives as well as cooperating local committees helped the new immigrants to secure employment and/or to find homes. The famous Galveston Movement was also a part of the program and work of the Industrial Removal Office, if unofficially.

## 1910–1911

In 1910–1911, West Virginia had 3 agencies of the Industrial Removal Office. These were located in the following cities:

Charleston        Huntington        Wheeling

(*AJYB*, 1911–1912 [5672 A.M.], page 228).

## 1911–1912

In 1911–1912, West Virginia still had its three agencies of the Industrial Removal Office, i. e., those located in Charleston, Huntington, and Wheeling.

## 1912–1913

In 1912–1913, there were, in West Virginia, four agencies of the Industrial Removal Office, with the agency in Parkersburg restored after two years of disuse. These 4 agencies were, in that year, located in:

Charleston        Parkersburg
Huntington        Wheeling

*(AJYB, 1913–1914 [5674], page 375).*

### 1914–1915

In the year 1914–1915, the Industrial Removal Office had the same four agencies in West Virginia in 1914–1915, i. e., those in Charleston, Huntington, Parkersburg, and Wheeling.

These four agencies of the Industrial Removal Office functioned in these four cities of West Virginia until the year 1922, when the Industrial Removal Office was closed down, since it was definitely established that all immigration into the United States was to be greatly restricted. Some small Jewish immigration into some of the cities of West Virginia continued until late in the 1940's, as to other parts of the United States.

### BiWEEKLY STUDENT RABBIS IN WEST VIRGINIA CONGREGATIONS

### (1943 to 1959)

(From the records supplied by Richard Bluestein and Dora Aaronsohn, of the Hebrew Union College-Jewish Institute of Religion, in Cincinnati)

The following rabbinical students (or "student rabbis," as they are usually called) from the Hebrew Union College, in Cincinnati, served the smaller Jewish congregations in West Virginia, those which were not large enough to maintain a resident or permanent rabbi, as part-time, biweekly "rabbis" or as High Holy Day officiants, during the period from 1943 to 1959. (For the details of these student rabbis' services and careers, and for complete data on these congregations, see the sections dealing with the individual cities and communities.)

*Beckley* (Beth El Congregation)

| | |
|---|---|
| 1948 | Josef Zeitin (for the High Holy Days only) |
| 1948–1949 | Richard G. Hirsch |
| 1949 | Donald Harris (for the High Holy Days only) |
| 1949–1950 | Norman Kahan |

1956        Dr. Elias Epstein (for the High Holy Days
            only)
1956–1957   Frank N. Sundheim
1959–1960   Gerald H. Schuster

*Bluefield* (Congregation Ahavath Sholom)
1943–1944   A.[lfred] Stanley Dreyfus
1944–1945   Sanford E. Rosen
1945–1946   Jerome W. Grollman

*Fairmont* (Fairmont Jewish Community Center)
1957–1958   Edwin Friedman
1958–1959   Robert Samuels

*Logan* (B'nai El Congregation)
1943–1944   Martin I. Hinchin
1944–1947   Sidney Akselrad
1947–1948   C. Melvyn Helfgott
1948–1949   Earl A. Grollman
1949–1950   Malcolm I. Cohen
1950        Alexander M. Schindler (for the High Holy
            Days only)
1950–1952   Wolfgang Hamburger
1952–1953   Stanley Kaplan
1953–1954   Frederick C. Schwartz
1954–1955   Isaac Jerusalmi
1955–1956   Nathaniel Zimskind
1956–1957   Walter Blumenthal
1957–1958   Joseph Levine
1958–1959   Joel Wittstein

*Martinsburg* (Beth Jacob Congregation)
1957–1958   Philip Schechter
1958–1959   David Kline

*Parkersburg* (B'nai Israel Congregation)
1942–1943   Irving A. Mandel
1944–1945   Jerome W. Grollman

1945–1946   Eugene Borowitz and Herbert M. Yarrish
1946–1948   Herbert M. Yarrish
1948–1949   Irwin M. Blank
1949–1950   Louis J. Sigel
1950–1951   Jerome B. Cohen
1951–1952   Richard S. Sternberger
1952–1953   Henry Cohen
1953–1954   Robert L. Lehman
1954–1955   Sanford M. Shapero
1955–1956   Sherwin Wine
1956–1957   Shimon Maslin
1957–1958   Harold Rubens
1958–1959   Alan Weitzman

*Welch* (Emanuel Congregation)

1943–1944   Alton Winters
1944–1945   Leonard H. Devine
1945–1947   Steven S. Schwarzschild
1947–1948   Max Podet
1948–1949   Rav A. Soloff
1949–1950   Jerome B. Cohen
1950–1955   Jakob J. Petuchowski
1955–1957   Leonard Kravitz
1957–1958   Rabbi M. Arthur Oles (a fellow at the Hebrew
            Union College)
1958        (September) Gerald Schuster (for the High
            Holy Days only)
1958–1959   Rabbi Stanley F. Chyet (biweekly)

*Williamson* (B'nai Israel Congregation)

1943–1945   H. Bruce Ehrmann
1945–1946   Murray Blackman
1946–1948   Jerome W. Grollman
1948–1949   Murray Blackman
1949–1950   Bernard Martin
1950–1952   Minard Klein

1952–1953   Alexander M. Schindler
1953–1954   Nathan Bark
1954–1955   Sherman Stein
1955–1957   Robert Blinder
1957–1958   William Leffler
1958–1959   William Leffler

In all cases, the services of the student rabbis from the Hebrew Union College, in Cincinnati, extended only throughout the so-called "religious year" or the "academic year," i. e., in each year from September or the beginning of the period of the High Holy Days, until the following June. The student rabbis did not function in the above communities during the summer months from June to September.

## The Jewish Chautauqua Society in West Virginia

A State Convention of Chautauqua [Jewish Chautauqua Society] Circles was founded in West Virginia, and was in existence for a number of years. Most of its representatives, over the years, came from Wheeling, where the Jewish community was the most greatly interested in the work of the older Jewish Chautauqua Society, which was founded by Rabbi Henry Berkowitz, of Philadelphia, and the aim of which was the spreading of Jewish culture and knowledge of Judaism among Jews and Jewish groups.

Thus, in the early years, those of the 1900's, Rabbi Harry Levi and I. [Israel] Isenberg, of Wheeling, were its representatives, or delegates, at the Summer Assemblies of the Jewish Chautauqua Society, held generally in the eastern part of the United States, in or near Philadelphia or Atlantic City, N. J. In several of these Summer Assemblies, Rabbi Harry Levi, up to the year 1911, when he moved to Boston, gave lecture courses for the teachers and other Jewish persons who attended.

JEWISH CHAUTAUQUA SOCIETY LECTURERS
IN WEST VIRGINIA

(1943–1959)

The following data on the visits paid by rabbis of the region to colleges, universities, summer camps, and church camps in West Virginia under the auspices of the later Jewish Chautauqua Society, in the interests of the understanding of Judaism by non-Jews, were either compiled by me from general knowledge and research; or were furnished to me through the kindness of Sylvan Lebow, executive director of the Jewish Chautauqua Society (formerly of Cincinnati, and later of New York City), and of Miss Ruth Kranz (Mrs. Ruth Kranz Simonson), his administrative assistant:

*Alderson-Broaddus College*, at Philippi, W. Va.

1946   Rabbi Louis J. Cashdan (then of Charleston, W. Va.)
1949   Rabbi Maurice Feuer (then of Goldsboro, N. C.)
1950   Rabbi Joseph H. Freedman (then of Wheeling, W. Va.)
1951   Rabbi A. Goodman (of Columbus, Ohio)
1952   Rabbi H. Goren Perlmutter (of Johnstown, Pa.)
1953   Rabbi Morris M. Rose (then of Morgantown, W. Va.)
1955   (April) Rabbi Morris M. Rose (then of Morgantown)
1957   (April 10) Rabbi Samuel Volkman (of Charleston, W. Va.)

*Beckley College*, at Beckley, W. Va.

1956   (May) Rabbi Abraham I. Shinedling (then of Beckley, W. Va.)

*Bethany College*, at Bethany, W. Va.

1945   Rabbi Samuel M. Gup (deceased; then of Columbus, Ohio)
1946   Rabbi Charles B. Lesser (then of Wheeling, W. Va.)
1947   Rabbi Louis J. Cashdan (then of Charleston, W. Va.)
1948   Rabbi Malcolm H. Stern (of Norfolk, Va.)

1950 Rabbi Harold L. Gelfman (then of Bluefield, W. Va.)
1954 (November) Rabbi Burton E. Levinson (then of Pittsburgh, Pa.)
1955 (December) Rabbi Harold Silver (of Pittsburgh, Pa.)

*Bluefield State Teachers College*, at Bluefield, W. Va.

1943 Rabbi Lawrence A. Block (then of Huntington, W. Va.)
1944 Rabbi Abraham Feinstein (of Chattanooga, Tenn.; formerly of Huntington)
1945 Rabbi Robert P. Jacobs (then of Asheville, N. C.)
1946 Rabbi Bernard Zeiger (then of Chapel Hill, N. C.)
1947 Rabbi Ezra Spicehandler (of the Hebrew Union College, Cincinnati)
1948 Rabbi Martin M. Perley (of Louisville, Ky.)
1949 Rabbi Eugene Hibshman (then of Huntington, W. Va.)
1950 Rabbi Louis J. Cashdan (then of Charleston, W. Va.)
1952 Rabbi Harold L. Gelfman (then of Bluefield, W. Va.)
1954 Rabbi Herbert J. Wilner (then of Bluefield)
1955 (April) Rabbi Samuel Volkman (of Charleston)
1956 (March) Rabbi Abraham I. Shinedling (then of Beckley, W. Va.)
1957 (March 5) Rabbi Samuel R. Shillman (of Roanoke, Va.)
1958 (March 11) Rabbi Arnold Shevlin (of Danville, Va.)
1959 (March 19) Rabbi George B. Lieberman (of Rockville Center, Long Island; formerly of Wheeling)

*Concord College*, at Athens, W. Va.

1943 Rabbi Lawrence A. Block (then of Huntington, W. Va.)
1944 Rabbi Frederick I. Rypins (then of Roanoke, Va.)
1945 Rabbi Louis J. Cashdan (then of Charleston, W. Va.)
1946 Rabbi Albert M. Lewis (then of Charlottesville, Va.)
1947 Rabbi Abraham I. Shinedling (then of Bluefield, W. Va.)

1948   Rabbi Eugene Hibshman (then of Huntington, W.
       Va.)
1955   (March) Rabbi Samuel R. Shillman (of Roanoke, Va.)
1956   (March) Rabbi Samuel Volkman (of Charleston, W.
       Va.)

*Davis and Elkins College,* at Elkins, W. Va.

1937   Rabbi Baruch Braunstein (then of Wheeling, W. Va.)
1945   Rabbi George B. Lieberman (then of Wheeling)
1946   Rabbi Abraham Shaw (of Baltimore, Md.)
1947   Rabbi A. [Abraham] Granowitz (Abram M. Granison)
       (of New York City)
1948   Rabbi Louis J. Cashdan (then of Charleston, W. Va.)
1949   Rabbi Albert T. Bilgray
1950   Rabbi Herbert J. Wilner (then of Bluefield, W. Va.)
1951   Rabbi Abraham I. Shinedling (then of Beckley, W.
       Va.)
1952   Rabbi Samuel Cooper (of Charleston)
1954   (March) Rabbi Abraham I. Shinedling (then of
       Beckley)
1955   (March) Rabbi Samuel Volkman (of Charleston)
1959   (April 8–9) Rabbi Theodore S. Levy (then of Hunt-
       ington)

*Fairmont Junior College,* at Fairmont, W. Va.

1948   Rabbi Louis J. Cashdan (then of Charleston)

*Glenville State College,* at Glenville, W. Va.

1942   Rabbi Alexander D. Goode (deceased)
1943   Rabbi Henry Tavel
1944   Rabbi Aaron Lefkowitz (formerly of Cumberland,
       Md.)
1945   Rabbi Samuel Cooper (of Charleston)
1947   Rabbi Louis J. Cashdan (then of Charleston)
1949   Rabbi Louis A. Josephson (then of Fairmont, W. Va.)
1950   Rabbi Leo Lichtenberg (then of Athens, Ohio)

1951 Rabbi Abraham I. Shinedling (then of Beckley, W. Va.) and Rabbi Eugene E. Hibshman (then of Huntington, W. Va.)
1952 Rabbi Abraham I. Shinedling (then of Beckley)
1953 Rabbi Samuel Volkman (of Charleston)
1954 (March) Rabbi Theodore S. Levy (of Huntington)
1955 (January) Rabbi Samuel Volkman (of Charleston)
1956 (March) Rabbi Joseph Levine (of Greensburg, Pa.)
1957 (March 20) Rabbi Samuel Volkman (of Charleston)

*Marshall College*, at Huntington, W. Va.

1940 Rabbi Samuel M. Gup (then of Columbus, Ohio) (deceased)
1949 Rabbi Abraham Feinstein (of Chattanooga, Tenn.)
1950 Rabbi Samuel Wohl (of Cincinnati, Ohio)
1951 Rabbi Stanley R. Brav (of Cincinnati)
1952 Rabbi Herbert S. Waller (of Louisville, Ky.)
1953 Rabbi Louis J. Cashdan (then of Charleston)
1954 (February) Rabbi Theodore S. Levy (of Huntington)
1955 (February) Rabbi Theodore S. Levy (of Huntington)
1956 (February) Rabbi Abraham Feinstein (of Chattanooga, Tenn.)
1958 (February 18) Rabbi Norman Diamond (of Springfield, Ohio)
1959 (March 1–4) Rabbi Joseph R. Rosenbloom (of Lexington, Ky.)

*Morris Harvey College*, at Charleston, W. Va.

1954 (February) Rabbi Joseph H. Freedman (then of Wheeling, W. Va.)

*Potomac State College of West Virginia University*, at Keyser, W. Va.

1951 Rabbi Herbert J. Wilner (then of Bluefield, W. Va.)
1957 (February 24 to 27) Rabbi David L. Schwartz (of Hagerstown, Md.)

1958   (February 23–26) Rabbi Leo J. Stillpass (of Johns-
       town, Pa.)
1959   (February 23–25) Rabbi Max Selinger (of Cumber-
       land, Md.)

*Salem College*, at Salem, W. Va.

   [year not given] Rabbi S. [Baruch?] Braunstein [then of
       Wheeling?]
1938   Rabbi Ariel L. Goldburg (then of Charleston, W. Va.)
1939   Rabbi S. Cook [Samuel Cook, then of Cincinnati?]
1940   Rabbi George B. Lieberman (then of Wheeling)
1941   Rabbi Hugo B. Schiff (then of Washington, D. C.)
1942   Rabbi Albert T. Bilgray
1943   Rabbi Israel J. Sarasohn
1944   Rabbi Irving M. Levey (of Princeton, N. J.)
1945   Rabbi Louis J. Cashdan (then of Charleston)
1946   Rabbi Victor E. Reichert (of Cincinnati)
1947   Rabbi Louis A. Josephson (then of Fairmont)
1948   Rabbi A. Goodman (of Columbus, Ohio)
1949   Rabbi M. Nathaniel Bension (then of Wheeling)
1950   Rabbi Herman E. Snyder (of Springfield, Mass.)
1951   Rabbi Louis J. Cashdan (then of Charleston)
1952   Rabbi C. Melvyn Helfgott (of Charlotte, N. C.)
1954   (February) Rabbi Samuel Volkman (of Charleston)
1955   Rabbi Robert A. Raab (of McKeesport, Pa.)

*Shepherd College*, at Shepherdstown, W. Va.

1942   Rabbi Alexander D. Goode (deceased)
1943   Rabbi Allan Tarshish (of Charleston, S. C.)
1944   Rabbi Joseph Klein (then of Philadelphia)
1945   Rabbi Nathan Kaber (of Altoona, Pa.)
1946   Rabbi Daniel L. Davis (of New York City)
1947   Rabbi Meir Lasker (of Philadelphia)
1948   Rabbi Abraham Shusterman (of Baltimore)
1949   Rabbi Lester W. Roubey (then of Lancaster, Pa.)
1950   Rabbi Philip D. Bookstaber (of Harrisburg, Pa.)
1951   Rabbi Wolli Kaelter (then of McKeesport, Pa.)

1952 Rabbi Marcus Kramer (then of York, Pa.)

1953 Rabbi David L. Schwartz (of Hagerstown, Md.)

1954 (February) Rabbi David Cardozo (of New York City)

1954 (May) Rabbi David L. Schwartz (of Hagerstown, Md.)

1956 (December 11) Rabbi David L. Schwartz (of Hagerstown, Md.)

1957 (April 3) Rabbi David L. Schwartz (of Hagerstown, Md.)

*Storer College*, at Harpers Ferry, W. Va.

1946 Rabbi Allan Tarshish (of Charleston, S. C.)

1947 Rabbi Meir Lasker (of Philadelphia)

1948 Rabbi Nathan Kaber (of Altoona, Pa.)

1949 Rabbi H. Goren Perelmuter (of Johnstown, Pa.)

1950 Rabbi M. Nathaniel Bension (then of Wheeling)

1951 Rabbi Aaron Seidman (of Washington, D. C.)

1952 Rabbi David L. Schwartz (of Hagerstown, Md.)

1954 (February) Rabbi David L. Schwartz (of Hagerstown, Md.)

1955 (February) Rabbi Emmet A. Frank (of Alexandria, Va.)

*West Liberty State College*, at West Liberty, W. Va.

1937 Rabbi Baruch Braunstein (then of Wheeling, W. Va.)

1938 Rabbi Ariel L. Goldburg (then of Charleston, W. Va.)

1939 Rabbi Abraham Shaw (of Baltimore)

1940 Rabbi Jacob M. Rothschild (of Atlanta, Ga.)

1941 Rabbi George B. Lieberman (then of Wheeling)

1942 Rabbi Aaron Lefkowitz (then of Cumberland, Md.)

1943 Rabbi Frederic A. Doppelt (of Fort Wayne, Ind.)

1944 Rabbi Abraham L. Feinberg (formerly of Wheeling)

1945 Rabbi Charles B. Lesser (then of Wheeling)

1946 Rabbi Louis J. Cashdan (then of Charleston, W. Va.)

1947 Rabbi Moshay P. Mann (then of Wheeling)

1948 Rabbi Eugene E. Hibshman (then of Charlottesville, Va.)

1949 Rabbi Harold B. Waintrup (of Philadelphia)

1950  Rabbi Murray I. Rothman (later of Newton, Mass.)
1951  Rabbi Burton E. Levinson (then of Pittsburgh, Pa.)
1952  Rabbi Joseph H. Freedman (then of Wheeling)
1955  (March) Rabbi Melvin S. Sands (of Steubenville,
      Ohio)
1956  (April) Rabbi Jakob J. Petuchowski (of the Hebrew
      Union College-Jewish Institute of Religion, Cincin-
      nati)
1957  (February 20) Rabbi Philip Gershon (of Pittsburgh)

In addition to the above, and not under the auspices of the
J. C. S., Rabbi George B. Lieberman, of Wheeling, served for a
time on the Faculty of West Liberty State College, as Professor
of World Literature and Comparative Literature, during the
years during which he served as the rabbi of Leshem Shomayim
Congregation, in Wheeling (1936–1943).

*West Virginia Institute of Technology*, at Montgomery, W. Va.

1947  Rabbi Lawrence A. Block (then of Huntington)
1948  Rabbi Louis J. Cashdan (then of Charleston)
1951  Rabbi Sidney Ballon (later of West Hempstead, Long
      Island)
1952  Rabbi Joseph Rauch (deceased; then of Louisville,
      Ky.)
1953  Rabbi Abraham I. Shinedling (then of Beckley)
1959  (March 17–18) Rabbi Samuel Volkman (of Charles-
      ton)

*West Virginia State College*, at Institute, W. Va.

1943  Rabbi Lawrence A. Block (then of Huntington)
1946  Rabbi Abraham Feinstein (of Chattanooga, Tenn.)
1947  Rabbi Samuel Wohl (of Cincinnati)
1948  Rabbi Louis J. Cashdan (then of Charleston)
1949  Rabbi Albert M. Lewis (then of Charlottesville, Va.)
1950  Rabbi Louis A. Josephson (formerly of Fairmont, W.
      Va.)
1951  Rabbi Eugene E. Hibshman (then of Huntington)

1952   Rabbi Abraham I. Shinedling (then of Beckley)
1953   Rabbi Samuel Volkman (of Charleston)
1954   (February) Rabbi Samuel Volkman (of Charleston) [Religious Emphasis Week]
1955   (March) Rabbi Theodore S. Levy (of Huntington) [Religious Emphasis Week]
1956   (March — four days) Rabbi Abraham I. Shinedling (then of Beckley) [Religious Emphasis Week]
1957   (March 12 to 14) Rabbi Samuel Volkman (of Charleston) [Religious Emphasis Week]
1958   (March 24–26) Rabbi Samuel Volkman (of Charleston) [Religious Emphasis Week]
1959   (March 16–18) Rabbi Leo J. Stillpass (of Johnstown, Pa.) [Religious Emphasis Week]

*West Virginia University*, at Morgantown, W. Va.

1937   Rabbi Victor E. Reichert (of Cincinnati)
1940   Rabbi Solomon N. Bazell (then of Louisville, Ky.)
1943   Rabbi George B. Lieberman (then of Wheeling)
1944   Rabbi Samuel Cook (later, of New York City; then of Cincinnati)
1945   Rabbi Aaron Lefkowitz (then of Cumberland, Md.)
1946   Rabbi Hugo B. Schiff (then of Washington, D. C.)
1947   Rabbi Joseph Klein (then of Philadelphia)
1948   Rabbi Burton E. Levinson (then of Pittsburgh)
1949   Rabbi Eugene J. Lipman (of New York City)

*West Virginia Wesleyan College*, at Buckhannon, W. Va.

1946   Rabbi Louis J. Cashdan (then of Charleston, W. Va.)
1947   Rabbi Sidney H. Brooks (then of Richmond, Va.)
1948   Rabbi Lawrence A. Block (then of Huntington, W. Va.)
1949   Rabbi Lester W. Roubey (then of Lancaster, Pa.)
1950   Rabbi Harold B. Waintrup (of Philadelphia)
1951   Rabbi Herbert J. Wilner (then of Cumberland, Md.)
1952   Rabbi Eugene E. Hibshman (then of Huntington)
1953   Rabbi Abraham I. Shinedling (then of Beckley, W. Va.)

1954   (January) Rabbi Morris M. Rose (then of Morgan-
       town, W. Va.)
1954   (December) Rabbi Samuel Volkman (of Charleston)
1955   (October) Rabbi Samuel Volkman (of Charleston)


SUMMER CAMPS OF THE METHODIST CHURCH
OF WEST VIRGINIA

Methodist Camp at Beckwith, W. Va., Rabbi Abraham I.
Shinedling (then of Beckley), in August, 1955

Methodist Camp, at West Virginia Wesleyan College, in Buckhannon, W. Va.

1955   (June) Rabbi Abraham I. Shinedling (then of Beckley)
1955   (June) Rabbi Tobias Rothenberg (of Roanoke, Va.)
1955   (July) Rabbi Harold Silver (of Pittsburgh)
1956   (June) Rabbi Abraham I. Shinedling (then of Beckley)
1956   (June) Rabbi David L. Schwartz (of Hagerstown, Md.)
1956   (June) Rabbi Tobias Rothenberg (of Roanoke, Va.)
1956   (July) Rabbi Joseph Levine (of Greensburg, Pa.)

Episcopal Peterkin Conference of the Episcopal Church of West
Virginia, at Romney, W. Va.

1957   (July 7 to 19) Rabbi David L. Schwartz (of Hagerstown,
       Md.


THE JEWISH POPULATION OF WEST VIRGINIA
(1877 TO 1959–1960)

In the following pages, for the sake of completeness, and of a
full bird's-eye view of the subject, I present a brief résumé of
the Jewish population of West Virginia from the earliest year,
i. e., the year 1877, for which any figure or estimate is available,
up to the present, i. e., the year 1959–1960. In some cases, the
data presented here duplicate the facts and figures given previously. Many of the facts, figures, and data have been culled

from the annual reports found in the volumes of the *AJYB*, or in other sources, or ascertained in the course of my researches.

| *Year* | *Jewish Population* |
|---|---|
| 1877 | 511 |
| 1897 | 6,000 |
| | (much too high an estimate, if not a wild guess; about 1,000 to 1,200 would be much more accurate for 1897) |
| 1905 | 1,500 |
| 1907 | 1,500 |
| 1910 | 1,827 |
| 1912 | 4,050 |
| 1916–1917 | 5,129 |
| 1917 | 5,129 |
| 1917–1918 | 5,129 |
| 1920 | 5,440 |
| 1927 | 7,471 |
| 1928–1929 | 7,471 |
| 1936–1937 | 7,980 |
| 1940–1941 | 7,213 [ca. 5,200 to 5,300?] |
| 1942 | 7,213 [5,391?] |
| 1950 | 7,000 (estimated) |
| 1955 | 6,000 (estimated; perhaps too low) |
| 1956 | 6,000 (estimated; perhaps too low) |
| 1957–1958 | 5,950 |
| 1959–1960 | 5,800 (estimated) |

## Miscellaneous Data on the Jewish Population of West Virginia

### (*AJYB*, 1914–1915 [5675 A.M.])

### 1877 to 1912

The following brief statistics of Jewish population for four cities of West Virginia were presented in the above volume of the *AJYB*: from 1877 to 1912:

| *Charleston* | *Jewish Population* |
|---|---|
| 1877 | 92 |
| 1905 | 142 |
| 1907 | 190 |
| 1912 | 3,000 |

| *Huntington* | |
|---|---|
| 1905 | 71 |
| 1907 | 100 |
| 1912 | 150 |

| *Parkersburg* | |
|---|---|
| 1905 | 150 (too high) |
| 1907 | 50 (too low) |
| 1912 | 400 (too high) |

| *Wheeling* | |
|---|---|
| 1877 | 300 |
| 1905 | 400 |
| 1907 | 550 |
| 1912 | 500 |

## 1916–1917

In 1916–1917, at a time when the Jewish population of West Virginia was estimated very closely at 5,129 (perhaps too high a figure), the estimated general population of the State was 1,439,165, so that the Jewish population of the State represented 0.35% (a little over one-third of one per cent) of the total State population. The Jewish population of 5,129 represented an increase of 3,629 over the estimated 1907 Jewish population of 1,500.

## 1917

Again, in 1917, the Jewish population of West Virginia was given as 5,129, out of a total State population of 1,412,602.

## 1917–1918

In a survey in the *AJYB*, "The Jewish Population of the United States," written in 1917–1918 for the *Year Book* for 1918–1919 [5679 A.M.] by Samson D. Oppenheim, and to be found on pages 31–74, the cities and towns of West Virginia were assigned the following Jewish populations, with the State at that time having a closely estimated total of 5,129 Jews:

| City or Town | Jewish Population |
|---|---|
| Bluefield | 152 |
| Bramwell | 5 |
| Charleston | 1,000 |
| | (purely an estimate) |
| Clarksburg | 245 |
| Elkins | 12 |
| Fairmont | 95 |
| Gary | 6 |
| Huntington | 310 |
| Kimball | 45 |
| Morgantown | 120 |
| Parkersburg | 440 |
| | (an estimate) |
| Wheeling | 1,000 |
| | (an estimate) |

The figures for Parkersburg and Wheeling given for the year 1917–1918 are much too high. To this day Parkersburg does not have anywhere near 400 or 440 Jews, but closer to 150 or 175 Jews. Wheeling, at that time, had perhaps 700 Jews.

Pocahontas, Va., then closely connected with the Bluefield Jewish community, had 81 Jews in 1916. Later, many of them moved to Bluefield when the Pocahontas, Va., Jewish community declined and then, later, disappeared.

Also, in the years 1916 to 1918, there were 92 smaller towns and localities of West Virginia which had small Jewish populations.

## 1920

The estimated Jewish population of West Virginia in 1920 was 5,440, out of a total general State population of 1,463,701 (1920 United States Census). Thus, in that year the Jewish population formed 0.4% (four-tenths of one per cent) of the total population of West Virginia.

## 1927

(*AJYB*, 1928–1929 [5689 A.M.], page 138)

In the year extending from 1927 to 1928, West Virginia had a total Jewish population of 7,471, out of a total general State population of 1,696,000. Thus, in that year, the Jewish population formed 0.44% (forty-four hundredths of one per cent) of the total general population of West Virginia.

## 1928

In 1928, urban places in West Virginia with a total general population of 222,066 reported having 3,310 Jews, or 1.49% of the total general population of those urban places.

83 incorporated places had a total of 5,517 Jews.

8 urban places of from 2,500 to 5,000 general population reported a total general population of 49,646, with 217 Jews. 6 places of from 5,000 to 10,000 general population reported having a total general population of 40,052, with 335 Jews. 6 places of from 10,000 to 25,000 general population, with a total general population of 88,494, reported having 1,344 Jews.

1 unincorporated place in West Virginia, with a general population of 1,763, reported having 36 Jews in 1928. 13 incorporated places with a general population of 18,299 reported having 311 Jews. No really complete reports of Jewish population for the State were obtainable at any time. Many reports over the years were at least in part estimates.

## 1936–1937

In 1936–1937, the Jewish population of the State was reported to be 7,980, out of a total State population of 1,865,000.

### THE 1936 CENSUS OF RELIGIOUS BODIES

The number of Jews, *by county*, in West Virginia, and also in the main centers of Jewish population, as listed by the *cities* in these counties, according to the last Census of Religious Bodies, taken in 1936, was as follows: (This census thus embraced only 15 of the 55 counties of West Virginia.)

| County | Number of Jews | Principal City |
|---|---|---|
| Berkeley | 120 | Martinsburg |
| Cabell | 810 | Huntington |
| Hancock | 350[1] | Weirton and Hollidays Cove |
| Harrison | 300 | Clarksburg |
| Kanawha | 1,500 | Charleston |
| Lewis | 31 | Weston |
| Logan | 83 | Logan |
| Marion | 235[2] | Fairmont |
| McDowell | 145 | Welch (including also the nearby localities of Keystone, Kimball, and North Fork) |
| Mercer | 210 | Bluefield (including also Princeton) |

---

[1] The figure of 350 population for Hancock County in 1936, for both Weirton and Hollidays Cove, later merged as one city, is perhaps too high.

[2] The figure of 235 for Fairmont's Jewish population for 1936 is without doubt much too high. In 1947, Fairmont is recorded as having then, more than a decade later, only 160 Jews, and in 1956 about 200 Jewish population. A more reasonable figure for the Jewish population of Fairmont in 1936 would be about 135 to 150 persons.

| County | Number of Jews | Principal City |
|--------|----------------|----------------|
| Mingo | 135 | Williamson |
| Monongalia | 132 | Morgantown |
| Ohio | 1,150[1] | Wheeling |
| Raleigh | 65[2] | Beckley |
| Wood | 125 | Parkersburg |

## 1940–1941

The figure for the Jewish population of West Virginia given in the *AJYB* for the year 5701 A.M. (page 228) was revised downward from 7,980 to 7,213.

## 1942

In the 1942 *West Virginia Blue Book*, the Jewish population of West Virginia was given as 5,391. The figure is, apparently, much too low.

## 1950

In 1950, the Jewish population of the State was estimated at 7,000, out of the total State population of 2,005,552.

## 1956

In 1956, the estimated Jewish population of West Virginia was 5,950, out of a total general population of 1,984,000 (thus, 0.3% of the general population).

---

[1] The figure of 1,150 for the Wheeling Jewish population in 1936 is too high by 200 or 300.

[2] This figure of 65 is almost certainly too low. Possibly 100 to 110 persons would be a more accurate Jewish population for Beckley in 1936, at a time when the then growing Jewish population of that city numbered some 30 families, and several individuals, and included also several Jewish families in nearby Mount Hope and Oak Hill, in Fayette County.

## 1957

In 1957, the Jewish population of the State was estimated at 5,900 (in a constant decline from 1950 on), out of a total general State population of 1,976,000 (or the same 0.3% of the total general population).

## 1959 (1959–1960)

(from the *AJYB*, Volume 61, 1960, page 10)

WEST VIRGINIA

| Estimated Jewish Population | Total Population | Estimated Jewish Percentage of the Total |
|---|---|---|
| 5,800 | 1,969,000 | 0.29 [i. e., less than 3/10 of 1%) |

According to the same volume of the *AJYB*, on page 8, the following 11 Jewish communities of West Virginia had a Jewish population of 100 or more persons in 1959 (estimated): Beckley, 230 (much too high); Bluefield-Princeton, 300; Charleston, 1,625; Clarksburg, 225; Fairmont, 175; Huntington, 925; Morgantown, 130; Parkersburg, 100 (much too low); Weirton, 350; Wheeling, 800; Williamson, 170 (perhaps too high).

## JEWS IN THE ACADEMIC LIFE OF WEST VIRGINIA

AARON ARKIN. Aaron Arkin, pathologist and college professor, born in Russia, in 1888; residence, Morgantown, W. Va. (University of West Virginia) (*AJYB*, Volume 24 [1922–1923; 5683 A.M.], page 115, in a list of "Jews of Prominence in the United States," compiled by I. George Dobsevage).

PHILIP CAPLAN. Philip Caplan served as assistant professor of business administration at Marshall College, in Huntington, from 1947 to 1953.

JULIUS COHEN. Julius Cohen served as associate professor of political science at West Virginia University, in Morgantown.

NATHAN DIAMANT. Nathan Diamant served as instructor of business administration at Marshall College, in Huntington, from 1948 to 1951.

C. C. FENTON. Dr. C. C. Fenton was a professor in the School of Medicine at West Virginia University, in Morgantown.

RICHARD HOMBERGER. Dr. Richard Homberger served as teacher of business administration at West Virginia State College, in Institute, W. Va., from 1946 to 1956. He then was appointed to a similar position at the University of Wichita.

FREDERICK LEHNER. Dr. Frederick Lehner (born in Vienna, Austria, on October 15, 1893) served as professor of German at West Virginia State College, in Institute, from 1939 to 1956. He retired in 1956, but continued to reside in Institute, and to teach an occasional course at the College.

JULIUS LIEBERMAN. Dr. Julius Lieberman became head of the German Department at Marshall College, in Huntington, in 1946. He was still serving in this position in 1958–1959.

MARVIN NEWMAN. Marvin Newman, whose home was in Charleston, W. Va., served as an instructor in mathematics at Glenville State College, in Glenville, W. Va., from 1949 to 1953. He then went to Philadelphia, as assistant professor of mathematics at the Drexel Institute of Technology.

MORTIN J. PLOTNICK. Dr. Mortin J. Plotnick served as associate professor of economics at Marshall College, in Huntington, from 1946 to 1947. He left in June, 1947, to accept a similar professorship at Blackburn College, in Carlinville, Ill.

JULES RIVLIN. Jules Rivlin became instructor in athletics and athletic coach at Marshall College, in Huntington, in 1955. He was still serving in this position in 1957–1958.

JACOB SAPOSNEKOW. Dr. Jacob Saposnekow served for a number of years as associate professor of sociology at the University of West Virginia, in Morgantown.

ROBERT WEISS. Dr. Robert Weiss became professor of German at West Virginia State College, in Institute, in 1957, in the position formerly held by Dr. Frederick Lehner.

## JEWS IN PUBLIC OFFICE IN WEST VIRGINIA

ANNA ABRAMSON. Anna Abramson (formerly of Piedmont, W. Va.; now of Baltimore, Md.) served in the Second World War in the Office of Price Administration, at Cleveland, Ohio, as a food rationing attorney. After the end of the Second World War, she was elected a justice of the peace in Piedmont.

VICTOR ABRAMSON. Dr. Victor Abramson (orginally from Piedmont, W. Va., and a brother of Anna Abramson) was, in 1957, an official in the United States Treasury Department, at Washington, D. C.

CHARLES BASS. Charles Bass (1889–1957), of Glenville, W. Va., served one term as mayor of Glenville, and three terms as a member of the City Council of Glenville.

MAX BUDNICK. Max Budnick, of Keystone, served as a member of the Keystone City Council in recent years.

FRED H. CAPLAN. Fred H. Caplan, of Clarksburg, W. Va., was serving, in 1956–1957, as assistant district attorney of West Virginia. He also served several terms as a member of the State House of Delegates.

HOWARD CAPLAN. Howard Caplan, of Clarksburg, served as United States Attorney for the Northern District of West Virginia. He served for a time also as the city attorney of Clarksburg.

LOUIS J. CASHDAN. Rabbi Louis J. Cashdan (then of Charleston, W. Va.) served as president of the Kanawha Welfare Council. (He was rabbi of the Virginia Street Temple, in Charleston, from 1945 to 1952.) He was appointed by the governor of the State as a member of the Advisory Board of the Department of Public Welfare, of West Virginia, serving from 1948 to 1952, when he left Charleston for Kansas City, Mo.

AARON CATZEN. The late Aaron Catzen, then a resident of Clark, W. Va., near Bluefield, but later a resident of North Fork, W. Va., served as mayor of the town of Clark for many years. Clark later was incorporated as a part of North Fork after Aaron Catzen's terms of office were over.

JULIUS COHEN. Julius Cohen, of Morgantown, W. Va., was appointed principal attorney of the War Manpower Commission, at Washington, D. C., in 1943, and served in this post during part of the period of the Second World War.

ADOLPH E. COOPER. Adolph E. Cooper, of Marlinton, W. Va., was elected city attorney of Marlinton in 1941, and in 1957 he was still serving in that post, having been elected continuously.

JACOB COOPER (died at Washington, D. C., in 1943), the father of Adolph E. Cooper, served for some time as a member of the Town Council of Cass, W. Va.

JACOB FISHER. Jacob [Jake] Fisher, of Wheeling, served as a State senator from 1901 to 1911. The *AJYB* for 1911–1912 [5672 A.M.], page 278, records one of his re-elections (the last) to this position as a State senator on November 8, 1910. Previously, Jacob Fisher had served in the House of Delegates, at Charleston, as a representative from Wheeling, from 1889 to 1901. From 1921 to 1927, he served as a judge in the Braxton County Court, in West Virginia.

DAVID FOX, JR. David Fox, Jr., was serving as a member of the Huntington City Council in 1956–1957.

HAROLD L. FRANKEL. Harold L. Frankel, of Huntington, was serving as mayor of the city in 1957–1958. In November, 1956, he was elected to the City Council.

NORA B. FRANKS. Mrs. Nora B. Franks entered the service of the Federal Government at Logan, W. Va., in the year 1940, serving there until 1948 with the Social Security Board, Old Age and Survivors Insurance. She has continued to serve with the Federal Government as manager of a Social Security Office in West Virginia, or as assistant manager, in Charleston, from 1948 to 1952 (as assistant manager), in Welch, from 1952 to 1954 (as manager), in Beckley, from 1954 to March, 1957 (as manager), and from March, 1957, to the present (May, 1959) in Parkersburg (as manager). She is the only woman, Jewish or otherwise, ever to serve as manager of a Social Security Office in West Virginia.

SAMUEL GIDEON. Samuel Gideon, one of the earliest Jewish

settlers in, and residents of, Huntington, served as the president of the Huntington Independent School District, and for several years he was a member of the City Council in Huntington. He was also president, for six years, of the Cabell County Court.

MAX GOLDBARTH. Max Goldbarth, of Charleston, W. Va. (died at Charleston, on November 3, 1911), was a member of the City Council of Charleston (*AJYB*, 1912–1913 [5673 A.M.], page 125).

ARIEL L. GOLDBURG. Rabbi Ariel L. Goldburg (then of Charleston, W. Va.; later of Richmond, Va.) was chairman of the State Board of the State Department of Public Assistance. (He served as rabbi of the Virginia Street Temple, in Charleston, from 1929 to 1945.)

HARRY GORDON. Harry Gordon, of Montgomery, W. Va., was elected a member of the City Council of Montgomery (in the 1950's).

WILLIAM GREENSPON. Dr. William Greenspon, of Bluefield, was a member of the original Bluefield City Park Commission.

JOSEPH HERZBRUN. Joseph Herzbrun, of Welch, served as a member of the City Council of Welch, in past decades.

MORRIS HORKHEIMER. Morris Horkheimer, of Wheeling (died in 1912), served as the commissary general of West Virginia from 1901 to 1905, under Governor Albert B. White.

MIKE KANDEL. Mike [Michael] Kandel was serving, in 1956–1957, as the city recorder of Montgomery, W. Va.

ABRAM KAPLON. Abram Kaplon, of Harpers Ferry (died on June 9, 1955), served as a member of the Town Council of Harpers Ferry for more than 25 years, and also served for many years as a road commissioner in Harpers Ferry.

JOSEPH KELLER. Joseph Keller, of Parkersburg, W. Va., held a city office in Parkersburg for some time.

SIDNEY J. KWASS. Sidney J. Kwass, of Bluefield, served as a United States Commissioner, District Court, Southern District, from 1946 to 1948.

LEO LOEB. Leo Loeb, of Charleston, served as the temporary president of the Charleston City Council, and as a member thereof in 1910.

ABRAM J. LUBLINER. Abram J. Lubliner, of Bluefield, served
as a member of the State Senate from 1931 to 1933. He was
also the assistant prosecuting attorney of Mercer County
for eight years; a member of the State Legislature from
1933 to 1947; and chairman of the Taxation, Labor, and
Finance Committee. He served as the chairman of the
Insurance Committee, and for several years he was a special
judge in the Mercer County Criminal Court.

ISIDORE MARGOLIS. Isidore Margolis, of Montgomery, was
elected a member of the City Council of Montgomery (in
the 1950's).

DANIEL MAYER. Daniel Mayer, of Charleston (died in 1910),
served as consul general of the United States at Buenos
Aires, Argentina. He served also for a while as commissioner
of immigration, and in 1889 he served as a member of the
West Virginia Legislature.

MEYER NEWBERGER. Meyer Newberger, of Parkersburg, served
as the secretary to Senator Camden.

BENJAMIN L. ROSENBLOOM. Benjamin L. [Louis] Rosenbloom,
of Wheeling (born in 1880), served as a member of the
United States House of Representatives from West Virginia,
in Washington, D. C., from 1921 to 1925. After his first
election, he was re-elected to this post on November 7,
1922. Later, he served as the vice mayor of Wheeling, from
1935 to 1939. He had previously served as a State senator
in the State Senate at Charleston from 1914 to 1918, his
first election to this office having taken place on November
3, 1914.

RUBY RUBENSTEIN. Ruby Rubenstein, of Thomas, W. Va. (who
celebrated his 77th birthday in April, 1959), served many
terms as the mayor of Thomas, from 1922 to 1937, and he
served also for four years as a member of the Board of
Education of Thomas. For twenty years he was a city
councilman.

[R. A. SALOMONS (SALMONS)] [R. A. SOLINS?]. R. A. Salomons, or
Salmons, of Wheeling, is recorded in the *AJYB* for 1911–1912
[5672 A.M.], page 287, as having served as a member of
the State Senate (a State senator) from 1911 to 1913, having

been elected to this office on November 8, 1910. According to the asterisk accompanying his name there, there is no indication as to his religious affiliation. All indications are to the effect that R. A. Salomons, or Salmons, if his name was correctly spelled, was not a Jew, and that his name was erroneously included in the above volume of the *AJYB*. [It is possibly an error for R. A. Solins. *See under* Welch.]

LEO SCHAFFER. Leo Schaffer, of Thurmond, W. Va. (born in Austria, in 1860), served as the mayor of Thurmond from 1906 to 1909, and possibly for several years before that, beginning as early as the year 1900.

DAVID SHEAR. David Shear, of Romney, was elected the mayor of Romney, in 1951. He was again serving in this post in 1957.

JOSEPH SHIELDS. Joseph Shields, of Charleston, served as collector of internal revenue for the United States Government at Charleston in the early days of the history of the Charleston community, during the Civil War. The *AJYB* for 1916–1917 [5677 A.M.], page 110, records his death at Cincinnati on April 7, 1916, at the age of 82.

HAROLD D. SLAVEN. Harold D. Slaven, of Morgantown, was elected to the House of Delegates of West Virginia in 1937, and was re-elected for a second term in 1939, thus serving for the four-year period from 1937 to 1941, as a representative from Monongalia County. From 1942 to 1945, during the Second World War, he served in Charleston in and with the Office of Price Administration.

SAMUEL SOLINS. Samuel Solins, of Welch, served as the first divorce commissioner of McDowell County, as well as assistant prosecuting attorney of the county. He served also for a time as a United States Commissioner.

SIDNEY THANHOUSER. Sidney Thanhouser, of Parkersburg, was on the staff of Governor Albert B. White.

HARRY WEISS. Harry Weiss, of Charleston, served as a member of the State Senate from 1913 to 1919.

ALBERT [AL] ZILENZIGER. Albert [Al] Zilenziger, of Parkersburg, served as a member of the City Council of Parkersburg from 1883 to 1885. Later he was elected city collector, and served for some time in that latter post.

## WEST VIRGINIA JEWS IN MILITARY SERVICE

(Some of the material contained in this section has as its source
the volume *American Jews in World War II* (Volume II) (published by the Dial Press), compiled by the Bureau of War
Records, of the National Jewish Welfare Board, under the
direction of Dr. Louis I. Dublin and Dr. Samuel C. Kohs. I
have corrected some of the inaccuracies which are to be found
in this volume with reference to West Virginia Jewish service
men, on the basis of my own researches. I have used also, as a
very good source for past wars, the various volumes of the
*American Jewish Year Book*, for which I am most grateful.)

Jews from West Virginia saw service in all the five major
wars of the United States since the Revolutionary War, i. e.,
the War of 1812, the Civil War, the Spanish-American War, the
First World War, and the Second World War. Their numbers
in the first three wars here mentioned were very small indeed.

## THE CIVIL WAR (1861–1865)

In the Civil War, there is record of 8 West Virginia Jews
who served in the Union Army, from what is now West Virginia
(1861–1865). These 8 included the three following:

LESSEMAN STRAUS, of Parkersburg, who served in the Union
Army. Lesseman Straus died at the age of 85 on November 10,
1912; he is recorded as "a Civil War veteran, from Parkersburg."

SAMUEL GIDEON, who later settled in Huntington, saw service
as a lieutenant in the Civil War, in the Illinois Infantry. In 1872,
he left his previous city of residence, Manchester, Ohio, and
lived for the rest of his life in Huntington, where he died on
June 13, 1923. Samuel Gideon was most prominent in the affairs
of his adopted city of Huntington.

DANIEL MAYER, of Charleston, served in the Fifth Infantry
of the Union Army in the Civil War, with the rank of captain.
His service and award have been mentioned previously in this
volume.

## THE SPANISH-AMERICAN WAR (1898–1899)

Four West Virginia Jews saw service in the Spanish-American War. These were:

JOSEPH HARBURGER, who served as a noncommissioned officer in the 41st United States Volunteer Infantry.

BENJAMIN GRAFF

JOSEPH KELLER, JR.

MAURICE RAUCH, who served in Company L of the 1st West Virginia Volunteer Infantry.

(Joseph Keller, Jr., and Maurice Rauch were from Parkersburg.)

In addition, Henry Altman, of neighboring Steubenville, Ohio, enlisted in the 2nd West Virginia Volunteer Infantry, serving in the Spanish-American War.

## THE TWO WORLD WARS (1917–1918 AND 1941–1945)

As far as can be ascertained, the following lists include all the Jewish men and women of West Virginia who saw service in the Armed Forces of the United States from the Civil War through the Second World War and beyond, including the four West Virginia Jewish participants in the Spanish-American War mentioned above, and arranged in alphabetical order.

A total of 226 Jews of West Virginia were in the United States Army and Navy in the period of the First World War, according to the *AJYB* for 1920–1921 [5681 A.M.], page 444.

A. DAVID ABRAMS. A. David Abrams, of Beckley, the son of Samuel I. Abrams, served in the United States Army and in the United States Navy as a dentist (with the rank of lieutenant) in the Second World War (1941–1945).

CHARLES ABRAMS. Charles Abrams, of Beckley, served in the United States Army in the Second World War (1943–1945).

IRVING ABRAMS. Irving Abrams, of Beckley, a cousin of A.

David Abrams, served in the United States Army, in the
Second World War, from 1941 to 1945.

LEONARD APPLEBAUM. Leonard Applebaum, of Beckley, served
in the United States Army in the Second World War
(1942–1945).

BENJAMIN ARDMAN. Benjamin Ardman, of Charleston, served in
the United States Army during the Second World War,
with the rank of 1st lieutenant. He was awarded the Air
Medal and the Purple Heart.

JACK M. BAKER. Jack M. Baker, of Charleston, served in the
United States Army, with the rank of captain, in the
Second World War. He died in the course of the War, in
non-combat service.

MAURICE BARBAKOW. Maurice Barbakow, then of Princeton,
the son of Harry Barbakow, served in the United States
Navy, with the rank of lieutenant senior grade, in the
Second World War. He served in the South Pacific Theatre
of the War.

YANKEE BARBAKOW. Yankee Barbakow, of Princeton, another
son of Harry Barbakow, and the brother of Maurice
Barbakow, enlisted in the United States Army in January,
1942, as a private, in the Second World War. He served in
Manila and other parts of the Philippine Islands, and was
honorably discharged in January, 1946, with the rank of
captain.

CHARLES BASS. Charles Bass (1889–1957), then of Glenville, W.
Va., served in France, as an infantryman, in the First
World War, in the 42nd (Rainbow) Division of the United
States Army.

CHARLES J. BEKENSTEIN. Charles J. Bekenstein, of Charleston,
served in the United States Army in the Second World
War, with the rank of technical corporal. He died in the
course of the War, in non-combat service.

NORMAN BEN BERGER. Norman Ben Berger, of Wheeling, served
in the United States Army in the Second World War, with
the rank of captain. He was the recipient of the Bronze
Star Medal and of the Purple Heart, 2 Oak Leaf Clusters.

HARRY BERMAN. Harry Berman, of Wheeling, served in the

United States Army in the Second World War, with the rank of captain. He was awarded the Silver Star and the Bronze Star Medal.

RALPH E. BERMAN. Ralph E. Berman, then of Beckley, served in the United States Army Medical Corps as a physician after the Second World War, from 1947 to 1949.

ROBERT J. BERMAN. Robert J. Berman, of Beckley, a younger brother of Dr. Ralph E. Berman, of Beckley, served as a sergeant in the United States Army in the Second World War, from 1943 to 1946. The two Berman brothers of Beckley were the sons of the late Nathan Berman.

O. B. BIERN. O. B. Biern (the name is incorrectly listed at times in the records as Bien), of Huntington, served as a lieutenant in the United States Army Medical Corps in the First World War (1917–1918).

BENJAMIN BINDERMAN. Benjamin Binderman, then of Beckley, the son of Jack Binderman, Sr., served in the United States Army in the Second World War.

JACK BINDERMAN, JR. Jack Binderman, Jr., of Beckley, the youngest son of Jack Binderman, Sr., served as a dentist in the United States Army in and shortly after the Second World War (1945–1947); and for two years thereafter (1952–1954). During his second term of service (1952–1954), he served as a dentist in the United States Navy, seeing service at San Diego, Calif., and in the Pacific region.

WILLIAM BINDERMAN. William Binderman, the oldest son of Jack Binderman, Sr., of Beckley, served in the United States Navy in the Second World War (1943–1945).

SAMUEL W. BLOCK. Samuel W. Block, of Hetzel, W. Va., served in the United States Army, as a private, in the Second World War. He was awarded the Purple Heart. He was killed in action against the enemy. (It is quite probable that Samuel W. Block was not a Jew, although of Jewish descent.)

RALPH H. BLUMENTHAL. Chaplain (Lieutenant Colonel) Ralph H. Blumenthal, of Huntington, who had been rabbi of Ohev Sholom Congregation, in Huntington, from 1939 until June, 1941, served as a chaplain in the United States

Army, in the Second World War, from 1941 on. In 1959 he was still in Army service as a chaplain, serving as Deputy Western Area Command Chaplain.

RICHARD M. BOCK. Richard M. Bock, later a resident for many years of White Sulphur Springs, W. Va., served in the United States Marines, in the Second World War, from September 4, 1942, to July 26, 1946.

JEROME L. BRECKSTEIN. Jerome L. Breckstein, of Richwood, served in the United States Army as a private first class in the Second World War, for 18 months, including ten months overseas. He was with the 65th Infantry Division.

JACOB BRONITSKY. Dr. Jacob Bronitsky, an orthopedic physician and surgeon, who lived in Martinsburg, W. Va., engaged as a Veterans Administration Hospital physician there, from 1949 to 1956, and then moved to Albuquerque, N. Mex., served for several years, during the Second World War, as a physician in the United States Army, being stationed in camps in Louisiana and other places.

MAX BURKA. Max Burka, of Clarksburg, served in the United States Army in the Second World War, with the rank of private. He was awarded the Purple Heart. He was killed in action against the enemy.

HAROLD M. CAPLAN. Harold M. Caplan, of Clarksburg, was serving in the United States Army in 1956–1957.

ALAN M. COHEN, JR. Alan M. Cohen, Jr., of Charleston, served in the United States Marine Corps in the Second World War, as a sergeant. He was awarded the Purple Heart.

EUGENE COHEN. Eugene Cohen, of Morgantown, served in the United States Navy in the Second World War with the rank of lieutenant, junior grade. He received a Commendation.

NELSON ROBERT COMBS. Nelson Robert Combs, of Wheeling, served in the United States Navy in the Second World War, with the rank of lieutenant commander. He was the recipient of the Purple Heart.

LEWIS COOPER. Lewis Cooper, originally of Cass, W. Va. (born in Cass, W. Va., on July 20, 1907), and later of Marlinton, W. Va., served in the United States Navy.

CALVIN DEITZ. Calvin Deitz, of Princeton, W. Va., the son of Henry Deitz, served in the United States Army for two years during the Korean War (1951–1953) as a sergeant in the Medical Corps. (He is a graduate pharmacist.)

LAWRENCE DE LYNN. Lawrence De Lynn, of Morgantown, served in the United States Army in the Second World War. He was awarded the Air Medal.

JOSEPH MAYER DREYFUSS. Joseph Mayer Dreyfuss, of Wheeling, served in the United States Army in the Second World War, with the rank of captain. He received the Bronze Star Medal.

ROBERT DUBIN. Robert Dubin, of Beckley, served in the United States Army in the Second World War.

MORRIS EDELMAN. Morris Edelman, of Wheeling, served in the United States Army in the Second World War, with the rank of 1st lieutenant. He was awarded the Purple Heart.

JACK EISENSCHIME. Jack Eisenschime, of Charleston, served as a corporal in the United States Army in the Second World War. He died a non-combat death in the course of the War.

HERBERT W. EMSHEIMER. Herbert W. Emsheimer, of Wheeling, served as a lieutenant in the United States Army in the First World War (1917–1918). He was appointed a lieutenant from the ranks in the course of the War.

LOUIS EPSTEIN. Louis Epstein, of Oak Hill, W. Va., served in the United States Army in the Second World War.

ALEXANDER ELIAS FARER. Alexander Elias Farer, of Wheeling, served in the United States Army in the Second World War with the rank of staff sergeant. He received the Presidential Unit Citation.

LAWRENCE W. FERGUSON. Lawrence W. Ferguson, of Charleston, served in the United States Army in the Second World War, with the rank of Flight Officer. He was awarded the Purple Heart. He was killed in action against the enemy.

HARRY C. FINE. Harry C. Fine, of Martinsburg, W. Va., served, in the First World War, from April, 1917, until June 6, 1919, as a supply sergeant with Battery E, 313th Field Artillery, of the United States Army, being a participant in the Battle of St. Mihiel and in that of the Meuse-Argonne.

MORIE FINK. Morie Fink, the younger brother of Sidney Fink
and the son of Louis J. Fink, of Beckley, served in the
United States Navy Medical Corps in the Second World
War, as a pharmacist's mate, 1st class, from 1942 to 1945.

SIDNEY FINK. Sidney Fink, of Beckley, the elder brother of
Morie Fink, and the son of Louis J. Fink, served as a
sergeant in the United States Army in the Second World
War, from 1942 to 1945.

LEONARD FIVERS. Leonard Fivers, of Beckley, served in the
United States Army in the Second World War, from 1942
10 1945. He entered the Army as a private in 1942, and
received the rank of sergeant before the end of the Second
World War.

DAVID FOX, JR. David Fox, Jr., of Huntington, served in the
Second World War as a 1st lieutenant in the United States
Army. He was the recipient of the Air Medal, 2 Oak Leaf
Clusters, and of the Purple Heart.

BERTRAM FRANKENBERGER. Bertram Frankenberger, of Charleston, served as a major in the United States Army, after the
First World War. In December, 1912, he had been appointed a 2nd lieutenant in the United States Army. In
the *AJYB* for 1922–1923 [5683 A.M.], page 141, Bertram
Frankenberger, of Charleston, is listed as a major in the
United States Army, residence, Camp Knox, Ky.

SAMUEL FRANKENBERGER. Samuel Frankenberger, of Charleston
(born on April 23, 1879, in West Virginia [Charleston?]),
served as a major in the United States Army after the First
World War. In 1898, he was appointed a cadet at the
United States Military Academy, in West Point, N. Y.,
and in 1902 he was graduated as a 2nd lieutenant in the
Artillery Corps of the United States Army. In the *AJYB*
for 1922–1923 [5683 A.M.], page 141, Samuel Frankenberger, of Charleston, is listed as a major in the United
States Army, residence in Washington, D. C.[1]

---

[1] The name of Samuel Frankenberger, of West Virginia [it should read in full:
Charleston, West Virginia], is listed as a second lieutenant in the Artillery Corps
of the United States Army, in the *AJYB*, 1904–1905 [5665 A.M.], page 94, in a

JOSEPH LEE FRANKLIN. Joseph Lee Franklin, of Wheeling, served as a staff sergeant in the United States Army in the Second World War. He received a Commendation.

JACOB HOWARD FRANZ. Jacob Howard Franz, of Charleston, served as a 1st lieutenant in the United States Army in the Second World War, and was awarded the Silver Star, the Distinguished Flying Cross, the Air Medal, 3 Oak Leaf Clusters, and a Commendation, 1 Oak Leaf Cluster. He saw service in the Southwest Pacific Theatre of the War.

JOSEPH H. FREEDMAN. Rabbi Joseph H. Freedman, who later served in Wheeling for half a dozen years or more, until 1957, as the rabbi of the Eoff Street Temple, served as a chaplain (with the rank of captain) in the United States Army in the Second World War, from 1942 to 1945.

STANLEY E. FRIEDMAN. Stanley E. Friedman, of Grafton, W. Va., served in the United States Army in the Second World War, as a private first class. He was awarded the Purple Heart.

HENRI E. FRONT. Rabbi Henri E. Front, of Wheeling, served from 1955 to 1957, for two years, as a chaplain in the United States Navy, first with the Second Marine Division at Camp Lejeune, and then with the Third Marine Division, FMF, on the island of Okinawa.

SIDNEY N. GHOLSEN. Sidney N. [Norman] Gholsen, of Huntington, served as a 1st lieutenant in the United States Army in the Second World War. He died a non-combat death in the course of the War, in 1942 or 1943, at Fort Meade, Md. His name is listed in the official records also as Norman Sidney Gholsen.

SAMUEL GIDEON. Samuel Gideon, later of Huntington, served as a lieutenant in the Illinois Infantry in the Civil War.

---

list of "Biographical Sketches of Jews Prominent in the Professions, etc., in the United States." Here it is stated that Samuel Frankenberger was born in West Virginia [Charleston] on April 23, 1879; in 1898 he was appointed a cadet in the United States Military Academy [at West Point, N. Y.]; and in 1902 he became a 2nd lieutenant in the Artillery Corps. At that time he was stationed in Washington, D. C., for army duty, or at least this was his official address.

He came to Huntington from Manchester, Ohio, in 1872, and died at Huntington on June 13, 1923.

HENNON GILBERT. Hennon Gilbert, of Bluefield, the son of Ezra Gilbert, and a first cousin of Fred Gilbert, served in the United States Army in the Second World War, with the rank of 1st lieutenant. He was awarded the Purple Heart and the Bronze Star Medal.

DAN [DANIEL] GLASSMAN. Dan [Daniel] Glassman, of Charleston, served in the United States Army in the Second World War, with the rank of captain. He was awarded the Presidential Unit Citation.

ARTHUR GOLDSTEIN. Arthur Goldstein, of Beckley, the son of Irving Goldstein, served as a sergeant in the United States Air Forces in the Second World War, from 1942 to 1946.

IRVING GOLDSTEIN. Irving Goldstein, of Beckley (previously of Brooklyn, N. Y.), served as a soldier in the United States Army in the First World War (1917–1918).

SIDNEY N. GOLDSTEIN.[1] Sidney N. Goldstein, of Huntington, served in the United States Army, in the Second World War. He died a non-combat death in the course of the War.

STANLEY D. GOTTLIEB. Stanley D. Gottlieb, of Bluefield, the son of William P. Gottlieb, served as a private first class in the United States Army in the Second World War. He was awarded the Presidential Unit Citation. He was hospitalized for a year or more, in the post-Second World War years, in Bluefield, from injuries and diseases contracted in the course of his War service.

JEROME GRAF. Jerome Graf, of Wheeling, served in the United States Army in the Second World War, with the rank of lieutenant. He was the recipient of the Purple Heart.

BENJAMIN GRAFF. Benjamin Graff, of West Virginia (his exact city or town in West Virginia has not been ascertained), served in Company L of the First West Virginia Volunteer Infantry in the Spanish-American War (1898–1899).

---

[1] The name of Sidney N. Goldstein is, apparently, an error, a duplication, or a dittography, for the Sidney N. Gholsen, or Norman Sidney Gholsen, listed above. The name of Sidney N. Goldstein, therefore, should be omitted as not being that of an actual soldier of the Jewish faith.

HENRY N. GRUNER. Henry N. Gruner, of Morgantown, served in the United States Army in the Second World War, with the rank of Seaman 1st Class. He received the Purple Heart and a Commendation. He was killed in action against the enemy.

MILTON G. HANDELSMAN. Milton G. Handelsman, of Charleston, served in the United States Army in the Second World War, with the rank of sergeant. He was awarded the Air Medal and the Purple Heart.

JOSEPH HARBURGER. Joseph Harburger, of West Virginia (the exact city or town of West Virginia from which he came is not known), served as a noncommissioned officer, or private, in the 41st United States Volunteer Infantry, in the Spanish-American War (1898–1899).

HAROLD E. HARVIT. Harold E. Harvit, of Beckley, the elder son of M. Edward Harvit, became a 2nd lieutenant in the United States Infantry in 1954, and was still serving in this position in 1958. He received his commission as a 2nd lieutenant at West Virginia University, in Morgantown, having served for four years in the R. O. T. C. there. He saw service at Fort Benning, Ga.

JACK HERMAN. Jack Herman, of Charleston, served in the United States Army in the Second World War, with the rank of private first class. He died a non-combat death in the course of the War.

HAROLD EMANUEL HIRSCH. Harold Emanuel Hirsch, of Fairmont, served in the United States Navy in the Second World War, with the rank of Petty Officer 3rd Class. He was the recipient of the Silver Star and the Purple Heart.

HARRY HOCHMAN. Harry Hochman, then of Beckley, the son of Morris Hochman, and the brother of Samuel Hochman, served in the United States Army in the Second World War,

SAMUEL HOCHMAN. Samuel Hochman, of Beckley, the brother of Harry Hochman, and the son of Morris Hochman, served in the United States Army in the Second World War, from 1943 to 1946.

ISAAC D. HORNBACK. Isaac D. Hornback, of Maud, W. Va., served in the United States Army in the Second World

War. He died a non-combat death in the course of the War. [It is now not believed that Isaac D. Hornback was a Jew.]

HARRY JACOBSON. Harry Jacobson, of Charleston, served in the United States Army as a sergeant in the Second World War. He was awarded the Purple Heart. He was killed in action against the enemy.

MYER E. KAHN. Myer E. Kahn, of Dunbar, served as a lieutenant in the Second World War in the United States Army. He was the recipient of the Purple Heart.

MAX L. KAMMER. Max L. Kammer, of Bluefield, the son of Harry Kammer, served in the United States Army in the Second World War, with the rank of captain. He was awarded the Bronze Star Medal, the Purple Heart, and the Croix de Guerre.

SAMUEL KANNER. Samuel Kanner, of Charleston, served as a 1st lieutenant in the United States Army in the Second World War. He was awarded the Purple Heart. He was killed in action against the enemy in North Africa.

HAROLD KATZ. Harold Katz, of Huntington, saw service in the United States Army in the Second World War. He was awarded the Purple Heart. He was killed in action against the enemy in the course of the War.

DANIEL KEISERMAN. Daniel Keiserman, then of Beckley, the son of Joseph Keiserman, served in the United States Army in the Second World War.

JOSEPH KELLER, JR. Joseph Keller, Jr., of Parkersburg [he is listed in the past official records as merely from West Virginia, but my later research disclosed the fact that his home city at the time was Parkersburg, W. Va.], served in the Spanish-American War (1898–1899) as a soldier in Company L of the First West Virginia Volunteer Infantry [Company E of the West Virginia National Guard].

EDWARD KLABAND. Edward Klaband, of Wheeling, served in the United States Army in the Second World War, with the rank of sergeant. He was the recipient of the Purple Heart.

JULIUS KRAVETZ. Rabbi Julius Kravetz, who, before his War service, had been the rabbi of Congregation Ahavath Sholom, in Bluefield (1936–1943), served as a chaplain in the United States Army, in the Second World War, from 1943 to 1945. In the course of the War, he attained the final rank of captain, rising from that of 1st lieutenant. At the end of the Second World War, despite his original intention of doing so, Rabbi Kravetz did not return to Bluefield.

JEROME KRIEGMAN. Jerome Kriegman, of Wheeling, served as a private in the United States Army, in the Second World War. He was awarded the Purple Heart.

ROBERT L. LEVENSON. Robert L. Levenson, of Wheeling, served in the United States Army in the Second World War. He was awarded the Distinguished Flying Cross, 1 Oak Leaf Cluster, the Air Medal, 4 Oak Leaf Clusters, and the Presidential Unit Citation, 1 Oak Leaf Cluster.

ROBERT H. LEVINE. Robert H. Levine, of Beckley, the son of Charles H. Levine, served as a 1st lieutenant in the United States Army in the Second World War, from 1943 to 1945.

MERRILL E. LEVY. Merrill E. Levy, of Hollidays Cove (Weirton), served as a staff sergeant in the United States Army in the Second World War. He was awarded the Air Medal, 1 Oak Leaf Cluster.

HARRY LEWIN. Harry Lewin, of Beckley, served in the United States Army in the Second World War.

BENJAMIN LEWIS. Benjamin Lewis, of Mount Hope, served in the United States Army Medical Corps in the Second World War (1943 to 1945).

FRANCES MAE LEWIS. Frances Mae Lewis, of Beckley, the daughter of Benjamin E. Lewis, served in the United States Armed Forces in the Second World War.

MILFORD LEWIS. Milford Lewis, of Beckley, the son of Benjamin E. Lewis, served in the United States Army in the Second World War.

ALFRED LOVITZ, JR. Alfred Lovitz, Jr., of Beckley (previously of Mount Hope), saw service in the United States Army in the Second World War.

BENSON LUBIN. Benson Lubin, of Huntington, served as a 2nd lieutenant in the United States Army in the First World War (1917–1918), under an official appointment to this post, as listed in the official records.

NORMAN J. MALLINGER. Norman J. Mallinger, of Wheeling, served as a 1st lieutenant in the United States Army in the Second World War. He was awarded the Soldiers Medal, the Air Medal, 3 Oak Leaf Clusters, the Purple Heart, 1 Oak Leaf Cluster, and the Presidential Unit Citation, 1 Oak Leaf Cluster.

JACOB R. MARCUS. Jacob R. Marcus, who in the 1910's was a resident of Wheeling and Farmington, W. Va., but later became Adolph S. Ochs Professor of American Jewish History at the Hebrew Union College, in Cincinnati, served as a 2nd lieutenant in the United States Infantry, in the First World War, from 1917 to 1919. As a theological student, he could have claimed exemption from military service.

WILLIAM W. MATTOX. William W. Mattox, of Bluefield, is listed in the official records as having served in the United States Army in the Second World War, as a staff sergeant. He was killed in action against the enemy.

However, no proof of his Jewishness has ever been found or proffered, and it is very likely that his being listed as a Jew in the official records is an error. I can find no record, after diligent search, that a Jewish family, or a Jewish individual, by the name of Mattox, ever lived in Bluefield, W. Va., or in the Bluefield area, or was ever a member of the Bluefield Congregation Ahavath Sholom.[1]

HUBERT MAY. Hubert May, of Charleston, served as a 1st lieutenant in the United States Army, in the infantry, in the First World War (1917–1918), under an official appointment to this rank, as listed in the records.

---

[1] A number of similar "misidentifications as Jews" have occurred in the so-called "official" War records for West Virginians, and also, presumably, for other States of the Union. Thus, Bernie H. Blankenship, of Crawley, W. Va., is supposed to have served in the United States Army in the Second World War, as a private first class, and to have been a member of the Jewish faith. He was awarded the Purple Heart. Bernie H. Blankenship was definitely not a Jew, nor was the Blankenship family ever Jewish, according to testimony received from his "home town" of Crawley, W. Va., where no Jewish families or individuals ever lived. I am totally unable to account for the making of these errors in identification.

DANIEL MAYER. Daniel Mayer, of Charleston, a physician, whose citation has been quoted in full above, served in the Fifth Infantry, in the Union Army, in the Civil War, with the rank of captain.

IRA W. MELTCHER. Ira W. Meltcher, then of Beckley, the son of Max Meltcher, served in the United States Army in the Second World War.

MORRIS ISIDORE MENDELOFF. Dr. Morris Isidore Mendeloff (of Charleston) was appointed a lieutenant in the Medical Reserve Corps of the United States Army, on August 9, 1916 (*AJYB*, 1917–1918 [5678 A.M.], page 260).

CHARLES W. MIDELBURG. Charles W. Midelburg, of Charleston, served in the United States Army in the Second World War, with the rank of lieutenant. He was the recipient of the Presidential Unit Citation.

SIGMUND MILFORD. Sigmund Milford, of Huntington, served in the Second World War in the United States Army, with the rank of major. He received a Commendation.

HENRY MILLER. Henry Miller, then of Beckley, but later of Baltimore, Md., served in the United States Army in the Second World War. He is the son of Mrs. Minnie M. Fink (Mrs. Louis J. Fink) and the stepson of Louis J. Fink, then of Beckley, but later of Baltimore.

ISADORE MILLER. Isadore Miller, of Beckley (not related to Henry Miller), served in the United States Army in the Second World War.

NATHAN E. MILLER. Nathan E. Miller, of Charleston, served in the United States Army in the Second World War, as a private. He was awarded the Purple Heart.

ISADORE NACHMAN. Isadore Nachman, then of Glenville, W. Va., the son of Max Nachman, served as a lieutenant in the United States Army in the Second World War.

SAMUEL NEWBERGER. Samuel Newberger, of Parkersburg, served as a lieutenant in the Home Guards at the beginning of the Civil War, before regular West Virginia troops were organized.

LEWIS NEWMAN. Cadet Lewis Newman, of Weirton, served as a lieutenant in the Second World War, in the United States

Army. He died in non-combat service in the course of the
War, at Prichert, Colo., in 1943.

DOLORES PICKUS. Dolores Pickus, of Beckley, the daughter of
Nathan Pickus, served in the United States Armed Forces
in the Second World War.

JAMES PICKUS. James Pickus, of Beckley, a brother of Nathan
and Louis Pickus, of Beckley, and the uncle of Dolores
Pickus, served in the United States Army, as a private, in
the First World War (1918). Before he immigrated into
the United States, in 1914, he had seen service in the
Czarist Army of Nicholas II, in Russia, from 1909 to 1912.

MALCOLM PICKUS. Malcolm Pickus, then of Beckley, the elder
son of Nathan Pickus, and the nephew of James Pickus,
served in the United States Air Force in the Second World
War, from 1942 to 1945.

MILTON PICKUS. Milton Pickus, then of Beckley, a cousin of
Malcolm Pickus, served in the United States Army in the
Second World War.

ABRAHAM PINSKY. Abraham Pinsky, of Follansbee, W. Va.,
served in the Second World War for about three and a half
years. He enlisted in the United States Army in September,
1942, and after graduating from the first enlisted men's
class, he (as an attorney) became a judge advocate in the
General's Department in history of corps in August, 1943,
and was commissioned a 2nd lieutenant. He served through
six campaigns from 1943 to 1946, in England, France,
Belgium, and Germany, and was first executive officer, staff
judge advocate, Ninth Tactical Air Command, and later
served as staff judge advocate, Ninth Air Force Service
Command, all in the E. T. O. [European Theatre of
Operations]. After three and a half years of such service,
Abraham Pinsky was separated from the Armed Services
in February, 1947, with the rank of lieutenant colonel.

C. M. RAUCH. C. [Charles] M. Rauch, of Parkersburg, served
in the 11th Infantry of the United States (the Union) Army
[in the Civil War].

MAURICE RAUCH. Maurice Rauch, of Parkersburg, served as a

soldier in Company L of the 1st West Virginia Volunteer Infantry (Company E of the 50th Infantry of the West Virginia National Guard), in the Spanish-American War. He was, presumably, related to C. M. Rauch, perhaps his son.

EDWARD M. RESNICK. Edward M. Resnick, of Wheeling, served in the United States Army as a lieutenant in the Second World War. He was awarded the Presidential Unit Citation.

MORRY [MORRIS] RITER. Morry [Morris] Riter, of Huntington, served in the United States Army in the Second World War, as a private first class. He was the recipient of the Purple Heart.

LEWIS W. ROSE. Lewis W. Rose, of Logan, served in the United States Army as a private, in the Second World War. He was awarded the Purple Heart. He was killed in the course of the War in action against the enemy.

KENNETH RUBENSTEIN. Kenneth Rubenstein, of Thomas, W. Va., the younger son of Ruby Rubenstein, served for four years in the United States Army in the Second World War, as an enlisted man.

DANIEL M. SAKS. Daniel M. Saks, of Beckley, a son of the late Abe Saks and of Mrs. Gussie B. Saks, served in the United States Navy in the Second World War, from 1941 to 1945, as an aviation chief radioman. His total military career in the United States Navy extended from February, 1937, to February, 1947, both before and after the Second World War.

ROBERT W. SAKS. Robert W. Saks, of Beckley, the younger brother of Daniel M. Saks, and the youngest son of the late Abe Saks and of Mrs. Gussie B. Saks, served in the United States Marine Corps in the Second World War, from 1942 to 1946. He sustained severe injuries on Saipan and Iwo Jimo islands. His rank was Petty Officer 1st Class. Robert W. Saks was awarded the Purple Heart.

PHILIP E. SCHAFFER. Philip E. Schaffer, of Charleston, served as a lieutenant in the United States Medical Corps, in the First World War, from 1917 to 1918.

WILLIAM SCHAFFER. William Schaffer, of Charleston, served as
a lieutenant in the United States Army Engineers' Corps in
the First World War, from 1917 to 1919.

RAYMOND D. SCHOENBAUM. Raymond D. Schoenbaum, of Huntington, served as a staff sergeant in the United States Army
in the Second World War. He was awarded the Purple
Heart and the Presidential Unit Citation. He was killed
in action against the enemy.

IRVIN SCHWABE. Irvin Schwabe, of Charleston, served as a
lieutenant in the United States Army, in the Infantry, in
the First World War, from 1918 to 1919.

CHARLES H. SILVER. Charles H. Silver, of Webster Springs, W.
Va., served as private first class in the United States Army,
in the Second World War. He was awarded the Purple
Heart.

MALCOLM SILVERBERG. Malcolm Silverberg, then of Beckley,
the son of Jacob Silverberg, served in the United States
Navy in the Second World War, as a quartermaster, from
1945 to 1946.

HOWARD A. SILVERMAN. Dr. Howard A. Silverman, then of
Beckley (son of the late Dr. Bernard E. Silverman, of
Beckley), served for two years (from October, 1956, to
October, 1958) as a physician with the United States Air
Force, being stationed in England during the entire period.
In 1959, he was practising medicine in Allentown, Pa.

HARRY SILVERSTEIN. Harry Silverstein, of Charleston, served as
a lieutenant colonel in the United States Army in the Second
World War. He died in War service on February 7, 1945.

PHILIP SILVERSTEIN. Philip Silverstein, of Charleston, served in
the United States Army in the Second World War, as a
private. He was awarded the Purple Heart.

SAMUEL SOLINS. Samuel Solins, of Welch, served as an officer
in the United States Army, in the First World War (1917–
1918).

JAMES THEODORE SOLOF. James Theodore Solof, of Huntington, served as a lieutenant in the United States Army in
the Second World War. He was awarded the Purple Heart.
He was killed in action against the enemy.

HAROLD A. SOPHER. Harold A. Sopher, of Beckley, served in the United States Air Force in the Second World War, from 1943 to 1944.

JESSE SPEYER. Jesse Speyer, of Wheeling, served as a lieutenant in the United States Army, in the First World War, from 1917 to 1918. He was appointed a lieutenant from the ranks in the course of the First World War. [Jesse Speyer's name is inadvertently misspelled as S*h*eyer several times in some of the records found in the *American Jewish Year Book.*]

MEYER J. SPIRO. Meyer J. Spiro, of Bluefield, served in the United States Army in the Second World War, and, after the end of the War, he was recalled to active duty for about two years, in the early 1950's.

DAVID S. STEINER. David S. Steiner, of Bluefield, served in the United States Army as a private first class in the Second World War. He was awarded the Purple Heart.

NORMAN STOKEN. Norman Stoken, then of Beckley, served in the United States Army in the Second World War, from 1942 to 1944.

LESSEMAN STRAUS. Lesseman Straus, of Parkersburg, a veteran of the Union Army in the Civil War, died at Parkersburg on November 10, 1912, at the age of 85.

HARRY STROMBERG. Harry (not Harold) Stromberg, then of Beckley, the elder son of Charles Stromberg, served in the United States Navy in the Second World War, and thereafter (from 1942 to 1947).

SIDNEY STROMBERG. Sidney Stromberg, then of Beckley, the younger son of Charles Stromberg, served in the United States Army in the Second World War.

ABRAHAM TOMCHIN. Abraham (Abe) Tomchin, then of Princeton, W. Va. (he later settled in Bluefield, W. Va.), the younger brother of Harold Tomchin, and a son of the late Joseph Tomchin, of Bluefield, served in the United States Navy as a 1st lieutenant in the Second World War.

HAROLD TOMCHIN. Harold Tomchin, of Princeton, W. Va., the older brother of Abraham Tomchin, and the eldest son of the late Joseph Tomchin, served in the United States Navy, for two years, in the Second World War.

HAROLD VOLKIN. Harold Volkin, of Princeton, W. Va., served in the United States Air Force, as a sergeant, for three and a half years in the Second World War. He was in the South Pacific Theatre of the War.

SAMUEL VOLKMAN. Rabbi Samuel Volkman, later the rabbi of the Virginia Street Temple, in Charleston (from 1952 on), served as a lieutenant junior grade (Chaplain) in the United States Navy, in the Second World War, from August, 1944, on (beyond the end of the War).

MILTON IRVIN WATZMAN. Milton Irvin Watzman, later of Steubenville, Ohio, the brother of Sanford Watzman, of Wellsburg, W. Va., left Beckley in 1942 to go with the Civilian Program at Patterson Field, near Dayton, Ohio, and then on to the Panama Canal Zone. In December, 1943, in the middle of the Second World War, having returned to the United States, he enlisted in the United States Army, serving with the 83rd Division in Europe, through five campaigns, until he was honorably discharged later in the year 1945. He apparently did not return to Beckley.

SANFORD WATZMAN. Sanford Watzman, of Wellsburg, W. Va., and formerly of Wheeling, the brother of Milton I. Watzman, enlisted in the United States Army Signal Corps in 1942, in the course of the Second World War, and served overseas for 27 months, through three campaigns. He was honorably discharged from the United States Army in January, 1946, and later settled in Wellsburg.

BERNARD WASSERKRUG. Bernard Wasserkrug, the son of Harry Wasserkrug, then of Oak Hill, W. Va., served in the United States Army in the Second World War.

ISADORE R. WEIN. Isadore R. Wein, of Beckley, served in the United States Navy in the Second World War, as a Rate-Specialist A, for 15 months, being stationed at the Great Lakes Naval Training Station and vicinity, near Chicago.

MORRI R. WEIN. Morri R. Wein, of Beckley (formerly of Newark, N. J.), the younger brother of Isadore R. Wein, served in the Signal Corps of the United States Army during the Second World War (from 1941 to 1945).

MORRIS S. WENDER, JR. Morris S. Wender, Jr., of Oak Hill,
W. Va., the younger brother of Ben H. and Max H.
Wender, of Beckley, served in the Second World War as a
1st lieutenant, in the United States Army Air Force, from
1942 to 1946. He was awarded the Air Medal, 2 Oak Leaf
Clusters, the Purple Heart, and the Presidential Unit
Citation.

ARTHUR WOLK. Arthur Wolk, then of Beckley, served in the
United States Army in the Second World War.

LESTER S. ZEFF. Lester S. Zeff, of Hollidays Cove (Weirton),
served in the United States Army in the Second World
War, with the rank of 1st lieutenant.[1] He was awarded the
Purple Heart, the Air Medal, 3 Oak Leaf Clusters, and the
Presidential Unit Citation.

## THE WEST VIRGINIA FEDERATION OF
## TEMPLE SISTERHOODS[2]

The West Virginia Federation of Temple Sisterhoods received
its charter from the National Federation of Temple Sisterhoods
(these two organizations are hereinafter most often referred to
as the W. V. F. T. S. and the N. F. T. S., respectively) on
January 19, 1922. It was founded and organized at Wheeling
in 1921 and 1922, and its First State Convention was held at
Charleston on April 17–19, 1923.

The W. V. F. T. S. is known as District No. 7 of the N. F. T. S.

---

[1] It is a fair inference that, wherever the rank of the above members of the Armed
Forces of the United States from West Virginia is not mentioned, or specified, the
rank was that of private.

[2] I am most deeply indebted for much of the following material on the West
Virginia Federation of Temple Sisterhoods (W. V. F. T. S.) to the four following
Jewish women, who supplied me with a tremendous wealth of data and facts from
which I was able to select the most important and noteworthy items of interest and
historical importance. The material presented herewith on the W. V. F. T. S.
represents only a small part of the large amount of data which they so generously
afforded me, and I take this opportunity of expressing my abiding gratitude to

In 1959, it included the following eleven local Sisterhoods, situated in various parts of the State:

| | |
|---|---|
| Beckley | Morgantown |
| Bluefield | Parkersburg |
| Charleston | Welch |
| Fairmont | Wheeling |
| Huntington | Williamson |
| Logan | |

In the *AJYB* for 1916–1917 [5677 A.M.], on page 249, there is an item to the effect that in 1915–1916, before the State Federation of Temple Sisterhoods was organized, West Virginia had three Sisterhoods which were affiliated with the N. F. T. S.:

Charleston: the Sisterhood of the Virginia Street Temple
Huntington: the Ladies' Hebrew Benevolent Society
Wheeling: the Ladies' Hebrew Benevolent Society.

The following nine Jewish women of West Virginia served on the National Board (the Executive Board) of the National Federation of Temple Sisterhoods:

Mrs. Garris I. Barkus, of Charleston (from 1922 to 1924)
Mrs. Louis J. (Eva S.) Cashdan, of Charleston (from 1950 to 1956)

---

them for their labors and work in my cause and in that of the history of West Virginia Jewry. These four women were:

Miss Miriam Wolfe, of New York City, assistant to the Director of the National Federation of Temple Sisterhoods, in New York

Mrs. Reba B. (Charles) Cohen, of Charleston, W. Va., an active member of the Virginia Street Temple, of the Charleston Temple Sisterhood, and of the State Federation, and a former president of the latter

Mrs. Helaine (Charles) Rotgin, also of Charleston, W. Va., then the 1st vice president of the State Federation, who in 1957 was elected president of the W. V. F. T. S.

Mrs. Milda G. (Sidney A.) Ardman, of Parkersburg, W. Va., who from 1955 to 1957 served a two-year term as president of the State Federation.

Also, Mrs. Charles J. (Janis) Stein was kind enough to send me, in time for this volume, data on the 31st General Assembly of the State Sisterhood, held at Wheeling, on April 14–15, 1959.

Mrs. Charles (Reba B.) Cohen, of Charleston (from 1941 to
    1947)
Mrs. Edward S. (Belle) Fields, of Morgantown (from 1955 to
    1957)
        (Later, Mrs. Belle Fields removed to Phoenix, Ariz., at
        the end of 1957 or in early 1958.)
Mrs. Max Frankenberger, of Charleston (from 1927 to 1933)
Mrs. Ralph (Gazella) Masinter, of Huntington (from 1955 to
    1959)
Mrs. L. A. Pollack, of Huntington (from 1926 to 1928)
Mrs. Charles (Helaine) Rotgin, of Charleston (serving as a
    member of the Executive Board of the N. F. T. S. in 1958–
    1959)
Mrs. Leo Wolf, of Wheeling (from 1924 to 1926)
    (Mrs. Eva S. Cashdan, in 1952, removed from Charleston
to Kansas City, Mo.)


In addition, these five National Board members served as
follows:

Mrs. Max Frankenberger, of Charleston, as a member of the
    N. F. T. S. Committee on Uniongrams; and as a past pres-
    ident of the West Virginia Federation of Temple Sister-
    hoods (1926–1928).
Mrs. Charles (Reba B.) Cohen, of Charleston, as a member of
    the N. F. T. S. Committee on Youth Activities; and as a
    past president of the W. V. F. T. S. (1928–1931).
Mrs. Louis J. (Eva S.) Cashdan, of Charleston, as chairman of
    the N. F. T. S. Committee on Interfaith Activities, from
    1953 to 1957, and as a member of the Department of
    Human Relations, from 1953 to 1957. Also, she served as
    vice chairman of the Committee on Interfaith Activities,
    from 1950 to 1953, for District No. 7, the Western Fed-
    eration of Temple Sisterhoods, Chairman on Interfaith
    Activities.
Mrs. Edward S. (Belle) Fields, of Morgantown, as a member of
    the Department of Membership and Administrative Serv-

ices, from 1953 to 1957; and as a past president of District No. 7, W. V. F. T. S. (1951–1953).

Mrs. Ralph (Gazella) Masinter, of Huntington, as a member of the Department of Human Relations, from 1955 to 1957. Also, she served as a past president of the W. V. F. T. S. (1949–1951).

Sporadic references to the periodical of the W. V. F. T. S. include the following two:

The editors of *The Sisterhood News of West Virginia* in 1936–1937, then published at Charleston monthly, were Mrs. A. M. Rosenblatt, editor; and Mrs. Grover Kaufman, assistant editor.

In 1939–1940, the *West Virginia Sisterhood News*, described as "a monthly publication devoted to the interests of Sisterhood," had the following editorial staff:

Editor: Mrs. Martha [William] Caplan, of Clarksburg;
Associate Editor: Eleanor Schiff, of Clarksburg; and
Associate Editor: Blanche Bear, of Clarksburg.

The various local Sisterhoods in West Virginia became affiliated with the State Federation and with the National Federation of Temple Sisterhoods as follows:

*Beckley*: The Beckley Sisterhood (later known as the Beckley Sisterhood, of Congregation Beth El) affiliated with the N. F. T. S. on December 3, 1925, with 11 members. The president of the Beckley Sisterhood at that time was Mrs. Nathan (Rose Y.) Pickus, and the secretary was Mrs. Sallye Waitzman.

*Bluefield*: The Bluefield Sisterhood (of Congregation Ahavath Sholom) affiliated with the N. F. T. S. on January 11, 1929, with 40 members. The president of the Bluefield Sisterhood at that time was Mrs. Ben Baker, and the secretary was Mrs. J. [Joseph] I. Kwass.

*Charleston*: The Charleston Sisterhood (of the Virginia Street
Temple, or B'nai Israel Congregation Sisterhood) became
affiliated with the N. F. T. S. on March 19, 1915, with 87
members. [The record, apparently, does not show the names
of the president and secretary of the Charleston Sisterhood
at that time.]

*Clarksburg*: The Clarksburg Sisterhood (of Tree of Life Congregation) became affiliated with the N. F. T. S. on March
1, 1916, with 40 members. (The Clarksburg Sisterhood
resigned from the N. F. T. S. and from the State Federation on September 19, 1955, to join a Conservative
congregational national Sisterhood group.)

*Fairmont*: The Fairmont Sisterhood (of the Fairmont Jewish
Community Center) joined the N. F. T. S. on May 14,
1920, with 21 members.

*Huntington*: The Huntington Sisterhood (of Oheb Sholom Congregation) joined the N. F. T. S. on October 13, 1913 [the
very year in which the N. F. T. S. was organized], with
38 members.

*Logan*: The Logan Sisterhood (of B'nai El Congregation) joined
the N. F. T. S. on December 11, 1922, with 14 members.

*Morgantown*: The Morgantown Sisterhood (of Tree of Life Congregation) joined the N. F. T. S. on November 12, 1922,
with 20 members.

*Parkersburg*: The Parkersburg Sisterhood (of B'nai Israel Congregation) joined the N. F. T. S. on March 22, 1920, with
25 members.

*Welch*: The Welch Sisterhood (of Congregation Emanuel) joined
the N. F. T. S. on October 11, 1923, with 34 members
(including many members from the neighboring and smaller
Jewish communities of War, Kimball, North Fork, and
Keystone).

*Wheeling*: The Wheeling Sisterhood (of the Eoff Street Temple, or Congregation Leshem [L'Shem] Shomayim) joined the N. F. T. S. on January 22, 1913, with 70 members. [Like the Huntington Sisterhood, it joined the national organization in the very year of its formation.]

*Williamson*: The Williamson Sisterhood (of B'nai Israel Congregation) joined the N. F. T. S. on June 9, 1922, with 12 members.

The West Virginia State Federation of Temple Sisterhoods serves only as a link between the local Sisterhoods and the N. F. T. S., in New York, and most of the work is done through the wants and needs of the national organization.

PRESIDENTS OF THE WEST VIRGINIA FEDERATION OF
TEMPLE SISTERHOODS SINCE ITS
ORGANIZATION IN 1923

(arranged in chronological order)

Mrs. Leo Wolf, of Wheeling (1923–1924)
Mrs. L. A. Pollack, of Huntington (1924–1926)
Mrs. Max Frankenberger, of Charleston (1926–1928)
Mrs. Charles (Reba B.) Cohen, of Charleston (1928–1931)
Mrs. Isadore (Anna H.) Katzen, of Welch (1931–1933)
Mrs. Eph [Ephraim] Broh, of Huntington (1933–1935)
Mrs. Abraham N. (Sarah A.) Schlossberg, of Bluefield (1935–1937)

(From 1937 to 1938 there is no record extant, and there appears to have been no State President during that year.)

Mrs. Paul Broida, of Parkersburg (1938–1940)
Mrs. William (Martha) Caplan, of Clarksburg (1940–1942)
Mrs. Ben (Lena) Shore, of Montgomery (1942–1944)
Mrs. Godfrey R. Millstone, of Morgantown (1944–1946)
Mrs. Nathan (Anna A.) Effron, of Bluefield (1946–1948)
Mrs. Anne A. Seletz, of Charleston (1948–1949)

Mrs. Ralph (Gazella) Masinter, of Huntington (1949–1951)
Mrs. Edward S. (Belle) Fields, of Morgantown (1951–1953)
Mrs. Irving (May) Albert, of Williamson (1953–1955)
Mrs. Sidney A. (Milda G.) Ardman, of Parkersburg (1955–1957)
Mrs. Charles (Helaine) Rotgin, of Charleston (1957–1959)

STATE SISTERHOOD ANNUAL OR BIENNIAL
CONVENTIONS HELD IN THE FOLLOWING
CITIES, FROM 1921 TO 1959

1921 and 1922 — Wheeling (organizational conventions; there
    are no records; the original minutes of these two
    meetings were lost)
1923 — First Convention: Charleston (April 17–19, 1923)
1924 — Second Convention: Fairmont (April 8–9, 1924)
1925 — Third Convention: Huntington (April 26–28, 1925)
1926 — Fourth Convention: Parkersburg (April 18–20, 1926)
1927 — Fifth Convention: Wheeling (March 28–30, 1927)
1928 — Sixth Convention: Charleston (April 30 to May 2, 1928)
1929 — Seventh Convention: Clarksburg (May 5–7, 1929)
1930 — Eighth Convention: Fairmont (April 28–30, 1930)
1931 — Ninth Convention: Williamson (October 18–20, 1931)
1932 — Tenth Convention — city of the convention now un-
    known; there are no records extant of the 1932
    Convention; the minutes were lost
1933 — Eleventh Convention: Welch (October 22–23, 1933)
1934 — Twelfth Convention: Huntington (October 21–22, 1934)
1935 — Thirteenth Convention: Parkersburg (October 27–28,
    1935)
1936 — Fourteenth Convention: Bluefield (October 11–12,
    1936)
1937 — Fifteenth Convention: Wheeling (October 17–18, 1937)
1938 — Sixteenth Convention: Charleston (October 23–24,
    1938)
1939 — Seventeenth Convention: Morgantown (October 15–16,
    1939)

1940 — Eighteenth Convention: Clarksburg (October 20–21, 1940)
1941 — Nineteenth Convention: Logan (October 19–20, 1941)
1942 — Twentieth Convention: Beckley (October 11–12, 1942)
1943 — Twenty-first Convention: Huntington (November 22–23, 1943)
1944 — Twenty-second Convention: Huntington (October 16, 1944)
1945 — Twenty-third Convention: Parkersburg (October 28–29, 1945)
1946 — Twenty-fourth Convention: Williamson (October 27, 1946)
1947 — Twenty-fifth Convention: Fairmont (October 26, 1947)
1948 — Twenty-sixth Convention: Wheeling (November 28, 1948)
1949 — Twenty-seventh Convention: Huntington (October 23, 1949)
1950 — Twenty-eighth Convention: Bluefield (November 19, 1950)
1951 — Twenty-ninth Convention: Charleston (September 23–24, 1951)

(Hereafter the State Conventions have been held only every two years.)

1953 — Thirtieth Convention: Beckley (the Beckley-Welch Convention) (October 11–12, 1953)
1955 — Thirty-first Convention: Morgantown (October 16–18, 1955)
1957 — Thirty-second Convention: Parkersburg (October 20–21, 1957)

(officially called the Thirtieth Assembly of the West Virginia Federation of Temple Sisterhoods)

1959 — Thirty-first Convention: Wheeling (April 14–15, 1959)

The term of office of the State Sisterhood president and of all State Sisterhood officers is now for two years, from October to October. Up to the year 1951, the State Sisterhood conventions used to be held every year, in the month of October, or in the month of November, in rotation among the various cities comprising the State Sisterhood. In September, 1951, at the Charleston Convention, by a change in the State Sisterhood Constitution, which went into effect beginning in 1952, a year in which no State Convention was held, the State Conventions were to be held only every other year, after the 1953 Convention (the Beckley-Welch convention), i. e., in alternate years to those in which conventions of the N. F. T. S. are held (the latter always in connection and jointly with the biennial conventions of the U. A. H. C., with which the N. F. T. S. is affiliated). In such alternate years, when State Conventions are not held, regional or district conventions of the State Sisterhood are held, for which purpose the eleven (originally twelve, but the Clarksburg Sisterhood severed its affiliation with the State Federation in October, 1955) local Temple Sisterhoods in West Virginia are divided into two regions, or districts (each of these two regions, or districts, having its own regional or district convention in the month of May, in alternate or rotating cities), as follows:

| *Northern Region or District*: | *Southern District or Region*: |
|---|---|
| Fairmont | Beckley |
| Huntington | Bluefield |
| Morgantown | Charleston |
| Parkersburg | Logan |
| Wheeling | Welch |
| | Williamson |

(Later, in the Newly Revised State Sisterhood Constitution of 1956, the Huntington Sisterhood was placed in the Southern Region.)

By the "unwritten law" of the State Sisterhood, the State President (or the State first vice president) always attends the N. F. T. S. Convention in October every two years, and both regional or district conventions held in alternate years, in the month of May, and presides at both district or regional meetings.

In October, 1955, the following were serving as the presidents of the eleven local Sisterhoods comprising the West Virginia Federation of Temple Sisterhoods:

Beckley: Mrs. William (Beatrice C.) Binderman
Bluefield: Mrs. Fred (Reva D.) Gilbert
Charleston: Mrs. Louis (Birdie R.) Cohen
Fairmont: Mrs. Joseph Levine
Huntington: Mrs. Harold Frankel
Logan: Mrs. Jack Moss
Morgantown: Mrs. Howard R. (Zelda S.) Weiss
Parkersburg: Mrs. Allan Staub
Welch: Mrs. Isadore (Anna H.) Katzen
Wheeling: Mrs. Kermit A. (Helen) Rosenberg
Williamson: Mrs. Alex H. Preiser

STATE COMMITTEE CHAIRMEN FOR 1955–1957

*Department No. 1: Religion and Education*

Chairman: Mrs. Charles (Helaine) Rotgin (of Charleston)
Religious School: Mrs. Paul Broida (of Parkersburg)
Jewish Ceremonials and Arts: Mrs. Joseph H. Freedman (of Wheeling)
Youth: Mrs. David Badner (of Charleston)
Program: Mrs. Samuel (Sally) Volkman (of Charleston)
Religious Extension: Mrs. Sidney (Mildred Jean) Schlossberg (of Bluefield)
Family Education: Mrs. Sidney (Helen B.) Rosenthal (of Bluefield)

*Department No. 2: Human Relations*

Chairman: Mrs. Philip (Fannie) Platnick (of Bluefield)
Emergency Services: Mrs. Henry Greenberg (of Parkersburg)
Interfaith: Mrs. Abraham I. (Helen L.) Shinedling (of Beckley)
   (She served until July, 1956, and then moved to Albuquerque, N. Mex.)

Peace and World Relations: Mrs. Abe Swartz (of Morgantown)
Braille: Mrs. Saul Cohen (of Charleston)

*Department No. 3: Advancement of Judaism*

Chairman: Mrs. Sam Weiner (of Logan)
World Union for Progressive Judaism: Mrs. David Baker (of Huntington)
YES (*Y*outh, *E*ducation, *S*isterhood): Mrs. Clarence (Frieda) Lovitch (of South Williamson, Ky.) (for the Williamson, W. Va., Sisterhood)
Uniongrams: Mrs. Henry Gruner (of Morgantown)

*Department No. 4: Membership and Administrative Services*

Chairman: Mrs. Charles (Janis) Stein (of Wheeling)
Cradle Roll: Mrs. Sidney Robbins (of Parkersburg)
Honor Roll: Mrs. Henry Hersch (of Parkersburg)
Newsletter: Mrs. Harry Golden (of Fairmont)
Stationery: Mrs. Jerome Vertman (of Wheeling)
By-Laws: Mrs. Charles (Reba B.) Cohen (of Charleston)

*National Board Members of the N. F. T. S. from West Virginia:*

Department of Membership and Administration: Mrs. Edward S. (Belle) Fields (of Morgantown)
Department of Human Relations: Mrs. Ralph (Gazella) Masinter (of Huntington)
Department of Advancement of Judaism: Mrs. Charles (Helaine) Rotgin (of Charleston)
Department of Religious Education: Mrs. Irving (May) Albert (of Williamson)

THE CONSTITUTION OF THE WEST VIRGINIA STATE
FEDERATION OF TEMPLE SISTERHOODS

REVISED COPY
of the
CONSTITUTION AND BY-LAWS
for the
WEST VIRGINIA FEDERATION OF
TEMPLE SISTERHOODS
1956

### ARTICLE I — NAME

The name of this organization shall be the West Virginia
Federation of Temple Sisterhoods.

### ARTICLE II — OBJECT

a. To promote the aims of the National Federation of Temple
Sisterhoods and to participate effectively and cooperatively in
its projects.

b. To bring the Sisterhoods of this State into closer cooperation and association with one another and to further their
respective activities.

c. To assist in the organization of new Sisterhoods within the
State.

### ARTICLE III — MEMBERSHIP

Any Sisterhood within the State and a member of the National
Federation of Temple Sisterhoods in good standing may apply
in writing to the Executive Board of the State Federation.

### ARTICLE IV — DUES

a. Every affiliated Sisterhood shall pay annually to the
Treasury of this Federation dues not to exceed .25 [25c] for

each of its dues-paying members. A Sisterhood whose dues are not paid shall not be eligible to representation at Conventions.

b. The fiscal year of the Federation shall be November 1 — October 31.

### ARTICLE V — OFFICERS

a. The officers of the Federation shall be a President, a First and a Second Vice President, a Recording Secretary, a Corresponding Secretary, a Treasurer, and an Auditor.

b. If necessary, because of the death or inability to serve by a President or vice-president, succession to the next higher office shall automatically take place from the numbered vice-presidents.

c. If the office of the second vice-president, or another office, becomes vacant, the filling of which is not covered by (b) above, it shall immediately be filled from among the members of the Executive Board. Officers thus chosen shall hold office for the balance of the unexpired term.

### ARTICLE VI — DUTIES

a. It shall be the duty of the President to preside at all meetings, to appoint the various committees and to cooperate with all committees in their work, to have general supervision of the interests of the Federation and to perform such duties as are incident to her office. She shall make an annual report to the Federation, a copy of which shall be sent to the N. F. T. S., and shall visit each Sisterhood once during the term of office.

b. The Vice-Presidents shall assist the President in the performance of her duties, shall perform the duties of President in case of her absence or inability to act, and shall preside over North and South regional fall meetings to be held [in] alternate years of Convention.

c. The Recording Secretary shall keep an accurate record of all meetings and shall have custody of the Constitution.

d. The Corresponding Secretary shall attend to all correspondence of the organization.

e. The Treasurer shall receive all monies of the Federation and deposit same in any Bank designated by the Executive Board. All checks shall be signed by the Treasurer, upon a voucher signed by the President. In the absence of the President, a duly authorized Vice-President shall be responsible for signing the voucher.

The Treasurer shall render a monthly statement of her finances to the President, and at the biennial meeting shall present a complete report of the same duly audited. All papers, monies, and other documents in her possession shall be delivered to her successor when installed. She shall make semi-annual reports in March and September to the N. F. T. S., giving the financial status of her [the] Federation.

f. The auditor shall make a biennial audit of all finances of the Federation.

### ARTICLE VII — EXECUTIVE BOARD

a. The Executive Board shall consist of the officers, chairmen of standing committees and the President or appointed representative of each affiliated Sisterhood. The immediate past President shall be an ex-officio member with power of voice and vote.

b. Every National Board member residing within the State shall by virtue of her membership on the National Executive Board be an ex-officio member of this Executive Board with power of voice and vote.

c. The Executive Board shall have authority over the affairs of the Federation during the interim between Conventions, excepting that of amending these By-Laws or modifying any action taken at the assembly.

d. The regular meeting of the Executive Board shall be held prior to the biennial. A special meeting may be called by the

President, and must be called upon written request of 8 members of the Executive Board.

e. Fifteen members of the Executive Board shall constitute a quorum.

f. The Executive Committee shall consist of the officers of the State Federation.

g. The Executive Committee shall manage the affairs of the Federation between meetings of the Executive Board and shall have the power to expend sums not to exceed $100.00 for any one purpose not included in the budget. The Executive Committee may not reverse or alter any decision of a convention or the Executive Board nor shall it have the power of amending these By-Laws.

h. The Executive Committee shall meet annually. Four members of the Executive Committee shall constitute a quorum. Special meetings may be called if necessary.

## ARTICLE VIII — COMMITTEES

a. The president shall appoint standing Committees corresponding to those of the N. F. T. S.

b. The President shall appoint such special Committees as are authorized by the Convention or Executive Board.

c. All Committee Chairmen shall submit annual reports to the President and to the N. F. T. S.

## ARTICLE IX — NOMINATIONS AND ELECTIONS

a. The President shall appoint a Committee on Nominations 6 months prior to the Biennial Convention. This committee shall consist of not more than 5, not [nor] less than 3 members; at least one shall be a member of the Executive Board.

b. Names of candidates endorsed by local Sisterhoods shall be submitted to the Chairman of the Committee on Nominations 5 months preceding the Biennial Convention.

c. The officers of the Federation shall be elected at the Biennial Convention. A majority of the votes cast shall be deemed necessary to elect.

d. The officers shall be elected for a term of two years. No officer shall be eligible for election to the same office for more than two consecutive terms.

### ARTICLE X — CONVENTIONS

a. A convention of this Federation shall be held biennially in the fall following the N. F. T. S. Biennial Assembly. In alternate years of the National Convention, State Regional meetings shall be held.

Sisterhoods shall be divided into two Regions.

| *Northern* | *Southern* |
|---|---|
| Morgantown | Bluefield |
| Fairmont | Beckley |
| Parkersburg | Williamson |
| Wheeling | Logan |
| | Huntington |
| | Charleston |
| | Welch |

b. The voting body of the Convention shall consist of the Executive Board, and the delegates or alternates appointed by each affiliated Sisterhood. Each person shall have one vote.

c. In addition to the members of the Executive Board, Sisterhoods shall be entitled to

2 delegates up to 50 members
4 delegates up to 150 members
6 delegates for 150 members or more

Sisterhoods shall be entitled to the same number of alternates as delegates. Alternates shall be entitled to vote in the absence of delegates.

PLATE V

The Old Scott Street Synagogue of Congregation Ahavath Sholom, Bluefield

(see pages 368–369)

PLATE VI

Rabbi A. Alan Steinbach
(formerly of Bluefield, W. Va.)
(see pages 391, 415, and 421)

The late Henry Rodgin
(of Bluefield, West Virginia)
(see page 507)

Isadore Cohen
(of Bluefield, W. Va.)
(see page 496)

Mrs. Nathan (Edna E.) Platnick
(of Bluefield, W. Va.)
For many years active in the Bluefield
Sisterhood, Hadassah, and Religious
School
(see page 506)

Nathan Platnick
(of Bluefield, W. Va.)
For many years president of Congregation Ahavath Sholom, in Bluefield
(see page 503)

d. A quorum, for the transaction of business at the general meeting, shall consist of 70% of the registered delegates at [the] Convention.

e. The expenses of [the] President and Corresponding Secretary shall be paid from the State Treasury to the State Biennial Convention. The State Budget shall also include funds to help defray the State President's expenses to the N. F. T. S. District President's Council meetings and toward her expenses to the National Biennial. Individual Sisterhoods shall assume the expenses of their permanent Rabbi.

f. The hostess convention City shall receive $200.00 from the State Treasury to help defray expenses.

g. A registration fee of $6.00 shall be paid by every member attending [the] Convention.

### ARTICLE XI — AMENDMENTS

Amendments to these By-Laws must be proposed in writing 35 days prior to the Biennial to each affiliated Sisterhood. Such amendments shall be acted upon by the Biennial Assembly and require a two-thirds vote of those present with voting privileges for adoption.

### ARTICLE XII — ARCHIVES

Permanent Archives shall be established in Charleston for systematically filing of all past records. A resident of that City shall be appointed to keep these archives.

### ARTICLE XIII

The authority governing the West Virginia Federation of Temple Sisterhoods shall be Roberts Rules of Order,[1] Revised. A State Parliamentarian shall be appointed by the President.

---

[1] The correct title of this work should be: *Robert's Rules of Order* [by Henry M. Robert].

HISTORY OF THE WEST VIRGINIA FEDERATION
OF TEMPLE SISTERHOODS

IMPORTANT EVENTS IN THE HISTORY OF
THE STATE FEDERATION[1]

1921 and 1922

The original minutes of the two organizational meetings, held at Wheeling in 1921 and 1922, have been lost.

*First Meeting: Charleston, April 17 to 19, 1923*

The first meeting (convention) of the State Federation of Temple Sisterhoods (of West Virginia) was held at Charleston, on April 17 to 19, 1923. A State fund was created by charging each local Sisterhood 10c per capita. Also, an Executive Board was created, to consist of State officers and of the Chairmen of all standing committees, as well as of the president of each local Sisterhood. The office of vice president was created, and that of financial secretary was abolished. The State was divided into districts, and district meetings were to be held at frequent intervals (later, annually).

Delegates were set up as follows to annual State Sisterhood conventions:

2 delegates for Sisterhoods with memberships of 25 or less
4 delegates for Sisterhoods with memberships of 25 to 50
6 delegates for Sisterhoods with memberships of over 50

---

[1] This section, dealing with the History of the West Virginia Federation of Temple Sisterhoods, is taken exclusively, in the form of excerpts, from data and minutes laboriously selected, copied out, and furnished to me by Mrs. Charles (Reba B.) Cohen and Mrs. Charles (Helaine) Rotgin, of Charleston; and by Mrs. Sidney A. (Milda G.) Ardman, of Parkersburg. To all three of these West Virginia Jewish ladies I herewith express my ample and grateful indebtedness and appreciation. The material which I herewith include in this section represents only about one-half of the data which they were kind and devoted enough to furnish to me.

In 1923, some of the Standing Committee chairmen were:

*Social Relations*: Mrs. S. A. Moses, of Charleston
*Religion*: Mrs. Herbert Sonneborn, of Wheeling
*Speakers' Bureau*: Mrs. Kraft
    [Her first name and the name of her city were not recorded
        in the minutes.]
*Programs*: Mrs. Max Frankenberger, of Charleston
*Uniongrams*: Mrs. M. Bachenheimer, of Wheeling
*Cooperation*: Mrs. Crone
    [Her first name and city were not recorded in the minutes.]

Other Standing Committees at that time included the District
Meetings Committee and the Scholarships Committee [for scholarships to the Hebrew Union College, in Cincinnati].

The following numbers of delegates attended this first State
Sisterhood Convention in Charleston, in April, 1923, from 9
local Sisterhoods:

| Charleston | 7 | Montgomery | 3 |
|------------|---|------------|---|
| Clarksburg | 2 | Parkersburg | 4 |
| Fairmont | 4 | Wheeling | 5 |
| Huntington | 28 | Williamson | 1 |
| Logan | 6 | | |

(Total, 60 delegates)

The names of these 60 delegates were not recorded in the
minutes.

Those nominated for office for the following year (1923–1924)
were as follows:

PRESIDENT: Mrs. Leo (Claudia) Wolf, of Wheeling
1ST VICE PRESIDENT: Mrs. G. [Garris] I. Barkus, of Charleston
2ND VICE PRESIDENT: Mrs. Philip O. Lipson, of Fairmont
CORRESPONDING SECRETARY: Mrs. M. Bachenheimer, of Wheel-
    ing
RECORDING SECRETARY: Mrs. S. Nusbaum, of Clarksburg
TREASURER: Mrs. Max Frankenberger, of Charleston
AUDITOR: Mrs. Ben Nathan, of Parkersburg
FIELD SECRETARY: Mrs. L. A. Pollock, of Huntington

The Beckley Sisterhood (of what was later, in 1934–1935, to be the Beckley Hebrew Association, or Congregation Beth El, of Beckley, W. Va.) joined the State Federation in 1923.

In 1923, the State Committees were combined as follows:

1. Department of Field Work
2. Department of District Meetings
3. Department of Social Relations
4. Department of Scholarships
   [for the Hebrew Union College, in Cincinnati]
5. Department of Religion
6. Program Department
7. Department of University Welfare
   [The forerunner, or predecessor, of the Hillel Foundations of the Union of American Hebrew Congregations and then, later, of the B'nai B'rith?]
8. Department of Uniongrams
9. Cooperation Department

In 1923, the West Virginia Federation of Temple Sisterhoods pledged the minimum [annual] sum of $350 for the State Federation scholarship (to the Hebrew Union College).

On October 11, 1923, the Welch Sisterhood (of Temple Emanuel) joined the West Virginia Federation of Temple Sisterhoods, and became affiliated with the N. F. T. S., with 34 members (including several such members from the neighboring towns and localities of McDowell County, W. Va., such as War, North Fork, Keystone, and Kimball).

The Original Claudia (Mrs. Leo) Wolf Prayer of the State Sisterhood read as follows:

"Before God's footstool to confess
A poor soul knelt, bowed his head.
    'I failed!' he cried.
The Master said:
    'Thou didst thy best, that is success.'
May we women of West Virginia be like unto this,
Successful in God's sight. So may it be!"

*The 2nd State Sisterhood Convention*
*Fairmont, April 8 to 9, 1924*

Thirty-four delegates, from 9 Sisterhoods, attended the 2nd annual meeting, or convention, of the W. V. F. T. S., held at Fairmont on April 8 to 9, 1924. The minutes of this meeting record their exact names:

*Charleston* (6 delegates)

Mrs. S. A. Moses
Mrs. Leo Loeb
Mrs. G. [Garris] I. Barkus
Mrs. Max Frankenberger
Mrs. Walter Builtman
Mrs. M. B. Goldman

*Clarksburg* (5 delegates)

Mrs. I. Aaron
Mrs. J. Jacobs
Mrs. B. Brown
Mrs. S. Nusbaum
Mrs. S. Newman

*Fairmont* (3 delegates)

Mrs. Baer [Her first name is not recorded.]
Mrs. Philip O. Lipson
Mrs. B. S. Finger

*Huntington* (3 delegates)

Mrs. Max Hirschman
Mrs. L. A. Pollock
Mrs. D. M. Osgood

*Logan* (2 delegates)

Mrs. [Sam] Weiner
Mrs. Ben Tobin

*Morgantown* (4 delegates)

Mrs. Samson [Lillian] Finn
Mrs. H. Silverman
Mrs. Lyons [Her first name is not recorded in the minutes.]
Miss Daisy Weil

*Parkersburg* (3 delegates)

Mrs. Bekenstein [Her first name is not recorded in the minutes.]
Mrs. J. S. Broida
Mrs. W. Goldstein

*Wheeling* (7 delegates)

Mrs. Leo Wolf
Mrs. D. Tyler
Mrs. H. [Herbert] Sonneborn
Mrs. J. Horkheimer
Miss Speyer [Her first name is not recorded in the minutes. She was, perhaps, a relative of Jesse Speyer.]
Mrs. M. Bachenheimer
Mrs. L. B. Stern

A total of 79 women, including the 34 delegates, alternate delegates, and interested observers, attended this 2nd convention.

*The Messenger*, the new State Sisterhood paper [a monthly], was adopted [approved of and initiated], at the price of 50c for an annual subscription. Its editors were Dena [Lena? Mrs. Ben] Shore (of Montgomery and Charleston) and Mrs. Charles (Reba B.) Cohen (of Charleston).

An increase in the amount of the annual Hebrew Union College Scholarship Fund from $350 to $500 was voted.

Mrs. J. Walter Freiberg, of Cincinnati, President of the N. F. T. S., whose husband had been president of the U. A. H. C., was the guest speaker at the 2nd Convention.

Nominated for office for the year 1924–1925 were the following:

HONORARY PRESIDENT: Mrs. Leo Wolf, of Wheeling
PRESIDENT: Mrs. L. A. Pollock, of Huntington
1ST VICE PRESIDENT: Mrs. Max Frankenberger, of Charleston
2ND VICE PRESIDENT: Mrs. Philip O. Lipson, of Fairmont
RECORDING SECRETARY: Mrs. I. Aaron, of Clarksburg
TREASURER: Mrs. J. S. Broida, of Parkersburg
CORRESPONDING SECRETARY: Mrs. Max Hirschman, of Huntington
FIELD SECRETARY: Mrs. M. Bachenheimer, of Wheeling
AUDITOR: Mrs. Ben Tobin, of Logan

*The 3rd State Convention*
*Huntington, April 26 to 28, 1925*

The 1925 (the 3rd) annual convention of the State Sisterhood Federation took place at Huntington, on April 26 to 28, 1925. Important decisions, data, or happenings at this 3rd convention included:

188 delegates were in attendance.
The State dues were increased to 10c per capita.
$25 was contributed by the State Sisterhood to the new Charles-

ton Community Center in memory of Morris Youngerman, rabbi of the Virginia Street Temple, who had passed away in Charleston during the preceding year.

The State Sisterhood Cradle Roll was started.

The State Speakers' Bureau was established.

Cooperation was pledged with the Morgantown Sisterhood in providing for the needs of the Jewish students at West Virginia University, in Morgantown, for a place of worship.

Mrs. Simon Moses and Mrs. Max Frankenberger were appointed the joint editors of *The Messenger*.

### The 4th State Convention
### Parkersburg, April 18 to 20, 1926

The 1926 convention, held at Parkersburg on April 18 to 20, 1926, was attended by 36 delegates from all 12 local Sisterhoods. Mrs. Max Frankenberger, of Charleston, was elected the new president for 1926–1927.

### The 5th State Convention
### Wheeling, March 28 to 30, 1927

The 1927 State Convention, held at Wheeling on March 28 to 30, 1927, was attended by 85 delegates. The sole important item acted on at this convention was the setting aside of $200 for the State Speakers' Bureau for the coming year.

### The 6th State Convention
### Charleston, April 30 to May 2, 1928

The 1928 State Convention was held at Charleston on April 30 to May 2, 1928. The general convention chairman was Mrs. Ben (Lena) Shore, of Montgomery and Charleston. The first printed program of a convention of the State Sisterhood is to be found in the minutes for 1928. Rabbi Maurice N. Eisendrath, the rabbi of the Virginia Street Temple, in Charleston, was appointed advisory chairman of the Convention.

*Sisterhood Song*

(Adopted in 1928, and sung to the tune of "America")

God bless our Sisterhood,        We pray as with one mind
Bless Jewish womanhood,          For peace for all mankind,
Throughout our land.             Great God, our King!
We pledge our lives to Thee;     Grant us the strength to be
We would of service be           Firm in our faith to Thee,
To Israel and humanity,          To serve Thee loyally
Sisterhood's high cause.         In love and truth.


42 delegates attended this 6th State Convention.

The convention favored a State Teachers' Organization, to be sponsored by the State Sisterhood.

Mrs. Charles (Reba B.) Cohen, of Charleston, was elected State President for 1928–1929.

Rabbi Charles E. Shulman, then of Wheeling, presented the sermon at the religious service. Mrs. Felix A. Levy, of Chicago, gave the main address at the banquet, her subject being "I and My Sisterhood." (She was the wife of the noted Chicago rabbi, then rabbi of Congregation Emanuel in that city.)


*The 7th State Convention*
*Clarksburg, May 5 to 7, 1929*

The 1929 State Convention, held at Clarksburg on May 5 to 7, 1929, was attended by 29 delegates. Rabbi Samuel H. Baron, director of the Hillel Foundation at Morgantown, delivered an address. Mrs. Maurice Steinfeld, of St. Louis, president of the N. F. T. S., spoke on the subject, "The Jewish Woman of Today."

A representative from each Sisterhood was appointed to form a Sabbath school association in West Virginia.

*The 8th State Convention*
*Fairmont, April 28 to 30, 1930*

At the 1930 State Convention, held at Fairmont on April 28 to 30, 1930, Mrs. Charles (Reba B.) Cohen, of Charleston, president of the State Federation, was in the chair. The religious service address was presented by Dr. Samuel H. Goldenson, noted scholar and philosopher, then rabbi of Rodef Shalom Congregation, of Pittsburgh.

A total of 66 delegates and visitors attended this 1930 State Convention. The time of State meetings was changed from the spring to the fall of each year.

*The 9th State Convention*
*Williamson, October 18 to 20, 1931*

The 1931 State Convention was held at Williamson on October 18 to 20, 1931. A historic note was struck at this convention, for in the minutes of this meeting the President's message refers "to the formation of the State Federation of Temple Sisterhoods ten years previously (in 1921) under the leadership of Mrs. Leo Wolf, of Wheeling."

The keynote of this decennial assembly was "A Program for the Expansion of Judaism." A Hillel Award to the West Virginia University student doing the best academic work was set up. The main speaker was Rabbi Jonah B. Wise (now deceased), of the Central Synagogue, of New York, the noted son of the famous American Reform Jewish leader and organizer, Rabbi Isaac Mayer Wise, of Cincinnati, founder of the Hebrew Union College; Jonah B. Wise's subject was, "Judaism in a Hostile World."

69 delegates and visitors attended the sessions at this convention.

*The 10th State Convention*

*1932*

The minutes of this State Convention were lost. Apparently, yet incredibly, it is not even remembered in what city this Tenth State Convention was held (presumably in late October, 1932).

*The 11th State Convention*

*Welch, October 22 to 23, 1933*

The 1933 State Convention, held at Welch on October 22 and 23, 1933, represented a joint enterprise of the Welch and North Fork Sisterhoods. [The North Fork Sisterhood was, apparently, a separate group not affiliated with the W. V. F. T. S., and later passed out of existence.] Mrs. Isadore (Anna H.) Katzen, of Welch, the State President (elected as the successor to Mrs. Charles Cohen, of Charleston, at a preceding State Convention), presided at the sessions. The convention keynote was "Modern Jewish Youth and Religion."

The main speaker was Rabbi Samuel D. Soskin, then rabbi of Ohev Sholom Congregation, of Huntington. He spoke on the subject, "You and I on the Job of Religion."

*The 12th State Convention*

*Huntington, October 21 to 22, 1934*

The 1934 State Convention was held at Huntington on October 21 and 22, 1934. Mrs. Eph Broh, of Huntington (apparently elected at the 1934 annual convention), president of the W. V. F. T. S., served in the chair at the convention. A total of 40 delegates were in attendance.

It was voted that a monthly bulletin containing Sisterhood news of the State be issued. [The previously published State Sisterhood bulletin had, obviously, been discontinued.] Rabbi James G. Heller, then the spiritual leader of the Isaac M. Wise

Temple, in Cincinnati, was the main speaker, delivering a sermon on the subject, "Judaism and the World Crisis."

Mrs. Ben (Lena) Shore, of Montgomery and Charleston, was appointed editor of the projected monthly bulletin. Mrs. Samson (Lillian) Finn, of Morgantown, was appointed the chairman of a committee which was created for the purpose of financing and supporting the Claudia Wolf Foundation at Morgantown. Each local Sisterhood in the State was supposed to raise $5 per capita for this fund.

Mrs. Leon Goodman addressed the convention on the subject, "The American Jewess Greets American Womanhood."

### The 13th State Convention
### Parkersburg, October 27 to 28, 1935

The 1935 State Convention also, held at Parkersburg on October 27 to 28, 1935, was presided over by Mrs. Eph Broh, of Huntington, the State President. 71 delegates and visitors were in attendance. The main address was given by Sidney G. Kusworm, of Dayton, Ohio, treasurer of the Supreme Grand Lodge of the B'nai B'rith. He spoke on the subject, "Religion of Life."

### The 14th State Convention
### Bluefield, October 11 to 12, 1936

The 1936 State Convention, held at Bluefield on October 11 to 12, 1936, was presided over by Mrs. Abraham N. (Sarah A.) Schlossberg, of Bluefield, the State President. A total of only 38 delegates attended the sessions. Resolutions were passed on the death of Claudia Wolf. The State Convention passed a motion to send the sum of $350 each year to the Hillel Foundation at West Virginia University, in Morgantown, for Hillel activities.

### The 15th State Convention
### Wheeling, October 17 to 18, 1937

The 1937 State Convention was held at Wheeling on October 17 to 18, 1937, and was presided over by the re-elected State

President, Mrs. Abraham N. (Sarah A.) Schlossberg, of Bluefield. There were 215 delegates and visitors in attendance at
the sessions. It was ordered that the monthly State Sisterhood
bulletin be maintained by means of an assessment of 10c per
annum, imposed on each member of every local Sisterhood in
the State.

For the first time in the history of the W. V. F. T. S. there
was felt the need for a State Parliamentarian. Mrs. Charles
(Reba B.) Cohen, of Charleston, was appointed to this post.
[It is of interest that Mrs. Charles Cohen still held this position,
uninterruptedly, in 1958, after more than twenty years of service
as State Parliamentarian.]

### The 16th State Convention
### Charleston, October 23 to 24, 1938

The 1938 State Convention was held at Charleston on October
23 to 24, 1938. Mrs. Paul Broida, of Parkersburg, the State
President, presided at these sessions. A total of 166 delegates
and visitors were in attendance. Rabbi Bertram Klausner, then
of the congregation in Fairmont, was a participant. For the
first time at any State Convention, a Sunday School Teachers'
Forum (later called the Religious School Teachers' Institute)
was ordered held, in Charleston, for all State religious school
teachers. [In 1958, such annual Religious School Teachers'
Institutes were still being held in various cities of West Virginia,
in rotation, under the auspices of the State Sisterhood Federation.]

The main speaker at the Convention was Rabbi Samuel H.
Markowitz, then of Achduth Veshalom Congregation, of Fort
Wayne, Ind.; his subject was, "Restoring Religion to Jewish
Life."

Dr. Jacob R. Marcus, Professor of Jewish History at the
Hebrew Union College, addressed and conducted the first State
Sunday School Teachers' Training Course, held at Charleston
in November, 1938.

## The 17th State Convention
### Morgantown, October 15 to 16, 1939

The 1939 State Convention, held at Morgantown on October 15 to 16, 1939, was presided over by Mrs. Paul Broida, of Parkersburg, the re-elected State President. A total of only 36 delegates attended the sessions. Rabbi Ariel L. Goldburg, then of the Virginia Street Temple, in Charleston, gave a résumé of the first Religious School Teachers' Training Course held at Charleston in November, 1938, under the leadership of Dr. Jacob R. Marcus, Professor of Jewish History at the Hebrew Union College. The Convention stressed the importance of youth groups for the present and the future of Judaism. Mrs. Albert J. May, the 2nd vice president of the N. F. T. S., addressed the delegates on the subject, "Some Jewish Problems of Our Day."

## The 18th State Convention
### Clarksburg, October 20 to 21, 1940

The 1940 State Convention was held at Clarksburg, on October 20 to 21, 1940. Mrs. Paul Broida, of Parkersburg, the again re-elected State President, again presided over the sessions. The Convention delegates voted that each immediate past president was to be made a member of the Executive Board. The Revised Constitution was accepted. [The State Sisterhood Constitution was revised for the third and last time in 1956; the text of this definitive Revised Constitution has been given in the preceding pages.] It was decided that a contribution of 75c per capita be made by all the local members of the twelve Sisterhoods of the State for the Hillel Student Foundation at West Virginia University, in Morgantown.

Mrs. Elma Ehrlich Levinger, of Columbus, Ohio, noted authoress in the field of Jewish books, and the wife of Rabbi Lee J. Levinger, then the Hillel Foundation director at Ohio State University, gave the main address, her subject being, "No Man Is An Island."

*The 19th State Convention*
*Logan, October 19 and 20, 1941*

The 1941 State Convention was held at Logan on October 19 to 20, 1941, and was presided over by Mrs. William (Martha) Caplan, of Clarksburg, the State President. At this convention regional conferences were organized. Seven rabbis and 24 delegates attended the sessions. The main speaker was Mrs. Louis A. Rosett, of New Rochelle, N. Y., the 1st national vice president of the N. F. T. S. The subject of her address was, "The National Federation of Temple Sisterhoods."

Another noted speaker at this Convention was Dr. Abram L. Sachar, noted historian who was then the national director of the Hillel Foundations, and later became the president of the new Brandeis University, at Waltham, Mass. Mrs. Louis A. Rosett also conducted a Leaders' Training Institute.

*The 20th State Convention*
*Beckley, October 11 to 12, 1942*

[According to the local Sisterhood records kept at Beckley, this 20th State Convention took place at Beckley on October 10 to 13, 1942.]

The 1942 State Convention was held at Beckley on October 11 to 12, 1942 [October 10 to 13, 1942]. Mrs. William (Martha) Caplan, of Clarksburg, the re-elected State President, was in the chair at these sessions. There were 106 delegates, visitors, and rabbis attending the Convention. [At all sessions of the State Conventions, rabbis in attendance were called upon for opening benedictions, for closing benedictions, and for comments on the work and activities of the Sisterhood, and suggestions for future action. The State Sisterhood has always fostered and encouraged the attendance of the rabbis of the State at its annual and biennial conventions.]

The State Sisterhood contribution for the Hebrew Union College scholarship was increased from $350 to $500. Mrs. Charles (Reba B.) Cohen, of Charleston, served as national chairman on youth activities during this year (1942–1943). Dr. Emanuel Gamoran, Education Director of the U. A. H. C., conducted a Teachers' [Training] Institute at the Convention. The main address was delivered by Mrs. Hugo Hartman, president of the N. F. T. S., who spoke at the annual banquet on the subject, "Rediscovering America," and also presented an outline for the work of the local Sisterhoods.

Mrs. Ben (Lena) Shore, of Montgomery and Charleston, was elected the new President of the State Federation.

The following additional data and notes on the 1942 (the 20th) State Convention, held at Beckley, were excerpted from the *History of the Beckley Jewish Community*, by Abraham I. Shinedling and Manuel Pickus (1955), pages 134–137:

The locale of the Convention was Temple Beth El, from October 10 to 13, 1942. The six State rabbis participating in this Convention were: Rabbi Elliot J. Einhorn, of Clarksburg; Rabbi Julius Kravetz, of Bluefield; Rabbi George B. Lieberman, of Wheeling; Rabbi Alfred Jospe, of Morgantown; Rabbi Lawrence A. Block, of Huntington; and Rabbi Ariel L. Goldburg, of Charleston. [Not one of these six rabbis was still serving in the State of West Virginia in 1959.]

The Beckley Sisterhood ladies who were chairman and cochairman, respectively, of the Convention were Mrs. Bernard E. (Faye R.) Silverman and Mrs. Abe (Gussie B.) Saks.

The theme of the Convention was "Sisterhood in Defense."

The following served as Chairmen of the Standing Committees of the State Federation of Temple Sisterhoods in 1941–1942:

STATE HONOR ROLL: Mrs. Sam Friedberg, of Williamson

UNIONGRAMS: Mrs. A. Fink, of Fairmont

AID TO REFUGEES: Mrs. Henry Hersch, of Parkersburg

PEACE AND WORLD RELATIONS: Mrs. Simon Penn, of Wheeling

YOUNG FOLKS TEMPLE LEAGUE: Mrs. Nathan (Rose Y.) Pickus, of Beckley

CRADLE ROLL: Mrs. Sidney A. (Milda G.) Ardman, of Parkersburg

STATIONERY: Mrs. Joe Bekenstein, of Charleston

JEWISH CEREMONIALS AND ART: Mrs. Bernard Miller, of Logan

PRESIDENT'S MESSAGE: Mrs. William (Martha) Caplan, of
   Clarksburg
STUDENT ACTIVITIES: Mrs. Godfrey Millstone, of Morgantown
CHILD STUDY AND PARENT EDUCATION: Mrs. Ralph (Gazella)
   Masinter, of Huntington
HEBREW UNION COLLEGE SCHOLARSHIP: Mrs. Max Michaelson,
   of Welch
SPEAKERS' BUREAU: Mrs. Frank Ohlman [city not given]
RELIGIOUS SCHOOLS: Mrs. Sam Rosen, of North Fork
BRAILLE: Mrs. Peter Front, of Wheeling
NEWS EDITOR: Mrs. Emanuel Bear, of Clarksburg
RELIGIOUS SCHOOL INSTITUTE: Mrs. Ariel L. (Fanny A.) Gold-
   burg, of Charleston
SPECIAL COMMITTEE ON THE WAR EFFORT: Mrs. Mark Melman,
   of Logan

Mrs. Louis Sherman, of Welch, delivered the opening prayer.
Religious services were conducted by Rabbi Julius Kravetz, of
Bluefield. An address was delivered by Rabbi George B. Lieber-
man, of Wheeling. Other benedictions were given by Rabbi
Julius Kravetz, by Rabbi Alfred Jospe, of Morgantown, and by
Mrs. Samson (Lillian) Finn, of Morgantown. The Claudia
Wolf Prayer was delivered by Mrs. Ben Shore, of Montgomery.
Mrs. Ben Shore also gave the report of the Field Secretary.
The incoming officers were installed by Rabbi Lawrence A.
Block, of Huntington. Rabbi Julius Kravetz served as the
toastmaster at the banquet session held on Monday evening,
October 12, 1942, at the Beckley Hotel. A major address was
delivered by Rabbi Ariel L. Goldburg, of Charleston. The
Sunday School Teachers' Training Institute, held at Temple
Beth El, was conducted by Dr. Emanuel Gamoran, of the
U. A. H. C. Department of Education, on Saturday afternoon,
October 10, 1942.

The State Sisterhood officers for the year 1941–1942 were:

PRESIDENT: Mrs. William (Martha) Caplan, of Clarksburg
1ST VICE PRESIDENT: Mrs. Joe Bekenstein, of Charleston

2ND VICE PRESIDENT: Mrs. Sidney J. (Edna D.) Kwass, of
 Bluefield
RECORDING SECRETARY: Mrs. Nathan (Rose C.) Matz, of
 Beckley
CORRESPONDING SECRETARY: Mrs. A. J. Rosenshine, of Clarks-
 burg
TREASURER: Mrs. Victor Wormser, of Huntington
AUDITOR: Mrs. Samson (Lillian) Finn, of Morgantown
FIELD SECRETARY: Mrs. Ben (Lena) Shore, of Montgomery

### The 21st State Convention
### Huntington, November 22 and 23, 1943

The 1943 State Sisterhood Convention was held at Huntington, on November 22 to 23, 1943. The chief subjects of discussion
and action were various aspects of War work (the Second World
War). Mrs. Ben Shore, of Montgomery and Charleston, the
State President, presided at the sessions.

### The 22nd State Convention
### Huntington, October 16, 1944

The 1944 State Convention was held at Huntington on
October 16, 1944, presided over by Mrs. Ben Shore, of Montgomery, the State President. At this convention, Mrs. Godfrey
Millstone, of Morgantown, was elected State President. There
were 19 Board members present; the principal matters discussed
were various aspects of work in the War services, and aid to
the Temples. The Hebrew Union College Scholarship Fund for
the year was $370.25. Emphasis was placed upon bond drive
efforts for the Second World War, and upon aid to the Red
Cross. The Red Cross work included sewing, canteen service,
the Grey Ladies, the sale of war bonds and stamps, local war
activities, surgical dressings, and local hospitality to service
people.

An Institute for Sunday School teachers and leaders was
held in Huntington on October 14 and 15, 1944, with Dr. Jacob

R. Marcus, Professor of Jewish History at the Hebrew Union College, giving a series of lectures on "Great Movements and Personalities in Jewish History."

The new officers for 1944–1945 were installed by Rabbi Ariel L. Goldburg, of Charleston.

### The 23rd State Convention
#### Parkersburg, October 28 and 29, 1945

The 1945 State Convention was held at Parkersburg on October 28 and 29, 1945. Twenty Board members and 27 delegates were in attendance at the sessions, which were presided over by the State President, Mrs. Godfrey Millstone, of Morgantown. Rabbi David Herson was introduced as the new Hillel Student Foundation director at West Virginia University, in Morgantown, for 1945–1946. He and Sidney Melnicoff, president of the State Council of the B'nai B'rith, requested financial aid from the State Sisterhood for the new Hillel House project on the campus at Morgantown.

An intensification of efforts on behalf of Braille was voted and pledged. One Hebrew Union College scholarship was voted. Tribute was paid to Mrs. Simon A. Moses, of Charleston, State Braille chairman, for her years of service in the Sisterhood; this tribute was presented by Mrs. Charles Cohen, of Charleston, a member of the National Board of the N. F. T. S.

Religious services were conducted in the Temple rooms of the Parkersburg congregation by Rabbi Louis J. Cashdan, newly elected rabbi of the Virginia Street Temple, of Charleston; by Rabbi David Herson, of Morgantown; by Rabbi Jacob Soshuk, of Beckley; and by Student Rabbi Eugene Borowitz, of Parkersburg.

It was reported at the convention that Mrs. David Tyler, of Wheeling, had Brailled Joseph Opatoshu's novel, *In Polish Woods*, for the Hebrew Institute. Mrs. Charles Cohen, of Charleston, served as the N. F. T. S. Chairman on Youth, and also as a N. F. T. S. National Board member, in 1945–1946.

It was reported that in the year 1945–1946, there were 6 permanent rabbis and 4 student rabbis in the State.

Dr. Emanuel Gamoran, Educational Director of the Commission on Jewish Education of the U. A. H. C., conducted a Religious Teachers' Institute, attended by a large number of religious (Sunday) school teachers and several rabbis.

The State Sisterhood voted not to support, financially, the Hillel Foundation project at Morgantown, but to render it moral support, urging the local Sisterhoods to contribute to its support and creation directly and individually. [Later, the State Council of the B'nai B'rith undertook the support of the Hillel Foundation project and building at Morgantown as one of its most important permanent projects, aided by District Grand Lodge, No. 3, of the B'nai B'rith.]

Rabbi Charles B. Lesser, then of Wheeling, installed the State officers elected for the year 1945–1946.

The main address, on the subject of "Loyalty in Peace Time," was delivered at the Convention by Mrs. Samuel Stone, 2nd vice president of the Ohio State Federation of Temple Sisterhoods.

*The 24th State Convention*
*Williamson, October 27, 1946*

The 1946 State Convention, under the presidency of Mrs. Godfrey Millstone, of Morgantown, was held at Williamson on October 27, 1946. There were 29 delegates and 5 rabbis in attendance. Mrs. Nathan (Anna A.) Effron, of Bluefield, was elected State President for the year 1946–1947. Rabbi Louis J. Cashdan, then of Charleston, installed the incoming officers. Student rabbis Jerome W. Grollman, of Bluefield (1946–1947), and Sidney Akselrad, of Logan, were present at the Convention.

Mrs. Sidney Wallens, of Buffalo, N. Y., National Chairman of the Peace and World Government Committee of the N. F. T. S., was the main speaker; her subject was, "Translating the Principles of Judaism into Everyday Life."

Discussion was had of the Sisterhood service performed at

Ashford General Hospital (War work), in White Sulphur Springs, W. Va. The sum of $100 was pledged annually for the support of the Temple Youth Conclave, to be held each year in the different cities of West Virginia.

*The 25th (Silver Anniversary) State Convention*
*Fairmont, October 26, 1947*

The 1947 State Convention, the 25th, or Silver Anniversary, Convention, was held in Fairmont on October 26, 1947, presided over by the State President, Mrs. Nathan (Anna A.) Effron, of Bluefield. There were 5 rabbis and 27 delegates in attendance, as well as many visitors. The sessions were held in the new Temple building of the Fairmont Jewish Community Center. Rabbi Abraham I. Shinedling, then the new permanent (full-time) rabbi of the Bluefield Congregation Ahavath Sholom, and a new arrival that fall in the State of West Virginia, was introduced to the convention, and delivered several invocations in its course.

Mrs. Charles Cohen, of Charleston, compiled and prepared a manual of instructions and duties for officers of the State Sisterhood. Dr. Emanuel Gamoran, of the Educational Department of the U. A. H. C., conducted a Teachers' Institute, with 25 persons in attendance, on the teaching of Jewish history and Bible, in the afternoon of the convention day.

The main address was delivered by Rabbi Arthur J. Lelyveld, then the National Director of the Hillel Foundations. Rabbi Lawrence A. Block, of Congregation Oheb Sholom, of Huntington, participated in the discussions, and delivered several benedictions.

*The 26th State Convention*
*Wheeling, November 28, 1948*

The 1948 State Convention was held at Wheeling on November 28, 1948. Mrs. Nathan (Anna A.) Effron, of Bluefield, the re-elected State President, presided over the sessions of the Convention. The theme of the Convention was, "To Promote the Spirit of Religion."

A total of 33 delegates and 5 rabbis of the State were in attendance. Mrs. C. C. Strassburger, of Knoxville, Tenn., the main speaker, and a member of the National Board of the N. F. T. S., spoke on the subject, "Living Our Religion through Sisterhood."

An important matter discussed was the contributions to be made by the local Sisterhoods of the State to the House of Living Judaism, the permanent home of the N. F. T. S. and the U. A. H. C., then being planned in New York City, at the southeast corner of Fifth Avenue and East 65th Street. Mrs. Simon A. Moses, the State Braille chairman, was honored by the State Sisterhood through its gift in her honor of the sum of $150 to the N. F. T. S. for the underwriting of Braille copy. The sum of $100, in addition, was voted to be sent to the House of Living Judaism by the State Federation, in honor of its past presidents.

Rabbi Eugene Hibshman, the newly elected rabbi of Ohev Sholom Congregation, of Huntington, was introduced to the State Convention, a new arrival in the State in the fall of 1948. He participated in the discussions and pronounced several benedictions.

Mrs. Anne A. Seletz, of Charleston, was elected State President for the year 1948–1949. She and the other newly elected officers were installed by Rabbi Eugene Hibshman, of Huntington.

Mrs. Sigmund (Libby) Braverman, of Cleveland, conducted a symposium on "Problems of the Religious School." Mrs. C. C. Strassburger conducted the "President's Problem Hour," speaking on the subject, "Qualifications and Responsibilities of Leadership." The address at the annual banquet was delivered by Forrest E. Kirkpatrick, Dean of Bethany College, at Bethany, W. Va.; his subject was, "Standing Up to the Future."

It was reported that during the past year a total of 5,642 Uniongrams had been sold by the local Sisterhoods throughout the State, an increase of 2,353 Uniongrams in one year.

*The 27th State Convention*
*Huntington, October 23, 1949*

The 1949 State Convention was held at Huntington on October 23, 1949, with Mrs. Anne A. Seletz, of Charleston, the State President, in the chair. There were 27 delegates and 4 rabbis in attendance.

Mrs. Harvey Steadman, of Lansing, Mich., was the N. F. T. S. speaker at that State Convention. The annual banquet speaker was Dr. Jacob R. Marcus, now Adolph S. Ochs Professor of American Jewish History at the Hebrew Union College, in Cincinnati; his subject was, "Old People in a New World."

Mrs. Ralph (Gazella) Masinter, of Huntington, was elected the new State President. She and the other newly elected officers for the year 1949–1950 were installed by Rabbi Eugene Hibshman, of Huntington.

The sum of $586.50 was raised for Braille work in the State during the preceding year; this was the largest amount ever raised for Braille by the State Federation.

[It was decided, at one of the State Conventions, that each local Sisterhood accept a quota of $10 per capita, no matter how raised, as the individual contributions of the local Sisterhoods to the House of Living Judaism, in New York.]

*The 28th State Convention*
*Bluefield, November 19, 1950*

The 1950 State Convention was held at Bluefield on November 19, 1950. The State President, Mrs. Ralph (Gazella) Masinter, of Huntington, presided over the sessions, most of which were held in the new synagogue building of Ahavath Sholom Congregation, at 632 Albemarle Street, which had been completed and dedicated in May, 1949; the annual banquet was held in the main ballroom of the West Virginian Hotel. Rabbi Harold L. Gelfman, then the newly elected rabbi of the Bluefield Congregation, was introduced to the Convention, and

Rabbi Abraham I. Shinedling, who had just left the Bluefield congregation and was, from September 1, 1950, on, the newly elected permanent rabbi of Congregation Beth El, in Beckley, attended, participating in the convention and delivering a benediction.

It was voted at this session that annual conventions were to be replaced by biennial conventions of the State Sisterhood, to meet in alternate years with the National Biennial Convention. Regional meetings were henceforth to be held in the year of the National Convention.

Two regions were therefore established for the local Sisterhoods of West Virginia:

| *The Northern Region* | *The Southern Region:* |
|---|---|
| Clarksburg | Beckley |
| Fairmont | Bluefield |
| Morgantown | Charleston |
| Parkersburg | Huntington |
| Wheeling | Logan |
| | Welch |
| | Williamson |

It was voted that the State Sisterhood Federation *Newsletter* be issued three times a year, and be devoted to outstanding Sisterhood activities, and not to social news.

The name of Mrs. Charles (Reba B.) Cohen, of Charleston, was ordered inscribed on the State Honor Roll in appreciation of her compilation of the Convention Manual.

Permanent Archives, in a fireproof, locked cabinet, for the State Sisterhood were set up at the Virginia Street Temple, in Charleston, and a resident of Charleston, it was voted, was to be appointed as the keeper of these State Sisterhood Archives.

Mrs. Eve (Louis J.) Cashdan, of Charleston, was elected a member of the National Executive Board of the N. F. T. S.

Mrs. Harold Baum, of Milwaukee, Wis., the National Interfaith Chairman of the N. F. T. S., was the National Sisterhood speaker at the Convention.

*The 29th State Convention*
*Charleston, September 23 and 24, 1951*

The 1951 State Convention was held at Charleston on September 23 and 24, 1951, with Mrs. Ralph (Gazella) Masinter, of Huntington, the State president, serving as chairman at all the sessions. The National representative of the Sisterhood at this convention was Mrs. C. C. Strassburger, of Knoxville, Tenn. It was voted by the delegates present that henceforth there were to be only bi-annual conventions, to meet in alternate years with the National Bi-Annual Assembly of the N. F. T. S. In the year of the National Sisterhood convention, it was decided, the State Federation of the West Virginia Sisterhoods would hold only regional meetings, one in the Northern region and one in the Southern region of the State.[1]

STATE SISTERHOOD OFFICERS IN 1951 TO 1953

PRESIDENT: Mrs. Edward S. (Belle) Fields, of Morgantown
1ST VICE PRESIDENT: Mrs. Irving (May) Albert, of Williamson
2ND VICE PRESIDENT: Mrs. Henry Hersch, of Parkersburg
CORRESPONDING SECRETARY: Mrs. Meyer Handmaker, of Morgantown
RECORDING SECRETARY: Mrs. David Badner, of Charleston
TREASURER: Mrs. Seymour Michael, of Wheeling
AUDITOR: Mrs. Robert Levenson, of Wheeling
PARLIAMENTARIAN: Mrs. Charles (Reba B.) Cohen, of Charleston

STATE CHAIRMEN OF COMMITTEES, IN 1951 TO 1953

RELIGIOUS SCHOOLS: Mrs. Helen L. (Abraham I.) Shinedling, of Beckley
INTERFAITH: Mrs. Bernard L. Miller, of Logan

---

[1] The data on the State Federation of Temple Sisterhoods from 1951 to 1957 were, in great measure, furnished by Mrs. Sidney A. (Milda G.) Ardman, of Parkersburg, who served as the State President from 1955 to 1957.

UNIONGRAMS: Mrs. Harry Golden, of Fairmont
PROGRAMS AND SPEAKERS' BUREAU: Mrs. Nathan (Anna A.)
Effron, of Bluefield
JEWISH LITERATURE FOR THE BLIND: Mrs. Simon Shein, of
Williamson
PEACE AND WORLD RELATIONS: Mrs. Leo Ziffer, of Huntington
TEMPLE YOUTH: Mrs. Harold Schradski, of Huntington
STATE BULLETIN: Mrs. Irving (May) Albert, of Williamson
CRADLE ROLL: Mrs. Joseph Levine, of Fairmont
HONOR ROLL: Mrs. Robert Weiner, of Clarksburg
STATIONERY: Mrs. E. M. Newman, of Welch

*The 30th State Convention*
(*The Beckley-Welch Convention*)
*Beckley, October 11 and 12, 1953*

The Beckley-Welch joint State Convention was held in
Beckley on October 11 and 12, 1953, with Mrs. Edward S.
(Belle) Fields, of Morgantown, the State President, in the chair.
At this Convention the delegates of the State Convention voted
to set aside the sum of $500 to subsidize a camping program
for the West Virginia Temple Youth group, a section of the
OVTY, or the Ohio Valley Federation of Temple Youth.
Also, it was voted at this Convention that the State Sisterhood
was to participate in aid to the Alderson, W. Va. (the Federal
Reformatory for Women), Jewish chaplaincy program being
conducted by Rabbi Abraham I. Shinedling, of Beckley [from
August, 1951, to September, 1954]. The sum of $200 was set
aside for this aid for the year 1953–1954. At the same time,
$100 was voted for the Hebrew Union College Scholarship and
Religious Fund of Education in observance of the fortieth
anniversary of the organizing of the N. F. T. S. in 1913.

The sessions of the Beckley-Welch State Convention were held
principally at Temple Beth El and at the Beckley Hotel, in
Beckley, on the above days (October 11 and 12, 1953). The
theme of this Convention was, "Our Hands Serve Humanity."
The Convention was held, jointly, and in full cooperation, by

the Beckley Sisterhood and by the Welch Temple Emanuel Sisterhood.

The Claudia Wolf Prayer was read by Mrs. Irving Albert, of Williamson. Invocations and blessings were delivered by Rabbi Abraham I. Shinedling, of Beckley; Rabbi Herbert J. Wilner, of Bluefield; and Rabbi Samuel Volkman; the religious service was read by Rabbi Shinedling; the sermon at the religious service was delivered by Rabbi Jakob J. Petuchowski, of the Hebrew Union College, then serving as the graduate part-time rabbi of the Welch Congregation Emanuel; the banquet address was delivered by Rabbi Morris M. Rose, of Morgantown; and the new officers elected for the term 1953–1955 were installed by Mrs. Abram Vossen Goodman, of New York, a member of the Executive Board of the N. F. T. S., who also conducted a workshop at the Convention.

### THE BECKLEY SISTERHOOD OFFICERS IN 1953

PRESIDENT: Mrs. Sidney (Irene B.) Fink
VICE PRESIDENT: Mrs. Joseph R. (Sylvia S.) Miller
RECORDING SECRETARY: Mrs. Bernard L. (Ruth W.) Saks
CORRESPONDING SECRETARY: Mrs. Archie (Dorothy) Ellenbogen
TREASURER: Mrs. Samuel (Zena Y.) Hochman
FINANCIAL SECRETARY: Mrs. Saul (Dorothy B.) Fortunoff

### THE WELCH TEMPLE EMANUEL SISTERHOOD OFFICERS IN 1953

PRESIDENT: Mrs. Julian Budnick
1ST VICE PRESIDENT: Mrs. Ellis Roston
2ND VICE PRESIDENT: Mrs. B. Herzbrun
RECORDING SECRETARY: Mrs. Morton (Hazel) Rosensweig
CORRESPONDING SECRETARY: Mrs. Isadore (Anna H.) Katzen
TREASURER: Mrs. M. [Milton] Gottlieb [of War, W. Va.]

### PRESIDENTS OF THE LOCAL SISTERHOODS OF WEST VIRGINIA IN 1953

BECKLEY: Mrs. Sidney (Irene B.) Fink
BLUEFIELD: Mrs. Harry (Josephine) Kammer

CHARLESTON: Mrs. Morton Hess
CLARKSBURG: Mrs. M. Lerner
FAIRMONT: Mrs. B. Bressler
HUNTINGTON: Mrs. L. Lerner
LOGAN: Mrs. J. T. Fish (vice president)
MORGANTOWN: Mrs. D. Friedman
PARKERSBURG: Mrs. H. Gottlieb
WELCH: Mrs. Julian Budnick
WHEELING: Mrs. S. Crone
WILLIAMSON: Mrs. W. M. Goodman

The chairmen of the 1953 State Convention were:

For Beckley: Mrs. Bernard E. (Faye R.) Silverman and Mrs. Herman (Minnie G.) Samans (co-chairmen)

For Welch: Mrs. Isadore (Anna H.) Katzen and Mrs. E. M. Newman (co-chairmen)

The treasurer of the 1953 Convention was Mrs. William (Beatrice C.) Binderman, of Beckley

The corresponding secretaries were:

For Beckley: Mrs. M. Edward (Anne K.) Harvit
For Welch: Mrs. Isadore (Anna H.) Katzen

*The 31st State Convention (1955)*
*Morgantown, October 16 to 18, 1955*

The 1955 State Convention, actually the 31st annual or biennial convention, but strangely (and inaccurately) called the 29th in the official program booklet of the State Sisterhood ("29th Biennial Convention of the West Virginia Federation of Temple Sisterhoods. Theme: Judaism: A Way of Life," Morgantown, W. Va., October 16–17–18, 1955"), was held at Morgantown, in the Tree of Life Congregation and at the Morgan Hotel, on October 16 to 18, 1955, under the auspices of the Tree of Life Temple Sisterhood. The general chairmen of the Convention were Mrs. Samson (Lillian) Finn and Mrs.

Edward S. (Belle) Fields. The sessions were presided over by Mrs. Irving (May) Albert, of Williamson, the State President for 1953–1955.

At this Convention, the By-Laws of the State Federation were revised for the first time since 1949, to conform more closely to the N. F. T. S. bylaws. At this same Convention, plans for a caravan were formulated, to visit and to help local Sisterhoods with their respective problems.

Mrs. Hugo (Helen M.) Dalsheimer, the N. F. T. S. President, and the Executive Committee of the N. F. T. S. appointed the following district members to serve in their respective national capacities for the biennial period extending from 1955 to 1957:

Mrs. Charles (Helaine) Rotgin, of Charleston — Member of the Department on Advancement of Judaism

Mrs. Irving (May) Albert, of Williamson — Member of the Department on Religion and Education

Mrs. Edward S. (Belle) Fields, of Morgantown — Member of the Department for Membership and Administrative Services

Mrs. Ralph (Gazella) Masinter, of Huntington — Member of the Department of Human Relations

The National Sisterhood representative at the Morgantown Convention in 1955 was Mrs. Albert Farber, of Elkins Park, Md., a National Executive Board member and Chairman of the National Committee on Peace and World Relations.

At the Sunday evening religious service (October 16, 1955) Rabbi Abraham I. Shinedling, then of Beckley, delivered the invocation, as well as the sermon, on the assigned Convention theme of "Judaism as a Way of Life." Other benedictions and invocations were pronounced by Mrs. Morris M. Rose, of Morgantown; Rabbi Theodore S. Levy, then of Huntington; and Rabbi Joseph H. Freedman, then of Wheeling.

On Monday afternoon, October 17, 1955, workshops were held in Religion and Education, Human Relations, Advancement of Judaism, and Administrative Services, with the following serving as the moderators for these four workshops, respectively: Mrs. Abraham I. (Helen L.) Shinedling, of Beckley; Mrs. Sidney A. (Milda G.) Ardman, of Parkersburg; Mrs. Irving (May) Albert, of Williamson; and Mrs. Louis W. ("Birdie")

Cohen, of Charleston. [Mrs. Louis Cohen, of Charleston, was the daughter of Mrs. Henry (Anna G.) Rodgin, of Bluefield.]

At the Monday night banquet, held on October 17, 1955, Rabbi Morris M. Rose, of Morgantown, served as toastmaster, and Rabbi Joseph Freedman, of Wheeling, delivered the main address. The main address at the Monday luncheon session was presented by Mrs. Albert Farber, of Elkins Park, Md. Mrs. Farber also installed the newly elected officers for the term 1955 to 1957.

## STATE SISTERHOOD OFFICERS FOR 1953–1955

(Elected in Beckley, on October 12, 1953)

PRESIDENT: Mrs. Irving (May) Albert, of Williamson
1ST VICE PRESIDENT: Mrs. Sidney A. (Milda G.) Ardman, of Parkersburg
2ND VICE PRESIDENT: Mrs. Julian Budnick, of Keystone (for the Welch Temple Emanuel Sisterhood)
CORRESPONDING SECRETARY: Mrs. Frank Bodenger, of Williamson
RECORDING SECRETARY: Mrs. Sy Bloom, of Logan
TREASURER: Mrs. Harry Tannenbaum, of Clarksburg
AUDITOR: Mrs. Harry Golden, of Fairmont
PARLIAMENTARIAN: Mrs. Charles (Reba B.) Cohen, of Charleston

## STATE SISTERHOOD COMMITTEE CHAIRMEN
### FOR 1953–1955

RELIGIOUS SCHOOL: Mrs. Abraham I. (Helen L.) Shinedling, of Beckley
UNIONGRAMS: Mrs. Lake Brown, of Charleston
BRAILLE: Mrs. Saul (Lucille J.) Cohen, of Bluefield
EMERGENCY SERVICE: Mrs. Ellis Roston, of Welch
JEWISH CEREMONIALS AND ARTS: Mrs. Ervin Goldsmith, of Morgantown
YOUTH: Mrs. H. Schradski, of Huntington
INTERFAITH, PEACE AND WORLD RELATIONS, AND WORLD UNION

FOR PROGRESSIVE JUDAISM: Mrs. Clarence Lovitch, of Williamson

PROGRAM AND SPEAKERS' BUREAU: Mrs. Harry Klayman, of Williamson

STATIONERY: Mrs. C. Dalton, of Clarksburg

CRADLE ROLL: Mrs. Sam Weiner, of Logan

HONOR ROLL: Mrs. Sidney (Helen B.) Rosenthal, of Bluefield

NEWSLETTER: Mrs. Martin Cremer, of Parkersburg

### LOCAL PRESIDENTS OF THE WEST VIRGINIA SISTERHOODS IN 1955 AND THE RABBIS OF THE STATE

| Local President | City | Rabbi |
|---|---|---|
| Mrs. William Binderman | Beckley | Abraham I. Shinedling |
| Mrs. Fred Gilbert | Bluefield | Herbert J. Wilner |
| Mrs. Louis Cohen | Charleston | Samuel Volkman |
| Mrs. Joseph Levine | Fairmont | Joseph S. Zuckerbram |
| Mrs. Harold Frankel | Huntington | Theodore S. Levy |
| Mrs. Jack Moss | Logan | Nathaniel H. Zimskind (student rabbi) |
| Mrs. Howard R. Weiss | Morgantown | Morris M. Rose |
| Mrs. Allan Staub | Parkersburg | Sherwin Wine (student rabbi) |
| Mrs. Isadore Katzen | Welch | Leonard Kravitz |
| Mrs. Kermit A. Rosenberg | Wheeling | Joseph H. Freedman |
| Mrs. Alexander H. Preiser | Williamson | Robert Blinder (student rabbi) |

[Of the seven permanent rabbis of the State in 1955, as mentioned above, only one, Samuel Volkman, of Charleston, was still serving in the State only four years later, in 1959.]

### OFFICERS OF THE MORGANTOWN TREE OF LIFE SISTERHOOD IN 1955

PRESIDENT: Mrs. Howard R. Weiss

1ST VICE PRESIDENT: Mrs. Stanley Manilla

2ND VICE PRESIDENT: Mrs. Donald Goldstein

RECORDING SECRETARY: Mrs. Leonard Brodsky
CORRESPONDING SECRETARY: Mrs. Ervin Goldsmith
TREASURER: Mrs. Samson Finn
AUDITOR: Mrs. Abe H. Swartz
PARLIAMENTARIAN: Mrs. Edward S. Fields

## OFFICERS OF THE STATE FEDERATION FOR
### 1955–1957

The following officers of the State Federation for 1955–1957 were elected at Morgantown on October 17, 1955:

PRESIDENT: Mrs. Sidney A. (Milda G.) Ardman, of Parkersburg
1ST VICE PRESIDENT: Mrs. Charles (Helaine) Rotgin, of Charleston
2ND VICE PRESIDENT: Mrs. Charles (Janis) Stein, of Wheeling
RECORDING SECRETARY: Mrs. Sam Weiner, of Logan
CORRESPONDING SECRETARY: Mrs. Ben C. Kart, of Parkersburg
TREASURER: Mrs. Sidney (Irene B.) Fink, of Beckley
AUDITOR: Mrs. Philip (Fanny) Platnick, of Bluefield
PARLIAMENTARIAN: Mrs. Charles (Reba B.) Cohen, of Charleston
[not elected, but "perennially" serving and reappointed]

## THE CARAVAN

In 1956 to 1957, the newly formed State Sisterhood Caravan made four trips: to Beckley and to Logan, in November, 1956, and later to Huntington and Parkersburg. The following Sisterhood women participated in these visits: Mrs. Sidney A. Ardman, Mrs. Charles Rotgin, Mrs. Charles Cohen, Mrs. Charles Stein, Mrs. Herbert Gottlieb, and Mrs. Sidney Rosenthal. The Caravan is an annual project, with different local Sisterhoods being visited every year, for meetings and for discussions of methods.

## SIXTH RELIGIOUS SCHOOL INSTITUTE

The Sixth Religious School Institute was held in Parkersburg in 1956, with Rabbi Jacob Tolochko, of Kinston, N. C., speaking on "Audio-Visual Aids."

### SEVENTH RELIGIOUS SCHOOL INSTITUTE

The Seventh Religious School Institute was held in Charleston, in 1957, with Albert Vorspan, of New York, addressing the delegates on the subject, "Teaching Social Justice."

### REGIONAL MEETINGS IN 1954 AND 1956

Regional meetings were held, in 1954, in Wheeling and in Williamson, as follows:

*Northern Regional Meeting*, in Wheeling, on September 21, 1954. Mrs. William Leffler, of New York, was the National Federation of Temple Sisterhoods representative.

*Southern Regional Meeting*, in Williamson, on September 23, 1954. Mrs. Leffler was again the National representative.

(In 1954–1955, Mrs. William Leffler was serving as the National Chairman of District Federations of the N. F. T. S.)

The regional meetings of 1956 were:

*The Northern District meeting*, held at Fairmont, on October 4, 1956, with Mrs. Elmer Moyer, of Dayton, Ohio, as the National representative.

*The Southern District meeting*, held at Bluefield, on October 2, 1956, with Mrs. Elmer Moyer, of Dayton, again as the National representative.

### LOCAL SISTERHOOD NEWSLETTER REPORTERS

In the year 1956 to 1957, the following Jewish women of West Virginia served as the *Newsletter* reporters for the various local Sisterhoods:

> Charleston: Mrs. Newton Margolis
> Beckley: Mrs. Albert (Marion M.) Schwartz
> Bluefield: Mrs. Edith (Abraham) Tomchin

PLATE VII

The Virginia Street Temple of Congregation B'nai Israel in Charleston, West Virginia
(see pages 559 and 573)

PLATE VIII

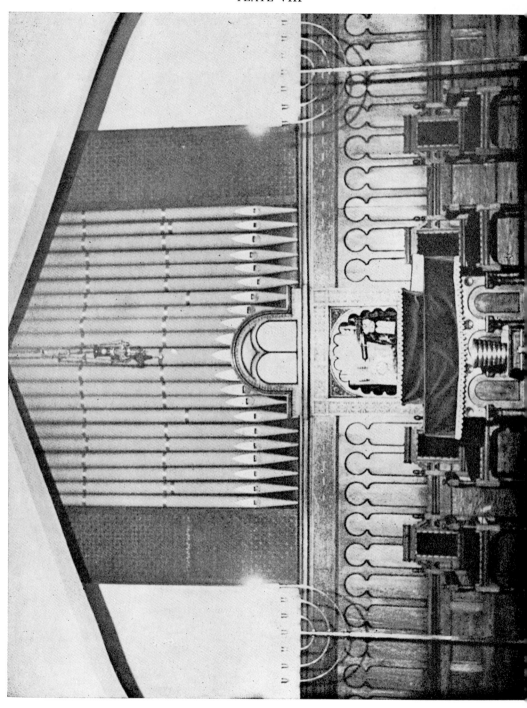

Fairmont: Mrs. Marvin Abrams
Huntington: Mrs. Arthur Weisberg
Logan: Mrs. Bernard L. Miller
Morgantown: Mrs. Ervin Goldsmith
Parkersburg: Mrs. Louis Cremer
Welch: Mrs. Milton Gottlieb
Wheeling: Mrs. Kermit A. Rosenberg
Williamson: Mrs. Charles Albert

## NATIONAL BOARD MEMBERS FROM WEST VIRGINIA, IN 1956

In 1956, the following four West Virginia Sisterhood women were serving as West Virginia National Board Members of the N. F. T. S.:

Mrs. Gazella S. (Ralph) Masinter, of Huntington
Mrs. May (Irving) Albert, of Williamson
Mrs. Helaine (Charles) Rotgin, of Charleston
Mrs. Belle (Edward S.) Fields, of Morgantown

## "AN EVALUATION OF SISTERHOOD"

The following article on "An Evaluation of Sisterhood" was written in April, 1956, by Mrs. Belle Fields, then of Morgantown, who in that year was serving as a National Board Member of the N. F. T. S., with the Department of Membership and Administration. The article was included in the Spring Issue, April, 1956, edition of the *Newsletter*, then under the editorship of Mrs. Sara Gail (Harry) Golden, of Fairmont:

"From time immemorial, one of the basic characteristics of human beings has been their desire to seek one another's company — to be gregarious. This has always been one of our virtues; and because the feeling of kinship, of working cooperatively, of playing in groups has resulted in constructive development, society has evolved many progressive consequences.

"A natural result of this group-craving participation was the sewing circle of the late 1800's. Soon, however, these women saw beyond their knitting of shawls and sweaters to broader vistas. The wider scope of business, of traveling potential, made busy men of their husbands; and it became evident that even the most continental of husbands came to rely gratefully on the energy of 'the little woman' who had time to include more than just passing interest in 'Kinder, Küche, and Kirche.' It became necessary for the women to shoulder more responsibilities in their synagogal affairs, to activate themselves more deeply in Sunday School functioning, and to become assimilated in the embryonic movement of public-minded consciousness.

"The pendulum swung a wider arc slowly, and eventually, in 1913 — on January 21st, to be exact — the Union of American Hebrew Congregations followed the example of alert menfolk to the realization that women were an entity unto themselves, and that this great potential of woman power could best serve Judaism if organized. And so the National Federation of Temple Sisterhoods, under its first President, Mrs. Abram [Carrie] Simon, of Washington, D. C., was founded in Cincinnati. Five thousand members within 49 Sisterhoods was [were] its first strength, but today [1956] — under the nurturing of the Union of American Hebrew Congregations, and under the wise leadership of strong presidential and executive direction — it has grown to more than 100,000 women in over 500 units [local Sisterhoods].

"As the years evaporated in the mist of time, the Federation enlarged its program to meet the increased diversification of atomic living. From assistance to the congregation in facilitating Temple functioning, to Uniongrams and the advancement of the Hebrew Union College, [the N. F. T. S. continued its activities] through furthering the enlightenment of the Braille Institute, adding the subsidization of the [Temple] Youth program, realizing the physical visualization of the House of Living Judaism to the ultimate in organizational expectation — enlisting its forces in combatting citizen lethargy in an effort to preserve universal peace.

"There is no man among them that does not recognize the

forces of woman power and its responsibilities. And we, who celebrate our 43rd year of existence, will never underestimate the value of our affiliation with an organization which is alert to the needs of humanity, adjusted to the tempo of rich Jewish lives among our compatriots, and attuned to the necessity of maintaining an ever vigilant watch on national and universal activities.

"We are proud to be an infinitesimal part of this informed group of women, and to accept the responsibilities of participating in its educational, cultural, and religious programs that have accomplished so much in so few years."

*The 30th [32nd?] General Assembly*
*Parkersburg, October 20 and 21, 1957*

The 30th General Assembly [it was actually the 32nd annual or biennial convention] of the West Virginia Federation of Temple Sisterhoods was held at Parkersburg on October 20 and 21, 1957. Mrs. Sidney A. (Milda G.) Ardman, of Parkersburg, the State President, was in the chair. The N. F. T. S. National Board representative was Mrs. Albert M. Shulman, of South Bend, Ind. [wife of Rabbi Albert M. Shulman, of Temple Beth-El, in South Bend]. Dr. Robert L. Katz, Professor of Human Relations at the Hebrew Union College — Jewish Institute of Religion, in Cincinnati, was the guest speaker.

Mrs. Charles (Helaine) Rotgin, of Charleston, was elected president of the W. V. F. T. S., to serve from October, 1957, to October, 1959.

Three *Newsletters* per annum were ordered published. It was voted that the 1959 Biennial Convention is to be held in Wheeling. Mrs. Albert M. Shulman spoke on "The Meaning of *YES* [*Y*outh, *E*ducation, *S*isterhood]," and installed the newly elected officers voted into office for the years 1957 to 1959.

In attendance at the Convention there were 71 persons, including 7 local Sisterhood presidents, 42 voting delegates, 3 rabbis (including one student rabbi), and 26 official visitors.

The only State rabbis present at the Convention were Rabbi Samuel Volkman, of Charleston, and Rabbi Theodore S. Levy, of Huntington.

The Convention theme was, "Sisterhood Serves Living Judaism." The religious service for the sessions, held at the Chancellor Hotel, was written by Student Rabbi Harold Rubens, of Parkersburg. The Beckley Sisterhood was not represented by delegates at this Convention.

The Executive Board decided, and it was approved, that a printed report of the work of State and Local Committees was to be compiled, and distributed at each State Convention.

The vital project of the State Sisterhood for the coming year was declared to be that of finding a camp site for the Temple Youth Camp. The sum of $1,500 was allocated for this youth camp in 1957–1958 by the State Federation.

### State Sisterhood Officers for 1957 to 1959

The officers and the Executive Board of the State Federation, elected for the two-year term 1957–1959 at the biennial convention held at Parkersburg on October 20 to 21, 1957, were as follows:

PRESIDENT: Mrs. Charles (Helaine) Rotgin, of Charleston

1ST VICE PRESIDENT: Mrs. Charles (Janis) Stein, of Wheeling

2ND VICE PRESIDENT: Mrs. Sidney (Mildred Jean) Schlossberg, of Bluefield

RECORDING SECRETARY: Mrs. Leonard (Marjorie) Lerner, of Huntington

CORRESPONDING SECRETARY: Mrs. Jay L. (Harriett) Margolis, of Charleston

TREASURER: Mrs. Martin (Belle) Cremer, of Parkersburg

AUDITOR: Mrs. Harry (Sara Gail) Golden, of Fairmont

PAST PRESIDENT: Mrs. Sidney A. (Milda G.) Ardman, of Parkersburg

NATIONAL BOARD MEMBERS: Mrs. Ralph (Gazella) Masinter, of Huntington, and Mrs. Charles (Helaine) Rotgin, of Charleston

## The State Sisterhood Executive Board for 1957–1959[1]

COMMITTEE CHAIRMEN

1.  DEPARTMENT OF RELIGION AND EDUCATION

Mrs. Charles (Janis) Stein, of Wheeling, Chairman
(1st Vice President)

CARAVAN COMMITTEE: Mrs. Sally (Samuel) Volkman, of Charleston

FAMILY EDUCATION COMMITTEE: Mrs. Barrett (Elaine) Skoll, of Huntington

JEWISH CEREMONIALS AND ART COMMITTEE: Mrs. Milton (Renee) Komito, of Parkersburg

PROGRAM COMMITTEE: Mrs. Lawrence (Shirley) Gang, of Huntington

RELIGIOUS SCHOOL COMMITTEE: Mrs. Kermit (Helen) Rosenberg, of Wheeling

YOUTH COMMITTEE: Mrs. Charles (Shirley) Broh, of Huntington

2.  DEPARTMENT OF MEMBERSHIP AND ADMINISTRATION

Mrs. Sidney (Mildred Jean) Schlossberg, of Bluefield, Chairman (2nd Vice President)

COMMITTEE AND DEPARTMENT ANALYSES: Mrs. Charles (Reba B.) Cohen, of Charleston

CONSTITUTIONAL REVISIONS COMMITTEE: Mrs. Louis W. (Bertie R.) Cohen, of Charleston

CRADLE ROLL COMMITTEE: Mrs. Samuel (Zena Y.) Hochman, of Beckley

FUND-RAISING COMMITTEE: Mrs. Robert (Helen) Levenson, of Wheeling

HONOR ROLL COMMITTEE: Mrs. Joseph (Debbie) Levine, of Fairmont

---

[1] These data were furnished to me by the newly elected State Sisterhood President, Mrs. Helaine (Charles) Rotgin, of Charleston.

NEWSLETTER COMMITTEE: Mrs. Sidney (Helen B.) Rosenthal, of Bluefield

STATIONERY COMMITTEE: Mrs. Walter (Jimmy) Goodman, of Williamson

3. DEPARTMENT OF ADVANCEMENT OF JUDAISM

Mrs. Leonard (Marjorie) Lerner, of Huntington, Chairman (Recording Secretary)

COMBINED CAMPAIGN COMMITTEE: Mrs. Morton (Helen) Hess, of Charleston (U. A. H. C. — H. U. C. — J. I. R.)

UNIONGRAMS COMMITTEE: Mrs. Alex (Mildred) Preiser, of Williamson

WORLD UNION FOR PROGRESSIVE JUDAISM: Mrs. Joseph T (Charlotte) Fish, of Logan

YES (YOUTH, EDUCATION, AND SISTERHOOD) COMMITTEE: Mrs. Abe (Molly) Swartz, of Morgantown

4. DEPARTMENT OF HUMAN RELATIONS

Mrs. Harry (Sara Gail) Golden, of Fairmont, Chairman (Auditor)

EMERGENCY SERVICES COMMITTEE: Mrs. William (Beatrice C.) Binderman, of Beckley

INTERFAITH COMMITTEE: Mrs. Robert (Hilda) Kaufman, of Morgantown [served only until September, 1958, and then left the State]

PEACE AND WORLD RELATIONS COMMITTEE: Mrs. David (Iris) Bressler, of Fairmont

SERVICE TO THE BLIND COMMITTEE: Mrs. Julian (Gertrude) Budnick, of Keystone [of the Welch Sisterhood]

### LOCAL SISTERHOOD PRESIDENTS IN 1957–1958

| City | Name of the Sisterhood | President |
|------|------------------------|-----------|
| Beckley | Beth El Temple Sisterhood | Mrs. Archie (Dorothy) Ellenbogen |
| Bluefield | Ahavath Sholom Temple Sisterhood | Mrs. Sidney (Mildred Jean) Schlossberg |

| City | Name of the Sisterhood | President |
|------|------------------------|-----------|
| Charleston | Virginia Street Temple Sisterhood | Mrs. Lake (Ruth) Brown |
| Fairmont | Temple Beth El Sisterhood | Mrs. Marvin (Marcia) Abrams |
| Huntington | Ohev Sholom Temple Sisterhood | Mrs. Leo (Julia) Ziffer |
| Logan | Logan [B'nai-El] Temple Sisterhood | Mrs. Bernard L. (Sylvia) Miller |
| Morgantown | Tree of Life Sisterhood | Mrs. Stanley (Marilyn) Manilla |
| Parkersburg | B'nai Israel Sisterhood | Mrs. Edwin (Dorothy) Yunker |
| Welch | Emanuel Sisterhood | Mrs. Isadore (Anna H.) Katzen |
| Wheeling | Woodsdale Temple Sisterhood | Mrs. Jerome (Myrna) Vertman |
| Williamson | Williamson Temple Sisterhood | Mrs. William H. (Betty) Rosen |

## STATE SISTERHOOD BUDGET FOR 1957 TO 1959

The State Sisterhood Convention at Parkersburg adopted the following Budget for 1957–1959 [for the entire two-year period] on October 20–21, 1957, the sums and data of which may prove of some historic interest in later years, as follows:

ESTIMATED DISBURSEMENTS

| | |
|---|---|
| Caravan | $ 100.00 |
| Honor Roll (printing names) | 20.00 |
| Nominating Committee | 30.00 |
| National Dues ($10.00 per year) | 20.00 |
| Newsletter (printing and mailing) | 200.00 |
| President's Expenses: National and State Conventions Presidents' Council Meeting | 275.00 |
| Religious School Teachers' Institutes | 250.00 |
| State Biennial Convention (for the hostess city) | 200.00 |
| Telephone, telegrams, printing, stamps, stationery, etc. | 200.00 |
| Youth (for the hostess city) [for the annual Youth Conclave] | 100.00 |
| Total | $1,395.00 |

ESTIMATED INCOME

| | | |
|---|---|---|
| Cradle Roll | $ | 225.00 |
| Honor Roll | | 150.00 |
| Stationery | | 500.00 |
| State Dues (739 members at 20¢ per member per annum) | | 295.60 |
| Youth Dues [for the Temple Youth Groups] (739 members at 15¢ per member per annum) | | 221.70 |
| Total | | $1,392.30 |

BALANCE IN THE CHECKING ACCOUNT AS OF
OCTOBER 1, 1957

CARAVAN FUND

| | | |
|---|---|---|
| Amount voted at the Biennial in Morgantown, in 1955 | $ | 350.00 |
| Expense in 1955 to 1957 | | 227.20 |
| | $ | 122.80 |
| Amount voted at the Biennial in Parkersburg in 1957 | | 100.00 |
| Balance | $ | 222.80 |

YOUTH CAMP FUND

| | | |
|---|---|---|
| Amount prior to the Biennial in Parkersburg in 1957 | $ | 500.00 |
| Amount voted at the Biennial in Parkersburg in 1957 | | 1,000.00 |
| Total amount in the Youth Camp Fund | | $1,500.00 |

BOND
$500.00

BUDGET COMMITTEE:  Mrs. Charles Stein, of Wheeling
Mrs. Charles Rotgin, of Charleston
Mrs. Sidney Fink, of Beckley

THE 31ST STATE CONVENTION OF THE SISTERHOOD
WHEELING, APRIL 14 AND 15, 1959

The 1959 State Convention, the 31st, of the W. V. F. T. S. was held at Wheeling, at the McLure Hotel and at the new Woodsdale Temple of Congregation Leshem Shomayim, on Tuesday and Wednesday, April 14 and 15, 1959. The sessions were presided over by the State Sisterhood president, Mrs. Charles (Helaine) Rotgin, of Charleston.

The attendance at this 31st State Convention, including delegates and visitors, was as follows (9 of the 11 local Sisterhoods of the State were represented, the Beckley and the Logan Sisterhoods alone sending no delegates):

*Delegates and Visitors*

| | | | |
|---|---|---|---|
| Bluefield-Princeton | 1 | Parkersburg | 4 |
| Charleston | 13 | Welch | 1 |
| Fairmont | 5 | Wheeling | 60 |
| Huntington | 6 | Williamson | 3 |
| Morgantown | 4 | | |

Total 97

*Delegates Alone*

(including local and past district (State) presidents, and district chairmen)

| | | | |
|---|---|---|---|
| Bluefield-Princeton | 1 | Parkersburg | 3 |
| Charleston | 8 | Welch | 1 |
| Fairmont | 5 | Wheeling | 7 |
| Huntington | 4 | Williamson | 3 |
| Morgantown | 3 | | |

Total number of delegates 35

(The State Sisterhood report shows a total of 37 voting delegates.) District chairmen, local presidents, and district officers 35. Visitors, rabbis (three) and guests 62.

Mrs. Irving E. Hollobow, of Evanston, Ill., 1st Vice President of the N. F. T. S., participated in this 31st State Convention, and was its principal speaker. Mrs. Charles (Helaine) Rotgin, of Charleston, who served as the State President for 1957–1959, presided at the sessions, and delivered a report on the work and progress of her administration.

Co-chairmen of the 31st State Convention were Mrs. Kermit (Helen) Rosenberg and Mrs. Jack (Joanne) Kaufman, of Wheeling. The Program Co-chairmen were Mrs. Joseph Strauss and Mrs. Seymour Michael, also of Wheeling.

### SISTERHOOD DELEGATES AND MEMBERS PRESENT
### AT THE 31ST STATE CONVENTION
### (APRIL 14–15, 1959)

The Sisterhood delegates and members present at the sessions, with several of the previously active and most interested members of the State Federation being absent, included the following 30 Jewish women of the State, representing a fair cross-section of the most active members of the local and State Sisterhoods, and thus perhaps a matter of historic interest:

Mrs. Marvin (Marcia) Abrams (of Fairmont)
Mrs. David (Evelyn) Badner (of Charleston)
Mrs. Leonard Brodsky (of Morgantown)
Mrs. Paul Broida (of Parkersburg)
Mrs. Lake (Ruth) Brown (of Charleston)
Mrs. Irwin Clark (of Wheeling)
Mrs. Samson (Lillian) Finn (of Morgantown)
Mrs. Harry (Sara Gail) Golden (of Fairmont)
Mrs. Morris Ginsburg (of Williamson)
Mrs. Harry Goldstein (of Morgantown)
Mrs. Morton (Helen) Hess (of Charleston)
Mrs. Isadore (Anna H.) Katzen (of Welch)
Mrs. Jack (Joanne) Kaufman (of Wheeling)
Mrs. Leonard (Marjorie) Lerner (of Huntington)
Mrs. Stanley Loewenstein (of Charleston)
Mrs. Clarence (Frieda) Lovitch (of Williamson)
Mrs. Ralph (Gazella) Masinter (of Huntington)
Mrs. Seymour Michael (of Wheeling)

Mrs. Harry N. Pollock (of Fairmont)
Mrs. David Reich (of Parkersburg)
Mrs. William H. (Betty) Rosen (of Williamson)
Mrs. Richard Rosenbaum (of Morgantown)
Mrs. Kermit (Helen) Rosenberg (of Wheeling)
Mrs. Sidney (Helen B.) Rosenthal (of Bluefield)
Mrs. Charles (Helaine) Rotgin (of Charleston)
Mrs. Stanley Silverstein (of Charleston)
Mrs. Charles J. (Janis) Stein (of Wheeling)
Mrs. Joseph Strauss (of Wheeling)
Mrs. Jerome (Myrna) Vertman (of Wheeling)
Mrs. Victor Wormser (of Huntington)

Three rabbis of the West Virginia congregations attended the convention, and participated in it, but there were no student rabbis of the smaller congregations. These three rabbis were:

Rabbi Samuel Volkman, of Charleston;
Rabbi Theodore S. Levy, then of Huntington;
Rabbi William A. Rosenthall, of Wheeling.

Members of the Credentials Committee who served at the 31st State Convention were:

Mrs. Victor Wormser, of Huntington, Chairman; and
Mrs. Leonard Brodsky, of Morgantown;
Mrs. Jack Kaufman, of Wheeling; and
Mrs. Stanley Loewenstein, of Charleston.

Mrs. Charles (Helaine) Rotgin, of Charleston, in her presidential message, presented this new definition of the Sisterhood as a goal towards which to work in the years to come, and of the philosophy of the work of the Sisterhood:

"To serve in Sisterhood is distinctly different from giving service through any other organization, for Sisterhood is not a social organization, nor is it a philanthropic organization. It is a religious group dedicated to the philosophy that the congregation is the logical unit of organization in Israel and that through congregational life the modern Jewess can most effectively express her influence upon Jewish and non-Jewish life."

A $100 Youth Scholarship for the summer of 1958 and for the summer of 1959 at the newly-purchased Ohio Valley Institute camp was voted by the delegates.

In 1958–1959, the State Sisterhood Caravan paid visits to the cities and the Sisterhoods of Bluefield, Fairmont, Morgantown, Welch, Wheeling, and Williamson. Serving as the State Sisterhood representatives were Mrs. Sally (Samuel) Volkman, of Charleston; Mrs. Janis (Charles J.) Stein, of Wheeling; Mrs. Elaine (Barrett) Skoll, of Huntington; and Mrs. Evelyn (David) Badner, of Charleston.

Eleanor Schwartz, Associate Director of the N. F. T. Y., during the week from October 10 to 16, 1958, met with Temple Youth Groups in Charleston, Huntington, Parkersburg, and Wheeling, and also addressed the Northern Regional Meeting of the State Sisterhood, at Morgantown, on October 12, 1958, and the Southern Regional Meeting, held at Charleston, on October 14, 1958. Panels were held in both areas, under the chairmanship of Shirley Broh, State Youth Activities Chairman, and with Rabbi Theodore S. Levy, of Huntington, and Rabbi Samuel Volkman, of Charleston, as well as Mrs. Clarence (Frieda) Lovitch, of Williamson, and Mrs. Iris Bressler, of Fairmont, serving as the local youth advisors; and with Gordon Sherman, Sylvia Bernstein, and Cookie Rotgin representing the Youth Group.

Under the auspices of the State Federation, the annual Religious School Institute, for 1958, was held in Huntington on September 7th. That for 1959 was held in Parkersburg on September 27, 1959.

In March, 1958, Mrs. Jay Margolis resigned as corresponding secretary of the State Sisterhood; and Mrs. Sidney (Mildred Jean) Schlossberg, of Bluefield, resigned as 2nd Vice President in June, 1958.

### Election of the Officers for 1959–1961

Officers of the W. V. F. T. S. for the two-year period 1959 to 1961 were elected as follows at the 31st State Convention, at Wheeling, on April 15, 1959:

PRESIDENT: Mrs. Charles J. (Janis) Stein (of Wheeling)
1ST VICE PRESIDENT: Mrs. Victor Wormser (of Huntington)
2ND VICE PRESIDENT: Mrs. Richard Rosenbaum (of Morgantown)
RECORDING SECRETARY: Mrs. Sidney (Helen B.) Rosenthal (of Bluefield)
CORRESPONDING SECRETARY: Mrs. Irwin Clark (of Wheeling)
TREASURER: Mrs. David (Evelyn) Badner (of Charleston)
AUDITOR: Mrs. Samson (Lillian) Finn (of Morgantown)

The 1961 State Convention is to be held in Williamson, with the Logan and the Williamson Sisterhoods acting as the co-hostesses.

### THE BUDGET FOR 1959–1961

The following budget, amounting to $1,970, was adopted for the two-year period from 1959 to 1961:

ESTIMATED DISBURSEMENTS

| | |
|---|---:|
| Caravan and Speakers' Bureau | $ 200.00 |
| Nominating Committee | 30.00 |
| National Dues (at $10.00 per annum) | 20.00 |
| American Association for the United Nations, Dues (West Virginia Division, at $10.00 per annum) | 20.00 |
| Newsletter | 200.00 |
| President's Expenses | 325.00 |
| N. F. T. S. Biennial and District Conventions and Meetings | |
| Religious School Teachers' Institute | 250.00 |
| Convention and Speaker (Hostess City) | 200.00 |
| Telephone, printing, stamps, stationery, telegrams, etc. | 300.00 |
| Youth Convention (Host City) (for 2 years) | 100.00 |
| Youth Scholarship (for 2 years) | 200.00 |
| Alderson Penitentiary Project | 100.00 |
| Miscellaneous | 25.00 |
| Total | $1,970.00 |

ESTIMATED INCOME

| | |
|---|---|
| Cradle Roll............................. | $ 200.00 |
| Honor Roll............................. | 100.00 |
| Stationery.............................. | 600.00 |
| State Dues (750 members) (25 cents per member per annum paid by the local Sisterhoods to the State Federation)...................... | 375.00 |
| Youth Dues (750 members) (15 cents per member paid by the local Sisterhoods to the State Federation per annum)................... | 225.00 |
| Total.............. | $1,500.00 |

*Balance in the Checking Account as of April 3, 1959* .. $ 755.50

THE BUDGET COMMITTEE IN 1959

Mrs. Martin Cremer (of Parkersburg)
Mrs. Sidney A. (Milda G.) Ardman (of Parkersburg)
Mrs. Charles J. (Janis) Stein (of Wheeling)
Mrs. Charles (Helaine) Rotgin (of Charleston)
Mrs. David (Evelyn) Badner (of Charleston).

*Luncheon Meeting*, at the McLure Hotel, on Tuesday, April 14, 1959

Mrs. Charles (Helaine) Rotgin, of Charleston, the State President for 1957–1959, presided at this and other functions at the Convention.

Mrs. Irving E. Hollobow, of Evanston, Ill., was the speaker, her subject being, "The Pattern for Sisterhood." In her address, she laid down the following five duties of the Sisterhoods: strengthening Jewish family life; bringing Judaism into each meeting; the improvement of human relations; the extending of hospitality; and helping to advance the entire Reform movement.

*Tuesday, April 14, 1959*

*6.30 P. M.: Religious Service*, at the Woodsdale Temple

*Participants*:

Opening Prayer: Mrs. Irving E. Hollobow, of Evanston, Ill.

Readers: Mrs. Ralph Masinter, of Huntington
  Mrs. Charles J. Stein, of Wheeling
  Mrs. Isadore Katzen, of Welch
  Mrs. Charles Rotgin, of Charleston

Torah Service and Sermonette: Rabbi William A. Rosenthall,
  of Wheeling
Adoration and Benediction: Rabbi Samuel Volkman, of Charleston
Music: The Woodsdale Temple Children's Choir, Mrs. Maurice
  Kaufman, Director

*7.15 P. M.: Buffet Supper* — Woodsdale Temple Social Hall

Invocation: Mrs. William A. Rosenthall, of Wheeling
Play: "The Case of the Mistaken Tuesday"
  Mrs. William A. Rosenthall, Director

               The Cast: Mrs. William A. Rosenthall
                         Mrs. Eugene Adelson
                         Mrs. Philip Eisenberg
                         Mrs. Arthur Gross
                         Mrs. Fred Horne
                         Mrs. Arnold Phillips
                         Mrs. Irving Gardner

*Wednesday, April 15, 1959*

*10.00 A. M.: Round-Table Discussion*

Subject: "Judaism: Something to Enjoy"
Moderator: Mrs. Charles J. (Janis) Stein

Presentations:

On Jewish Art, by Rabbi William A. Rosenthall, of
Wheeling

On Jewish Music, by Mrs. Vivien Richman, of Pittsburgh

On Jewish Literature, by Mrs. Alexander Wishnew, of
Wheeling (Librarian and organizer of the Woodsdale
Temple Library)

*Luncheon Meeting, Wednesday, April 15, 1959,* at the Woodsdale
Temple

Symposium: "What Are Some of the Social Problems Con-
fronting the Jewish Community?"

Moderator and Leader: Rabbi Samuel Volkman (of the Virginia
Street Temple, Charleston)

The Panel:

"The Constitutional Question: The Separation of Church
and State," paper prepared by Mrs. Richard Glaser
(of Charleston)

"The School Question: Religion and the Public Schools,"
by Mrs. Mose Boiarsky (of Charleston)

"The Separation of Church and State," by Rabbi Samuel
Volkman

Recorder: Mrs. Manuel Gersman (of Parkersburg)

*Wednesday Evening, April 15, 1959,* at the McLure Hotel

*7.30 P. M.: Banquet and Concluding Program*

Toastmistress: Mrs. Jerome (Myrna) Vertman, President of the
Woodsdale Temple Sisterhood, of Wheeling

Invocation: Rabbi Samuel Volkman (of Charleston)

Dinner:

Vivien Richman, Folk Singer, of Pittsburgh, Pa.

Greetings from the Woodsdale Temple Congregation:
Harry Robbin

Greetings from the Woodsdale Temple Youth: Karen Rosenberg, President

Motion Picture: "American Morning"; Introduction by Rabbi Theodore S. Levy (of Huntington)

Introduction of the Guest Speaker: by Mrs. Charles (Helaine) Rotgin, Retiring President of the W. V.-F. T. S.

Address: "Our Challenge," by Mrs. Irving E. Hollobow, of Evanston, 1st Vice President of the National Federation of Temple Sisterhoods

Special Presentation: of a Uniongram Booklet to Mrs. Irving E. Hollobow, by Mrs. Ralph Masinter (of Huntington)

Installation of the Officers for 1959–1961: by Mrs. Charles Rotgin

Remarks by the New President: by Mrs. Charles J. (Janis) Stein (of Wheeling)

Benediction: Rabbi William A. Rosenthall (of Wheeling).

### Text of the Sisterhood Installation Scroll

#### Ten Commandments of Leadership

1. Study well the Rules and Regulations, the accomplishments and the goals of the splendid organization which you serve.

2. Honor and add to the works of those who have preceded you, so that our Federation may continue to serve well Jewish and humanitarian causes.

3. You shall do everything in your power to increase the manifold services of our State projects.

4. Be gentle in the face of ingratitude or when idle tongues distort your noblest motives.

5. Reach the end of each new day with that inward feeling of satisfaction that you have used your gifts gratefully and faced its trials bravely.

6. Live so that your deeds will bless other lives and leave behind you the heritage of a good name.

7. You shall encourage all members to make sanctuaries of their homes by having them reflect the light of love and religious truth.

8. You shall do everything within your power to strengthen our religious loyalties and those of our children.

9. You shall create a clean heart within you and renew steadfastness of spirit. [This "commandment" is a citation from the *Union Prayer Book*.]

10. The works of your hands shall be truth and justice.

### The B'nai B'rith in West Virginia

### The B'nai B'rith Council of West Virginia
#### and the
### B'nai B'rith Hillel Foundation at Morgantown

#### 1907–1908

In the year 1907 to 1908, there were only two B'nai B'rith local lodges in the entire State of West Virginia. These were:

Bluefield Lodge, No. 617, with I. Aaron as its secretary.
Wheeling Lodge, No. 615, with Joseph Raduziner as its secretary.

#### 1913

[*American Jewish Year Book*, 1913–1914 (5674 A.M.), page 370]

In 1913, the B'nai B'rith (founded in New York City, in 1843) had four [five?] lodges in West Virginia, as follows:

| | |
|---|---|
| Clarksburg | Huntington |
| Fairmont | Wheeling[1] |

---

[1] Mention of the Bluefield Lodge, listed above as in existence as early as the year 1907–1908, was apparently omitted through inadvertence.

## 1916–1917

According to the *AJYB* for 1916–1917 [5677 A.M.], page 234, there were in West Virginia, in the year 1915–1916 and presumably in the following year also, the following seven [eight] B'nai B'rith local lodges in District No. 3 [District Grand Lodge, No. 3]:

| | |
|---|---|
| [Bluefield] | Huntington |
| Charleston | Morgantown |
| Clarksburg | Parkersburg |
| Fairmont | Wheeling[1] |

## 1943

In 1943, W. [William] Walder, of Charleston, was president, and Lawrence M. Brile, of Fairmont, honorary president, of the West Virginia Council of the B'nai B'rith, belonging to District Grand Lodge, No. 3.

## 1955

In 1955, there were 13 local lodges of the B'nai B'rith in West Virginia, as follows:

Beckley — Beckley Lodge, No. 1360
Bluefield — Bluefield Lodge, No. 617[2]
Charleston — Charleston Lodge, No. 788
Clarksburg — Louis Hiller Lodge, No. 727
Fairmont — Simon Goodman Lodge, No. 726
Huntington — Huntington Lodge, No. 795
Logan — Logan Lodge, No. 1236
Morgantown — Morgantown Lodge, No. 1321

---

[1] Again, apparently, mention of the still existent Bluefield Lodge was omitted by mistake.

[2] Apparently, later, its number was changed to 967. It is possible that for some years the Bluefield Lodge went out of existence, and that when it was reorganized it was given a new number, No. 967.

McDowell County (Welch) — McDowell County Lodge, No.
   1265
Parkersburg — Parkersburg Lodge, No. 767
Weirton — Weirton Lodge, No. 1658
Wheeling — Herman Cooper Lodge, No. 615
Williamson — Williamson Lodge, No. 1040

## STATE COUNCIL OFFICERS FOR 1955 TO 1956

The State officers of the B'nai B'rith Council of West Virginia
for the year extending from May, 1955, to May, 1956, were:

PRESIDENT: Herman Fetter, of Huntington
1ST VICE PRESIDENT: Leo Levey, of Parkersburg
2ND VICE PRESIDENT: A. David Abrams, of Beckley
3RD VICE PRESIDENT: Dr. David Thompson, of Weirton
SECRETARY-TREASURER: Jerome Cantor, of Huntington
DELEGATES-AT-LARGE:
   Harry N. Barton, of Charleston     (The General Committee
   Bernard Gottlieb, of Clarksburg       of District Grand Lodge,
                                          No. 3)

In 1955 to 1956, I. Edward Adler, of Pittsburgh, served as
the Regional Director of D. G. L., No. 3. The West Virginia
State Council is a part of District Grand Lodge, No. 3, of the
B'nai B'rith (Independent Order of B'nai B'rith, or I. O. B. B.),
which includes the four states of West Virginia, Delaware,
Pennsylvania, and New Jersey.

## STATE COUNCIL OFFICERS FOR 1956 TO 1957

The State Council officers for 1956–1957, elected at the State
Council meeting held in Parkersburg on May 20, 1956, were
as follows:

PRESIDENT: Leo Levey, of Parkersburg
1ST VICE PRESIDENT: A. David Abrams, of Beckley
2ND VICE PRESIDENT: Dr. David Thompson, of Weirton
3RD VICE PRESIDENT: Harry J. Berman, of Clarksburg

SECRETARY-TREASURER: Herbert Gottlieb, of Parkersburg
DELEGATES-AT-LARGE:

Harry N. Barton, of Charleston  (The General Committee
Herman Fetter, of Huntington  of D. G. L., No. 3)

### STATE COUNCIL OFFICERS FOR 1957 TO 1958

The officers of the B'nai B'rith Council of West Virginia for the year 1957–1958, elected at the Spring Council meeting held in May, 1957, were as follows:

PRESIDENT: A. David Abrams, of Beckley
1ST VICE PRESIDENT: Dr. David Thompson, of Weirton
2ND VICE PRESIDENT: Harry J. Berman, of Clarksburg
3RD VICE PRESIDENT: Jerome Cantor, of Huntington
SECRETARY-TREASURER: Aaron Cohen, of Clarksburg
GENERAL COMMITTEEMEN:

Harry N. Barton, of Charleston
Bernard Gottlieb, of Clarksburg

In 1957, the State Council had approximately 850 members in 13 local Lodges throughout the State. Two of the lodges were practically inoperative at that time.

The Honorary Presidents of the State Council in 1957 were:

Lawrence M. Brile, of Fairmont
[He moved to Brooklyn, N. Y., in February, 1958.]
Dr. I. I. Hirschman, of Huntington
Isadore Cohen, of Bluefield
Albert Schlossberg, of Huntington

### PAST PRESIDENTS OF THE WEST VIRGINIA STATE COUNCIL

[Budd L. Moser, of Huntington, and Lawrence M. Brile, then of Fairmont, served also a term each as president of District Grand Lodge, No. 3.]

The complete list of the Past Presidents of the State Council, with their year or years of office being given in parentheses, is as follows:

Budd L. Moser, of Huntington [year of office not recorded]
Lawrence M. Brile, then of Fairmont (1937–1939)
Isadore Cohen, of Bluefield (1939–1941)
Sidney Swartz, of Wheeling (1941–1943)
William A. Walder, of Charleston (1943–1945)
Sidney Melnicoff, of Morgantown (1945–1947)
Albert Schlossberg, of Huntington (1947–1949)
Walter H. Adler, of Clarksburg (1949–1951)
    [Walter H. Adler later moved to Phoenix, Ariz.]
Harry N. Barton, of Charleston (1951–1953)
Robert H. Levine, of Beckley (1953–1954)
Bernard Gottlieb, of Clarksburg (1954–1955)
Herman Fetter, of Huntington (1955–1956)
Leo Levey, of Parkersburg (1956–1957)

The B'nai B'rith Council of West Virginia holds two sessions annually: the Spring Council session, generally in May; and the Fall Council session, generally in October. The place of these two annual sessions rotates among the various cities of the State.

At each State Council session, memorial services are conducted by the rabbis of the State who are members of the local lodges for members in the State who have passed away during the six-month interval between Council meetings. When no rabbi is present, a lay member of the lodge conducts the ritual of the memorial service.

The State Council contributes an annual sum towards the maintenance of, and the reduction of the mortgage on, the Hillel Foundation building at West Virginia University, in Morgantown. [The D. G. L., No. 3, also contributes to the maintenance fund of the Hillel Foundation.] In 1956, there were 63 Jewish students at the University in Morgantown. More than 90% of these students are natives of West Virginia, for whose cultural and religious welfare, therefore, provision is made through the State Council of the B'nai B'rith. The State Council also contributed to the erection of the National Hillel Building — the Henry Monsky Foundation Building — in Washington, D. C.

Budd L. Moser, of Huntington, Louis Hiller, of Clarksburg, and Lawrence M. Brile, of Fairmont, also served a term each as president of District Grand Lodge, No. 3, of the B'nai B'rith. They were the only West Virginians ever to do so.

In 1955–1956, Lawrence M. Brile, then of Fairmont (but who later removed to Brooklyn, N. Y., in early 1958), was chairman of the Hillel Maintenance Fund, with Harry N. Pollock, also of Fairmont, and with Nathan (Nat) Harrison, of Wheeling, also serving on this important State committee. In that same year, Bernard Gottlieb, of Clarksburg, served as chairman of the special Hillel Foundation Mortgage Fund.

The Council publishes a State Bulletin, issued from two to four times a year. Aaron Cohen, of Clarksburg, was State bulletin editor in 1955–1956 and again in 1956–1957; during the latter year, six issues of the State Bulletin were published (in mimeographed form) and distributed to the membership. Its official name is *The West Virginia State Council B'nai B'rith News Bulletin*, and it was the only State publication for the Jewry of West Virginia containing news and events of the Jewish communities of the entire State.

## Data on Semi-Annual State B'nai B'rith Conventions

### State Convention, May 2, 1954, at Clarksburg, at the Stonewall Jackson Hotel

Address of Welcome: By Harry J. Berman, president of the Louis Hiller Lodge, No. 727, of Clarksburg

Response by Robert H. Levine, of Beckley, president of the West Virginia State Council

Principal speaker, Milton K. Susman

Invocations by Rabbi Solomon Poupko, of Clarksburg, and by Rabbi Abraham I. Shinedling, of Beckley

Installation of the new officers, by Budd L. Moser, of Huntington

Toastmaster: Maxwell Samuel

### THE CLARKSBURG CONVENTION COMMITTEE

| | |
|---|---|
| Abraham Chapnick | Donald Berman |
| Aaron Cohen | Harry Berman |
| Bernard Gottlieb | Edward Levy |
| Marc Selman | Sidney Rosenthal |
| Maxwell Samuel | Isadore Moshein |

Robert Dellen

### SPRING COUNCIL CONVENTION: AT HUNTINGTON, ON APRIL 22, 1955 AT THE PRICHARD HOTEL

Invocation by Rabbi Jacob M. Danziger, of Bnai Israel Congregation, Huntington

Installation of the new officers of the State Council by Theodore H. Cook, of Philadelphia, secretary of D. G. L., No. 3

Main address by Philip M. Klutznick, of Park Forest, Ill., president of the Supreme Grand Lodge of the B'nai B'rith

Benediction by Rabbi Theodore S. Levy, rabbi of Ohev Sholom Congregation, Huntington

### STATE COUNCIL MEETING: AT FAIRMONT, ON NOVEMBER 6, 1955 AT THE FAIRMONT HOTEL

Toastmaster: Lawrence M. Brile, of Fairmont

Invocation by Rabbi Joseph S. Zuckerbram, of Temple Beth El, Fairmont

Address of Welcome: Emanuel Levine, president of Simon D. Goodman Lodge, No. 726, of Fairmont

Response: by Herman Fetter, of Huntington, president of the West Virginia State Council

Principal speaker: Max U. Appelbaum, 2nd vice president of D. G. L., No. 3, B'nai B'rith

Benediction by Rabbi Morris M. Rose, rabbi of Tree of Life Congregation, Morgantown

The Hillel Mortgage at West Virginia University, in Morgantown, was reported reduced to $5,000 in 1955.

THE FAIRMONT STATE COUNCIL COMMITTEE:

Marvin Abrams        Emanuel Levine
Max Fields           Rudolph Romberg
            Carl Susskind


SPRING COUNCIL MEETING, SUNDAY, MAY 20, 1956, AT
PARKERSBURG, IN THE CHANCELLOR HOTEL

Invocation by Student Rabbi Sherwin Wine, of Congregation
    B'nai Israel, of Parkersburg
Toastmaster: Paul Broida, of Parkersburg
Address of Welcome, by Harry J. Berman, of Clarksburg
Response, by Herman Fetter, of Huntington
Speakers:  Dr. Irvin Stewart, president of West Virginia Univer-
                sity; and
            Benjamin R. Epstein, National Chairman of the
            Anti-Defamation League of the B'nai B'rith
Presentation of the Humanities Award to Dr. Irvin Stewart
Installation of the newly elected officers by Budd L. Moser, of
    Huntington
Benedictions by Rabbi Abraham I. Shinedling, of Congrega-
    tion Beth El, Beckley; and Rabbi Morris M. Rose, of
    Morgantown


THE PARKERSBURG COMMITTEE FOR THE STATE COUNCIL
    MEETING:

Co-Chairmen: Martin Cremer and Manuel Cremer

Committee Chairmen: David Reich        Leo Levey
                    Manuel Gersman    Manuel Cremer
                    Arthur Ardman     Max Yunker
                    Milton Komito     Herbert Gottlieb
                        Murray Salsitz

A Sample Program of a Spring or Fall B'nai B'rith
State Council Meeting

Program for the Spring Council Convention, held on
Sunday, April 22, 1955, at Huntington, W. Va., at
the Prichard Hotel

9.00 A. M.  Registration      Mezzanine
10.30 A. M.  Business Session    Mezzanine
12.15 P. M.  Luncheon      Dining Room, Main Lobby
1.30 P. M.  Business Session    Dining Room, Main Lobby
2.00 P. M.  Women's Tour
6.00 P. M.  Social Hour      Mezzanine
7.00 P. M.  Grand Banquet      Main Ballroom, Mezzanine

### Evening Banquet Program

| | |
|---|---|
| Invocation...................... | Rabbi Jacob M. Danziger, of Bnai Israel Synagogue, Huntington |
| Pledge of Allegiance to the Flag....... | The Assembly |
| "God Bless America"................ | Led by Mrs. Budd L. Moser |
| Master of Ceremonies............... | Lawrence I. Glick, of Huntington |
| Welcome......................... | Leonard A. Lerner, Convention Chairman |
| Installation of the Officers of the Huntington B'nai B'rith Lodge.......... | Theodore H. Cook, Secretary, D. G.-L., No. 3, B'nai B'rith, of Philadelphia |
| Installation of the Officers of the West Virginia Council of the B'nai B'rith.. | Theodore H. Cook |
| Presentation of the West Virginia B'nai B'rith Council Awards............. | Harry J. Berman, Chairman |
| Musical Interlude.................. | Marshall College Men's Concert Choir, under the direction of R. Wayne Hugoboom |
| Presentation of the West Virginia B'nai B'rith Council Humanities Award... | Budd L. Moser, President, D. G. L., No. 3, B'nai B'rith |
| Introduction of the Supreme Grand Lodge President.................. | Budd L. Moser, of Huntington |
| Address.......................... | Philip M. Klutznick, President of the Supreme Grand Lodge of the B'nai B'rith |
| Benediction...................... | Rabbi Theodore S. Levy, of Ohev Sholom Congregation, Huntington |
| "America"....................... | The Assembly |

## STATE ACTIVITIES OF THE B'NAI B'RITH IN WEST VIRGINIA

Aid to Israel Committee
Anti-Defamation League Committee
Armed Forces and Veterans Committee
B. B. Y. O. [B'nai B'rith Youth Organization]
Athletics
Hillel Foundation Committee
Membership and Retention Committee
Social Service Committee
Vocational Service Committee
Civic Affairs and Americanization Committee

## WEST VIRGINIA PAST PRESIDENTS OF D. G. L., No. 3

West Virginia had three B'nai B'rith members who served as past presidents of District Grand Lodge, No. 3:

Louis Hiller (of Clarksburg)
Lawrence M. Brile (of Fairmont)
Budd L. Moser (of Huntington)

From 1953 to 1954, Budd L. Moser, of Huntington, served as the 1st vice president of D. G. L., No. 3.

## LIFE MEMBERS OF DISTRICT GRAND LODGE, No. 3, FROM WEST VIRGINIA

Harry N. Pollock, of Simon D. Goodman Lodge No. 726, Fairmont
Albert Schlossberg, of Huntington Lodge, No. 795, Huntington

## GENERAL COMMITTEE, IN 1953–1954

On the General Committee of D. G. L., No. 3, from West Virginia, there were serving, in 1953–1954:

Harry N. Barton, of Charleston
Nathan Harrison, of Wheeling

Harry N. Barton, of Charleston, was also, in 1953–1954, chairman of the D. G. L., No. 3, Constitution Committee.

MEMBERSHIP OF THE WEST VIRGINIA B'NAI
B'RITH LODGES IN 1953–1954

| City | Name of the Lodge | Number of Members |
|---|---|---|
| Beckley | Beckley Lodge, No. 1360 | 41 |
| Bluefield | Bluefield Lodge, No. 967 | 66 |
| Charleston | Charleston Lodge, No. 788 | 246 |
| Clarksburg | Louis Hiller Lodge, No. 727 | 62 |
| Fairmont | Simon D. Goodman Lodge, No. 726 | 34 |
| Huntington | Huntington Lodge, No. 795 | 202 |
| Logan | Logan Lodge, No. 1236 | 23 |
| McDowell County (Welch) | McDowell [County] Lodge, No. 1265 | 23 |
| Morgantown | Morgantown Lodge, No. 1321 | 25 |
| Parkersburg | Parkersburg Lodge, No. 767 | 54 |
| Weirton | Weirton Lodge, No. 1658 | 44 |
| Williamson | Williamson Lodge, No. 1040 | 42 |
| Wheeling | Herman Cooper Lodge, No. 615 | 76 |
| | Total Membership for the State in 1953–1954 | 938 |

CONSTITUTION OF THE B'NAI B'RITH
COUNCIL OF WEST VIRGINIA

[Revised at the B'nai B'rith Council of West Virginia Spring Convention, held at Parkersburg, on May 20, 1956.]

[The Constitution Committee consisted of the following three men:

Aaron Cohen, Chairman (of Clarksburg)
Jerome Cantor (of Huntington)
Bernard Gottlieb (of Clarksburg)]

PREAMBLE AND PURPOSES

The B'nai B'rith Council of West Virginia has taken upon itself the mission of uniting the Jewish People of the State of West Virginia in the work of promoting their highest interests and those of humanity; of developing and elevating the mental and moral character of the people of our faith; of inculcating the purest principles of philanthropy, honor and patriotism; of supporting science and art; alleviating the sick; coming to the rescue of victims of persecution; providing for, protecting, and assisting the widow and orphan on the broadest principles of humanity.

## ARTICLE I

### NAME AND JURISDICTION

Section 1. This [organization] shall be known as [the] B'nai B'rith Council of West Virginia.

Section 2. The jurisdiction of this Council shall be over all B'nai B'rith Lodges within the state of West Virginia.

## ARTICLE II

### MEMBERSHIP

Section 1. The B'nai B'rith Council of West Virginia shall be composed of the following:

Section 1 (a) Delegates elected to represent the Local Lodges in accordance with Section 2 of this Article.

Section 1 (b) "Life Delegates" to the District Grand Lodge No. 3, B'nai B'rith.

Section 1 (c) Past Presidents of this Council and those upon whom the rights of a Past President have been conferred by it.

Section 1 (d) Members of the General Committee of the District Grand Lodge, No. 3, B'nai B'rith, during their incumbency as members of the General Committee.

Section 1 (e) Past Presidents of the District Grand Lodge, No. 3, B'nai B'rith, who reside within the jurisdiction of the B'nai B'rith Council of West Virginia.

Section 2. Each Lodge which is a member of the B'nai B'rith Council of West Virginia shall be represented by a minimum of Five (5) Delegates including the Local Lodge President and Secretary. Any Lodge having more than fifty (50) members shall be entitled to one (1) additional delegate for each twenty-five (25) members above the first fifty (50) or a major fraction thereof.

Section 3. All Past Presidents of the Council, Past Presidents of District Grand Lodge No. 3, B'nai B'rith, residing within the jurisdiction of the Council, District General Committeemen, and District "Life Delegates" shall be entitled to attend the meetings of the State Council as Delegates at Large with the same rights and privileges of [as] duly elected delegates including the privilege of voice and vote.

Section 4. Each Local Lodge shall select one alternate for each delegate in the event of the inability of [the] said delegate to attend.

Section 5. The term of office of any delegate shall commence with the opening of a Council Meeting and continue until he is replaced by the Local Lodge.

## ARTICLE III

### MEETINGS

Section 1. The Council shall hold two (2) regular meetings during each calendar year, one (1) in the Spring, and one (1) in the Fall.

Section 1 (a) [The] exact time and place of [the] meeting is [are] to be decided by the Executive Committee of the B'nai B'rith Council of West Virginia.

Section 2. The President shall call special meetings at any time he deems it proper to do so.

Section 2 (a) The President shall call a special meeting at any time when requested to do so by motion or resolution adopted by at least five (5) Lodges having their permanent seats of government in the State of West Virginia, provided that such motion or resolutions shall state the purpose of such special meeting. Upon receipt of such request the President shall immediately call such special meeting, which shall be held within fourteen (14) days from the receipt of such motion or resolution.

Section 3. Only such business shall be transacted at a special meeting as shall be stated in the motion resolution referred to in Section 2 of this Article, or in the call by the President, and written notices for such special meetings stating the nature of the business to be transacted and the time and place for the holding of such special meeting to be given [by] the United States Mail to the President and Secretary of each B'nai B'rith Lodge whose permanent seat of government is situated in the State of West Virginia.

Section 4. Written notices of all regular meetings, stating the time and place of the holding thereof, shall be given by United States Mail to the President and Secretary of each B'nai B'rith Lodge whose permanent seat of government is situated in the State of West Virginia.

Section 5. Fifteen (15) Delegates, having the right to vote provided in Article II of this Constitution, shall constitute a quorum for the transacting [of] business of any meeting of the B'nai B'rith Council of West Virginia.

Section 6. Roberts Rules of Order shall be the Governing rules of Order for all Council meetings unless otherwise provided for by this Constitution.[1]

## ARTICLE IV

### ELECTIONS

Section 1. (a) At the Spring Council Meeting there shall be elected from the Delegates to the B'nai B'rith Council of West Virginia a President, a First Vice President, a Second

---

[1] Robert's, not Roberts. The correct title of this work is: *Robert's Rules of Order* [by Henry M. Robert].

Vice President, a Third Vice President, and a Secretary-Treasurer.

Section 1. (b) There shall also be nominated for recommendation to the District Grand Lodge two general committeemen, or such number of general committeemen as the B'nai B'rith Council of West Virginia is entitled thereto by the District Grand Lodge No. 3 to represent the B'nai B'rith Council of West Virginia in the said district.

Section 2. No officer shall succeed himself in office.

Section 3. At the Spring Meeting the President shall appoint Three (3) tellers, none of whom shall be a candidate for office, whose duty it shall be to distribute ballots properly prepared, to collect such ballots after they have been marked by the voters, to count and tabulate them and report to the President[,] who shall forthwith make the announcement of such findings to the Council assembled.

Section 4. Whenever a candidate shall receive a majority of the entire number of votes cast, he shall be declared elected. However, if, on the first ballot, no candidate shall receive a majority of the entire number of votes cast, then the candidate receiving the lowest number of votes shall be eliminated, and further balloting shall continue until one candidate receives a majority of the entire number of votes cast.

Section 5. In the event of death, removal, resignation, or disqualification of any officer, the order of succession shall be the same with respect to succession of officers [as] in the said District Grand Lodge No. 3, B'nai B'rith.


## ARTICLE V

### Duties of Officers

Section 1. (a) The President shall preside at all meetings of the B'nai B'rith Council of West Virginia and all Executive Committee Meetings of the B'nai B'rith Council of West Virginia.

Section 1. (b) The President shall enforce all laws, decisions, resolutions of the Supreme Lodge, District Grand Lodge No. 3, B'nai B'rith, and the B'nai B'rith Council of West Virginia.

Section 1. (c) The President shall sign all proper orders drawn on the Treasury.

Section 1. (d) The President shall appoint all State Committees and make any assignments to the Vice Presidents [that] he shall desire.

Section 1. (e) The President shall from time to time visit Local Lodges within the Council.

Section 1. (f) The President shall prepare and submit a report and message to the State Council at each meeting.

Section 2. (a) The First Vice President shall act as President during the absence or inability of the latter to perform the duties of his office.

Section 2. (b) The First Vice President shall make visitations to Local Lodges assigned to him by the President.

Section 3. (a) The Second Vice President shall act as President during the absence or disability of the President and First Vice President.

Section 3. (b) The Second Vice President shall be the coordinator between the Council Committees and the Local Committees dealing with external activities, that is, activities which do not directly benefit the members of the Local Lodges.

Section 3. (c) The Second Vice President shall make visitations to Local Lodges assigned to him by the President.

Section 4. (a) The Third Vice President shall act as President during the absence or disability of the President, the First Vice President, and the Second Vice President.

Section 4. (b) The Third Vice President shall be the coordinator between the Council Committees and the Local Committees dealing with internal activities, that is, activities which are especially for the members and benefit of the Local Lodges.

Section 4. (c) The Third Vice President shall make visitations to Local Lodges assigned to him by the President.

Section 5. (a) The Secretary-Treasurer shall keep the minutes of the proceedings of the Council Meetings and Executive [Committee] Meetings, and prepare them for Council Meetings. A copy of the minutes of such proceedings [shall] be sent to the Secretary of [District] Grand Lodge No. 3, B'nai B'rith.

Section 5. (b) The Secretary-Treasurer shall keep an account of all monies received and paid out and report same at each Council Meeting.

Section 5. (c) The Secretary-Treasurer shall keep all the books and accounts of the B'nai B'rith Council of West Virginia.

Section 5. (d) The Secretary-Treasurer shall perform such other duties as may appertain to his office or which may be imposed upon him by the B'nai B'rith Council of West Virginia.

Section 6. (a) The Two (2) General Committeemen shall represent the B'nai B'rith Council of West Virginia at all meetings of the [District] Grand Lodge No. 3 B'nai B'rith General Committee, and serve to the best interest of the Council and the Order.

## ARTICLE VI

### COMMITTEES

Section 1. There shall be the following standing committees of the B'nai B'rith Council of West Virginia:

Section 1. (a) External Activities Committees
   (1) Citizenship and Civic Affairs
   (2) B. B. Y. O. [B'nai B'rith Youth Organization] and Youth Activities
   (3) Hillel [Foundations]
   (4) Hillel Maintenance
   (5) Veterans' Affairs
   (6) Vocational Guidance

Section 1. (b) Internal Activities Committees
   (1) Adult Education
   (2) Anti-Defamation
   (3) Awards

(4) Laws
(5) Membership
(6) Program
(7) Publicity

Section 2. The Humanities Award Committee shall be a Special Committee appointed by the President.

Section 3. At the Spring Meeting of the B'nai B'rith Council of West Virginia, or within Thirty (30) days after assuming office, the President shall appoint such sub-committees and special committees as in his judgment may be necessary. The Chairman of each committee shall report regularly to the Executive and shall submit a written annual report to the Council at its Spring Meeting.

## ARTICLE VII

### DUTIES OF COMMITTEE CHAIRMEN

Section 1. The Chairman of the Citizenship and Civic Affairs Committee shall encourage and assist aliens, both within and without [outside of] the Order, to become citizens of the United States and try to inculcate the true spirit of Americanism in them, and impress upon them the necessity of performing their civic duties where they reside. He shall foster the establishment of local committees in each lodge within the Council and shall cooperate with the National Americanism Commission of the Supreme Lodge and the Citizenship and Civic Affairs Committee of the [District] Grand Lodge No. 3 B'nai B'rith, and shall have such further duties relating to Citizenship and Civic Affairs and to cooperate with the National Defense Program as assigned from time to time by the President.

Section 2. The Chairman of the B. B. Y. O. [B'nai B'rith Youth Organization] and Youth Activities shall promote the establishment and retention of B. B. Y. O. Chapters within the Council and shall supervise the organization and activities of each chapter. He shall foster cooperation between all Youth Organizations within the Council.

Section 3. The Chairman of the Hillel [Foundation] Committee shall be charged with the responsibility of furthering the work and program of Hillel within the Council.

Section 4. The Chairman of the Hillel Maintenance Committee shall supervise and see that the Hillel Foundation and its properties at West Virginia University are maintained.

Section 5. The Chairman of the Veterans' Affairs Committee shall be concerned with the general welfare of veterans of our Armed Forces, with particular concern to hospitalize[d] veterans, and shall encourage cooperation of the lodge committees within the Council.

Section 6. The Chairman of the Vocational Guidance Committee shall encourage the creation of Vocational Guidance or Vocational Service Committees in the Lodges within the Council, and assist them in carrying out the program of the National B'nai B'rith Vocational Service Program [Commission].

Section 7. The Chairman of the Adult Education Committee shall encourage the dissemination of educational material to the Lodges within the Council and the supervision of fireside chats [and] class programs, and urge lodges within the Council to encourage their members to attend the Institute of Judaism.

Section 8. The Chairman of the Anti-Defamation Committee shall keep in touch and cooperate with the Anti-Defamation Committee of the Council and [the] Anti-Defamation Commission of the Order, and shall see that there is formed an Anti-Defamation Committee in each Lodge within the Council. He shall encourage them to carry out within their respective localities and [the] purposes of the Anti-Defamation League, and direct and assist them in their work.

Section 9. The Chairman of the Awards Committee shall be charged with the duty of setting up the rules for the Council Awards Program. It is his duty to arrange for the judging of all entries and obtain the necessary trophies for the Council program.

Section 10. The Chairman of the Laws Committee shall act as

Parliamentarian for the Council, and his committee shall examine the Constitution and By-Laws and recommend any amendments or modifications they deem necessary.

Section 11. The Chairman of the Membership Committee shall be charged with the duty of increasing, retention, and conservation of membership in Lodges within the Council. He shall concern himself with the revivification of dormant Lodges and shall make available to the Lodges such plans and suggestions which may be beneficial to the Lodges in retaining their members.

Section 12. The Chairman of the Program Committee shall arrange programs and suggest lodge activities so as to render lodge meetings and functions more attractive and beneficial. He shall encourage and assist the lodges within the Council in the promotion of programs and activities and proper observance of religious occasions.

Section 13. The Chairman of the Publicity Committee shall keep in touch with the activities of the Council and the various Lodges within the Council, and shall endeavor to secure publicity matter of public interest. He shall, when reasonable, edit and have published a Council Bulletin.

Section 14. The Special Humanities Award Committee Chairman shall arrange for the submitting of nominees and [shall] arrange for the judging of the nominees for the Humanities Award for the B'nai B'rith Council of West Virginia.

## ARTICLE VIII

### THE EXECUTIVE COMMITTEE

Section 1. The Executive Committee of the B'nai B'rith Council of West Virginia shall consist of the following members:

Section 1. (a) All duly elected officers of the B'nai B'rith Council of West Virginia.

Section 1. (b) All Presidents and Secretaries of Local Lodges within the B'nai B'rith Council of West Virginia.

Section 1. (c) All Council Committee Chairmen.

Section 1. (d) All Life Delegates and Past Presidents of District
    Grand Lodge No. 3, B'nai B'rith, residing within the
    Council.

Section 2. The Executive Committee shall meet at least two (2)
    times during each year at the call of the Council President.

Section 3. The Executive Committee may be called into session
    upon petition of at least 5 members of the said Executive
    Committee.


## ARTICLE IX

### DUES

Section 1. Each Lodge shall pay dues to the B'nai B'rith Council
    of West Virginia in the following manner:

Section 1. (a) One Dollar ($1.00) per member annually for
    each of the first fifty (50) members of the respective Lodge.

Section 1. (b) Seventy-five cents (75¢) per member annually
    for the next one hundred (100) members of the respective
    Lodge.

Section 1. (c) Fifty cents (50¢) per member annually for all
    over one hundred fifty (150) members of the respective
    Lodge.

Section 2. No Lodge shall pay less than twenty-five dollars
    ($25.00) annually.

Section 3. (a) Each Lodge shall also pay to the B'nai B'rith
    Council of West Virginia six dollars ($6.00) per member
    annually for the District Grand Lodge No. 3, B'nai B'rith,
    Service Fund.

Section 3. (b) The six dollars ($6.00) per member shall be
    billed and collected by the Secretary-Treasurer of the B'nai
    B'rith Council of West Virginia.

Section 3. (c) The amount collected by the Secretary-Treasurer
    of the B'nai B'rith Council of West Virginia for the District
    Grand Lodge No. 3, B'nai B'rith, Service Fund shall be
    divided in the following manner:
    (1) Five dollars ($5.00) per member of the amount collected

shall be sent to the Hillel Maintenance Chairman, who will keep records of the income and disbursements of the Hillel Maintenance Fund.

(2) One dollar ($1.00) per member of the amount collected shall be forwarded to the District Grand Lodge No. 3, B'nai B'rith, Service Fund.

Section 4. The Secretary-Treasurer of the B'nai B'rith Council of West Virginia shall use the number of members for each Lodge as are on the records of District Grand Lodge No. 3, B'nai B'rith, as of December 1st, prior to his election and installation in office, in determining the dues for each Lodge within the B'nai B'rith Council of West Virginia.

Section 5. Any Lodge which shall not have paid the dues according to Article IX by the Spring Council Meeting shall be considered [in] arrears.

## ARTICLE X

### Relation of [the] Council to District
### Grand Lodge No. 3, B'nai B'rith, and
### [the] Local B'nai B'rith Lodges

Section 1. The B'nai B'rith Council of West Virginia shall take no action or pass any resolutions or legislation on any political matter or controversial matters affecting or determining B'nai B'rith policy.

Section 2. The B'nai B'rith Council of West Virginia shall have the right to memorialize the District Grand Lodge No. 3, B'nai B'rith, with respect to matters of B'nai B'rith Policy, but may not make public and/or print pronouncements of any resolution or action on any matter affecting B'nai B'rith Policy without the consent of the District Grand Lodge No. 3, B'nai B'rith, or its General Committee. All resolutions of memorialization directed to the District Grand Lodge No. 3, B'nai B'rith, or its General Committee pursuant to this Section shall be accompanied by a statement showing the number of Lodges represented and the number of those voting for and against the resolution at the time the resolution was considered by the Council.

Section 3. No action of the B'nai B'rith Council of West Virginia shall be deemed to effect [affect] the autonomy of any member Lodge.

## ARTICLE XI

### AMENDMENTS TO THIS CONSTITUTION

Section 1. This Constitution of the B'nai B'rith Council of West Virginia shall not be altered, amended, or repealed unless such changes, alterations, amendments, or repeal be proposed in writing by no less than two delegates or those entitled to transact business of the Council, as provided in Article II of this Constitution, or by any Lodge within the Council, attested by the President and Secretary under its proper seal and presented to the President and Secretary of the Council at least thirty (30) days before a Council Meeting. Copies of the same shall be forwarded to the Lodges within the Council, and if such proposed changes, alterations, amendments, or repeal receive the affirmative vote of two-thirds (2/3) of the delegates and those entitled to transact the business of the B'nai B'rith Council of West Virginia present when same are acted and voted upon by the Council, such change, alteration, amendment, or repeal shall be declared adopted.

Section 2. The Report of a committee appointed by the Council President to revise the laws shall be adopted or rejected in whole or in part by a majority vote of delegates present, and action thereon may be held [taken] at a regular or [a] special session.

Section 3. All laws, resolutions, enactments, or parts thereof inconsistent with these laws are hereby repealed.

Section 4. These laws shall become effective immediately after adoption.

THE B'NAI B'RITH HILLEL FOUNDATION AT
MORGANTOWN, WEST VIRGINIA (AT WEST
VIRGINIA UNIVERSITY)[1]

The only B'nai B'rith Hillel Foundation which has ever been in existence in the State of West Virginia (as distinguished from a Hillel Counsellorship, which is a part-time operation) has been at West Virginia University, in Morgantown. Its existence is recorded in the files of the National B'nai B'rith Hillel Foundations, in New York City, for the first time in 1930. From 1930 to 1940, the Foundation had no resident full-time Director of its own, but was served by the rabbis of the congregations in Uniontown, Pa., and Fairmont, W. Va.

Between 1930 and 1939, the following rabbis served the Foundation:

Samuel Halevi Baron      Avery J. Grossfield
Henry A. Kagan      Bertram Klausner

They were followed, in the period from 1939 to 1956, by the following full-time resident Directors, of whom four served, also, at the same time, as the rabbis of Tree of Life Congregation, in Morgantown:

1939–1940: Meyer Miller      1950–1952: Edwin Schoffmann
1940–1944: Alfred Jospe*      1953 (for only part of the year):
1944–1945: David Herson*          Morrison D. Bial*
1945–1948: Justin Hofmann    1953–1956: Morris M. Rose*
1948–1950: Norman Samson

---

[1] Many of the data contained in this section were generously supplied to me by Dr. Alfred Jospe, director of the Department of Program and Resources of the B'nai B'rith Hillel Foundations, and formerly a Hillel Director at West Virginia University, in Morgantown; by Rabbi George B. Lieberman, formerly of Wheeling, W. Va.; and by Rabbi Avery J. Grossfield, formerly of Fairmont. Both the latter also served for a time as Hillel Directors in Morgantown.

* These four rabbis, Alfred Jospe, David Herson, Morrison D. Bial, and Morris M. Rose, served also, at the same time, as the rabbis of the Tree of Life Congregation, in Morgantown. All the others during this period (1940–1956) were full-time Hillel Directors in Morgantown, but were not associated with the ministry to the congregation.

In September, 1960, Rabbi Bernard A. Silverblatt (ordained by the H. U. C. - J. I. R., in New York, in 1954) was appointed Director of the Hillel Foundation at West Virginia University, in Morgantown. He had previously served as the rabbi of Temple Beth Zion, in Bradford, Pa.

The number of Jewish students at West Virginia University since 1930 has undergone considerable variations. Between 1930 and 1939, the Jewish enrollment averaged 150 students, and on occasions it reached as high as 225. In 1939, there were 125 Jewish students. Between 1940 and 1945, the period of the Second World War, Jewish civilian student enrollment gradually dropped to about 60. However, throughout this War period, West Virginia University participated in the military training program (Army and Air Force), and between 75 to 150 military students were served by Hillel annually during that period. Since the end of the War (1945), the Jewish enrollment has remained relatively constant, fluctuating between 60 and 80 students, both boys and girls.

Due to the economic recession in 1936, the number of Jewish students at West Virginia University suffered a severe decline, with the result that there were not enough Jewish students to warrant the continued maintenance of the Hillel Foundation there. The Hillel Foundations of the B'nai B'rith, therefore, in that year, suspended operations in Morgantown. However, in order to assist the remaining Jewish students at West Virginia University, at a time when there was no resident rabbi in Morgantown, Rabbi Avery J. Grossfield, then (1936–1937) rabbi of the congregation in Fairmont (the Fairmont Jewish Community Center; Avery J. Grossfield supplied me with a great deal of the data on this and on the following pages, from his memory and from his files), interested the West Virginia Federation of Temple Sisterhoods and the West Virginia Council of the B'nai B'rith in the matter, and induced them to organize and maintain, jointly, the Jewish Student Foundation of West Virginia University, as an organization totally separate from and independent of the Hillel Foundations. The Jewish Student Foundation was governed by an Administrative Committee consisting of the following:

the president of the State Council of the B'nai B'rith, as president, representing the State B'nai B'rith Council;

George B. Lieberman, rabbi of Congregation Leshem Shomayim, in Wheeling, at the time, representing the rabbis of West Virginia, as vice president;

Mrs. Samson (Lillian) Finn, of Morgantown, representing the State Federation of Temple Sisterhoods, as treasurer;

the president of the Jewish Student Group at West Virginia University, representing the students of the University, as secretary;

and Rabbi Avery J. Grossfield, of Fairmont, as the executive director.

This arrangement lasted from September-October, 1936, until the end of June, 1939. There were many programs arranged for during this period of almost three years, chief among them a several-day session with Professor Abraham Cronbach, of the Hebrew Union College, in Cincinnati, as the guest speaker.

BOARD OF GOVERNORS OF THE [JEWISH] STUDENT
FOUNDATION AT THE UNIVERSITY OF WEST
VIRGINIA IN APRIL, 1942[1]

PRESIDENT: Rabbi George B. Lieberman, of Wheeling
Samuel Stein (of Morgantown)
Lawrence M. Brile (of Fairmont)
W. A. Walters[2]
Mrs. Samson (Lillian) Finn (of Morgantown)
DIRECTOR: Rabbi Alfred Jospe (of Morgantown)

The budget for 1942–1943 was set at $2,688.

---

[1] Rabbi George B. Lieberman, of Rockville Center, Long Island, N. Y., then (1936–1943) rabbi of Congregation Leshem Shomayim, of Wheeling, furnished me, most generously, with a great many of the data and details contained in this and in the following pages.

[2] In all likelihood, the name W. A. Walters, on this page and on page 244, represents an error (a misrecollection) for William A. Walder, of Charleston, who was most active in the B'nai B'rith in Charleston and in the State Council.

OFFICERS FOR 1942–1943

PRESIDENT: Rabbi George B. Lieberman (of Wheeling)
VICE PRESIDENT: Samuel Stein (of Morgantown)
SECRETARY: Mrs. Samson (Lillian) Finn (of Morgantown)
TREASURER: Lawrence M. Brile (of Fairmont)
DIRECTOR: Rabbi Alfred Jospe
(Re-elected director. He served in this position until October,
1944.)

EXECUTIVE BOARD OF THE HILLEL FOUNDATION,
AT MORGANTOWN, IN APRIL, 1943

PRESIDENT: Rabbi George B. Lieberman
SECRETARY: Mrs. Samson (Lillian) Finn
TREASURER: Lawrence M. Brile

    Mrs. William (Martha) Caplan (of Clarksburg)
    Mrs. Godfrey Millstone (of Morgantown)
    Samuel Stein (of Morgantown)
    Rabbi Lawrence A. Block (of Huntington)
    W. A. Walters

Jewish soldiers were stationed at West Virginia University,
for study, in this year.
The budget for 1943–1944: $2,651.
The above officers were re-elected for 1943–1944.

1944

In October, 1944, Rabbi Eugene Hibshman, then rabbi of
the Reform congregation in Uniontown, Pa., was elected part-
time director of the Hillel Foundation in Morgantown.

[1943–1944]

OFFICERS OF THE JEWISH STUDENT FOUNDATION
OF WEST VIRGINIA UNIVERSITY

PRESIDENT: Rabbi George B. Lieberman
TREASURER: Lawrence M. Brile

SECRETARY: Mrs. Samson (Lillian) Finn
[VICE PRESIDENT?] Sidney Melnicoff

## 1944-1945

### OFFICERS OF THE JEWISH STUDENT FOUNDATION
### AT WEST VIRGINIA UNIVERSITY FOR 1944-1945

PRESIDENT: Rabbi George B. Lieberman
VICE PRESIDENT: Sidney Melnicoff
SECRETARY: Sidney Goldberg (of Morgantown)
TREASURER: Lawrence M. Brile (of Fairmont)

BOARD MEMBERS:

Mrs. Godfrey Millstone (of Morgantown), representing the
Morgantown Temple Sisterhood
Harry N. Pollock (of Fairmont), representing the West
Virginia State Council of the B'nai B'rith
Sidney Melnicoff    Lawrence M. Brile (of Fairmont)
Mrs. Samson Finn and Sidney Goldberg (both of Morgan-
town), representing the Jewish community of Mor-
gantown
Rabbi George B. Lieberman (of Wheeling) and Rabbi
Lawrence A. Block (of Huntington), representing the
rabbis of the State

## 1953-1957

Rabbi Morris M. Rose, of the Morgantown Tree of Life
Congregation, served from September, 1953, to the end of
August, 1956, as the Hillel director in Morgantown. Max
Levine, a noted Jewish businessman of Morgantown, was active
in the work of the Hillel Foundation as adviser to Rabbi Rose
and as his assistant; the secretary of the Foundation during part
of Rabbi Rose's term of office in Morgantown was his daughter,
Naomi Rose.

In July, 1957, Rabbi Robert A. Kaufman, formerly Jewish
Post Chaplain and assistant Post Chaplain at Fort Bragg, in
North Carolina, was called to Morgantown to be director of
the Hillel Foundation and also the rabbi of Tree of Life Con-

gregation, replacing Rabbi Rose, who left his positions in
Morgantown in August, 1956, to become rabbi in the Garden
City, Long Island, Reform congregation. Rabbi Kaufman was
ordained at the New York School of the H. U. C. - J. I. R. in
June, 1955. He served in Morgantown for only a little more
than a year, from July, 1957, to the end of August, 1958, and
then left for Rochester, Minn.

In the interval of almost one year which elapsed between the
departure of Rabbi Rose in August, 1956, and the arrival of
Rabbi Kaufman in July, 1957, the Hillel Foundation at Morgantown was taken charge of by Max Levine and by several members of the Tree of Life Sisterhood in Morgantown, as well as by
several Jewish graduate students at the University.

Beginning with the year 1948, most of the local Lodges of
the B'nai B'rith in West Virginia, and many of their individual
members, obligated themselves to contribute the sum of $5.00
each per annum to the maintenance fund of the Hillel Foundation in Morgantown, as well as an extra sum of $5.00 annually
towards the reduction of the mortgage on the building of the
Hillel Foundation in Morgantown, located at 1420 University
Avenue. Edward T. Buff, of Huntington, was for years in charge
of the collection of these two funds. By July, 1957, this building
mortgage had been reduced from an original sum of about
$14,000 to less than $5,000. The Hillel Foundation building in
Morgantown is not a new building, but an older building
purchased and remodeled for its present use, and owned by
the State B'nai B'rith Council and lodges, under the general
supervision of both the State Council and of District Grand
Lodge, No. 3. Those most actively interested among the State
Council members in the maintenance and mortgage reduction
of the building of the Hillel Foundation, throughout the 1950's,
were Edward T. Buff, of Huntington; Max Levine, of Morgantown; Lawrence M. Brile and Harry N. Pollock, of Fairmont;
and Nathan Harrison, of Wheeling.

From 1940 to 1950 the national B'nai B'rith Hillel Foundations also maintained a B'nai B'rith Hillel Foundation Counselorship at Marshall College, in Huntington. The Jewish en-

rollment averaged about eight students per annum at Marshall College, was never more than fifteen, and finally sank to four in 1950. The counselorship service there was discontinued at that time. The Counselorship at Marshall College was always in charge of the respective rabbis of the Reform Congregation (Ohev Sholom) in Huntington.

The B'nai B'rith Hillel Foundations never maintained official Hillel service at any of the other schools or colleges in the State. However, the Hillel Directors in Morgantown occasionally visited some of the colleges with larger Jewish enrollments, such as West Virginia Wesleyan College, in Buckhannon, and Davis and Elkins College, in Elkins, in order to meet informally with the students. They have always been on call for any services which they could render to students and to college authorities.

## The Jewish Student Foundation, at Morgantown, of West Virginia University

Report by Rabbi Avery J. Grossfield, then of the Fairmont Temple Beth El, who in 1936 was appointed part-time director of the Jewish Student Foundation:

PURPOSES: to create a center for the advancement of the religious, cultural, and social life of the Jewish students on the campus;

To interpret Judaism and Jewry to their fellow-students of the Christian faith, and, in co-operation with them, to foster interreligious understanding and mutual good will;

To help promote, in co-operation with their Christian fellow-students, the best interests of student life on the campus and of the University in general.

The genesis of the Jewish Student Foundation of West Virginia University is due to the cooperative interest of the West Virginia State Federation of Temple Sisterhoods and the West Virginia Council of the B'nai B'rith. The organizational committee met at Morgantown on December 6, 1936, and consisted of the following members:

Mrs. Samson (Lillian) Finn (of Morgantown)
Rabbi George B. Lieberman (of Wheeling)
Lawrence M. Brile (of Fairmont)
Harry N. Pollock (of Fairmont)
Jack Friedlander (of Clarksburg)
L. A. Goldstein (of Parkersburg)
B. Kahn (of Williamson)
Harry Kammer (of Bluefield)
Isadore Cohen (of Bluefield)

The project was approved by Dr. C. E. Boucher, president of West Virginia University, and Dr. Richard Aspinall, his assistant. It was agreed that the Jewish Student Foundation was to be supported and governed jointly by the West Virginia State Federation of Temple Sisterhoods and the State Council of the B'nai B'rith.

The first Administrative Board was composed of the following elected members for the year 1937–1938:

CHAIRMAN and TREASURER: Lawrence M. Brile (of Fairmont)
VICE CHAIRMAN: Rabbi George B. Lieberman (of Wheeling)
SECRETARY: Mrs. Samson (Lillian) Finn (of Morgantown)

Also on the Administrative Board, regularly, was to be the president of the Jewish Student Foundation Council at the University.

DIRECTOR: Rabbi Avery J. Grossfield (of Fairmont).

### THE HILLEL FOUNDATION AT WEST VIRGINIA STATE UNIVERSITY

Excerpts from the Report of Dr. Alfred Jospe, Director, to the West Virginia State Council of the B'nai B'rith, dated Morgantown, April 12, 1942:

West Virginia University, in Morgantown, W. Va., is attended, at present [1941–1942], by about 2,600 students. 77 of these are Jewish; 54 are boys, and 23 are girls. 50 Jewish students belong to 2 fraternities and 1 sorority (37 boys and 13 girls), and 27 are independent [unaffiliated with any fraternity or sorority] (17 boys and 10 girls). There was a decrease in the number of Jewish students over the previous year. 72 out of 77 potential members enrolled as members, and participated in the programs and activities.

The Hillel Foundation at West Virginia University is headed by a student executive council consisting of five students representing the two fraternities, the sorority, and the organization of the independent students. Dr. Alfred Jospe serves in an advisory capacity. The main objective of the Hillel Foundation is "to bring a more adequate knowledge of their heritage to the Jewish students and to make Jewish religious and cultural values vital and relevant for the college generation."

To implement this program, the activities of the Hillel Foundation at West Virginia University include Jewish education, interfaith activities, and social activities. The educational program includes regular Sunday night meetings for the discussion of vital Jewish or general questions, with students, professors of the University, rabbis, ministers, and other outstanding personages of the State addressing the group; joint meetings with the Protestant Westminster Foundation, or open forums; book reviews by the director; and student services, both on the Hillel campus and at the Tree of Life Congregation, with students conducting the services and giving the sermons. Also observance of the high holy days and holidays.

Chanukah and Purim celebrations, and a student Seder on Passover. Arrangements for Seder on the first eve of the Passover for the students at the homes of members of the Morgantown Jewish Congregation Tree of Life. Debates on pertinent Jewish questions. Hillel, in its interfaith activities, brought to the Morgantown campus as speakers and lecturers such noted personages as Erica Mann, Louis Adamic, Clarence Streit, Max Lerner, John Metcalfe, and John Haynes Holmes. The Hillel also has a student loan fund, an employment service, and a library.

EXCERPTS FROM THE REPORT PRESENTED IN
APRIL, 1943 FOR THE YEAR 1942–1943

By Dr. Alfred Jospe, Director

West Virginia University, in the year 1942 to 1943, had 2,200 students, of whom, on April 1, 1943, 68 were Jewish (47 boys and 21 girls); on September 15, 1942, the number of the Jewish students was 78 (56 boys and 22 girls).

In addition to the regular students, there were 17 Jewish air cadet trainees, and 29 Jewish engineering students. Hillel on the campus contributed to the War effort [World War II]. The director conducted religious services for the Jewish trainees on every Sunday night, alternating between the Conservative and the Reform ritual, and including a short sermon, or a discussion of Jewish interest. On Friday nights from 2 to 40 students attended religious services at Tree of Life Congregation. The Sisterhood gave a buffet supper once a month on Sunday nights for the Jewish trainees. The Annual Student Service was held on March 26, 1943. Three students served Tree of Life Congregation as teachers in the Religious School.

Norman Thomas, Yolanda Barnett, Dr. B. Tower, Dr. George B. Lieberman, Miss Kung Pu Shing, Erwin Jospe, Reverend H. Wilson, Reverend A. Beckett, and Mrs. E. Reed participated in the Town-Hall meetings and the Sunday night meetings at the Hillel Foundation.

## THE BUDGET OF THE MORGANTOWN HILLEL
## FOUNDATION FOR 1942–1943

| *Income* | *1942–1943* | *For 1943–1944* (estimated) |
|---|---|---|
| Rent from the Morgantown Congregation (for 12 months) [before the Tree of Life Synagogue was erected] | $ 420 | $ 420 |
| District [Grand Lodge], No. 3 [of the B'nai B'rith] | 500 | 500 |
| 12 B'nai B'rith lodges, $50 each | 600 | 650 |
| United Welfare Drives of Charleston, Huntington, and Wheeling | 300 | 500 |
| Sisterhoods of the State (75¢ per capita) | 480 | 481 |
| B'nai B'rith War Service Fund | | 100 |
| TOTAL | $2,300 | $2,651 |

| *Expenditures* | | |
|---|---|---|
| Rent — 12 months [This was before the Hillel Foundation secured and remodeled its own building with the aid of D. G. L., No. 3, and the West Virginia Council of the B'nai B'rith] | $ 600 | $ 600 |
| Director (salary, 12 months) | 900 | 900 |
| Assistants — 9 months (2 students at $16 each per month) | 288 | 385 |
| Janitor and supplies — 9 months | 162 | 216 |
| Utilities, approximately | 150 | 200 |
| Petty cash, for socials, office supplies, Hi-Lites [bulletins], etc. | 200 | 250 |
| Miscellaneous | | 100 |
| TOTAL | $2,300 | $2,601 |

EXCERPTS FROM THE REPORT OF THE B'NAI B'RITH
HILLEL FOUNDATION AT WEST VIRGINIA
UNIVERSITY FOR 1943 TO 1944

by Dr. Alfred Jospe, Director

BUDGET, 1943 TO 1944

*Income*

| | |
|---|---:|
| Rent from [the] Morgantown Congregation [Tree of Life] | $ 420 |
| National Hillel Office | 500 |
| West Virginia [B'nai B'rith] Lodges | 400 |
| West Virginia Sisterhoods | 322 |
| United Welfare Drives (Fairmont, Wheeling, Parkersburg, Charleston, and Huntington) | 700 |
| War Service Fund of the B'nai B'rith (for service to military students) | 250 |
| TOTAL | $2,592 |

*Expenditures*

| | |
|---|---:|
| Rent | $ 600 |
| Director (salary) | 900 |
| Janitor and supplies — 12 months | 210 |
| Student assistants | 282 |
| (secretary: $17 monthly for 12 months; warden: $10 monthly for 9 months) | |
| Utilities | 150 |
| Programs, speakers, food, office, Hi-Lites [bulletins], etc. | 450 |
| TOTAL | $2,592 |

On March 30, 1944, with the Second World War causing a decrease in the enrollment of civilian students throughout the colleges of the nation, but with an increasing number of Jewish military students who were stationed at West Virginia University, the enrollment was:

(a) Civilian students 46
(b) Military students:
    ASTP engineers 81
    ASTP pre-profess.[ional] 9
    Air cadets 23

making a total of 159 students. The wives of 17 trainees, in addition, lived in Morgantown during the past year, and participated regularly in Hillel's activities. This number was the largest number of Jewish students there ever was on the campus since Hillel was re-established in Morgantown in 1935.

The established and well-tested pattern of Hillel work had to be modified in order to make the Foundation more serviceable to civilian and military students alike. Instead of operating for 9 months a year, during the academic season, the Hillel Foundation operated during that year on a 12-month basis. The number of regular meetings was greatly increased, one meeting a week at least being held for the entire group on the average. Hillel's Executive Council was enlarged in order to give full representation to the trainees. Two military students selected by their own group were appointed to the Executive Board. All regular activities of Hillel had to be changed over to the weekends. All Jewish students were released from duty and study periods on Sunday nights and were encouraged to attend Hillel every Sunday night for services and cultural or social activities. For military discipline and a rigid schedule made it impossible for many soldiers to attend religious services on Friday nights.

The Hillel director was appointed civilian chaplain for the Jewish soldiers. Religious activities during the year from April 1, 1943, to April 1, 1944, included High Holy Day services, the Friday night services of the congregation, a public Passover Seder, attended by 109 persons, Chanukah and Purim programs, the Annual Student Service (March 10, 1944), including addresses by Lucille Kraus and Private Gilbert Degelman, Sunday night services, and special Yahrzeit services. The cultural activities included addresses by Dr. Paul Elbin, president of

West Liberty College, on "Jews and Christians"; group discussions of intermarriage, the Jews as the chosen people, the role of Palestine for the solution of Jewish post-War problems, Judaism and Christianity, a Jewish view of Jesus, anti-Semitism, and a wide variety of lectures and addresses on personal, political, and social problems, given by Professor Quinn Curtis, Dr. L. B. Deatrick, Raymond Ratcliffe, Dr. DeLancy, and Dr. Jacob Saposnekow. Public forums were held, with Dr. Louis Wirth and Langston Hughes as the speakers. Many social activities were arranged, in addition to the Sunday night social hour after the weekly religious service and meeting.

In operation, again, were the Hillel Library, the Hillel Loan Fund, and the Hillel publication, the *Hi-Lites*.

In September, 1960, Rabbi Bernard A. Silverblatt (H. U. C. - J. I. R., New York, 1954) became Hillel Foundation Director at West Virginia University, in Morgantown.

In September, 1961, Rabbi Herbert J. Wilner, formerly (1952–1957) rabbi of Ahavath Sholom Congregation, of Bluefield, W. Va., and later the rabbi of a congregation in Levittown, Pa., was appointed Director of the Hillel Foundation at West Virginia University, in Morgantown; and he was elected also, at that time, rabbi of The Tree of Life Congregation, in Morgantown.

# III

# The Jewish Communities of West Virginia

ALDERSON is a residential town in Greenbrier and Monroe Counties, in southeastern (southern) West Virginia, on the Greenbrier River, 15 miles east of Hinton, and 51 miles northeast of Beckley. It is located on the main line of the Chesapeake & Ohio Railroad. It was settled in 1777. Alderson is the site of the Federal Industrial Institution for Women (known also as the Federal Reformatory for Women), which was established in 1926, and which, for many years, was the only Federal penitentiary for women in the United States, until a second one was established in California about the year 1955.

The United States Census for 1950 gave Alderson a general population of 1,489. Previous general population reports were 1,458 in 1935, and 1,493 in 1940.

The only Jewish resident of Alderson of whom there is a personal record is M. [Meyer] Levy, a brother of Frank H. Levy, of Ronceverte. Meyer Levy came to Alderson about the same time that his brother settled in Ronceverte, i. e., in the year 1903 or 1904, and lived there until about 1913 or 1914, earning his living as a merchant. He then left the town. He had a wife and family, about whom no record has been left.

There were no Jews living in Alderson in 1958–1959. Previously, several Jews appear to have lived in Alderson. For a contribution was made, in 1906–1907, by the Jewish community of Alderson, or at least by local Jews living there at that time, to the Fund Collected for the Relief of the Sufferers by the Russian Outrages of October to November, 1905. Also, there were several Jewish physicians and dentists from other cities who, from time to time, from the 1930's on, served as members of the staff of the Federal Reformatory for Women, in Alderson. Thus, from December, 1937, to April, 1945, Dr. H. Viola Shlickerman

255

served as acting assistant dental surgeon in the United States Public Health Service in the Alderson Institution, after which she settled in Beckley; Dr. Belle Abrams, of New York, served as dentist there in the early 1950's; and a Dr. Laster and two or three other Jewish physicians served on the staff of the Institution in Alderson in the early 1950's.

From September, 1951, to September, 1954, Rabbi Abraham I. Shinedling, then rabbi of Beth El Congregation, in Beckley, made monthly (and occasionally even more frequent) visits, as well as on some of the holy days, to the Federal Reformatory for Women, in Alderson, under the auspices of the Synagogue Council of America, of New York, and under the sponsorship of the Beckley Sisterhood (1951–1953) and of the West Virginia Federation of Temple Sisterhoods (1953–1954). During this three-year period he conducted religious services and preached sermons to the Jewish women inmates, who in that period numbered from 7 to 10 inmates in a total prison population of 500 to 550 women, and gave private interviews and held personal consultations with the Jewish inmates, for a total of four hours of service on each visit. In 1951 the Beckley Sisterhood presented a large supply of Jewish Bible translations, Union Prayer Books, and more traditional prayer books to the Library of the Federal Reformatory for Women, for the use specifically of the Jewish inmates and more generally of the rest of the inmates; and the Synagogue Council of America donated a constant supply of religious objects for gifts to those Jewish women who desired them.

In the fall of 1958, the State Sisterhood Federation revived its service to Alderson, and from 1958 to 1959, under its auspices, Rabbi Amos Schauss, of Bluefield, served as part-time Jewish chaplain at the Federal Reformatory for Women.

## ANAWALT (JEANETTE)

Anawalt is a town situated in the extreme southwestern part of West Virginia, near Welch, and above Gary, in McDowell County, in the direction of Pocahontas. A branch line of the Norfolk & Western Railway from Gary to Anawalt was of considerable aid in the development of the town of Anawalt. In 1940, its population was about 450. It was originally called by the name of Jeanette, but it was later renamed Anawalt, after one of the officials of the United Supply Company, one of whose stores was located in Anawalt. The original name of Jeanette was connected with the Block family of Pocahontas, an early Jewish family in that nearby Virginia town.

According to the 1950 United States Census, the population of Anawalt was 1,383. Later sources indicate that in 1959, including the immediate surrounding area, Anawalt had a general population of about 1,350.

In June, 1955, Israel Forman [Foreman], living in Anawalt, was a member of the Welch Congregation Emanuel. Israel Forman [Foreman], as well as the Kasdin Brothers, who may possibly have been Jewish, were among the early merchants who settled in Anawalt and its area. Anawalt never had a Jewish organization of its own of any kind, and there were no other Jews living in the town in 1959.

[Some of the data about Anawalt were, like some of those concerning other communities of McDowell County, excerpted from the *McDowell County History* of Mrs. Samuel Solins and Mrs. Paul W. Jones, of Welch.]

## ATHENS

Athens is a town in Mercer County, located about 6 miles northeast of Princeton. Its population in 1957 was 682. It is the seat of Concord College (founded in 1872), a coeducational teachers' (State) college. In 1957 there were no Jewish residents in the town of Athens.

Concord College, in 1957, had two Jewish men on its faculty. These were: Dr. Frank Stein, instructor in speech and English, who came to Concord College in 1948, and resides in nearby Princeton, of which community he is a member; and Harry Finkelman (a Certified Public Accountant), who, a teacher of business subjects, also came to Concord College in 1948. From 1948 to 1949, Harry Shaffer served as instructor in economics, leaving in 1949 to teach at the University of Alabama.

Harry Finkelman, who, together with his wife, also lives in Princeton, and served for several years as a teacher in the Congregation Ahavath Sholom Religious School, in Bluefield, in the late 1940's and early 1950's, was, in June, 1956, elected president of the Athens Lions Club, serving until June, 1957. Both Harry Finkelman and Dr. Frank Stein were, in 1957–1958, members of the Princeton Jewish community, which in turn formed an integral part of the Bluefield Jewish congregation and community.

Concord College, in 1957, had no Jewish students at all. In the past five-year period there were only two students of the Jewish faith at Concord College, one from Pennsylvania and one from Maryland. There has never been any Hillel Foundation activity on the campus of Concord College, but from 1943 to 1956 eight rabbis from the surrounding areas visited the College and lectured and paid classroom visits under the auspices of the Jewish Chautauqua Society.

Concord College was formerly the Concord State Normal School and Concord State Teachers College. It is coeducational, and was established by act of the State Legislature on February 28, 1872. The College was opened on May 10, 1875, with Captain James Harvey French as the principal, and with William M. Reynolds as his assistant. In the early 1950's, Virgil H. Stewart was president of Concord College.

Its total enrollment of full-time students for the year 1953–1954 was 709; it had also some 300 part-time students. In 1956, there were 1,064 full-time students, in addition to part-time and off-campus classes and students. The College grants the degrees of Bachelor of Science in Education, Bachelor of Science in Business Administration, Bachelor of Science in Music Education, Bachelor of Science in Vocational Home Economics, also the degrees of Bachelor of Arts and Bachelor of Science, and it provides instruction in vocational education, under the supervision of the State Board of Education. It also provides special courses in art, music, home economics, business education, physical education, and library science. In addition, it provides preprofessional courses of two or more years for students of engineering, medicine, dentistry, law, nursing, commerce, and pharmacy. It furthermore prepares teachers for public elementary and secondary schools. In July, 1952, the West Virginia Board of Education gave approval to Concord College to operate a special program in bequests, endowments, and scholarships.

The Concord College plant consists of about 70 acres and 16 modern buildings, including the Administration Building, the J. Franklin Marsh Library, the Music Hall, the Physical Education Building, the new and the old Science Hall, the Sam Holroyd Hall, and a number of men's and women's residence halls.

In the period from 1943 to 1956, the following eight rabbis visited and addressed assemblies at Concord College, under the auspices of the Jewish Chautauqua Society, which presented the Concord College Library with gifts of a number of volumes of Jewish interest:

1943: Rabbi Lawrence A. Block (then of Huntington)
1944: Rabbi Frederick I. Rypins (then of Roanoke, Va.)
1945: Rabbi Louis J. Cashdan (then of Charleston)
1946: Rabbi Albert M. Lewis (then of Charlottesville, Va.)
1947: Rabbi Abraham I. Shinedling (then of Bluefield)
1948: Rabbi Eugene Hibshman (then of Huntington)
1955: Rabbi Samuel R. Shillman (of Roanoke, Va.)
1956: Rabbi Samuel Volkman (of Charleston)

So far as can now be ascertained, no Jewish families or persons have ever resided in Athens, W. Va.

*Concord College*, Athens, W. Va.

In 1961, Gerald E. Platnick, the younger son of Nathan and Edna E. Platnick, of Bluefield, became a student at Concord College, and remained there until early 1962, when he went to work for Platnick Brothers, in Bluefield, Va.

## BARBOURSVILLE

Barboursville is a town in Cabell County, in western West Virginia, located at the confluence of the Mud and Guyandot

Rivers, near Huntington. In 1950, it had a general population of 1,943 (1950 United States Census). There were no Jews living in Barboursville in 1957, and, so far as it can now be ascertained, no Jews have ever resided in the town.

Barboursville was chartered in 1813. It was the scene of a Federal (Union Army) victory during the Civil War, on July 13, 1861. There is also a state hospital located in the town. Morris Harvey College (founded in 1888) was located in Barboursville until 1934, when it was removed to, and relocated in, Charleston.

## BATH (BERKELEY SPRINGS)

Bath (Bath District), in Morgan County, is the legal name for Berkeley Springs. According to the 1950 United States Census, Bath had a total general population at that time of 1,213. There were no Jews living in Bath, or Berkeley Springs, in 1957.

Bath (to give it its legal name), or, as it is also known and as it was formerly called, Berkeley Springs, is a town, and a noted health resort, in Morgan County, of which it is the county seat, located in northeastern West Virginia, near the Potomac River, 18 miles northwest of Martinsburg. It was chartered as a town in 1776. In 1957, its general population was recorded as 1,145.

An entry in the 1927 volume of the *American Jewish Year Book* reads to the following effect:

> Bath District (Hancock), Morgan County
> 1927        36 Jews

and a similar entry is to be found in the *AJYB* for 1937, giving the same Jewish population, in that year, of 36 persons, which is, in all likelihood, much too high a figure, and based on mere conjecture.

According to another entry in the *AJYB* for both 1927 and 1937, Berkeley Springs had a Jewish population of ten persons or less.

# Beckley[1]

## GENERAL

Beckley is a city, the county seat of Raleigh County, located in the southern part of West Virginia, 51 miles north of Bluefield, and 72 miles southeast of Charleston, the State capital. In 1955, Beckley had an approximate general population of 22,000, and at that time it had a Jewish population of some 50 families. In 1950, according to the United States Census of that year, it had a general population of 19,397.

The population of the city, according to other United States Census reports and unofficial reports, was as follows in past years:

| 1920 | 1930 | 1940 | 1956 |
|------|------|------|------|
| 4,149 | 9,357 | 12,852 | 22,500 |

Beckley is located in the heart, or at least in "one of the several hearts," of the bituminous (soft) coal industry of West Virginia, and there are also many lumbering operations in its immediate vicinity. It manufactures clothing, wool products, and mining machinery, as well as electronics materials, and is noted countrywide as a great soft-coal-mining center. It is one of the half-dozen or more chief business centers of West Virginia. Beckley refers to itself as "the Smokeless Coal Capital of the World."

The city is situated on a broad plateau of the Allegheny Mountains, about 2,500 feet above sea level. Beckley has only freight railroad lines of the Chesapeake & Ohio Railway, but it is provided with through and local railroad passenger service by the Chesapeake & Ohio Railroad at and through its station at Prince, W. Va., in the valley about 11 miles north of Beckley.

---

[1] For further details of the Beckley Congregation Beth El and of the Beckley Sisterhood, the Beckley Temple Youth Group, the Beckley B'nai B'rith Lodge, and the Beckley Hadassah, see the *History of the Beckley Jewish Community* (1955), by Abraham I. Shinedling and Manuel Pickus. Also, for more detailed biographies of Beckley Jewish residents whose names are included in this volume, as well as for brief biographical sketches of Jewish residents of past and present who are not included in this section on Beckley, see *ibidem*, pages 19 to 76.

The city of Beckley was started by General Alfred Beckley (1802–1888), who came to Raleigh County (then a part of Fayette County) from Philadelphia in 1836. Alfred Beckley was self-styled, and was also designated by other persons, as "the founder" of the city of Beckley and as "the Father of Raleigh County." Beckley thus is believed to have begun to be settled in the year 1837. In 1848, Alfred Beckley made the first map of what is now Beckley. Two years later, Raleigh County itself was founded, and began actually to be settled (January 23, 1850). In the summer of 1950, the city of Beckley and Raleigh County both celebrated their centennials. In 1850 there were as yet no Jews either in Beckley or in the whole of Raleigh County.

Alfred Beckley (later a general) was the son of John Beckley, who had served as the librarian of the House of Representatives, in Washington, D. C., for several years, and also as a clerk in the House of Representatives in Washington, during the presidencies of George Washington and John Adams, and during part of the administration of Thomas Jefferson. Alfred Beckley named the city of Beckley after, and in memory of, his father (not after himself, as is sometimes erroneously believed and stated), who had died at Philadelphia in 1807. Alfred Beckley served briefly, for about a year, as a minor Confederate Army general during the Civil War, after which he was then captured and later paroled during the balance of the Civil War.

The Virginia Assembly met on April 4, 1838, and chartered thirty acres "of wilderness" which was called Beckley. Alfred Beckley, some years after the founding of the city and county, served as the first clerk of the Circuit Court of Raleigh County, and in 1872 he served as the county superintendent of schools.

On February 14, 1908, the West Virginia Legislature declared Beckley to be a city, and on April 26, 1927, the Legislature put into effect the second charter of the city, adding a considerable area to the territory of the city. In 1850, when Beckley became the county seat of Raleigh County, Alfred Beckley "conveyed to the people of Raleigh County their present beautiful courthouse plot of two acres as well as one-half the building lots of his town, providing [provided that] the people would establish the seat of justice in and at the town of Beckley forever." The third and last Raleigh County Court House, replacing the smaller, less expensive, and earlier ones dating from, and built in, 1852 and 1893, respectively, was completed in 1937, and cost about half a million dollars.

Nathan Street, in Beckley, one block long, and extending from Fairlawn Avenue to Beckley Place, in back of the telephone company's building on Woodlawn Avenue, close to the business section of the town (Neville Street), was named after Nathan Pickus, a long-time Jewish resident of the city, who came to Beckley from Monongah, W. Va., in 1911, and was still resident there in 1959. The name was given to the street in 1920, after Nathan Pickus had helped to divide it (and other nearby streets) up into street lots, subsequent to his purchasing of the property in conjunction with other local Jewish men.

By 1960, according to the United States Census, the general population of Raleigh County had decreased to about 77,000, from its 1950 Federal Census total of about 96,000.

## THE JEWISH COMMUNITY OF BECKLEY

According to the *American Jewish Year Book*, the Jewish population of Beckley was estimated, or was given, as follows in the following years:

1927: 51
1936: Census of Religious Bodies, 1936
1936: Beckley (by county: Raleigh) is listed as having a
      Jewish population of 65 persons in 1936. [This
      is an estimate which is perhaps too low. At
      this time the congregation had long since been
      in existence, and the Temple had already been
      completed, so that possibly a figure of 100 to
      110 Jewish individuals would be more accurate,
      the Beckley Jewish community then having
      about 30 families.]
1937: 65 [again perhaps too low an estimate. As above
      mentioned, at this time Beckley already had

an organized congregation with a synagogue
building]

1948: 142
[142 is probably once more too low an estimate.
Beckley, in all likelihood, had a Jewish population of from 175 to 200 persons in 1948]
1950: 228 (including three or four Jewish families in
nearby Mount Hope and Oak Hill, W. Va.)
1954–1955: 228 Jews (including the several Jewish families in
Mount Hope and Oak Hill) [perhaps slightly
too high a figure]
1956 and 1957: 175 (including Mount Hope and Oak Hill)

[The official and same count of 228 (estimated) for Beckley for
1956–1957 is too high.]

1957–1958: 175 (estimated Jewish population)
1959: 230 (estimated Jewish population, *AJYB* for 1960)
[Volume 61, page 8] [much too high]

From 1952 on, at least a dozen Jewish families left Beckley
and settled in Florida; in other cities of West Virginia, for
example Charleston, Huntington, and Parkersburg; and in other
states, especially Virginia. Thus, in the period from 1952 to
1958, Charles H. Levine, Robert H. Levine, Jack Binderman,
Jr., Malcolm Pickus, Gerald A. Pickus, Israel Fink, Harold
Rudin, Isadore Rich (Reichenthal), Harry and Sidney Stromberg,
and Calvin J. Schildkraut left Beckley, and also several others;
and in 1958–1959, Samuel Hochman (and, in 1961, Edward
Saymen), Dr. H. Viola Shlickerman, Morri R. Wein, and
others, left Beckley and resettled elsewhere.

The figure for the Beckley Jewish population, to be found in
the *AJYB* (Volume 58, 1957), of 228 Jewish population in 1956,
is too high, and should have been revised downward, on the
basis of personal inquiry which could have easily been answered,
to about 175, as above mentioned. This figure of 175 for 1956
included two Jewish families remaining in Oak Hill (six persons)
and three Jewish families in Mount Hope (seven persons).

PLATE IX

RABBI LOUIS J. CASHDAN

Rabbi of the Virginia Street Temple,
in Charleston, W. Va.
(1945–1952)
(see pages 599, 651, and 746)

RABBI SAMUEL VOLKMAN

Rabbi of B'nai Israel Congregation
(The Virginia Street Temple)
in Charleston, W. Va.
(1952–    )
(see pages 615 and 658)

FRANK A. BAER
(of Charleston, W. Va.)

A Former President of the
Virginia Street Temple
(B'nai Israel Congregation),
of Charleston
(see pages 590, 608,
and 626)

MRS. CHARLES (REBA B.) COHEN
of Charleston, W. Va.

For many years active in the State Sisterhood of West Virginia, and in the
Religious School of the Virginia Street
Temple, in Charleston, as superintendent and teacher
(see pages 625–626, 744, and 746)

PLATE X

Dr. Morris I. Mendeloff, *President*
(see page 600)

Sidney M. Kleeman, *Vice President*
(see pages 600, 608, and 748)

Fred A. Bloomberg, *Treasurer*
(see page 600)

M. M. Margolis, *Secretary*
(see page 600)

Officers of the Virginia Street Temple of Charleston, West Virginia, in April, 1948

## The First Jewish Settlers

It is generally believed that the first Jew ever to live in
Beckley was Ben Hurvitz, who formerly resided and had a
business in Scarbro, W. Va. Before the year 1910 (or at least
some time after 1900), Ben Hurvitz, a partner in the firm of
Hurvitz and Lopinsky (Joseph M. Lopinsky), opened a general
merchandise store also in Beckley, on Main Street, which was a
branch of their original store in Sewell, W. Va. The Beckley
store was located at the northwest corner of Heber and Neville
Streets, where the Watkins Drug Store was located in 1958.
Ben Hurvitz later owned and operated a shoe store in the
Beckley building at 324 Neville Street in which Nobil's Shoe
Store was located in 1958. About the year 1918, Ben Hurvitz
sold out his general store in Beckley to Aaron Totz, and moved
to Charleston, where he died on April 19, 1942, at the age
of 75.

Other Beckley "old-timers" declare that the first Jewish
settler in the city of Beckley was Louis Fine (at some unstated
and now unascertainable time before 1911). The available
records and the recollections of some of the earlier Beckley
Jewish settlers indicate that the following were the earliest
Jewish settlers and residents in Beckley: (The presumable year
of their arrival in Beckley is given in parentheses.)

Max Sager (1909 or 1910)
Samuel Fisher (before 1910)
Louis Fine (before 1911)
Nathan Pickus and Louis
  Pickus (brothers) (1911)
Samuel Scharlow (1913 or
  1914)
Louis J. Fink (1914)
James Pickus (a younger
  brother of Louis and
  Nathan Pickus) (1914)

Nathan Berman (1915)
Jack Shechtman (1918)
Jack Hart (before 1920)
Louis Roth (before 1920)
Hyman Roth (before 1920)
Irving Goldstein (1920)
Jack Plain (1920)
Samuel Wasserkrug (before
  1921)
Abe Saks (1921)
Jacob Silverberg (1921)

## THE BECKLEY JEWISH COMMUNITY IN 1921

In 1921, the following 13 Jewish men or families (some had, in the interim, departed from the city) were resident in Beckley:

| | |
|---|---|
| Nathan Berman | Nathan Pickus |
| Louis J. Fink | Jack Plain |
| Samuel Fisher | Jack Shechtman |
| Irving Goldstein | Max Sager |
| Jack Hart | Jacob Silverberg |
| James Pickus | Samuel Wasserkrug |
| Louis Pickus | |

There was no congregation or other Jewish organization in Beckley in the year 1920. However, a religious school was begun about this time (1921), with about a dozen Jewish children receiving instruction, in private homes. The first religious services were held in September, 1921, for the High Holy Days, in the old Beckley Presbyterian Church, on South Kanawha Street. A student from the Hebrew Union College, in Cincinnati, of whose name there exists today no record or remembrance, conducted these Rosh Hashanah and Yom Kippur services. The occasion was the arrival in Beckley, from the "Old Country" (Russia), of Mrs. Sana (Mendel) Pickus, the mother of the three brothers James, Louis, and Nathan Pickus, who had just emigrated to Beckley with her daughter and her son-in-law, Jacob and Anna Pickus Silverberg.

## THE FORMING OF THE CONGREGATION AND THE ERECTION OF THE SYNAGOGUE (1935–1936)

In 1925, there were, at the most, about 15 Jewish families in Beckley proper. Sophia, Mount Hope, and Oak Hill, at that time, each had also a few Jewish families. By the early part of the year 1935, however, there were perhaps 30 to 35 Jewish families in Beckley, including Albert and Harry Abel, brothers, in Mount Hope. As a result, the Beth El Congregation (known early, in its first years, as the Beckley Hebrew Association, or the B. H. A.) was formed, in April, 1935, by ten men who met at the home of Irving Goldstein, at 215 Woodlawn Avenue (a house later sold by him to James and Naomi A. Pickus, who were still living in it in 1959).

These ten founding members were:

| | |
|---|---|
| Samuel I. Abrams | James Pickus |
| Nathan Berman | Louis Pickus |
| Louis J. Fink | Nathan Pickus |
| Irving Goldstein | Abe Saks |
| William Klein | Jacob Silverberg |

The first officers of the new congregation, elected at that time, were as follows: (The congregation was originally known as the Beckley Hebrew Association, but from 1948 on it was known officially as Beth El Congregation [House of God], and unofficially as the Beckley Hebrew Congregation, or the B. H. A.)

PRESIDENT: Nathan Berman (1935–1937)
SECRETARY: William Klein (1935–1938)
TREASURER: Irving Goldstein (1935–1936)

The building of Beth El Congregation was erected in 1935–1936 at the northeast corner of Bellevue Lane and Second Street, at a cost of slightly less than $6,000. The trustees of the Beckley Hebrew Association, at that time, who arranged for its building, were Harry Abel (of Mount Hope), Nathan Berman, David Freed, Irving Goldstein, and Benjamin E. Lewis. The architect was Samuel H. Bridge, who was still actively engaged in work in Beckley in 1956.

The new synagogue (referred to nowadays either as the Synagogue or as the Temple) (the congregation in those early years of the 1930's was still, in part at least, Conservative) was dedicated on Sunday evening, November 29, 1936, by Rabbi Julius Kravetz, of Congregation Ahavath Sholom, in Bluefield, and by Rabbi Samuel Cooper, of B'nai Jacob Congregation, in Charleston. Its constitution was adopted in 1935. A Sefer Torah, secondhand, was purchased in New York that same year, by the congregation, and for 22 years it was the only Sefer Torah which the congregation owned. On Sunday, April 14, 1958, the second Sefer Torah of Beth El Congregation, a gift of

the collective members, was dedicated at the Temple by the
then Rabbi Abraham A. Kertes, in the presence of a large
congregation of members and of non-Jewish persons of the
community.

## THE CHARTER MEMBERS OF CONGREGATION BETH EL

The Charter Members of the Beckley Hebrew Association,
in 1935–1936, included 29 men, two of whom (Harry and
Albert Abel, brothers) lived in Mount Hope at the time. Their
names are as follows (those marked with an asterisk* were still
living in Beckley in 1957):

Albert Abel (still living in Mount Hope in 1959)
Harry Abel (deceased)
Samuel I. Abrams (deceased)
David Arnstein (deceased)
Nathan Berman (deceased)
*Jack Binderman, Sr.
Israel Fink (no longer resident in Beckley)
*Louis J. Fink (he moved to Baltimore in early 1957)
*Sidney Fink
David Freed
Edward Gilbert (deceased)
*Irving Goldstein
Charles Greenfield (deceased)
I. J. [Jerry] Greenfield
Ben Harris
*M. Edward Harvit
Joseph B. Heller (deceased)
Joseph Keiserman
*William Klein
*Benjamin E. Lewis
Abe Lovitz (died in Florida, in 1958)
Ben Myers
*James Pickus
Louis Pickus (deceased)
*Nathan Pickus

Abe Saks (deceased)
*Jacob Silverberg
Thomas Sopher (deceased)
Samuel Wasserkrug

### PRESIDENTS OF BETH EL CONGREGATION

Nathan Berman (1935–1937)
Irving Goldstein (1937–1938)
Joseph Keiserman (1938–1939)
Joseph B. Heller (1940–1941)
Jack Binderman, Sr. (1941–1942)
William Klein (1942–1943)
J. Leonard Baer (1944–1945)
Isadore R. Wein (1945–1946 and 1951–1957, and serving
    continuously from 1957 to 1959)
Samuel I. Abrams (1946–1947) (thereafter vice president,
    from 1947 until his death in April, 1952)
Sidney Fink (1947–1948)
M. Edward Harvit (1948–1950)
Charles H. Levine (1950–1951)

### CONGREGATIONAL SECRETARIES AND TREASURERS

(The offices of secretary and treasurer were combined most
of the time.)

Irving Goldstein (1935–1936)
Benjamin E. Lewis (several terms)
Jack Binderman, Sr.
Eric Rosenbaum
Isadore R. Wein (1950–1957)
Mrs. Herman (Minnie G.) Samans (1957–1959)

## 1936–1937

In September, 1936, Beckley Congregation Beth El had a
student rabbi (theological student) from the Hebrew Union
College, in Cincinnati, for the High Holy Days.

In the year 1936–1937, the Jewish children of the congregation organized a Young Judea society, which was in existence for a number of years, and was then disbanded. It was presumably succeeded by the First Temple Youth Group (in the early 1940's).

In 1936–1937, Mrs. Irving (Edna B.) Goldstein was the Beckley correspondent for *The Sisterhood News of West Virginia*.

### 1937–1938

In 1937–1938, Mrs. David (Reba) Freed, formerly of Beckley, but later resident in Charleston, served as the 2nd vice president of the West Virginia Federation of Temple Sisterhoods.

### BOARD OF DIRECTORS OF THE CONGREGATION
### 1954 TO 1955

PRESIDENT: Isadore R. Wein
SECRETARY-TREASURER: Isadore R. Wein

DIRECTORS:
    A. David Abrams
    William Binderman
    Sidney Fink
    Irving Goldstein
    M. Edward Harvit
    Nathan Pickus
    Jacob Silverberg

### BOARD OF DIRECTORS, 1955 TO 1958

(re-elected in May, 1956, and in May, 1957, to additional one-year terms)

PRESIDENT: Isadore R. Wein (Chairman of the Board of Directors)

SECRETARY-TREASURER: Isadore R. Wein (only until May, 1957, when Mrs. Minnie G. [Herman] Samans, as above-mentioned, was elected the new secretary of the congregation; and Joseph R. Miller, in May, 1957, was elected treasurer)

A. David Abrams          Sidney Fink
William Binderman        Mrs. Nora B. Franks

(Mrs. Nora B. Franks was elected to the Board of Directors in May, 1956, but she served only until March, 1957, when she was transferred to Parkersburg.)

Irving Goldstein         Eric Rosenbaum
Harry Lewin              Edward Saymen


OFFICERS OF THE CONGREGATION IN 1957–1958

PRESIDENT (Chairman of the Board): Isadore R. Wein
SECRETARY: Mrs. Minnie G. (Herman) Samans
TREASURER: Joseph R. Miller
RABBI: Abraham A. Kertes (served until July, 1959)


PAST MEMBERS OF THE CONGREGATION AND COMMUNITY
OF BECKLEY (AS OF JULY, 1956)

(Those marked with an asterisk* are deceased.)

*Harry Abel (of Mount       Jacob Bloom
   Hope)                    *Harry Burk
Charles Abrams              Benjamin Cohen
*Samuel I. Abrams           Herbert E. Cohen
*David Arnstein             *Sidney Danbury
*J. Leonard Baer            Charles Darvin
Marcus Berman               *Larry [Lawrence] Davis
Milford Berman              Robert Dubin
*Nathan Berman              Louis Epstein (of Oak Hill)
Ralph E. Berman             Sylvia Favish
Robert J. Berman            Mrs. Mayme M. (George)
Benjamin Binderman            Favish
Isadore Binderman           *Louis Fine
Jack Binderman, Jr.         Israel Fink

Jack Fink
*Mrs. Annie W. Fink
  (first wife of Louis J.
  Fink)
*Hyman Fisher
*Max Fisher
*Samuel Fisher
Leonard Fivers (Fivars)
*Marc L. Front
David Freed
Joseph Freed
Aaron Friedman
Sidney Friedman
*Edward Gilbert
Melvin Goldberg
Abraham Goldstein
*Charles Greenfield
I. J. (Jerry) Greenfield
Ben Harris
Jack Hart
Harold E. Harvit
Dr. Lee Hedson
*Joseph B. Heller
Charles Heller
Jack Heyman
Nathan Hirsch
Harry Hochman
*Adele Holz
Arthur Horowitz
*Ben Hurvitz
*Charles Hurvitz
Ernest Jaffee
*Tom [Thomas] Jaffee
Morris Jaffee
*Blossom (Mrs. Edwin)
  Kamen
Edwin Kamen
Dr. Robert Karpat

Daniel Keiserman
Joseph Keiserman
Isadore Klein
*Eugene Lopinsky
Henry Lopinsky
*Joseph M. Lopinsky
*Morris Lopinsky
Robert H. Levine
Milford Lewis
*Abe S. Lovitz
*Mollie (Mrs. Abe S.)
  Lovitz
Morris Markowitz
Dr. Samuel Martin
Ira W. Meltcher
Max Meltcher
*Joseph Mendel
Morris Mendel
Henry Miller
Isadore Miller
*Jacob Miller
Samuel Milstein
*Morris Morgan (Morgan-
  stern)
Benjamin Myers
William Newman
Eric Paige
Gerald A. Pickus
Malcolm Pickus
*Louis Pickus
Milton Pickus
  *Sarah Ethel Snow Pickus
  (Mrs. Louis Pickus)
Jack Plain
*Rabbi Bertrand E. Pollans
Isadore Rich (Reichenthal)
Hans Rosenbaum
Hyman Roth

Louis Roth
Milton Rubenstein
Samuel Rudin
Max Sager
*Abe Saks
Bernard L. Saks
Robert W. Saks
*Sam Scharlow
*Jack Shechtman
Calvin J. Schildkraut
Albert Schwartz
Dr. Leo Sherman
*Isadore Shubinski
Malcolm Silverberg
Sonia Silverberg
Dr. Howard A. Silverman
Joan M. Silverman (Mrs.
Martin Bogarad)
*Thomas Sopher
Dora Steiner

Arthur Stern
Norman Stoken
Harry Stromberg
Sidney Stromberg
Aaron Totz
Sidney Tucker
Henry Waitsman
*Mrs. Sallye Waitsman
Bernard Wasserkrug (of
Oak Hill)
Harry Wasserkrug (of Oak
Hill)
Samuel Wasserkrug
Milton Watzman
Samuel Weber
*Dora Fisher Wender (Mrs.
Morris H. Wender, Sr.)
*Morris H. Wender, Sr.
Arthur Wolk
Murray Wolk

(All those whose names are not marked with an asterisk in the above list lived in Beckley in past years, but by July, 1956, had moved away from the city or its vicinity, and were no longer resident in Beckley, except Bernard L. Saks, who resettled in Beckley in 1959.)

## Jewish Residents in Beckley (1910–1955)

A. David Abrams (1932)
Charles Abrams (1935) (no longer resident in Beckley in 1957)
*David Arnstein (1934)
*J. Leonard Baer (1940)
*Nathan Berman (1915)

---

Those marked with an asterisk * are deceased.
The year of their arrival in Beckley, when known, is given in parentheses following the name.

Dr. Ralph E. Berman (1923; born in Beckley; no longer resident in Beckley in 1957)

Robert J. Berman (1925; born in Beckley; no longer resident in Beckley in 1957)

Isadore Binderman (1941)

Jack Binderman, Sr. (1928)

Dr. Jack Binderman, Jr. (1928)) (moved to San Diego, Calif., in 1955)

William Binderman (1928)

*Harry Burk (1924)

Alfred E. Cohen (1940)

Herbert E. Cohen (moved to Florida in 1952)

*Sidney Danbury (1934)

Charles Darvin (1937) (no longer resident in Beckley in 1957)

Robert Davis (no longer resident in Beckley in 1957)

Archie Ellenbogen

*Louis Fine (1914 or before)

Jack Fink (1925) (no longer resident in Beckley)

Louis J. Fink (1914) (moved to Baltimore in 1957)

Morie Fink (1920; born in Beckley; moved to New York in 1956)

Sidney Fink (1915)

Samuel Fisher (1910) (no longer resident in Beckley)

Dr. Saul Fortunoff (1951) (He left Beckley in 1956.)

Mrs. Nora B. Franks (1954) (She moved to Parkersburg in 1957.)

David Freed (1934) (He moved to Charleston later in the 1930's.)

Joseph Freed (1936) (He moved to Parkersburg in 1955.)

Aaron Friedman (1931) (no longer resident in Beckley in 1957)

Sidney Friedman (1929–1930) (no longer resident in Beckley in 1957)

*Marc L. Front (1942)

Dr. Abraham Gellar (1951)

*Edward Gilbert (1924)

Abraham Goldstein (1949) (He moved to Brooklyn, N. Y., in 1951.)

Arthur Goldstein (1921)

Irving Goldstein (1920)
*Charles Greenfield (1935)
I. J. (Jerry) Greenfield (1935) (He moved to Cincinnati.)
Ben Harris (no longer living in Beckley in 1957)
Jack Hart (1920) (no longer in Beckley)
M. Edward Harvit (1933)
Harold E. Harvit (1933) (no longer resident in Beckley)
Charles Heller (1931) (moved to New York)
*Joseph B. Heller (1931)
Morris Hochman (1938)
Samuel Hochman (1938) (He moved to Hammond, Ind.,
    in 1959.)
Arthur Horowitz (1952) (He moved to Charleston, W. Va.,
    in 1954.)
Edward M. Kandell (1946) (He moved to Lexington, Ky.,
    in 1956.)
Daniel Keiserman (1932) (no longer resident in Beckley
    in 1957)
Joseph Keiserman (1932) (no longer resident in Beckley
    in 1957)
Dr. Benjamin Kishony (1952) (no longer resident in Beckley
    in 1959)
William Klein (1934)
Sidney Labovitz (1942) (no longer resident in Beckley in 1957)
Charles H. Levine (1939) (He moved to Charleston in 1957.)
Robert H. Levine (1939) (He moved to Charleston in 1955.)
Dr. Paul Levison (1950)
Fred Lewin (1954)
Harry Lewin (1938)
Max Lewin (1946)
Benjamin E. Lewis (1929)
Morris Markowitz (1938) (no longer resident in Beckley in
    1957)
Nathan Matz (1938)
Ira Meltcher (1944) (no longer resident in Beckley in 1957)
Max Meltcher (1944) (no longer resident in Beckley in 1957)
*Joseph Mendel (1925)
*Jacob Miller (1934)

Joseph R. Miller (1934)

*Morris Morgan (1941) (originally, Morganstern)

Benjamin Myers (1930) (no longer resident in Beckley in 1957)

Gerald A. Pickus (1928; born in Beckley) (In 1957, he was living in Bluefield.)

James Pickus (1914)

*Louis Pickus (1911) (He lived in Richmond, Va., for several years, until November, in 1958, when he died there.)

Malcolm Pickus (1924; born in Beckley) (living in Waynesboro, Va., in 1957)

Manuel Pickus (1931) (He moved to Charleston in 1956.)

Nathan Pickus (1911)

Dolores Pickus (later, Mrs. Monroe Bayer, of Baltimore)

*Sana Moskovitch Pickus (1921)

Jack Plain (1920) (no longer living in Beckley in 1957)

*Rabbi Bertrand E. Pollans (1946)

Isadore Reichenthal (Rich) (1938) (He moved to Norfolk, Va., in 1955.)

Eric Rosenbaum (1939)

Hans Rosenbaum (1941) (He later moved to Washington, D. C.)

Theodore Rosenbaum (1940)

Louis Roth (1920) (no longer living in Beckley in 1957)

Milton Rubenstein (1936) (no longer living in Beckley in 1957)

Jacob Rubin (1932)

Harold Rudin (1949) (He moved to Huntington in 1956.)

Samuel Rudin (1932) (He later moved to Charleston.)

Max Sager (1909 or 1910) (no longer living in Beckley in 1957)

*Abe Saks (1921)

Bernard L. Saks (1922) (In the early 1950's, he moved to Waynesboro, Va., but in early 1959 he returned to Beckley.)

Daniel M. Saks (1922)

Robert W. Saks (1924) (born in Beckley) (He moved to Washington, D. C., in 1957.)

Herman Samans (1944)

Edward Saymen (1940)

*Sam Scharlow (1913)

Calvin J. Schildkraut (1952) (He moved to Milwaukee in 1954.)

Albert Schwartz (1934) (He moved to Pittsburgh about the year 1954 or 1955.)

Harry Seidman (1930)

Maurice Selden (1948)

*Jack Shechtman (1918)

Rabbi Abraham I. Shinedling (1950) (He moved to Albuquerque, N. Mex., in late July, 1956.)

Dr. H. Viola Shlickerman (1945) (She moved to Hollywood, Fla., in March, 1959.)

Jacob Silverberg (1921)

Malcolm Silverberg (1927) (He moved to Charleston in the late 1940's.)

*Dr. Bernard E. Silverman (1939) (He died at Beckley in July, 1959.)

Harold A. Sopher (1942) (He moved to Baltimore in 1959.)

Ira B. Sopher (1942)

Arthur Stern (1943) (He was no longer resident in Beckley in 1957.)

Norman Stoken (1938 or 1939) (no longer living in Beckley in 1957)

Charles Stromberg (1939)

Harry Stromberg (1939) (no longer resident in Beckley in 1957, but in Albany, N. Y.)

Sidney Stromberg (1939) (no longer resident in Beckley in 1957)

Henry Waitsman (1936–1937) (no longer resident in Beckley in 1957)

Samuel Wasserkrug (1921) (He moved to Washington, D. C., but in 1959 he still operated a store in Beckley.)

Milton Watzman (1937) (He was no longer resident in Beckley in 1957.)

Isadore R. Wein (1940)

Morri R. Wein (1946) (He moved to Elizabethton, Tenn., in 1960.)

Ben H. Wender (1952)

Max H. Wender (1937)

Nathan Wolf (1934) (He was no longer living in Beckley in 1957.)

Arthur Wolk (1939) (no longer resident in Beckley in 1957)

Louis Wolman (1952)

## THE MEMBERSHIP OF CONGREGATION BETH EL IN 1954–1955

(69 families or members in 1954–1955)

Albert Abel (of Mount Hope)

*Harry Abel (of Mount Hope)

A. David Abrams

Mrs. Samuel I. (Esther B.) Abrams

*David Arnstein

Mrs. Rose R. (J. Leonard) Baer

Mrs. Nathan (Dorothy B.) Berman

Robert J. Berman

Jack Binderman, Sr.

Dr. Jack Binderman, Jr.

William Binderman

Hugo Bornheim (of Oak Hill)

Alfred E. Cohen

Archie Ellenbogen

Louis J. Fink

Morie Fink

Sidney Fink

Dr. Saul Fortunoff

Joseph Freed

Mrs. Nora B. Franks

Dr. Abraham Gellar

Mrs. Marc L. (Dora C.) Front

Arthur Goldstein

Irving Goldstein

M. Edward Harvit

Morris Hochman

Samuel Hochman

Arthur Horowitz

Edward M. Kandell

William Klein

Charles H. Levine

Robert H. Levine

Dr. Paul Levison

Fred Lewin[1]

Harry Lewin

Max Lewin

Benjamin Lewis (of Mount Hope)

Benjamin E. Lewis

Nathan Matz

Joseph R. Miller

Those marked with an asterisk * were deceased in 1957.

In 1950, Edward Saymen, William Binderman, Mrs. Nathan (Dorothy B.) Berman, and Jacob Rubin were also members of the Conservative B'nai Jacob Congregation, of Charleston.

[1] Fred Lewin died at Beckley on April 1, 1960. He was the first person to be buried in the new Jewish section of the Beckley cemetery on Harper Road.

James Pickus
Manuel Pickus
Nathan Pickus
Isadore Reichenthal (Rich)
Eric Rosenbaum
Theodore Rosenbaum
Jacob Rubin
Harold Rudin
Mrs. Abe (Gussie B.) Saks
Bernard L. Saks
Daniel M. Saks
Herman Samans
Edward Saymen
Harry Seidman
Maurice Selden
Rabbi Abraham I.
    Shinedling

Dr. H. Viola Shlickerman
Jacob Silverberg
*Dr. Bernard E. Silverman
    (died at Beckley, in early
    July, 1959)
Harold A. Sopher
Ira B. Sopher
Charles Stromberg
Harry Stromberg
Isadore R. Wein
Morri R. Wein
Ben H. Wender
Max H. Wender
Morris S. Wender (of Oak
    Hill)
Louis Wolman

In addition, about a dozen Jewish families living in Beckley were members of the Jewish community, and participated in some of the community functions and activities, but were not members of Congregation Beth El.

In September, 1959, the Beckley Congregation Beth El became affiliated with the U. A. H. C., with its headquarters in New York City.

In November, 1959, Isadore R. Wein was still serving as Chairman of the Board (president) of Congregation Beth El, for the year 1959–1960, and at that time the congregation numbered the following 33 families and 10 individual members: [There were perhaps a dozen other Jewish families in the city at this time, who held no membership in the congregation or in its two other organizations, the Beckley Sisterhood and the Beckley Lodge, No. 1360, of the B'nai B'rith.]

A. David Abrams (Ruth L.)[1]
Albert Abel (of Mount Hope)
Mrs. Esther B. (Samuel I.) Abrams
Mrs. Minnie (Minerva; David) Arnstein

[1] The name of the member's wife is given in parentheses.

Mrs. Rose R. (J. Leonard) Baer
Mrs. Dorothy B. (Nathan) Berman
Jack Binderman, Sr. (Manya S.)
William Binderman (Beatrice C.)
Archie Ellenbogen (Dorothy)
Sidney L. Fink (Irene B.)
Mrs. Dora C. (Marc L.) Front
Arthur Goldstein (Shirley M.)
Irving Goldstein (Edna B.)
M. Edward Harvit (Anne K.)
Robert B. Harvit (Stephanie S.)
Morris Hochman (Tillie M.)
Dr. Albert Kistin
William Klein (Ida M.)
Harry Lewin (Louise G.)
Max Lewin
Benjamin Lewis (Harriet L.) (of Mount Hope)
Benjamin E. Lewis (Ida)
Joseph R. Miller (Sylvia S.)
Nathan Matz (Rose C.)
James Pickus (Naomi A.)
Nathan Pickus (Rose Y.)
Eric Rosenbaum (Millie G.)
Theodore Rosenbaum (Martha B.)
Bernard L. Saks (Ruth W.)
Daniel M. Saks
Mrs. Gussie B. (Abe) Saks
Herman Samans (Minnie G.)
Edward Saymen (Ruth B.)
Maurice Selden (Hannah H.)
Jacob Silverberg (Anna P.)
Ira B. Sopher (Mary J.)
Alan Susman (Sally M.)
Isadore R. Wein (Jeanette A.)
Morri R. Wein
Ben H. Wender (Sadie)
Max H. Wender (Frieda L.)
Morris S. Wender, Jr. (Dolores) (of Oak Hill)
Louis Wolman (Sarah P.)

In 1961–1962, Beth El Congregation had no student rabbi, and there were no regular Friday night religious services held in the Temple. Services were held in the Religious School only on Sunday mornings, in connection with the Religious School sessions.

On Saturday morning, September 1, 1962, Isadore R. Wein officiated at the Bar Mitzvah of his youngest son, Gary A. Wein, at Temple Beth El.

### The Cemetery of Congregation Beth El

Up to May, 1954, Beth El Congregation did not have a cemetery of its own. The Jewish dead of the congregation and community were buried in cemeteries in Baltimore, Md.; Charleston, W. Va.; New York City; Brooklyn, N. Y.; in various other cemeteries on Long Island, N. Y.; or in the Monte Vista Cemetery of the Bluefield-Princeton Congregation Ahavath Sholom, situated between Bluefield and Princeton, W. Va., on the new road linking these two cities; or in Cincinnati, Ohio, and other cities.

In May, 1954, an agreement was reached between the Cemetery Committee (consisting of Nathan Pickus, Isadore R. Wein, Irving Goldstein, and Rabbi Abraham I. Shinedling) and the Homeseekers Land and Building Company, of Beckley (represented by O. F. Cook and Lacy Trump), whereby the Cemetery Committee, for the Congregation, purchased a section of the Sunset Memorial Cemetery, on Harper Road, about three miles north of the business section of Beckley, for use as a Jewish Cemetery, with perpetual care. This new Jewish Section of the Cemetery was dedicated on Sunday, May 30, 1954 (Memorial Day), in the presence of men and women of the Congregation, by Rabbi Abraham I. Shinedling and by Isadore R. Wein, president of the Congregation.

### The Religious School of Congregation Beth El

Early teachers in the Beth El Religious School, the sessions of which have always been held on Sunday mornings, included:

Janet Berman (now Mrs. Robert H. Levine, of Charleston)
Nathan Berman

M. B. Cohen
Dolores Pickus (now Mrs. Monroe Bayer, of Baltimore)
Mrs. Naomi A. (James) Pickus
Mrs. Rose Y. (Nathan) Pickus
Mrs. Selma Rubenstein
Dora Steiner (later of Bluefield)

The beginnings of the Beckley Religious School go back to the year 1921 or 1922, and in 1925 the newly established Beckley Sisterhood took over the conduct of the School. Before the founding of the congregation and the building of the Temple structure, in 1935–1936, the sessions of the Religious School were held in private homes or in local buildings, such as the Institute School on Park Avenue and the American Legion Hall on South Kanawha Street.

In 1921, the Religious School had only 12 children. In 1953, it had 40 children and 5 teachers, but by 1956 the enrollment had dropped to 32 pupils, with 5 teachers. Sessions were held on Sunday mornings from 10.00 A. M. to 12.00 noon, with a half-hour assembly and brief religious service preceding the one and one-half hours of classroom study.

The curriculum always included the following subjects in the 1940's and 1950's:

Bible                           Customs and Ceremonies
Jewish History                  The Jewish Holidays
Jewish Religion                 Hebrew (but not on
Jewish Current Events               Sunday mornings)
Music and Hymns

In the period from 1936 to 1956, the teaching staff of the Beth El Congregation Religious School included the following:

Student Rabbi Morton M. Applebaum
Bernice L. Arnstein
Rabbi Maxwell Berger
Mrs. Beatrice C. (William) Binderman
Philip M. Binderman
Leonard Fivers

Rabbi Harold L. Gelfman
Mrs. Anne K. (M. Edward) Harvit
Student Rabbi Richard G. Hirsch
Student Rabbi Norman Kahan
Bernard Lande
Manuel Pickus
Mrs. Naomi A. (James) Pickus
Rabbi Bertrand Pollans
Mrs. Ruth W. (Bernard L.) Saks
Edward Saymen
Mrs. Ruth B. (Edward) Saymen
Calvin J. Schildkraut
Maurice Selden
Mrs. Maurice (Hannah H.) Selden
Rabbi Abraham I. Shinedling
Mrs. Helen L. (Abraham I.) Shinedling
Sidney T. Shinedling
Sonia Silverberg
Joan M. Silverman
Mrs. Faye R. (Bernard E.) Silverman
Howard A. Silverman
Mrs. Maxine B. (Harold A.) Sopher
Rabbi Jacob G. Soshuk
Isadore R. Wein
Mrs. Sarah P. (Louis) Wolman

In the Religious School year from September, 1955, to June, 1956, the five teachers of the Beth El Religious School faculty were:

Mrs. Rose R. (J. Leonard) Baer
Philip M. Binderman
Rabbi Abraham I. Shinedling (also superintendent)
Mrs. Helen L. (Abraham I.) Shinedling
Sidney T. Shinedling

Substitute teachers: Mrs. Esther B. (Samuel I.) Abrams, Edward Saymen, Maurice Selden.

STUDENTS OF THE RELIGIOUS SCHOOL IN 1954–1955

(35 pupils)

Richard Abrams
David Abrams
Paul Henry Arnstein
Ruth Ann Arnstein
Philip M. Binderman
Valerie Binderman
Kenneth M. Fink
Leonard B. Fink
Rita Harvit
Robert B. Harvit
Alan Hochman
Richard Hochman
Robert S. Klein
Natalie Jo Levine
Gordon Lewis (of Mount Hope)
Paul D. Lewis (of Mount Hope)
Jeffrey D. Miller

Franklin M. Rosenbaum
Thomas S. Rosenbaum
Vicki Rudin
Jerome H. Saks
Dennis G. Saymen
Jeri Lynn Saymen
Sidney T. Shinedling
Russell Sopher
Averie Faye Stromberg
Esther Lee Stromberg
Alan J. Wein
Gary A. Wein
Robert M. Wein
Lynda D. Wender
Matthew Wender (of Oak Hill)
Michele E. Wender
Jack Wolman
Marsha Wolman

Additional pupils of the Religious School in 1955–1956, who entered in September, 1955, included:

Joel Hochman
Sheila J. Selden
Paul Roodin

Marjorie Roodin
Judith Roodin

SUBSTITUTE TEACHERS IN THE RELIGIOUS
SCHOOL (1950–1956)

Mrs. Esther B. Abrams
Sylvia Favish
Mrs. Naomi A. Pickus

Edward Saymen
Maurice Selden

TEACHERS IN THE RELIGIOUS SCHOOL IN 1957–1959,
UNDER RABBI ABRAHAM A. KERTES

Rabbi Abraham A. Kertes
Mrs. Abraham A. (Margaret) Kertes
Mrs. Samuel (Zena Y.) Hochman
Mrs. Joseph R. (Sylvia S.) Miller
Mrs. Rose R. (J. Leonard) Baer
Mrs. Alan (Sally M.) Susman
Mrs. Eva (Benjamin) Kishony (substitute teacher)

In 1959–1960, the following were the teachers in Congregation Beth El's Religious School:

Class 1: Ruth Ann Arnstein  Class 4: Dennis G. Saymen
Class 2: Louis Wolman       Class 5: Eric Rosenbaum
Class 3: Bernard L. Saks

There were 35 children in the Religious School in 1957–1958. Also, in 1957–1958, Rabbi Kertes conducted an adult education course embracing the three subjects of Jewish history, Jewish customs and ceremonies, and Judaism and Christianity (comparative religion).

In 1959–1960, the following 23 boys and girls were pupils in Congregation Beth El's Religious School, divided into five classes, as follows:

Class 1: Teacher, Ruth Ann
  Arnstein
    Stanley Selden
    Robin Susman
    Gail Goldstein
    Nicki Wender (of Oak
      Hill)

Class 2: Teacher, Louis
  Wolman
    Sheila J. Selden

Samuel I. Abrams
Dennis Miller

Class 3: Teacher, Bernard L.
  Saks
    Leonard B. Fink
    Dennis Abrams
    Jeffrey Miller
    Marsha Wolman

Class 4: Teacher, Dennis G.        Class 5: Teacher, Eric
  Saymen                              Rosenbaum
    Gary Wein                            Robert M. Wein
    Richard Abrams                       Thomas Rosenbaum
    Matthew Wender                       Franklin Rosenbaum
      (of Oak Hill)                     Paul H. Arnstein
    Naomi Kistin                         Kenneth M. Fink
    David Lewin                          Jerome H. Saks
                                         Martin Kistin

## BAR MITZVAHS IN CONGREGATION BETH EL

Since its organization as a congregation in the year 1935–
1936, Beth El Congregation has always practised the Bar
Mitzvah ceremony of boys at the age of thirteen, in the synagogue, when desired by parents, according to the Reform
ritual and manner. Apparently, there were no Bar Mitzvahs
at all held in the Beckley community before the erection of the
Temple in the year 1935–1936. On occasions, when the congregation had no rabbi, Isadore R. Wein prepared the boys for
their Bar Mitzvah, in the period after 1940, when he settled in
Beckley, and he conducted the actual Bar Mitzvah ceremony.

The following is a list of boys Bar Mitzvahed in Temple Beth
El from its beginnings as a congregation until 1959. (There were
no Bar Mitzvah ceremonies at all held in the congregation or by
individual Jews until the year 1940, so far as could be
ascertained.)

Malcolm Silverberg (August, 1940, by Rabbi Maxwell Berger)
Charles Heller (October, 1941, by Rabbi Berger)
Manuel Pickus (August, 1944, by Isadore R. Wein)
Howard A. Silverman (1945, by Rabbi Jacob G. Soshuk)
Harold E. Harvit (July, 1945, by Rabbi Soshuk)
Milford Berman (1947, by Isadore R. Wein)
Peter E. Ellenbogen (1948, by Isadore R. Wein)
Robert B. Harvit (February 2, 1951, by Rabbi Abraham I.
  Shinedling)

Sidney T. Shinedling (January 25, 1952, by his father, Rabbi
    Abraham I. Shinedling)
Philip M. Binderman (March 7, 1952, by Rabbi Shinedling)
Robert S. Klein (September 25, 1953, by Rabbi Shinedling)
Paul D. Lewis (of Mount Hope) (November 13, 1953, by Rabbi
    Shinedling)
Alan J. Wein (December 25, 1954, by Rabbi Shinedling)
Dennis G. Saymen (October 14, 1955, by Rabbi Shinedling)
Jack Wolman (January, 1957, by Isadore R. Wein)
A. David Abrams, Jr. (April 25, 1958, by Rabbi Abraham A.
    Kertes)
Paul Henry Arnstein (January 30, 1959, by Rabbi Kertes)
Franklin M. Rosenbaum and Thomas S. Rosenbaum (twins)
    (April 3, 1959, by Rabbi Abraham A. Kertes)
Kenneth Martin Fink (on November 7, 1959, by Rabbi Abra-
    ham I. Shinedling, who made a special trip from his new
    home in Albuquerque, N. Mex., to Beckley, for this Bar
    Mitzvah, at the request of Sidney L. and Irene B. Fink, in
    the absence of a permanent rabbi in Beckley at that time).

In the earlier days, the congregation used to hold Bar Mitzvah
ceremonies at the Saturday morning services (in the 1930's and
early 1940's). Later, for economic reasons, and because many
of the members of the congregation had to be in their stores and
places of business on Saturday mornings, the time for the holding
of Bar Mitzvahs was changed over to the main weekly service of
the congregation, i. e., that on Friday night. The one exception
was the Bar Mitzvah of Alan J. Wein, which was held on a
Saturday morning which coincided with Christmas Day on
December 25, 1954.

> Jerome H. Saks (May, 1960)
> Robert M. Wein (June 18, 1960)

### CONFIRMATIONS IN BETH EL CONGREGATION

The congregation, since its beginnings in 1935–1936, has
always believed in, and practised, the rite of confirmation for
boys and girls on Shabuoth (The Feast of Weeks), in addition

to Bar Mitzvahs for boys. The age of confirmation is usually
set at 16 or 17, and the time is the Festival of Shabuoth, either
at the evening or the morning service of this holiday.

The first recorded confirmation in the congregation is that of
Howard A. Silverman and Bernice L. Arnstein, which was held
at the Temple on May 20, 1945, with Rabbi Jacob G. Soshuk
as the officiant. Subsequent confirmations held at the Temple
through the year 1955 were as follows:

Shirley R. Klein ⎫ all three were confirmed on Friday
Joan M. Silverman ⎬ night, June 3, 1949, by Student
Sonia Silverberg ⎭ Rabbi Richard G. Hirsch

Philip M. Binderman ⎫ all three were confirmed on Friday
Robert B. Harvit ⎬ night, May 27, 1955, with Rabbi
Sidney T. Shinedling ⎭ Abraham I. Shinedling as the
                          officiant

### Rabbis and Student Rabbis (Part-Time Rabbis) of Congregation Beth El

The earlier student rabbis, or part-time students who served
as rabbis of the congregation, and who came from the Hebrew
Union College, in Cincinnati, serving the congregation over the
years up to 1939, have been totally forgotten; there is no record
of their names, and not even the oldest Jewish inhabitants of the
city recall them. The first student rabbi, or rabbinical student,
from the Hebrew Union College of whom there is record was
Morton M. Applebaum, who served the congregation on a
biweekly basis from 1939 to 1940.

The complete list of the rabbis who served Congregation Beth
El from 1939 to 1959 is as follows:

(Short biographical sketches of these rabbis and student rabbis,
the latter now all ordained, follow the list.)

Morton M. Applebaum, student rabbi (1939–1940)
Maxwell Berger (1940–1942)
Harold L. Gelfman (1942–1943)

Jacob G. Soshuk (1944–1946)

Bertrand E. Pollans (1946–1947)

Joseph Zeitin (for the High Holy Day services of 1948)

Richard G. Hirsch, student rabbi (1948–1949)

Donald Harris, student rabbi (for the High Holy Day services of 1949)

Norman Kahan, student rabbi (1949–1950)

Abraham I. Shinedling (1950–1956)

Dr. Elias L. Epstein (a professor at the Hebrew Union College-Jewish Institute of Religion, in Cincinnati) (for the High Holy Day services of 1956)

Frank N. Sundheim, student rabbi (1956–1957)

Abraham A. Kertes (1957–1959)

Gerald H. Schuster, triweekly [every third week] student rabbi (1959–1960)

MORTON M. APPLEBAUM (1939–1940). Morton M. Applebaum, who served the congregation from 1939 to 1940, was the first bi-weekly student rabbi whom the congregation ever had, so far as the records show. Born in Toronto, Canada, on August 25, 1911, he was ordained by the Hebrew Union College, in Cincinnati, in June, 1940. In 1959, he was serving as the rabbi of Temple Israel, in Akron, Ohio.

MAXWELL BERGER (1940–1942). Originally a Conservative rabbi, Maxwell Berger came to Beckley from Shamokin, Pa., in September, 1940, as the first permanent, full-time rabbi of the congregation. He remained in Beckley for two years, and left the city in August, 1942, retiring from the active rabbinate. Some years thereafter he settled in Washington, Pa., where he engaged in business.

HAROLD L. GELFMAN (1942–1943). Harold L. Gelfman served as the full-time rabbi of the congregation from 1942 to 1943. He was born at Springfield, Mass., on November 11, 1910, and was ordained by the Hebrew Union College in June, 1938. Some years after leaving Beckley he served for two years (1950–1952) as the rabbi of Congregation Ahavath Sholom of Bluefield-Princeton. From 1952 to 1956 he was rabbi of Temple Beth Israel, of Jackson, Mich., and from

1956 to 1957 he served as the rabbi of the Cape Cod Synagogue, in Hyannis, Mass. In September, 1957, he was elected rabbi of Temple Beth El, in Macon, Ga.

JACOB G. SOSHUK (1944–1946). The congregation apparently had no rabbi from 1943 to 1944. Jacob G. Soshuk (born at New York City, on March 10, 1912) served as the rabbi of the congregation from 1944 to 1946. He was ordained by the Jewish Institute of Religion, in New York, in 1945. In 1946, he left Beckley to return to New York, and in 1957 he was still serving as a teacher of Hebrew at Erasmus Hall High School, in Brooklyn, N. Y.

BERTRAND E. POLLANS (1946–1947). Bertrand E. Pollans served the congregation as rabbi from 1946 to 1947. He was ordained by the Jewish Institute of Religion, in New York, in 1932. Shortly after leaving Beckley, due to illness, he returned to New York City, where he died in November, 1947.

JOSEPH ZEITIN. Again, from 1947 to 1948, the congregation had no rabbi. Rabbi Joseph Zeitin was in Beckley only for the High Holy Day services of the year 1948. In 1959, he was living in San Francisco, Calif., where he was engaged in literary work as well as in part-time congregational work. In 1948, Isadore R. Wein was serving as the chairman of the Religious Committee, and officiated at the religious services.

Rabbi Joseph Zeitin was born in Mainz (Mayence), Germany, in 1907, and emigrated to the United States from Shanghai, China, in July, 1947. From 1949 to 1953, following his brief interlude in Beckley, he served as rabbi of B'nai David Congregation, in San Francisco, and from 1953 to 1954 he was rabbi of B'nai Israel Congregation, in East Liverpool, Ohio. In 1957 to 1959, at San Francisco, he was doing research for a projected history of the Jewish community of Shanghai from 1850 to 1950, and on a study of the concept of citizenship in the German constitutions of the 19th and 20th centuries. Joseph Zeitin was ordained at the Far Eastern Rabbinical College, in Shanghai, and received the Ph.D. degree from the University of Cologne,

Germany. Deeply interested in the history of his native city of Mainz, he published a history of that city in 1935 (German), and wrote also a volume entitled *Die Entwicklung der Mainzer Presse.*

RICHARD G. HIRSCH (1948–1949). Richard G. Hirsch, who served the congregation as student rabbi, on a bi-weekly basis, from 1948 to 1949, was born at Cleveland, Ohio, on September 13, 1926. He attended Western Reserve University, in Cleveland, and received the B.A. degree from the University of Cincinnati (1947). He was ordained by the Hebrew Union College-Jewish Institute of Religion, in Cincinnati, in 1951, after two years spent in Israel, where he studied at Jerusalem from 1949 to 1950 under a scholarship granted to him by the Zionist Organization of America. Thereafter he served as a rabbi in Chicago, from September, 1951, to 1953, and as the assistant rabbi of Temple Emanuel, in Denver, Colo., from 1953 to March, 1956, and in April, 1956, he was appointed director of the Chicago Federation of the Union of American Hebrew Congregations. He also served as a Hillel Counsellor at the University of Denver during the period from September, 1953, to March, 1956. In 1954, he married Bella Rosencweig, of Tel-Aviv, Israel.

DONALD HARRIS. Donald Harris, then a student at the Hebrew Union College, conducted the religious services in Beckley during the High Holy Days of September, 1949. He did not complete his rabbinical course at the Hebrew Union College.

NORMAN KAHAN (1949–1950). Norman Kahan (originally, Kahanowitch) (born in Mozyr, Russia, on January 2, 1922) served as the biweekly student rabbi of the Beckley congregation from September, 1949, to June, 1950. He was ordained in 1952 by the Hebrew Union College-Jewish Institute of Religion, in Cincinnati, and from 1952 to 1956 he served as the rabbi of Temple Beth Israel, in Lima, Ohio. In September, 1956, he was elected rabbi of Beth Jacob Congregation, in Newburgh, N. Y. In 1957, he was appointed the Jewish chaplain at the United States

Military Academy, at West Point, N. Y. He still occupied both positions in 1959.

ABRAHAM I. SHINEDLING (1950–1956). Rabbi Abraham I. Shinedling came to Beth El Congregation, in Beckley, from Bluefield, W. Va., on September 1, 1950, and served as its rabbi until the end of July, 1956. In August, 1956, he settled in Albuquerque, N. Mex., retiring from the active rabbinate and devoting himself thereafter to literary work and to research in the fields of biography and American Jewish history, serving as a full-time member of the staff of the American Jewish Archives, which is an affiliate of the Hebrew Union College-Jewish Institute of Religion, in Cincinnati.

In September, 1956, he accepted the position of part-time bi-weekly "commuting rabbi" of the Los Alamos Jewish Center, in Los Alamos, N. Mex., serving in this position until the end of August, 1957, and then was compelled to give it up, because of the pressure of his other work, and for other reasons.

During his six years of rabbinical service with the Beckley congregation, he paid a large number of visits to colleges, universities, and Christian summer church camps in and near West Virginia (in West Virginia, Ohio, Tennessee, and Kentucky) in the interests of, and under the aegis of, the Jewish Chautauqua Society. His visit to Beckley (Junior) College, in May, 1956, was the first paid to that institution under the auspices of the Jewish Chautauqua Society. Another "first" was his visit, in August, 1955, to Camp Beckwith, near Fayetteville, W. Va., a Methodist summer camp, under the auspices of the Jewish Chautauqua Society. From September, 1951, to September, 1954, he served as the part-time Jewish chaplain of the Federal Reformatory for Women, in Alderson, W. Va., and from 1951 to 1956 as the part-time Jewish chaplain at the Veterans Administration Hospital, in Beckley, under the auspices of the National Jewish Welfare Board.

In 1955, Rabbi Abraham I. Shinedling and Manuel Pickus published, in cooperation, the *History of the Beckley*

*Jewish Community*, and in 1958, at Albuquerque, he published his *History of the Los Alamos Jewish Center*, dealing with the Jewish community in Los Alamos, New Mexico.

On June 6, 1959, at Cincinnati, Rabbi Abraham I. Shinedling was awarded the degree of Doctor of Divinity *honoris causa* by the Hebrew Union College-Jewish Institute of Religion "for his many contributions to America's religious, civic, and scholarly life," in the words of the citation read and published by Dr. Nelson Glueck, president of the H.U.C.-J.I.R., and a former fellow student of his at the College in Cincinnati from 1914 to 1920.

Further details of the biography of Abraham I. Shinedling may be found in the Beckley Jewish history, on pages 64 to 66.

ELIAS L. EPSTEIN (High Holy Days, 1956). Dr. Elias L. Epstein, Professor of Hebrew Language and Literature at the Hebrew Union College-Jewish Institute of Religion, in Cincinnati, conducted the High Holy Day services for the Beckley congregation in September, 1956, when the congregation did not have a permanent rabbi.

FRANK N. SUNDHEIM (1956–1957). Frank N. Sundheim, of Philadelphia, an upper-class student at the Hebrew Union College, served the Beckley congregation as its part-time, bi-weekly student rabbi from late September, 1956, to early June, 1957. He was ordained by the H.U.C.-J.I.R., in Cincinnati, on June 7, 1958, after receiving the M.H.L. degree there, and in the latter part of 1958 he entered the United States Army as a chaplain, stationed at Fort Sill, Okla., in which position he was still serving in July, 1959.

In early 1960, Frank N. Sundheim was elected rabbi of Ohev Sholom Congregation, in Huntington, to succeed Rabbi Theodore S. Levy. For his complete biography, *see under* Huntington.

ABRAHAM A. KERTES (1957–1959). Rabbi Abraham A. Kertes, previously rabbi of B'nai Jacob Congregation, in East Liverpool, Ohio, came to Beckley in September, 1957, to become the full-time, resident rabbi of Beth El Congregation. Rabbi Kertes, a native of Hungary, came to the

United States in 1947 (by way of the Dominican Republic,
to which country he was sent in 1947 to aid Jewish refugees
awaiting transportation to Israel), from Israel, where he
lived from 1934 to 1947, and served both as a rabbi and
also as an *Orech Din Rabbani* (rabbinical counsellor), li-
censed by the chief rabbinate of Jerusalem, as a special
expert in all matters pertaining to the problem of the
"Agunah." He has written articles on the difficult problem
of the "Agunah" and on other rabbinical legal subjects.
Rabbi Abraham A. Kertes has also a diploma as a lawyer.

Before coming to Beckley from East Liverpool, Ohio,
in September, 1957, Rabbi Kertes had served also as rabbi
in Portsmouth, N. H., in Rochester, N. Y., and in Aberdeen,
S. Dak. He left the Beckley congregation in July, 1959, to
become, for the second time, the rabbi of the congregation
in Aberdeen, S. Dak.

GERALD H. SCHUSTER. Gerald H. Schuster, of Milwaukee, Wis.,
a student at the H. U. C. - J. I. R., in Cincinnati, served
as the part-time (triweekly) student rabbi of Congregation
Beth El, in 1959–1960.

### THE BECKLEY SISTERHOOD (OF CONGREGATION BETH EL)

The Beckley Sisterhood was founded in 1925, under the
auspices and aegis of Mrs. Claudia (Leo) Wolf, of Wheeling,
who at that time was the president of the West Virginia Federation of Temple Sisterhoods. It had 17 charter members,
as follows:

Mrs. Dora S. (Harry) Abel (of Mount Hope)
Mrs. Dorothy B. (Nathan) Berman
Mrs. Gussie (Robert) Davis
Mrs. Annie W. (Louis J.) Fink
Mrs. Lillie (Hyman) Fisher (of Scarbro)
Mrs. Edna B. (Irving) Goldstein
Mrs. Anna (Jacob) Hart
Mrs. Mollie (Abe S.) Lovitz (of Mount Hope)
Mrs. Rose Y. (Nathan) Pickus
Mrs. Sana M. (Mendel) Pickus

Mrs. Sarah S. (Louis) Pickus
Mrs. Max Sager
Mrs. Gussie B. (Abe) Saks
Mrs. Anna P. (Jacob) Silverberg
Mrs. Dora (Aaron) Totz
Mrs. Marie (Samuel) Wasserkrug
Mrs. Dora F. (Morris H.) Wender (of Oak Hill)[1]

The Constitution of the Beckley Sisterhood states that it is the purpose of that organization "to bind [Jewish women] together for religious, philanthropic, civic, cultural, social, educational, and recreational purposes. It is to be an auxiliary of the Beth El Temple, of Beckley, W. Va."

The Beckley Sisterhood affiliated with the National Federation of Temple Sisterhoods on December 3, 1925, with 11 members [obviously, a decline from the number of its original charter members in the earlier part of that same year 1925]. Its president at that time was Mrs. Nathan (Rose Y.) Pickus, and its secretary was Mrs. Sallye Waitsman. It joined the W. V. F. T. S. presumably at the same time (in December, 1925), although in some of its official records this date is given as the year 1923 (presumably erroneous, for this was before the Beckley Sisterhood was organized).

The Beckley Sisterhood's original officers (1925–1926) (the name of its 1st vice president is not recorded) included:

PRESIDENT: Mrs. Dora (Aaron) Totz
TREASURER: Mrs. Gussie (Robert) Davis
SECRETARY: Mrs. Rose Y. (Nathan) Pickus

The Beckley Sisterhood disbanded in the fall of 1926, due to a serious loss of its membership, but it was reorganized in the fall of 1927, and has been in continual existence since then. Mrs. Leah (Joseph) Mendel served as its president from 1927 to 1928, and Mrs. Rose Y. Pickus served as its president during that year of reorganization. The reorganization of the Beckley

---

[1] Mrs. Sallye Waitsman also would appear to have been a charter member of the Beckley Sisterhood, in 1925, although her name is not found in the official records of the Sisterhood as such.

Sisterhood in 1927 was aided by Mrs. Joseph Bekenstein, of Charleston, who was prominent in the State Sisterhood work.

## PRESIDENTS OF THE BECKLEY SISTERHOOD (1934 TO 1957)

The names of the presidents of the Beckley Sisterhood in the years from 1928 to 1934 have been lost, together with most of the records of those six years. The following Beckley and vicinity Jewish women served as its presidents in the years from 1934 to 1957:

Mrs. Edna B. (Irving) Goldstein (1934–1935)
Mrs. Ida (Benjamin E.) Lewis (1935–1936)
Mrs. Bertha B. (Thomas) Sopher (1936–1937)
Mrs. Rose Y. (Nathan) Pickus (1937–1938)
Mrs. Rose (Abe S.) Lovitz (1938–1940)
Mrs. Anne K. (M. Edward) Harvit (1940–1941 and 1943–1944)
Mrs. Faye R. (Bernard E.) Silverman (1941–1942, 1944–1945, and 1948–1949)
Mrs. Violet G. (Charles H.) Levine (1942–1943)
Mrs. Beatrice C. (William) Binderman (1945–1946 and 1955–1956)
Mrs. Minnie G. (Herman) Samans (1946–1947 and 1949–1950)
Mrs. Ruth L. (A. David) Abrams (1947–1948)
Mrs. Dorothy (Archie) Ellenbogen (1950–1951; re-elected president in May, 1957, for the term 1957–1958)
Dr. H. Viola Shlickerman (1951–1952)
Mrs. Irene B. (Sidney) Fink (1952–1954)
Mrs. Zena Y. (Samuel) Hochman (1956–1957)

In 1959–1960, Mrs. Joseph R. (Sylvia S.) Miller served as the president of the Beckley Sisterhood.

In 1961–1962, Mrs. Shirley M. (Arthur) Goldstein served as the president of the Beckley Sisterhood.

## VICE PRESIDENTS OF THE BECKLEY SISTERHOOD

The Beckley Sisterhood vice presidents, over the years from 1934 to the present, have included:

PLATE XI

Temple Israel, Charleston, W. Va. (B'nai Israel Congregation), Dedicated in September, 1960

(see pages 629 and 630)

PLATE XII

Mrs. Mary Frances (Herbert E.) Cohen
Mrs. Anne K. Harvit
Mrs. Violet G. Levine
Mrs. Sylvia S. (Joseph R.) Miller
Mrs. Gussie B. (Abe) Saks
Mrs. Ruth W. (Bernard L.) Saks
Dr. H. Viola Shlickerman
Mrs. Bertha B. Sopher

### SISTERHOOD TREASURERS

Treasurers of the Beckley Sisterhood in the past two decades and more have included the following:

Mrs. Beatrice C. Binderman
Mrs. Manya S. (Jack, Sr.) Binderman
Mrs. Herbert E. Cohen
Mrs. Anne K. Harvit
Mrs. Zena Y. Hochman
Mrs. Sylvia (Benjamin) Myers
Mrs. Gussie B. Saks
Mrs. Sarah P. (Louis) Wolman

### BECKLEY SISTERHOOD SECRETARIES

The secretaries of the Beckley Sisterhood have included:

Mrs. Beatrice C. Binderman
Mrs. Herbert E. Cohen
Mrs. Dorothy Ellenbogen
Mrs. Reba (David) Freed
Mrs. Dorothy B. (Saul) Fortunoff
Mrs. May (Joseph) Keiserman
Mrs. Violet G. Levine
Mrs. Mildred (Samuel) Milstein
Mrs. Morris Morganstern [Morganstern, originally; later, Morgan)
Mrs. Naomi A. (James) Pickus

Mrs. Ruth W. Saks
Mrs. Minnie G. Samans
Mrs. Ruth B. (Edward) Saymen
Mrs. Faye R. Silverman

### STATE SISTERHOOD CONVENTIONS IN BECKLEY

State Sisterhood conventions were held in Beckley on October 10 to 13, 1942 (the 20th), and on October 11 to 12, 1953 (the 28th). The 20th annual State Convention was presided over by Mrs. William (Martha) Caplan, of Clarksburg, its president. Dr. Emanuel Gamoran, director of education of the U. A. H. C., conducted a Religious Teachers' Institute at the Convention, and Mrs. Hugo Hartman, then the national president of the N. F. T. S., was the main speaker, her subject being, "Rediscovering America."

The 1953 annual State Convention (the 28th) was the Beckley-Welch Convention, and its co-chairmen were Mrs. Faye R. Silverman and Mrs. Minnie G. Samans, for Beckley; and Mrs. Anna H. Katzen and Mrs. E. Newman for Welch. Its sessions were presided over by the State President, Mrs. Belle (Edward S.) Fields, of Morgantown. The main sermon of the Convention was delivered by Rabbi Jakob J. Petuchowski, then the part-time rabbi of the Welch Congregation Emanuel, but later appointed Assistant and then Associate Professor of Rabbinic Literature at the H. U. C. - J. I. R., in Cincinnati. Mrs. Abram Vossen Goodman, of Long Island, New York, a member of the Executive Board of the N. F. T. S., was the main Sisterhood speaker, and installed the new officers of the State Sisterhood. Rabbi Morris M. Rose, of Morgantown, was the main speaker at the banquet session.

### PERMANENT ACTIVITIES OF THE BECKLEY SISTERHOOD

The annual, constant activities, as well as the special and occasional projects, of the Beckley Sisterhood include the following:

Support of the Religious School of Beth El Congregation
Financial aid to Congregation Beth El
Community Canteen service (in World War II)
Local charities, hospitals, and other organizations (aid and service)
Raleigh County Cancer Society
Raleigh County Blood Bank
House of Living Judaism, in New York (an N. F. T. S. project)
V. A. V. S. (Veterans Administration [Hospital] Volunteer Service Committee of the Beckley V. A. Hospital)
Women's Committee of the National Jewish Welfare Board
Temple Youth Group
Pinecrest Sanitarium, in Beckley (a State tuberculosis sanitarium)

The Beckley Sisterhood, in 1955–1956, together with some of the other local church groups, took part in the collection of money for UNICEF (the United Nations International Children's Emergency Fund), for the first time in Beckley. It helped with the Tuberculosis Association Christmas seal drive, donated Bibles to the new United Mine Workers' Hospital, near Beckley, and aided the Pinecrest Sanitarium and the V. A. V. S. work.

## OFFICERS OF THE BECKLEY SISTERHOOD IN 1956–1957

The Beckley Sisterhood officers for the year 1956 to 1957, elected in May, 1956, and installed in that same month by Rabbi Abraham I. Shinedling, were the following:

PRESIDENT: Mrs. Zena Y. (Samuel) Hochman
1ST VICE PRESIDENT: Dr. H. Viola Shlickerman
2ND VICE PRESIDENT: Mrs. Anne K. (M. Edward) Harvit
TREASURER: Mrs. Sarah P. (Louis) Wolman
RECORDING SECRETARY: Mrs. Shirley M. (Arthur) Goldstein
CORRESPONDING SECRETARY: Mrs. Sylvia S. (Joseph R.) Miller
FINANCIAL SECRETARY: Mrs. Beatrice C. (William) Binderman

In May, 1957, Mrs. Dorothy (Archie) Ellenbogen was elected its president, to serve for the year 1957–1958.

BECKLEY SISTERHOOD OFFICERS FOR 1957–1958

PRESIDENT: Mrs. Archie (Dorothy) Ellenbogen
1ST VICE PRESIDENT: Mrs. Sidney (Irene B.) Fink
2ND VICE PRESIDENT: Mrs. Eric (Millie G.) Rosenbaum
TREASURER: Mrs. Louis (Sarah P.) Wolman)
RECORDING SECRETARY: Mrs. Arthur (Shirley M.) Goldstein
CORRESPONDING SECRETARY: Mrs. Joseph R. (Sylvia S.) Miller
FINANCIAL SECRETARY: Mrs. William (Beatrice C.) Binderman

In 1957–1959, Mrs. Samuel (Zena Y.) Hochman served also as the chairman of the Cradle Roll Committee of the State Sisterhood. During the same two-year period (1957–1959) Mrs. William (Beatrice C.) Binderman served also as chairman of the Emergency Services Committee of the State Sisterhood.

MEMBERSHIP ROSTER OF THE BECKLEY
SISTERHOOD IN 1945 TO 1946

(72 members)

The 1945–1946 *First Annual Yearbook* of the Beckley Sisterhood lists the following members and former members of the organization:

(The former members, as of 1945–1946, have an asterisk * before their names.)

> Mrs. Harry (Dora S.) Abel (of Mount Hope)
> Mrs. Samuel I. (Esther B.) Abrams
> *Mrs. Berta Adams
> Mrs. David (Minerva [Minnie]) Arnstein
> Mrs. J. Leonard (Rose R.) Baer
> Mrs. Nathan (Dorothy B.) Berman
> *Mrs. Isadore Binderman
> Mrs. Jack (Manya S.) Binderman
> Mrs. William (Beatrice C.) Binderman
> *Mrs. Jacob Bloom

Mrs. Hugo (Meta A.) Bornheim (of Oak Hill)
*Mrs. Ida Burk
Mrs. Alfred [E.] (Betty) Cohen
Mrs. Herbert [E.] (Mary Frances) Cohen
*Mrs. Louis Colton
Mrs. Sydney Danbury
*Mrs. Robert Davis
*Mrs. Robert Dubin
Mrs. Archie (Dorothy) Ellenbogen
*Mrs. Israel (Sophie W.) Fink
*Mrs. Hyman (Lillie) Fisher
*Mrs. Aaron (Edna F.) Friedman
*Mrs. Sydney Friedman
*Mrs. David (Reba) Freed
Mrs. Marc L. (Dora C.) Front
Mrs. Irving (Edna B.) Goldstein
*Mrs. Charles Greenfield
Mrs. I. J. [Jerry] Greenfield
Mrs. M. Edward (Anne K.) Harvit
Mrs. Joseph B. (Sadie P.) Heller
*Mrs. Sylvia (Jack) Heyman
Mrs. Morris (Tillie M.) Hochman
*Mrs. Adele Holz
*Mrs. Helmut Holz
Mrs. Joseph (May) Keiserman
Mrs. William (Ida M.) Klein
Mrs. Sydney (Esther) Labovitz
Mrs. Charles (Violet G.) Levine
Mrs. Benjamin E. (Ida) Lewis
*Mrs. Abe Lovitz (of Mount Hope)
Mrs. Alfred Lovitz (of Mount Hope)
Mrs. Nathan (Rose C.) Matz
Mrs. Max Meltcher
*Mrs. Leah Mendel
*Mrs. Maurice Mendel
Mrs. Henry Miller
Mrs. Jacob [Dora] Miller
Mrs. Morris Morgan (of Whitesville)

*Mrs. Ben Myers
Mrs. James (Naomi A.) Pickus
Mrs. Louis (Sarah S.) Pickus
Mrs. Nathan (Rose Y.) Pickus
Mrs. Isadore (Sarah A.) Rich (Reichenthal)
Mrs. Eric (Millie G.) Rosenbaum
Mrs. Theodore (Martha) Rosenbaum
*Mrs. Selma Rubenstein
Mrs. Abe (Gussie B.) Saks
Mrs. Herman (Minnie G.) Samans
Mrs. Edward (Ruth B.) Saymen
Dr. H. Viola Shlickerman
Mrs. Jacob (Anna P.) Silverberg
Mrs. Bernard E. (Faye R.) Silverman
Mrs. Arthur Stern
Mrs. Thomas (Bertha B.) Sopher
Mrs. Charles (Gussie M.) Stromberg
Mrs. Harry (Shirley F.) Stromberg
*Mrs. Aaron (Dora) Totz
*Mrs. Harry (Celia) Wasserkrug [of Oak Hill]
*Mrs. Samuel (Marie) Wasserkrug
Mrs. Isadore R. (Jeanette A.) Wein
Mrs. Max H. (Frieda L.) Wender
*Mrs. Nathan Wolfe

## MEMBERSHIP ROSTER OF THE BECKLEY
## SISTERHOOD IN 1955

(47 members)

Mrs. Dora S. (Harry) Abel (of Mount Hope)
Mrs. Esther B. (Samuel I.) Abrams
Mrs. Ruth L. (A. David) Abrams
Mrs. Rose R. (J. Leonard) Baer
Mrs. Dorothy B. (Nathan) Berman
Mrs. Beatrice C. (William) Binderman
Mrs. Manya S. (Jack, Sr.) Binderman
Mrs. Meta A. (Hugo) Bornheim (of Oak Hill)
Mrs. Dorothy (Archie) Ellenbogen

Mrs. Irene B. (Sidney) Fink
Mrs. Minnie (Louis J.) Fink
Mrs. Dorothy B. (Saul) Fortunoff
Mrs. Nora B. Franks
Mrs. Dora C. (Marc L.) Front
Mrs. Edna B. (Irving) Goldstein
Mrs. Shirley M. (Arthur) Goldstein
Mrs. Anne K. (M. Edward) Harvit
Mrs. Tillie M. (Morris) Hochman
Mrs. Zena Y. (Samuel) Hochman
Mrs. Ida M. (William) Klein
Mrs. Janet B. (Robert H.) Levine
Mrs. Violet G. (Charles H.) Levine
Mrs. Harriet L. (Benjamin) Lewis (of Mount Hope)
Mrs. Ida (Benjamin E.) Lewis
Mrs. Rose C. (Nathan) Matz
Mrs. Sylvia S. (Joseph R.) Miller
Mrs. Naomi A. (James) Pickus
Mrs. Rose Y. (Nathan) Pickus
Mrs. Martha B. (Theodore) Rosenbaum
Mrs. Millie G. (Eric) Rosenbaum
Mrs. Zeena B. (Harold) Rudin
Mrs. Gussie B. (Abe) Saks
Mrs. Ruth W. (Bernard L.) Saks
Mrs. Minnie G. (Herman) Samans
Mrs. Ruth B. (Edward) Saymen
Mrs. Hannah H. (Maurice) Selden
Mrs. Helen L. (Abraham I.) Shinedling
Dr. H. Viola Shlickerman
Mrs. Anna P. (Jacob) Silverberg
Mrs. Faye R. (Bernard E.) Silverman
Mrs. Maxine B. (Harold A.) Sopher
Mrs. Gussie M. (Charles) Stromberg
Mrs. Shirley F. (Harry) Stromberg
Mrs. Jeanette A. (Isadore R.) Wein
Mrs. Freda [Frieda] L. (Max H.) Wender
Mrs. Dolores (Morris S., Jr.) Wender (of Oak Hill)
Mrs. Sarah P. (Louis) Wolman

Not all the Jewish women residing in Beckley in 1955 were members of the Sisterhood in that year. Some, disaffected, had dropped their previous memberships. Others, for various reasons, failed or refused to join. In September, 1955, some 10 Jewish women residents of Beckley were nonmembers of the Beckley Sisterhood. There were losses, also, in the period from 1952 to 1958, through deaths in the community and through removals from the city.

In 1959, at the regular annual May election, Mrs. Sylvia S. (Joseph R.) Miller was elected president of the Beckley Sisterhood, to serve for the year 1959–1960. At this time, the Sisterhood was reorganized and its activities were curtailed, as the result of a loss in membership during the preceding period.

## THE BECKLEY CHAPTER OF HADASSAH

The Beckley Chapter of Hadassah (the Women's Zionist Organization of America) was organized on April 13, 1948, by a group of 15 Jewish women of the community, with Mrs. Ezra Shapiro, of Cleveland, as the guest speaker at the organizational meeting. In May, 1948, the charter of the Beckley Chapter was presented to the first president, Mrs. Violet G. (Charles H.) Levine, by Mrs. Jacob B. Hurwitz, of Cleveland, the vice president of the Central States Region of Hadassah, of which the Beckley Chapter of Hadassah is [was] a member and an affiliate.

The first officers of the Beckley Hadassah, for the year 1948–1949, were as follows:

PRESIDENT: Mrs. Violet G. (Charles H.) Levine
1ST VICE PRESIDENT: Mrs. Beatrice C. (William) Binderman
2ND VICE PRESIDENT: Mrs. Shirley F. (Harry) Stromberg
TREASURER: Mrs. Anne K. (M. Edward) Harvit
RECORDING SECRETARY: Mrs. Minnie G. (Herman) Samans
FINANCIAL SECRETARY: Mrs. Estelle (Sidney) Stromberg
CORRESPONDING SECRETARY: Mrs. Janet B. (Robert H.) Levine

### CHARTER MEMBERS OF THE BECKLEY HADASSAH
### (APRIL, 1948)

The 35 charter members of the Beckley Chapter of Hadassah, in April, 1948, were:

Mrs. Dora S. Abel (of Mount Hope)
Mrs. Ruth L. Abrams
Mrs. Samuel I. Abrams
Mrs. David Arnstein
Mrs. Manya S. Binderman
Mrs. William Binderman
Mrs. Alfred E. Cohen
Mrs. Herbert E. Cohen
Mrs. Dorothy Ellenbogen
Mrs. Israel Fink
Mrs. Minnie Fink
Mrs. Sidney Fink
Mrs. Anne K. Harvit
Mrs. Samuel Hochman
Mrs. Edwin Kamen
Mrs. William Klein
Mrs. Charles H. Levine

Mrs. Robert H. Levine
Mrs. Samuel M. Milstein
Mrs. Rose Y. Pickus
Mrs. Naomi A. Pickus
Mrs. Isadore Rich
Mrs. Marilyn Rose
Mrs. Bernard L. Saks
Mrs. Herman Samans
Mrs. Edward Saymen
Mrs. Jacob Silverberg
Mrs. Bertha B. Sopher
Mrs. Maxine B. Sopher
Mrs. Charles Stromberg
Mrs. Harry Stromberg
Mrs. Sidney Stromberg
Mrs. Isadore R. Wein
Mrs. J. H. Wolfe

### PAST PRESIDENTS OF THE BECKLEY CHAPTER OF HADASSAH

Mrs. Violet G. Levine (1948–1951 and 1953–1955)
Mrs. Zena Y. Hochman (1951–1953)
Mrs. Hannah H. Selden (1955–1956)

### OFFICERS OF THE BECKLEY HADASSAH FOR 1954–1956

PRESIDENT: Mrs. Violet G. Levine and Mrs. Hannah H. Selden
1ST VICE PRESIDENT: Mrs. Zena Y. Hochman
2ND VICE PRESIDENT: Mrs. Hannah H. Selden
TREASURER: Mrs. Ruth B. Saymen

RECORDING SECRETARY: Mrs. Beatrice C. Binderman
FINANCIAL SECRETARY: Mrs. Ida M. Klein
CORRESPONDING SECRETARY: Mrs. Dorothy B. Fortunoff

### OFFICERS IN 1957–1958

PRESIDENT: Mrs. Hannah H. (Maurice) Selden
VICE PRESIDENT: Mrs. Samuel (Zena Y.) Hochman
TREASURER: Mrs. Edward (Ruth B.) Saymen
SECRETARY: Mrs. Benjamin (Eva) Kishony

### MEMBERSHIP OF THE BECKLEY CHAPTER OF HADASSAH IN 1948–1949

(62 members)

The peak membership of the Beckley Chapter of Hadassah was 62 women in 1948–1949, the year following its organization. In the period from 1952 to 1955, its membership suffered a severe decline, to only 24 women, due in part to loss of membership through removals from the city, and partly due also to the deaths of husbands of members, and also, in part, as the result of the adverse economic situation in the coal fields of Raleigh County, which still prevailed in the period from 1957 to 1959.

The peak membership of 62 in 1948–1949 consisted of the following Jewish women:

*Mrs. Harry (Dora S.) Abel (of Mount Hope)
Mrs. A. David (Ruth L.) Abrams
Mrs. Samuel I. (Esther B.) Abrams
*Mrs. Mervin Ameles
Mrs. J. Leonard (Rose R.) Baer
Mrs. Dorothy B. (Nathan) Berman
Mrs. Jack, Sr. (Manya S.) Binderman
Mrs. William (Beatrice C.) Binderman

---

Those names marked with an asterisk * were members who were no longer living in Beckley or in the Beckley region in 1956–1957. Two women who were members in 1948–1949 were deceased by 1957. Jewish women who left Beckley in the period from 1956 to 1959 are indicated in parentheses following the name.

Mrs. Hugo (Meta A.) Bornheim (of Oak Hill)
Mrs. Alfred E. (Betty) Cohen
*Mrs. Herbert E. (Mary Frances) Cohen
*Mrs. Theodore S. Decker
Mrs. Archie (Dorothy) Ellenbogen
*Mrs. Mayme (George) Favish
*Mrs. Israel (Sophie W.) Fink
Mrs. Louis J. (Minnie M.) Fink
Mrs. Sidney (Irene B.) Fink
Mrs. Marc L. (Dora C.) Front
*Mrs. Abraham (Helen S.) Goldstein
Mrs. Irving (Edna B.) Goldstein
Mrs. M. Edward (Anne K.) Harvit
*Mrs. Joseph B. (Sadie P.) Heller
Mrs. Morris (Tillie M.) Hochman
Mrs. Samuel (Zena Y.) Hochman
*Mrs. Edwin (Blossom) Kamen (deceased)
*Mrs. Jerry Kamen
*Mrs. Edward M. (Mary [Patricia]) Kandell
*Mrs. Daniel Keiserman
*Mrs. Joseph (May) Keiserman
Mrs. William (Ida M.) Klein
Mrs. Charles H. (Violet G.) Levine
*Mrs. Robert H. (Janet B.) Levine
Mrs. Benjamin (Harriet L.) Lewis (of Mount Hope)
Mrs. Benjamin E. (Ida) Lewis
Mrs. Alfred Lovitz, Sr. (of Mount Hope)
Mrs. Nathan (Rose C.) Matz
*Mrs. Max Meltcher
*Mrs. Samuel M. Milstein
Mrs. James (Naomi A.) Pickus
Mrs. Louis (Sarah S.) Pickus (deceased)
Mrs. Nathan (Rose Y.) Pickus
Mrs. Eric (Millie G.) Rosenbaum
Mrs. Theodore (Martha A.) Rosenbaum
Mrs. Abe (Gussie B.) Saks
*Mrs. Bernard L. (Ruth W.) Saks
    (Returned to Beckley in 1959)

Mrs. Herman (Minnie G.) Samans
Mrs. Edward (Ruth B.) Saymen
*Mrs. Albert (Marion M.) Schwartz
*Mrs. Abraham I. (Helen L.) Shinedling
　　　(She was a member of the Beckley Hadassah from
　　　　　September, 1950, to July, 1956)
Dr. H. Viola Shlickerman
　　　(Removed from Beckley in March, 1959)
Mrs. Jacob (Anna P.) Silverberg
Mrs. Bernard E. (Faye R.) Silverman
Mrs. Harold A. (Maxine B.) Sopher
　　　(Removed to Columbus, Ohio, in 1959)
*Mrs. Thomas (Bertha B.) Sopher
Mrs. Charles (Gussie M.) Stromberg
*Mrs. Harry (Shirley F.) Stromberg
*Mrs. Sidney (Estelle) Stromberg
*Mrs. Harry (Celia) Wasserkrug (of Oak Hill)
Mrs. Isadore R. (Jeanette A.) Wein
*Mrs. Morri R. (Sylvia F.) Wein
Mrs. Ben H. (Sadie) Wender
Mrs. Max H. (Frieda L.) Wender

## THE 24 MEMBERS OF THE BECKLEY CHAPTER
## OF HADASSAH IN 1954–1955

Mrs. Dora S. Abel (of Mount
　　Hope)
Mrs. Esther B. Abrams
Mrs. Ruth L. Abrams
Mrs. Beatrice C. Binderman
Mrs. Manya S. Binderman
Mrs. Minnie (Louis J.) Fink
Mrs. Dorothy B. Fortunoff
Mrs. Tillie M. Hochman
Mrs. Zena Y. Hochman
Mrs. Eva (Benjamin)
　　Kishony
Mrs. Ida M. Klein

Mrs. Violet G. Levine
Mrs. Janet B. Levine
Mrs. Rose C. Matz
Mrs. Sylvia S. Miller
Mrs. Naomi A. Pickus
Mrs. Rose Y. Pickus
Mrs. Ruth B. Saymen
Mrs. Hannah H. Selden
Mrs. Helen L. Shinedling
Dr. H. Viola Shlickerman
Mrs. Anna P. Silverberg
Mrs. Gussie M. Stromberg
Mrs. Jeanette A. Wein

## The Work of the Beckley Hadassah

During the years from 1948 through 1955, the Beckley Chapter of Hadassah raised and contributed an average of $600 per annum for the following projects and work of Hadassah on behalf of the State of Israel:

Youth Aliyah ($300)
Hadassah-Rothschild-Hebrew University Hospital ($225)
Hadassah Medical Organization (HMO) ($450)
Youth activities ($25)
Vocational education in Israel, and other projects there ($100)
Jewish National Fund

The peak contribution was in 1952–1953, when the Beckley Hadassah donated a total of $1,100 for Hadassah projects and work in the new State of Israel. In 1955, its contribution for National Hadassah work and projects was $500. Hadassah in Beckley supported also the Trees for Israel Fund, the Jewish National Fund (Keren Kayemeth Leyisrael), and the Hadassah-Rothschild-Hebrew University hospital building project in Jerusalem.

In 1959, as the result of removals from the city and other serious loss in membership, the Beckley Chapter of Hadassah disbanded, and its membership became affiliated with the Bluefield Chapter.

## The Temple Beth El Youth Group

The first Temple Beth El Youth Group was formed in 1946–1947, by a group of young teen-age people of the congregation, which included the following:

| | |
|---|---|
| Milford Berman | Shirley R. Klein |
| Peter E. Ellenbogen | Manuel Pickus |
| Jack Front | Sonia Silverberg |
| Harold E. Harvit | Joan M. Silverman |

Its purposes were partly religious, partly cultural, and partly social. Most active in its organization and in its work, and its president from 1946–1947 until 1951, when it was disbanded, was Harold E. Harvit, the elder son of M. Edward and Anne K. Harvit. When most of its members had graduated from Woodrow Wilson High School, in Beckley — by June, 1951 — and had gone off to universities, away from Beckley, this first Temple Youth Group went out of existence. It was affiliated with the National Federation of Temple Youth, and was associated in most of its endeavors and projects with the nearby and equally small Bluefield Temple Youth Group, holding many of its dinner and other meetings and various projects together in both cities, alternately.

The second Temple Youth Group of Congregation Beth El was formed in September, 1951, by Harmon Cohen, of Bluefield, then president of the Bluefield Temple Youth Group as well as president of the Tri-State Subregion of the Ohio Valley Federation of Temple Youth (OVTY). It is affiliated with the OVTY as well as with the National Federation of Temple Youth, whose headquarters are in New York.

Charter members of the Second Beckley Temple Youth group, and members of it until 1956, were:

| | |
|---|---|
| Philip M. Binderman | Beverly Samans |
| Robert B. Harvit | Sidney T. Shinedling |
| Manuel Pickus | |

Later members who joined in the period from 1952 to 1956 were:

| | |
|---|---|
| Robert S. Klein | Valerie Binderman |
| Paul D. Lewis (of Mount Hope) | Rita Harvit |
| Sandra Schwartz | Dennis G. Saymen |
| Michele E. Wender | Alan J. Wein |

Robert B. Harvit, like his elder brother, Harold E. Harvit, before him, was greatly interested in the work and projects of the Second Temple Beth El Youth Group. He served as its president from 1951 to 1954. He was succeeded in this post by Philip M. Binderman (1954–1955), and the latter was followed in this office by Robert S. Klein (1955–1956). Robert B. Harvit served also, from April, 1954, to April, 1955, as president of

the Tri-State Subregion of the OVTY, and as a vice president
of the OVTY, remaining active in all three organizations until
he went away to college in September, 1955. Sidney T.
Shinedling was a member from 1952 to 1956, when he left the
city and went off to college.

### Temple Youth Group Officers Elected in May, 1956

The following officers of the second Beth El Temple Youth
Group (which, incidentally, did not form an affiliation with the
second Bluefield Temple Youth Group at any time) were elected
in May, 1956, and were installed in their offices on May 27,
1956, at a dinner meeting attended also by all the parents of
the members:

> President: Philip M. Binderman
> Vice President: Robert S. Klein
> Recording Secretary: Rita Harvit
> Corresponding Secretary: Dennis G. Saymen
> Treasurer: Robert S. Klein
> Publicity Chairman: Valerie Binderman
> Adult Adviser: Mrs. Ida M. Klein

### Members in 1956–1957

| | |
|---|---|
| Ruth Ann Arnstein | Robert S. Klein |
| Valerie Binderman | Paul D. Lewis (of Mount Hope) |
| Philip M. Binderman | Dennis G. Saymen |
| Rita Harvit | Alan J. Wein |
| Robert B. Harvit | Jack Wolman |

In 1956–1957, Mrs. Ida M. (William) Klein served as advisor
to the Temple Youth Group. Three of its members that year
taught in the Religious School, and one of them, Dennis G.
Saymen, a student of piano and organ, played the organ at the
religious services in the Temple on Friday nights, after the
departure from the city of the organist who served from 1950
to 1956 (Mrs. Helen L. Shinedling). For several years, from
1951 on, the second Temple Youth Group conducted an annual

religious service, replete with a sermon presented by one of its members, on one Friday night a year, in the Temple, and thus earned "Mitzvoth" from the N. F. T. Y. Robert S. Klein served as the president of the group from 1957 to 1958. Dennis G. Saymen was president of the Beth El Temple Youth Group in 1959–1960. Previous adult advisers of both Temple Youth Groups included: Morri R. Wein, Manuel Pickus, Mrs. William Binderman, and Edward Saymen.

In 1959–1960, the officers and members of the Beth El Temple Youth Group were as follows:

PRESIDENT: Dennis G. Saymen
VICE PRESIDENT and TREASURER: Ruth Ann Arnstein
SECRETARY: Jeri Lynn Saymen
LIBRARIANS: Paul H. Arnstein
             Jerome H. Saks
CALLING COMMITTEE: Martin Kistin

Other Members:

| | |
|---|---|
| Kenneth M. Fink | Robert M. Wein |
| Franklin Rosenbaum | Jack Wolman |
| Thomas Rosenbaum | |

In September, 1960, Dennis G. Saymen, long active in the Temple Youth Group, left Beckley for Cincinnati, to enroll in the McMicken College of Arts and Sciences of the University of Cincinnati as a pre-medical student.

In 1962, Rita Harvit (born at Beckley, on January 28, 1942) was a student at Ohio University, in Athens, Ohio, where she was preparing to become a teacher of speech in high school. She had previously studied for two years at West Virginia University, in Morgantown.


THE JUNIOR CONGREGATION OF TEMPLE BETH EL

A distinctive feature and phenomenon of Congregation Beth El was its active Junior Congregation, established in September, 1950, by Charles H. Levine, then president of the Congregation, and by Rabbi Abraham I. Shinedling, and still in existence at the end of the religious year 1955–1956. The members of the Junior Congregation, recruited on a voluntary basis from among the pupils of the Religious School who are eight years of age and older, adopted their own Constitution and By-Laws in November, 1950, and the Junior Congregation has the following as its main purposes:

(*a*)   the collection and distribution of contributions for charitable causes: local, national, and Jewish

(*b*)   the conducting of religious services and programs in the weekly Sunday morning assembly of the Religious School

(*c*)   assisting in the Saturday morning Sabbath services, through the reading of parts of the religious service and the reading of the translation of the Torah and Haftarah portions

(*d*)   the creation and maintenance of a Religious School Library (including a full membership in the Jewish Publication Society of America), from contributions by children and adults

(*e*)   assisting in the celebration of the Jewish holidays of Purim, Chanukah, Pesach, and Sukkoth, as well as in the holding of the annual Religious School picnic at the close of each Religious School year

The members of the Junior Congregation, in the years from 1950 to 1956, through their regular attendance and participation in the Sabbath morning religious service in the Temple, actually made such regular services (lacking in many other Reform congregations) possible and successful.

The presidents of the Junior Congregation have included Dennis G. Saymen (1954–1955) and Rita Harvit (1955–1956), and other members of the group also served as presidents for the limited time of three to six months laid down by the constitution.

Adult advisers have included: A. David Abrams, Rabbi Abraham I. Shinedling, and Mrs. Maxine B. Sopher.

In 1954–1955 the membership of the Junior Congregation consisted of the following 16 pupils of the Religious School:

David Abrams

Paul Henry Arnstein

Ruth Ann Arnstein

Valerie Binderman

Kenneth M. Fink

Rita Harvit

Franklin Rosenbaum

Thomas Rosenbaum

Jerome H. Saks

Dennis G. Saymen

Jeri Lynn Saymen

Sidney T. Shinedling

Esther Lee Stromberg

Alan J. Wein

Robert M. Wein

Lynda D. Wender

[Many of the parents of the children, and many of the members of the congregation, realized that the "*Junior* Congregation" of today will be the *senior* congregation of tomorrow, and supported its efforts wholeheartedly; some of the parents of the eligible children, however, were woefully negligent and indifferent, in the years 1950 to 1956, in their appreciation and support of the unique "Junior Congregation" of Temple Beth El.]

In the course of the years, as pupils of the Religious School became old enough to join the Temple Youth Group, some of them dropped their membership in the Junior Congregation; however, others retained membership in both these valuable young Jewish organizations.

The Junior Congregation of Temple Beth El has, since September, 1950, been a Library Member of the Jewish Publication Society of America, Philadelphia, purchasing each year all the new books (generally ten in number) published by the Society.

At the end of September, 1955, the following 15 children of the Religious School of Temple Beth El were members of the Junior Congregation, which is an autonomous, self-electing, and independent organization of the Religious School and of the congregation, and which holds its weekly meetings, for about half an hour each week, on Sundays after the end of the regular sessions of the Religious School:

David Abrams

Paul Henry Arnstein

Ruth Ann Arnstein

Valerie Binderman

Alan Hochman

Rita Harvit

Marjorie Roodin

Paul Roodin

Franklin Rosenbaum          Jeri Lynn Saymen
Thomas Rosenbaum           Robert M. Wein
Vicki Rudin                Lynda D. Wender
Dennis G. Saymen

BECKLEY LODGE, NO. 1360, OF THE B'NAI B'RITH

Beckley Lodge, No. 1360, of the B'nai B'rith (the only Jewish fraternal order ever organized in Beckley), was chartered on April 3, 1939, by District Grand Lodge, No. 3, with its head-quarters in Philadelphia. The original charter of the Lodge, which hangs in the Vestry Rooms of Temple Beth El, was signed by Charles H. Roemer, of Paterson, N. J., who in 1939 was president of District Grand Lodge, No. 3; and by the late Henry Monsky, of Omaha, Neb., who was then serving as president of the Supreme Grand Lodge of the B'nai B'rith (I.O.B.B.). The Beckley Lodge underwent a reorganization in March and April, 1941, and has remained in active and continuous existence since that time.

The reorganization of the year 1941 was aided by Lawrence C. Kaufman and Marcus Smith, who were at that time officers of the Charleston (West Virginia) Lodge, No. 788. The Beckley Lodge is affiliated with the West Virginia Council of the B'nai B'rith, and also with District Grand Lodge, No. 3, in the affairs of which two groups it has taken an active part since the early 1940's.

At the Fall State Council meeting held in Fairmont in November, 1955, A. David Abrams, of Beckley, was elected 1st vice president of the State Council. In May, 1957, he was elected president of the State Council for the year 1957 to 1958. Previously, Robert H. Levine, then of Beckley, had served as the president of the State Council (1953–1954), and in May, 1954, he was elected Committeeman-at-Large for West Virginia of D. G. L., No. 3. Malcolm Pickus, also then a resident of Beckley, had previously served as secretary of the State Council during the administration of Robert H. Levine (1953–1954).

The following paragraph, taken from the new *Constitution and By-Laws of Beckley Lodge, Number 1360, B'nai B'rith*, adopted in April-May, 1953, states the aims and purposes of the Lodge, as follows:

"The B'nai B'rith has taken upon itself the mission of uniting Jews in the work of promoting their highest interests and those of humanity; of developing and elevating the mental and moral character of the people of our faith; of inculcating the purest principles of philanthropy, science, and art; alleviating the wants of the poor and needy; visiting and attending the sick; coming to the rescue of victims of persecution; providing for, protecting, and assisting the widow and the orphan on the broadest principles of humanity."

(For the complete text of this latest [1953] *Constitution and By-Laws* of the Beckley B'nai B'rith Lodge, *see* Abraham I. Shinedling and Manuel Pickus, *History of the Beckley Jewish Community* [Beckley, 1955], pages 182–192.)

## THE CHARTER MEMBERS OF BECKLEY LODGE
## No. 1360, B'NAI B'RITH

(1939) (26 members)

*Abe Saks
Ben Myers
James Pickus
*Tom [Thomas] Sopher
Leonard Applebaum
I. J. [Jerry] Greenfield
*Harry Abel (of Mount
   Hope)
*Nathan Berman
Milton Rubenstein
Ben Harris
Harry Jacobson
Morton M. Applebaum
(Then the student rabbi of
   Congregation Beth El)

*Charles Greenfield
Edward Berman
Jacob Silverberg
William Binderman
Jack Binderman [, Sr.]
M. Edward Harvit
Irving Goldstein
Israel Fink
Benjamin E. Lewis
Dr. A. R. Korensky
Harry Wasserkrug (of Oak
   Hill)
William Klein
Joseph Keiserman
*Joseph B. Heller

Those persons whose names are marked with an asterisk are now deceased.

(These names are not in alphabetical order. They are given in the exact order in which they are inscribed on the Charter of the Beckley Lodge, which hangs in the front of the Assembly and Vestry Rooms of Congregation Beth El, where the Beckley Lodge holds most of its meetings, generally every two weeks except in the summer months, when the meetings are held monthly. Occasional dinner meetings, and State Council meetings, as well as special Executive Board meetings, are held in other Beckley places, such as the El Chico Restaurant, the Beckley Hotel, and the Moose Club. In the preceding and following lists, the names of members who, in 1959, were deceased, are preceded by an asterisk.)

## CHARTER MEMBERS OF 1941 (ADDITIONAL)
### (AT THE TIME OF THE REORGANIZING OF THE LODGE)

| | |
|---|---|
| *Samuel [I.] Abrams | *Louis Pickus |
| *Edward Gilbert | Nathan Pickus |
| Harry Lewin | Samuel Rudin |
| Nathan Matz | *Dr. Bernard E. Silverman |

One of the chief functions of the Beckley B'nai B'rith Lodge, No. 1360, has been its Americanization program, for the preparation of the foreign-born, or aliens, in Raleigh County, both Jewish as well as non-Jewish, for becoming naturalized citizens of the United States of America. Several Beckley Jewish residents were thus aided by the Lodge to become citizens of the United States, as a result of these efforts of the members of the active Americanization Committee of the Beckley Lodge; in this respect, the Beckley Lodge initiated a pioneering movement among the thirteen B'nai B'rith Lodges of the entire State. Since the inception of this program in 1948, Malcolm Pickus, Archie Ellenbogen, Arthur Goldstein, and Robert H. Levine have been, or were, active in it as instructors (members of the Lodge's Americanization Committee) in Beckley; and Edward Saymen and Morris S. Wender, Jr., in Oak Hill (from 1955 to 1959).

The Beckley Lodge also assists in a vocational guidance program at the two local high schools; maintains an Emergency Fund; maintains an annual Travelers' Aid Fund (for Jewish transients passing through the city); makes annual contributions to the Leo N. Levi Memorial Hospital, in Hot Springs, Ark., and to the National Jewish Hospital, in Denver, Colo. (both of these institutions originally B'nai B'rith projects); contributes annually to the Anti-Defamation League of the B'nai B'rith (A. D. L.); contributes annually to the Building Fund and the Maintenance Fund of the Hillel Foundation at West Virginia University, in Morgantown; and assists several local charities, civic programs, cultural programs, the Beckley V. A. Hospital, and non-Jewish youth groups, annually.

Several semiannual meetings of the State Council of the B'nai B'rith were held in Beckley in the late 1940's and the early 1950's.

The peak membership of the Beckley Lodge was 64, on September 1, 1950. By October 1, 1955, the membership of the Beckley B'nai B'rith Lodge had declined to 40, chiefly as a result of several deaths of Jewish residents of the community, and of the removal of members from Beckley to other cities because of the unfavorable economic conditions prevailing in the city (the decline in the production and use of bituminous coal) from 1952 on; also because of the resignation and withdrawal of a number of members from membership in the Lodge in the years 1950 to 1955. In 1959, under the presidency of Ben H. Wender (1958–1959), as a result of further removals from the city in the four-year period from 1955 to 1959, and three or four deaths of members, it was reported that the Lodge membership numbered about 30 active members.

THE 1951–1952 *Program Booklet*

Of rare and unusual interest, because copies of it are now so very scarce, is the *Program Booklet* of the Beckley Lodge for the Year 1951–1952, at the time of its greatest membership and activity, from which the following data have been excerpted:

OFFICERS OF THE BECKLEY LODGE FOR 1951–1952:

PRESIDENT: Harold Rudin
1ST VICE PRESIDENT: Israel Fink
2ND VICE PRESIDENT: Malcolm Pickus
SECRETARY: Robert [H.] Levine
TREASURER: Samuel Hochman
WARDEN: William Binderman
MONITOR [CHAPLAIN]: Rabbi Abraham I. Shinedling

BOARD OF TRUSTEES:

    Sidney Fink
    William Klein
    Eric Rosenbaum

MEMBERS OF LODGE NO. 1360, OF BECKLEY,
WEST VIRGINIA (1951–1952)

*Harry Abel (of Mount Hope)
David Abrams
*Sam [Samuel I.] Abrams
*Dave [David] Arnstein
Jack Binderman, Jr.
Jack Binderman, Sr.
William Binderman
Alfred [E.] Cohen
Herbert [E.] Cohen
Lewis Cohen
Archie Ellenbogen
Louis Epstein (of Oak Hill)
Sidney Fink
Louis J. Fink
Joseph Freed

*Marc [L.] Front
I. [Israel] Fink
Arthur Goldstein
I. [Irving] Goldstein
[M.] Edward Harvit
Sam [Samuel] Hochman
*Joseph [B.] Heller
William Klein
Edward [M.] Kandell
Charles [H.] Levine
Robert [H.] Levine
Harry Lewin
Benjamin Lewis (of Mount Hope)
Benjamin E. Lewis
Nathan Matz
Joseph [R.] Miller

The names of those members marked with an asterisk are those of now-deceased members.

James Pickus
Malcolm Pickus
Nathan Pickus
Eric Rosenbaum
Harold Rudin
Daniel [M.] Saks
Bernard [L.] Saks
Robert [W.] Saks
Herman Samans
Edward Saymen
Albert Schwartz
Maurice Selden

Rabbi Abraham I.
  Shinedling
Jacob Silverberg
Harold A. Sopher
Ira B. Sopher
Charles Stromberg
Harry Stromberg
Isadore R. Wein
Morri [R.] Wein
Max [H.] Wender
Morris S. Wender (of Oak
  Hill)

(Jacob Silverberg passed away in Beckley in May, 1961, and Bernard L. Saks in September of the same year.)

[In addition to the five deceased members indicated above, the following Beckley B'nai B'rith members were no longer resident in the city or vicinity in or by late 1959: Jack Binderman, Jr.; Jack Binderman, Sr.; Herbert E. Cohen, Lewis Cohen, Louis Epstein, Louis J. Fink, Joseph Freed, Israel Fink, Samuel Hochman, Edward M. Kandell, Charles H. Levine, Robert H. Levine, Malcolm Pickus, Harold Rudin, Robert W. Saks, Albert Schwartz, and Harry Stromberg, a total of seventeen members.]

PROGRAM AND MEETING SCHEDULE FOR 1951–1952:

*1951*

September 13th: Dinner Meeting. District [Grand] Lodge Speaker, Robert H. Levine

September 27th: Business Meeting. Report on Americanism. Host: Malcolm Pickus

October 11th: Business Meeting. Host: Harry Stromberg

October 25th: Business Meeting. Guest speaker on the Korean War. War film. Host: Harold Rudin

October 30th: Halloween Ball. Hosts: David Abrams, Maurice
　　Selden, and Bernard L. Saks

November 8th: Business Meeting. Host: Robert [W.] Saks

November 22nd: Business Meeting. Hillel [Foundation at Mor-
　　gantown, W. Va.] Report. Host: William Klein

December 6th: Business Meeting. Fall Council Report (State).

*1952*

January 1st: Annual New Year Affair

January 3rd: Business Meeting. Book review. Host: Rabbi
　　Abraham I. Shinedling

January 17th: Business Meeting. Host: David Abrams

January 20th: B'nai B'rith Follies of 1952. Director: Sam
　　Hochman

January 31st: Business Meeting. Host: Jack Binderman

February 14th: Business Meeting. Brotherhood Observance.
　　Host: Isadore R. Wein

February 28th: Joint meeting of the men's and the ladies'
　　(Sisterhood and Hadassah) Groups

March 14th: Business Meeting. New Member Program

March 28th: Business Meeting. B'nai B'rith Duty to the Teen
　　Ager. Host: Eric Rosenbaum

April 11th: Past President and Charter Member Dinner. Hosts:
　　Edward Harvit and William Klein

April 25th: Business Meeting. Anti-Defamation League Report
　　by Edward M. Kandell

May 9th: Business Meeting. Host: Daniel M. Saks

May 23rd: Installation Dinner Meeting. Host: Isadore R. Wein,
　　Chairman

Plans after this date include the Spring Council Meeting for
this district. [In June, July, and August, annually, one meeting
a month was held by the Beckley Lodge, for business and social
purposes.]

## Active Lodge Committees in 1951–1952

(The first person named is Chairman of the Committee)

*Auditing Committee*

Charles Levine
Irving Goldstein
Louis J. Fink

*Adult Education Committee*

Rabbi Abraham I.
   Shinedling
William Binderman
Charles Levine
Charles Stromberg
Nathan Pickus

*Anti-Defamation League
   Committee*

Edward M. Kandell
Malcolm Pickus
William Binderman
Daniel M. Saks
Jack Binderman, Jr.

*United Jewish Appeal Committee*

Samuel I. Abrams
Isadore R. Wein
Charles Levine
Jacob Silverberg

*Program Committee*

Samuel Hochman
Edward Saymen
Robert W. Saks
Sidney Fink
Isadore R. Wein

*Membership Committee*

Harry Stromberg
Eric Rosenbaum
Benjamin Lewis (of Mount
   Hope)
Maurice Selden

*Sick Committee*

James Pickus
Samuel I. Abrams
Herman Samans
Rabbi Abraham I.
   Shinedling

*Publicity and Publications
   Committee*

Robert W. Saks
Jack Binderman, Jr.
Bernard L. Saks
Robert Levine
Morri R. Wein

*Athletics Committee*

Malcolm Pickus
Robert W. Saks
Samuel Hochman
William Klein
Joseph R. Miller

*Hillel Building Fund Committee*

Isadore R. Wein
Robert Levine
Edward Saymen

*Telephone Committee*

Rabbi Abraham I.
  Shinedling
Robert W. Saks
Harold Rudin
William Klein
Benjamin Lewis
William Binderman
Joseph R. Miller

*Americanism Committee*

Malcolm Pickus
Harold Sopher
Robert W. Saks
Joseph Freed
David Abrams
Max Wender
Arthur Goldstein

*V. A. V. S. Committee (Veterans
  Administration [Hospital]
  Volunteer Service Committee)*

Irving Goldstein
Harry Lewin

*B. B. Y. O. (B'nai B'rith Youth
  Organization) Committee*

David Abrams
Bernard L. Saks
Edward Saymen

*Hillel Foundation Committee*

[M.] Edward Harvit
Archie Ellenbogen
Robert Levine
Robert W. Saks
Jacob Silverberg
James Pickus
Marc L. Front

ROSTER OF MEMBERS IN SEPTEMBER, 1954

(49 members)

*Harry Abel (of Mount
  Hope)
A. David Abrams
#Dr. Jack Binderman, Jr.
#Jack Binderman, Sr.
William Binderman
Archie Ellenbogen
#Louis J. Fink
#Morie Fink

#Dr. Saul Fortunoff
#Joseph Freed
Arthur Goldstein
Irving Goldstein
M. Edward Harvit
Morris Hochman
Samuel Hochman
#Arthur Horowitz
#Bernard Lande

---

Those names marked with an asterisk * represent members who are deceased,
and those marked with the symbol # are no longer, as of July 1, 1959, living in
Beckley or in the Beckley area.

William Klein
#Charles H. Levine
#Robert H. Levine
Harry Lewin
Max Lewin
Benjamin Lewis (of Mount
    Hope)
Benjamin E. Lewis
Nathan Matz
Joseph R. Miller
James Pickus
#Malcolm Pickus
#Manuel Pickus
Nathan Pickus
Eric Rosenbaum
Theodore Rosenbaum
#Harold Rudin
Bernard L. Saks

Daniel M. Saks
Herman Samans
Edward Saymen
Maurice Selden
#Rabbi Abraham I.
    Shinedling
Jacob Silverberg
*Dr. Bernard E. Silverman
Harold A. Sopher
Ira B. Sopher
Charles Stromberg
#Harry Stromberg
Isadore R. Wein
Morri R. Wein
Max H. Wender
Morris S. Wender, Jr.
    (of Oak Hill)
Louis Wolman

In September, 1954, the Beckley Lodge had 49 members. In the three-year period from September 1, 1954, to September 1, 1957, of these 49 members:

1 had passed away
14 had moved to other cities
2 had withdrawn or dropped their membership in the Lodge
32 were still living in Beckley and were members of the Lodge
    and, in addition, two or three new members had joined.

In the slightly less than two-year period from September 1, 1957, to July 1, 1959, there was one more death of a member of the Lodge; 1 member had returned to the city to live, and had rejoined the lodge; two new members had joined the Lodge; and two more members had removed from the city.

## Past Members of the Beckley B'nai B'rith Lodge
### (Before 1954)

*David Arnstein
*Samuel I. Abrams
Sidney Fink
Dr. Lee Hedson
*Joseph B. Heller
Edward M. Kandell
Daniel Keiserman
Joseph Keiserman
Gerald A. Pickus

Malcolm Pickus
Calvin J. Schildkraut
Dr. Leo Sherman
Sidney Stromberg
Maurice Baer
Alfred E. Cohen
*Marc L. Front
Albert Schwartz

## Past Officers of the Beckley Lodge

*Past Presidents*

Benjamin E. Lewis (1939–1940)
Irving Goldstein (1940–1941)
M. Edward Harvit (1941–1943)
William Klein (1943–1945)
A. David Abrams (1945–1947)
Edward Saymen (1947–1948)
Robert H. Levine (1948–1949)
Isadore R. Wein (1949–1950)
Eric Rosenbaum (1950–1951 and 1955–1956)
Harold Rudin (1951–1953)
Malcolm Pickus (1953–1954)
Arthur Goldstein (1954–1955)
Daniel M. Saks (1956–1957)

*Past Secretaries*

William Binderman (1939–1940)
Ben Myers (1940)
M. Edward Harvit (1941)

---

An asterisk * preceding a name means that the person is deceased.

Eric Rosenbaum (1941–1944)
Robert H. Levine (1950–1951)
William Klein (1951–1953)
Abraham I. Shinedling (1953–1956)

*Past Treasurers*

Abe Saks (1939–1940)
William Klein (1940–1941)
Joseph B. Heller (served as treasurer for several
    years, intermittently, from 1941 on)
Samuel Hochman (1950–1953)
William Binderman (1953–1955)
Bernard E. Silverman (1955–1956)

OFFICERS OF THE LODGE IN 1955–1956

PRESIDENT: Eric Rosenbaum
1ST VICE PRESIDENT: Manuel Pickus
2ND VICE PRESIDENT: Daniel M. Saks
SECRETARY: Rabbi Abraham I. Shinedling
TREASURER: Max H. Wender and Bernard E. Silverman
    (Each served for part of the year.)
GUARDIAN: Edward Saymen
WARDEN: Louis Wolman
MONITOR (CHAPLAIN): Arthur Goldstein
PARLIAMENTARIAN: William Klein

TRUSTEES:

William Klein
Arthur Goldstein
Harold Rudin

OFFICERS OF THE LODGE IN 1956–1957

(Elected in April, 1956, and installed on May 27, 1956, by
Herman Fetter, of Huntington, retiring president of the West
Virginia Council of the B'nai B'rith.)

PRESIDENT: Daniel M. Saks
1ST VICE PRESIDENT: William Klein
2ND VICE PRESIDENT: Harry Lewin
SECRETARY: Robert W. Saks
TREASURER: William Binderman
PARLIAMENTARIAN: William Klein
CHAPLAIN (MONITOR): Eric Rosenbaum
WARDEN: Joseph R. Miller
GUARDIAN: Samuel Hochman

TRUSTEES:

Arthur Goldstein
William Klein
Eric Rosenbaum

In May, 1957, William Klein was elected president of the Lodge, to serve for the year 1957 to 1958. He has been, re-elected time and time again, the parliamentarian of the Lodge "from time immemorial."

OFFICERS OF BECKLEY LODGE, No. 1360,
B'NAI B'RITH, IN 1957–1958

PRESIDENT (and PARLIAMENTARIAN): William Klein
1ST VICE PRESIDENT: Harry Lewin
2ND VICE PRESIDENT: Isadore R. Wein
SECRETARY: Robert W. Saks
TREASURER: William Binderman
CHAPLAIN: Daniel M. Saks
GUARDIAN: Samuel Hochman

TRUSTEES:

Arthur Goldstein
Eric Rosenbaum
Daniel M. Saks

In May, 1958, Ben H. (Hyman) Wender was elected president of the Lodge, for the year 1958–1959.
In November, 1959, after the Beckley B'nai B'rith Lodge had

suffered a decline, due to loss of membership, and after a period of inactivity lasting for several months, the Lodge was again reactivated and reorganized. On November 8, 1959, at a time when the Lodge had about 25 members, the following officers were elected for the year 1959–1960:

PRESIDENT: Isadore R. Wein
VICE PRESIDENT: Maurice Selden
SECRETARY: Max H. Wender
TREASURER: Arthur Goldstein

### THE EMERGENCY FUND OF THE BECKLEY B'NAI B'RITH LODGE

On January 15, 1953, the Beckley B'nai B'rith Lodge established the B'nai B'rith Emergency Fund, with an initial capital of $600, for the purpose of helping members of the Jewish community (not just members of the Lodge or of the congregation) who may be in financial distress. Isadore R. Wein served as its chairman from 1953 to 1957, and Abraham I. Shinedling as its secretary from 1953 to 1956. Sidney Fink was its treasurer in 1953 to 1954; in the latter year, he was succeeded in that post by Edward Saymen.

In the years from 1953 to 1957, the members of the Board of Directors of the Emergency Fund included:

| | |
|---|---|
| A. David Abrams | M. Edward Harvit |
| William Binderman | Robert H. Levine |
| Archie Ellenbogen | Nathan Pickus |
| Sidney Fink | Edward Saymen |
| Dr. Saul Fortunoff | Isadore R. Wein |
| Irving Goldstein | |

### BECKLEY MEMBERS OF THE JEWISH PUBLICATION SOCIETY OF AMERICA

There is no indication or record that any Beckley Jewish residents were ever members of the J. P. S. A. before 1950. In September of that year the Junior Congregation of Temple

Beth El enrolled, under the treasurership of Dennis G. Saymen, and has retained its membership to the present day. Abraham I. Shinedling, the rabbi of the congregation, also became a member of the J. P. S. A. in September, 1950, being a member of that Society during the six years of his service as rabbi of Beth El Congregation, in Beckley.

In 1958–1959 the only two members of the J. P. S. A. from Beckley were the Junior Congregation and Captain Lee H. Trachtenberg, of the Beckley Memorial Hospital (from October, 1957, on).

BECKLEY JEWISH MEN AND WOMEN IN MILITARY SERVICE

The following members of the Jewish community in Beckley, including Jewish residents of nearby Mount Hope and Oak Hill, in Fayette County, saw service in the United States Armed Forces in World War II:

(A Memorial Plaque containing all their names hangs on the south wall of the Vestry Rooms of the Temple.)

#Charles Abrams
A. David Abrams
#Maurice Baer
#Dr. Ralph Berman
Robert J. Berman
#Benjamin Binderman
#Jack Binderman, Jr.
William Binderman
#Robert Dubin
#Louis Epstein (of Oak Hill)
#Morie Fink
Sidney Fink

#Leonard Fivers
Arthur Goldstein
#Harry Hochman
#Samuel Hochman
#Daniel Keiserman
#Robert H. Levine
Harry Lewin
Benjamin Lewis (of Mount Hope)
#Frances Mae Lewis
#Milford Lewis
Alfred Lovitz, Jr.
#Henry Miller

---

Those names marked with the symbol # are the names of persons no longer living in Beckley, as of 1959.

#Isadore Miller

#Ira W. Meltcher

#Dolores Pickus (Bayer)

#Malcolm Pickus

#Milton Pickus

Daniel M. Saks

#Robert W. Saks

(Robert W. Saks served as a Petty Officer, 1st class, in the United States Marine Corps. He was awarded the Purple Heart.)

#Malcolm Silverberg

#Harold A. Sopher

#Norman Stoken

#Harry Stromberg

#Sidney Stromberg

#Bernard Wasserkrug (of Oak Hill)

#Milton Watzman

Isadore R. Wein

(Isadore R. Wein served for 15 months, with the rank of Specialist A, in the United States Navy, at the Great Lakes Naval Training Station, in the Second World War.)

Morri R. Wein

(Morri R. Wein, the younger brother of Isadore R. Wein, formerly of Newark, N. J., before he settled in Beckley in 1946, served in the Signal Corps of the United States Army from 1941 to 1945.)

Morris S. Wender, Jr. (of Oak Hill)

#Arthur Wolk

A. David Abrams and Jack Binderman, Jr., both graduate dentists, served in the United States Armed Forces as dentists in World War II, the latter also for two additional years in the early 1950's.

Two Beckley Jewish residents saw service in the First World War:

Irving Goldstein (before he settled in Beckley)
and
James Pickus

(James Pickus saw service in the First World War in the United States Army in 1918. He had previously served in the Russian Czarist Army in the years before the outbreak of the First World War, in 1909 to 1912, before coming to the United States in 1914.)

### Beckley Jews in Local Service Organizations

In 1959, Nathan Matz was the only Beckley Jewish resident who was a member of the local Rotary Club. At the same time, Sidney L. Fink was a member of the local Kiwanis Club.

In November, 1959, the Beckley Civitans Club had five Jewish members: A. David Abrams, William Klein, Daniel M. Saks, Isadore R. Wein, and Morri R. Wein. Isadore R. Wein served as president of the Beckley Civitans Club from May, 1956, to May, 1957, and in 1959–1960 he served as the district lieutenant governor of the Civitans, for the District of West Virginia.

### Noteworthy Persons of the Beckley Jewish Community
#### (Brief Biographical Sketches)

A. David Abrams. A. David Abrams, the only son of the late Samuel I. and Esther Block Abrams, was born in Brooklyn, N. Y., on November 19, 1919. His parents moved to Beckley from Scarbro, W. Va., in 1932. After being graduated as a dentist from the University of Maryland, at College Park, Md., he served in both the United States Army and the Navy as a dentist. In 1944, together with his brother-in-law, Isadore R. Wein, he took over the Modern Furniture Company from his father, after the latter's retirement from the business which he had founded. A. David Abrams and Isadore R. Wein were still engaged in this business (furniture and clothing) in 1959, and conducting also its three branches in nearby Mount Hope, Oak Hill, and Sophia. (The Oak Hill branch was, reportedly, closed down in or about 1959.)

In early 1962, A. David Abrams was serving as a member of the West Virginia House of Delegates, under appointment by the Governor, during its last session, to fill a vacancy. In the November, 1962, elections, he was scheduled to run for that office for an elective seat.

From 1948 to 1956, A. David Abrams served as a director of Congregation Beth El. Active in the work of the Civitans

Club of Beckley, he was elected to its Board of Directors in May, 1955. He served for several years (from 1954 on) as the chairman of the Civitans Bowl Football Game Committee, arranging and having charge of the annual football game played in Woodrow Wilson High School Stadium between West Virginia Tech, of Montgomery, W. Va., and Concord College, of Athens, W. Va. From 1945 to 1947 he was president of the Beckley Lodge of the B'nai B'rith, No. 1360. In 1948 he was president of the Beckley Junior Chamber of Commerce. In May, 1955, he was elected 3rd vice president, in May, 1956, 2nd vice president, and later 1st vice president, and in May, 1957, he was elected president (for 1957–1958), of the West Virginia State Council of the B'nai B'rith. He served from 1956 to 1957 as president of the Beckley Business Bureau.

SAMUEL I. ABRAMS. Samuel I. Abrams (born in Yanova, Province of Kovno, Lithuania, in 1887) at first lived in Brooklyn, N. Y., after emigrating to the United States. In 1912, he left Brooklyn, and came to Scarbro, W. Va., and at first worked there for his cousins, Eugene and Morris Lopinsky, in their department store. (Samuel I. Abrams was a first cousin of all the Lopinsky family members of West Virginia.) After a brief return to Brooklyn, he came back to West Virginia for good in 1918, and from that time until 1932, when he settled for the rest of his life in Beckley, he lived in Scarbro, Oak Hill, Mullens, and other West Virginia towns, successively, engaged in the furniture and clothing business. In Beckley, he founded the Modern Furniture Store, on Neville Street, with branches, later, in Oak Hill, Sophia, and Mount Hope, which he conducted until his retirement in 1944.

Samuel I. Abrams was a charter member of the Beckley Hebrew Association (later Congregation Beth El) in 1935–1936, and served from 1948 until his death at Newark, N. J., on April 12, 1952, as its vice president and as a member of its Board of Directors. From 1946 to 1947, he served as the president of Congregation Beth El. From 1944 until his death in 1952 he was active in all the affairs of the congregation, especially the Religious School and the choir.

J. LEONARD BAER. J. Leonard Baer, the only Jewish attorney ever to live and practise law in Beckley, was born in Baltimore on July 1, 1888. In 1940 he came to Beckley from Wheeling. After his graduation from the University of Maryland Law School, J. Leonard Baer practised law from 1912 to 1940 in Keyser, W. Va., and in Wheeling. From 1944 to 1945 he served as the president of the Beckley Hebrew Association. In Beckley, he practised law from 1940 until his death in Beckley on December 7, 1948, and was a member of the West Virginia Bar Association and of the Raleigh County Bar Association.

NATHAN BERMAN. Nathan (Nat) Berman (born in Easton, Pa., on November 29, 1899) came to Beckley to settle about the year 1915. Engaged at first in the furniture business, as the owner of the Union Furniture Store, he later entered the junk metal and scrap iron business in Beckley, which he conducted until his death in that city on June 9, 1942. Nathan Berman supplied the steel which was used in the construction of the synagogue of Temple Beth El in 1935–1936.

Nathan Berman was a charter member of the Beckley Hebrew Association, and instrumental in its formation and in the erection of the synagogue building (1935–1936). From 1936 to 1937 he served as the first president of the congregation, and he served also for several years as a teacher in the Religious School. He was a charter member of Beckley Lodge, No. 1360, B'nai B'rith. A plaque dedicated to his memory is affixed to the rear wall of the sanctuary of Temple Beth El.

JACK BINDERMAN, JR. Jack Binderman, Jr., the younger brother of William Binderman, and the only practising private dentist whom the Beckley Jewish community ever had, was born at Harlan, Ky., in 1924, and four years later he was brought to Beckley by his parents, Jack, Sr., and Manya S. Binderman, from Hazleton, Pa., to which city they had moved shortly after his birth. Graduated from the Dental College of the University of Maryland in 1947, he saw service (1945–1947) in the United States Army even before that, and from 1947 to 1952 he practised as a dentist in Beckley. From 1952 to 1954, he served, under recall, once more as a dentist in the United States Navy, in Japan, as a lieutenant, junior grade. In mid-1954 he returned to Beckley, again resuming his private practice of dentistry, but in December, 1954, he settled in San Diego, Calif., where he opened a dental office.

WILLIAM BINDERMAN. William Binderman (born in New York City, on March 15, 1916), the oldest son of Jack Binderman, Sr., came with his parents to Beckley from Hazleton, Pa., in 1928. After service in the United States Navy from 1943 to 1945 in the Second World War, he took over the ownership of the People's Credit Clothing Store, on Neville Street, and was still operating this business in 1959.

William Binderman was a charter member of Congregation Beth El in 1935–1936, and also of Beckley Lodge, No. 1360, B'nai B'rith, in 1939. From 1948 to 1956 he served as a member of the Board of Directors of the Congregation; from 1953 to 1955, and again from 1955 to 1957, he served as treasurer of the local B'nai B'rith Lodge, and as the lodge secretary from 1939 to 1940.

MRS. BEATRICE COHEN BINDERMAN. Beatrice Cohen Binderman, the wife of William Binderman, was president of the Beckley Sisterhood from 1945 to 1946, and again from 1955 to 1956. She also served a one-year term as its treasurer, and one year as its recording secretary. From 1954 on, she served also as the recording secretary of the Beckley Hadassah, and served also as a teacher in the Religious School of the Congregation for several years. In April, 1948, she became a charter member of the Beckley Hadassah, and she was always active in its work.

ISRAEL FINK. Israel Fink (born in Brooklyn, N. Y., in 1895) moved to Beckley from Bluefield in 1948, and operated first the Cavalier Cut Rate (drug) Store on Prince Street, and then the Prince Jewelry and Loan Company, on Prince Street also. In January, 1954, due to ill-health, he settled in Newport News, Va., retiring from business. Israel Fink was a charter member of the Beckley Hebrew Association in 1935–1936, and also of Beckley Lodge, No. 1360, B'nai B'rith, in 1939. From 1950 to 1951 he served as the 1st vice president of the Beckley Lodge. From 1952 to 1953, he served as a director of Beth El Congregation.

LOUIS J. FINK. Louis J. Fink, noted Beckley merchant and financier, was born in Miluten, Province of Volhynia, Ukraine, Russia, on February 7, 1883. After his emigration to the United States in 1903, he at first settled in Baltimore, Md. He came to Beckley in 1914, being one of the first Jewish settlers in Raleigh County. In that same year he opened the Hub Store, a ladies' ready-to-wear business, on Neville Street, and in 1932 also the Vogue Store; in these two stores, for several years, he was in partnership with his two sons, Sidney L. and Morie Fink. In 1956, Morie Fink, the younger son, withdrew from the business partnership, and moved to New York, but Sidney Fink remained in the commercial partnership with his father, in both stores. In early 1957, Louis J. Fink returned to Baltimore, his original American home, to live, retaining his business interests in Beckley.

In 1935–1936, Louis J. (most often known as L. J.) Fink was a charter member of the Beckley Hebrew Association. He served as [a] director of the Beckley National Bank for several years, and also as a member of its Discount Board. In 1953, also, he aided greatly in the financing of the Beckley Medical Arts, Inc., Center, which was erected in East Beckley. In 1953, the occasion of his seventieth birthday was celebrated in the Beckley Jewish community, and served as the scene of a generous gift to the cause of the Hadassah, in which he and his second wife were deeply interested.

MRS. MINNIE MILLER FINK, originally from Baltimore, the second wife of Louis J. Fink, was noted, during the entire period of her residence in Beckley until early 1957, as a prime fosterer of the Beckley Chapter of Hadassah, and as a philanthropist in the Jewish community. Louis J. Fink's first wife was Annie Wasserkrug Fink, an older sister of Samuel and Harry Wasserkrug.

SIDNEY L. FINK. Sidney L. Fink, the elder son of Louis J. Fink, was born in Baltimore on September 20, 1914. He was brought to Beckley in that same year by his parents, Louis

J. and Annie Wasserkrug Fink. From 1942 to 1945 he
served in the United States Army as a sergeant, in the
Second World War. In 1946, he became associated with
his father as a partner in the Hub and Vogue ladies'
ready-to-wear stores, and in 1954 he became manager of
the Vogue Store. He is noted as a generous contributor to
philanthropic causes, and as one of the prominent and
progressive younger businessmen of Beckley, together with
such Jewish merchants as Isadore R. Wein, Eric Rosenbaum, Nathan and James Pickus, A. David Abrams, Harry
Lewin, and William Binderman.

In 1959, Sidney L. Fink was a member of the Beckley
Kiwanis Club.

The elder son of Sidney L. and Irene B. Fink, Kenneth
M. Fink, was Bar Mitzvahed at Temple Beth El on Saturday
morning, November 7, 1959, in a ceremony which saw the
former rabbi of the congregation, Abraham I. Shinedling,
of Beckley, come from Albuquerque, N. Mex., his new
home, to officiate at the Bar Mitzvah of his former pupil.

Sidney L. Fink was a charter member of Congregation
Beth El in 1935–1936, and served as its president from 1947
to 1948. From 1947 to 1956, he served as a member of the
congregational Board of Directors. He served also as a
member of a number of important committees in the
Beckley Jewish community.

IRENE BESSO FINK. Irene Besso Fink, the wife of Sidney L.
Fink, was president of the Beckley Sisterhood from 1952 to
1954. From October, 1955, to October, 1957, she served
as the treasurer of the West Virginia Federation of Temple
Sisterhoods.

DR. SAUL FORTUNOFF. Dr. Saul Fortunoff (born at New York
City, on March 5, 1905) came to Beckley in January, 1951,
from Butler, Pa., to become the chief of the medical service
of the Beckley Veterans Administration Hospital. He retained this position until early 1956, when he left to become
the administrator of the Veterans Administration Hospital
in Altoona, Pa. He had served as a physician on the staff
of the V. A. Hospital in Butler, Pa., from 1947 to 1951.
Saul Fortunoff received his M.D. degree from the New

York Medical College in 1928, served as a physician in the United States Army from 1942 to 1946, after being in private practice in New Rochelle, N. Y., for a number of years, and in 1946 he entered the service of the Veterans Administration. He is a Service Fellow of the American Medical Association. [1]

DOROTHY BAER FORTUNOFF. Dorothy Baer Fortunoff, the wife of Dr. Saul Fortunoff, served from 1954 to 1956 as the corresponding secretary of the Beckley Chapter of Hadassah. From 1953 to 1956, she served as the financial secretary of the Beckley Sisterhood.

MRS. NORA B. FRANKS. Mrs. Nora B. Franks (born in Detroit, Mich.) entered the service of the Federal Government in 1940, and served with the Social Security Board, Old Age and Survivors Insurance, in Logan, W. Va., from 1948 to 1952, and in Welch, W. Va., from 1952 to 1954. She was then transferred to Beckley, where she served as the manager of the Social Security Office from 1954 to March, 1957, when she went to Parkersburg, W. Va., to which place she was transferred to become the manager of the Parkersburg Social Security Office. She is the only woman who is a Social Security Office manager in West Virginia.

During her residence both in Welch and in Beckley, Nora B. Franks was active in the work of the Temple Sisterhoods. She was one of the founders of the Public Library in Welch, in the years from 1952 to 1954. In Beckley, she served from 1954 to 1956 as a co-chairman of the Sisterhood Planning Committee. From May, 1956, until her departure for Parkersburg in March, 1957, she served as an elected member of the Board of Directors of Congregation Beth El, being the first woman to be elected to the Board of Directors of the congregation in Beckley. In 1955–1956, together with Mrs. Rose Y. [Nathan] Pickus, she was instrumental in the founding of the Beckley Golden

---

[1] From 1957 to 1961, Dr. Saul Fortunoff served as the manager or administrator of the V. A. Hospital in Dwight, Ill., and his son, Stephen Fortunoff, having finished his medical studies and received his M.D. degree, was serving as resident physician, in 1961, in the Bronx, N. Y., Veterans Administration Hospital.

Age Club, for Beckley residents over sixty years of age, and was a founder and a director of the Raleigh County Mental Health Association.

IRVING GOLDSTEIN. Irving Goldstein (born at Makava, Poland, on July 13, 1891) came to the United States at an early age, and at first he lived in Brooklyn, N. Y., until November, 1920. He had served in the United States Army in the First World War, as a resident of Brooklyn. In late 1920, he settled in Beckley, at first operating a clothing store and a dollar store, but later he entered the finance business, opening the small loans firm known as the People's Finance Company, on Prince Street. He had also previously been in the department store business in Beckley. In 1959, he was still in this business, in partnership with his son, Arthur Goldstein.

For many years Irving Goldstein was a noted figure in the civic and the athletic life of Beckley. He is a past commander of the American Legion Post of the city, and served as its Finance Officer for seventeen years. From 1953 on, he served as the president of the Warren Williams Junior Baseball League, in Beckley. In the 1930's and 1940's, when Beckley had a team in minor professional baseball leagues, Irving Goldstein was an ardent fosterer and supporter of organized baseball.

In 1935–1936, he became a charter member of Congregation Beth El, and served as its president from 1937 to 1938. From 1935 to 1936 he was also the first treasurer of the Congregation. He was a member of the Board of Directors of the Congregation from 1948 to 1956, and in 1939 he became a charter member also of Beckley Lodge, No. 1360, B'nai B'rith. From 1952 to 1956, he was a member of the Cemetery Committee of the Congregation, playing an important role in the laying out and the acquisition of the first cemetery of the Congregation.

EDNA BRODKIN GOLDSTEIN. Edna Brodkin Goldstein, the wife of Irving Goldstein, was president of the Beckley Sisterhood from 1934 to 1935. She became a charter member of the Sisterhood in 1925.

ARTHUR GOLDSTEIN. Arthur Goldstein (born in Brooklyn,

N. Y., on November 12, 1921), the son of Irving and Edna
B. Goldstein, served as a sergeant in the United States
Army in the Second World War, from 1942 to 1946, and
in the latter year, upon his return to Beckley, he became
associated with his father in the People's Finance Company.
He served as the president of the Beckley B'nai B'rith Lodge
from 1954 to 1955, after serving for two years previously as
one of the vice presidents of the Lodge. For several years
beginning with 1952, he was an active member of the
Americanism Committee of the Lodge, instructing the
foreign-born of Raleigh County so that they might become
naturalized citizens of the United States.

M. EDWARD HARVIT. M. Edward Harvit (born in Montreal,
Canada, on May 8, 1906) at first lived in Mount Hope,
W. Va., after leaving New York, in which city he had
settled after his immigration into the United States from
Montreal. His residence in Mount Hope embraced the
years 1931 to 1933, and he was in the clothing business
there. He settled in Beckley in 1933. In 1935–1936 he
became a charter member of the Beckley Hebrew Association, and also, in 1939, of Beckley Lodge, No. 1360, of
the B'nai B'rith. From 1948 to 1950, he served as the
president of Beth El Congregation, and as a member of its
Board of Directors from 1948 to 1956. After being in the
clothing business in Beckley for some years, he entered the
ladies' ready-to-wear business in Whitesville, W. Va., and
remained in that business until early 1959, when he gave
up his store there as a result of the poor economic conditions prevailing in many sections of West Virginia at that
time. Thereafter he worked as a salesman of jewelry and
shoes in Raleigh County and in the State, part of the time
in partnership with Benjamin Lewis, of Mount Hope. For
some years M. Edward Harvit was connected with the
West Virginia State Board of Control [the liquor control
Board], and in 1954 to 1956 he was connected with the
West Virginia State administration politically.

His two sons, HAROLD E. HARVIT and ROBERT B.
HARVIT, were both prominent in the organization and the
maintenance of the Temple Beth El Youth Group. In

1955, Harold E. Harvit became a lieutenant in the United States Army, and served for a while (as a graduate of West Virginia University, in Morgantown) as an instructor in the United States Army. On September 6, 1959, at B'nai Jacob Congregation, in Charleston, Robert B. Harvit was married to Stephanie Sloman, of Charleston, with Rabbi Samuel Cooper as the officiant. In that same year he had become program director of Radio Station WWNR, in Beckley, serving under Richard Booth, station manager.

In March, 1962, Robert B. Harvit moved from Beckley to Williamson, where he became manager of Radio Station WBTH. Previously, in November, 1957, his elder brother, Harold E. Harvit, had moved to Williamson, after three years of service in the United States Army as a 2nd lieutenant. In Williamson, he became the manager of a credit clothing store.

MRS. ANNE KANDELL HARVIT. Mrs. Anne Kandell Harvit, the wife of M. Edward Harvit, was active in the work of the Beckley Sisterhood. From 1940 to 1941 and again from 1943 to 1944 she was president of the Beckley Sisterhood. She also served a term as its treasurer. She is the permanent custodian and chairman of the Sisterhood's congregational Book of Life. In 1948, she served as the first treasurer of the Beckley Hadassah. For several years, always active in the work of the local Sisterhood, she served as a co-chairman (together with Mrs. Nora B. Franks) of the Planning Committee of the Beckley Sisterhood.

SAMUEL HOCHMAN. Samuel ("Sam") Hochman has the distinction, among all the members of the Beckley Jewish community, of having been "born at sea," on February 2, 1921, on the S. S. "Manoa," near the Azores Islands, while his parents, Morris and Tillie Morayniss Hochman, were on their way to the United States, from their native Russia, to settle. In 1938, Samuel Hochman settled in Beckley with his parents, and at first worked as a salesman for his uncle, Charles Stromberg, who operated the Leader Furniture Store. He saw service, from 1943 to 1946, in the United States Army during the Second World War, and in the latter year he returned to Beckley, opening up the Capitol

Home Furnishing Company, which business he operated until early 1959, when he left Beckley and settled in Hammond, Ind., where he accepted an administrative position in a hospital, as assistant business manager of the Kuhn Clinic, in Hammond. In 1954, also, he became a special agent for the Lincoln National Life Insurance Company, of Fort Wayne, Ind.

Samuel Hochman served from 1948 to 1950 as the secretary of Beckley Lodge, No. 1360, B'nai B'rith, and from 1950 to 1953 as its treasurer. From 1953 to 1955, he was a vice president of the Lodge.

In 1950, he became a member of the American Contract Bridge League, and, together with William Klein, who also is a member of the Beckley congregation, played in many State and Tri-State bridge tournaments. He also lectured on, and gave private lessons in, contract bridge for many years. His wife, Zena Y. Hochman, also is noted as a bridge expert locally and in West Virginia. Sam Hochman was the winner of several State bridge tournaments in the period from 1950 to 1956.

ZENA Y. HOCHMAN. Mrs. Zena Y. Hochman, the wife of Samuel Hochman, served from 1950 to 1954 as the treasurer of the Beckley Sisterhood, and from 1956 to 1957 she served as its president. From 1951 to 1953 she was president of the Beckley Hadassah, and from 1954 to 1956 she was its vice president. She was a charter member of the Beckley Hadassah in 1948. In April, 1955, she was elected to a one-year term as president of the Southern West Virginia Bridge League.

WILLIAM KLEIN. William Klein (born at New York City, on November 27, 1907) came to Beckley in April, 1934, from Huntington, W. Va. After working as the credit manager of the Lewis Furniture Company for ten years, he became an insurance agent (later district agent) for the Lincoln National Life Insurance Company, of Fort Wayne, Ind. He was a charter member of the Beckley Tennis Club. He was a charter member also of Beth El Congregation (1935–1936) and of Beckley Lodge, No. 1360, of the B'nai B'rith (1939). He was also a founder of the Beckley Life Underwriters Association, and served as its secretary and as a member of its Board of Directors.

From 1936 to 1938, William Klein served as the first secretary of the Beckley Hebrew Association (Congregation Beth El), and as its president from 1942 to 1943. He served as president of the local B'nai B'rith Lodge from 1943 to 1945, as its treasurer from 1940 to 1941, as its secretary from 1951 to 1953, again as its president from 1957 to 1958, and he is the permanent parliamentarian of the Beckley Lodge.

William Klein is also a national committeeman of the American Contract Bridge League, and in September, 1955, he was elected a life master by the American Contract Bridge League. He participated in several State and Tri-State tournaments, both alone and with Samuel Hochman, and enjoys a State-wide-and-beyond reputation as an excellent contract bridge player and theorist of the game.

IDA MANDEL KLEIN. Mrs. Ida Mandel Klein, the wife of William Klein, is the daughter of the late Rabbi Samuel Mandel, who served for many years as the rabbi of the Orthodox Synagogue (B'nai Israel Congregation) in Huntington, W. Va. She served as financial secretary of the Beckley Hadassah (1954–1956), and is also noted in local and State contract bridge circles as an excellent player. In April, 1948, Ida M. Klein became a charter member of the local Hadassah chapter.

CHARLES H. LEVINE. Charles H. Levine was born in Hoosick Falls, N. Y., on March 31, 1891. His original home thereafter was New Castle, Pa. He graduated from the Carnegie Institute of Technology, at Pittsburgh, Pa., in 1913, and he is a graduate also of Harvard University (1917). He came to Beckley in 1939 from Morgantown, where he had lived and worked for several years, and founded (in nearby Mabscott, W. Va.) the Raleigh Junk Company, dealing in scrap iron and metals. He and his son, Robert H. Levine, still conducted that business in 1959, although by that time they had both moved away from Beckley to Charleston, the former in early 1957, and the latter in late 1954. In Charleston, in 1953, they opened a branch of the Raleigh

Junk Company, at Reed, W. Va., which later became the main seat of the business.

Charles H. Levine was, from 1939 to 1957, active in the general charitable field in Beckley, and served for years as the chairman of the United Jewish Appeal drives in Beckley. From 1950 to 1951 he served as the president of Beth El Congregation, and from 1948 to 1951 as a member of its Board of Directors. In 1950 his contribution of a large sum of money aided the congregation in the purchase of the electric organ of the Temple. He was a popular figure in Beckley for many years, being affectionately known as, and advertising as, "Poor Charlie," an endearing title or name by which he perhaps intended to symbolize, or memorialize, the early struggles through which he went, for years, in New Castle, Pa., in Morgantown, and in Beckley, before he attained to material competence in his business in the last-named city.

VIOLET G. LEVINE. Mrs. Violet Greenwald Levine, the wife of Charles H. Levine, was corresponding secretary of the Beckley Sisterhood (1941–1942), and its president from 1942 to 1943. She was a charter member of the Beckley Chapter of Hadassah in April, 1948, and very instrumental in its organization, serving as president of the Beckley Hadassah from 1948 to 1951 and again from 1953 to 1955.[1]

ROBERT H. LEVINE. Robert H. Levine, the son of Charles H. and Violet G. Levine, was born at New Castle, Pa., on July 23, 1923. He came to Beckley from Morgantown with his parents in 1939. After graduating from Virginia Polytechnic Institute, at Blacksburg, Va., with the B.S. degree, in 1945, and after serving in the United States Army as a 1st lieutenant in the Second World War (1943–1945), he entered his father's firm, the Raleigh Junk Company, in 1946, and was still associated with it in 1959. In 1954, he moved to Charleston, W. Va., to become the manager of the branch of the business established at Reed, W. Va., in 1953.

Robert H. Levine was extremely active in the work of the Beckley B'nai B'rith Lodge, No. 1360, both locally and

---

[1] Mrs. Violet G. Levine died at Charleston in the latter part of the year 1961.

on a State and District Grand Lodge level, from 1946 on. From 1948 to 1949 he was president of the Beckley Lodge, and served as its secretary from 1950 to 1951. From 1953 to 1954 he served as president of the West Virginia Council of the B'nai B'rith, and in May, 1954, he was elected a Committeeman-at-Large for West Virginia of District Grand Lodge, No. 3. He was active in the support of the Hillel Foundation at West Virginia University, in Morgantown. For several years before he left Beckley in 1954, Robert H. Levine served as an instructor on the Lodge's Americanism Committee, preparing aliens in Raleigh County for naturalization as American citizens, performing outstanding service along this line.

JANET B. LEVINE. Mrs. Janet B. Levine, the wife of Robert H. Levine, and the daughter of Nathan Berman, served as the first corresponding secretary of the Beckley Chapter of Hadassah, from 1948 on. Robert H. and Janet B. Levine were the first couple to be married, as an "all-Beckley couple," in Temple Beth El, with Rabbi Samuel Cooper, of the Conservative B'nai Jacob Congregation, of Charleston, as the officiant, on June 29, 1947. They attained to yet another "distinction" in Beckley, as the only Jewish parents of twin girls, Marilyn Lou and Caroline Sue Levine; the only other Jewish twins in Beckley, the sons of Eric and Millie G. Rosenbaum, were Franklin and Thomas Rosenbaum.

HARRY LEWIN. Harry Lewin was born in Lipnishok, near Lida, Poland, on October 8, 1910. He came to Beckley from Logan, W. Va., in 1938, to settle permanently. In Logan he had worked for two years for the Silver Brand Clothing Store. In Beckley, too, he worked for the Silver Brand Clothing Store until 1947, when he opened up his own clothing store, Harry's Men's Shop, on Neville Street, which business he was still operating in 1959.

In 1954, Harry Lewin took over a wooded area on Eisenhower Drive, near the State Police headquarters, and, with local aid, converted it into a recreational and baseball field for the Babe Ruth Baseball League, of which he had been one of the organizers. In 1954, this recreational field was named Lewin Field, in his honor. Harry Lewin paid a great part of the cost of the lighting and other features of the field.

Harry Lewin was active in many United Jewish Appeal drives in Beckley, and served from 1955 to 1958 as a member of the Board of Directors of Congregation Beth El. In May, 1956, he was elected a vice president of Beckley Lodge, No. 1360, B'nai B'rith.

BENJAMIN E. LEWIS. Benjamin E. Lewis (born in Baltimore, Md., on June 3, 1898) came to Mount Hope from Washington, D. C., in 1919. Here he at first worked for Harry Abel in the latter's clothing store, but in 1929 he moved to Beckley, where he opened up Ben's Army Store, on Neville Street. He still conducted this business in Beckley in 1959, residing part of the time in Beckley each year, and part of the time in Washington, D. C., where he also developed business interests.

In 1935–1936, Benjamin E. Lewis was a charter member of the Beckley Hebrew Association, and served as its treasurer from 1936 to 1947, but not continuously. In 1939, he became a charter member also of Beckley Lodge, No. 1360, B'nai B'rith, and served as the first president of the lodge (1939–1940).

JAMES PICKUS. James Pickus was born in Uzda, Province of Minsk, Russia, in 1890. He is the younger brother of Nathan and the late Louis Pickus, and he settled in Beckley at the age of 24 in 1914, coming to the city directly from his native Russia. He had served for three years as a soldier in the Czarist Russian Army (1909–1912). From 1914 to 1918, in Beckley, he worked as a clerk in the store owned by his two older brothers, Louis and Nathan Pickus. In 1918 to 1919 he served as a soldier in the United States Army, part of the time in the First World War, and then, after residing in Paducah, Ky., for about a year, he returned to Beckley, in 1920, worked again for his two brothers until 1925, and then he opened up the Quality Shop, a ladies' ready-to-wear store, on Main Street, near North Kanawha Street, which business he was still operating in 1959.

James Pickus was a charter member of the Beckley

Hebrew Association, in 1935–1936, and also of the Beckley Lodge, No. 1360, B'nai B'rith, in 1939. He has served continuously, since 1920, as the *Baal Tokea*, or Shofar blower, of Congregation Beth El.

NAOMI A. PICKUS. Mrs. Naomi Aronson Pickus, the wife of James Pickus, served as an early secretary of the Beckley Sisterhood, and as a teacher in the Religious School. Active in the work of the Beckley Chapter of Hadassah, she was one of its charter members in April, 1948.

MANUEL PICKUS. Manuel Pickus, the son of James and Naomi A. Pickus (born at Baltimore, on August 14, 1931), served for two years (1954–1956) as an officer and a vice president of the local B'nai B'rith Lodge, No. 1360, and also taught for a while in the Religious School of the congregation. He is the co-author (with Rabbi Abraham I. Shinedling) of the *History of the Beckley Jewish Community* (Beckley, 1955). Manuel Pickus was associated with his father in the latter's Quality Shop for several years (1951–1956) as assistant manager and buyer. In July, 1956, with his father as his partner, he moved to Charleston, W.Va., and opened up a similar ladies' ready-to-wear store, Manuel's. [1]

MALCOLM PICKUS. Malcolm Pickus, the elder son of Nathan and Rose Y. Pickus, was born in Beckley on April 17, 1924. After three years of service in the United States Army in the Second World War, he entered the wholesale jewelry business with his brother, Gerald A. Pickus, and then entered his father's business, the Budget Shop (a women's clothing store), on North Fayette Street, remaining here from 1951 until 1954. In the latter year he moved to Waynesboro, Va., where he opened up a ladies' ready-to-wear store.

Malcolm Pickus was president of the Beckley B'nai B'rith Lodge from 1953 to 1954. From 1951 to 1953 he served as a vice president of the Lodge. In 1953 he was elected secretary of the West Virginia Council of the B'nai B'rith, serving until 1954 with Robert H. Levine as the president of the

---

[1] By the year 1961, Manuel Pickus had given up his store in Charleston and, still living in that city, was employed as a life insurance agent.

State Council. He was active for several years on the Beckley Lodge's Americanism Committee, instructing the foreign-born to become naturalized American citizens; he was active also in B'nai B'rith athletics, especially in basketball, as a player and as the manager of the Beckley Lodge- Congregation Beth El basketball team in the Beckley Church League, for several years.

NATHAN PICKUS. Nathan Pickus, the middle one of the three Pickus (Louis, Nathan, and James Pickus) brothers, of Beckley, was born in Uzda, Province of Minsk, Russia, on September 15, 1887. In 1911 he settled in Beckley, after living in Monongah and Fairmont, W. Va., from 1905, when he first arrived in the United States as an immigrant from his native Russia, until 1911. In these two cities he was engaged in the retail clothing business, and in 1911, after his removal to Beckley with his older brother, Louis Pickus, he also engaged in the clothing business, later opening up the Budget Shop, on North Fayette Street, a ladies' ready-to-wear store, in which business he was still engaged in 1959.

Nathan Pickus was a charter member of the Beckley Hebrew Association in 1935–1936, and he served from 1952 to 1955 as a member of its Board of Directors. In 1952 he became chairman of the Beth El Temple Cemetery Committee, and still held this office in 1958. He was active, together with Irving Goldstein and Isadore R. Wein, in 1953, in the creation of the Temple Beth El Jewish Cemetery, in Sunset Memorial Park. Engaged in the real estate business in his early years in Beckley, he had bought, together with co-owners, a tract of land, and from 1917 on he developed this land into streets and lots, which the partners later sold off. Nathan Street, running for one block parallel to Woodlawn Avenue, behind the Post Office and the Telephone Company Building, was named after him, being part of the tract which he helped to develop.

ROSE Y. PICKUS. Mrs. Rose Y. Pickus, the wife of Nathan Pickus, served as president of the Beckley Sisterhood from 1937 to 1938. From 1925 to 1926, and again from 1927 to 1928, she had served as its first secretary. From 1922 on, for a number of years, she was a teacher in the first Sunday School organized by the Jews of Beckley. Since 1921 she has been a member of the Beckley Women's Club, and was one of the charter members of the Beckley Chapter of the League of Women Voters. She founded the Pinecrest Sanitarium Library, and since 1941 she has been the State Hospital Chairman of the American Legion Auxiliary at Pinecrest Sanitarium, in Beckley.

In 1925, Rose Y. Pickus was one of the charter members of the Beckley Sisterhood, and in April, 1948, she became a charter member also of the Beckley Chapter of Hadassah. In October, 1955, she and Nora B. Franks helped to organize the Beckley "Golden Age" Club for local persons over sixty years of age.

ERIC ROSENBAUM. Eric Rosenbaum (born in Buende, Westphalia, Germany, on March 31, 1902) came to the United States in 1938, and lived for one year in Tarboro, N. C. In 1939, he settled permanently in Beckley. From 1939 to 1944, he worked as a bookkeeper in Samuel I. Abrams' Modern Furniture Store, and then he entered the jewelry business, establishing Eric's Jewelry Store on Neville Street (for a few years it was located on nearby McCreery Street), which business he was still conducting in 1959.

Eric Rosenbaum was president of Beckley Lodge, No. 1360, of the B'nai B'rith, from 1950 to 1951, and again from 1955 to 1956. From 1941 to 1944 he served as the secretary of the Lodge, from 1947 to 1948 as the treasurer of Congregation Beth El, and from 1956 to 1958 he was a member of the Board of Directors of the congregation, being re-elected in May, 1957. An extraordinary affair in the life of the Beckley congregation was the Bar Mitzvah, in early 1959, of the twin sons (and only children) of Eric and Millie G. Rosenbaum, under the direction of Rabbi Abraham A. Kertes, the only such twins ever to be Bar Mitzvahed in the entire history of the Beckley community; these were Franklin and Thomas Rosenbaum.

THEODORE and MARTHA BORNHEIM ROSENBAUM. Theodore and Martha Bornheim Rosenbaum, the parents of Eric Rosenbaum, were, in 1959, the oldest Jewish residents in the city of Beckley. Theodore Rosenbaum was born at Halle, Westphalia, Germany, on July 30, 1867 (being 92 years old in 1959), and Martha Bornheim Rosenbaum was born in Leopoldshoehe, Lippe, Germany, on December 2, 1876, thus being 83 years old in 1959. They celebrated their golden wedding at Temple Beth El in 1951, the only Jewish couple to do so in the history of the community. The elder Rosenbaums settled in Beckley in 1940, coming from Tarboro, N. C. Theodore Rosenbaum is noted for his German and English calligraphy.

HAROLD RUDIN. Harold Rudin was born in Pittsburgh, Pa., on April 8, 1915, and he came to Beckley from Parkersburg, W. Va., in 1949. Here he worked for seven years as the manager of his father-in-law's (Charles Barrack) Barrack's Auto Supply Company, and held this position until February, 1956, when he moved to Huntington, W. Va., to assume a similar position in his father-in-law's establishment.

Harold Rudin was an active worker in the Beckley B'nai B'rith Lodge, serving as president of the Lodge from 1951 to 1953.

ABE SAKS. Abe Saks (born in Dvinsk, Latvia, on December 28, 1895) came to Beckley from Norfolk, Va., in 1921. At first (1924–1945) he operated an army and navy clothing store, under the name of Abe's Army Store. He then entered the jewelry business on Neville Street, and, after his death, on October 7, 1947, at Norfolk, his three sons, Bernard L. Saks, Daniel M. Saks, and Robert W. Saks, continued the business, under the name of Saks Jewelers. In 1959, Robert W. Saks moved to Washington, D. C., and the business was being operated by the two other sons, Bernard L. Saks having returned in the early part of that year from Waynesboro, Va., where he had operated a children's clothing store for several years. [1]

Abe Saks was a charter member of the Beckley Hebrew Association (1935–1936) and of Beckley Lodge, No. 1360, B'nai B'rith (1939). From 1939 to 1940 he served as the treasurer of the Lodge.

---

[1] Bernard L. Saks died at Beckley in September, 1961. He was the second person to be interred in the new Jewish cemetery on Harper Road.

GUSSIE B. SAKS. Mrs. Gussie Burk Saks, the wife of Abe Saks, was treasurer of the Beckley Sisterhood for several years, and from 1955 to 1956 she served as its vice president. She became a charter member of the Beckley Sisterhood in 1925.

HERMAN SAMANS. Herman Samans (born in Philadelphia, on June 17, 1906) settled in Beckley in 1944, after living and working in Welch, W. Va., for several years subsequent to his removal to West Virginia from Philadelphia. Until 1950, in Beckley, he worked as a salesman and clerk for the non-locally owned and operated Berman Jewelry Store, and then he entered business for himself in nearby Sophia, W. Va., opening up a music store. In 1952, he transferred this business to Beckley, adding several other lines and enlarging it, and changing its name to the Beckley Wholesale Mart.

Herman Samans was vice president of Beth El Congregation from 1947 to 1948. He is noted in the Beckley area as a violinist of ability. He and his daughter, Beverly Samans, served for many years in the congregational choir, and in 1958 she was known as a student of voice and as a singer in Raleigh County, attending a college in Boston in order to receive a degree in music.

MINNIE GEALT SAMANS. Mrs. Minnie Gealt Samans, the wife of Herman Samans, and a native of Philadelphia, was president of the Beckley Sisterhood from 1946 to 1947, and again from 1949 to 1950. She was always active in Beckley Sisterhood work, serving for years on several of its important committees. She was the first recording secretary (from 1948 on) of the Beckley Hadassah.

In May, 1957, Mrs. Minnie G. Samans was elected secretary of Congregation Beth El, and she was still serving in this position in 1959.

EDWARD SAYMEN. Edward Saymen was born in Newport, Ky., on April 1, 1919. He is the son-in-law of Jack Binderman, Sr., and the brother-in-law of William Binderman. In July, 1940, he left Cincinnati, where he was then residing, and settled in Beckley, and in 1947 he entered the credit clothing business with Jack Binderman, Sr., and William Binderman.

In 1950 he bought out the People's Clothing Store, in Oak Hill, W. Va., In 1959, although residing in Beckley, he was still engaged in business as the owner of the People's Clothing Store, in Oak Hill. [1]

Edward Saymen and his wife, RUTH BINDERMAN SAYMEN, were always active in the religious and organizational life of the Beckley Jewish community. He served as vice president and then president (1947–1948) of the Beckley B'nai B'rith Lodge, and from 1954 to 1959 he conducted courses in Americanism for aliens desiring naturalization in Oak Hill, for Fayette County, with the aid of Morris S. Wender, Jr., of Oak Hill. From 1955 to 1958 he served as a member of the Board of Directors of Congregation Beth El, being re-elected in May, 1957. In 1954, he was elected a director and treasurer of the B'nai B'rith Emergency Fund. He and Ruth B. Saymen taught for years in the Religious School of the congregation, and they also served in the Temple Choir for many years. Mrs. Ruth B. Saymen also served for several years (from 1954 on) as the treasurer of the Beckley Hadassah. She became a charter member of the Beckley Hadassah in 1948.

RABBI ABRAHAM I. SHINEDLING. Rabbi Abraham I. Shinedling (born in Menominee, Mich., on September 8, 1897) came to Beckley on September 1, 1950, from Bluefield, W. Va., where he had served for three years (1947–1950) as the rabbi of Ahavath Sholom Congregation. He was ordained in June, 1920, by the Hebrew Union College, in Cincinnati, which on June 6, 1959, conferred upon him the degree of Doctor of Divinity, *honoris causa*. He received his B.A. degree from the University of Cincinnati in 1919, and his M.A. degree from Columbia University, New York, in 1928.

In Beckley, he served from 1953 to 1956 as the secretary of Beckley Lodge, No. 1360, B'nai B'rith; as secretary-treasurer of the Beckley Ministerial Association (1953 and 1954); as Jewish chaplain at the Beckley V. A. Hospital (1951–1956); as Jewish chaplain at Pinecrest Sanatorium

---

[1] In 1961, Edward and Ruth B. Saymen left Beckley, and settled in South Bend, Ind., having given up their clothing store in Oak Hill.

(a State tuberculosis hospital), in Beckley (1950–1956); as Jewish chaplain at the Federal Reformatory for Women, at Alderson, W. Va. (1951–1954); as secretary of the B'nai B'rith Emergency Fund (1953–1956); and as a member of the Cemetery Committee of Congregation Beth El (1952–1956).

At the very end of July, 1956, Rabbi Abraham I. Shinedling left Beckley, and retired from the active rabbinate, settling in Albuquerque, N. Mex. Here he became a full-time member of the staff of the American Jewish Archives, affiliated with the Hebrew Union College-Jewish Institute of Religion, of Cincinnati (of which he had served as a part-time member of the staff from August 1, 1952, on), working in the field of American Jewish history under the direction of his colleague and classmate, Dr. Jacob R. Marcus, who is the Adolph S. Ochs Professor of American Jewish History at the Hebrew Union College. (Dr. Marcus himself is a long-time resident of West Virginia, having previously lived for more than ten years in Wheeling and Farmington, W. Va.)

From September, 1956, to August, 1957, Rabbi Abraham I. Shinedling served as part-time rabbi of the Los Alamos, N. Mex., Jewish Center, and from 1956 to 1959 he served also as a teacher of Hebrew in the two Albuquerque Jewish congregations. In July, 1958, he published, at Albuquerque, the *History of the Los Alamos Jewish Center*, and since he arrived at Albuquerque in August, 1956, he was engaged in the compilation and writing of his history of West Virginia Jewry, and in the writing of Memoirs on several members of his family, including his father, Moses Shinedling. While he was living in Beckley, he and Manuel Pickus wrote and published the *History of the Beckley Jewish Community* (Beckley, W. Va., 1955).

HELEN L. SHINEDLING. Mrs. Helen L. Shinedling, the wife of Abraham I. Shinedling, while in Beckley, was active in the work of the congregation, the Beckley Sisterhood, and the general community. From 1950 to 1956 she served as the organist of the congregation, and as a Religious School and Hebrew teacher. From 1951 to 1955 she was State Chairman of Religion of the W. V. F. T. S. She served as the local chairman of religion of the Sisterhood from 1950 to 1956. From 1954 to 1956 she was treasurer of the Beckley Branch of the League of Women Voters. From 1955 to 1956 she served as the Interfaith Chairman of the State Federation of Temple Sisterhoods.

DR. H. VIOLA SHLICKERMAN. Dr. H. Viola Shlickerman (born at Buffalo, N. Y., on March 7, 1892) settled in Beckley in April, 1945, as a dentist on the staff of Pinecrest Sanitarium, a State tuberculosis institution. She had served previously, from December, 1937, to April, 1945, as the acting assistant dental surgeon of the United States Public Health Service in the Federal Reformatory for Women at Alderson, W. Va. In 1914 she graduated from the University of Buffalo Dental Department. In March, 1959, she retired from her position as the dentist at Pinecrest Sanitarium, and moved to Hollywood, Fla.

Dr. H. Viola Shlickerman had always been active in the work of the Beckley Sisterhood, serving as its president from 1951 to 1952, and as its corresponding secretary from 1946 to 1948. She was a member of the Ethics Committee of the New River Dental Society, in West Virginia. One of her sons, Dr. Leo Sherman (formerly Shlickerman), served, in the 1950's, for a couple of years as a physician for one of the large coal companies in the Beckley area.

JACOB SILVERBERG. Jacob Silverberg, a brother-in-law of the three Pickus brothers of Beckley (Nathan, Louis, and James Pickus), was born in Warsaw, Poland, on October 10, 1898, and in 1921 he emigrated to the United States, settling directly in Beckley. After clerking as a salesman in clothing stores for five years, he opened up the Sample Shop, a ladies' ready-to-wear store, on Neville Street, near the corner of Heber Street, in 1926. He was still conducting this business in 1959.

In 1935–1936, Jacob Silverberg became a charter member of the Beckley Hebrew Association, and in 1939 he became a charter member also of the Beckley B'nai B'rith

Lodge. From 1948 to 1955 he served as a member of the congregational Board of Directors. [1]

DR. BERNARD E. SILVERMAN. Dr. Bernard E. Silverman (born in Kishinev, Russia, on July 4, 1902; died at Beckley, on July 13, 1959) was brought to the United States in 1904 or 1905 by his parents, who settled in Chicago. In 1939, he settled in Beckley, after having practised chiropody in Chicago from 1926 to 1939. He received his D.S.C. (Doctor of Surgical Chiropody) degree from the Illinois College of Chiropody in 1926. Until his death at Beckley in early July, 1959, he was noted as the only practising chiropodist in Beckley and in the whole of Raleigh County, as well as in the surrounding counties, and he practised his profession also in the nearby towns of Welch, Hinton, Williamson, Logan, and Mullens (all in West Virginia), one or two days each month.

Dr. Bernard E. Silverman was noted in Raleigh County as a chess player. In early 1957, he was invited by the *Raleigh Register* (Sunday edition) to conduct and write a weekly chess column, called "Royal Game." In 1941, he became a charter member of the Beckley B'nai B'rith Lodge, and served as its treasurer in 1955–1956.

FAYE R. SILVERMAN. Mrs. Faye Rosen Silverman, the wife of Dr. Bernard E. Silverman, has always been active in the work of the Beckley Sisterhood, serving as its president from 1941 to 1942, from 1944 to 1946, and from 1948 to 1949. She taught in the Religious School of the congregation from 1939 to 1943, and was active for years on the Board of Directors of the Raleigh County Chapter of the American Red Cross. She was co-chairman of the two State Sisterhood Conventions which were held in Beckley, in 1942 and in 1953.

DR. HOWARD A. SILVERMAN, son of the late Dr. Bernard E. Silverman (born in Chicago, on May 31, 1931), who lived in Beckley from 1939 to 1955, served from October, 1956, to October, 1958, as a physician with the United

---

[1] Jacob Silverberg died at Beckley in late May, 1961, and was buried in a Jewish cemetery in Charleston, W. Va.

States Air Force, being stationed in England. He then opened up a medical office in Allentown, Pa.

THOMAS SOPHER. Thomas Sopher (born at Baltimore, in May, 1891) moved to Mount Hope from Baltimore in 1923, working at first as a clerk and salesman in the store of his brother-in-law, Harry Abel. He later entered business for himself in Mount Hope. However, in 1942, he moved to Beckley, and, together with his two sons, Harold A. Sopher and Ira B. Sopher, he opened up the Best Furniture Store, on South Fayette Street. After his death in Beckley on April 8, 1949, this business was continued by his sons. In early 1959, Harold A. Sopher moved to Baltimore, Md.; his brother, Ira B. Sopher, continued to operate the Best Furniture Store in Beckley.

Thomas Sopher was a charter member of both the Beckley Hebrew Association (1935–1936) and of the Beckley Lodge of the B'nai B'rith (1939). His wife, BERTHA BERMAN SOPHER, was, from 1936 to 1937, president of the Beckley Sisterhood.

MILTON I. WATZMAN. Milton I. Watzman (born in Martins Ferry, Ohio, on April 3, 1917) is a nephew of Mrs. Nathan (Rose C.) Matz and of Mrs. Marc L. (Dora C.) Front, of Beckley. Milton Watzman attended West Virginia University, at Morgantown, and came to Beckley from Wheeling in February, 1938; here, for several years (1938–1942), he conducted a cigar stand at the President Hotel, in Beckley, which was leased and operated by his uncle, Nathan Matz. He left Beckley in 1942 to go with the civilian program at Patterson Field, in Dayton, Ohio, and then on to the Panama Canal Zone. He then returned to the United States, and enlisted in the United States Army, in December, 1943. Having served with the Eighty-Third Division through five campaigns in Europe, he was honorably discharged from the United States Army in 1945.

Then Milton Watzman, together with his brother, Sanford Watzman, in August, 1946, went to Wellsburg, W. Va., where they opened up a men's clothing store, known as Watzman's, at 707–709 Charles Street. In June, 1946, he married, and made his home in Wellsburg, but in 1959,

although engaged in the same business in Wellsburg, he
was living in nearby Steubenville, Ohio, to which city he
had moved in 1954.

ISADORE R. WEIN. Isadore R. Wein has been the most outstanding Jewish religious, communal, civic, and public
figure whom the Beckley Jewish community has ever
produced. He was born in Harrison, New Jersey, in 1914,
and in 1940 he settled in Beckley, after being graduated
as a registered pharmacist. Previously, he had worked as a
pharmacist and conducted a pharmacy for several years
in Irvington, N. J., near Newark. He married Jeanette
Abrams, the daughter of Samuel I. Abrams, of Beckley,
and several years later, in 1940, he moved to Beckley,
where he entered the Modern Furniture Store business
with his father-in-law; in 1944, upon the latter's retirement,
Isadore R. Wein, together with his brother-in-law, A. David
Abrams, took over this business, as well as its three branches
in nearby Sophia, Mount Hope, and Oak Hill.

Isadore R. Wein saw service in the United States Navy
for fifteen months in the Second World War; he was a
Rate Specialist A, and served in the Great Lakes Naval
Training Station and vicinity, near Chicago.

From 1945 to 1946, and again from 1951 to 1957, Isadore
R. Wein served as president (Chairman of the Board of
Directors) of Beth El Congregation, being re-elected for
another year in May, 1957. He was also secretary-treasurer
of the congregation from 1948 to 1957, and a member of its
Board of Directors during this same period (1948–1958).
He assisted in the conducting of the religious services and
in the Bar Mitzvahing of boys in the Temple whenever
the congregation was without a rabbi. From 1949 to 1950,
he was president of Beckley Lodge, No. 1360, B'nai B'rith;
in the 1940's and 1950's he was active in the raising of
funds for the benefit of the United Jewish Appeal in Beckley.
From 1953 on he served as chairman of the B'nai B'rith
Emergency Fund, as well as a trustee of this Fund. From
May, 1954, on, he served as a member of the Congregation
Beth El Cemetery Committee, which set up the new cemetery (the Jewish Section) in Sunset Memorial Cemetery,
north of Beckley, on Harper Road; he helped to dedicate

this Jewish Section in May, 1954. Several times, in the absence of a rabbi in Congregation Beth El, he conducted services and preached on the High Holy Days for the congregation. In September, 1958, thus, due to the illness of Rabbi Abraham A. Kertes, Isadore R. Wein conducted the High Holy Day services and preached the sermons in Temple Beth El.

In 1960, Isadore R. Wein was still serving as the Chairman of the Board of Directors (president) of Congregation Beth El, having been re-elected both in 1958 and in 1959. In November, 1959, upon the reorganization of Beckley Lodge, No. 1360, B'nai B'rith, he was again elected its president, for the year 1959–1960.

In the general community, Isadore R. Wein served for a number of years as the president and a director of the Raleigh County Cancer Society. From 1948 to 1956, he was chairman of the Civitans' Dental Health Committee. He served as vice president of the Beckley Civitans Club from 1950 to 1951 and from 1954 to 1956; in April, 1956, he was elected to a one-year term as its president. From 1947 to 1951 and again from 1953 to 1954 he was a member of its Board of Directors. In 1959–1960, Isadore R. Wein served as the lieutenant governor of the Civitans Clubs, for the District of West Virginia. His biography is included in *Who's Who in World Jewry* (1955).

For a number of years he was a teacher in the congregational Religious School. He is noted as a contributor to, and a fosterer of, all worthwhile philanthropies and institutions.

On Sunday, September 2, 1962, Isadore R. Wein's eldest son, Alan J. Wein, was married to Lynne Sheila Abrams, of Newark, N. J., at Temple Beth El, with Rabbi Frank N. Sundheim, of Huntington, as the officiant. Alan J. Wein was graduated, in June, 1962, from Princeton University, in Princeton, N. J., and thereafter entered the University of Pennsylvania, in Philadelphia, as a medical student, in its Medical School.

JEANETTE ABRAMS WEIN. Mrs. Jeanette Abrams Wein, the wife of Isadore R. Wein, became a charter member of the Beckley Hadassah in 1948.

## BELINGTON

Belington is a shipping city in northern West Virginia, located eight miles north northwest of Elkins, in Barbour County. It is in a coal mining and forest area. Belington, incorporated in 1905, had a population of 1,517 in 1957. In 1950, according to the United States Census, it had a total general population of 1,699. A great deal of farming is also carried on in the region.

Early records of Jewish residents in Belington are few and far between. In 1901 to 1902 D. K. Walker, of Belington (presumably a non-Jew), was listed in the *AJYB* as a member of the Jewish Publication Society of America. There were no Jewish residents in Belington in 1957.

Dr. Jacob Lazarus, a Baltimore dentist, and a former resident of Belington, is the source for much of the data herewith presented on Belington. His parents, Alex [Alexander] and Celia Klein Lazarus, moved to Belington in 1901. The Lazarus family was the only Jewish family in Belington. At that time there were four children in the Lazarus family, and three more children were born to Alex and Celia Klein Lazarus in Belington; thus Jacob Lazarus had four brothers and two sisters, all of whom moved away to other cities from Belington after they grew up. Alex Lazarus conducted a business in Belington for 31 years, and died in Belington in 1932; he was brought to Baltimore for burial. Celia Klein Lazarus died in Belington in 1938. The Lazarus family took an active part in the civic and general affairs of the city; several members of this family were still residing in nearby towns in 1957.

Mrs. Sara Schwartz [Simon] Schuchat, formerly of Marlinton, W. Va., is authority for the following two biographical items on former Jewish residents of Belington:

"Ephriam Lazarus, a first cousin of Mrs. Sara Schwartz [Simon] Schuchat, of Marlinton, and a son of Alex Lazarus, of Belington, taught high school in Belington for a number of years."

"Celia Klein, a maternal aunt of Mrs. Sara Schwartz [Simon] Schuchat, of Marlinton, married Alex Lazarus, of Belington. Celia Klein Lazarus and Alex Lazarus, of Belington, had two daughters and four sons. Louis Lazarus later moved to Wheeling; Morris [Lazarus] moved to Wheeling, and died there several years ago; Jack [Jacob] Lazarus became a dentist, and moved to Baltimore. Ephriam Lazarus taught high school for many years in Belington, and then moved to Baltimore. The two Lazarus girls later married, and settled in Baltimore."

## BENWOOD

Benwood is a city in Marshall County, in northern West Virginia, situated on the Ohio River, three miles south of Wheeling. It is in the Northern Panhandle of West Virginia. It was chartered in 1853. Benwood is noted for its steel industries (the manufacturing of steel), and it has coal mining. In 1950, according to the United States Census, it had a general population of 3,485. On its official stationery Benwood advertises itself as "the iron and steel center of West Virginia."

There were no Jewish residents in Benwood in 1958. Only two Jewish families ever lived in Benwood, according to the records. These were the Lando family and the Moidel family, both of them engaged in the clothing business. Albert Moidel, a resident of Wheeling in 1958, and Morris H. Lando, who in 1958 lived in Bellaire, Ohio, where he was engaged in the business of janitorial supplies (the Morlan Chemical Company, together with his brother, Louis Lando), were members of these two above-mentioned families.

MORRIS H. LANDO (born in Bellaire, Ohio, on December 14, 1897) was the son of Charles and Shina Esther Lando. His parents, who passed away (presumably in Benwood) in previous years, had seven sons and two daughters, all of whom at one time lived in Benwood. Two of the Lando sons are now deceased. The two Jewish families of Benwood (the Moidel and Lando families) had social relations with the nearby Jewish community of Wheeling.

## BERKELEY SPRINGS (BATH)

Berkeley Springs is a town and a health resort, the county seat of Morgan County, in northeastern West Virginia, near the Potomac River, 18 miles northwest of Martinsburg. Its legal name is Bath. It was chartered in 1776. In 1957, Berkeley Springs had a total general population of 1,145. There were, seemingly, no Jews at all resident in the town in 1957.

However, in 1927, it was reported that there were ten or fewer Jews living in Berkeley Springs, or Bath, and the same number, without any specific details, was again reported in 1937.

It is of interest that the famous Baltimore rabbi, Dr. Benjamin Szold (1829–1902), rabbi of Oheb Shalom Congregation, of Baltimore, and father of Henrietta Szold, died at Berkeley Springs, on July 31, 1902, to which place he had, presumably, gone for a rest, or for health reasons.

*See also* under Bath.

## BETHANY

Bethany is a town in Brooke County, in the Northern Panhandle of West Virginia, situated about 12 miles north northeast of Wheeling, and near the Pennsylvania State line. In 1957, it was reported to have a general population of only 410 persons, although the United States Census of 1950 listed it as having a population of 1,063. No Jewish residents were living in Bethany in 1957, nor, so far as could be ascertained, had any Jews ever lived in the town throughout the entire course of its history.

Bethany is the seat of Bethany College, a coeducational institution chartered (founded) in 1840, and opened by Alexander Campbell in 1841. Bethany College is the oldest college in the entire State of West Virginia. Its chartering in 1840 took place under the Old Dominion (Virginia). Alexander Campbell was its founder and the first president of the College; its second president was William Kimbrough Pendleton. Perry Epler Gresham, the kindly source of much of the information about Bethany and Bethany College, became president of the College on October 23, 1953.

Perry Epler Gresham furnished the following succinct picture of Bethany College, of its Jewish students, and of the visits paid to it by rabbis in the years from 1945 to 1955, under the auspices of the Jewish Chautauqua Society, of Cincinnati and, later, of New York:

"The early leadership of the religious communion known as the Disciples of Christ, the Christian Church, or the Church of Christ, is identical with that of Bethany College. Alexander Campbell was the principal influence in both, who was educated in the universities of Scotland and in the University of Virginia.

"The college is closely affiliated with the Disciples of Christ, or Alexander Campbell's movement, which has now about 2,000,000 adult communicants. The broad pattern of non-sectarian Christian education prevailing at Bethany College was set by the broad undenominational emphasis of Alexander Campbell's faith. The first trustees of Bethany College had the strong conviction that the spirit of the institution should be totally non-sectarian, and they directed 'that in the religious instruction of the youths of this college, no sectarian or denominational doctrines are to be imparted.'

"It is a liberal arts college, devoted to the arts and science. Enrollment is limited to about 600 students, co-educational. Bethany College is situated in the Northern Panhandle of West Virginia, in Buffalo Valley, in the western foothills of the Alleghenies, three miles from the Pennsylvania border, seven miles from the Ohio border, and 35 miles north of the Mason and Dixon line, northeast of Wheeling."

On July 12, 1956, in a letter to me, the president, Dr. Perry Epler Gresham, reported:

". . . there were 17 Jewish students in our student body for the academic year 1955-1956. Most of them came from the areas of New York City and northern New Jersey. We do not have at the present time any faculty members who are of the Jewish faith. We always have a Rabbi join our Christian Living Emphasis Week programs. The [Jewish] students attend services at nearby synagogues."

Visits to Bethany College under the auspices of the Jewish Chautauqua Society were paid as follows:

1945: Rabbi Samuel M. Gup (deceased; then of Columbus, Ohio)
1946: Rabbi Charles B. Lesser (then of Wheeling)
1947: Rabbi Louis J. Cashdan (then of Charleston)
1948: Rabbi Malcolm H. Stern (of Norfolk, Va.)
1950: Rabbi Harold L. Gelfman (then of Bluefield)
1954: Rabbi Burton Levinson (then of Pittsburgh)
1955: Rabbi Harold Silver (of Pittsburgh)

In March, 1958, in a list of smaller colleges in the United States, prepared by the U. A. H. C., the following data were given for Bethany College, for the academic year 1957–1958:

"Bethany College, in Bethany, W. Va. Rural. Co-educational. Private control. General enrollment, about 500. Jewish students, about 50. Jewish facilities."

## BLUEFIELD

### GENERAL

Bluefield is a city in Mercer County, in southern West Virginia, on the southern boundary of the State, in the Blue Ridge (Appalachian) Mountains. It is one of the main business centers of West Virginia (about 12 miles distant from the nearest coal fields), and in its vicinity there are coal, iron, silica, and limestone mines. It is situated near one of the very large coal fields of West Virginia. The city, which has an elevation of 2,600 feet above sea level, has also several lumber mills, and manufactures beverages, bedding, and mine equipment.

Bluefield, settled in the year 1777, is the shipping point for the Pocahontas, Va., coal field, which contributed essentially to the growth of the city. It is located on the main line of the Norfolk & Western Railroad running between Norfolk, Va., and Cincinnati and Columbus, Ohio. In 1940, its population was listed as 20,641. The United States Census for 1950 gave Bluefield a general population of 21,506. Bluefield, W. Va., is contiguous to, and continuous with, Bluefield, Va., with its population of about 3,900 persons. According to the *Encyclopaedia Britannica*, "in 1883, when the first shipment of the famous 'smokeless' coal was made, the site of the city was covered with the bluegrass fields which gave it its name." The locally owned Consolidated Bus Lines, which serve a number of the other cities of the State as well, and which are owned by Jack and Paul Craft, father and son, have painted on each of their busses the legend: "Serving West Virginia's Billion-Dollar Coal Fields."

Bluefield is the site of Bluefield State College, formerly a Negro (but now a fully integrated) co-educational State college, organized (founded) in 1895. Bluefield College, a junior college belonging to the Baptist denomination, is situated right across the Virginia line in Bluefield, Va. Bluefield, W. Va., is ten miles southwest of Princeton, and 51 miles due south of Beckley. The city was incorporated in 1889, and in 1921 it adopted a city manager form of government.

The nearby and contiguous city of Bluefield, Va., has only two or three Jewish families (1959).

### GENERAL POPULATION OF BLUEFIELD IN PREVIOUS YEARS

| 1920 | 1930 | 1940 | 1950 | 1956 |
|------|------|------|------|------|
| 15,282 | 19,339 | 20,641 | 21,506 (according to other figures, 25,718 in 1950) | 22,000 |

### THE BLUEFIELD JEWISH COMMUNITY AND CONGREGATION

Brief excerpts referring to the Bluefield Jewish community and to the population of the city of Bluefield generally, as found in the various year books of the Jewish Publication Society of America, as well as in other early sources, present the following data:

### 1906–1907

A contribution was made in 1906–1907 by the Jewish community or by Jewish individuals in Bluefield to the Fund Collected for the Relief of the Sufferers by the Russian Outrages of October to November, 1905.

### 1907–1908

In 1907–1908 there was a B'nai B'rith Lodge in Bluefield, called Bluefield Lodge No. 617, of which I. Aaron was the secretary.

Directory of Jewish Local Organizations in the United States (*AJYB*, 5668 A.M. [1907–1908], pp. 424–425):

*Bluefield*: Ahavas Sholem Congregation, [later spelled always as Ahavath Sholom Congregation]
    Cantor: Kalman Slifkin
    Services held on Sabbath and holidays.
    At this time there was a B'nai B'rith Lodge, Bluefield Lodge, No. 617, whose secretary was I. Aaron.

## 1916–1917

In 1916–1917, the Jewish population of Bluefield was 152.

## 1917

152 Jews in Bluefield in 1917

## 1919–1922

In the years between 1919 and 1922, Bluefield had a Jewish population of 152. [The figure is slightly inaccurate, being merely repeated from the year 1916–1917.] Its local organization was Congregation Ahavath Sholom, on Scott Street, organized in 1905. Rabbi Kalman Slifkin, whose address was listed as 119 Giles Street, [conducted] Hebrew services. There was a religious school in the congregation, with 1 teacher and 27 pupils.

## 1927

1 congregation, with 220 Jews

## 1936

Census of Religious Bodies, 1936
Bluefield (by county: Mercer) is listed as having 210 Jews.

## 1936–1937

In 1936–1937, the Rae Matz School of Dancing flourished in Bluefield.

## 1937

1 congregation, with 210 Jews (estimated)

## 1941–1942

Bluefield-Princeton Jewish Charities, including [the rest of] Mercer County. Organized in 1939. Max Matz, president; Rabbi Julius Kravetz, secretary.

Rabbi Julius Kravetz served in this position until early 1943, when he left the city to become a chaplain in the United States Army in the Second World War.

## 1943–1944

In 1943–1944, Ezra Gilbert was a member of the American Jewish Committee, of New York, representing the Bluefield-Princeton Jewish Welfare Fund.

## 1948

300 the estimated Jewish population of Bluefield

## 1950

300 the estimated Jewish population
Bluefield city: 21,506 population (1950 United States Census)

## 1954

Estimated Jewish population, 300

## 1954–1955

310 Jews

## 1956–1957

Estimated Jewish population, 300 (including Princeton, W. Va.) (in 1956)

## 1959

300 Jews
    (according to the *AJYB* for 1960, Volume 61, page 8, estimated Jewish population)

## POCAHONTAS, VIRGINIA

(*AJYB*, 1903–1904 [5664 A.M.], page 98)

Tobias H. Schwartz was rabbi in [nearby] Pocahontas, Va. In the above *AJYB*, on the same page, in an article entitled:

"Biographical Sketches of Rabbis and Cantors Officiating in the United States":

TOBIAS H. SCHWARTZ. Minister of Congregation Adath Jeshu-
run, Newport News, Va. Born in 1863, at Kovno, Russia
[Lithuania]. Son of Jacob Schwartz. Educated at Kovno
and Vilna. Rabbinical diploma conferred by Rabbi Isaac
Elchanan Spector, at Kovno. Held positions in Kibarten,
Poland, and Pocahontas, Va. [an Orthodox congregation].
Address: 232 28th [St.], Newport News, Va.

(*AJYB*, 1903–1904 [5664 A.M.], page 84)
POCAHONTAS, VA.

E. M. Mosinter is mentioned as the former rabbi at
Pocahontas, Va.

From data in a list entitled "Biographical Sketches of
Rabbis and Cantors Officiating in the United States," in the
*AJYB*, as above:

E. M. MOSINTER. Rabbi of Congregation Chased Shel Emeth,
Springfield, Ohio. Born in Russia in 1865. Son of Ralph
Mosinter. Educated in Kovno [Lithuania]. Rabbinical
diploma conferred by Rabbi M. Ziew, and Rabbi L. S.
Schapiere. Was rabbi at Pocahontas, Va., and Marietta,
Ohio. Address: 137 East Main Street, Springfield, Ohio.[1]

In 1916–1917, Pocahontas had a Jewish population of 81
persons.

### CONGREGATION AHAVATH SHOLOM

Ahavath Sholom Congregation, of Bluefield-Princeton, W.
Va., in November, 1957, celebrated the fiftieth anniversary of

---

[1] Apparently, Rabbi E. M. Mosinter (possibly a relation of the present-day Masinter
families of Huntington, W. Va.) was not a member of the C. C. A. R.; he was an
Orthodox rabbi, in all likelihood, as the congregations in Pocahontas, Va., and
Marietta, Ohio, were always Orthodox. The Pocahontas congregation has by now
(1959) totally disappeared; the Marietta, Ohio, congregation was still in existence
in 1959, but has had no rabbi for many years.

its founding. It is believed to have been founded in the year 1907. This is in accordance with certain records of the congregation and of the local newspapers, which appear to convey the idea that the Bluefield congregation was founded in 1907. However, the best and most accredited date for the actual founding or organizing of the congregation is the year 1904, rather than 1907, and if this is the case, the congregation simply overlooked the actual, proper fiftieth anniversary, or passed it by through inadvertence, and made up for this error by means of the jubilee observance about two or three years later. Somewhere in the congregational records there is this brief notation:

"On August 20, 1905, the members of the new Jewish congregation [Ahavath Sholom] arranged to purchase a church building from the Presbyterians, the Scott Street church, which the Presbyterians were abandoning . . . . They moved in immediately."

Thus, since its organization in 1904–1905, Congregation Ahavath Sholom has used, or had, or worshipped in, the following four buildings:

   *1.* The Scott Street "Shul" (as it was called [Synagogue])

   *2.* The Masonic Temple on Federal Street (used for the High Holy Day services in several years)

   *3.* The Consolidated Bus Terminal building, running through from Federal to Bland Streets, about two blocks south of Princeton Avenue and the Norfolk & Western Railroad tracks. The congregation used the second floor of this bus terminal as its sanctuary, and the Bluefield Sisterhood and the B'nai B'rith Lodge as their meeting rooms, and also as the Sunday School headquarters, for several years, between the time when the Scott Street "Shul" was sold (1941), and the year 1948 (September), when the Social Hall and the Religious School sections of the new Albemarle Street Temple (at 632 Albemarle Street) were ready for occupancy, and the congregation moved in, even before the main sanctuary had been completed. [This latter took place in April or May, 1949.]

[In late 1958, the old Consolidated Bus Terminal building, whose second storey was thus used as a "Temple" by Ahavath

Sholom Congregation, for seven years, from 1941 to 1948, before the new Albemarle Street Temple was completed in 1948–1949, was torn down, and was replaced by a modern J. C. Penney store.]

4. The new, modern red-brick synagogue (Temple) at 632 Albemarle Street, in the southern residential section of the city, partly completed in September, 1948, and fully completed in April or May, 1949.

Thus, according to the best, definitive records in the possession of the congregation, the congregation was actually founded and organized in 1904; in August, 1905, after it had been in existence without any place of meeting for about a year (except, possibly, for the private homes of members), the members of the new congregation bought the Scott Street church from the Presbyterians of the city, fitted it out and fixed it up as a synagogue, and moved in that same month. However, it is not known where the congregation worshipped during the year which elapsed between the time of its organization and August, 1905, when it moved into the Scott Street church building; probably services were held in the homes of individual members, and these services were, undoubtedly, strictly Orthodox in nature.

Nonetheless, despite the discrepancy in the dates of the organizing or founding of the congregation, the Bluefield Congregation celebrated its fiftieth anniversary on Friday to Sunday, November 8 to 10, 1957, with a commemorative religious service conducted by one of its former rabbis, Julius Kravetz (on Friday night, November 8, 1957), and with an anniversary banquet (on Sunday, November 10, 1957), with Rabbi Alexander Alan Steinbach, of Brooklyn, N. Y., another former rabbi, as guest speaker, at the West Virginian Hotel. Many non-Jews of Bluefield and of Princeton were invited to the anniversary celebration as the guests of the congregation.

Co-chairmen of the 50th Anniversary Committee were Fred Gilbert, Alfred E. Land, and Meyer J. Spiro. Sidney J. Kwass was the historian of the 50th Anniversary Committee; below are presented his reports on the history of the Bluefield-Princeton Congregation Ahavath Sholom.

The records of the congregation indicate further: "In 1941, after thirty-six years of continuous use, the Scott Street Synagogue, 'the little white Shule on the hill,' was sold, and from then on the congregation held services in the B'nai B'rith quarters, partly above the Consolidated Bus Terminal, on Federal-Bland Streets, from 1941 to 1948. In September, 1948, the new Temple building on Albemarle Street was ready for services and occupancy."

A notation in the congregational records indicates that the Scott Street Synagogue was in use in 1935–1936. It was repaired and improved several times between the time of its purchase in 1905 and the time when it was sold, in 1941.

A further congregational record contains the following data:

"The Scott Street Synagogue was sold, as being too small for the congregation, in the year 1941, and for seven years thereafter the congregation worshipped in an apartment [flat] made into a synagogue and Sunday School rooms and B'nai B'rith Lodge headquarters above the Consolidated Bus Terminal in Bland Street, above [south of] Princeton Avenue, until 1948, when the new synagogue of the congregation, located at 632 Albemarle Street, was finished, and was first used for religious worship at the high holy days of 1948. [From 1941 through 1947, for the most part, the High Holy Day services were held in the Masonic Temple, on the third floor of its headquarters in the business section of the city, on Federal Street, about half a block south of Princeton Avenue.]

"Conductors of the Orthodox services during these years were Louis Diamond and Benjamin Matz. [Benjamin Bernhard Matz, the father of Nathan Matz, of Beckley, died at Bluefield on December 19, 1951.] The conductor of the Conservative high holy day services in those years was Philip Platnick. Conductors of the Reform services on the high holy days in those years [from 1941 to 1948 and beyond] were Rabbi Julius Kravetz, the several student rabbis of the congregation, Rabbi Abraham I. Shinedling, Rabbi Harold L. Gelfman, and Rabbi Herbert J. Wilner. On the high holy days of each of these years [from 1941 and before that to 1948 and beyond] the Orthodox services were the earliest services, both in the evening and in the morning, followed by the Conservative services [both these services were without sermons], and, finally, the Reform services concluded the religious observance on each occasion, replete with sermons. On the second day of Rosh Hashanah, each year, there was no Reform service, but only an Orthodox and a Conservative service."

The cornerstone for the new Albemarle Street Temple was laid in November, 1947. Rabbi Abraham I. Shinedling, then the new rabbi of the Congregation, Isadore Cohen, William P. Gottlieb, treasurer of the congregation and chairman of the Building Committee, and Nathan Platnick, president of the congregation, participated in the program. The dedication of the completely finished new Temple Ahavath Sholom was held on Friday night, May 5, 1949, with Isadore Cohen chairman of the occasion, and Rabbi Ariel L. Goldburg, of Richmond, Va. (formerly of the Charleston Reform synagogue), as the principal speaker. The religious services and the invocations were read and presented by Rabbi Abraham I. Shinedling.

The following account of Congregation Ahavath Sholom, of Bluefield, and of its early history and founding, is excerpted from the Semi-Centennial Anniversary edition of the *Bluefield Sunset-News* and *Daily Telegraph*, in 1939:

"The Bluefield Congregation Ahavath Sholom (Love of Peace) was founded in 1904, by a group of ten prominent Bluefield Jews: Henry Rodgin, Samuel Turk, Solomon Greenspon, Samuel Matz, Morris Rosenberg, I. Aaron, Jacob Baker, Barney M. Cohen, Saul Turk, and Louis Kaufman. At first the congregation worshipped in the hall of the Pocahontas Fuel Company building. [The Pocahontas Fuel Company building was located at the corner of Princeton Avenue and Scott Street.] On August 20, 1905, the Jews of Bluefield arranged to purchase from the Presbyterian Church of Bluefield, which had built its own building, in South Bluefield, the frame building on Scott Street which the Presbyterians had thitherto been using as a house of worship. The Jewish congregation remodeled the building as a synagogue. [The new church building of the Presbyterian Congregation is located at the southeast corner of Washington and Albemarle Streets.]

"The first rabbi of the congregation was the Reverend M. Levinson. Then came Kalman Slifkin, who as late as 1939 was serving as assistant rabbi."

Subsequent rabbis of the Bluefield congregation were:

Alexander Alan Steinbach, later of Brooklyn, N. Y.

Nathan A. Perilman, later associate rabbi of Temple Emanu-El, in New York.

Colman A. Zwitman (deceased), who later served as rabbi in Miami, Fla.

Julius Kravetz, who served as its rabbi from 1936 to 1943, when he went into the chaplaincy service in the United States Army in the Second World War, and did not return to Bluefield at the end of the War.

Alfred [A.] Stanley Dreyfus, then a student at the Hebrew Union College, in Cincinnati, who served from 1943 to 1944, and again from 1946 to 1947.

Sanford E. Rosen (1944–1945), part-time student rabbi.

Jerome W. Grollman (1945–1946), part-time student rabbi.

Abraham I. Shinedling, who served from 1947 to 1950, and later became rabbi of the Beckley Congregation Beth El (1950–1956).

Harold L. Gelfman, who served from 1950 to 1952.

Herbert J. Wilner, who served from 1952 to August, 1957.

Amos Schauss, who began his service with the congregation in the fall of 1957, and was still the incumbent in August, 1959.

[Biographical data about all the above and other (student) rabbis are presented below.]

In the above-mentioned Semi-Centennial Anniversary year of the city of Bluefield (which was founded and incorporated as a city in 1889), i. e., in 1939, the Bluefield Congregation had 65 member families. Rabbi Julius Kravetz and other rabbis, including some of the student rabbis, served also the North Fork [North Fork-Keystone] and the Welch (Congregation Emanuel) congregations in West Virginia for some years, but beginning with 1943 the Welch congregation secured its own part-time student or graduate rabbi from the Hebrew Union College, in Cincinnati.

Rabbi Herbert J. Wilner, who did considerable research in the congregational records in 1957 in preparation for the celebration of the fiftieth anniversary of the founding of the congregation, which was held in Bluefield in November, 1957, on the above-given dates (but which he did not witness, since before November, 1957, he had left Bluefield to become rabbi of Congregation Temple Shalom, in Levittown, Pa.), arrived at the following conclusions, and sent me the following memorandum in the early spring of 1957:

The Bluefield Congregation Ahavath Sholom was founded in the year 1904, and not in the year 1907.

However, the year 1907 marks the date of the first acquisition of a permanent sanctuary, in accordance with the following:

'On June 17, 1907, a deed was made for the sale of the Presbyterian Church Building [on Scott Street, "on the hill"] to the trustees of the Jewish congregation. (Morris Rosenber*ry* [sic. This is indubitably an error and a misprint for Morris Rosenberg], Saul [not the same as Sol, or Solomon] Greenspon, Samuel Matz), $1,000 cash, $2,800 total. This was recorded on July 10, 1907, in the Deed Book 63, page 129 (Princeton, [West Virginia,] M. W. Sterne and wife). Sold for $4,500 in 1941.'[1]

Work on the new (632 Albemarle Street) synagogue of Congregation Ahavath Sholom was not begun until six years after the sale of the old Scott Street Synagogue, i. e., in early 1947. The work of building was hampered and delayed by the difficulty of obtaining needed steel, in that early post-Second World War period. The cornerstone [as mentioned above] was laid in November, 1947, and the completed synagogue was dedicated in May, 1949 [May 5, 1949], with Rabbi Ariel L. Goldburg, of Beth Ahabah Congregation, Richmond, Va., giving the consecration sermon. Rabbi Abraham I. Shinedling (Hebrew Union College, 1920) was rabbi of the congregation at the time (1947–1950), and he read the religious services at the consecration ceremony, and introduced the principal speaker. Isadore Cohen, also, who was active in the erection of the new synagogue, and was on the dedication committee, also participated in the consecration program. (Thus far the memorandum of Rabbi Herbert J. Wilner, in 1957.)

---

[1] However, it has been indicated above, more than once, that it was in August, 1905, that the Scott Street church building was purchased and moved into by the congregation, and not in 1907. The year 1907 indicates merely the belated presentation or handing over of the deed to the Jewish congregation.

THE CHARTER MEMBERS OF THE
BLUEFIELD CONGREGATION

A corrected, or at least a different, list of the charter members
(nine in number) of the Bluefield Congregation Ahavath Sholom,
on Scott Street, dating perhaps from the year 1905, is as follows:

I. AARON. I. Aaron came to Bluefield in the 1890's. He was
the father of Mrs. Sarah (Abraham N.) Schlossberg. [His
full first name is never found in the congregational records.
It was, perhaps, Isaac.]

JACOB BAKER. Jacob Baker came to Bluefield in the early
1890's. In later years, the business known as Baker's Furs
was established in the city.

SIMON BAKER. Simon Baker, a brother of Jacob Baker, also
came to Bluefield in the early 1890's.

BARNEY M. COHEN. Barney M. Cohen, the elder brother of
Isadore Cohen, came to Bluefield in the middle 1880's.
[Isadore Cohen settled in Bluefield in 1905, apparently
just a few months too late to become or be a charter member
of the congregation.]

ISAAC L. COHEN. Isaac L. Cohen came to Bluefield in the early
1890's.

SAUL GREENSPON. Saul Greenspon arrived in Bluefield in the
1890's.

SOLOMON GREENSPON. Solomon Greenspon, who later became
the father-in-law of Isadore Cohen, came to Bluefield in
the middle 1880's. [It is presumed that Saul and Solomon
Greenspon were brothers, or cousins.]

LOUIS KAUFMAN. Louis Kaufman came to Bluefield in the
1890's.

HENRY RODGIN. Henry Rodgin came to Bluefield in the early
1890's. Later he became the husband of Anna Grollman
Rodgin and the father of Dr. Joseph I. [Jay] Rodgin.[1]

---

[1] It will be observed that not mentioned in the above list, but given in the above-
presented newspaper account, as of the year 1904, as founders and thus presumably
as charter members of the congregation, are the following four men: Samuel Turk,
Samuel Matz, Morris Rosenberg, and Saul Turk.
It is most probable that all sixteen of these men, those mentioned in both lists, were

## "Old Timers" of the Bluefield Community

In late 1958, Isaac L. ("Ike") Diamond, an active member of the Bluefield congregation and community, after research in the congregational records of that city, and after consultation with the "old timers" still resident in the community, prepared the following list of

### "Bluefield Old Timers"[1]

S. Aaron (it should be I. Aaron)
S. Catzen
Ben F. Baker
Jacob Baker
Simon Baker
Barney M. Cohen
Harry Cohen
Ike L. [Isaac] Cohen
Isadore Cohen
Philip Cohen
Sam [Samuel] Cohen
Rabbi Simon Cohen
Charles Diamond
Louis Diamond [father of Isaac L. Diamond]
Morris Diamond
J. Goldman
A. Greenspon

Isaac Greenspon
Solomon Greenspon
Sol [Solomon] Hyman
Louis Kaufman
Morris Lisagor
Samuel Matz
Henry Rodgin
Morris Rosenberg
Morris Sameth
Rabbi Kalman Slifkin
Louis Snurman
Nathan Sohn
Sam Story
Samuel Tuch [should be Turk]
Saul Tuch [should be Turk]
Harry Weinberg

The above-mentioned nine men are declared to have founded the congregation several months before the Scott Street "Shul"

---

the charter members and founders of Congregation Ahavath Sholom, since ten men would have been rather a small number of charter members or founders of any organization, especially of a synagogue or congregation of that size. Both lists of charter members are, therefore, to be regarded as incomplete, and as supplementary the one to the other.

[1] Many of these names do not appear in any of the preceding or following lists of Bluefield residents or congregational or organizational members.

of Ahavath Sholom Congregation was purchased. This original "Scott Street Shul," as it was often called, was, as above mentioned, previously a Presbyterian church, a small, unimpressive, frame structure, and the above charter members encompassed the purchase of it in 1905, as described above. In 1957, this Scott Street "Shul" was still standing, and was still in use as a church, at the top of the Scott Street Hill, surmounting a quite steep and long flight of stairs, having been sold to a Negro congregation as a church building seven years before the new synagogue building of Ahavath Sholom Congregation, at 632 Albemarle Street, was occupied for the first time in September, 1948.

The following account, taken in its entirety from the *Bluefield Sunset News* of May 5, 1949, as written by Frank Green, a reporter, presents the story of the dedication ceremony of the new Albemarle Street Temple [Synagogue] of the congregation, as well as some of the anterior history of the congregation:

[All bracketed insertions are by Abraham I. Shinedling.]

New Temple Completed. The new Temple Ahavath Sholom, on Albemarle Street, will be dedicated tonight in ceremonies conducted by Rabbi Abraham Shinedling. The structure was begun in 1946 [1947].

TEMPLE AHAVATH SHOLOM DEDICATION
RITES TONIGHT

New Structure is the Result of Many Years of Hard Work

By Frank Green

The new Temple Ahavath Sholom on Albemarle Street will be dedicated tonight in a simple service at eight o'clock [Friday night, May 5, 1949].

Rabbi Abraham Shinedling will conduct the rites, which will include a program of music and a dedication sermon by Dr. Ariel L. Goldburg, Rabbi of Congregation Beth Ahabah in Richmond.

William P. Gottlieb, chairman of the building committee, will present the keys of the Temple to Nathan Platnick, president of the Bluefield-Princeton congregation.

Following the lighting of the perpetual lamp by Mrs. Joseph [Ethel J.] Tomchin [then president of the Bluefield Temple Sisterhood], and the invocation by Rabbi Shinedling, Henry Fortune, Bluefield baritone, will sing 'Psalm 23,' accompanied by Mrs. Lewis [Sarah] Reiland at the organ.

Rabbi Shinedling will then conduct the [Sabbath] evening service, which will be followed by greetings from the Union of American Hebrew Congregations, brought by Sidney Kleeman, president of the Virginia Street Temple in Charleston.

Dr. Goldburg's dedication sermon will be next, after which another solo, 'My Covenant,' will be sung by Henry Fortune.

The concluding service will be conducted by Rabbi Shinedling, with Dr. Goldburg asking the benediction.

Isadore Cohen, the brother of one of the founders of the congregation [Barney M. Cohen], and Harry Kammer [a former vice president of the congregation] headed the committee in charge of arrangements for the program.

Headed by [William P.] Gottlieb, the building committee is made up of Julius Land, George Frehling, Max Turk, Dr. William Greenspon, Jerome Katz, Mrs. Edna Platnick [Edna E. Platnick, wife of the president, Nathan Platnick], Mrs. Joseph [Ethel J.] Tomchin, Mrs. Esther [Max] Auerbach, Mrs. Henry [Anna G.] Rodgin, Jack [I. Jacob] Blank, Arthur Weiss, and Sam [Samuel] Slifkin [a son of the early rabbi of the congregation, the Reverend Kalman Slifkin].

Tonight's dedication is the culmination of eight years of determined effort on the part of the entire congregation. The fine-looking [red-] brick Temple is the result of the tireless effort and selfless financial support of only about 90 people [Jewish families of the congregation.]

It has cost in the neighborhood of $100,000 [actually, over $125,000 including the fixtures and equipment], and every member of the Jewish communities of both Bluefield and Princeton [united into one joint congregation] has contributed his personal share.

With the building completed and the congregation installed, there is left only some $10,000 to be paid off. [It was in the form of a loan, unsecured, given to the trustees of the congregation by one of the three local Bluefield banks.]

The Temple was built section by section as the money was raised. [Actually, the Temple was built in only two sections, as above described, and the raising of the money had nothing to do with the progress on the actual construction of the synagogue, except that the completion of the sanctuary or Temple half of the building was delayed by about eight months, from September, 1948, to the end of April, 1949, until more funds could be secured.] Ground was broken, after four years of careful planning, in 1946 [1947]. The cornerstone was laid in 1948. [This is an error, also. The date for the laying of the cornerstone should be November, 1947.] Then the shell of the building was completed, and the west wing, or the 'community center,' was finished. With this last operation complete, the congregation was able to sponsor various profitable projects in the community center, all of the proceeds from which went to the finishing of the Temple proper, or the east wing. This work was started just eight months ago.

The Congregation Ahavath Sholom was organized in 1897 by Louis Kaufman, Barney M. Cohen, and Samuel Matz. [The date 1897 given by Reporter Frank Green is in error. The best and most accurate date for the founding of the actual group, or congregation, as mentioned above, although at that time it did not as yet have a synagogue building, is the year 1904. The exact month and date of the founding of the congregation, in the sense of the original group of men who were associated together in it, are no longer ascertainable, and the congregational records make no mention thereof. Besides the three men mentioned in this paragraph, there were at least six other, and possibly as many as thirteen other, founding or charter members, whose names are given above.]

[Samuel] Matz is the only member of the trio still living. He is now [1949] living in Florida, and although the congregation made every effort to have him here for the dedication, his advanced age prevented him from coming. [Samuel Matz is the only one of the nine original founding members still alive in 1957. He is the father of Max Matz, owner of the Matz Hotel, in Bluefield.]

For years the congregation met in the old temple on Scott Street. This was sold in 1939 [an error for 1941, as mentioned above], the funds gained thereby being immediately allocated to the new Temple, which was then hardly in the planning stage. Since then the members [of the Temple] have met in a number of places wherever they could get the room.

The Temple is of brick-faced masonry construction with a reinforced concrete floor. The sills and copings are of limestone. The Temple section seats 110 persons, and the recreation room can be thrown open to provide an auditorium accommodating a total of 250. Stained glass windows look out on Albemarle Street. [Also, now, on the parking lot in the rear, towards College Avenue.] The recreation room is lighted by fluorescent lights, while the Temple is illuminated with indirect 'cove-lights' installed in hidden fixtures.

A parking lot with facilities for some thirty automobiles is in the rear.

Lewis A. Nixon, local [he moved to Beckley in 1953] architect, designed the building, and supervised its construction.

Other officers of the congregation assisting President [Nathan] Platnick are Max Turk, vice president; Abe Angrist, secretary; and [William P.] Gottlieb, treasurer.

The president of Congregation Ahavath Sholom in 1945–1946 was Sidney J. Kwass. After the end of the Second World War, Rabbi Julius Kravetz did not return to Bluefield, because of the serious illness of his then aged parents who needed a more clement climate, but he became rabbi in Tallahassee, Florida, and also director of the Hillel Foundation at Florida State University, which positions he held for several years before moving first to Gainesville, Fla., and then to New York, where he retired from the active congregational rabbinate. A more complete biography of Rabbi Julius Kravetz, who played an important role in the life of the congregation for some seven years, is to be found below.]

Nathan Platnick served as congregational president from 1946 to 1951, and in April, 1956, he was re-elected once more as the president of Congregation Ahavath Sholom. In 1959, he was still the incumbent in that post. During his first administration, on December 8, 1947, Congregation Ahavath Sholom joined the Union of American Hebrew Congregations. In December, 1955, it had a total of 85 contributing members.

### PRESIDENTS OF CONGREGATION AHAVATH SHOLOM

So far as can now be ascertained, the following men have served as presidents of the congregation:

Henry Rodgin (from 1930 on)
I. [Isidore] Steckler
Max Turk (for 1 year)
Nathan Platnick (1935–1936, 1946–1951, and 1956 to 1959)
Sidney J. Kwass (1945–1946 and 1951–1953)
Fred Gilbert (1953–1955)
Ben [Benjamin] Lazer (1955–1956)

### OFFICERS OF THE CONGREGATION IN 1948–1950

The congregational officers and members of the Board of Directors for the two-year period extending from May, 1948, to May, 1950, were:

PRESIDENT: Nathan Platnick
VICE PRESIDENT: Frank Nelson (of Princeton)
TREASURER: William P. Gottlieb
ASSISTANT TREASURER: Frank Klauber
SECRETARY: Joe [Joseph] Nathan and Abe [Abraham] Angrist

BOARD OF DIRECTORS:

Yankee Barbakow
   (of Princeton)
I. J. [Jack] Blank
Fred Gilbert
William P. Gottlieb
Sidney J. Kwass
Alfred E. Land

Joe [Joseph] Nathan
Frank Nelson (of Princeton)
Nathan Platnick
Dr. J. [Joseph] I. Rodgin
Samuel Shaman
Max Turk

Abraham I. Shinedling was the rabbi of the congregation in 1947–1950.

### OFFICERS AND BOARD OF DIRECTORS IN 1956–1957

PRESIDENT: Nathan Platnick
1ST VICE PRESIDENT: Emanuel Borinsky (of Princeton)
2ND VICE PRESIDENT: Meyer J. Spiro
SECRETARY: Mrs. Ruth (Joseph) Jason
TREASURER: Jesse B. Michelson

BOARD OF DIRECTORS:

Emanuel Borinsky
   (of Princeton)
Stanley D. Gottlieb
Mrs. Ruth (Joseph) Jason
Sidney J. Kwass
Alfred E. Land
Samuel Laufer
   (of Princeton)

Jesse B. Michelson
Alvin Platnick
Nathan Platnick
Jacob R. Siegel
Meyer J. Spiro
Arthur Weiss
Ben Lazer (Immediate Past
   President)

Herbert J. Wilner was rabbi of the congregation in 1952–1957.

In May, 1959, at the expiration of his final term of office, Nathan Platnick was succeeded by Benjamin Lazer as president of Congregation Ahavath Sholom. The complete list of officers of the congregation elected at that time for the year 1959–1960 was:

## OFFICERS AND BOARD OF DIRECTORS IN 1959–1960

*Officers*:

PRESIDENT: Benjamin Lazer
1ST VICE PRESIDENT: Sidney J. Kwass (for Bluefield)
2ND VICE PRESIDENT: Yankee Barbakow (for Princeton)
SECRETARY: Harry Finkelman (of Princeton)
TREASURER: Fred Gilbert
RABBI: Amos Schauss

BOARD OF DIRECTORS:

| | |
|---|---|
| Yankee Barbakow | Philip Platnick |
| (of Princeton) | Robert Rosenthal |
| Marvin Effron | Irving E. Selig (of Princeton) |
| Harry Finkelman | Eugene Solomon |
| (of Princeton) | Eli Weinberg (of Princeton) |
| Dr. Gerald Frank | Fred Gilbert |
| Mrs. Ruth (Joseph) Jason | Nathan Platnick (Immediate |
| Sidney J. Kwass | Past President) |
| Benjamin Lazer | |

Amos Schauss came to the congregation as rabbi in December, 1957, and was still the incumbent in 1959–1960.

## THE BLUEFIELD CEMETERY

The cemetery of the congregation is known as the Bluefield [and Princeton] Ahavath Sholom Section of the Monte Vista Cemetery, managed by Ray Graham (a non-Jew) and located on the new Bluefield-Princeton road, halfway between Bluefield and Princeton. In both past and present, some of the Jewish dead from Beckley have been buried in the Bluefield Monte Vista Cemetery, with the rabbi from either Bluefield or Beckley officiating. A number of graves and tombstones have been transferred, during the past decade, from the nearby and no longer used Pocahontas, Va., cemetery, after their removal from that abandoned cemetery.

## POCAHONTAS, VIRGINIA

Even though nearby Pocahontas (about fourteen miles from Bluefield) is located in Virginia, not very far from the West Virginia line, its Jewish history is closely connected with that of Bluefield and the Bluefield congregation. Pocahontas, Va., was a lusty and thriving frontier town in the olden days (up to about the year 1916), when liquor used to be sold there, and in those years some 40 to 50 Jewish families lived in Pocahontas, including:

Joseph I. Kwass (the father of Sidney J. Kwass)
Joseph (Joe) Matz (living in Bluefield in 1959)
Harry Matz
Max Matz (living in Bluefield in 1959, and operator of the Matz Hotel, on Princeton Avenue, in that year, and for many years before that)
Sidney Block (who died in Pocahontas several years ago)
the Magrill family, which included Carl and Esther Magrill, brother and sister, and their parents, Mr. and Mrs. L. Magrill, both of whom died at Pocahontas, the latter in the late 1940's, and the former previously

as well as many other families and persons. Sidney J. Kwass was born in Pocahontas (on November 11, 1908), as was, in all probability, also his brother, Meyer Kwass, now resident in Charleston, W. Va.

For several years the Pocahontas congregation, as mentioned above, had its own rabbi, always Orthodox, and the congregation was chiefly Orthodox in those years.

A large percentage of the Jewish men of Pocahontas operated liquor stores in the 1900's and 1910's, and the community and

the city itself were thriving. However, when liquor was pro-
hibited in Virginia some time before the year 1920 (about the
year 1916), many of these Jewish families in Pocahontas moved
to Bluefield, W. Va., and some went to Baltimore; a few also
went to Charleston. As late as 1957, Max Auerbach, of Bluefield, who for many years conducted a hardware and household
appliance store in Pocahontas, gave up this store, and moved to
Florida. By 1957, there was hardly a single Jewish family left in
Pocahontas, aside from Carl and Esther Magrill, who were then
still conducting a clothing and general store in the much smaller
town; this store had been founded by their father, L. Magrill.

The Pocahontas congregation at one time had a small synagogue, which was sold about the year 1951 to the Women's
Club there; also a small Jewish cemetery, which was in a bad
state of repair in 1955. In 1948 and 1949, Max Auerbach and
Rabbi Abraham I. Shinedling visited this old Pocahontas Jewish
cemetery several times, listing all the names of the Jewish dead
on the tombstones and headstones there, and turning all these
data over to the Bluefield congregation as part of its permanent
record. They made an unsuccessful attempt either to have the
living relatives of the Jewish dead buried there improve and
repair the cemetery and the fences, tombstones, and headstones; or to remove the graves and tombstones to the Monte
Vista Cemetery. Most of their letters to the relatives of the
Jewish dead buried in the Pocahontas cemetery went unan-
swered, and the few who did reply eventually approved the
transfer of their deceased kin to the Monte Vista Cemetery.

### Rabbi Julius Kravetz' Reminiscences of Bluefield

The following interesting data and bits of information about
the Bluefield congregation are excerpted from two letters (dated
February 16 and 27, 1957) written to me by the former rabbi of
the congregation, Julius Kravetz, who served as rabbi there
from 1936 until 1943, and who, in 1959, had long since given
up the active congregational rabbinate, and was living and
teaching in New York. The period in which Rabbi Julius
Kravetz served, from 1936 to 1943, was a formative period of the

congregation, and his notes and memoirs contain valuable side-lights on the history of the congregation. His rabbinate in Blue-field was outstanding in many respects.[1]

I was ordained at the Jewish Institute of Religion, [in New York,] in 1934, and after serving at the Floral Park Jewish Center, in Floral Park, N. Y., I came to Bluefield in 1936, and stayed until 1943. (Seven years, without even a Leah.) [The reference is to *Genesis* 29:18–30. Julius Kravetz to this time has not married.] I am a graduate of the University of Rochester (B.A.), and have the Master of Hebrew Literature degree from the Jewish Institute of Religion. I. [Isidore] Steckler, Nathan Platnick, and Henry Rodgin were the only three presidents I had, unless I am mistaken. Among my Religious School teachers were Mrs. Max [Esther L.] Auerbach, Miss Miriam Cohen [daughter of Isadore Cohen], Miss Selma Lubliner [the sister of Esther Lubliner Auerbach and of Abram J. Lubliner; Selma Lubliner taught high school for many years at Beaver High School, in Bluefield, before she removed to Florida in the 1950's], Ben Lazer, Honey [Roslyn] Weinberg [later Mrs. Joseph Nathan; Joe and Roslyn W. Nathan moved to Ashland, Ky., in the early 1950's], Miss Bertie Rodgin [Bertie Rodgin, the daughter of the late Henry Rodgin and of Mrs. Anna Grollman Rodgin, is now Mrs. Louis W. Cohen, of Charleston, W. Va.], Mrs. Nathan [Anna A.] Effron, and Dora Steiner.

When I arrived in Bluefield [in 1936], services were held in an ancient, soot-covered [frame] building at the top of the hill on Commerce Street. [Actually, it was on Scott Street, one block south of Commerce Street.] Before I left, the building was sold, and plans were made for a new structure. Temporary services were held in a panelled suite of rooms formerly used by the radio station [on Federal Street]. The B'nai B'rith Lodge also met there, and one room was set aside for . . . card games and social purposes . . . .

I was active in B'nai B'rith work. I attended all meetings of the Lodge and all State meetings [of the West Virginia B'nai B'rith Council]. I served [for] one year as the secretary of the Lodge, and in the following year as president. I was also active in the Bluefield Ministerial Association as a regular member, as chairman of the Program Committee, and as president. [Julius Kravetz served also, for years, up to the very month of his leaving Bluefield, in April, 1943, as the secretary of the Bluefield-Princeton Jewish Charities (Welfare

---

[1] Relevant material included in these two letters, and dealing with North Fork, Princeton, and Welch, W. Va., is not included here, but is given in the sections on those three localities.

Fund).] I served the Jewish communities of Welch, W. Va., and Northfork-Keystone-Kimball. I would visit Welch [the Welch Congregation Emanuel] on alternate Sundays, and Keystone on alternate Sundays [There was a small Orthodox synagogue in Keystone in those years.], and I conducted services there. I engaged in the same extracurricular activities as most other rabbis: book reviews and addresses before civic groups, luncheon clubs, church study groups, Parent-Teachers' Associations, Brotherhood Week services, etc.

I volunteered for the chaplaincy in 1943 [in the United States Army, in the Second World War], and remained in it until 1947. I served in Camp Adair, Oregon, in 1943–1944, in the Southwest Pacific (the New Hebrides, Guadalcanal, and the Philippine Islands) from 1944 to 1946, and at Fort Dix, N. J., [from] 1946–1947. I had originally intended to return to Bluefield, but the serious illness of both my parents (who were living in Rochester, N. Y.) made it necessary for me to seek a situation in Florida, and therefore I moved with them to Tallahassee in the fall of 1947. There I was rabbi of Temple Israel and Director of the Hillel Foundation (Florida State University). I moved to Gainesville, Fla., in 1954 (serving as the Hillel Director at the University of Florida) and remained there until May, 1956. My mother passed away in Tallahassee in 1948. My father died in Gainesville in March, 1956. I am now living in New York City [1957], taking graduate courses at the Jewish Institute of Religion [presumably for his Doctor of Divinity degree], and teaching a class there in Talmud. I am not serving as a rabbi.[1]

Among the old-timers in Bluefield, I guess Isadore Cohen can supply many details of local Jewish history.[2] Mrs. Nathan [Edna E.] Platnick, Mrs. Henry [Anna G.] Rodgin, Mrs. Abe [Sarah A.] Schlossberg, and Mrs. Nathan [Anna A.] Effron . . . . were important workers in the Bluefield Sisterhood . . . . As for Hadassah in that area, Mrs. Rodgin and Mrs. Max [Esther L.] Auerbach were important workers. Isaac Diamond is now [1957] head of the local B'nai B'rith. He also has

---

[1] In the summer of 1958, Rabbi Julius Kravetz, in addition to teaching his class in Talmud at the Jewish Institute of Religion, in New York, was also appointed religious adviser to the Jewish students at Dartmouth College, in Hanover, N. H., conducting High Holy Day services there, and coming to the Dartmouth College campus every other weekend to conduct religious services and to counsel the Jewish students there.

[2] Indeed, Isadore Cohen was most generous and gracious in supplying me, both before and after the receipt of Julius Kravetz' letters in February, 1957, with a great deal of data with reference to the early history of the Bluefield, North Fork, and Keystone Jewish communities and biographical data on some of their Jewish residents, all incorporated into this volume.

access to the United Jewish Appeal material.[1] I was secretary of the Bluefield-Princeton Charities for a number of years.

Of course, I served the Princeton Jewish Community throughout my stay in Bluefield. They [the members of Congregation Ahavath Sholom who lived in Princeton, ten miles northeast of Bluefield] would drive to Bluefield for services. I would go there [to Princeton] for Hebrew instruction and for adult education classes. (I also conducted these in Bluefield.) I also addressed church and civic groups in Princeton. During my last year in Bluefield, an arrangement was made whereby I spent one Friday evening a month in Princeton.

The Reverend Kalman Slifkin was serving the area as Shochet and Bluefield as cantor [also as Mohel] for the [High] Holy Days when I came there [in 1936]. He passed away in 1940. Mrs. Jack Blank [Toby S. Blank] is his daughter. One of the most active workers in my day for a new Temple structure was Ezra Gilbert. Hennon Gilbert is his son . . . . Sam Slifkin and Ike [Isaac] Slifkin were sons of Reverend Kalman Slifkin. [Isaac Slifkin had moved away from Bluefield to New England by the year 1947. Sam Slifkin was still living in Bluefield in 1959. He had served a term or two previously as president of the Bluefield B'nai B'rith Lodge.]

Other old-timers of Bluefield are Harry Clark, A. [Abe] Effron [father of Nathan Effron and Hyman Effron, of Bluefield, and of Robert Effron, of Princeton], S. Angrist, and Max Turk, the son of Samuel Turk.

THE "GOLDEN JUBILEE" OF THE CONGREGATION:

REPORT BY SIDNEY J. KWASS

On the occasion of the "Golden Jubilee" celebration (1907–1957) of Congregation Ahavath Sholom, of Bluefield-Princeton, West Virginia, Sidney J. Kwass, appointed historian of the congregation for the jubilee celebration, held in Bluefield in November, 1957, compiled the following report, which is herewith presented in two sections:

---

[1] I did get, a year or two later, a great deal of valuable and useful data and material on the Bluefield B'nai B'rith Lodge and on the United Jewish Appeal, in the late 1940's and early 1950's, from Isaac L. Diamond.

(A) Report by Sidney J. Kwass, Historian for the Golden Jubilee Celebration, Congregation Ahavath Sholom, Bluefield-Princeton, West Virginia (November, 1957)

*To the Board of Directors:*

The undersigned [Sidney J. Kwass, an attorney at law, of Bluefield, W. Va.] first called a meeting of those residents of Bluefield and Princeton who have lived in those communities for many years and in order to check the recollection[s] of one against the other. They were: Mr. and Mrs. Abraham N. [Sarah A.] Schlossberg; Dr. William Greenspon; Abe Effron; Nathan Effron; Anna [Effron] Hall; Isadore Cohen; Mrs. Anna [Henry] Rodgin; Mr. and Mrs. Harry [Rose A.] Clark; Abe Angrist; Mrs. I. J. [Toby S.] Blank; Ben Platnick; H. [Harry] Barbakow [of Princeton]; Boris Borinsky [of Princeton]; and Joseph Lisagor [of Princeton]. With the exception of Dr. [William] Greenspon, who was out of the city, and of Mrs. [Anna E.] Hall and Mr. [Joseph] Lisagor, all were present.

A history was prepared and presented at the banquet meeting on November 10, 1957, two copies of which are hereto attached. (Parenthetically, only notes were used in [the] delivery, so that the wording of the delivery varied, although the facts did not.)

According to the recollection of those present at the meeting of long-time residents, the families of the following were probably living in Bluefield in 1907 when the first Synagogue was purchased:

Samuel [I. ?] Aaron  
Simon Baker  
J. [Jacob] Baker  
Isadore Cohen  
Henry Rodgin  
Kalman Slifkin  
Solomon Greenspon  
Saul Greenspon  
B. [Barney] M. Cohen  
Morris Rosenberg  
Samuel Matz  

I. [Isaac] L. Cohen  
J. Goldman  
Ben [Benjamin] Baker  
Sam [Samuel] Stern  
M. Legum  
Harry Weinberg  
S. Catzen  
Morris Diamond  
Charles Diamond  
Rabbi Simon Cohen

Other residents who came shortly afterwards were:

> S. Angrist
> H. [Harry] Barbakow (at Princeton)
> B. [Boris] Borinsky (at Princeton)
> J. [Joseph] Lisagor (possibly) (at Princeton)
> William Steiner (for a time at Princeton)
> the Platnick family
> the Effron family
> Harry Clark
> B. S. Block
> Samuel Turk
> Saul Turk
> Nathan Sohn
> Abe [Abraham N.] Schlossberg
> David Schlossberg

and certainly many others in all categories.


With regard to Rabbis of the Congregation, the following is near to a chronological list:

Dr. Alexander Alan Steinbach, now of Congregation Ahavath Sholom, of Brooklyn

Harry Kellman (who was a student at the Jewish Theological Seminary [of America, in New York]

Rabbi Joseph Marcus

Rabbi Harrison [Bernard Harrison?]

Rabbi Nathan [A.] Perilman, now of Temple Emanu-El in New York City

Rabbi Avery [J.] Grossfield

Rabbi John Russkind

Rabbi Coleman [A.] Zwitman

Rabbi Julius Kravetz [1936–1943]

[A.] Stanley Dreyfus and Sanford [E.] Rosen [1943–1947]
   (both of these were students at the Hebrew Union College,
      in Cincinnati, during the war years) (World War II)

Rabbi Abraham I. Shinedling [1947–1950]

Rabbi Harold [L.] Gelfman [1950–1952]

Rabbi Herbert J. Wilner [1952–1957]
Amos Schauss (the new rabbi, not here yet)
    [Rabbi Amos Schauss arrived at Bluefield in December, 1957.]

The first public record in the coal-field area which I have been able to find is in Tazewell County, Virginia, and is a deed made [on] November 20, 1888, to my grandfather, Meyer Kwass. (Deed Book 24, page 86.) Other records followed shortly in both Mercer County, West Virginia, and Tazewell County.

From my own standpoint it was interesting to note that the first public ceremony of which anyone knew in the old Synagogue on Scott Street was the wedding of my parents [Mr. and Mrs. Joseph I. Kwass] in January, 1908, and that the first public ceremony in the new Temple, [that on Albemarle Street,] held in the west wing before the completion of the entire structure, was the Bar Mitzvah of my son Robert in September, 1948 [with Rabbi Abraham I. Shinedling as the officiant].

It has been impossible to determine all the past presidents of the congregation, but the following, at least, are still living:

| | |
|---|---|
| Samuel L. Matz, reported to be the first president | David Platnick |
| | Ben [Benjamin] Lazer |
| Max Matz | Fred Gilbert |
| Harry Clark | and the undersigned |
| Nathan Platnick | [Sidney J. Kwass] |

We know that for many years [the late] Henry Rodgin and I. [Isidore] Steckler served in that capacity, and that the late Ezra Gilbert likely also did so.

As a result of talking with a number of members, the undersigned [Sidney J. Kwass] respectfully recommends that the Board: (1) provide a permanent filing system and place for records; (2) direct that the original copy of minutes of Board and Congregation be placed in that place; and (3) provide a plaque in the Temple on which the names of successive presidents be inscribed, undertaking, if possible, to determine and place thereon the names of all past presidents.

Submitted this 14th day of November, 1957.
SIDNEY J. KWASS, Historian.

(B) BRIEF HISTORY OF BLUEFIELD-PRINCETON CONGREGATION
AHAVATH SHOLOM

Records in the Clerks' offices in Tazewell County, Virginia, and Mercer County, West Virginia, disclose that there were citizens of [the] Jewish faith in these coal fields at least as early as the advent of the Norfolk & Western [Railroad] to the area in 1888. The Princeton community probably began with the entry of the Virginian Railway about 1907.

The history of a congregation is necessarily a record of the people who comprise the community. Nevertheless, it quickly became apparent that if I would attempt to call names over the 50-year period, even if [those names were] confined to those who have descendants among our present membership, the time required would soon go beyond the bounds of that alloted to me this evening. There was also the danger of omitting some which should be called, or calling some which should be omitted.

For that which I say — or leave unsaid — here this evening I take full responsibility. I do, however, want you to know that an advisory committee of "old-timers" has checked my factual material, and approved the necessary decision to eliminate personal references to members — past or present.[1]

Inquiry of those "old-timers" discloses that High Holy Day, Minyan, and Yahrzeit services were held in Bluefield at various homes, stores, and other locations in the 15- or 20-year period prior to 1907. Early that year the community arranged for Rabbi Kalman Slifkin to come to Bluefield and serve the area in such ceremonials as marriages, brisses [circumcisions], funerals and the supervision of slaying [slaughtering] of kosher meats and fowls.

In that year the building on Scott Street at the head of Commerce [Street] which had formerly been a Presbyterian church became available, and the Jewish people of Bluefield purchased it, with deed being made [on] June 17, 1907, to the Trustees of Jewish Congregation Ahavath Sholom, that deed

---

[1] In my opinion, this was a definite error on the part of the chairman and the committee, and represents a possible loss of valuable facts and material.

being the first record of a definite organized Congregation, with the name still used.

You may be interested to know that the total price paid for the property was $2,800, of which $1,000 was cash, and that when the property was sold in 1941 it was purchased by the Catholic Bishop of Wheeling to be used as a place of worship for colored members of the Catholic Church at a price of $4,500. We understand that it is now being used for Greek Orthodox worship.

As near as can be recalled, there were perhaps two dozen Jewish families in Bluefield when the Congregation was formed and the synagogue established. During the period from 1907 to about 1921, services were conducted along Orthodox lines by Mr. [Kalman] Slifkin, with the assistance of the lay members of the Congregation. Even after rabbis with training in this country came to Bluefield, Mr. Slifkin continued his association with the Congregation in cantorial and "kashra" [kashruth] capacities until his death in the year 1940.

For that same period, that is, from 1907 until 1921, numerous teachers of Hebrew and [of] Jewish history lived in Bluefield for respective short times, and some of our long-time residents recollect attendance at the schools conducted by them.

The community at Princeton began with the entry of the Virginian Railway into the coal fields in 1907, but because of the difficulties of travel and communication did not join with Bluefield to make up the Mercer County Congregation until about the end of World War I, at which time the predecessor organization to [the] United Jewish Appeal first introduced them to communal efforts.

The first full-time Rabbi of American training at Bluefield is our honored speaker tonight, Dr. Alexander Alan Steinbach, who came to Bluefield early in 1921 and remained until 1922, and even survived preparing me for my Bar Mitzvah. One summer when we had student rabbis only during the school year, Dr. Steinbach returned to Bluefield for the funeral of one of our old residents and, remaining over a few days to visit, performed a wedding ceremony which I hope my wife regrets only at long-spaced intervals.

The first organized Sunday School of this Congregation was established during Dr. Steinbach's tenure here. Today there are fourth-generation graduates. The Sisterhood, organized about the same time, was first affiliated with the Orthodox Women's League of the United Synagogues [Synagogue] of America until 1928, and then became affiliated with the National Federation of Temple Sisterhoods.[1]

Following Dr. Steinbach's departure to more fertile fields of endeavor, the Congregation had in its pulpit almost a dozen full-time Rabbis and perhaps a half-dozen or more students on [a] part-time basis. We can be proud to note that despite depressions, difficulties of obtaining rabbis, and the small number in our community, throughout the past 26 [36?] years since 1921, this Congregation has never been without a rabbi.

Limitation of time this evening prevents my listing all who served in the pulpit of this Congregation, but it is interesting to note that our small community has been a stepping-stone to prominence in the rabbinate, including, though certainly not limited to, Rabbi Nathan Perilman, a native West Virginian presently rabbi of perhaps the largest and wealthiest congregation in this country, Temple Emanu-El at New York; Rabbi Coleman [Colman] Zwitman, who was at Miami when he became a chaplain in World War II and in the Pacific contracted the unusual disease which took his life shortly after his return to this country; and of course the good rabbi who conducted our past High Holy Day services, those [services] Friday night, and who is with us here tonight, Julius Kravetz. It is unfortunate that our new rabbi, Amos Schauss, could not be here tonight by reason of [his] honoring his agreement to give his present congregation time within which to find a replacement.

A Temple Youth Group was first organized about ten years

---

[1] It is most probable that Sidney J. Kwass here meant to write "*third*-generation graduates." It is difficult to see how Jewish boys and girls who attended the Steinbach-Ahavath Sholom Congregation Sunday School in 1921–1922 could have had *great*-grandchildren, or even, for that matter, *grand*children, by the year 1957, only 35 or 36 years later. If Sidney J. Kwass meant "fourth-generation graduates" (or, better, *pupils*) of the earliest Congregation Ahavath Sholom religious school, perhaps of the 1890's or the earliest of the 1900–1910 years, his statement might be correct.

PLATE XIII

The House on Bibby Street, in Charleston, W. Va., the residence of the Julius Nearmans, used as the first meeting place for Orthodox Jewish religious services around the year 1890

(see page 665)

PLATE XIV

The house originally situated on State Street (now Lee Street), in Charleston, W. Va., used by the Virginia Street Temple (Congregation B'nai Israel) until 1894. The Orthodox congregation (B'nai Jacob) first rented and then purchased this house from the Virginia Street Temple for its own use as a place of worship, and moved the building to its present location at the corner of

ago and has been active in the tri-state region as well as nationally, having sent several of its members to Wisconsin, Ohio, and elsewhere for camps and training. As you know, we do not have a Temple Brotherhood, but [we] call upon the local chapter [lodge] of [the] B'nai B'rith, which was organized about 1923, for the work which would normally come from the Brotherhood. The active local Hadassah chapter, which has been in existence since 1918, is also an integral part of the community life.

In the late 30's [1930's] the inadequacy of the old synagogue on the hill became apparent and efforts to raise funds for a new temple to be constructed in South Bluefield were instituted. After the sale of the synagogue in the spring of 1941 and following consideration of numerous locations in South Bluefield, the present site [at 632 Albemarle Street] was selected and 75 feet of the frontage presently owned [were] purchased. When the imminency of World War II became apparent and the government requested that out of patriotism only buildings imperatively needed be constructed, plans for the new temple were shelved and funds collected [were] invested in government bonds. Services and Sunday School were conducted in makeshift locations all over town.

In June, 1945, the remaining 75 feet of the property on Albemarle Street was [were] purchased, an architect was employed, and new efforts [were] made to obtain the funds necessary to begin construction. Our new building was actually under way by the spring of 1946, and services [were] held in the West Wing, which was first completed, in the fall of 1948. The East Wing was finally completed in the spring of 1950 [1949], and the Temple then [was] formally dedicated. The community is justifiably proud of the Temple, which was completed principally with funds raised as it proceeded and with only a very small amount of the final construction costs borrowed and then without mortgaging the building. Already the facilities, particularly for Sunday School, are proving inadequate, and plans are afoot to add space to the Sunday School section.

So much for the brief history of our Congregation. It is entirely fitting and proper that we should mark this 50th anniversary of its formal creation. More important, however, is the work of the future, and in that connection we proudly point to the fact that this year, as in many years past, our Board of Directors includes many of the younger men of the community whose interest is as deep and sincere as any of the older people, and are undoubtedly physically and mentally more capable of continuing the progress of the group. In them and in the youth of this community we place our abiding trust for future operations, with the sincere belief that fifty years from now those who will celebrate the Congregation's 100th anniversary will have great progress to report.

November 10, 1957

[Bluefield, West Virginia]                                    SIDNEY J. KWASS.

MEMBERS OF THE BLUEFIELD-PRINCETON CONGREGATION
AHAVATH SHOLOM[1]

(1950–1957)

Abe Angrist
Ben Angrist
Harry Angrist
S. Angrist[2]
Max Auerbach (Esther Lubliner Auerbach)
    [moved to Florida in 1957]
Hugo Benjamin
I. Jack Blank (Toby Slifkin Blank)
Morris (Max) Braum (deceased) (Rose Steiner Braum)
Isadore Cohen (Flora Greenspon Cohen)
William Cohen
Saul Cohen (Lucille Jaffe Cohen)

---

[1] Members living in Princeton, W. Va., will be found listed under Princeton. Names in parentheses are those of the members' wives, when known.

[2] S. Angrist, father of the preceding three Angrist brothers, died at Bluefield in the latter part of 1958, at the age of 94. He and Abe Effron were the oldest Jewish residents in the city for all the preceding years.

Harry Clark (Rose Angrist Clark)

Samuel DeLott (Sarah) [father of Mrs. Edna D. (Sidney J.) Kwass]

Herman Diamond

Isaac L. Diamond

Louis Diamond (Sarah Turk Diamond) [the father of the two preceding Diamond brothers]

Abe Effron [the father of the two following Effron brothers]

Hyman Effron (Sylvia Forman Effron)

Nathan Effron (Anna Abrahamson Effron)

Marvin Effron (Amy)

Samuel Fine (Nell)

Israel Fink (Sophie Winer Fink)
[They moved to Beckley in 1948.]

Philip Fliegelman (Elizabeth Burton Fliegelman)

Mrs. Abe Forman [mother of Mrs. Hyman Effron]

Mrs. Freda A. Frank

George Frehling (Marjory)

Rabbi Harold L. Gelfman (Hilda) [1950–1952]

Fred Gilbert (Reva Deem Gilbert)

Hennon Gilbert (Antoinette)
[In 1959, Hennon Gilbert moved to Fort Worth, Tex.]

Stanley D. Gottlieb [son of William P. Gottlieb]

William P. Gottlieb [living in Miami Beach, Fla., in 1957]

Lillian Greenspon [daughter of Isaac Greenspon, deceased]

Minna Greenspon [daughter of Isaac Greenspon, deceased]

Dr. William Greenspon (Bernice Rothschild Greenspon)

Solomon Gross

Mrs. Anna E. Hall [daughter of Abe Effron]

Solomon Hyman (Frieda) [He later moved to Columbus, Ohio.]

Joseph Jason (Ruth)

Harry Kammer (Josephine)

Max L. Kammer

Jerome Katz (Hilda)

Leroy Katz

Mrs. Rose Katz

Morris Kaufman (Dora Platnick Kaufman)

Frank Klauber
Sidney J. Kwass (Edna DeLott Kwass)
Alfred E. Land (Gladys Garten Land)
Julius Land (Minnie)
Ben Lazer (Lois)
Morris Lorber
Abram J. Lubliner (Claudine)
Selma Lubliner [moved to Florida]
Philip Maltzman
Benjamin B. Matz [deceased]
Joseph I. Matz
Max Matz
M. Medwin
Jesse B. Michelson (Marie Steckler Michelson)
Samuel Milchin
Joseph Nathan (Roslyn Weinberg Nathan)
     [moved to Ashland, Ky.]
Alvin Platnick
Benjamin Platnick (Sadie)
David Platnick (Gertrude)
Nathan Platnick (Edna Effron Platnick)
Philip Platnick (Fannie) [The four Platnick men are brothers.]
Gerald A. Pickus (Gloria Blank Pickus)
Lester Robinson
Dr. J. [Joseph] I. Rodgin
Mrs. Anna G. (Henry) Rodgin
Albert Rosenfeld (Mary)
Harry Rosenthal (Sadie)
Robert Rosenthal (Millicent Shaman Rosenthal)
Sidney Rosenthal (Helen Baum Rosenthal)
Mordy Ross
Jessel S. Salzberg (Beatrice) [They moved to California.]
Bernhard Schicke (Shik) (Adele)
Jonas Schicke (Shik)
Abraham N. Schlossberg (Sarah Aaron Schlossberg)
Sidney Schlossberg (Mildred Jean)
Alexander Segal (Lillian Brown Segal)

Raymond Seligman (of North Fork) (deceased) (Dina)

Samuel Shaman (Ida)

    [In 1959, Samuel (Sam) Shaman was living in Florida]

Harry I. Sherrin (Minnie)

    [Harry I. Sherrin died at Bluefield, in early 1960.]

Rabbi Abraham I. Shinedling (Helen Lowenstein Shinedling)
    [1947–1950]

Jacob R. Siegel (Edith Robinson Siegel)

Samuel Slifkin [son of Kalman Slifkin)

Bernard Snyder (Miriam Fink Snyder)

    [They moved to Norfolk, Va., in the early 1950's.]

Meyer J. Spiro

Mrs. Isidor[e] Steckler

Ben Steiner

David Steiner

Max Steiner

Morris Steiner

Theodore Steiner (Bertie Cohen Steiner)

Harry Stolch

Mrs. Ann [Land] Susman

Martin Thames

Abe [Abraham] S. Tomchin (Edith)

Joseph Tomchin (Ethel J.) [Joseph Tomchin died at Bluefield
    in the first half of 1959.]

Isadore Tucker [no longer resident in Bluefield]

Sidney Tucker (Lillian Kohn Tucker)

Max Turk (Trudy) [They moved to Florida.]

Maurice Weinberg

Mrs. Sadie Weinberg

Arthur Weiss (Edith Fine Weiss)

Samuel Werfel (of Bluefield, Va.)

[Sidney Werfel, of Bluefield, Va.] (son of Samuel Werfel)

Rabbi Herbert J. Wilner (Helen Abramowitz Wilner) [1952–
    1957]

Jacob Wilson (Rebecca Land Wilson, deceased)

Louis Zaltzman

FORMER MEMBERS OF THE BLUEFIELD JEWISH COMMUNITY
OR OF
CONGREGATION AHAVATH SHOLOM[1]

(1880–1950)

I. Aaron [father of Mrs. Sarah Aaron Schlossberg (Mrs. Abraham N. Schlossberg)]
I. [E.?] Alifeld
Isadore Baker (before 1942) [deceased]
Jacob Baker
Simon Baker
J. I. Blake
B. [Ben] S. Block [deceased]
Barney M. Cohen (brother of Isadore Cohen) [deceased]
Ben Cohen
Isaac Cohen
Philip Cohen
William Cohen (father of Mrs. Theodore [Bertie Cohen] Steiner)
Leon (Leo) Diamond
Albert Ehudin (Uhdin?)
Bernard Effron (brother of Mrs. Nathan [Edna Effron] Platnick) [moved to Orlando, Fla.]
Julius Fink (before 1942) [deceased]
Rabbi Harold L. (Hilda) Gelfman [1950–1952]
Philip Gerard (a student at Bluefield College; his original home city was Philadelphia)
        [Philip Gerard died at Bluefield in June, 1948]
Edward Gilbert (before 1942) [deceased]
Ezra Gilbert (father of Hennon Gilbert) [deceased]
M. B. Goldman
Norman Gradsky
Harry Greenspon (before 1942)

---

[1] In part this list was prepared by Nathan Platnick, and in part it was compiled by Isaac L. Diamond, who has done considerable research in the history of the Bluefield Jewish community, and has kept some of its records over the past twenty years; it is based, also, in part, on my own personal records, researches, and observations as rabbi of the congregation from 1947 to 1950.

Isaac Greenspon

Isador Greenspon (before 1942)

Saul Greenspon

Solomon Greenspon (before 1942) (father of Mrs. Isadore [Flora Greenspon] Cohen)

Harry Gross (before 1942) [deceased]

J. Harris

I. Hirschberger

S. Holswieg

Mr. Isaacson (first name now unknown)

David Katz (deceased) (before 1942) [David Katz was the father of Jerome and Leroy Katz, and the husband of Mrs. Rose Katz]

Louis Kaufman (before 1942) [deceased]

Rabbi Julius Kravetz (1936–1943)

Joseph I. Kwass (before 1942) (father of Sidney J. Kwass)

S. Lazar

Ben Lennett (before 1942)

Sidney Lennett

J. Lowenstein

H. Lubliner [perhaps the father of Abram J. Lubliner]

L. Magrill (of Pocahontas, Va.)

Meyer Marcus

Mark Masters

I. Matz

Nathan Matz
   [He moved to Beckley, and was still living there in 1959.]

Samuel Matz (father of Max Matz)

H. Meyers

Harry Miller [before 1942]

Gilbert Orin

Mrs. Ida (Joseph) Platnick [mother of Benjamin, Nathan, David, and Philip Platnick, of Bluefield, and of Mrs. Morris (Dora) Kaufman, of that city] [deceased]

Henry Rodgin [deceased]

Morris Rosenberg

D. Schlossberg

Goodwin Schlossberg (son of Abraham N. Schlossberg)

Rabbi Abraham I. [and Helen L.] Shinedling (1947–1950)
D. Silber
Isaac L. Slifkin (son of the Reverend Kalman Slifkin) (before
1942)
Reverend Kalman Slifkin [father of Mrs. Toby [I. Jack] Blank,
and of Samuel Slifkin and Isaac L. Slifkin) [deceased]
Mr. Sorin [first name not known. This name is possibly an error
for Gilbert *Orin.*]
L. H. Taschman
J. H. Todd
Henry Tucker
Isadore Tucker
Samuel Turk (father of Max Turk)
Saul Turk (before 1942)
Bernard J. Wagner (before 1942)
Harry Weinberg (before 1942) [deceased]
Sidney Weiss (brother of Arthur Weiss)
Rabbi Herbert J. (and Helen A.) Wilner (1952–1957)
I. Wohlmuth
Tony Zappan (before 1942)

MEMBERS OF AHAVATH SHOLOM CONGREGATION
FROM PRINCETON, W. VA.[1]

(1950–1957)

Harry Barbakow (Lilly) (father of Yankee Barbakow) [Mrs.
Lilly Barbakow died at Princeton, in early 1958.]
Yankee Barbakow (Libby Mervis Barbakow)
Oscar Baum (died at Radford, Va., in May, 1956]
Boris Borinsky (father of Emanuel Borinsky)
Emanuel Borinsky
Calvin R. Deitz
Henry Deitz (father of Calvin R. Deitz)
Robert Effron (Charlotte)
Samuel Laufer (Frances)
Joseph Lisagor

---

[1] These members are listed also in the section on Princeton, W. Va.

Frank Nelson (Beatrice Effron Nelson)
Moe Nelson (Moses) (Shirley Mervis Nelson) (brother of Frank
    Nelson) [Moe Nelson moved to Bluefield in the early 1950's.]
Irving Selig (son-in-law of Boris Borinsky)
Abe S. Tomchin (Edith) [moved to Bluefield in 1949]
Harold Tomchin (Sylvia Forman Tomchin)
Harold Volkin
Ralph Weinberg (Ida Effron Weinberg) (father of Eli Weinberg)
    [Ralph Weinberg died about the year 1952.]
Eli Weinberg

### Former Members of Congregation Ahavath Sholom from Princeton
### (1900–1950)

Abe Borinsky (son of Boris Borinsky)
B. Barbakow
Maurice Barbakow (son of Harry Barbakow)
Leon (Leo) Feingold
S. Goodstein
L. Meron

### List of Members of, and Contributors to, the Bluefield-Princeton United Jewish Charities[1]
### (October, 1957)

Abe Angrist
Ben Angrist

---

[1] 114 contributors and members from Bluefield and Princeton, W. Va. This list is practically tantamount to a list of the membership of the Bluefield-Princeton Congregation Ahavath Sholom, in October, 1957; those persons who were then living in Bluefield and were presumably not members of the congregation itself, as well as those persons then living outside of Bluefield and Princeton, and also, presumably, not members of the congregation itself, have an asterisk * preceding their names. The name of the wife, when known to me, is given in parentheses after the name of the individual member. The symbol # before the name of a member or contributor indicates that such person is married, but that I do not know or have forgotten the first name of the wife.

Harry Angrist
[S. Angrist] [died in Bluefield in 1958]
Harry Barbakow (Lilly) (of Princeton)
       [Lilly Barbakow died at Princeton early in 1958.]
Yankee Barbakow (Libby Mervis Barbakow) (of Princeton)
Mrs. Oscar Baum (of Princeton)
I. Jack [Jacob] Blank (Toby Slifkin Blank)
#Boris Borinsky (of Princeton)
#Emanuel Borinsky (of Princeton)
Mrs. Rose Steiner (Mrs. Morris) Braum
#*Carl Carp (of Wytheville, Va.)
Harry Clark (Rose Angrist Clark)
Isadore Cohen (Flora Greenspon Cohen)
#Calvin R. Deitz (of Princeton)
#Henry Deitz (of Princeton)
Samuel DeLott (Sarah) [now of Coral Gables, Fla.]
Emory Deutsch
Herman Diamond
Isaac L. Diamond (Elizabeth Klein Diamond)
Louis Diamond (Sarah Turk Diamond)
Abe Effron
Hyman Effron (Sylvia Forman Effron)
Marvin Effron (Amy)
Nathan Effron (Anna Abrahamson Effron)
Robert Effron (Charlotte) (of Princeton)
Sam Fine (Nell)
#Harry Finkelman (of Athens, W. Va.) [lives in Princeton]
Philip Fliegelman (Elizabeth Burton Fliegelman)
Louis Forman
Mrs. Freda A. Frank
Dr. Gerald Frank
Fred Gilbert (Reva D.)
Hennon Gilbert (Antoinette)
#Stanley D. Gottlieb
William P. Gottlieb (Marie)
       [living in Miami Beach, Fla., in 1959]
Edith Greenspon
Lillian Greenspon

Minna Greenspon
Dr. William Greenspon (Bernice Rothschild Greenspon)
Joseph Jason (Ruth)
Harry Kammer (Josephine)
#Max L. Kammer
Jerome Katz (Hilda C.)
#Leroy Katz
  Morris Kaufman (Dora Platnick Kaufman)
  Frank Klauber
  Ira Kleiman (Rose Katz Kleiman)
  Elizabeth Klein [in December, 1957, she married Isaac L.
      Diamond.]
  Henry Klein
  Sidney J. Kwass (Edna DeLott Kwass)
  Alfred E. Land (Gladys Garten Land)
  Julius C. Land (Minnie)
  Samuel Laufer (Frances) (of Princeton)
  Ben Lazer (Lois)
 *B. D. Lenett (of Wytheville, Va.)
#*Marvin S. Lenett (of Pulaski, Va.)
#*Sidney J. Lenett (of Wytheville, Va.)
  Morton M. Lipman (Dorothy Grace Rowe Lipman)
#Joseph Lisagor (of Princeton)
#Maurice Lisagor (of Princeton)
#Morris Lorber
  Abram J. Lubliner (Claudine)
  Carl H. Magrill (of Pocahontas, Va.)
#Philip H. Maltzman
#Selig Markowitz (of Mullens, W. Va.)
#Joseph Matz
#Max Matz
#Milton Medwin
  Jesse B. Michelson (Marie Steckler Michelson)
#Dr. Samuel Milchin
  Frank Nelson (Beatrice Effron Nelson) (of Princeton)
  Moses [Moe] L. Nelson (Shirley Mervis Nelson)
  Gerald A. Pickus (Gloria Blank Pickus)
#Alvin Platnick

Ben Platnick (Sadie)
David Platnick (Gertrude)
Nathan Platnick (Edna Effron Platnick)
Philip Platnick (Fannie)
Mrs. Henry (Anna G.) Rodgin
#Dr. Joseph I. Rodgin
Harry Rosenthal (Sadie)
Robert Rosenthal (Millicent Shaman Rosenthal)
Sidney Rosenthal (Helen Baum Rosenthal)
#Mordy Ross
Mrs. Mary Ruby
Rabbi Amos Schauss
Abraham N. Schlossberg (Sarah Aaron Schlossberg)
Sidney Schlossberg (Mildred Jean Schlossberg)
#Irving Selig (of Princeton)
#Samuel Shaman
Philip Shapiro
Harry I. Sherrin (Minnie) [deceased]
#Joe [Jonas] Shik [Schicke]
Bernard [Bruno, Ben] Shik [Schicke] (Adele)
Jacob R. Siegel (Edith Robinson Siegel)
Samuel I. Slifkin
#Meyer J. Spiro
Mrs. I. [Isidore] Steckler
Dr. Frank Stein (of Athens, W. Va.) [lives in Princeton]
Harry Stolch
#Eugene Solomon
*Ben Steiner
*David Steiner
*Leo Steiner
*Max Steiner
*Morris Steiner
Mrs. Ann Land Susman
#Dr. B. L. Susman (of Tazewell, Va.)
Abe [Abraham S.] Tomchin (Edith)
Harold Tomchin (Sylvia Forman Tomchin) (of Princeton)
Joseph Tomchin (Ethel J.)
   [Joseph Tomchin died at Bluefield in July, 1959.]

#Milton Tomchin
Sidney Tucker (Lillian Kohn Tucker)
Max Turk (Trudy) [living in Miami Beach, Fla., in 1959]
Harold Volkin (of Princeton)
#Maurice Weinberg
#Eli Weinberg (of Princeton)
Mrs. Ralph (Ida Effron) Weinberg (of Princeton)
Arthur Weiss (Edith Fine Weiss)
Jacob Wilson (of Welch, W. Va.)
Louis Zaltzman

In 1957, Mrs. Sara B. (Lewis) Reiland, of Bluefield, was
the organist of the congregation. Harry C. Hopkins was the
building custodian (*Shammash*) of the synagogue.

CONSTITUTION AND BY-LAWS OF CONGREGATION AHAVATH
SHOLOM (OF BLUEFIELD AND PRINCETON, W. VA.)[1]

## ARTICLE I

### ORGANIZATION

Section 1 — This organization shall be known by the name of
Congregation Ahavath Sholom.
Section 2 — Membership shall consist of men and women who
desire to practice and perpetuate the teachings of Judaism,
and who meet the other requirements fixed by the Board
of Directors pursuant to these by-laws.

---

[1] Adopted in 1949–1950. The Constitution Committee of the Congregation, at that
time, consisted of Sidney J. Kwass, Max Turk, I. Jacob Blank, Rabbi Abraham I.
Shinedling, and Nathan Platnick. With one amendment. Based in large measure,
with some variations, on the U. A. H. C. Model Constitution for Reform Jewish
Congregations, and as such of interest to Reform Jewish congregations in the
United States, as a typical, or model, Reform Jewish congregational constitution.

## ARTICLE II

### OFFICERS AND ELECTIONS

Section 1 — The affairs of the Congregation shall be administered by the Board of Directors.

Section 2 — The Board of Directors shall consist of twelve members; in addition, the retiring president of the Board, unless already a member, shall automatically become a member of the Board for one year. Six of said members shall be elected at each annual meeting [of the Congregation] by written ballot on [a] plurality vote and [they are] to hold office for two years, or until their successors are elected.

Section 3 — The officers of the Board shall be a President, First Vice-President, Second Vice-President, Secretary, Treasurer, and Assistant Treasurer. The Assistant Treasurer shall be compensated for his services in [an] amount as fixed by the Board. Said officers shall be elected by the Board by [a] plurality vote on written ballot and shall, with the exception of the Assistant Treasurer, be members of the Board. The term of office shall be one year.

Section 4 — The retiring President shall call a meeting of the new Board within two weeks after the annual meeting for the purpose of organization and election of officers.

Section 5 — A Nominating Committee of three members of the Congregation shall be appointed by the President at the February meeting of the Board of Directors, which Committee shall nominate six or more candidates for election to the Board of Directors, depending on the number of vacancies to be filled. The Nominating Committee shall report its nominations to the Board of Directors at the March meeting of said Board. The President shall then direct the Secretary to circulate these nominations, together with the notice of the Annual Congregation Meeting. Further nominations may be made from the floor at the Annual Congregation Meeting.

Section 6 — The Rabbi of the Congregation shall, ex officio, be an advisory member of the Board, but shall not be entitled to a vote.

Section 7 — The office of any member of the Board who shall absent himself from three consecutive meetings without cause shall be declared vacant by the Board. In [the] event of such vacancy, or any vacancies created by other causes, the Board shall call a special meeting of the Congregation for the purpose of filling the vacancies.

## ARTICLE III

### ANNUAL MEETING

Section 1 — The annual meeting of the Congregation shall be held in the month of April at such time as the Board shall fix and upon at least two weeks' notice to the membership.

## ARTICLE IV

### DUTIES OF OFFICERS

Section 1 — It shall be the duty of the President to preside over all business meetings of the Congregation and the Board. He shall decide all points of order and cast the deciding vote in [the] event of a tie. He shall execute any documents for the Congregation. He shall appoint all committees with the advice and consent of the Board. He shall perform all other duties incident to his office.

Section 2 — The First Vice President shall assume and perform the duties of the President during the latter's absence or disability.

Section 3 — The Second Vice-President shall assume and perform the duties of the First Vice-President during the latter's absence or disability.

Section 4 — The Secretary shall act as secretary of the Board and of the Congregation and shall keep minutes of the meetings of both. He shall be responsible for the giving of all notices required by these by-laws. He shall be responsible for all minutes and records of the Board and the Congregation and for the delivery of [the] same to his successor.

Section 5 — All funds of the Congregation shall be delivered to the Treasurer and by him deposited in such banking institution as may be designated by the Board, subject to withdrawal on his signature with the counter-signature of the Assistant Treasurer or the President. He shall keep a record of receipts and disbursements, furnish annual reports to the Congregation and such special reports as requested by the Board. He shall be responsible for [the] delivery of all funds and records to his successor.

Section 6 — The Assistant Treasurer shall approve all bills, mail statements of dues and other obligations of the membership and act in the place of the Treasurer in [the] event of the absence or disability of the Treasurer.


## ARTICLE V

### POWERS AND DUTIES OF THE BOARD

Section 1 — The Board shall be entrusted with the administration and executive business of the Congregation and shall act in all matters involving membership in the Congregation.

Section 2 — The Board shall prepare an annual budget estimate of the amount of money to be raised for the operation of the Congregation, including payment to the Rabbi and any other employees of the Congregation, and determine the method of raising those funds.

Section 3 — The Board shall hold meetings at least [once] monthly and at such times as it shall fix. A quorum shall consist of seven members.


## ARTICLE VI

### COMMITTEES

Section 1 — The President shall, with the consent and approval of the Board, appoint for one year the following standing committees: Temple Maintenance; Auditing; Membership; Religious Services; Choir; Sunday School; Social Activities; Ushers; Attendance; Parking; Funeral Arrangements and Cemetery; Grievances; Welfare and Visitation; Memorials; Publicity; By-Laws; and such other committees as the Board may from time to time determine [to be] necessary. Each of the committees shall consist of at least three members; the President, Rabbi, and Secretary shall be ex officio members of all committees.

Section 2 — [The] Temple Maintenance Committee shall have the Temple real and personal property in its care and under its supervision.

Section 3 — [The] Auditing Committee shall annually audit the books of the Treasurer and Assistant Treasurer, compare their accounts with all bills and vouchers, and report in writing to the Board.

Section 4 — [The] Membership Committee shall have charge of all efforts toward the increase in membership, and visit and welcome new arrivals in the community.

Section 5 — [The] Religious Services Committee shall have general charge of the public worship, after consultation with the Rabbi, and subject to [the] approval of the Board.

Section 6 — [The] Choir Committee shall have general supervision of the music of the congregation.

Section 7 — [The] Sunday School Committee shall be an advisory group to the Superintendent of the Sunday School and the Rabbi in matters pertaining to such school.

Section 8 — [The] Social Activities Committee shall, in cooperation with the Sisterhood, plan all social activities to be undertaken by the Congregation during the year.

Section 9 — [The] Welfare and Visitation Committee shall visit the sick and render assistance to any member requiring aid.

Section 10 — [The] Ushers Committee shall act as ushers at Congregational services and at various affairs.

Section 11 — [The] Attendance Committee shall use every possible means to obtain the maximum possible attendance at all religious services and Congregational meetings and affairs.

Section 12 — [The] Parking Committee shall insure maximum use of the parking area at the rear of the Temple.

Section 13 — [The] Funeral Arrangements and Cemetery Committee shall assist member families and out-of-town families in matters pertaining to death and burial, and shall exercise control of the Cemetery Fund. They shall provide for the burial of any indigent persons when necessary.

Section 14 — [The] Grievances Committee shall hear and arbitrate all grievances and complaints arising from the general operation of the Congregation.

Section 15 — [The] Memorials Committee shall have charge of selecting, placing and assigning present remaining Temple memorials or future memorials.

Section 16 — [The] Publicity Committee shall, upon request of the Board, the Rabbi, or any committee chairmen, publicize any activity or facts properly and in good taste.

Section 17 — [The] By-Laws Committee shall keep in permanent form the by-laws and make additions to [the] same when properly amended; a copy shall be available at every Congregation and Board meeting.


## ARTICLE VII

### MEMBERSHIP

Section 1 — The Board shall have the power to fix the terms and conditions of membership.

Section 2 — Members of the Congregation shall have the following privileges:

(a) to attend all Congregational services and activities;

(b) to vote at all Congregational meetings. Each membership shall carry only one vote.

(c) to be elected or appointed to office;

(d) to have the use of the Religious and Sunday Schools for their children without additional charge;

(e) to attend all meetings of the Board and express opinions, but without the right to vote;

(f) to receive all rabbinical services without additional charge, such as Kaddish or Minyan services, Bar Mitzvah and Confirmation services and instruction, weddings, funerals, unveilings, [and] consultations with the Rabbi. This does not prohibit the giving of voluntary gifts to [the] Temple or Rabbi.

Section 3 — Membership dues shall be due and payable in advance at the beginning of each fiscal year. The fiscal year shall begin October 1st.

Section 4 — Non-members may purchase tickets for [the] High Holy Days and be provided with other services rendered by the Congregation, or its Rabbi, at fees determined by the Board.

## ARTICLE VIII

### QUORUMS AND SPECIAL MEETINGS

Section 1 — Twenty-five voting members of the Congregation shall constitute a quorum at any Congregational meeting.

Section 2 — Special meetings of the Board or Congregation may be called by the President whenever he deems them necessary. He shall call a special Board meeting upon written request of not less than three Board members. He shall call a special Congregation[al] meeting upon written request of not less than ten members, and within ten days of such request, provided [that] the object of the meeting be set forth in the request. No other business shall be presented at such special Congregational meeting[s].

## ARTICLE IX

### THE RABBI

Section 1 — Employment of the Rabbi shall be recommended by the Board to the annual meeting of the Congregation or a special meeting called for that purpose, and he shall be elected by the Congregation at such meeting for not less than one year.

Section 2 — The Rabbi shall be present and officiate at every religious service in the Temple. He shall perform all religious ceremonies pertaining to his office, such as funeral services, weddings, Bar Mitzvahs, Confirmations, unveilings, circumcisions, and the like.[1] He shall keep a permanent record of such ceremonies in a book provided by the Congregation. He shall superintend the instruction of the children in the religious and Sunday schools.

## ARTICLE X

General procedure at Congregation and Board meetings shall be governed by the manual of Roberts' [Henry M. Robert's] Rules of Order.

## ARTICLE XI

These by-laws may be amended by a two-thirds vote of the members of the Congregation present at any annual meeting or any special meeting called for that purpose.

### Congregation Ahavath Sholom, of Bluefield and Princeton

#### Officers and Board of Directors, 1957–1958

President: Nathan Platnick
1st Vice President: Emanuel Borinsky (of Princeton)
2nd Vice President: Meyer J. Spiro
Secretary: Abraham S. Tomchin
Treasurer: Frank Klauber

Directors:

Mrs. Sylvia F. (Hyman) Effron     Samuel Laufer (of Princeton)
Fred Gilbert                      Sidney Schlossberg
Stanley D. Gottlieb              Jacob R. Siegel
Leroy Katz

---

[1] This is strangely and inaccurately expressed. It undoubtedly means not that the rabbi shall act as a Mohel and actually perform circumcisions, for which function no rabbi is trained, but that he shall conduct, perform, or read the religious ritual or ceremonial service connected with a circumcision performed by a Mohel or by a surgeon.

OFFICERS OF THE BLUEFIELD-PRINCETON UNITED JEWISH
CHARITIES (FOR THE YEAR 1957–1958)

OFFICERS

PRESIDENT: Fred Gilbert
CAMPAIGN CHAIRMAN: Fred Gilbert
VICE PRESIDENT: Meyer J. Spiro (for Bluefield)
VICE PRESIDENT: Yankee Barbakow (for Princeton)
EXECUTIVE SECRETARY AND IMMEDIATE PAST PRESIDENT: Isaac
L. Diamond
TREASURER: Frank Klauber

BOARD OF DIRECTORS (1956–1958)

Yankee Barbakow (of Princeton)   Frank Klauber
Emanuel Borinsky (of Princeton)  Alfred E. Land
Isaac L. Diamond                 Frank Nelson (of Princeton)
Fred Gilbert                     Joseph Tomchin

BOARD OF DIRECTORS (1957–1959)

Isadore Cohen                    Harry Rosenthal
Samuel Laufer (of Princeton)     Samuel Slifkin
Benjamin Lazer                   Meyer J. Spiro
Nathan Platnick                  Abraham S. Tomchin

TEAM CAPTAINS

Yankee Barbakow                  Nathan Platnick
Isaac L. Diamond                 Meyer J. Spiro

Early in 1958, Congregation Ahavath Sholom (according to
the *U. A. H. C. Handbook*) was affiliated with the Ohio-Valley
Region of the U. A. H. C., with Nathan Platnick as its president,
and Amos Schauss as its rabbi; at that time it was listed as having
82 members, a slight decline from its membership of 85 as
given in the *U. A. H. C. Year Book* published in December, 1955.

THE RABBIS AND STUDENT (PART-TIME) RABBIS
OF CONGREGATION AHAVATH SHOLOM
(1930 to 1959)

Perhaps the first rabbi, Chazan, or Shochet of the congregation, whose mere name (with no data) is found in the congregational records, was Simon Cohen. Nothing further is known about him. He was, evidently, not a Hebrew Union College student, nor was he Simon R. Cohen (H. U. C., 1899), who later became rabbi in Brooklyn, N. Y. Simon Cohen was, in all likelihood, an Orthodox rabbi, otherwise unknown, who served the congregation perhaps sometime in the period from 1904 to 1907. As mentioned below, the records indicate that he was a resident of Bluefield in and before the year 1907. Also, perhaps sometime during this three-year period (1904 to 1907), a rabbi, cantor, or Shochet by the name of M. Levinson served the congregation briefly; nothing further is known or recorded about him.

It is possible that "Rabbi" Simon Cohen was Simon Aaron Cohen, the father of Isadore Cohen, who settled in Bluefield in 1905. It is possible that Simon A. Cohen — if he actually lived in Bluefield — served for a year or two as the unofficial "rabbi" and *Melammed* (Hebrew teacher) of the congregation, and that he was a considerable Hebrew student, as was also his son Isadore Cohen.[1]

The first permanent, long-term Chazan, Shochet, Mohel, and rabbi of the Bluefield congregation was the Reverend Kalman Slifkin, who served, so far as the data found in the records indicate, from about the year 1906 until the year 1930 or 1931, in which latter year he appears to have retired from his several offices, except when occasionally called on to perform religious services in his post-retirement years, in the absence of a per-

---

[1] Simon Cohen was indeed the father of Isadore and Barney Cohen. In a communication sent to me by the then more-than-75-year-old Isadore Cohen in mid-January, 1961, from Bluefield, he stated as follows: "My father was not a rabbi, but he did serve the congregation in Bluefield prior to the coming of the Reverend Mr. Kalman Slifkin to Bluefield, which was about 1907. He did serve the congregation in rabbinical work, but, of course, only on a purely voluntary and unpaid basis."

manent rabbi. He lived in Bluefield, in retirement, until his death there in 1940. He was buried in the Monte Vista Cemetery.

Following him, there came to the congregation the first Hebrew Union College (of Cincinnati) student rabbi of record, i. e., Avery J. Grossfield, who came to the Bluefield-Princeton Congregation Ahavath Sholom every other weekend, on a part-time basis, beginning in September, 1930, and serving until June, 1931. He was then a senior student at the Hebrew Union College.

Even before Avery J. Grossfield came to the congregation in September, 1930, the congregation had had a full-time Conservative rabbi for one year, from 1921 to 1922. This was Alexander Alan Steinbach, who served as the Conservative rabbi of the congregation prior to his going to a Conservative congregation in Norfolk, Va., as rabbi. In the days of the joint service of Kalman Slifkin and Alexander Alan Steinbach (as Chazan-Shochet-Mohel and as rabbi, respectively) and for some years after 1922, the Bluefield congregation engaged a student rabbi from the Jewish Theological Seminary of America (Conservative), of New York, for the High Holy Days. [The names of these Conservative student rabbis are now unknown.] In the 1930's and also in the early 1940's, the congregation was Conservative; beginning with the middle and late 1940's, the Reform element in the congregation came to predominate, but from that day to the present there was always a strong Orthodox element of perhaps a dozen or more families, and a smaller Conservative group of half a dozen or more families (see below).

Alexander Alan Steinbach, after serving for several years in Norfolk, Va., later became rabbi of Temple Ahavath Sholom, in Brooklyn, N. Y., where he is still serving (1959).

Avery J. Grossfield was succeeded in his office by Nathan A. Perilman, who served as the graduate, full-time rabbi from September, 1931, to August, 1932. Rabbi Perilman then left Bluefield to become associated with Temple Emanu-El, New York, which position he still (1959) occupies.

Following Nathan A. Perilman, Nathaniel S. Share, later rabbi of Congregation Gates of Prayer, in New Orleans, became the full-time rabbi of the Bluefield congregation, serving for a little less than a complete year, from 1932 to 1933. After Rabbi Share, there was a rabbi named John Ruskin, or Russkind, who later moved to California, after serving as the full-time rabbi of the congregation from [September,] 1933 to August, 1934. Rabbi Ruskin died in California a short time after leaving Bluefield.

After the departure of Rabbi Ruskin, late in August, 1934, the congregation resumed its bi-weekly arrangement with students from the Hebrew Union College, of Cincinnati, from September, 1934, to June, 1936, until Rabbi Julius Kravetz came to Bluefield as the full-time congregational rabbi in September, 1936, serving until April, 1943. It was perhaps during this "interregnum" or interval that Bernard [?] Harrison, an H. U. C. student, served as a part-time student rabbi, or it may have been earlier. The congregational records are uncertain and incomplete for the period of the 1920's and 1930's. (See below.) From 1943 (with the departure of Julius Kravetz from the city to serve as an Army chaplain in the Second World War) until June, 1947, there were again only student rabbis, three in number, i. e., A. Stanley Dreyfus, Jerome W. Grollman, and Sanford E. Rosen, who served successively for one year each from September, 1943, to June, 1947 (one of them, A. Stanley Dreyfus, served for two years, not in succession), until just before Abraham I. Shinedling came, to be once more the full-time rabbi of the congregation, serving until September 1, 1950. From 1947 to the present (1959), except for a few months in the latter part of the year 1957, the congregation has had, continuously, the services and the ministrations of full-time graduate rabbis. Harold L. Gelfman served as rabbi from 1950 to 1952; Herbert J. Wilner from 1952 to 1957; and Amos Schauss, the present incumbent, from December, 1957, on.

As briefly indicated above, by the year 1945 and thereafter the congregation was preponderantly Reform, some half-dozen or more of its member families being Conservative, and a small group, numbering hardly more than a dozen families, still remaining Orthodox. Up to that time, in the 1920's and 1930's, fully half or more of the congregation had consisted of Conservative and Orthodox families, but many of these passed away

or left the city for Charleston, W. Va., as well as for Eastern
cities. The congregation, overwhelmingly (perhaps as high as
75%) Reform by 1947, and by that time using only the Reform
*Union Prayer Book* for all Sabbath, holiday, and High Holy Day
religious services (in addition to the Conservative and Orthodox
*Machzorim* used at extra Conservative and Orthodox services on
both days of Rosh Hashanah and on Yom Kippur), joined the
Union of American Hebrew Congregations on December 8,
1947, at the instance of Rabbi Abraham I. Shinedling and after
a visit paid to the congregation by Rabbi Leo J. Stillpass, then
a regional representative of the U. A. H. C. and rabbi of the
Reform Congregation Beth-El, of Knoxville, Tenn. Thus, from
1945 on, and perhaps also for a few years previously, there has
always been, in Congregation Ahavath Sholom, a Conservative
service, as well as an Orthodox service, each year, in the Temple,
but only on the High Holy Days (two days of Rosh Hashanah
and on Yom Kippur), in addition to the Reform Jewish services.
The weekly Sabbath evening and morning services, as well as
the services on all other Jewish holidays, have always been Reform, with the exception that in some years, on the first and
second days of Pesach and on the first two and last two days of
Sukkoth, or on the first and eighth days of Sukkoth, a handful
of Orthodox and Conservative members (all of them men) held
occasional Orthodox religious services during the past fifteen
years.

For the most part, Philip Platnick, the older brother of
Nathan Platnick, was the leader of the small Conservative group
in the congregation, and he conducted the evening and morning
Conservative religious services on Rosh Hashanah (one day)
and on Yom Kippur, in the years from about 1945 to the present.
Louis Diamond, his two sons Isaac and Herman Diamond,
Solomon Hyman (deceased), Isaac Greenspon (deceased), Raymond Seligman of North Fork (deceased); the Kaufman
brothers of Kimball, W. Va.; Joseph Matz, and Benjamin
Bernhard Matz (deceased) represented the small Orthodox
group remaining in the congregation after the year 1945. Louis
Diamond and Benjamin B. Matz conducted the Orthodox
services for a number of years after 1945 on the High Holy Days;

the Orthodox members of the congregation residing in Princeton conduct their own High Holy Day services. Minyan services for Yahrzeit and for mourners were held in the Temple building at any time, by request, conducted by the rabbi or by some lay member of the congregation.

Isadore Cohen, Nathan Platnick, William P. Gottlieb, and Sidney J. Kwass were leaders of the Reform element. Isadore Cohen served for years, especially during the rabbinates of Abraham I. Shinedling, Harold L. Gelfman, and Herbert J. Wilner, as chairman of the Committee on Religion, whose duty it was to arrange for, and set the time of, the successive Orthodox, Conservative, and Reform services on the eve and in the morning of the first day of Rosh Hashanah and on Yom Kippur, and during the all-day religious services for Yom Kippur day. Frank Nelson was the representative of the Reform group of the Princeton members of the congregation.

### COMPLETE LIST OF THE RABBIS AND STUDENT RABBIS IN BLUEFIELD

M. Levinson (exact dates now unknown)

Simon Cohen (exact dates now unknown)

Kalman Slifkin (1907–1931) — full-time — rabbi, Shochet, Mohel, and Chazan — Orthodox

Alexander A. Steinbach (1921–1922) — full-time — Conservative (Reform ?)

Avery J. Grossfield (1930–1931) — part-time — Reform

Nathan A. Perilman (1931–1932) — part-time — Reform

Nathaniel S. Share (1932–1933) — full-time — Reform

John Ruskin (Russkind) (1933–1934) — full-time — Conservative

Bernard [?] Harrison (dates now unknown) — Reform

Colman A. Zwitman (1934–1936) — full-time — Reform[1]

---

[1] There is a conflict here in the records of the congregation. According to some of the congregational records, as above stated, there was no full-time rabbi, but there were only student rabbis, from 1934 to 1936. However, this is the exact period assigned, in other records of the congregation, to the rabbinate of Colman A. Zwitman, who is recorded as having served as the full-time rabbi of the congrega-

Julius Kravetz (1936–1943) — full-time — Reform

A. [Alfred] Stanley Dreyfus (1943–1944 and 1946–1947) — part-time student rabbi, Reform, in his first year of service in Bluefield; in his second year as part-time rabbi, he was a graduate rabbi, taking additional studies at the Hebrew Union College, in Cincinnati, in preparation for his doctorate.

Sanford E. Rosen (1944–1945) — part-time student rabbi — Reform

Jerome W. Grollman (1945–1946) — part-time student rabbi — Reform

Aaron Kammerling (of Chicago) (September, 1946, only for the High Holy Days)

Abraham I. Shinedling (September 1, 1947, to September 1, 1950)— full-time — Reform

Harold L. Gelfman (September, 1950, to August, 1952) — full-time — Reform

Herbert J. Wilner (September, 1952, to August, 1957) — full-time — Reform

Amos Schauss (December, 1957) — full-time — Reform (still the incumbent in 1959)

### Brief Biographical Sketches of the Bluefield Congregation Rabbis and Student Rabbis

M. Levinson. According to the congregational records, M. Levinson was the first-known rabbi of Ahavath Sholom Congregation, serving, apparently, in the early 1900's, for perhaps two or three years, or even less, before the arrival of the Reverend Kalman Slifkin in 1907 [1906?]. He may have been the immediate predecessor of Kalman Slifkin. His full first name is now unknown. It may have been Morris or Moses Levinson. He was an Orthodox rabbi.

---

tion then (1934–1936), and whose ministry is well-remembered by some of the old-time members of the congregation. Later, after leaving Bluefield, Colman A. Zwitman became a chaplain in the Armed Forces of the United States, and died in 1950 of a tropical disease contracted in the course of his Army service, after serving with distinction, for several years after his return, as rabbi of Temple Israel, in Miami, Fla.

SIMON COHEN. Simon Cohen was also an early rabbi of the congregation, whose period of service may have come between that of M. Levinson and Kalman Slifkin. No data on his rabbinate are recorded in the congregational files. In and before 1907 he is mentioned as living, or residing, in Bluefield. He was not the same as the Simon R. Cohen who, ordained by the Hebrew Union College, in Cincinnati (Reform), in 1899, later served in Brooklyn, N. Y., for many years as the rabbi of Union Temple, and died at Brooklyn in 1943. The Bluefield Simon Cohen was Orthodox.

As has been mentioned above, it is quite possible that this early "Rabbi" Simon Cohen was, in actuality, Simon A. [Aaron] Cohen, the father of Isadore Cohen. If this "theory" is correct, then Simon A. Cohen came to Bluefield in 1905, from his native Lithuania, together with his son Isadore Cohen and other members of the Cohen family, and he served unofficially as the "rabbi" and as the Hebrew teacher of the congregation for a year or two, perhaps until 1906 or 1907, when Kalman Slifkin came to the city as rabbi of the congregation. [1]

KALMAN SLIFKIN. Kalman Slifkin was born in Russia in 1871, and died at Bluefield, W. Va., in 1940. He emigrated from Russia to Ireland in 1905, and only about one year later, in either 1906 or 1907, he left Ireland and settled in Bluefield, where he remained for the rest of his life, having been called to Bluefield to be the first permanent rabbi, Chazan, and Shochet of the congregation. For either 33 or 34 years he served as rabbi in Bluefield, from 1906 or 1907 to 1940, part of the time, from 1921 to 1922, and from 1930 to 1940, in cooperation, as Mohel and assistant after his retirement, with the active Conservative or Reform rabbis of the congregation. Rabbi Slifkin himself always remained an undeviating and strictly Orthodox rabbi.

In 1907, a year or less after his settlement in Bluefield, he sent to Ireland for his wife and four children to join him

---

[1] See Note 1, page 414, for confirmation of the "theory" that Simon A. Cohen, the father of Isadore and Barney Cohen, actually served as the unofficial rabbi and as the Hebrew teacher of the Bluefield congregation from 1905 to 1907.

in Bluefield. In 1907, that same year, one of his daughters was born in Bluefield.

From September, 1936, until his death in 1940, Rabbi Kalman Slifkin lived in Bluefield as the retired, or semi-retired, rabbi, Chazan, Shochet, and Mohel of the congregation (the only Chazan, Shochet and Mohel, apparently, whom the congregation ever had), on occasions assisting Julius Kravetz, who had come to the congregation as the full-time rabbi in September, 1936. From 1906 or 1907 until 1936 (and, when needed and called upon, also from 1936 to 1940), Kalman Slifkin served the entire Bluefield area, including the whole of McDowell County (Welch, North Fork, Keystone, and Kimball), Princeton, the rest of Mercer County, and Pocahontas, Va., as Shochet, and as a Mohel, and served also as cantor (Chazan) on the High Holy Days.

Of his children, Toby (Mrs. I. Jacob) Blank and Samuel Slifkin still reside in Bluefield; Isaac L. Slifkin, a former Bluefielder, now lives in New England.

ALEXANDER ALAN STEINBACH. Rabbi Alexander A. Steinbach became rabbi of Congregation Ahavath Sholom in May, 1921, and served until August 31, 1922, when he left the city to become rabbi of Temple Beth El, in Norfolk, Va. Bluefield was his first congregation after his ordination, and at that time the late Henry Rodgin was president of the congregation. In September, 1934, he left Norfolk to become rabbi of Temple Ahavath Sholom, in Flatbush (Brooklyn), N. Y.; in May, 1952, he was given life tenure.

Alexander A. Steinbach was born in Baltimore, Md., on February 2, 1894. He was ordained by the Hebrew Union College in 1930, from which he later received the honorary degree of Doctor of Divinity. He is a graduate of Johns Hopkins University, in Baltimore. He served as a United States Army chaplain in the Eighth Service Command during the Second World War, and is editor of the *Jewish Book Annual* of the National Jewish Book Council. In Brooklyn, he was president of the Metropolitan Jewish Book Council, and the first president of the Brooklyn Association of Reform Rabbis. A member of the Commission on Ceremonies and also of the Liturgical Committee of the C. C. A. R., he is the author of seven books, including *Sabbath Queen; What Is Judaism?; Musings and Meditations; In Search of the Permanent;* and *Bitter-Sweet.*

AVERY J. GROSSFIELD. Avery J. Grossfield was the first student rabbi from the Hebrew Union College, to serve the Bluefield-Princeton congregation. He acted as student rabbi on a bi-weekly basis from September, 1930, to June, 1931, when he was ordained. He was succeeded by Nathan A. Perilman, on a part-time basis (1931–1932).

Avery J. Grossfield, born in New York City, was awarded the earned degree of Doctor of Hebrew Literature in Jewish social studies, his thesis subject having been, "Some Juvenile Delinquents — A Study of Three Hundred Cases." After serving for several years as rabbi of Beth Israel Congregation, in Florence, S. C., he was called, in September, 1957, to be rabbi of Temple Beth Avodah, in Westbury, N. Y. In September, 1959, Rabbi Avery J. Grossfield left Westbury, L. I., to become rabbi of Temple Rodef Sholom, in Port Arthur, Tex.

NATHAN A. PERILMAN. Nathan A. Perilman (born in Marietta, Ohio, on June 2, 1905) served as the student rabbi of the Bluefield-Princeton congregation from 1931 to 1932. He received the B.A. degree from the University of Pittsburgh in 1926, and was ordained by the Hebrew Union College in 1932. In the very month of his ordination (June, 1932) he was elected to the position of assistant rabbi of Temple Emanu-El, in New York; in 1938 he became associate rabbi of that congregation, and in 1948 its rabbi. In 1959 he still held the position of Rabbi of Emanu-El Congregation, New York, together with Rabbi Julius Mark, the Senior Rabbi.

NATHANIEL S. SHARE. Nathaniel S. Share served as the full-time rabbi of Congregation Ahavath Sholom, of Bluefield-Princeton, from 1932 to 1933. Born in Montreal, Canada, on May 12, 1908, he came to the United States in 1917. He received the B.A. degree from the University of Cincinnati in 1931, and was ordained by the Hebrew Union College in 1932. Since 1934 he has served as rabbi of Congregation Gates of Prayer, in New Orleans.

BERNARD [?] HARRISON. A rabbi by the last name of Harrison, according to the congregational records, served as a student rabbi of the congregation, at an unspecified time. It is possible that he was the Bernard Harrison who, ordained by the Jewish Institute of Religion, of New York, in 1938, died at Beverly Hills, Calif., in 1957.[1]

JULIUS KRAVETZ. Julius Kravetz (born in Poland, on March 9, 1908) served as the full-time, permanent rabbi of Congregation Ahavath Sholom from September, 1936, until April or May, 1943, when he left the city to become a chaplain in the United States Army in the Second World War, attaining the final rank of captain. He was brought to the United States from Poland in the very year of his birth by his parents, who then settled in Rochester, N. Y.

Julius Kravetz received the B.A. degree from the University of Rochester in 1930, and was ordained, and was awarded the degree of Master of Hebrew Literature, by the Jewish Institute of Religion, in New York, in 1934. During his close to seven years of service as rabbi in Bluefield, he served also the Welch Congregation Emanuel, as well as B'nai Israel Congregation, in Keystone, on a part-time basis. He served also the Princeton group of Ahavath Sholom Congregation. As an Army chaplain, he saw service in the Pacific theatre of war.

In 1947, at the end of his volunteer chaplaincy service with the United States Army, Julius Kravetz did not return to Bluefield, due to the adverse condition of his parents' health, but accepted a position as rabbi of a congregation in Tallahassee, Fla. Later he went to Gainesville, Fla., to become Hillel Director at the University of Florida, and still later he served as the rabbi of Temple Beth El, in Bainbridge, Ga. In 1956 he left the active congregational rabbinate and moved to New York, where he pursued advanced studies and taught a course in Talmud at the New York School of the H. U. C. - J. I. R. (1956–1959).

---

[1] No data at all about the brief rabbinates of M. Levinson, Simon Cohen, and [Bernard?] Harrison survive in the congregational records.

Beginning in September, 1958, with the High Holy Days,
Rabbi Kravetz was appointed religious adviser to the Jewish
students in Dartmouth College, at Hanover, N. H., coming
to the campus on every other weekend to conduct religious
services and to counsel the students. His appointment to
that position is the first in the history of Dartmouth College.
At the same time, he continued his work and courses at the
J. I. R., in New York, as well as his duties as an instructor
in Talmud at the New York School.

A. [ALFRED] STANLEY DREYFUS. Rabbi Alfred Stanley Dreyfus
(more usually known as Stanley Dreyfus) was born in
Youngstown, Ohio, on January 31, 1921. He served as
rabbi of Congregation Ahavath Sholom for two non-
successive years, the first time as a part-time student rabbi
(1943–1944), and the second time (1946–1947) as a part-
time graduate rabbi. He was ordained by the Hebrew
Union College in 1946, and in 1951 he received the Ph.D.
degree there; he had received the B.A. degree from the
University of Cincinnati in 1942.

After his ordination in 1946, A. Stanley Dreyfus did
post-graduate study at the H. U. C. for several years, and
then became rabbi of the congregation at Beaver Falls, Pa.
A year or two later he was elected rabbi of the United
Hebrew Congregation in Terre Haute, Ind. (1951), serving
until September, 1956, with a leave of absence for about
two years, from 1953 to 1955, for service as a chaplain in
the United States Army. From 1951 to 1953 he served also
as the Jewish chaplain in the United States Penitentiary in
Terre Haute. In September, 1956, he became rabbi of
Temple B'nai Israel, in Galveston, Tex. It is of interest
that the wife of A. Stanley Dreyfus, the former Marianne
Berlak, is a granddaughter of the famous Rabbi Leo Baeck
(now deceased), formerly of Germany, and of German
Nazi concentration camp fame, who later became a professor at the Hebrew Union College, in Cincinnati.

SANFORD E. ROSEN. Sanford E. Rosen (born on May 13, 1920,
at Cleveland, Ohio) served as the part-time student rabbi
of Congregation Ahavath Sholom from 1944 to 1945. He

PLATE XV

The Synagogue at the corner of Lee and Court Streets, Charleston, W. Va., formerly the State Street Methodist Church, the home of B'nai Jacob Congregation from 1908 to 1949.

(see page 666)

PLATE XVI

The Ark and Interior of the Main Section of the new B'nai Jacob Synagogue of Charleston, West Virginia

was ordained by the Hebrew Union College in 1947. In 1951 he became the rabbi of the Peninsula Temple Beth El, in San Mateo, Calif., and was still serving in this position in 1959. In 1956–1957 he served also as visiting lecturer on the humanities at Stanford University.

The following excerpts are taken from a long and interesting letter written to me by Sanford E. Rosen on March 29, 1957, from San Mateo, Calif., which I cite because of its intense human interest, and as the résumé, or summary, of a Reform rabbinical career, including a considerable amount of moving from pulpit to pulpit, which is, unfortunately, only too often, the lot of rabbis, of all branches of Judaism:

.... It is difficult now to recollect details of the [my] experience in Bluefield when, as you know, that occurred more than 12 years ago, and so much has happened in the interim ....

I was born in Cleveland, Ohio, on May 13, 1920.[1] I received my Bachelor of Arts degree from Adelbert College of Western Reserve University, in Cleveland, in 1941; the Bachelor of Hebrew Letters [degree] at the Hebrew Union College in 1944; [and the] Master of Hebrew Letters [degree] and [my] ordination [the degree of Rabbi] at the Hebrew Union College (1947).

I was still a student entering my Junior year when I left Bluefield in 1945 for Shreveport, Louisiana, where I occupied the pulpit as a licensee of Congregation B'nai Zion during David Lefkowitz Jr.'s absence for military duty. I returned to the Hebrew Union College in early 1946 to complete my studies and served the congregation at Kokomo, Indiana, on a bi-weekly basis during my Senior year.

Upon ordination I became the first and founding Rabbi of Temple Beth El, [in] Bakersfield, California. Four years later (1951) I became the first and founding Rabbi of Peninsula Temple Beth El, [in] San Mateo, [California]. Our congregation here is just now completing a $500,000 building program.

I suspect that if I looked through my files I would find the names of congregational officers, school teachers, etc. [of Bluefield], but I am afraid that this would require more time .... But I do recollect that at the time I served in Bluefield, the congregation had recently sold

---

[1] My younger colleague, Sanford E. Rosen, then, was born exactly four weeks before my ordination at the Hebrew Union College, on June 10, 1920. Indeed, as far as rabbis, at least, go, the old Biblical proverb (*Ecclesiastes* 1:4), *dor holech vedor ba*, "One generation comes, and another generation goes," still applies.

their Temple and were using the B'nai B'rith meeting rooms for services. Of course, you know that Julius Kravitz [Kravetz], who was overseas, was the official Rabbi, and that I was merely serving as a replacement of [for] him on a bi-weekly student basis . . . . The B'nai B'rith . . . would use the same premises for their meetings and [card] games, but this equipment was all covered up for the Sabbath eve services . . . . The outstanding event of the year in Bluefield was a community-wide Thanksgiving [Day] observance in which the local ministers were extremely cooperative.

JEROME W. GROLLMAN. A more complete biography of Jerome W. Grollman will be found in the section on Williamson. He served as the student rabbi of Congregation Ahavath Sholom, in Bluefield, for one year, from 1945 to 1946, before he was ordained at the Hebrew Union College, in Cincinnati, in 1948. In 1956 to 1957, and until May, 1958, Jerome W. Grollman served as associate rabbi of United Hebrew Congregation, in St. Louis. In May, 1958, he was formally installed as rabbi of that congregation. In Bluefield, in August, 1945, he participated, as the representative of the Jewish community, in V-J Day services, celebrating the surrender of Japan and the end of the Second World War. He is a maternal nephew of Mrs. Henry (Anna Grollman) Rodgin, of Bluefield.

ABRAHAM I. SHINEDLING. A fuller biography of Rabbi Abraham I. Shinedling will be found in the section on Beckley. He came to Bluefield as the rabbi of Congregation Ahavath Sholom on September 1, 1947, from his previous position in Selma, Alabama, where he had served from September, 1944, to August 31, 1947, as the rabbi of Congregation Mishkan Israel. Services in Bluefield for the High Holy Days of September, 1947, were conducted by him at the Masonic Temple, on Federal Street, with the assistance of Philip Platnick (for the Conservative services) and of Louis Diamond and Benjamin B. Matz (for the Orthodox services); thereafter the new Temple on Albemarle Street was used for the High Holy Day services. From September, 1947, to the end of August, 1948, during his entire first year in Bluefield, the Friday night and the Saturday morning services and the sessions of the Religious School were held in the old (Consolidated) Bus Terminal building, on the second floor, running through most of the way from Bland Street to Federal Street.

During Abraham I. Shinedling's three-year stay in Bluefield as rabbi, until he left on September 1, 1950, to become rabbi of Congregation Beth El, in nearby Beckley, Mrs. Nathan (Edna E.) Platnick served as superintendent of the Religious School, and NATHAN PLATNICK was the PRESIDENT of the congregation. Other Religious School teachers in the period from September, 1947, to June, 1950, were:

Philip Gerard
Samuel Laufer (of Princeton)
Benjamin Lazer
Selma Lubliner
Bert Rappoport

Mrs. Helen L. (Abraham I.)
   Shinedling
Meyer J. Spiro
Harold Tomchin (of Princeton)

Sisterhood presidents during his rabbinate in Bluefield were:

1947–1948: Mrs. Jessel S. (Beatrice) Salzberg
1948–1950: Mrs. Joseph (Ethel J.) Tomchin

Other congregational officers during that three-year period from 1947 to 1950 included the following:

VICE PRESIDENT: Frank Nelson (of Princeton)
TREASURER: William P. Gottlieb
ASSISTANT TREASURER: Frank Klauber
SECRETARY: Abe Angrist (following Joseph Nathan)

DIRECTORS:

Fred Gilbert
Sidney J. Kwass
Yankee Barbakow (of Princeton)

Jerome Katz
Sidney Rosenthal

Into the Bluefield congregational Religious School Abraham I. Shinedling and Mrs. Nathan Platnick successfully introduced, as the originators, the Junior Congregation, which held assembly programs every Sunday morning in the Religious School; assisted in the conducting of the regular Saturday morning Temple services, including the reading of the translation of the Torah and Haftarah portions; and collected and dispensed charity and book fund money.

While in Bluefield, Rabbi Abraham I. Shinedling served frequently as a Jewish Chautauqua Society lecturer at universities and colleges in West Virginia, Virginia, Kentucky, and Tennessee; and served as the treasurer of the Bluefield Ministerial Association in 1948 to 1950. On June 6, 1959, the Hebrew Union College-Jewish Institute of Religion awarded him the degree of Doctor of Divinity *honoris causa* in Cincinnati.

HAROLD L. GELFMAN. Harold L. Gelfman was born on November 11, 1910, at Springfield, Mass. He was ordained by the Hebrew Union College in 1938. On September 1, 1950, he succeeded Abraham I. Shinedling as the rabbi of the Bluefield congregation, and remained with the congregation for two years, until August, 1952. He came to Bluefield from Elmira, N. Y., where he had served as rabbi of Temple B'nai Israel. In September, 1952, he went to Jackson, Mich., as rabbi of Temple Beth Israel; from September, 1956, to September, 1958, he served as rabbi of The Cape Cod Synagogue, in Hyannis, Mass.; and in September, 1958, he was elected rabbi of Congregation Beth Israel, in Macon, Ga. From 1941 to 1942 Harold L. Gelfman had served as the rabbi of Congregation Beth El, in Beckley.

HERBERT J. WILNER. Herbert J. Wilner (born on December 10, 1913, in Pittsburgh, Pa.) succeeded Harold L. Gelfman as rabbi of Congregation Ahavath Sholom, in Bluefield, in early September, 1952. In early September, 1957, after five years with the congregation, he left Bluefield to become rabbi of Temple Shalom, in Levittown, Pa. He came to Bluefield from Cumberland, Md., where he had served as rabbi of B'er Chayim Congregation from 1948 to 1952.

Herbert J. Wilner was ordained by the Jewish Institute of Religion, in New York City, in 1940. He had received the B.A. degree from the University of Rochester in 1935, and he received the earned degree of Doctor of Hebrew Literature from the H. U. C. - J. I. R., in Cincinnati, in 1953. From 1941 to 1948 he had served as rabbi of Temple

Beth-El, in St. Petersburg, Fla.; in 1948, he was Jewish chaplain for the United States Veterans Administration [Hospital] at Bay Pines, Fla.[1]

While in Bluefield, Herbert J. Wilner served as a lecturer for the Jewish Chautauqua Society, and also as the first chairman of the Bluefield Human Relations Committee. In 1957 he was the first treasurer of the West Virginia Association for Mental Health (whose name was officially changed upon its affiliation with the National Association for Mental Health, having been known previously as the West Virginia Mental Health Society, of which Rabbi Wilner was the second treasurer). He served also as the first treasurer of the Mercer County Mental Health Society.

AMOS SCHAUSS. Amos Schauss (ordained by the H. U. C. - J. I. R., in Cincinnati, in June, 1953) came to Bluefield in December, 1957, to succeed Herbert J. Wilner as the rabbi of Congregation Ahavath Sholom. (He was born at New York City, on September 24, 1925.) He had previously been rabbi of Temple B'nai Israel, in Butte, Mont. From 1958 to 1959, and continuing thereafter, Rabbi Amos Schauss served as part-time Jewish chaplain at the Federal Reformatory for Women, at Alderson, W. Va., under the auspices of the W. V. F. T. S. He is the son of Hayyim Schauss (1884–1953), historian and author, who died at Los Angeles on October 4, 1953, and was the author of *Jewish Festivals* and of a number of works on Jewish history.

## THE BLUEFIELD TEMPLE SISTERHOOD [2]

The Bluefield Temple Sisterhood (the Bluefield-Princeton Sisterhood) of Congregation Ahavath Sholom was organized in June, 1921. The list of the charter members has, apparently,

---

[1] In September, 1961, Rabbi Herbert J. Wilner moved to Morgantown, where he was appointed Director of the Hillel Foundation at West Virginia University, and was elected rabbi of The Tree of Life Congregation.

[2] Much of the material presented in the following section on the Bluefield Temple Sisterhood was furnished to me by my old and friendly Bluefield congregants Mrs. Edna E. (Nathan) Platnick, Mrs. Anna A. (Nathan) Effron, and Mrs. Fannie (Philip) Platnick, all three of them most active workers in the cause and work of the Bluefield Sisterhood and Congregation.

not been preserved. The Bluefield Sisterhood affiliated with the
N. F. T. S. on January 11, 1929, with 40 members. The president
of the Sisterhood at that time was Mrs. Ben Baker, and the
secretary was Mrs. J. [Joseph] I. Kwass [the mother of Sidney J.
Kwass]. It is affiliated also with the W. V. F. T. S.

Permanent committees of the Bluefield Sisterhood are:

| | |
|---|---|
| Uniongrams | Publicity |
| Programs | Cemetery |
| Temple Youth | Telephone |
| Sunday School | P. T. A. [Parent-Teachers' |
| Honor Roll | Association] |
| Cradle Roll | Membership |
| Synagogue | Friday Night Social |
| Stationery | Hostesses |
| Sisterhood News | |

The Bluefield (Bluefield-Princeton) Sisterhood has six active
circles for fund-raising and social affairs. The Sisterhood also
contributed more than $250 to the House of Living Judaism, in
New York City, as well as a total of $300 to the Hillel Foundation
in Morgantown. It maintains and sponsors the Religious [Sun-
day] School, contributes to the maintenance of the Temple, and
pays the salaries of the teachers of the Religious School.

From September, 1946, to the end of August, 1948, when the
B'nai B'rith rooms above the Consolidated Bus Terminal, on
Bland Street, were used for the temporary site of the Sunday
School and of the Temple, many of the Sisterhood meetings also
were held there, until the new Temple at 632 Albemarle Street
was opened for use in early September, 1948. The Bluefield
Sisterhood contributed $250 towards the cost of renovating these
temporary quarters, in November, 1946. During the years before
the Albemarle Street Temple building was completed, and after
the Scott Street Synagogue was sold (1941), many of the major
Sisterhood meetings and functions were held in the Appalachian
Electric Company's hospitality and assembly rooms, on Bland
Street.

A chronological record of Sisterhood membership, officers, events and activities for the period from 1935 to 1959 follows:[1]

## 1935

The president of the Bluefield Sisterhood from 1935 to 1936 was Mrs. Nathan (Anna A.) Effron; the secretary during that year was Mrs. Jerome (Hilda) Katz. In July, 1935, the Sisterhood "labored to pay off an $800 note, or mortgage, due on the Scott Street Synagogue."

Sisterhood members of record in the year 1935 [not all-inclusive] included also the following:

Mrs. B. Block
Mrs. Leon (Leo) Feingold
Mrs. Freda A. Frank
Mrs. Ezra Gilbert
Mrs. Solomon [Frieda]
   Hyman
Mrs. B. [Ben D.] Lennett
Mrs. H. Lubliner

Mrs. I. [Joseph I. ?] Matz
Mrs. D. Schlossberg
Mrs. Goodwin Schlossberg
Mrs. Isaac L. Slifkin
Mrs. Harry Stolch
Mrs. Rebecca (B. J.)
   Wagner

## 1935–1936

Members in 1935–1936 included:

Mrs. Hugo Benjamin
Mrs. Solomon [Frieda] Hyman
Mrs. Ben Lennett
Mrs. H. Lubliner
Mrs. Mark Masters
Mrs. Nathan [Rose C.] Matz
Mrs. Joseph I. Matz
Mrs. Ida [Joseph] Platnick [mother of Nathan Platnick]
Mrs. Isaac L. Slifkin

---

[1] There are no records at all available, or extant, for the period of 15 years from 1921 to 1935. These records were either lost, although they most certainly existed originally, or they were inadvertently destroyed.

New members in 1936 are recorded as follows:

Mrs. Sarah [T.] [Louis] Diamond
Mrs. Ben (Lois) Lazer
Mrs. M. [Mark] Masters

In December, 1936, "as the result of a successful cabaret party conducted by the Sisterhood at the West Virginian Hotel, the note on the Scott Street Synagogue was reduced from $800 to $200."

## 1936–1937

The State Sisterhood Convention was held in Bluefield on October 11 and 12, 1936. The guest speaker was Rabbi Alexander Alan Steinbach, of Brooklyn, N. Y., formerly a rabbi of the congregation. Mrs. Harry (Rose A.) Clark was State corresponding secretary from 1935 to 1937, and again, in 1937 to 1938, she served as the corresponding secretary of the W. V. F. T. S.

### OFFICERS FOR 1936–1937

In 1936–1937, MRS. NATHAN EFFRON again served as the local president, having been re-elected. During that year, MRS. ROSE C. (NATHAN) Matz served as its secretary.

Other officers for 1936–1937 included:

1ST VICE PRESIDENT: Mrs. Sam [Nell] Fine
2ND VICE PRESIDENT: Mrs. H. Lubliner
TREASURER: Mrs. Goodwin Schlossberg

### NEW SISTERHOOD MEMBERS IN 1937 WERE:

Mrs. S. Goodstein
Mrs. S. Holswieg

In 1936–1937, Mrs. Freda A. Frank was correspondent, from Bluefield, of the *Sisterhood News of West Virginia*.

## 1937–1938

The Sisterhood officers for 1937–1938:

PRESIDENT: Mrs. Henry (Anna G.) Rodgin
1ST VICE PRESIDENT: Mrs. Sam [Nell] Fine (re-elected)
2ND VICE PRESIDENT: Mrs. Boris Borinsky (of Princeton)
SECRETARY: Mrs. Sidney J. [Edna D.] Kwass
TREASURER: Mrs. Hugo Benjamin

### PRINCETON MEMBERS OF THE AHAVATH SHOLOM CONGREGATION SISTERHOOD IN 1937–1938

| | |
|---|---|
| Mrs. B. Barbakow | Mrs. S. Goodstein |
| Mrs. Oscar Baum | Mrs. Frank [Beatrice E.] Nelson |
| Mrs. Boris Borinsky | Mrs. Joseph [Ethel J.] Tomchin |
| Mrs. Sam [Sarah] DeLott | Mrs. Ralph [Ida E.] Weinberg |
| Mrs. Henry Deitz | Mrs. Robert [Charlotte] Effron |
| Mrs. Leon Feingold | |

Mrs. Henry Rodgin served for several years (1938–1941) as chairman of the Sisterhood Sunday School Committee. In December, 1938, Mrs. Sydney [Lillian K.] Tucker was elected to fill the unexpired term as secretary of Mrs. Sidney J. [Edna D.] Kwass, who had resigned her office.

In 1937–1938, Mrs. Abraham N. [Sarah Aaron] Schlossberg was president of the W. V. F. T. S.

## 1938–1939

### SISTERHOOD OFFICERS FOR 1938–1939:

PRESIDENT: Mrs. Henry [Anna G.] Rodgin [re-elected]
1ST VICE PRESIDENT: Mrs. Sam [Nell] Fine [re-elected]
2ND VICE PRESIDENT: Mrs. Boris Borinsky (of Princeton) (re-elected)
SECRETARY: Mrs. Sidney J. Kwass (replaced in December, 1938, by Mrs. Sydney Tucker)
TREASURER: Mrs. Ezra Gilbert (re-elected)

## New Sisterhood Members in 1938–1940

Mrs. I. J. [Jack] [Toby S.] Blank     Mrs. Meyer Marcus
Mrs. Philip Cohen                     Mrs. D. Silber
Mrs. Bernard Effron                   Mrs. J. H. Todd
Mrs. J. Harris                        Mrs. Henry (Helen) Tucker

## Sisterhood Officers in 1939–1940

PRESIDENT: Mrs. Abraham N. [Sarah A.] Schlossberg
1ST VICE PRESIDENT: Mrs. Sam [Nell] Fine
2ND VICE PRESIDENT: Mrs. Oscar Baum (of Princeton)
SECRETARY: Mrs. Freda A. Frank
TREASURER: Mrs. Ezra Gilbert

## Sisterhood Officers for 1940–1941:

PRESIDENT: Mrs. Max [Trudy] Turk
1ST VICE PRESIDENT: Mrs. Joseph I. Matz
2ND VICE PRESIDENT: Mrs. Oscar Baum (of Princeton)
SECRETARY: Mrs. Freda A. Frank
TREASURER: Mrs. Hugo Benjamin

## Sisterhood [New Members] in 1940–1945 [1]

Mrs. E. Alifeld (1940)
Mrs. J. I. Blake (1940)
Mrs. William Cohen (1940)
Mrs. Henry Deitz (of Princeton) (1940)
Mrs. Rose (Philip) Fliegelman (1940)
Mrs. M. B. Goldman (1940)
Mrs. Joseph Lisagor (of Princeton) (1940)
Mrs. L. Magrill (of Pocahontas, Va.) (1940)
Mrs. Benjamin B. Matz (1940)
Mrs. L. Meron (1940)

---

[1] The figure in parentheses indicates the year in which the member joined the Temple Sisterhood.

Mrs. H. Meyers (1940)
Mrs. Gilbert Orin (1941–1942)
Mrs. Stella Pritchard (1943–1944)
Mrs. Isidor Steckler (1940)
Mrs. Theodore (Bertie Cohen) Steiner (1940)
Mrs. Albert Uhdin (1941)
  [spelled in the records often also as Ehudin]

## SISTERHOOD OFFICERS FOR 1941–1942

PRESIDENT: Mrs. Harry [Rose A.] Clark
1ST VICE PRESIDENT: Mrs. Freda A. Frank (Mrs. Louis
  Zaltzman)
2ND VICE PRESIDENT: Mrs. Joseph [Ethel J.] Tomchin
SECRETARY: Mrs. Hyman [Sylvia F.] Effron
TREASURER: Mrs. Sidney J. [Edna D.] Kwass

## SISTERHOOD MEMBERS LISTED AS AFFILIATED IN 1941–1942 AND EARLIER

Mrs. S. Angrist
Mrs. B. Barbakow (of Princeton)
Mrs. Hugo Benjamin
Mrs. Abe Borinsky (of Princeton)
Mrs. Ben Cohen
Mrs. S. [Henry] Deitz (of Princeton)
Mrs. Louis [Sarah Turk] Diamond
Mrs. Albert Ehudin [Uhdin]
Mrs. Ezra Gilbert
Mrs. L. Magrill (of Pocahontas, Va.)
Mrs. D. Silber
Mrs. Sorin
  [In all likelihood, a scribal error for Mrs. G.
  (Gilbert) Orin]
Mrs. Goodwin Schlossberg
Mrs. Theodore [Bertie Cohen] Steiner
Mrs. Ralph (Ida E.) Weinberg
Mrs. Louis (Freda A. Frank) Zaltzman

Mrs. Roberta [Bertie; Mrs. Theodore] Steiner served as secretary of the local Sisterhood in 1942–1943. Otherwise there is no record extant of the other Sisterhood officers who served in the year 1942–1943. In 1943–1944, also, Mrs. Roberta Steiner served as the local Sisterhood secretary pro tempore.

### SISTERHOOD OFFICERS FOR 1943–1944

PRESIDENT: Mrs. Louis Zaltzman (Freda Frank Zaltzman)
1ST VICE PRESIDENT: Mrs. Sidney J. (Edna D.) Kwass
2ND VICE PRESIDENT: Mrs. Hyman (Sylvia F.) Effron
SECRETARY: Mrs. Jessel S. (Beatrice) Salzberg
TREASURER: Mrs. David (Gertrude) Platnick

### SISTERHOOD OFFICERS FOR 1944–1945

PRESIDENT: Mrs. Sidney J. Kwass
1ST VICE PRESIDENT: Mrs. Max (Esther L.) Auerbach
2ND VICE PRESIDENT: Mrs. Hyman Effron
SECRETARY: Mrs. Jessel S. (Beatrice) Salzberg
TREASURER: Mrs. David (Gertrude) Platnick

### SISTERHOOD OFFICERS FOR 1945–1946

PRESIDENT: Mrs. Max (Esther L.) Auerbach
1ST VICE PRESIDENT: Mrs. Hyman Effron
2ND VICE PRESIDENT: Mrs. Sidney (Helen B.) Rosenthal
SECRETARY: Mrs. Jessel S. (Beatrice) Salzberg
TREASURER: Mrs. David Platnick

### COMPLETE ROSTER OF THE MEMBERS OF THE BLUEFIELD-PRINCETON SISTERHOOD IN 1945–1946

[73 members]

Mrs. A. [S.] Angrist
Mrs. Max [Esther L.] Auerbach
Mrs. I. Alifeld
Mrs. Jack [I. J.] (Toby S.) Blank

Mrs. Hugo Benjamin
Mrs. Harry Barbakow (of Princeton)
Mrs. Oscar Baum (of Princeton)
Mrs. Boris Borinsky (of Princeton)
Mrs. Harry (Rose A.) Clark
Mrs. Isadore (Flora G.) Cohen
Mrs. William Cohen
Mrs. Saul (Lucille J.) Cohen
Mrs. Henry Deitz (of Princeton)
Mrs. Samuel (Sarah) DeLott
Mrs. Leon Diamond
Mrs. Louis [Sarah T.] Diamond
Mrs. Hyman (Sylvia F.) Effron
Mrs. Nathan (Anna A.) Effron
Mrs. Robert (Charlotte) Effron (of Princeton)
Mrs. Philip (Rose) Fliegelman
Mrs. Abe Forman
Mrs. Sam (Nell) Fine
Mrs. Fred (Reva D.) Gilbert
Mrs. Hennon (Phyllis) Gilbert
Mrs. William P. (Marie) Gottlieb
Mrs. William (Bernice R.) Greenspon
Mrs. Solomon [Frieda] Hyman
Mrs. Joseph (Ruth) Jason
Mrs. Jerome (Hilda C.) Katz
Mrs. Leroy Katz
Mrs. Rose Katz
Mrs. S. Kay
Mrs. Sidney J. (Edna D.) Kwass
Mrs. Harry (Josephine) Kammer
Mrs. Julius (Minnie) Land
Mrs. Ben (Lois) Lazer
Mrs. Joseph Lisagor (of Princeton)
Mrs. Abram J. (Claudine) Lubliner
Mrs. Samuel (Frances) Laufer (of Princeton)
Mrs. Jesse B. (Marie S.) Michelson
Mrs. Benjamin B. Matz
Mrs. Joseph Matz

Mrs. Max Matz
Mrs. L. Magrill (of Pocahontas, Va.)
Mrs. L. Meron (of Princeton)
Mrs. H. Meyers
Mrs. Joseph (Roslyn W.) Nathan
Mrs. Frank (Beatrice E.) Nelson (of Princeton)
Mrs. Ben (Sadie) Platnick
Mrs. David (Gertrude) Platnick
Mrs. Nathan (Edna E.) Platnick
Mrs. Philip (Fannie) Platnick
Mrs. Henry (Anna G.) Rodgin
Mrs. Harry (Sadie) Rosenthal
Mrs. Sidney L. (Helen B.) Rosenthal
Mrs. Abraham N. (Sarah A.) Schlossberg
Mrs. Sidney (Mildred Jean) Schlossberg
        [a new member in that year]
Mrs. Jessel S. (Beatrice) Salzberg
Mrs. Samuel (Ida) Shaman [deceased]
Mrs. Isadore Steckler
Mrs. Albert L. (Mary) Rosenfeld
Mrs. Harry (Minnie) Sherrin
Mrs. Theodore (Roberta [Bertie] C.) Steiner
Mrs. Ann L. Susman
Mrs. Max (Trudy) Turk
Mrs. Sidney (Lillian K.) Tucker
Mrs. Joseph (Ethel J.) Tomchin
Mrs. Sadie Weinberg
Mrs. Ralph (Ida E.) Weinberg (of Princeton)
Mrs. Arthur (Edith F.) Weiss
Mrs. Sidney Weiss
Mrs. Jacob (Rebecca L.) Wilson
Mrs. Louis (Freda A. Frank) Zaltzman

### SISTERHOOD OFFICERS FOR 1946–1947

PRESIDENT: Mrs. Hyman (Sylvia F.) Effron
1ST VICE PRESIDENT: Mrs. Sidney L. (Helen B.) Rosenthal
2ND VICE PRESIDENT: Mrs. Arthur (Edith F.) Weiss

Treasurer: Mrs. Fred (Reva D.) Gilbert
Secretary: Mrs. Jessel S. (Beatrice) Salzberg

### Sisterhood Officers in 1947–1948

President: Mrs. Jessel S. (Beatrice) Salzberg
Vice President: Mrs. Gertrude (David) Platnick
Secretary: Mrs. Sidney L. (Helen B.) Rosenthal
Treasurer: Mrs. Saul (Lucille J.) Cohen

In December, 1947, an annual Interfaith Meeting was held in Bluefield, at the Appalachian Electric Power Company's hospitality rooms, by the Bluefield Sisterhood, under the auspices of the State Sisterhood. A program dealing with Chanukah was presented by the eight members of the Confirmation Class of 1949, and an address on the Feast of Lights was given by the then new rabbi of the Bluefield congregation, Abraham I. Shinedling. This program, which was continued annually thereafter, was usually a Chanukah program held in a public hall in the month of December.

### New Sisterhood Members in 1947–1948

Mrs. Israel (Sophie W.) Fink
Mrs. B. Forman
Mrs. George (Marjorie) Frehling
Mrs. Norman Gradsky
Mrs. Alfred E. (Gladys G.) Land
Mrs. Abraham I. (Helen L.) Shinedling
Mrs. Bernard (Miriam F.) Snyder
Mrs. Harold (Sylvia F.) Tomchin (of Princeton)
Mrs. Martin Thames

In 1948, the Bluefield-Princeton Sisterhood had a total of 55 members, which was about one-half of the total number of Jewish women then living in Bluefield and Princeton. Mrs. Jessel S. (Beatrice) Salzberg resigned as president in October, 1948, for reasons of health, and Mrs. David (Gertrude) Platnick, the vice president, was elected to replace her in the head office for the balance of the year 1948–1949.

## 1948–1949

In 1949, the Bluefield Sisterhood had 54 members. Mrs. Samuel (Sarah) DeLott and Mrs. Max (Esther L.) Auerbach were elected to the Executive Board (Board of Directors) of Congregation Ahavath Sholom, from the Sisterhood, according to the provisions of the new Constitution adopted by the congregation in that year.

### Sisterhood Officers for the Year 1948–1949

PRESIDENT: Mrs. Jessel S. (Beatrice) Salzberg
    (replaced in midterm by Mrs. David [Gertrude] Platnick)
VICE PRESIDENT: Mrs. David (Gertrude) Platnick
SECRETARY: Mrs. Sidney L. (Helen B.) Rosenthal
TREASURER: Mrs. Saul (Lucille J.) Cohen

EXECUTIVE BOARD MEMBERS

Mrs. Harry (Rose A.) Clark
Mrs. Frank (Beatrice E.) Nelson (of Princeton)
Mrs. Nathan (Edna E.) Platnick
Mrs. Abraham N. (Sarah A.) Schlossberg

Mrs. S. Lazar became a new member of the Sisterhood in 1949.

### Officers of the Bluefield-Princeton Sisterhood for 1949–1950

(re-elected in May, 1950, to serve for an additional year, from 1950–1951)

PRESIDENT: Mrs. Ethel J. (Joseph) Tomchin
VICE PRESIDENT: Mrs. Max (Esther L.) Auerbach
SECRETARY: Mrs. Sidney L. (Helen B.) Rosenthal
TREASURER: Mrs. Saul (Lucille J.) Cohen

EXECUTIVE BOARD FOR 1949–1950

Mrs. Nathan Platnick
Mrs. Abraham N. Schlossberg

EXECUTIVE BOARD FOR 1950–1951

Mrs. Hyman (Sylvia F.) Effron
Mrs. Frank (Beatrice E.) Nelson (of Princeton)
Mrs. Bernard (Miriam F.) Snyder
Mrs. Sidney (Lillian K.) Tucker

## 1951–1953

### SISTERHOOD OFFICERS IN THE TWO-YEAR PERIOD EXTENDING FROM 1951 to 1953

PRESIDENT: Mrs. Harry (Josephine) Kammer
VICE PRESIDENT: Mrs. Sidney L. (Helen B.) Rosenthal
SECRETARY: Mrs. Albert L. (Mary) Rosenfeld
TREASURER: Mrs. Sidney (Lillian K.) Tucker

EXECUTIVE BOARD MEMBERS

Mrs. Nathan (Anna A.) Effron
Mrs. Fred (Reva D.) Gilbert
Mrs. Sidney J. (Edna D.) Kwass
Mrs. Samuel (Frances) Laufer (of Princeton)
Mrs. Nathan (Edna E.) Platnick

## 1953–1955

### SISTERHOOD OFFICERS IN THE PERIOD FROM 1953 to 1955

PRESIDENT: Mrs. Sidney L. (Helen B.) Rosenthal
VICE PRESIDENT: Mrs. Fred (Reva D.) Gilbert
SECRETARY: Mrs. Sidney (Mildred Jean) Schlossberg
TREASURER: Mrs. Philip (Fannie) Platnick

EXECUTIVE BOARD MEMBERS

Mrs. Saul (Lucille J.) Cohen
Mrs. Harry (Josephine) Kammer
Mrs. Sidney J. (Edna D.) Kwass
Mrs. Jesse B. (Marie S.) Michelson

SISTERHOOD MEMBERS IN THE PERIOD FROM 1950 to 1956

(culled from the Sisterhood records and minutes)

Mrs. Esther L. (Max) Auerbach
Mrs. Harry (Lillie] Barbakow (of Princeton)
Mrs. Yankee (Libby M.) Barbakow (of Princeton)
Mrs. Oscar Baum (of Princeton)
Mrs. I. Jack (Toby S.) Blank
Mrs. Boris Borinsky (of Princeton)
Mrs. H. Borinsky (of Princeton)
Mrs. Max (Rose S.) Braum
Mrs. Harry (Rose A.) Clark
Mrs. Isadore (Flora G.) Cohen
Mrs. Saul (Lucille J.) Cohen
Mrs. Samuel (Sarah) DeLott
Mrs. Louis (Sarah T.) Diamond
Mrs. Hyman (Sylvia F.) Effron
Mrs. Marvin (Amy) Effron
Mrs. Nathan (Anna A.) Effron
Mrs. Robert (Charlotte) Effron (of Princeton)
Mrs. Samuel (Nell) Fine
Mrs. Philip (Elizabeth B.) Fliegelman
Mrs. B. Forman
Mrs. Freda A. Frank
Mrs. George (Marjorie) Frehling
Mrs. Harold L. (Hilda) Gelfman
Mrs. Fred (Reva D.) Gilbert
Mrs. Hennon (Antoinette) Gilbert
Mrs. Stanley D. Gottlieb
Mrs. William P. (Marie) Gottlieb
Mrs. William (Bernice R.) Greenspon
Mrs. Solomon Gross
Mrs. Ruth (Joseph) Jason
Mrs. Harry (Josephine) Kammer
Mrs. Max L. Kammer
Mrs. Jerome (Hilda C.) Katz
Mrs. Leroy Katz

Mrs. Rose Katz
Mrs. Morris (Dora P.) Kaufman
Mrs. Sidney J. (Edna) Kwass
Mrs. Alfred E. (Gladys G.) Land
Mrs. Julius (Minnie) Land
Mrs. Samuel (Frances) Laufer (of Princeton)
Mrs. Benjamin (Lois) Lazer
Mrs. Abram J. (Claudine) Lubliner
Mrs. Philip Maltzman
Mrs. Joseph Matz
Mrs. Max Matz
Mrs. Jesse B. (Marie S.) Michelson
Mrs. Samuel Milchin
Mrs. Joseph (Roslyn W.) Nathan
Mrs. Beatrice E. (Frank) Nelson (of Princeton)
Mrs. Edna E. (Nathan) Platnick
Mrs. Fannie (Philip) Platnick
Mrs. Gertrude (David) Platnick
Mrs. Sadie (Benjamin) Platnick
Mrs. Anna G. (Henry) Rodgin
Mrs. Albert L. (Mary) Rosenfeld
Mrs. Harry (Sadie) Rosenthal
Mrs. Robert (Millicent S.) Rosenthal
Mrs. Sidney L. (Helen B.) Rosenthal
Mrs. Mordy Ross
Mrs. Jessel S. (Beatrice) Salzberg
Mrs. Sarah A. (Abraham N.) Schlossberg
Mrs. Sidney (Mildred Jean) Schlossberg
Mrs. Alexander (Lillian B.) Segall [Segal]
Mrs. Irving Selig (of Princeton)
Mrs. Raymond (Dena) Seligman (of North Fork)
Mrs. Samuel (Ida) Shaman (deceased)
Mrs. Harry (Minnie) Sherrin
Mrs. Helen L. (Abraham I.) Shinedling
Mrs. Edith R. (Jack [Jacob]) Siegel
Mrs. Bernard (Miriam F.) Snyder
Mrs. M. Steiner
Mrs. Max Steiner

Mrs. Isidor Steckler
Mrs. Ann L. Susman
Mrs. Martin Thames
Mrs. Abraham S. (Edith) Tomchin
Mrs. Ethel J. (Joseph) Tomchin
Mrs. Harold (Sylvia F.) Tomchin (of Princeton)
Mrs. Isadore Tucker
Mrs. Sidney (Lillian K.) Tucker
Mrs. Max (Trudy) Turk
Mrs. Eli Weinberg (of Princeton)
Mrs. Ralph (Ida E.) Weinberg (of Princeton)
Mrs. Sadie Weinberg
Mrs. Arthur (Edith F.) Weiss
Mrs. Herbert J. (Helen A.) Wilner


ROSTER OF MEMBERS OF THE BLUEFIELD-PRINCETON
SISTERHOOD IN 1954–1955

[65 members]

Mrs. Max (Esther L.) Auerbach
        [moved to Florida in 1957]
Mrs. Yankee (Libby M.) Barbakow (of Princeton)
Mrs. Arnold Barrick (of Princeton)
Mrs. Oscar Baum (of Princeton)
Mrs. I. Jack [Jacob] (Toby S.) Blank
Mrs. Boris Borinsky (of Princeton)
Mrs. Emanuel Borinsky (of Princeton)
Mrs. Harry [Lilly] Barbakow (of Princeton)
        [Mrs. Lilly Barbakow died at Princeton in 1958.]
Mrs. Rose A. (Max) Braum
Mrs. Harry (Rose A.) Clark
Mrs. Isadore (Flora G.) Cohen
Mrs. Saul (Lucille J.) Cohen
Mrs. Calvin Deitz (of Princeton)
Mrs. Samuel (Sarah) DeLott
        [reported to be living in Florida in 1959]
Mrs. Louis (Sarah T.) Diamond

Mrs. Hyman (Sylvia F.) Effron
Mrs. Marvin (Amy) Effron
Mrs. Nathan (Anna A.) Effron
Mrs. Robert (Charlotte) Effron (of Princeton)
Mrs. Samuel (Nell) Fine
Mrs. B. Forman
Mrs. Freda A. Frank
Mrs. Hennon (Antoinette) Gilbert
    [living in Fort Worth, Tex., in 1959]
Mrs. Fred (Reva D.) Gilbert
Mrs. Stanley D. Gottlieb
Mrs. William P. (Marie) Gottlieb
    [living in Florida in 1959]
Mrs. William (Bernice R.) Greenspon
Mrs. Joseph (Ruth) Jason
Mrs. Harry (Josephine) Kammer
Mrs. Max L. Kammer
Mrs. Jerome (Hilda C.) Katz
Mrs. Leroy Katz
Mrs. Rose Katz
Mrs. Morris (Dora P.) Kaufman
Mrs. Sidney J. (Edna D.) Kwass
Mrs. Alfred E. (Gladys G.) Land
Mrs. Julius (Minnie) Land
Mrs. Samuel (Frances) Laufer (of Princeton)
Mrs. Benjamin (Lois) Lazer
Mrs. Joseph Lisagor (of Princeton)
Mrs. Morris Lorber
Mrs. Abram J. (Claudine) Lubliner
Mrs. M. Medwin
Mrs. Jesse B. (Marie S.) Michelson
Mrs. Samuel Milchin
Mrs. Frank (Beatrice F.) Nelson (of Princeton)
Mrs. Moses (Shirley M.) Nelson
Mrs. Alvin Platnick
Mrs. Benjamin (Sadie) Platnick
Mrs. David (Gertrude) Platnick
Mrs. Nathan (Edna E.) Platnick

Mrs. Philip (Fannie) Platnick
Mrs. Henry (Anna G.) Rodgin
Mrs. Albert L. (Mary) Rosenfeld
Mrs. Harry (Sadie) Rosenthal
Mrs. Robert (Millicent S.) Rosenthal
Mrs. Sidney L. (Helen B.) Rosenthal
Mrs. Mordy Ross
Mrs. Jessel S. (Beatrice) Salzberg
 [moved to California in the early 1950's]
Mrs. Jonas Schicke (Shik)
Mrs. Bernard Schicke (Shik)
Mrs. Abraham N. (Sarah A.) Schlossberg
Mrs. Sidney (Mildred Jean) Schlossberg
Mrs. Alex [Alexander] (Lillian B.) Segall
Mrs. Irving Selig (of Princeton)
Mrs. Raymond (Dena) Seligman (of North Fork)
 [moved to Chicago in the early 1950's)
Mrs. Samuel (Ida) Shaman (deceased)
Mrs. Harry (Minnie) Sherrin
Mrs. Jacob (Edith R.) Siegel
Mrs. Isidor Steckler
Mrs. Alan (Sally Matz) Susman
 [moved to Beckley in 1955]
Mrs. Ann L. Susman
Mrs. Martin Thames
Mrs. Abraham S. (Edith) Tomchin
Mrs. Harold (Sylvia F.) Tomchin (of Princeton)
Mrs. Joseph (Ethel J.) Tomchin
Mrs. Milton Tomchin
Mrs. Sidney (Lillian K.) Tucker
Mrs. Isadore Tucker
 [later moved away from Bluefield to northern West
  Virginia]
Mrs. Ralph (Ida E.) Weinberg (of Princeton)
Mrs. Eli Weinberg (of Princeton)
Mrs. Arthur (Edith F.) Weiss
Mrs. Herbert J. (Helen A.) Wilner
 [moved to Levittown, Pa., in August, 1957]

AHAVATH SHOLOM CONGREGATION SISTERHOOD
OFFICERS FOR 1957–1958

PRESIDENT: Mrs. Sidney (Mildred Jean) Schlossberg
VICE PRESIDENT: Mrs. Jack (Jacob R.) (Edith R.) Siegel
SECRETARY: Mrs. Alfred E. (Gladys G.) Land
TREASURER: Mrs. Stanley D. Gottlieb

In 1957–1958, Mrs. Sidney Schlossberg served also as chairman of the Department of Membership and Administration of the State Sisterhood, and in that same year Mrs. Helen B. (Sidney L.) Rosenthal served as chairman of the Newsletter Committee of the State Sisterhood.

## 1957–1959

At the Biennial State Sisterhood Convention held at Parkersburg (October 20–21, 1957), Mrs. Sidney (Mildred Jean) Schlossberg, of Bluefield, was elected 2nd Vice President for 1957–1959; however, she served in this post only until June, 1958, when she resigned.

At the 31st General Assembly of the W. V. F. T. S., held at Wheeling, on April 14–15, 1959, Mrs. Sidney L. (Helen B.) Rosenthal, of Bluefield, was elected recording secretary. Mrs. Fannie (Philip) Platnick served a two-year term as State auditor (1955–1957), and Mrs. Nathan (Anna A.) Effron served as State President from 1946 to 1948. Previously, Mrs. Sarah A. [Abraham N.] Schlossberg had served as State President from 1935 to 1937.

THE BLUEFIELD-PRINCETON JEWISH COMMUNITY, 1949–1956
A SPECIAL PRESENTATION WRITTEN BY MRS. NATHAN
(ANNA A.) EFFRON

*1*. AHAVATH SHOLOM CONGREGATION, OF BLUEFIELD AND PRINCETON

In 1952, the Congregation added an amendment to its Constitution which states that a Sisterhood member of the Bluefield-Princeton Sisterhood is to be added to the Temple

Board [of Directors], to serve accordingly for a two-year term. Such Board member from the Sisterhood is to be elected by the Congregation. Those who served up to 1956 in this post included Mrs. Max (Esther L.) Auerbach, Mrs. Nathan (Anna A.) Effron, and Mrs. Joseph (Ruth) Jason.

### 2. THE BLUEFIELD-PRINCETON SISTERHOOD

The Sisterhood passed an amendment to its Constitution, which requires that officers be elected for a term of two years, with the vice president succeeding the president in office. On June 9, 1956, a five-foot brass Menorah was set up in the sanctuary of the Temple by the Sisterhood, in memory of deceased Sisterhood members. It was accompanied by an impressive religious service.

In 1956, the following were serving their second term (1956–1957) as the Sisterhood officers:

PRESIDENT: Mrs. Fred (Reva D.) Gilbert
VICE PRESIDENT: Mrs. Sidney (Mildred Jean) Schlossberg
SECRETARY: Mrs. Abraham S. (Edith) Tomchin
TREASURER: Mrs. Philip (Fannie) Platnick

### 3. THE BLUEFIELD-PRINCETON CHAPTER OF HADASSAH, 1956–1957

#### OFFICERS FOR THE YEAR 1956–1957

PRESIDENT: Mrs. Irving Selig (of Princeton)
1ST VICE PRESIDENT: Mrs. Sidney L. (Helen B.) Rosenthal
2ND VICE PRESIDENT: Mrs. Harry (Josephine) Kammer
SECRETARY: Mrs. Marvin (Amy) Effron
TREASURER: Mrs. Meyer J. Spiro

### 4. COMMUNITY ACTIVITIES

The women of the Bluefield Jewish community play an important role in such activities as: the Cancer Society, the Women's Club, the Quota Club, the music clubs, the Red Cross Organization, and the Community Chest. Those active in the above clubs or organizations in the 1950's included:

*Cancer Society*

Mrs. Marvin (Amy) Effron
Mrs. Arthur (Edith F.) Weiss

*Women's Club*

Mrs. Esther L. (Max) Auerbach
Mrs. Samuel (Sarah) DeLott
Mrs. Sidney J. (Edna D.) Kwass
Mrs. Alvin Platnick
Mrs. Nathan (Edna E.) Platnick
Mrs. Robert (Millicent S.) Rosenthal

*Community Chest and Red Cross*

Mrs. Leroy Katz
Mrs. Jesse (Marie S.) Michelson

*Music Clubs*

Mrs. Nathan (Anna A.) Effron
Mrs. Gertrude (David) Platnick
Mrs. Henry (Anna G.) Rodgin
Mrs. Meyer J. Spiro

*Quota Club*

Mrs. Harry (Rose A.) Clark
Mrs. William P. (Marie) Gottlieb
Miss Edith Greenspon
Mrs. Harry (Josephine) Kammer
Mrs. Jesse B. (Marie S.) Michelson
Mrs. Jacob R. (Edith R.) Siegel

## The Bluefield-Princeton Sisterhood in the State Federation of Temple Sisterhoods

State Sisterhood Conventions were held in Bluefield in the two years 1936 and 1950. Previously, at the 13th annual State Convention of the W. V. F. T. S., held at Parkersburg on

October 27–28, 1935, Mrs. Abraham N. (Sarah A.) Schlossberg, of Bluefield, was elected president of the State Federation for the year 1935–1936, and Mrs. Harry (Rose A.) Clark, also of Bluefield, was elected its secretary for that year. Mrs. Sarah A. Schlossberg was re-elected president for the year 1936–1937 at the 14th annual State Convention, held in Bluefield on October 11–12, 1936.

112 visitors and delegates, including those from Bluefield, were registered at this 14th State Convention in Bluefield (October 11–12, 1936). The roster of delegates showed an out-of-town total of 46 actual delegates, as follows:

| | | | |
|---|---|---|---|
| Beckley | 3 | Logan | 7 |
| Charleston | 9 | Roanoke (Va.) | 2 |
| Bristol (Va.) | 3 | Welch | 11 |
| Huntington | 4 | Williamson | 2 |
| Kimball and Northfork | 5 | | |

For the Bluefield Sisterhood, the late Mrs. Samuel (Ida) Shaman was chairman of registration, and the president, Mrs. Abraham N. Schlossberg, presided at all the sessions.

Mrs. Nathan (Anna A.) Effron, of Bluefield, was elected president of the W. V. F. T. S. for the year 1946–1947, at the 24th annual State Convention, held in Williamson on October 28–29, 1946. She was re-elected president for the year 1947–1948 at the 25th annual State Convention held at Fairmont on October 26, 1947.

The 28th annual State Convention was held in Bluefield on November 19, 1950, with Mrs. Ralph (Gazella) Masinter, of Huntington, its president, in the chair. The main speaker for the N. F. T. S. was Mrs. Harold Baum, of Milwaukee, then the National Interfaith Chairman of the N. F. T. S.

Mrs. Philip (Fannie) Platnick was elected auditor of the State Federation for the two-year term 1955 to 1957 at the Convention held in Morgantown on October 16–17, 1955.

From 1955 to 1957, Mrs. Sidney (Mildred Jean) Schlossberg served as chairman of the Religious Extension Committee, and Mrs. Sidney L. (Helen B.) Rosenthal as chairman of the Family

Education Committee of the State Federation. Also, in that same two-year period, Mrs. Philip (Fannie) Platnick served as chairman of Department No. 2, Human Relations, of the W. V. F. T. S.

The Southern Regional meeting of the State Sisterhood for 1956 was held in Bluefield on October 2, 1956, with Mrs. Elmer Moyer, of Dayton, Ohio, as the N. F. T. S. representative.

### The Bluefield Sisterhood Cradle Roll

An important religious and philanthropic project of both the local Sisterhoods and the State Sisterhood of West Virginia is the Cradle Roll, listing the names of children of pre-Religious School age in the community. In later years, as these children grow up and take their place in the religious life of the Jewish congregation, their names as recorded in the earlier years of their lives assume some retrospective and historic value and interest.

The following Cradle Roll names are found in the incomplete records of the Bluefield-Princeton Sisterhood:

### Cradle Roll for 1945–1946[1]

*Harry A. Aronson
*Catherine Hanna Baum
   (of Princeton)
Alan Braum
David Braum
*Henry Rodgin Cohen
   (of Charleston)
Richard Jaffee Cohen
Terry Lynn Cohen

David Meyer Katz
Carol [Karel A.] Kwass
Linda Hope Matz
Gerald E. Platnick
Jerry (Gerald) Rosenthal
*Hanley Schwartzman
Judith Steiner
Jane Lewis Turk

---

[1] Some of the names listed below are those of children of relatives of members of the Bluefield-Princeton community living in other cities. These are indicated with an asterisk preceding their names.

CRADLE ROLL OF YOUNG CHILDREN FOR THE YEAR 1948
(May 12, 1948)

Allen Sanders Auerbach
Robert Hanna Auerbach
Bonnie Nannette Barbakow
(of Princeton)
Elaine Beth Effron
Susan Gaye Effron
Vivian Lynn Effron
Joan Beatrice Gilbert
Edward Barry Laufer
(of Princeton)
Jerry Stuart Laufer
(of Princeton)
Judith Elaine Laufer
(of Princeton)

Joel Hanna Lubliner
Michael Joseph Nathan
Daniel Melton Platnick
Ivan Martin Platnick
Steven Jeffry Rosenthal
Harriet Faye Snyder
Jeffrey Lee Snyder
Mark Neal Snyder
Judith Rae Steiner
David L. Tomchin
Edward Rodgin Tomchin
Alice Kathryn Turk

THE BLUEFIELD-PRINCETON CONGREGATIONAL
RELIGIOUS SCHOOL

There are no records extant of the Bluefield-Princeton Congregation Ahavath Sholom Religious (Sunday) School before the year 1935, although the Religious School existed for many years before then. In 1935–1936, under the auspices of the Bluefield-Princeton Sisterhood, Mrs. Max (Esther L.) Auerbach served as the Sunday School chairman (superintendent). Other teachers in that same year included Roslyn Weinberg (later Mrs. Joseph Nathan) and Sidney Lennett.

The Religious School has always had a paid superintendent. The Bluefield-Princeton Sisterhood has always paid its teachers and superintendent a modest monthly salary, and given them appropriate Purim and Chanukah gifts annually.

In November, 1936, according to the preserved Sisterhood records, Mrs. Max (Esther L.) Auerbach was still chairman and superintendent of the Religious School. At that time there were 30 pupils and 5 teachers, including the rabbi of the congregation. The teachers were:

Mrs. Esther L. (Max) Auerbach
Miss [first name not recorded] Borinsky (of Princeton)
Rabbi Julius Kravetz
Benjamin Lazer
Marvin Lennett

The names of three pupils in the year 1936–1937 are mentioned in the Sisterhood records:

Miriam Cohen (daughter of Isadore Cohen)
Jerry (Gerald) Frank (son of Mrs. Freda A. Frank)
  [later an optometrist in Bluefield]
Laurence Slifkin (son of Isaac L. Slifkin)

In the year 1937 to 1938, the Religious (Sunday) School had four teachers:

Miss Borinsky (of Princeton) (presumably the daughter of Boris
  Borinsky)
Rabbi Julius Kravetz
Benjamin Lazer
Miss Roslyn Weinberg (later Mrs. Joseph Nathan)

The teachers from 1938 to 1939, again 4 in number, were:

Mr. Isaacson [first name not recorded]
Miss Roslyn Kammer (daughter of Harry Kammer)
Rabbi Julius Kravetz
Mrs. Max (Trudy) Turk

In the year extending from 1938 to 1939, there was a Children's Choir in the Religious School, trained by Mrs. Nathan (Anna A.) Effron and Mrs. Joseph I. Matz.

In 1941–1942, there were 17 pupils in the Sunday School. There were only 3 teachers, as follows:

Helen Baum (of Princeton)
  [later Mrs. Sidney L. Rosenthal, of Bluefield]
Rabbi Julius Kravetz
Leona Silverman

Teachers in the year 1943 (presumably for the period 1942–1943) were 5 in number, as follows:

Justine Cohen [daughter of Isadore Cohen]
M. B. Goldman
Benjamin Lazer
Mrs. Henry (Anna G.) Rodgin, Hebrew instructor
Millicent Shaman (later Mrs. Robert Rosenthal)

In the year 1943 to 1944, with A. Stanley Dreyfus as the student rabbi (from the H. U. C., of Cincinnati) of the congregation, there were 5 classes and 32 pupils in the Religious School. There were 6 teachers in that year, as follows:

Justine Cohen
Student Rabbi Alfred Stanley Dreyfus
[only every other Sunday]
Mrs. M. B. Goldman
Benjamin Lazer
Mrs. Henry (Anna G.) Rodgin
Millicent Shaman

In January, 1943, after Leona Silverman had left the city to reside elsewhere, she was replaced as a teacher by Mrs. Esther L. (Max) Auerbach.

The first confirmation service in the history of Congregation Ahavath Sholom of which there is any record was that of Richard Salzberg (son of Jessel S. and Beatrice Salzberg) and Calvin Deitz (son of Mr. and Mrs. Henry Deitz, of Princeton). This took place on May 9, 1943, with Rabbi Julius Kravetz as the officiant.

In 1944–1945 there were 3 teachers of record in the Religious School, as follows:

Benjamin Lazer
Nathan Platnick
Millicent Shaman

Rabbi Kravetz had left at the end of the Religious School year 1942 to 1943 to become a chaplain in the Armed Forces of the United States.

In the religious year 1945–1946, Alfred E. Land joined the faculty of the Religious School as a teacher (October, 1945). In that year, under the aegis of Student Rabbi Jerome W. Grollman, there were 5 classes and 45 pupils; the pupils ranged in age from 4 to 16 years. There were six teachers in the Religious School, including the new superintendent, Mrs. Nathan (Edna E.) Platnick, who was to serve as such until 1951. Mrs. Philip (Fannie) Platnick served as Sunday School Chairman for the Bluefield Sisterhood, and Mrs. Nathan Platnick served also as substitute teacher. The six teachers were:

> Student Rabbi Jerome W. Grollman
> Alfred E. Land
> Mrs. Fannie (Philip) Platnick
> Mrs. Nathan (Edna E.) Platnick
> Millicent Shaman
> Dora Steiner

In the several years preceding 1947, perhaps from about 1943 to 1946, the following served as substitute teachers:

[Their years of service are not given in the official records.]

> Mrs. Landsman [first name not recorded]
> Mrs. Edith R. (Jacob R.) Siegel
> Mrs. Joseph (Ethel J.) Tomchin

In early 1947 the following four teachers are listed in the Sisterhood records as teachers in the Religious School, presumably for the religious year extending from September, 1946, to June, 1947:

Philip Gerard (a student at Bluefield College)
Mrs. Nathan (Edna E.) Platnick (superintendent and teacher)
Bertram Rappaport (a student at Bluefield College)
Meyer [J.] Spiro

Mrs. Nathan Platnick continued as superintendent and substitute teacher of the Religious School until June, 1951.

In the year 1947 to 1948, under the aegis of Rabbi Abraham I. Shinedling, who had come to the Bluefield-Princeton congregation in September, 1947, there were six classes and 51 pupils in the Religious School, as well as the following 7 teachers:

> Samuel Laufer (of Princeton)
> Mrs. Edna E. (Nathan) Platnick
> (superintendent and substitute teacher)
> Bertram Rappaport
> Rabbi Abraham I. Shinedling
> Mrs. Abraham I. (Helen L.) Shinedling
> Mrs. Jacob R. (Edith R.) Siegel
> Meyer J. Spiro

Philip Gerard also served as a substitute teacher, until his death at Bluefield in June, 1948.

Benjamin [Ben] Lazer and Harold Tomchin (of Princeton) joined the teaching staff of the Religious School in 1948, at which time Bertram Rappaport and Meyer J. Spiro retired as teachers.

In the year 1947 to 1948, at the suggestion of Mrs. Nathan Platnick, a Parent-Teachers Association was formed within the Bluefield Sisterhood. A Junior Congregation, which held its meetings in the Sunday morning Religious School Assembly, also was formed, at the suggestion of Rabbi Abraham I. Shinedling and of Mrs. Nathan Platnick, which organization collected and distributed small donations from the pupils each week, in the assembly, for charitable purposes and for the purchase of books for the Temple Library. For the first time, it is believed, in the history of the congregation, Saturday morning religious services, mainly for the children of the Religious School, but also for adults, were introduced into the congregation, under the aegis of Rabbi Shinedling and Mrs. Nathan Platnick, and the Hebrew classes were transferred from Sunday morning to Saturday morning, with Rabbi Shinedling and Mrs. Helen L. Shinedling conducting a total of five Hebrew classes of one hour each for the various age groups, both before and after the Temple services, in which some of the older children participated each Saturday morning, on a voluntary basis. This arrangement was continued by the two subsequent rabbis, Harold L. Gelfman

PLATE XVII

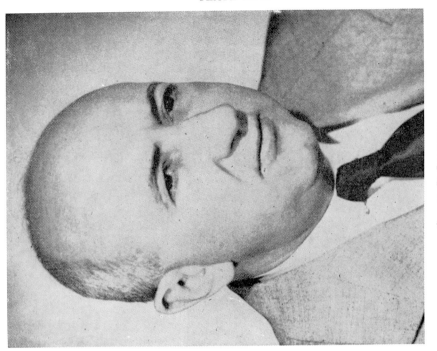

SAMUEL D. LOPINSKY
President of B'nai Jacob Congregation
of Charleston, West Virginia
in 1950
(see pages 706 and 748)

RABBI SAMUEL COOPER
of B'nai Jacob Congregation, Charleston, West Virginia
(see pages 669 and 672)

PLATE XVIII

Mrs. Ben Preiser

of B'nai Jacob Congregation
of Charleston, West Virginia

(see pages 689 and 718)

Simon Meyer

Historian of B'nai Jacob Congregation
of Charleston, West Virginia

(see pages 663 and 720)

(1950–1952) and Herbert J. Wilner (1952–1957). The annual picnic of the Religious School, at the close of the Religious School year in June, previously celebrated, continued to be held from 1947 on, under the auspices of Mrs. Nathan Platnick.

With the approval of the Board of Directors, headed by Nathan Platnick and Frank Nelson (of Princeton), then president and vice president, respectively, of the congregation, stricter requirements in both Hebrew and other subjects, as well as in attendance, were laid down for Bar Mitzvah boys and for confirmation children. The first Bar Mitzvah celebrated in the new Albemarle Street Synagogue of the congregation, held in September, 1948, was that of Robert M. Kwass, son of Sidney J. and Edna D. Kwass, with Rabbi Shinedling as the officiant. The still part-Orthodox quality of the congregation even in the late 1940's is indicated by the fact that Harmon Cohen, elder son of Saul and Lucille J. Cohen, was Bar Mitzvahed in the Orthodox style in the Temple in the spring of 1949, with Benjamin B. Matz, leader of the Orthodox group of the congregation, as the officiant and as his teacher in the strictly Orthodox mode.

The second confirmation of the Religious School of which there is record was that of the year 1949, held under the auspices of Rabbi Abraham I. Shinedling and Mrs. Nathan Platnick. This was also the first confirmation service to be held in the new Albemarle Street Synagogue of the congregation. The following brief description of this class, and of its individual members, was written for this volume by Mrs. Nathan (Anna A.) Effron, the mother of one of the confirmands, and an active worker in the Bluefield Sisterhood and in the State Sisterhood. It is cited herewith in full because of its human interest, because it shows the vicissitudes of human life that occur within only a few short years of confirmation, and because it illustrates the rapid leaving of small Jewish communities by religious school pupils after their confirmation and their graduation from the local high schools, and the fact that very seldom do they return to their former cities of residence to reside after their university and college days are over:

"The confirmation class of June, 1949, will always be remembered as one of outstanding note, mainly because of the thorough training of their brilliant teacher, Rabbi Abraham I. Shinedling. This class consisted of eight members: three boys and five girls. It is of interest to know that all the girls in this class (five in number) are now (1956) married, namely:

Gloria H. Blank (now Mrs. Gerald A. Pickus, of Bluefield)
    (daughter of I. Jacob and Toby S. Blank)
Gloria Effron (now Mrs. Milton J. Subit)
    (daughter of Nathan and Anna A. Effron)
Doris Sue Katz (now Mrs. Morris Kantor; married on June 17,
    1956) (daughter of Jerome and Hilda Katz)
Yetta Faye Nelson (of Princeton) (now Mrs. Norman Rosenbaum) (daughter of Frank and Beatrice E. Nelson)
Barbara Sherrin (now Mrs. Marvin Fink)
    (daughter of Harry and Minnie Sherrin)

"The three boy members of the class, of whom one (Alan Susman) was confirmed in absentia, since at the time he was a student at Duke University, in Durham, N. C., and could not attend to participate in the service, were as follows:

Alan Susman (living in Beckley in 1956)
    (son of Mrs. Ann Land Susman)
Richard Wilson
    (son of Jacob and Rebecca Wilson)
Arthur Wilson
    (son of Jacob and Rebecca Wilson)

"Arthur Wilson, nicknamed 'Sandy,' has just (1956) returned from two years of service in the United States Army in Korea."

In the year 1949 to 1950, there were 50 pupils in the Religious School, a faculty of 6 teachers, and 6 classes. The faculty was again headed by Mrs. Nathan Platnick as superintendent, and included, in addition, the following:

Harry Finkelman (an instructor at Concord College, in Athens,
    W. Va., who lived in Princeton) (he joined the faculty in
    September, 1949)

Rabbi Abraham I. Shinedling
Mrs. Helen L. Shinedling
Martin Thames (joined the faculty in September, 1949)
Harold Tomchin (of Princeton)
    (joined the faculty in September, 1949)

In addition, under the aegis of Mrs. Nathan Platnick, boys and girls who had passed the more rigorous confirmation requirements were welcomed back into the Religious School as substitute teachers, later to become full teachers. In the year 1949 to 1950 the following three confirmation girls of the preceding June, 1949, thus became substitute teachers in the lower classes of the Religious School:

    Doris Sue Katz
    Yetta Faye Nelson (of Princeton)
    Barbara Sherrin

Rabbi Harold L. Gelfman came to the congregation as rabbi in September, 1950. The records fail to show the names of the teachers of the Religious School in his first year in Bluefield (1950–1951), but in addition to him there were, it is known, also Harry Finkelman, Martin Thames, and Harold Tomchin, as well as the three girl substitute teachers mentioned above, and Mrs. Edna E. (Nathan) Platnick served her last year as school superintendent in that year. Under Rabbi Gelfman, in June, 1951, there was another confirmation, whose members included:

Harriet Salzberg
    (daughter of Jessel S. and Beatrice Salzberg, now living in
       California)
Edna Faye Tucker
    (daughter of Sidney and Lillian K. Tucker)
Barbara Rosenfeld
    (daughter of Albert L. and Mary Rosenfeld)
    [In 1956 she was a student at Duke University, in Dur-
       ham, N. C.]

Other members of the original class who were scheduled to be confirmed in June, 1951, but who had previously left for private schools or for college, or whose parents felt that Bar Mitzvah had precluded the necessity for their confirmation, included:

| | |
|---|---|
| Robert M. Kwass | Harmon Cohen |
| Ellis Joe Seligman | Laura Lee Michelson |
| (of North Fork) | Joye Sue Weiss |

In the year 1952–1953, the Sunday school teachers were eight in number:

| | |
|---|---|
| Mrs. Rose S. (Max) Braum | Mrs. Irving Selig |
| Harmon Cohen | (of Princeton) |
| Selma Lubliner | Edna Faye Tucker |
| Mrs. Joseph (Roslyn W.) Nathan | Rabbi Herbert J. Wilner |
| Mrs. Sidney (Mildred Jean) Schlossberg | |

Rabbi Herbert J. Wilner came to the congregation in September, 1952, and remained until August, 1957.

The presentation of the above lists of teachers in the Religious School of just Congregation Ahavath Sholom in Bluefield, W. Va., alone, in the various years from about 1940 to 1953, illustrates one of the serious defects and evils of Jewish religious education and of Reform Jewish congregational Religious or Sunday Schools: the too frequent turnover of teachers, and the failure of Religious School teachers to remain in their teaching posts for more than a year or two, for the most part, i. e., the lack of continuity of the individual teachers, with few exceptions, and their resignation from their positions soon after they have acquired a little experience as teachers.

In June, 1955, under the aegis of Rabbi Herbert J. Wilner, the following pupils of the Religious School were confirmed:

Naomi Kaufman
  (daughter of Morris and Dora P. Kaufman)
Adeline Platnick
  (daughter of Ben and Sadie Platnick)

In September, 1955, Mrs. Fannie (Philip) Platnick became superintendent of the Religious School, In that year (1955–1956), there was an enrollment of 54 children in the Religious School, with 7 teachers for the 7 classes.

The Confirmation Class of 1956, confirmed on June 3, 1956, included the following ten boys and girls of the Religious School:

Allen Sanders Auerbach
    (son of Max and Esther L. Auerbach)
Alan Steiner Braum
    (son of Mrs. Rose S. [Max] Braum)
Robert Mayer Jason
    (son of Joseph and Ruth Jason)
Helen Kay Kammer
    (granddaughter of Harry and Josephine Kammer)
Karel Ann Kwass
    (daughter of Sidney J. and Edna D. Kwass)
David Mayer Katz
    (son of Jerome and Hilda Katz)
Alan Cecil Lazer
    (son of Benjamin and Lois Lazer)
Gerald Effron Platnick
    (son of Nathan and Edna E. Platnick)
Roberta Lee Platnick
    (daughter of Philip and Fannie Platnick)
Neil Allen Tucker
    (son of Sidney and Lillian K. Tucker)

The following program of the 1956 Confirmation service may prove of interest to the future "religious historian":

### CONFIRMATION

June 3, 1956        8.oo P. M.
Sivan 25, 5716
Ahavath Sholom Congregation
Bluefield, West Virginia

[The parents of the confirmands invite you to a reception in the Social Hall following the Services.]

## Order of the Service

Organ Prelude.................Mrs. Sarah Reiland
Anthem No. 146, Union Hymnal....The Choir
Processional.....................The Confirmands
Meditation........The Parents and Rabbi Herbert J. Wilner
Opening Prayer..................David M. Katz

## Floral Service

Floral Prayer....................Karel A. Kwass
Floral Dedication ...............Helen Kay Kammer
Floral Offering..................Roberta L. Platnick
Greetings to the Parents...........Robert M. Jason
Hymn No. 150, Union Hymnal.....The Choir
Union Prayer Book..............pages 288–297
 (Read by Roberta L. Platnick and Alan C. Lazer)

## Torah Service

Akdamuth — Poem of Praise — ....Alan S. Braum
And It Shall Come to Pass........Karel A. Kwass
The Proclamation................Neil A. Tucker
Hebrew Blessings and the Reading of
 the Decalogue...............Gerald E. Platnick
Proverbs 4:1–13.................Allen S. Auerbach

## Addresses

Our God.........................Allen S. Auerbach
Our People......................David M. Katz
Our Torah.......................Roberta L. Platnick
Our Holy Writings...............Neil A. Tucker
Our Faith.......................Helen Kay Kammer
Our Country.....................Gerald E. Platnick
Our View of Science.............Alan C. Lazer

Presentations

Mrs. Fred Gilbert
Nathan Platnick
Charge and Blessing of the Confir-
    mands......................Rabbi Herbert J. Wilner
Adoration and Kaddish............Rabbi Wilner
Closing Prayer...................Robert M. Jason
Hymn No. 76, Union Hymnal......The Congregation
Recessional.....................Mrs. Sarah Reiland
                                          [Organist]

REPORT OF MRS. FANNIE [PHILIP] PLATNICK,
SUPERINTENDENT OF THE RELIGIOUS SCHOOL

[for the Year 1955–1956] (Dated April 30, 1956)

"The Religious School of the Bluefield-Princeton Temple
Ahavath Sholom enjoyed for the year 1955–1956 an enrollment
of 54 students, who were divided into 7 groups. Heading those
groups there were the rabbi and 6 teachers, whose names were
as follows:

    1. Rabbi Herbert J. Wilner
    2. Alfred [E.] Land
    3. Arthur Weiss
    4. Alan [C.] Lazer
    5. Milton Medwin
    6. Mrs. Irving (Beatrice) Selig (of Princeton)
    7. Mrs. Moe [Moses] (Shirley M.) Nelson

"I, Mrs. Philip Platnick, served as the Sunday School Superintendent.

"Official registration was on September 25th [1955], preceded
by children's Rosh Hashanah and Yom Kippur services. During
the year, besides classroom activities, we had a consecration
service for the younger children, and also the usual model
Succah, a Chanukah and a Purim party, and a model Seder.
During assembly, interesting movies were shown, and also film

strips on current events. The ladies of the Sisterhood also helped us serve lunch for the whole Sunday School a few times during the year.

"Our Sunday School also originated something this year: each child gets a Uniongram on his or her birthday. In this way the children feel remembered, and we also help the Sisterhood meet the Uniongram quota. We are also very proud to have been able to contribute, in the past year, towards the United Jewish Appeal, the Huntington Orthopedic Hospital, the American Jewish Archives, the Jewish Chautauqua Society, the Jewish National Fund (when we planted ten trees in the union forest), and also the Combined Campaign [of the U. A. H. C. and the H. U. C. - J. I. R.].

"As our Sunday School year draws to its close, we are all looking forward to our yearly picnic and, last but not least, to our Confirmation exercises, which will be held on June 3rd [1956]. At this time I want to thank the ladies of the Sisterhood, Rabbi Wilner, and all the teachers for their efforts and their help, which have made the success of the passing school year possible.

"Respectfully submitted,

"Fannie Platnick
"[Mrs. Philip Platnick]."

ROSTER OF STUDENTS OF THE RELIGIOUS SCHOOL OF
AHAVATH SHOLOM CONGREGATION FOR THE YEAR
1955–1956

(54 Students)

| | |
|---|---|
| Alan Sanders Auerbach | David Braum |
| Robbie Auerbach | Edward Effron |
| Bonnie Barbakow | (of Princeton) |
| (of Princeton) | Elaine Beth Effron |
| Dennis Barbakow | Lynn Effron |
| (of Princeton) | Susan Gay Effron |
| Alan S. Braum | Karen Jean Gilbert |

Robert M. Jason
Helen Kay Kammer
David M. Katz
Douglas Katz
Karel A. Kwass
Kathy Kwass
Sara Ann Land
Steven Gordon Land
Edward Barry Laufer
(of Princeton)
Jerry Laufer (of Princeton)
Judith Elaine Laufer
(of Princeton)
Joel Harman Lubliner
Alan Medwin
Marcia Medwin
Gerald Milchin
Sharon Diane Milchin
Susan Rebecca Milchin
Bruce Nelson
Gerald E. Platnick
Ivan Platnick
Norman Ira Platnick
Roberta L. Platnick
Dan Rosenthal
Deborah Faye Rosenthal

Gerald Rosenthal
Janice Rosenthal
Steven Rosenthal
Alan Lewis Schlossberg
Frances Selig (of Princeton)
Philip Selig (of Princeton)
Alan Siegel
Barbara Swerdloff
(of Ripplemead, Va.)
Judy Swerdloff
(of Ripplemead, Va.)
Robert Charles Swerdloff
(of Ripplemead, Va.)
Stephanie Swerdloff
(of Ripplemead, Va.)
David Tomchin
(of Princeton)
Edward Tomchin
(of Princeton)
Ellen Beth Tomchin
Sara Tomchin
(of Princeton)
Neil Tucker
Robert Gerry Weiss
Charlotte Wilner
John Wilner

## 1956–1957

Mrs. Fannie Platnick continued as the superintendent of the Religious School in the year 1956–1957. In that year the number of pupils declined to 44, chiefly as the result of the graduation and confirmation of the large class of ten boys and girls in June, 1956, and also because the four Swerdloff children, of Ripplemead, Va., did not return to the School for the year 1956–1957.

The teaching staff, in addition to Rabbi Herbert J. Wilner and Mrs. Fannie Platnick, the superintendent, included the following 7 persons, of whom those marked with an asterisk (four in number) were former pupils and recent graduates (confirmands) of the Religious School:

*Alan S. Braum (substitute teacher)      Dr. S. Susman
*Karel A. Kwass                          *Neil Tucker
 Mrs. Milton Medwin                       Arthur Weiss
*Roberta L. Platnick

In addition, Alan C. Lazer, a member of the Bluefield Temple Youth Group, taught in the Religious School in 1956–1957.

The roster of students for the year 1956–1957 shows the following five new pupils (as well as the loss of the four Swerdloff children and of the ten confirmands of June, 1956):

Daniel Carp                     Henry Rosenthal
Stephen Lennett                 Arlene Weinberg (of Princeton)
Marsha Ann Lennett

## THE TEMPLE AHAVATH SHOLOM YOUTH GROUP

The Ahavath Sholom Temple Youth Group was organized in September, 1947, with a membership of 9 boys and girls, of high school age. Dr. Joseph I. [Jay] Rodgin and Meyer J. Spiro were the adult advisors, or counsellors, of this first Temple Youth Group. The work and activities of this so-called "First" Temple Youth Group continued for two years, from 1947 to the summer of 1949, when eight of its members had already been confirmed (May, 1949). In the latter year (1948–1949), with the accretion of seven of the younger group of Temple Religious School students, the First Temple Youth Group attained a membership of 16, with Mrs. Bernice R. (William) Greenspon as its adult adviser, assisted by Rabbi Abraham I. Shinedling (ex officio). One of its members ([Yetta] Faye Nelson) was from Princeton, W. Va.

The First Temple Youth Group was affiliated with, and under the auspices of, the N. F. T. Y., which had its headquarters then in Cincinnati (later transferred to New York). Its affiliation dated from March, 1948. This group issued a Youth Group newspaper, under the editorship of Richard

Salzberg, who then, as a high school student, worked part-time as a reporter and staff writer for the Bluefield newspapers.

The officers of this First Bluefield-Princeton Temple Youth Group for the year 1947–1948 were:

PRESIDENT: Yetta Faye Nelson (of Princeton)
SECRETARY: Gloria Effron
TREASURER: Gloria H. Blank

The other members in that year were:

| | |
|---|---|
| Doris Sue Katz | Alan Susman |
| Richard Salzberg | Arthur Wilson |
| Barbara Sherrin | Richard Wilson |

During the period from 1948 through 1951, what might be called the second Bluefield-Princeton Temple Youth Group was affiliated with the Beckley Temple Youth Group; the two Youth Groups held joint business and dinner-program meetings alternately in Bluefield and in Beckley. This Bluefield-Princeton Temple Youth Group ceased its activities at the end of June, 1951, most of its members now being away from the city.

## 1951–1957

From 1951 to 1952, the adult advisers of the second (actually, the third) and newest Bluefield-Princeton Temple Youth Group which was formed were Mrs. Lucille J. (Saul) Cohen and Mrs. Henry (Anna G.) Rodgin. The roster of members for that year including the following 17 young people of the congregation:

| | |
|---|---|
| Harmon Cohen | Kenneth B. Platnick |
| Robert M. Jason | Barbara Rosenfeld |
| David M. Katz | Harriet Salzberg |
| Doris Sue Katz | Susan Salzberg |
| Robert M. Kwass | Ellis Joe Seligman |
| Naomi Kaufman | (of North Fork) |
| Alan C. Lazer | Edna Faye Tucker |
| Stanley Nelson | Neil A. Tucker |
| (of Princeton) | Joy[e] Sue Weiss |
| Adeline Platnick | |

In the five years from 1952 on, the following 7 additional members joined the last-formed and still existent Temple Youth Group:

Alan Sanders Auerbach          Karel A. Kwass
Alan S. Braum                       Gerald E. Platnick
Arnold Effron                       Roberta L. Platnick

In 1956 to 1957, Mrs. Edythe R. (Jacob R.) Siegel served as the adult adviser to the Temple Youth Group.

In 1957 to 1958, Mrs. Sidney (Lillian K.) Tucker was the Temple Youth Group adult adviser. In that year, three members of the group were teachers in the Religious School of the Congregation.

In 1956 to 1957, the Temple Youth Group had a total of 17 members, but this membership declined in the following year.


## THE BLUEFIELD COLLEGES

### ACTIVITIES OF THE JEWISH CHAUTAUQUA SOCIETY

There is a record that in September, 1936, three Jewish students were enrolled at Bluefield College (in Bluefield, Va.), all of them young men. In the period from 1946 to 1948, there were two Jewish boys enrolled there, both of whom taught for those two years in the Religious School of Congregation Ahavath Sholom, in Bluefield. These were Philip Gerard and Bertram Rappaport.

The various successive rabbis of the Bluefield congregation paid a number of visits to nearby colleges in West Virginia, Virginia, Kentucky, and Tennessee, under the auspices of the Jewish Chautauqua Society. Also, the J. C. S. sent a number of rabbis into Bluefield to speak at both Bluefield College and Bluefield State College, the former in Bluefield, Va., and the latter in Bluefield, W. Va. Rabbi Abraham I. Shinedling, while in Bluefield (1947–1950), addressed the Bluefield College assembly twice. Rabbi Herbert J. Wilner, who later served (1952–1957) as rabbi of the Bluefield congregation, served as lecturer at the Potomac State College of West Virginia (1951), under

J. C. S. auspices; and Rabbi Abraham I. Shinedling and Herbert J. Wilner, as well as Rabbi Harold L. Gelfman (1950–52), visited Concord College, in nearby Athens, W. Va., and also Bluefield State College, as well as several colleges in Kentucky, Tennessee, and Virginia, under J. C. S. auspices. Rabbis Gelfman and Wilner also visited Bluefield College under the same auspices.

## BLUEFIELD STATE TEACHERS COLLEGE

The following represents a complete list of J. C. S. lecturers who visited Bluefield State Teachers College in the period from 1943 to 1958:

1943: Rabbi Lawrence A. Block (then of Huntington)
1944: Rabbi Abraham Feinstein (of Chattanooga, Tenn.)
1945: Rabbi Robert P. Jacobs (then of Asheville, N. C.)
1946: Rabbi Bernard Zeiger (then of Chapel Hill, N. C.)
1947: Rabbi Ezra Spicehandler (of the Hebrew Union College)
1948: Rabbi Martin M. Perley (of Louisville)
1949: Rabbi Eugene Hibshman (then of Huntington)
1950: Rabbi Louis J. Cashdan (then of Charleston)
1952: Rabbi Harold L. Gelfman (then of Bluefield)
1953: Rabbi Herbert J. Wilner (then of Bluefield)
1955 (April 8): Rabbi Samuel Volkman (of Charleston)
1956 (March): Rabbi Abraham I. Shinedling (then of Beckley)
1957 (March 5): Rabbi Samuel R. Shillman (of Roanoke, Va.)
1958 (March 11): Rabbi Arnold Shevlin (of Danville, Va.)

## BLUEFIELD COLLEGE

The following interesting and historic data were furnished to me, and by me were excerpted from the material supplied by, James Zambus, Dean of Bluefield College, a Baptist junior college, in Bluefield, Va., in his letter of October 22, 1956:

"Last year (1955–1956) and the year before that (1954–1955) we did not have any Jewish students in our student body, though the year before [1953–1954] we did have two young ladies who were of the Jewish faith . . . .

"Of course, you will be interested to know that two or three of the men who were instrumental in getting Bluefield College located in Bluefield [Virginia] were men who belonged to the Jewish Synagogue here [Bluefield, W. Va.] in the city, and served on the Committee to go to the Virginia Baptist General Association when it was known that Baptists were going to build a school somewhere in this area.

"Jewish Students at Bluefield College:

("I am sorry that our records are not complete.)

1931–1932: Sidney Len[n]ett, of Wytheville, Va.

1934–1935: four Jewish students; one was David Cohen, of Brooklyn, N. Y.

1935:–1936:

Bert Benjamin                          Jerome Weinberg
Marvin Len[n]ett (of Pulaski, Va.)     John Woodward
Earl Schrier

1938–1939: Joel Sameth (of Welch, W. Va.)

1939–1940:

Louis Lazero (of New London, Conn.)
Benjamin Goodstein (of Meriden, Conn.)

1940–1941: 14 Jewish students (their names are not recorded)

1941–1942:

Leonard Barrack (of Revere,        Daniel Frederick
    Mass.)                         Morris Gladstein (of Jersey
Irving Burness (of West                City, N. J.)
    Hartford, Conn.)               Norman Horowitz
Alvin Berger                       Milton Medwin (of
Milton Fein                            Bluefield)
Arthur Feldman                     Richard Rosenberg

Charlotte Schlossberg (now Mrs. B. A. Mollen, of Richmond, Va.)

1943–1944: Charles R. Schlossberg (of Roanoke, Va.)

1946–1947: Seymour Mermelstein (of Irvington, N. J.)

1946–1948: Philip L. Gerard [then of Philadelphia; died at
Bluefield by his own hand in June, 1948]
Bertram Rap[p]aport (of Jersey City, N. J.]
Melvin Goldberg (then of Mount Vernon, N. Y.)

1947–1948: Stanley C. Baker (formerly of Bluefield; then of
Washington, D. C.)

1953–1954: Mrs. Harry (Rose A.) Clark (of Bluefield, W. Va.;
an adult student)
Nathan Platnick (of Bluefield, W. Va.; an adult
student) [in this and the following years,
Nathan Platnick's wife, Edna E. Platnick, was
pursuing courses at Bluefield State College]

1954–1955: Mrs. Harry (Rose A.) Clark (of Bluefield, W. Va.)

"In the years not listed, there were no Jewish students in
Bluefield College."

In 1949, Rabbi Abraham I. Shinedling spoke at Bluefield
College under the auspices of the J. C. S., and visited the college
a number of other times.

In May, 1956, Mr. and Mrs. Isadore Cohen, of Bluefield,
presented to Bluefield College, for the new Library, a picture
entitled, "Music and Literature," by William N. Harnett.

## The Bluefield B'nai B'rith Lodge, No. 617

According to the *AJYB* for 1907–1908 [5668 A.M.], Bluefield
Lodge, No. 617, of the B'nai B'rith, was in existence as early as
1907, with I. Aaron [father of Mrs. Sarah A. (Abraham N.)
Schlossberg] as its secretary. In the early years of its existence,
the Bluefield Lodge met regularly in rented rooms in various
parts of downtown Bluefield. For several years in the 1940's,
before the new Albemarle Street Temple of Congregation
Ahavath Sholom was completed [1948; the west wing], the
members of the Lodge met in rooms which it fitted out in the
Consolidated Bus Terminal building on Bland Street, as above
mentioned, or in a commercial building on Princeton Avenue.

After 1948, it held its meetings and had its headquarters in the Albemarle Street Temple.

No further earlier records of the Lodge are extant until 1942, except for the fact that Sidney J. Kwass served as president of the Lodge from 1933 to 1934. Isaac L. Diamond is the authority (on March 8, 1957) for the statement that "the minutes of the B'nai B'rith of past years were lost in the basement of the congregation."

Besides Sidney J. Kwass, other presidents of the Bluefield Lodge have included the following:

[the list in the records of the Lodge is not complete even for the period from 1947 to 1958]

Nathan Platnick                    Jesse B. Michelson (1951–1953)
Dr. Joseph I. Rodgin               Isaac L. Diamond (1955–1957)
William P. Gottlieb (1947–         Eli Weinberg (of Princeton)
    1949)                             (1957–1958)
Samuel Slifkin (1949–1951)

In 1937–1938, Isadore Cohen, of Bluefield, served as 1st vice president of the West Virginia Council of the B'nai B'rith, and in the following year he served one term as the president of the State Council. He is listed on the official stationery and records of the State Council and of the local Lodge as a past president of the State Council.

The presently existent Bluefield Lodge, No. 967, of the B'nai B'rith, now known as Bluefield-Princeton Lodge, No. 967 (apparently, the Lodge was reorganized at the time, and its original number 617 was changed to 967), was chartered in the year 1923 by District Grand Lodge, No. 3, of the B'nai B'rith, which had its headquarters in Philadelphia. The Lodge is a constituent member also of the West Virginia Council of the B'nai B'rith.

The officers of Bluefield-Princeton Lodge, No. 967, in 1957–1958, were as follows:

PRESIDENT: Eli Weinberg (of Princeton)
1ST VICE PRESIDENT: Arthur Weiss
2ND VICE PRESIDENT: Isaac L. Diamond

TREASURER: Harold Tomchin (of Princeton)
RECORDING SECRETARY: Sidney L. Rosenthal
FINANCIAL SECRETARY: Frank Klauber


## THE LATER HISTORY OF THE BLUEFIELD-
## PRINCETON B'NAI B'RITH LODGE[1]

Bluefield Lodge, No. 967, of the B'nai B'rith, was organized [it was a reorganization of an earlier lodge which had been founded some twenty years previously, in the early 1900's] in April, 1923. The early minutes of the lodge, not only those from 1900 on to 1923, but also those from April, 1923, the year of its founding [reorganization], until early 1942, were either lost, misplaced, or inadvertently destroyed, according to Volume 1, No. 2, of the B'nai B'rith Lodge Bulletin of January 28, 1942.

In 1923, Samuel Shaman and Harry Miller planned to organize a local Young Men's Hebrew Association group. They conducted a survey, and found that a sufficient number of Jewish men were interested in the project. In the meantime, Albert Schlossberg, of Huntington, W. Va., the brother of Abraham N. Schlossberg, of Bluefield, and an active member of the local Huntington, W. Va., lodge, and a past president of the State Council, heard of the plan, paid a visit to Bluefield, and persuaded the leaders and the community to organize a B'nai B'rith Lodge instead. An application for a charter was filed with the Third District Grand Lodge [with its headquarters in Philadelphia], and in April, 1923, the D. G. L., No. 3, granted the Bluefield group a charter, the lodge to be known as the Bluefield Lodge, No. 967. [Obviously, the previous charter of the earlier Bluefield Lodge, No. 617, had lapsed, and was recalled by the D. G. L., No. 3, sometime, perhaps, in the 1910's, although there is no record of this anywhere.] [In later years, a number of members joined Bluefield Lodge, No. 967, from Princeton.]

---

[1] From the files and records of Isaac L. Diamond, graciously made available to me by him.

In the election for officers, Harry Gross [now (January, 1942) deceased] was elected the first president of the Lodge. It may be assumed that Harry Greenspon was elected vice president, for he became the second president of the Lodge in the following year [1924]. The names of the other officers of the Lodge in the year of its organization [1923–1924] can no longer be ascertained, because of the loss or destruction of the early lodge records and its early minutes for about the first two decades of its existence.

The following charter members of the Bluefield Lodge, No. 967, were still members of the Lodge in January, 1942:

*Harry Barbakow
   (of Princeton)
*Boris Borinsky
   (of Princeton)
*Harry Clark
*Abe Effron
*Nathan Effron
#Ezra Gilbert
*Dr. William Greenspon
*Benjamin Lazer
*Benjamin Platnick
*David Platnick

*Nathan Platnick
#Henry Rodgin
*Abraham N. Schlossberg
#Goodwin Schlossberg
*Harry Stolch
##Samuel Shaman
#Joseph Tomchin [died in July, 1959] (then of Princeton)
##Samuel Turk
*Louis Zaltzman

Benjamin [Ben] Lennett served as president of the Lodge for two years, and Hyman Effron for a year and a half. [The years of their service are no longer known.]

A bulletin issued by the local Lodge on January 28, 1942, contained the following historic data:

"Of the 18 past presidents [who served before 1942], nine are still [in January, 1942] active members of the Bluefield [-Princeton] Lodge:

Harry Clark
Sidney J. Kwass

Jerome Katz
Nathan Platnick

---

* indicates still resident in Bluefield or Princeton in 1959
# deceased
## indicates no longer resident in Bluefield in 1959

Hyman Effron
  [served as Lodge president
  for a year and a half)
Abe Angrist

Ben [Benjamin] Lazer
Sidney Tucker
Dr. William Greenspon

"Four past presidents of the Lodge have moved away from the city:

    Harry Greenspon (to Charleston, W. Va.)
    Joe [Joseph I.] Kwass (moved to Charleston)
    Bernard Wagner (moved to Miami, Fla.)
    Ben Lennett (moved to Pulaski, Va.)
      [served as Lodge president for two years]

"Three past presidents of the Lodge have died [up to 1942]:

      Harry Gross
      Harry Weinberg
      Julius Fink

"Two other past presidents have ceased to be members of the Lodge:

      Abram J. Lubliner
      Harry Kleiman

"The first meetings of the Bluefield Lodge, No. 967, of the B'nai B'rith were held in a club room over Blank's [I. Jack Blank's] shop [a paint store], on Princeton Avenue [near Mercer Street]. For many years thereafter the Lodge met in a hall on the mezzanine floor of the Matz Hotel [also on Princeton Avenue], and it was only last year [in 1941] that the present [1942] quarters were leased [in the building occupied by Radio Station WHIS on Federal Street]. Previously the three wood-panelled rooms and wood-panelled reception hall were used by Radio Station WHIS as its broadcasting studio and business office. Small alterations made them suitable for club uses, and the Bluefield Lodge now [1942] has one of the best meeting places in this area. After 1942, the B'nai B'rith Lodge of Bluefield had club and meeting rooms on the second floor of the old Consolidated Bus Terminal building [now no longer extant], extending from Bland Street most of the way to Federal Street, near Princeton Avenue; then it next occupied clubrooms on the third floor of a building on Princeton Avenue, near Bland Street; and finally, after the completion of the Albemarle Street Temple in 1948–1949, it transferred its lodge meetings to the Temple vestry rooms."

## Charter Members of the Bluefield-Princeton B'nai B'rith Lodge

"Death [by January 1, 1942] had claimed several charter members of the Lodge:

| | |
|---|---|
| Rabbi [The Reverend] | David Katz |
| Kalman Slifkin | [the father of Jerome and |
| Harry Gross | Leroy Katz] |
| Ben Block | Julius Fink |
| Saul Greenspon | Isador Baker |
| Harry Weinberg | Louis Kaufman |

"By January, 1942, also, the following other charter members of the Lodge had moved away from Bluefield to other cities:

Isaac Slifkin (to New York City)
[later he moved to New England]
Saul Turk (to Philadelphia)
Harry Greenspon (to Charleston, W. Va.)
Ben Lennett (to Pulaski, Va.)
Edward Gilbert (to Beckley)
[now deceased]
Tony Zappan (to Williamson)
Isador Greenspon (to New York)."

## The Bluefield Zionist Organization of America

A branch of the Zionist Organization of America (Z. O. A.) was active in Bluefield for a number of years, especially in the period from 1945 to 1950. Dr. Joseph I. Rodgin served for several years as its president. Isaac L. (Ike) Diamond was also its president in the early 1950's. In 1956–1957, Isaac L. Diamond served as the secretary of the Bluefield-Princeton chapter of the Z. O. A. Dr. Joseph I. Rodgin served also as the president of the Southern West Virginia district of the Zionist Organization of America. The establishment of the State of Israel in May, 1948, and its admission to the United Nations organization as an integral member, stimulated interest in, and the activities and the reactivation of, the previously existent chapter of the Z. O. A. in Bluefield, with its several active Princeton members.

OFFICERS IN 1958–1959 OF THE SOUTHERN WEST
VIRGINIA ZIONIST DISTRICT [OF THE] ZIONIST
ORGANIZATION OF AMERICA
in Bluefield, West Virginia

(Bluefield-Princeton, West Virginia)

PRESIDENT: Emanuel Borinsky (of Princeton)
VICE PRESIDENT: Alvin Platnick
TREASURER: Samuel I. Slifkin
SECRETARY: Isaac L. Diamond

EXECUTIVE COMMITTEE

Yankee Barbakow
   (of Princeton)
Jack [I. Jacob] Blank
Isadore Cohen
Jesse B. Michelson
Harry Clark
Robert Effron
   (of Princeton)
Fred Gilbert

Jerome Katz
Frank Klauber
Frank Nelson
   (of Princeton)
Nathan Platnick
Harry Rosenthal
Joseph Tomchin
   [died in July, 1959]
Sidney Tucker

Isadore Cohen, Lifetime Honorary Chairman (in Bluefield, W. Va.).

Inscribed in the Golden Book:

Ezra Gilbert (deceased)
Rabbi Julius Kravetz (now of New York City)

PREVIOUS OFFICERS AND EXECUTIVE COMMITTEE

(before 1958)

PRESIDENT: Samuel I. Slifkin
VICE PRESIDENT: Dr. Joseph I. Rodgin
TREASURER: Samuel I. Slifkin
SECRETARY: Isaac L. Diamond

EXECUTIVE COMMITTEE:

[in addition to the 14 members of the Executive Committee listed above]

> Oscar Baum (of Princeton) [deceased]
> William P. Gottlieb [now living in Florida]
> Albert L. Rosenfeld
> Samuel Shaman [now living in Florida]

PAST PRESIDENTS OF THE SOUTHERN WEST VIRGINIA ZIONIST DISTRICT OF THE ZIONIST ORGANIZATION OF AMERICA IN BLUEFIELD-PRINCETON

| | |
|---|---|
| Yankee Barbakow (of Princeton) | Alfred E. Land |
| Abraham S. Tomchin | Samuel Shaman |
| Isaac L. Diamond | Jesse B. Michelson |
| Harry Rosenthal | Isadore Cohen |

THE BLUEFIELD-PRINCETON UNITED JEWISH CHARITIES

The Bluefield-Princeton United Jewish Charities (which includes in its scope, service, and collections the whole of Mercer County, W. Va., of which Princeton is the county seat) was organized in 1939, for the administration of local social services; for the support of affiliated local organizations, as well as for the support of national welfare programs; and for the support of overseas (international, especially European and in the State of Israel, later, but then Palestine) welfare programs. In the year 1941–1942 Max Matz served as its president, and Rabbi Julius Kravetz served as its secretary. The fifteen or sixteen

Jewish families of Princeton have always, since its organizing, been constituent and contributing members of the Bluefield-Princeton United Jewish Charities, and several Princetonians have served as its officers.

There is no official record of the officers of the United Jewish Charities from 1939 to 1941, but it is known that Rabbi Julius Kravetz served as its secretary from 1939 to 1941, and also from 1942 to early 1943, when he left for service, in May, 1943, as a chaplain in the United States Army in the Second World War. The name of Rabbi Julius Kravetz was erroneously carried in the annual reports in the *AJYB* as the secretary of the Bluefield-Princeton United Jewish Charities for several years [ten in actual number until 1953] after his departure from Bluefield in 1943; also, from 1953 through 1959, and equally erroneously, and through some inadvertence, the name and the report of the Bluefield-Princeton United Jewish Charities, still in existence in 1959 and continuously since 1939, failed to be mentioned or listed in the *AJYB*, on page 332 (*AJYB*, 1959, Volume 60), where the other three Jewish federations and welfare funds of West Virginia, those of Charleston, Huntington, and Wheeling, are faithfully and safely listed.

Again, in 1960, the name of the Bluefield-Princeton United Jewish Charities was omitted from Volume 61 of the *AJYB* (1960, page 395), although I several times called the attention of the editors of the *AJYB* to this inexplicable omission in both 1958 and 1959, and also apprised some of the officials of the Bluefield community of this strange and erroneous omission.

Thereafter (after 1943), the president of Congregation Ahavath Sholom and the secretary of the congregation generally, and automatically, became the president and the secretary, respectively, also of the Bluefield-Princeton United Jewish Charities, but not in every year. Also, the membership of (or list of contributors to) the United Jewish Charities is tantamount to a complete list of the congregational membership, with the proviso that a number of local (Bluefield, but not Princeton) Jewish men and women who are not members of the congregation are nonetheless members of and contributors to the United Jewish Charities.

The following valuable, informative, and historical data and statistics were furnished to me, in the form of a series of letters and reports, by Isaac L. (Ike) Diamond, who in 1956–1957 was president and campaign chairman of the Bluefield-Princeton United Jewish Charities. From his letters and reports, which evidenced a considerable amount of generous and painstaking research work on the part of Isaac L. Diamond over the period of at least six months, I have excerpted what I believe to be the following indispensable data and material:

Max Matz was the chairman of the United Jewish Charities of Bluefield-Princeton in the year 1944–1945 (in addition to his previous chairmanship or presidency of the organization in 1941–1942). In that year the Jewish contributors to the United Jewish Charities gave a total of $7,079.50, and the Christian contributors [always on a strictly volunteer basis, and most generously, an indication of the fine mutual relations which have always existed in Bluefield-Princeton between Jewish and Christian fellow citizens] donated $421, making a joint total for the year of $7,500.50.

The first drive, or campaign for funds, in Bluefield took place in the year 1917, on the Eve of Yom Kippur, more than 20 years before the actual and official organizing of the United Jewish Charities. This drive was for the American Jewish Relief Committee, and Isadore Cohen and Gus Kahn were the local chairmen. Louis Marshall, noted Jewish lawyer and congregational and Jewish communal personage of New York City, was the national chairman. In 1917, Isadore Cohen attended the meeting of this Committee in Pittsburgh, Pa. Over $16,000 was raised in Bluefield and in Princeton in that year for this first campaign of 1917. Sol [Solomon] and Abe [Abraham] Hyman, of Huntington, W. Va., and Max Frankenberger, of Charleston, W. Va., were active in the State campaign in that selfsame year.

The earliest year for which definite and detailed names and statistics are available, with reference to the United Jewish Appeal and the general campaign of the Bluefield-Princeton United Jewish Charities, held annually, for many other national and overseas causes and institutions, is the year 1946–1947, seven years after the founding of the United Jewish Charities.

[All previous records up to 1946–1947 have, apparently, been misplaced, lost, or destroyed.] In that year 1946–1947, at a time when the National Goal of the United Jewish Appeal was $100,000,000, the Bluefield-Princeton quota was set at $25,000.

At that time (1946–1947) the officers of the Bluefield-Princeton United Jewish Charities were as follows:

CHAIRMAN: Isadore Cohen
VICE-CHAIRMAN: Nathan Platnick (for Bluefield)
VICE-CHAIRMAN: Joseph Tomchin (for Princeton)
    [Later, Joseph Tomchin moved to Bluefield.]
TREASURER: William P. Gottlieb

CAMPAIGN MANAGERS:

    Joseph Nathan
    Frank Klauber

SECRETARY: Hennon Gilbert

COMMITTEES [COMMITTEE CHAIRMEN]:

Publicity: Sidney J. Kwass
Campaign Letters: Sidney Weiss
Banquet: Harry Rosenthal
Program: Dr. Jay [Joseph I.] Rodgin
Initial Gifts: Nathan Platnick

SPONSORS:

Harry Barbakow (of Princeton)
Oscar Baum (of Princeton)
Jack [I. Jacob] Blank
Boris Borinsky (of Princeton)
Harry Clark
Isadore Cohen
Henry Deitz (of Princeton)

Abe Effron
Robert Effron (of Princeton)
Samuel Fine
Fred Gilbert
Hennon Gilbert
William P. Gottlieb
Philip H. Green
Dr. William Greenspon
Harry Kammer
Jerome Katz
Sidney J. Kwass
Alfred E. Land
Joseph Lisagor (of Princeton)
Max Matz
Paul Markowitz (of Mullens)
Selig Markowitz (of Mullens)

Frank Nelson (of Princeton)
Ben Platnick
David Platnick
Nathan Platnick
Mrs. Henry (Anna G.)
    Rodgin
Albert [L.] Rosenfeld
Harry Rosenthal
Sidney [L.] Rosenthal

Jessel [S.] Salzberg
Abraham N. Schlossberg
Samuel Shaman
I. [Isador] Steckler
Theodore Steiner
Joseph Tomchin (then of
    Princeton)
Sidney Tucker
Max Turk

## THE BLUEFIELD-PRINCETON CHRISTIAN COMMITTEE
### (1946–1947)

J. L. Alexander
F. M. Archer
W. Oris Barton
Joseph H. Bowen
C. I. Cheyney
The Honorable D. M.
    Easley (a judge)
Frank S. Easley
J. Taylor Frazier
Harry A. Goodykuntz
J. Hudson Huffard
Herman Kirchner
W. E. O. Koepler

C. A. Lilly
Herbert Markle
Sam [D.] May
J. C. Newbold
E. G. Otey
Lon M. Rish
Hugh Shott, Jr.
C. G. Taylor
Laurence E. Tierney
The Honorable F. Morton
    Wagner (a judge)
Jim Ed Wagner
R. [Russell] A. Yarbrough

### 1952–1953

The 1952–1953 goal was $151,500,000 nationally for the United Jewish Appeal. In that year the personnel of the Jewish Committee in Bluefield-Princeton was as follows:

## THE JEWISH COMMITTEE (1952–1953)

CHAIRMAN: Isadore Cohen (for Bluefield)
CO-CHAIRMAN: Yankee Barbakow (for Princeton)

VICE-CHAIRMEN:

Harry Clark
Fred Gilbert
William P. Gottlieb

Frank Nelson (of Princeton)
Nathan Platnick
Sidney [L.] Rosenthal

## THE CHRISTIAN COMMITTEE (1952–1953)[1]

CHAIRMAN: J. Hudson Huffard
CO-CHAIRMAN: Joseph H. Bowen, Sr.
TREASURER: Russell A. Yarbrough

THE COMMITTEE:

Lindsey Alley
Sydnor Barksdale
Charles E. Belcher
James C. Borden
Carl Brunner
Reverend Father G.
   [George] J. Burke
C. I. Cheney [Cheyney]
W. [William] J. Cole
Paul Craft
Carl E. Creasy
The Honorable
   D. M. Easley
F. Tyler Easley
H. L. Godschalk
Charles McD. Harrell
Dr. Upshur Higginbotham
Albert Kemper
Roland C. Luther
Alex B. Mahood
Sam D. May
David V. McGonagle

E. G. Otey
W. S. Owen
George Richardson, Jr.
Lon M. Rish
The Reverend Frank
   Rowley
The Reverend Paul L.
   Royer
Lynn C. Seyler
Dr. R. V. Shanklin
Hugh Shott, Jr.
Merriman S. Smith
H. Edward Steele
The Reverend Glenn W.
   Stewart
C. G. Taylor
L. [Laurence] E. Tierney, Jr.
E. C. Wade
The Honorable F. Morton
   Wagner
J. E. [Jim Ed] Wagner

---

[1] The comparison of the 1946–1947 and the 1952–1953 Jewish and Christian Committees will give an indication of the constant shifting of population to and from and between cities in the United States. Many of the Committee members of both Committees in 1952–1953 were not even living in Bluefield and Princeton in 1946–1947.

## 1953–1954

### The Jewish Committee (1953–1954)

PRESIDENT and CAMPAIGN CHAIRMAN: Isadore Cohen
VICE PRESIDENT: Fred Gilbert (for Bluefield)
VICE-PRESIDENT: Yankee Barbakow (for Princeton)
SECRETARY: Samuel I. Slifkin
TREASURER: Frank Klauber

BOARD OF DIRECTORS:

### 1953–1954

| | |
|---|---|
| Yankee Barbakow (of Princeton) | William P. Gottlieb |
| Boris Borinsky (of Princeton) | Frank Klauber |
| Isaac [L.] Diamond | Benjamin Platnick |
| Fred Gilbert | Sidney [L.] Rosenthal |

### 1953–1955

| | |
|---|---|
| Oscar Baum (of Princeton) | Nathan Platnick |
| Jack [I. Jacob] Blank | Dr. J. [Joseph] I. Rodgin |
| Isadore Cohen | Samuel [I.] Slifkin |
| Samuel Fine | Joseph Tomchin |

### COMMITTEES

INITIAL GIFTS:

| | |
|---|---|
| Harry Clark | David Platnick |
| Isaac [L.] Diamond | Nathan Platnick |
| Hennon Gilbert | Sidney [L.] Rosenthal |
| William P. Gottlieb | Abraham S. Tomchin |

CAMPAIGN DIRECTORS:

| | |
|---|---|
| Jack [I. Jacob] Blank | Frank Nelson (of Princeton) |
| Samuel Fine | Dr. J. [Joseph] I. Rodgin |
| Jerome Katz | Joseph Tomchin |

ADVISORY COMMITTEE:

Oscar Baum (of Princeton)    Joseph Lisagor (of Princeton)
Boris Borinsky (of Princeton)  Benjamin Platnick
Abe Effron

FINANCE COMMITTEE:

Sidney J. Kwass      Sidney Tucker
Max Matz

WOMEN'S DIVISION:

Mrs. Nathan (Edna E.) Platnick
Mrs. Joseph (Ethel J.) Tomchin

BANQUET ARRANGEMENTS:

Mrs. Fred (Reva D.) Gilbert
Mrs. Henry (Anna G.) Rodgin

BANQUET ATTENDANCE:

Samuel DeLott

RECEPTION:

Dr. and Mrs. William (Bernice R.) Greenspon
Mr. and Mrs. Jesse B. (Marie S.) Michelson
Dr. and Mrs. Samuel Milchin

BANQUET PROGRAM:

Jesse B. Michelson

PUBLICITY:

Alfred E. Land
Samuel Shaman

THE CHRISTIAN COMMITTEE (1953-1954)[1]

CHAIRMAN: Dr. R. V. Shanklin
TREASURER: Russell A. Yarbrough

COMMITTEE:

Lindsey Alley
Sydnor Barksdale
Charles E. Belcher
James C. Borden
Joseph H. Bowen, Sr.
Carl Brunner
Reverend Father G.
  [George] J. Burke
C. I. Cheney [Cheyney]
W. [William] J. Cole
Paul Craft
Carl E. Creasy
The Honorable D. M.
  Easley
F. Tyler Easley
H. L. Godschalk
Charles McD. Harrell
J. T. (Bundy) Harvey
Dr. Upshur Higginbotham
J. Hudson Huffard
Albert Kemper
Roland C. Luther
Alex B. Mahood

Samuel D. May
David V. McGonagle
R. R. McLaughlin
E. G. Otey
W. S. Owen
George Richardson, Jr.
Lon M. Rish
The Reverend Frank
  Rowley
The Reverend Paul L.
  Royer
Lynn C. Seyler
Hugh Shott, Jr.
Merriman S. Smith
H. Edward Steele
The Reverend Glenn W.
  Stewart
C. G. Taylor
Laurence E. Tierney, Jr.
E. C. Wade
The Honorable F. Morton
  Wagner
Jim Ed Wagner

---

[1] Many of these members of the Christian Committee I knew well, as fellow Rotarians during my three years in Bluefield, from 1947 to 1950; or from my speaking and other appearances in Christian churches and before various Christian groups of Bluefield; or from my general and civic activities and contacts in that city. In view of their continuing and sincere interest in the cause of Jewish relief and welfare, and of their contributions to our Jewish cause, I have chronicled their names herewith, and I believe that their names were worth recording in this history.

## 1954–1955

### Officers

PRESIDENT and CAMPAIGN CHAIRMAN: Fred Gilbert
VICE PRESIDENT: Harry Barbakow (for Princeton)
VICE PRESIDENT: Isaac [L.] Diamond (for Bluefield)
SECRETARY: Samuel I. Slifkin
TREASURER: Frank Klauber
IMMEDIATE PAST PRESIDENT: Isadore Cohen

BOARD OF DIRECTORS:

### 1953–1955

| | |
|---|---|
| Oscar Baum (of Princeton) | Nathan Platnick |
| Jack [I. Jacob] Blank | Dr. J. [Joseph] I. Rodgin |
| Isadore Cohen | Samuel I. Slifkin |
| Samuel Fine | Joseph Tomchin |

### 1954–1956

| | |
|---|---|
| Harry Barbakow (of Princeton) | Frank Klauber |
| Boris Borinsky (of Princeton) | Jerome Katz |
| Isaac [L.] Diamond | Joseph Lisagor (of Princeton) |
| Fred Gilbert | Abraham S. Tomchin |

### Committee Chairmen

INITIAL GIFTS: Nathan Platnick
ADVISORY COMMITTEE: Harry Barbakow (of Princeton)
SOCIAL COMMITTEE: Mrs. Max (Esther L.) Auerbach
PUBLICITY COMMITTEE: Dr. Joseph I. Rodgin

## 1955–1956

### Officers

PRESIDENT and CAMPAIGN CHAIRMAN: Nathan Platnick
VICE PRESIDENT: Irving E. Selig (for Princeton)
VICE PRESIDENT: Isaac [L.] Diamond (for Bluefield)

SECRETARY: Samuel I. Slifkin
TREASURER: Frank Klauber
IMMEDIATE PAST PRESIDENT: Fred Gilbert

BOARD OF DIRECTORS:

## 1954–1956

Harry Barbakow (of Princeton)   Frank Klauber
Boris Borinsky (of Princeton)   Jerome Katz
Isaac [L.] Diamond              Joseph Lisagor (of Princeton)
Fred Gilbert                    Abraham S. Tomchin

## 1955–1957

Isadore Cohen          Dr. Joseph I. Rodgin
Morris Kaufman         Irving E. Selig (of Princeton)
Jesse B. Michelson     Samuel I. Slifkin
Nathan Platnick        Meyer J. Spiro

PROGRAM OF THE BLUEFIELD-PRINCETON UNITED JEWISH
CHARITIES ANNUAL DINNER
ON BEHALF OF THE UNITED JEWISH APPEAL

NATHAN PLATNICK, *Chairman*

at the West Virginian Hotel
on Sunday, November 27, 1955
at 6.30 P. M.
Bluefield, West Virginia

Song: "America"................The Assembly
Invocation....................Rabbi Herbert J. Wilner
Introduction of the Speaker.......Benjamin Lazer
Address:......................Leo Lania (of New York)
Remarks.......................Nathan Platnick
                                   (Chairman)
Benediction...................Rabbi Herbert J. Wilner

(Organ selections during the five-course dinner, by James
Worden)

PLATE XIX

The Board of Trustees of B'nai Jacob Congregation of Charleston, West Virginia, in 1950

Seated, left to right: George Sklar, secretary; Mrs. Philip Preiser, Sam Sloman, Charles Kerstein, vice-president; Samuel D. Lopinsky, president; Jacob Wells, Mrs. Louis Lovett, Philip Wells, Joe Rubin, David Abrams. Standing, left to right: Max Roth, Louis Lovett, Morris Steiger, Simon Meyer, Harry Cohen, Mose Pushkin, Zundel Hark, financial secretary; Ben Preiser, David Ogrin, Dr. Max Koenigsberg. Absent when picture was taken: Sidney Cohen, treasurer; Joseph Hearst.

PLATE XX

The Board of Trustees of the Ladies' Auxiliary of B'nai Jacob Congregation of Charleston, West Virginia, in 1950

Seated, left to right: Mrs. Joseph Hearst, Mrs. Samuel Cooper, Mrs. Philip Nearman, Mrs. Zundel Hark, recording secretary; Mrs. Fred Marks, auditor; Mrs. Joe Miller, 1st vice-president; Mrs. Louis Lovett, president; Mrs. Leon Wells, 2nd vice-president; Mrs. Ben Lovett, financial secretary; Mrs. Harry Galinsky, corresponding secretary; Mrs. Simon Meyer, Mrs. Ben Preiser. Standing, left to right: Mrs. Fred Goldman, Mrs. Jack Koppelman, Mrs. Irving Abrams, Mrs. Philip Preiser, Mrs. Michael Kosmin, Mrs. Sam Fixler, Mrs. Armond Levy, Mrs. Paul Reiss, Mrs. Joe Boiarsky, Mrs. Hyman Cohn, and Mrs. Irving Blumenthal. Absent when the picture was taken: Mrs. D. Leonard Gordon, Mrs. Louis Jaffe, Mrs. L. K. Landau, and Mrs. Benjamin Samuels.

(see pages 685–688)

PROGRAM OF THE 1956–1957 ANNUAL MEETING OF THE
BLUEFIELD-PRINCETON UNITED JEWISH CHARITIES
ON BEHALF OF THE UNITED JEWISH APPEAL

on Sunday, November 25, 1956
at The Temple, Albemarle Street
Bluefield, West Virginia
at 8.00 P. M.

Songs: "The Star-Spangled Banner"
and "Hatikvah"............The Assembly
Invocation...................Rabbi Herbert J. Wilner
Songs.........................Charles Julian
Introduction of the Speaker......Dr. Joseph I. Rodgin
Address......................Paul Kollek
Remarks.....................Isaac Diamond
                                   (Chairman)
Benediction...................Rabbi Herbert J. Wilner
Reception............By the Bluefield Chapter of Hadassah


OFFICERS AND BOARD OF DIRECTORS OF THE BLUEFIELD-
PRINCETON UNITED JEWISH CHARITIES FOR THE
YEAR 1956–1957

### OFFICERS

PRESIDENT and CAMPAIGN CHAIRMAN: Isaac L. Diamond
VICE PRESIDENT: Joseph Tomchin (for Bluefield)
VICE PRESIDENT: Yankee Barbakow (for Princeton)
SECRETARY: Samuel I. Slifkin
TREASURER: Frank Klauber
IMMEDIATE PAST PRESIDENT: Nathan Platnick

BOARD OF DIRECTORS

### 1956–1958

| | |
|---|---|
| Yankee Barbakow (of Princeton) | Frank Klauber |
| Emanuel Borinsky (of Princeton) | Alfred E. Land |
| Isaac L. Diamond | Frank Nelson (of Princeton) |
| Fred Gilbert | Joseph Tomchin |

1955–1957

| Isadore Cohen | Dr. Joseph I. Rodgin |
| Morris Kaufman | Irving E. Selig (of Princeton) |
| Jesse B. Michelson | Samuel I. Slifkin |
| Nathan Platnick | Meyer J. Spiro |

## THE BLUEFIELD-PRINCETON UNITED JEWISH CHARITIES

## A FEW FINANCIAL FIGURES REGARDING RECEIPTS AND DISBURSEMENTS

## THE 1955–1956 CAMPAIGN
## ALLOCATION MEETING, OCTOBER 9, 1956

| CHAIRMAN: | Isadore Cohen 1953–1954 Drive | Fred Gilbert 1954–1955 Drive | Nathan Platnick 1955–1956 Drive |
|---|---|---|---|
| *Receipts:* | | | |
| Jewish Contributions........... | $10,596.50 | $10,471.50 | $11,793.38 (+$3,395, special emergency drive) |
| Christian Contributions........ | 1,652.00 | 1,308.00 | 1,062.50 |
| Subtotal................. | 12,248.50 | 11,779.50 | 12,855.88 |
| Less: Expenses............ | 454.10 | 102.67 | 281.68 |
| Available for Allocation......... | $11,794.40 | 11,676.83 | 12,574.20 |
| *Disbursements:* | | | |
| (1) National Institutions........ | $ 1,500.00 | 1,550.00 | 1,560.00 |
| (2) Theological Seminaries, Welfare Homes, and Israel Institutions............... (about 15 items) | 155.00 | 155.00 | 165.00 |
| (3) Local Transient Fund....... | 150.00 | 150.00 | 150.00 |
| (4) United Jewish Appeal....... | 9,989.40 | 9,821.83 | |
| Total Disbursements............... | | 11,676.83 | 12,574.20 (+ the proceeds of the special emergency drive of 1956–1957, i. e.: $ 3,395.00) |
| Total: | | | $15,969.20 |

BLUEFIELD-PRINCETON UNITED JEWISH CHARITIES
DISBURSEMENTS TO NATIONAL INSTITUTIONS
IN THE FISCAL YEAR 1954–1955

( 1) Combined Campaign of the Hebrew Union
College-Jewish Institute of Religion, and the
Union of American Hebrew Congregations..... $   225
( 2) Jewish Theological Seminary of America, New
York........................................          50
( 3) Yeshiva University, New York.................          50
( 4) Hebrew University — Technion — Joint Maintenance Appeal.............................          50
( 5) Jewish Chautauqua Society [New York].........         100
( 6) Joint Defense Appeal of the Anti-Defamation
League of the B'nai B'rith and the American
Jewish Committee..........................         350
( 7) B'nai B'rith National Youth Service (formerly,
Wider Scope)..............................         100
( 8) HIAS (Hebrew Sheltering and Immigrant Aid
Society, New York)........................         175
( 9) National Jewish Welfare Board................          50
(10) American Jewish Congress and World Jewish
Congress..................................          25
(11) Jewish Consumptive Relief Society.............          50
(12) Leo N. Levi Memorial Hospital................          50
(13) National Jewish Hospital.....................          50
(14) Jewish National Home for Asthmatic Children...          50
(15) American Fund for Israel Institutions..........          50
(16) American Red Mogen Dovid for Israel, Inc......          50
(17) Committee on Solicitation of Funds, of the Central
Conference of American Rabbis..............          25
(18) Histadrut...................................          50
                                              —————
                         Total............. $1,550

($1,560 in 1955–1956)

### BLUEFIELD-PRINCETON UNITED JEWISH CHARITIES
### COMPARATIVE ANALYSIS OF RECEIPTS AND DISBURSEMENTS
### (1945–1946 TO 1952–1953)

| | 1945–1946 CHAIRMAN William P. Gottlieb | 1946–1947 CHAIRMAN Isadore Cohen | 1947–1948 CHAIRMAN Alfred E. Land |
|---|---|---|---|
| *Receipts:* | | | |
| Jewish Contributions............... | $ 9,395.00 | 18,070.50 | 25,217.00 |
| Christian Contributions............ | 1,320.00 | 2,683.50 | 3,928.50 |
| *Total Receipts:* | 10,715.00 | 20,754.00 | 29,145.50 |
| *Disposition of the Funds Collected:* | | | |
| (1) United Jewish Appeal.......... | 8,589.53 | 17,510.50 | 23,919.18 |
| % of the Total................ | 80.16% | 84.37% | 82.07% |
| (2) National Institutions.......... | 1,500.00 | 2,400.00 | 3,945.00 |
| (3) Theological Seminaries, Welfare Homes, and Palestinian Institutions...................... | 232.50 | 182.50 | 225.00 |
| (4) Local Transient Fund.......... | 38.00 | 23.75 | 300.00 |
| (5) Expenses..................... | 354.97 | 637.25 | 756.32 |
| *Total Disbursements:* | $10,715.00 | 20,754.00 | 29,145.50 |

| | 1948–1949 CHAIRMAN Isadore Cohen | 1949–1950 CHAIRMAN Dr. Joseph I. Rodgin | 1950–1951 CHAIRMAN Fred Gilbert | 1951–1952 CHAIRMAN Jessel S. Salzberg | 1952–1953 CHAIRMAN Isadore Cohen |
|---|---|---|---|---|---|
| *Receipts:* | | | | | |
| Jewish Contributions........ | $20,847.00 | 17,132.50 | 15,308.00 | 11,790.00 | 13,164.50 |
| Christian Contributions...... | 3,183.50 | 376.00 | 1,465.00 | 1,436.50 | 1,628.50 |
| *Total Receipts:* | $24,030.50 | 17,508.50 | 16,773.00 | 13,226.50 | 14,792.50 |
| *Disposition of the Funds Collected:* | | | | | |
| (1) United Jewish Appeal.... | $19,718.70 | 14,548.90 | 14,468.47 | 11,165.48 | 12,381.02 |
| % of the Total.......... | 82.06% | 83.10% | 86.26% | 84.42% | 83.70% |
| (2) National Institutions..... | 3,425.00 | 2,350.00 | 1,925.00 | 1,645.00 | 1,785.00 |
| (3) Theological Seminaries, Welfare Homes and Palestinian Institutions.... | 165.00 | 175.00 | 150.00 | 147.50 | 155.00 |
| (4) Local Transient Fund.... | 122.42 | 100.00 | 100.00 | 100.00 | 100.00 |
| (5) Expenses.............. | 599.38 | 334.60 | 129.53 | 168.52 | 371.48 |
| *Total Disbursements:* | $24,030.50 | 17,508.50 | 16,773.00 | 13,226.50 | 14,792.50 |

(For the complete list of contributors to, and members of, the Bluefield-Princeton United Jewish Charities, as of October, 1957, see above.)

Contributions of the Bluefield-Princeton United
Jewish Charities to the C. C. A. R. Relief
and Subvention Fund (1950–1959)

From 1950 to 1959, the Bluefield-Princeton United Jewish
Charities was one of the few West Virginia Jewish organizations
which made annual contributions to the Relief and Subvention
Fund of the Central Conference of American Rabbis. Such
contributions were recorded as follows in the *CCAR*:

1950

$10.00 (*CCAR*, LX [1950], page 421)

1952–1953

$10.00 in each of these two years (*CCAR*, LXII [1952], 562;
LXIII [1953], 559)

1954

$25.00 (*CCAR*, LXIV [1954], 248)

1955–1958

$25.00 in each of these four years.

1958–1959

In 1958–1959, the Bluefield-Princeton United Jewish Charities
made a contribution of $25.00 to the C. C. A. R. Relief and
Subvention Fund (*CCAR*, LXIX [1959], 302).

Bluefield Members of the Jewish Publication Society
of America (1915 to 1959)

1915–1916 (5676 A.M.)

B. S. Block
Isadore Cohen
I. [Isaac] Greenspon
Mrs. S. [Solomon] Greenspon

L. Hirshberger
Mrs. L. Kaufman
L. H. Taschman
I. Wohlmuth

1916-1917 (5677 A.M.)

Mrs. Henry (Anna G.) Rodgin (joined as a new member)

1917-1918 (5678 A.M.)

Reverend Kalman Slifkin (joined as a new member)

1918-1919 (5679 A.M.)

Mrs. S. (Solomon) Greenspon (rejoined as a new member)

1922-1923

Isadore Cohen                    J. Lowenstein
Mrs. S. (Solomon) Greenspon  Mrs. Henry (Anna G.) Rodgin
Mrs. L. Kaufman                  Harry Stoltz [Stolch]
  (rejoined as a new member)

1930-1935

Mrs. Henry (Anna G.) Rodgin
G. Schlossberg
B. J. Wagner (also in 1935-1936)

1947-1948

Isadore Cohen (rejoined as a new member)

1955-1956

Isadore Cohen
Congregation Ahavath Sholom Religious School
Isadore Tucker[1]

1958-1959

Isadore Cohen
Congregation Ahavath Sholom Religious School

BLUEFIELD JEWS IN THE UNITED STATES MILITARY SERVICE

FRED GILBERT. Fred Gilbert, of Bluefield, served in the United
  States Army in the Second World War, from 1943 to 1945.
HENNON GILBERT. Hennon Gilbert, of Bluefield, a cousin and

---

[1] Formerly of Bluefield, and in 1957 living in Ellenboro, W. Va., in Ritchie County,
east of Parkersburg. A brother of Sidney Tucker, Isadore Tucker left Bluefield in
1950, after a residence there of three or four years.

former business partner of Fred Gilbert, served in the United States Army in the Second World War as a 1st lieutenant. He was awarded the Purple Heart and the Bronze Star Medal. [Hennon Gilbert moved to Fort Worth, Tex., in 1959.]

STANLEY D. GOTTLIEB. Stanley D. Gottlieb, of Bluefield, the son of William P. Gottlieb, served in the United States Army during the Second World War as a Private 1st Class. He received the Presidential Unit Citation. He was wounded in the course of the War.

MAX L. KAMMER. Max L. Kammer, of Bluefield, the son of Harry Kammer, served in the United States Army in the Second World War with the rank of captain. He was awarded the Bronze Star Medal, the Purple Heart, and the Croix de Guerre.

JOSEPH I. RODGIN. Dr. Joseph I. Rodgin, of Bluefield, the son of Mrs. Henry [Anna G.] Rodgin, served in the Second World War, for four years, in the Medical Department of the United States Air Corps.

MEYER J. SPIRO. Meyer J. Spiro, of Bluefield, served in the United States Army, after the end of the Second World War, from 1951 to 1953.

DAVID S. STEINER. David S. Steiner, of Bluefield, served in the United States Army in the Second World War with the rank of Private 1st Class. He was wounded in action, and received the Purple Heart.

ARTHUR WILSON. Arthur Wilson, of Bluefield, the younger son of Jacob Wilson, served in the United States Army, in Korea, from 1954 to 1956.

A boy named William W. Mattox, of Bluefield, is listed in the Second World War records as having served in the United States Army with the rank of staff sergeant, and as also having been of the Jewish faith. He was killed in action. However, there is no proof that he was Jewish. The probability is very great that he was not a Jew, and that his being listed in the records as Jewish is an error. No Jewish boy of Bluefield, so far as I ever heard while I served as congregational rabbi in Bluefield, or from my researches learned thereafter, lost his life in the service of his country in the Second World War. In the course of my three years in Bluefield, from 1947 to 1950, I never heard of any family of or near Bluefield, either Jewish or non-Jewish, by the name of Mattox, nor did I ever hear anything to the effect that a Jewish boy by that name, or any Jewish boy, had lost his life in the War.

## NOTED BLUEFIELD JEWS

I. AARON. I. Aaron, one of the early pioneers of the Bluefield Jewish community, had two daughters. One daughter was Sarah Aaron, who later married Abraham N. (Abe) Schlossberg, a Bluefield jeweler, who still (1959) resided in Bluefield. Mrs. Sarah A. Schlossberg has been active in the Bluefield and State Sisterhood, and in communal work in Bluefield. A second daughter of I. Aaron married Louis Schuchat, of Lewisburg, W. Va., where she still resided in 1958. Her husband, a merchant in Lewisburg, retired from business in 1955. Mrs. Louis Schuchat had been a school-teacher in Bluefield before her marriage to Louis Schuchat and her removal to Lewisburg.

S. ANGRIST. S. [Samuel?] Angrist, the oldest Jewish resident of Bluefield, died in Bluefield in late 1958, at the age of over 90. He was the father of the brother clothing merchants Abe, Ben, and Harry Angrist, and of Mrs. Rose A. (Harry) Clark and of Mrs. Freda A. Frank.

HARRY and ROSE A. CLARK. Harry Clark, a long-time "old settler" in Bluefield, was a past director and officer of the Bluefield congregation, and was noted for his service on behalf of the Jewish community over a period of many years. He was the owner of a shoe store on Princeton Avenue, in Bluefield, for many years, and retired from business in June, 1958. Harry Clark's wife, Rose Angrist Clark, was active in the Bluefield Sisterhood for many years.

ISADORE COHEN. Isadore Cohen was born in Zagor (Zagarren), Lithuania, on May 11, 1885. His parents were Simon Aaron Cohen and Amelia Cohen. He received the D.M.D. degree at the University of Kiev, Russia, in 1904, and in the following year he emigrated to the United States, settling in Bluefield in that same year (1905). He was a jeweler and a motion picture theatre owner and operator for a number of years, and then he later (in 1930) went into the insurance business, as an agent, and as a life insurance counsellor, with the Sun Life Insurance Company, of Canada.[1]

Isadore Cohen has for several decades been prominently identified with the civic and communal undertakings of Bluefield, and with all Jewish activities, locally and state-wide, in West Virginia. He served as the president of the West Virginia Council of the B'nai B'rith from 1939 to 1941, after serving as the 1st vice president of the State Council from 1937 to 1938. In 1959, he was serving as an honorary president of the State Council. He was one of the founders and organizers of the Bluefield Symphony Orchestra, and served as its first president. In 1956, he was still honorary president of the Bluefield Symphony Orchestra. In 1952, he was awarded a certificate by the State B'nai B'rith Council of West Virginia for his services to the community. In December, 1954, he was given an honorary life membership in the Bluefield Chamber of Commerce. On February 11, 1954, Isadore Cohen was elected a member of the Board of Directors of the West Virginia Cancer Society (a member since 1940). He was a charter member of the Bluefield Rotary Club.

In the earlier days of Bluefield, Isadore Cohen was a founder of the Old Playground Association, and served as vice president of the Bluefield Chamber of Commerce. He served also as a member of the Council of the National

---

[1] As we have already mentioned above, it is evident that Isadore Cohen's father, Simon A. [Aaron] Cohen, was the otherwise unknown "rabbi" who is recorded as having lived in Bluefield in 1907 and as having served as the "rabbi" of the congregation for an undetermined period of time around that date. It is possible that Simon A. Cohen was a considerable Hebrew scholar previously in Lithuania, before his presumable immigration to the United States and to Bluefield, perhaps in 1905.

Chamber of Commerce. In the First World War he was appointed, and served as, a member of the Mercer County Committee of the Federal Fuel Administration.

Isadore Cohen served a term as president of Ahavath Sholom Congregation, and for several years he served as the president of the Bluefield-Princeton United Jewish Charities organization and campaign. He has always been prominent in the work of Congregation Ahavath Sholom, served for years as chairman or as co-chairman of its Religious Committee, and played a prominent role in the ceremony of the cornerstone laying (November, 1947) and in that of the dedication (May, 1949) of the new Albemarle Street Synagogue of the congregation. He is a past president of the Bluefield Zionist Organization of America. His name is recorded *in Who's Who in World Jewry* (1955).[1]

ISRAEL FINK. Israel Fink (born in Brooklyn, N. Y., in 1895) settled in Bluefield in 1946, coming from Newport News, Va. In Bluefield, together with his son-in-law, Bernard Snyder, he operated the Cavalier Cut Rate (drug) Store, on Princeton Avenue. In 1948, he moved to Beckley.

EDWARD GILBERT. Edward Gilbert, who lived in Beckley from 1924 until his death there in June, 1947, originally operated a men's clothing store in Bluefield, until 1924. In Beckley, too, after having operated a jewelry store for a few years, he operated a clothing store.

EZRA GILBERT. Ezra Gilbert, the father of Hennon Gilbert, played a prominent role in the religious and communal life of the Bluefield Jewish community, and was most active in its philanthropic activities. An early settler and "pioneer" of the Bluefield Jewish congregation, Ezra Gilbert assisted greatly, and was one of the "prime movers," in the impetus towards the building of the new Albemarle Street Temple, whose completion, however, he did not live to see.

FRED GILBERT. Fred Gilbert was born in Wilno (Vilna), Poland [Lithuania], on December 10, 1906, and was brought to the United States in that same year by his parents, Morris

---

[1] By mid-1961, Isadore Cohen and his wife, Flora Greenspon Cohen, had left Bluefield, and were residing in Washington, D. C., where their two married daughters lived.

and Eva Horowitz Gilbert. He came to Bluefield in 1928. His father, Morris Gilbert, was the brother of Ezra Gilbert. Fred Gilbert is noted in Bluefield as a merchant and as a Jewish communal worker. Since 1933, he has been either a partner in, or the sole owner of, the People's Loan Company, in Bluefield, a small loans business. He was formerly in partnership in that business with his cousin, Hennon Gilbert.

Fred Gilbert served in the United States Army, from 1943 to 1945, during the Second World War. Upon his return to Bluefield, he served as the treasurer of the Bluefield B'nai B'rith Lodge, from 1946 to 1957. From 1952 to 1956, he served as the vice president of the Bluefield-Princeton United Jewish Charities. He was chairman of the United Jewish Appeal and of the Bluefield-Princeton United Jewish Charities in 1950 to 1951. From 1950 to 1952, he served as the treasurer of Congregation Ahavath Sholom, and he served as the president of the congregation from 1953 to 1956. His biography is recorded in *Who's Who in World Jewry* (1955).

WILLIAM P. GOTTLIEB. William P. Gottlieb, owner and operator of the Vogue Fur Store, on Federal Street, served for many years as the treasurer of Congregation Ahavath Sholom, and was chairman of the Building Committee which erected the new Albemarle Street Temple, in 1947 to 1949. In 1958–1959, William P. Gottlieb was still a member of the Bluefield Congregation, but was living in Miami Beach, Fla.[1] His son, Stanley D. Gottlieb,[2] was operating the Vogue Fur store in his absence. William P. Gottlieb served from 1946 to 1948 as president of the Bluefield-Princeton B'nai B'rith Lodge, No. 967, and he was active for many years in civic affairs and in the work of the congregation.

WILLIAM GREENSPON. Dr. William Greenspon is the son of Saul and Marie Greenspon, who were pioneer settlers in Bluefield in 1889. Saul Greenspon was one of the ten [sixteen?] founders of Congregation Ahavath Sholom.

---

[1] William P. Gottlieb died in Florida about the latter part of the year 1959, or in early 1960.

[2] In 1961, Stanley D. Gottlieb was living in Miami Beach, Fla.

William Greenspon was born in Bluefield, W. Va., on May 11, 1897. He was graduated from the Philadelphia Optical College in 1916, and from the University of Pennsylvania in 1921, and took post-graduate work at the West Virginia University Extension. He received the O.D. (Doctor of Optometry) degree. In 1917, he attended the United States Naval Officers' School, as an ensign in the United States Naval Reserve.

In his field of optometry, Dr. William Greenspon has held many offices. He served as chairman of the Council on Optometric Education of the American Optometric Association (a member since 1943); as past president of the International Association of the Boards of Examiners in Optometry (1948–1950); as past president of the West Virginia Optometric Association (five terms as president, and a member thereof for 36 years); and as past president of the Southeastern Congress of Optometry (1947). He is a member of the Research Council of the American Optometric Foundation, a member of the Executive Council of the American Academy of Optometry, and was a fellow (1942–1946), and past State chairman, of the Optometric Extension Program, as well as a member of the "20 Year Planning Commission" of the American Optometric Association. He also represents the profession of optometry on the National Commission on Accrediting (Universities and Colleges). He is visual safety consultant to several area industrial plants, on visual problems in the schools, and to the American Gas and Electric Company subsidiaries.

William Greenspon was a member of the original City Park Commission, and served as past president of the Board of Directors of the Union Mission and of the Bluefield Symphony Orchestra. He served a term as president of the Bluefield B'nai B'rith Lodge, No. 967. He is also an officer or a director of several utilities and business firms in Bluefield.

William Greenspon married the former Bernice Rothschild, of Washington, D. C. Their son, William Stuart Greenspon, received the M.D. degree from the University of Virginia (1952), and in 1957 he was resident physician in psychiatry at Bellevue Hospital, New York.

FRANK KLAUBER. Frank Klauber was born in Vienna, Austria, on January 3, 1915. After completing elementary school and high school in Vienna, he attended the University of Vienna for two years, and then immigrated to the United States, in 1939. He settled in Bluefield in 1940; here he opened an accounting office in 1941, and he has practised as a public accountant ever since that year.

For several years (in the late 1940's and early 1950's) Frank Klauber served as assistant treasurer of Congregation Ahavath Sholom. He was then elected treasurer of the congregation, and in 1959 he was still serving in that position. He served also as treasurer of the Bluefield-Princeton United Jewish Charities for a number of years, and as financial secretary of Bluefield-Princeton Lodge, No. 967, B'nai B'rith; he was still serving in the latter post in 1957-1958.

SIDNEY J. KWASS. Sidney J. Kwass, the son of Joseph I. Kwass, was born in Pocahontas, Va., on November 11, 1908. He received the LL.B. degree from the University of West Virginia in 1931, and served as the city attorney of Bluefield from 1933 to 1937, and as a commissioner in chancery of the Circuit Court from 1938 to 1946. From 1942 to 1946 he served as a referee in bankruptcy. From 1942 to 1946 he was also commissioner of accounts of the County Court of Mercer County, W. Va. From 1946 to 1948 he served as United States Commissioner of the District Court, in the Southern District. In 1951, he was president of the Mercer County Bar Association.

Sidney J. Kwass served as president of the Bluefield Lodge of the B'nai B'rith in 1933. He was president of Congregation Ahavath Sholom from 1945 to 1946, and again from 1951 to 1953, served on the Religious Committee of the congregation, was active in the Bluefield-Princeton United Jewish Charities, and was prominent in all affairs of the Jewish community. His biography is included in *Who's Who in World Jewry* (1955).

ABRAM J. LUBLINER. Abram J. Lubliner (born in Virginia, on October 25, 1900) was admitted to the bar in West Virginia and Virginia in 1922. He attended Emory and

Henry College, in Emory, Va., and in 1922 he received the
LL.B degree from Washington and Lee University. He was
a member of the State Senate from 1931 to 1933. He served
for eight years as assistant prosecuting attorney of Mercer
County; as a Commissioner in Chancery; and as a member
of the State Legislature from 1933 to 1947. He was chairman of the Taxation and Finance Committee, chairman of
the Labor Committee, and served as chairman of the
Insurance Committee, and as Government appeal agent for
selective service from 1940 to 1957. He also served as Special
Judge of the Criminal Court of Mercer County. Abram J.
Lubliner received a Congressional citation and medals as
authorized by the President of the United States.

BENJAMIN BERNHARD MATZ. Benjamin Bernhard Matz, father
of Nathan Matz, of Bluefield, was born in Libau, Russia
(Latvia), in 1873. He died in Bluefield on December 19,
1951. A Hebraist of note, as well as a rabbinic scholar, and a
well-known Baal Kore (Chazan, or reader) in the Orthodox
manner, Benjamin B. Matz prepared Jewish boys of Bluefield for Bar Mitzvah and taught them Hebrew in the years
before the Bluefield Jews had permanent rabbis in their
congregation. He also conducted the Orthodox religious
services for the High Holy Days in Ahavath Sholom Congregation (frequently together with Louis Diamond, father
of Isaac L. Diamond and himself a staunch member of
the Orthodox segment of the Bluefield Jewish community)
for a number of years, until the very year of his death.
(Philip Platnick usually conducted the Conservative services, and the congregational rabbi or student rabbi conducted the Reform services, on Rosh Hashanah and Yom
Kippur, as successive religious services.) Benjamin B. Matz
and Louis Diamond also officiated at Passover and Feast
of Tabernacles services in Congregation Ahavath Sholom,
both in the Scott Street "Shul" and in the new Albemarle
Street Temple, for some years.

By occupation, Benjamin B. Matz was a Jewish baker,
the only one in the history of the Bluefield Jewish community, before his retirement from the trade about the year
1945. His son, Nathan Matz, came from Bluefield, in 1938,

to Beckley, where he became the lessee and operator of the President Hotel.

NATHAN PLATNICK (and the PLATNICK BROTHERS). Nathan Platnick was born in Kielem, Lithuania, near the East Prussian border, on July 8, 1899. He is the second oldest of the noted four Platnick brothers of Bluefield who are prominent in the business, religious, and civic life of that city. Philip Platnick is the oldest, and Benjamin and David Platnick are, respectively, the third oldest and the youngest. Nathan Platnick has been co-owner, together with two of his three brothers in Bluefield (Benjamin and David Platnick), of the firm of Platnick Brothers, scrap iron and steel fabricators, as well as metal dealers, in Bluefield, Va., since 1915.

Nathan Platnick, the son of Joseph and Ida Mary Goldman Platnick, arrived in the United States from his native Lithuania in October, 1913, when he was only 14 years of age. His father, Joseph Platnick, died in the "Old Country" when he was only four years of age. Joseph Platnick had been an Orthodox rabbi. In the "Old Country" the young Nathan attended a Hebrew parochial school as well as the Yeshiva in his native Lithuanian town. Nathan Platnick and his mother, who were enabled to come to the United States through the aid of an uncle in this country, settled in Bluefield in October, 1913, a few weeks after their arrival in America. His two younger brothers, Benjamin (always nicknamed "Ben") and David (always known as "Dave") Platnick, came to the United States in April, 1914, and settled at once in Bluefield, W. Va.

Nathan Platnick first went to work for Isaac Greenspon (father of Minna, Lillian, and David Greenspon), who at that time operated a soft drink manufacturing plant where W. R. Keesee is now located. He continued to go to school, and worked after school and in his spare time for a small sum. Ben Platnick went to work in the small junk yard which had been owned by his uncle, but which, after the uncle's death in January, 1914, had been sold to a new owner. In the following year (1915), the man who had bought the junk business from the Platnick brothers' uncle turned it over to Ben Platnick for a small sum, to be paid off in small installments, and so the three brothers entered the junk and scrap iron business in 1915. Originally the business was located on the North Side of Bluefield, W. Va., but in 1938 the three brothers moved their business to the much smaller city of Bluefield, Va., operating at the old furnace property, which the brothers had bought in 1928.

Gradually, also, the firm entered the structural new-steel business, and in 1957, Alvin Platnick, the son of Benjamin Platnick, who is a graduate engineer, was in charge of the steel-fabricating end of the business, which the brothers at that time were rapidly expanding. In 1957, the firm's new steel-fabricating plant was almost completed. The firm of Platnick Brothers is active also in the dismantling field. In 1957, the firm completed a dismantling job for the Appalachian Electric Power Company in Roanoke, Va., and also a previous job for the United States Steel Company at Gary, W. Va., and at the present time (mid-1957), the firm was doing a dismantling job in Richmond, Va. It also, some ten or more years ago, did the considerable job of dismantling and removing the old street car tracks (about ten miles) running between Bluefield and Princeton.

Morris Kaufman, the brother-in-law of the four Platnick brothers, who married the only Platnick sister, the former Dora Platnick, was still serving, in 1959–1960, as a foreman in the plant of Platnick Brothers, which position he had occupied for close to 20 years. Morris Kaufman is a considerable Yiddish student, as is also his noted brother-in-law, Nathan Platnick. The latter is known also, locally, as a capable occasional public speaker, and as a considerable philanthropist in all general and Jewish causes.

Nathan Platnick served as president of Ahavath Sholom Congregation from 1937 to 1938 and from 1946 to 1951, and was re-elected in September, 1956; in 1959, he was still serving in this position, having been re-elected several times. He was president of the Bluefield Lodge of the B'nai B'rith in 1936. He served also as State Chairman of the Joint

Defense Appeal in 1947 to 1948; and as a member of the Board of Directors of the Cincinnati Chapter of the Institute of Scrap Iron and Steel. He was instrumental in the erection of the new Albemarle Street Temple of the congregation (1947–1949), and served several terms as president and chairman of the United Jewish Appeal campaigns and of the Bluefield-Princeton United Jewish Charities. He is affiliated with a number of local civic and cultural organizations, being very active in the local Kiwanis Club. Possessed of a cultural drive, he has made up for his lack of childhood and youthful education by obtaining the equivalent of a high school and of a Junior College diploma in the Graham High School, in Bluefield, Va., and in Bluefield College, in that same city. Nathan Platnick's biography in included in *Who's Who in World Jewry* (1955).

Of personal interest is the following brief description, written in the third person, of his belated schooling: "As evidence of his desire to imbibe some of the education and culture which he had missed, and never secured, and which he felt the lack of most grievously as a grown man, culture and education which he had failed to receive when he was young and had to go to work at much too early an age, Nathan Platnick, for about two years, took private lessons in Latin and English from Rabbi Abraham I. Shinedling, while the latter was rabbi of the Bluefield Congregation (1948–1950), in order to help him with his knowledge and use of English; and after 1950 he took several courses at Graham High School, in Bluefield, Va., and at Bluefield College, which resulted in his being awarded his belated high school diploma. Since then he has continued his college studies in Bluefield College."

On May 30, 1960, Nathan Platnick was awarded the honorary degree of Bachelor of Literature by Bluefield State College, the first honorary degree ever bestowed by this College; the honorary degree emphasized the "intellectual growth and the persistent and continuing search for knowledge as typified by the recipient, and the place in education of strong, sturdy character and responsible citizenship."

His wife, Mrs. Edna E. Platnick, at the same commence-
ment exercises of Bluefield State College, was awarded the
earned degree of Bachelor of Science, *magna cum laude*.

EDNA EFFRON PLATNICK (Mrs. Nathan Platnick). Edna Effron
Platnick (the sister of the eminent Cincinnati violinist
Sigmund Effron), originally a native of Cincinnati, the wife
of Nathan Platnick, has been active for years in the Bluefield
Sisterhood and in the Bluefield Chapter of Hadassah, and
served for years as an officer and director of the Bluefield
Sisterhood. She collated and gathered much of the material
and data on the Bluefield Sisterhood which have been
incorporated into this volume. She also served for a number
of years, from 1945 or 1946 to 1951, as the superintendent
of the Religious School of the congregation, and as one of
its substitute and regular teachers for some years before and
after that period of time. She and her sister-in-law, Mrs.
Gertrude (Mrs. David) Platnick, were for some years co-
organists of the Temple. Edna E. Platnick is noted in the
Bluefield congregation and community for her many Jewish
and non-Jewish charitable acts and contributions, and, like
many other Jewish women of the community, including
Mrs. Nathan (Anna A.) Effron, Mrs. Abraham N. (Sarah
A.) Schlossberg, Mrs. Ethel J. (Joseph) Tomchin, contributed greatly to all philanthropic, social, religious, civic,
and cultural projects and groups in the city. In 1947, with
the aid of Rabbi Abraham I. Shinedling, and most enthusiastically, she introduced into the Religious School the
Junior Congregation project which has worked so well in
the congregation in the past twelve years, and founded the
Temple Library and Museum.

PHILIP PLATNICK. Philip Platnick, the oldest brother of Nathan
Platnick, Benjamin Platnick, and David Platnick, served for
years as the conductor (Baal Tefillah) of the Conservative
religious services in the Bluefield congregation on the High
Holy Days, and also as a teacher in the Religious School
of the congregation. He is noted as a Hebraist and as a
Jewish scholar, having been originally quite Orthodox.
Philip Platnick was born in Lithuania, in the same town as

witnessed the birth of his three younger brothers, and came to the United States in his later years, after he had graduated from a dental school in the "Old Country" and practised as a dentist for years in Latvia. After his arrival in Bluefield, he at first operated a ladies' ready-to-wear store, known as the Glamour Shop, on South Bland Street, but after a number of years in this store, and in another clothing store on Bland Street, he gave up the merchandising business, in 1950, and entered the scrap iron and metal business in Princeton, in which he was still engaged in 1959.

FANNIE PLATNICK. Fannie Platnick, the wife of Philip Platnick, also served for years as a teacher in the congregational Religious School, and served as its superintendent from 1955 to 1957. Active also in local and State Sisterhood affairs, Mrs. Fannie Platnick served also as an officer in the Bluefield Sisterhood and, from 1953 to 1955, she served as the auditor of the West Virginia Federation of Temple Sisterhoods. Like her husband, she is noted in Bluefield as a Hebraist of note, and for years taught Hebrew in the Religious School.

HENRY RODGIN. Henry Rodgin, who died at Bluefield, W. Va., at the age of sixty on March 24, 1944, was not only a businessman, but also a pioneer of Bluefield who rose from a street vendor of newspapers to a successful career as a merchant in the city. He played an important role in the upbuilding of Bluefield, strongly supporting all those institutions, movements, and civic projects which were designed to build a better community and to improve the general welfare of the city and of the community.

Henry Rodgin was born in Lithuania in 1884, and was brought to the United States by his parents when he was three years old. The Rodgin family settled in Bluefield soon after the city was incorporated. Henry Rodgin started his career as a businessman as a newspaper salesman while still hardly more than a boy, becoming the first route boy for the *Bluefield Daily Telegraph*. This was about the year 1895, when he was about eleven years of age.

In 1902, from savings accumulated from his earnings on his newspaper route, Henry Rodgin began his merchandising career in the jewelry business, which some years later developed into the leading jewelry firm in southern West Virginia.

For many years, Henry Rodgin was interested in educational affairs in Bluefield, and gave scholarships at Beaver High School, in Bluefield, at Bluefield College, and at Bluefield State College. He was one of the founders of Ahavath Sholom Congregation, and served as its president for a number of years.

His daughter, Bertie Rodgin, married Louis W. Cohen, owner of a widespread and successful chain of drug stores operating in Bluefield, Beckley, Charleston, and other cities of West Virginia.

ANNA GROLLMAN RODGIN. Anna Grollman Rodgin, the wife of Henry Rodgin, taught for years in the Congregation Ahavath Sholom Sunday School, and took an active part in the women's organizations of the city, both Jewish and non-Jewish. She is noted in Bluefield as a generous contributor to all philanthropic causes, like Henry Rodgin during his lifetime. In 1948, she donated a new organ to the new Temple of the congregation in memory of her departed husband. Mrs. Anna G. Rodgin is the maternal aunt of Rabbi Jerome W. Grollman and of his younger brother, Rabbi Earl A. Grollman, both ordained by the Hebrew Union College, in Cincinnati.

JOSEPH I. RODGIN. Dr. Joseph I. Rodgin (generally known by the familiar and affectionate nickname of "Jay" Rodgin), the son of Henry and Anna G. Rodgin, was born in Bluefield, and was graduated from Bluefield College. He then entered the Columbia University School of Optometry, in New York, from which he was graduated in 1940 with a degree in optometry. He received the Andrew Jay Cross Memorial Award. He served for four years in the Medical Department of the United States Air Corps during the Second World War, and then returned to Bluefield, where he resumed his practice of optometry. Noted in the field of optometry in Bluefield and its vicinity, where he has practised his profession for almost fifteen years, Joseph I. Rodgin designed a controlled exposure shutter test object for use in perimetric work, and has written articles on this subject, on Slit-lamp biomicroscopy, and on industrial vision. A past director of the Bluefield Rotary Club, and a member of the Narrows, Va., Lions Club, in which city, also, he practises optometry one or two days a week, he was chosen by the latter organization as the Man-of-the-Year in 1953, in recognition of his gratuitous work with visually handicapped children. He is a fellow of the American Academy of Optometry, and a member of the West Virginia Board of Optometry.

Active in local civic and communal work, Dr. Joseph I. Rodgin served as secretary of the Bluefield Junior Chamber of Commerce, as president of the Bluefield College Alumni Association, as secretary of Congregation Ahavath Sholom and as a member of its Board of Directors, as president of the Bluefield B'nai B'rith Lodge, and as president of the Southern West Virginia District of the Zionist Organization of America. He also has been active, for years, in the annual "campaigns" or "drives" for funds of the United Jewish Appeal and of the Bluefield-Princeton United Jewish Charities, serving as a trustee and committee member for years. He was also, together with Meyer J. Spiro, one of the original sponsors and adult counsellors of the Bluefield Temple Youth Group.

JOSEPH TOMCHIN. Joseph Tomchin, who died at Bluefield in the early part of July, 1959, came to West Virginia from New York, and at first he settled in Princeton, as one of the "later Jewish pioneers" of that city. In Princeton, he founded the large Tomchin Furniture Company, whose store was, in 1959, located on Mercer Street. In that year the Tomchin Furniture Company had two or three branches in Mullens and in other cities of southern West Virginia. His two sons, Harold Tomchin, of Princeton, and Abraham S. Tomchin, of Bluefield, as well as his nephew, Milton Tomchin, of Bluefield, were associated with him in the furniture business, the former managing the Princeton store. Joseph Tomchin moved to Bluefield from Princeton about the year 1942, after many years of residence in Princeton. In both cities he served for some years as a member of the Board of Directors of the Bluefield-Princeton United Jewish Charities, in the 1940's and 1950's, and took an active part in the work of the congregation, especially in the erection of the new Albemarle Street Synagogue, in 1947 to 1949.

Joseph Tomchin and his wife, ETHEL J. TOMCHIN, both took a most active part in the religious and communal life of the Bluefield Jewish community. Mrs. Ethel J. Tomchin served from 1948 to 1950 as the president of the Bluefield Temple Sisterhood. For some years she sang in the Bluefield Temple choir, being noted locally as a singer of ability.

The following biographical sketch of Joseph Tomchin was written for this volume by his elder son, Harold Tomchin, of Princeton, W. Va., in early 1961:

Joseph Tomchin (1894–1959) was born in Pilchovitz, Russia, a village in the Province of Minsk in that country. At the age of 14 he came to the United States, in the year 1908, arriving on July the Fourth. Because of the fireworks displays which he viewed from the ship bringing him into New York harbor, the young immigrant boy actually thought that every day was a holiday in this new land. [Joseph Tomchin — or Joe, as his intimates and best friends generally called him — had a considerable knowledge of Hebrew, possessed a fund of humor and narrative ability, and in his early days in his native Russia, apparently, had received a good education in Hebrew studies. He also knew the Yiddish language well. He was a modern Orthodox Jew in his many years spent in Princeton and in Bluefield.]

After working as a shipping clerk for $3.00 a week in the clothing business, he took a notion to head west for Chicago, where he had learned that wages were higher than in New York. While working in that city in the same type of job, he decided to establish himself as a peddler of dress goods and dress patterns. He toured large parts of the Middle West at this occupation.

About the year 1912 he had begun to peddle into West Virginia. He settled in Princeton, and in 1914 he married Ida Rodgin, of Bluefield, who died in 1919.

From the grocery and clothing business begun with almost no

capital, he entered the hardware business in Princeton, and later, together with his sons, Harold and Abraham Tomchin, he entered the furniture business, which later was expanded to three stores, his company's name being the Tomchin Furniture Company, Incorporated, of 423 Mercer Street, Princeton.

In 1943, Joseph Tomchin married Ethel Judelson, of Brooklyn, N. Y., who survived him. [About 1942, as above mentioned, he removed from Princeton, and settled in Bluefield, W. Va.]

In 1960, a short time after the death of Joseph Tomchin, Mrs. Ethel J. Tomchin left Bluefield, and returned to New York City, her original home.

In May, 1962, KENNETH B. PLATNICK, the elder son of Nathan Platnick and Edna E. Platnick, was working for *The New York Times*, in New York City, after having graduated from Dartmouth College and after having done considerable post-graduate study in universities in New York City. He was born in Bluefield, W. Va., in December, 1937, and in December, 1950, he was Bar Mitzvahed in Temple Ahavath Sholom in Bluefield by Rabbis Harold L. Gelfman and Abraham I. Shinedling.

Their younger son, GERALD E. PLATNICK, after being a student at Concord College, in Athens, W. Va., for some time, joined the Platnick Brothers firm in Bluefield, Va. He is his brother's junior by about two years.

In September, 1962, Gerald E. Platnick became a teacher in the Ahavath Sholom Congregation Religious School, in Bluefield, W. Va.

## BRAMWELL

Bramwell is a residential town in Mercer County, in southern West Virginia, eight miles southwest of Bluefield. It is in a coal-mining section of the State, and was incorporated in the year 1888. In 1940–1945, the town of Bramwell had a general population of 1,494. The United States Census for 1940 gave it a general population of 1,587. In 1957, its general population was estimated to be about 2,000.

According to the records found in the *American Jewish Year Book* for various years, there resided in Bramwell in the following years the following very small number of Jews:

1916–1917:  5 Jews
    1917:  5 Jews
    1927:  10 or fewer Jews
    1937:  10 or fewer Jews

There were no Jews living in Bramwell in 1958–1959.

However, Miss Edith Jameson, a high school teacher of Bramwell, and a student of the local history, who was the source of many of the following data about the interesting general and Jewish history of Bramwell, reported that her mother, who was still living in Bramwell in March, 1957, had stated that the Abrahamson family (the family of Mr. and Mrs. Mendel Abrahamson, who were the parents of Mrs. Nathan [Anna Abrahamson] Effron, of Bluefield) had been the only Jewish family whom she could remember as ever residing in Bramwell. In 1957, D. W. McCormick, the principal of the public schools of the town, was also its mayor.

I am greatly indebted to Miss Edith Jameson for the following account of the Abrahamson family and of their residence in Bramwell:

Mr. and Mrs. Mendel Abrahamson came to Bramwell from Pocahontas, Va. Mendel Abrahamson was a dry goods merchant, and for years he operated such a store in the town. Both the elder Abrahamsons died in Bramwell, and they were buried ın the Jewish Section of the Monte Vista Cemetery (on the new Bluefield-Princeton road).

Mendel Abrahamson and his wife had three children, all daughters:

Mrs. Rae Abrahamson Seigle (Mrs. William Seigle), now of New York City. She had taught in the Bramwell Elementary School (a public school) until her marriage to William Seigle, and thereafter she went to New York City to live.

Mrs. Gertrude Abrahamson Mohr, now the wife of Dr. Samuel Mohr, of New York. Gertrude Abrahamson assisted her father in his dry goods store in Bramwell until his death. She then went to New York, worked there for some time, and later married Dr. Samuel Mohr in that city.

Mrs. Anna Abrahamson Effron, the wife of Nathan Effron, of Bluefield, also taught in the Bramwell Elementary School until her marriage to Nathan Effron, a Bluefield clothing and general store merchant. After her marriage, she moved to Blue-field, where she became active in the work of the local and State Sisterhood, serving from 1946 to 1948 as the State Sisterhood president, and both she and her husband being most active in the work of the congregation, the latter also as a member of the Temple Board of Directors for some years.

The Abrahamson family resided in Bramwell for approx-imately twenty years.

The following copious excerpts dealing with the most in-teresting general history of the town of Bramwell (cf. also under Welch) were taken from an article or account compiled by a West Virginia History Class in the Bramwell High School about the year 1955, and going up to the year 1935; it was prepared under the aegis of Miss Edith Jameson:

## "HISTORY OF BRAMWELL

When the first surveys were being made, preparatory for the opening of Mercer County's coal industry, the site of Bramwell was picked out by the surveyors for a residential town. Major C. H. Duhring, local manager of the Flat-Top Coal Land Association, established the head-quarters of the land company and built the first house of the new town on the banks of the Bluestone River.

This territory was named for Mr. J. H. Bramwell, who came from New York about 1883, with Captain I. A. Welch [after whom the city of Welch, in nearby McDowell County, was named], as a civil engineer and mine promoter. The enterprise which gave life to the community was the opening of the Mill Creek Coal and Coke Company by John Cooper at Cooper[s] in 1884; [the] Caswell Creek Coal and Coke Company by John Freeman and Jenkin Jones [after whom the town of Jenkinjones, in West Virginia, was named]; [the] Booth-Bowen Coal and Coke Company opened by Jonathan Bowen, Senior, and William and James Booth. In 1886, John D. Hewitt, Senior, B. Moore, J. B. Stevenson, and William D. Mullin opened [the] Buckeye Coal and Coke Company. The opening of these companies brought many fine families to the section, and the payrolls of the operations gave financial background to the building of the town. The homes of the early Bramwell settlers were primitive in construction, most of them only a story and a half high. Among the early settlers were Captain I. A. Welch, Major Duhring, Captain George Belcher, Philip Goodwill, Robert Goodwill, J. [John] J. Tierney, H. H. Tabor, and J. Collins; in addition . . . [there were] the heads of the first coal operators [operations] mentioned above.[1]

In the year 1884, the Norfolk and Western Railway was extended from Bluestone Junction to the mouth of Simmons Creek.

In 1886, where the town of Bramwell now stands, there were only a half dozen buildings. Major Duhring, president of the Bluestone Land Company, with his family; Captain I. A. Welch, purchasing agent for the Land Company; and Captain George Belcher and [his] family resided there and entertained all newcomers. Mr. Bernheim [possibly, and almost certainly, a Jew] conducted a mercantile business where (shortly afterwards) the Masonic Temple was erected. John J. Tierney was chief engineer for the land company. One of the old residents worthy of mention was H. H. Tabor, whose generous hospitality aided much in those days to establish the town. Mr. Spicer, for whom Spicer Town (now Simmons and incorporated with Bramwell) was named, was also an early pioneer.

The Bank of Bramwell, chartered by the State and with a capital of $100,000.00, was organized in 1889. J. H. Bramwell was its first president.

---

[1] The beginnings of the history and settlement of the town of Bramwell are parallel to, and reminiscent of, those of many other smaller towns of West Virginia into which Jewish settlers, in smaller or larger numbers, came to settle, including Welch, Kimball, North Fork, Beckley, Mount Hope, Oak Hill, Mullens, Keystone, and many other cities and towns of the State; hence the interest in this detailed account, nowhere else available, of the beginnings of the town of Bramwell, even though not particularly typical.

Many stores [in my opinion, at least a few of them started and conducted by Jewish merchants, whose names have been lost] began to be established to meet the needs of the growing community. Lee, Ellwood, & Hunt had one of the early stores of the town. In 1893, J. C. Pack became a partner in this business. Mr. Pack soon took up other lines of work, but [a] Mr. Peters continued in the mercantile business until April, 1927. In November, 1896, [a] Mr. Fristoe, owner of a store in Bluefield, opened a branch establishment in Bramwell, in which there was carried a stock of goods equal in size to that in the Bluefield store.

The progressive citizens of Bramwell now began to initiate further steps of progress. In 1895, A. C. Godfrey was given a contract 'to construct a good and substantial road . . . not less than 16 feet in width' . . . a connection of South Block St. with the Bramwell-Pocahontas Road. In August, 1895, the Bramwell Water Company was organized, and was granted a franchise to furnish water to the town of Bramwell. Arrangements were soon made for the installation of electric lights for [in] the town. The Bramwell Accident Insurance Company was organized on April 20, 1895. On May 13, 1896, W. D. Tyler, B. Moore, F. L. Paddock, J. P. Parker, J. B. Kirk, and Isreal Myers [Israel Myers, who would appear to have been undoubtedly a Jew] bound 'themselves, heirs, executors and administrators to the town of Bramwell for the sum of five thousand dollars.' The town was on its way to prosperity. Bramwell was incorporated in 1889 under a special charter granted by the Circuit Court of Mercer County, and Colonel John C. Hewitt was elected as its first mayor. The succeeding mayors included, in rotation [succession?]: James Booth, Joseph Young, R. T. Little, Joseph Day, E. M. Keately, Thomas F. Burke, A. F. Godfrey, James A. Waddell, T. M. Ginnegan, and R. L. Parsons (1918–1935).

The thriving community took an early interest in the establishment of churches. The town of Cooper (founded by John Cooper), later to be incorporated with Bramwell, founded a Methodist Church in 1884; the Reverend Tyler B. Frazier was the pastor. Bramwell's first church was built (early in the 1890's) by the united efforts of the land company, the coal operators, and the residents. Because of the predominance and the initiative work of the Presbyterians, this church was dedicated to that denomination. The building was erected a short distance across the railroad from the Bramwell station. In 1903, the Honorable Isaac T. Mann erected and donated a beautiful bluestone church to the Presbyterian congregation. The latter soon installed a beautiful pipe organ. The Methodist Church was organized in 1876. In 1905 and 1906 the Methodist denomination erected a commodious church building with modern equipment. The Ladies Aid Society installed a pipe organ. Reverend Sidney B. Vaught became the pastor of the new church. The Baptist church and the Episcopal church were soon established. After the erection of the new Methodist church, the Baptist congregation moved into the church vacated by the Methodists.

In 1896, Bramwell, with 4,000 residents, was the headquarters for the general manager of the Flat-Top Coal Land Association, its engineers, draftsmen, mining engineers, and the like. It was also the home of two presidents and superintendents of coal and coke plants, it had four churches, eight stores for the sale of general merchandise, an excellent school building, and several modern conveniences.

In 1909, the main part of the town suffered a severe loss, [in a conflagration] which destroyed every house from the railroad station to the Bank of Bramwell, with the exception of the Bluestone Inn and the home of Edward Cooper. None of the buildings were replaced on these sites.

The Bramwell of today has the distinction of having three post offices within its corporate limits: Bramwell, Cooper[s], and Freeman. The town proper, 2,300 feet above sea level, is situated in a horseshoe bend on the Bluestone River and the Norfolk and Western Railroad, surrounded by picturesque mountain ridges which rise up like great statues, marking the scene of the greatest coal development of the State of West Virginia.

Bramwell, in the 1920 census, recorded 1,696 inhabitants. Two important enterprises are missing from Bramwell, now [1935], which were of long duration in the town. The Bank of Bramwell, established in 1889, closed down in 1933; and the Bluestone Inn, long a favorite resort for travelers, was torn down in 1933. While the population of Bramwell is less than half of what it was in 1896, the community is still a progressive one. The Bramwell of today [1955] has paved streets, fine churches, efficient consolidated schools, a high school, many palatial homes, and all modern church conveniences. The four original coal companies, the enterprises which caused the founding of the town and upon which Bramwell chiefly depends for its existence, are still in operation.

None of the descendants of J. H. Bramwell, for whom the town was named, are still [1935] living in Bramwell, due to the fact that, after acquiring his fortune in real estate, J. H. Bramwell moved to Switzerland, where he died in the early 1890's.

Harry Bowen and E. S. Baker are the only ones of the early prominent settlers who still [1935] reside in the town. The descendants of many of the early and prominent settlers of Bramwell, however, live within the precincts of the town. Among the early settlers whose descendants still [1955] reside in Bramwell are: Harry Bowen, J. P. Bowen, John Cooper, Philip Goodwill, Robert Goodwill, John D. Hewitt, H. H. Tabor, W. S. Freeman, J. C. Pack, R. T. Little, B. Moore, and E. S. Baker.

A small factory engaged in the manufacture of children's clothing is now [1955] in operation at the old Mill Creek Store in Coopers (a part of the corporation of Bramwell). This factory employs about thirty persons. The home office of the Newhold-Keesling Theatre Chain is located in the old Bank Building on the Main Street of Bramwell."

[The full name of Captain I. A. Welch, always given in the above historical account as I. A. Welch, was Isaiah A. Welch. *See also* under Welch.]

## BRIDGEPORT

Bridgeport is a cattle-shipping town located in Harrison County, in northern West Virginia, five miles east of Clarksburg. It is a grazing area. The town was chartered in 1816. It is the site of the beautiful cathedral-like Methodist Church built by Michael L. Benedum, head of the noted Benedum Family, formerly resident in Bridgeport but now living in Pittsburgh, Pa. Michael L. Benedum died in Pittsburgh, on July 30, 1959, at the age of ninety.

*The New York Times,* under date of July 30, 1959, reporting on its obituary page the death of Michael L. Benedum, presented a longer account of his life and deeds from which the following brief excerpts are taken:

Michael L. Benedum, last of the great oil wildcatters, died today [July 30, 1959] at his home, Greystone, in Pittsburgh's old East End section. He was 90 years old. Mr. Benedum was said to have discovered more oil than any single man in the industry. His fortune at his death was said to be near $100,000,000 . . . .

Mr. Benedum was as well known for his philanthropy as for his amazing success as an oil wildcatter. During his lifetime he set up a foundation destined to devote most of his wealth to philanthropy. It was named for his son, killed in World War I. In setting up the foundation, Mr. Benedum indicated [that] he expected to leave it the bulk of his fortune. Its charter specified [that] it is to be used for the advancement of religious, charitable, scientific, literary, and educational interests and for the prevention of cruelty to animals.

Besides the foundation, Mr. Benedum's gifts during his lifetime totaled many millions of dollars. To his home town of Bridgeport, W. Va., he gave $4,500,000 to build a new civic center and a new Methodist Church and to restore a community cemetery.

In 1956, the general population of Bridgeport was estimated at 1,581. The 1950 United States Census gave Bridgeport a general population of 2,414.

So far as can be ascertained, no Jews ever lived in Bridgeport, or at least there is no record of such. This was in spite of, or perhaps because of, its proximity to Clarksburg, where Jews coming into the area preferred to settle, instead. In 1959, there were no Jews living in Bridgeport.

## BUCKHANNON

Buckhannon is a city located in Upshur County, in north-eastern central West Virginia, fourteen miles east of Weston, on the Buckhannon River, and south of Clarksburg. Buckhannon, which is located at an elevation of 1,400 feet above sea level, is served by a branch line of the Baltimore and Ohio Railroad, but with no passenger service. The city is the county seat of Upshur County.

Buckhannon is situated in a cattle and mineral region, and possesses natural gas. It was settled in 1770. (Other historians give the date of its settlement as 1764.) In 1851, it was incorporated as a city. Its population in 1957 was 4,450. The United States Census for 1950 gave Buckhannon a total general population of 6,016. Buckhannon is known, in particular, as the seat of West Virginia Wesleyan College, a Methodist coeducational institution, which was founded in 1890. Several manufacturing plants are located in the city.

According to the *AJYB*, three volumes of which contain brief references to the city of Buckhannon, there were 10 or fewer Jews living in Buckhannon in 1927, and in 1937 there were 15 Jews (others, 13 Jews) living in the city. In the 1915–1916 *AJYB*, for the Jewish calendar year 5676 A.M., Earle O. Karickhoff is listed as a member of the Jewish Publication Society of America for that year (1915–1916).

R. R. Colinder, secretary of the Buckhannon Chamber of Commerce, in 1956, wrote as follows with reference to former Jewish residents of Buckhannon, in a letter sent to me early in June, 1956:

Simon Levinstein came to Buckhannon more than sixty years ago as a pack peddler. Later he went into the men's clothing business, which he conducted for more than forty years. He finally moved from Buckhannon to Baltimore, where he died.

Max Schindler came here with his wife eighteen years ago (1936), and went into business. He handled men's clothing, and his wife conducted the Smart Shop for Ladies. This spring (1956) Mrs. Max [Rae Rubenstein] Schindler passed away, and he then sold out his store and moved to North Carolina. I think that he is the last of our

Jewish families. We have several Jewish boys here in [West Virginia Wesleyan] College.

Thus, according to R. R. Colinder's statement, there were no Jews any longer living in Buckhannon in 1956.

Max Schindler was the most prominent and the most noted Jewish resident of Buckhannon, and an eminent merchant of the city. Theodore Cooperman, of New York, who for three years (1953–1956) was a student at West Virginia Wesleyan College, and who knew Max Schindler well, gave me the following account of this personage in June, 1956, on the occasion of my second visit to Buckhannon for a Methodist summer camp session at the College under the auspices of the Methodist Conference of West Virginia and of the Jewish Chautauqua Society:

Max Schindler came to Buckhannon about the year 1926 [note this conflict in date with the year 1936 given above by R. R. Colinder] from Hagerstown, Md. He was born in Hagerstown about the year 1900. He was a merchant, operating a men's clothing store. Max Schindler moved to Wilmington, N. C., in May, 1956, following the death of his wife, Rae Rubenstein Schindler (who died on February 22, 1956, at Buckhannon, at the age of 53; she was born in 1903). [Mrs. Rae Rubenstein Schindler was a sister of Ruby Rubenstein, the former mayor of Thomas, W. Va., which town was her original home.] Rae Rubenstein Schindler, for a number of years, operated a dress shop in Buckhannon, very successfully.

Max Schindler asserted that at one time (in the late 1920's and early 1930's), there were some thirty Jewish families living in Buckhannon. In 1956, after Max Schindler moved away from the city, not one of these several Jewish families still remained in Buckhannon. There never was a synagogue or any other Jewish communal building in Buckhannon. The Jewish residents of the city used to go to Clarksburg, to the Tree of Life Synagogue, for the High Holy Days of Rosh Hashanah and Yom Kippur, and many of them were dues-paying members of this Clarksburg Conservative congregation.

The other Jewish residents living in Buckhannon in previous years were chiefly merchants, operating stores of various kinds.

Max Schindler was for a term an elected member of the City Council of Buckhannon.

The Victor Rubenstein family of Thomas, W. Va., including their notable son Ruby Rubenstein, who later served for fifteen years as the mayor of Thomas, lived for a short period of time in Buckhannon, after settling in West Virginia, before moving permanently to Thomas (1894). Rae Rubenstein, also a daughter of Victor and Anne [Annie] Cohen Rubenstein, and a sister of Ruby Rubenstein, of Thomas, lived in Buckhannon for several years, and after her death she was buried in Hagerstown, Md. Rae Rubenstein (Mrs. Max) Schindler was born in Thomas in 1903.

## OTHER FORMER JEWISH RESIDENTS OF BUCKHANNON

The following brief data are known also about four other former Jewish residents of Buckhannon:

SAMUEL ABEL. Samuel Abel, a brother of Harry Abel and of Albert Abel, of Mount Hope, W. Va., lived in Buckhannon until 1914, and then moved to Mount Hope.

MAX BERNSTEIN. Max Bernstein came to Sutton, W. Va., from Buckhannon in 1904 or 1905, after residing in the latter city for a number of years. By occupation, he was a bottler of soft beverages. (*See* under Sutton, W. Va., for further details.)

SIMON M. LEVENSTEIN [Levinstein]. Simon M. Levenstein (briefly mentioned above by R. R. Colinder), a noted merchant of Buckhannon, was, in 1927, elected director of the Chamber of Commerce of the city. He held this position for a number of years.

RAE RUBENSTEIN. Rae Rubenstein (also mentioned above), a daughter of Victor Rubenstein, of Thomas, and a sister of Ruby Rubenstein, the former mayor of Thomas, lived in Buckhannon for a number of years after leaving Thomas. She was buried in Hagerstown, Md., from which city many of the former Jewish residents of Buckhannon, besides Max Schindler, came to Buckhannon to settle and to enter business. Rae Rubenstein was married to Max Schindler, of Buckhannon, who survived her. (*See above.*)

## West Virginia Wesleyan College, at Buckhannon

Buckhannon is the site of West Virginia Wesleyan College, a coeducational institution which was founded in 1890 by the West Virginia Conference of the Methodist Episcopal Church under the title of the West Virginia Conference Seminary. In 1886, the Conference organized the Board of Trustees of the West Virginia Conference Seminary, which chose Buckhannon as the site of the new school. A building was erected, and the college opened for its first term in September, 1890. For fourteen years, until 1904, the West Virginia Conference Seminary was operated as an academy, or preparatory school. In that year, however, it became an institution of collegiate rank, and has since been known as West Virginia Wesleyan College. Its academic (academy-like) or secondary courses were dropped after a number of years, as a result of the increase throughout the State of the number of public high (academic) schools.

In 1941, the West Virginia Conference of the Methodist Church, constituted by the unification of the Methodist Episcopal Church, the Methodist Episcopal Church, South, and the Methodist Protestant Church, decreed that West Virginia Wesleyan College should be the only educational institution to be operated under its auspices. As a result of this action, Morris Harvey College, in Charleston, which had been owned and operated by the Methodist Episcopal Church, South, since 1889, became an independent institution. The chief aim of West Virginia Wesleyan College is "to help her students to synthesize scholarship and Christianity in the good life."

B. W. Hutchinson was the president of the College from 1890 to 1898. He was succeeded, among others, by: John Wier (1900–1907), Wallace B. Fleming (1915–1922), Homer E. Wark (1926–1931), Roy McCluskey (1931–1941), and William J. Scarborough (1946–    ).

For many years in the past there has been a moderate number of Jewish students, for the most part men, in West Virginia Wesleyan College, chiefly from New York City and the eastern states. In 1955–1956 there were 63 Jewish students at the College in Buckhannon, mostly from New York City. During the academic school year these students conducted Minyan services every Friday evening in the Brown Chapel, the students themselves reading the services. Various rabbis of West Virginia for the most part, but some from outside of the State, visited and spoke at the College, and to the Jewish students, under the auspices of the Jewish Chautauqua Society, as well as visited the College during the months of June and July for various assemblies of the Methodist youth of the West Virginia Conference.

From 1946 to 1959, the following rabbis visited the campus of the College under J. C. S. auspices during the academic year:

1946: Rabbi Louis J. Cashdan (formerly of Charleston)
1947: Rabbi Sidney Brooks (formerly of Richmond, Va.)
1948: Rabbi Lawrence A. Block (formerly of Huntington)
1949: Rabbi Lester W. Roubey (formerly of Lancaster, Pa.)
1950: Rabbi Harold B. Waintrup (of Philadelphia)
1951: Rabbi Herbert J. Wilner (later of Bluefield)
1952: Rabbi Eugene Hibshman (then of Huntington)
1953: Rabbi Abraham I. Shinedling (then of Beckley)
1954: Rabbi Morris M. Rose (then of Morgantown)
1954 (December): Rabbi Samuel Volkman (of Charleston)
1955: Rabbi Samuel Volkman (of Charleston)
1959: (March 19th) Rabbi George B. Lieberman, of Rockville
       Center, Long Island; formerly of Wheeling)

Rabbi Abraham I. Shinedling and other West Virginia rabbis, as well as several rabbis from nearby Pennsylvania, visited West Virginia Wesleyan College in the summer, in the early 1950's, under J. C. S. auspices and under the aegis of the West Virginia Conference of the Methodist Church, and presented requested courses of lectures on the Hebrew Prophets and on other Judaic subjects to summer camp students of high school and university age, for one week or two weeks at a time.

In earlier years, Rabbi Charles E. Shulman, who served for four years (1927–1931) as the rabbi of the Eoff Street Temple, in Wheeling, also paid visits to West Virginia Wesleyan College, and spoke there before the student body, under J. C. S. auspices. Other State rabbis did the same in earlier years before 1946, but all record of their visits has been lost.

## CAMERON

Cameron is a city in Marshall County, in northern West Virginia, 12 miles southeast of Moundsville. Located in a rich farming section of the Northern Panhandle of West Virginia, Cameron was settled in 1788. In 1950, according to the United States Census of that year, the city had a general population of 1,736.

There were no Jews living in Cameron in the year 1957, nor had there been any Jews residing in the city for a considerable number of years before that. However, there were several families of Jews resident in the city in former years, according to statistics and names furnished by Miss Helen Ray, clerk of the city of Cameron, who wrote: "The following Jewish families did live in Cameron several years ago . . . . However, they have all moved away from here so long ago. Their names are as follows:

"Minor Grossman — moved to Cincinnati. He operated a clothing store.

Abraham Brody — moved to Wheeling. He operated a restaurant.

Louis Lazarus — moved to Wheeling. He operated a clothing store.

Louis Lando — moved to Bellaire, Ohio. He operated a clothing store.

Louis Goodman — moved to Moundsville, W. Va. He operated a clothing store.

Abraham Lazure — moved to Pittsburgh. He operated a clothing store.

"There was also Dr. George L. Joseph, an eye specialist, who came to Cameron from Wheeling, one day a week, until some years ago, when he ceased his medical visits."

## CASS

Cass is a town in east central West Virginia, located in Pocahontas County, on the Greenbrier River, 25 miles northeast of Marlinton. It is situated southeast of Webster Springs. In

1937, its general population was 708. In 1917, the *AJYB* stated that in 1917–1918, Caso (Cass), W. Va., had a population of ten Jews, out of a general population of less than 1,000 persons.

The only Jewish family who ever resided in Cass, of whom there is record, is the Jacob Cooper family. In 1959, there were no Jewish residents in Cass. Jacob and Maggie Gordon Cooper came to Cass from Washington, D. C., about the year 1905, and lived in Cass until 1930. Jacob Cooper was a merchant, operating Cooper's Department Store. In 1930, he moved his store to Durbin, W. Va., and continued in business there until 1932, when he moved back to Washington, D. C. Jacob Cooper died in Washington in 1943, and his wife, Maggie Gordon Cooper, passed away in 1947.

Jacob Cooper served for several years as a member of the Town Council of Cass. Two of his sons, Adolph E. Cooper, of Marlinton, W. Va., and Lewis Cooper, of Washington, D. C., were born in Cass, Adolph E. Cooper on June 7, 1906, and Lewis Cooper on July 20, 1907. During all the years that they lived in Cass, the Cooper family members were the only Jewish family in Cass. In 1957, Adolph E. Cooper still retained his affiliation with the lodge of the Masonic Order in Cass. Lewis Cooper served in the United States Navy.

(For further details on the Cooper family, *see under* Marlinton.)

## CEDAR GROVE

Cedar Grove is a town in southern West Virginia, located on the Kanawha River, southeast of Charleston. It was settled in 1773. Cedar Grove is located in a coal-mining region. In 1950, according to the United States Census of that year, Cedar Grove had a general population of 1,738.

In 1937, according to a report in the *AJYB*, Cedar Grove had a Jewish population of ten or fewer persons. So far as can be ascertained, there were no Jews living in Cedar Grove in 1958.

The site of Booker T. Washington's boyhood home, it is of interest to observe, is near Cedar Grove, W. Va.

## CEREDO

Ceredo is a town located in Wayne County, in western West Virginia, a few miles southwest of Huntington. It is situated in a farming area. The town was founded in 1857. The 1950 United States Census gave Ceredo a general population of 1,399.

There were no Jews living in Ceredo in 1958, and, so far as can be ascertained, no Jews ever lived in the town, perhaps because of the existence of the city of Huntington just a few miles away, with its large Jewish community and its several Jewish communal institutions and organizations.

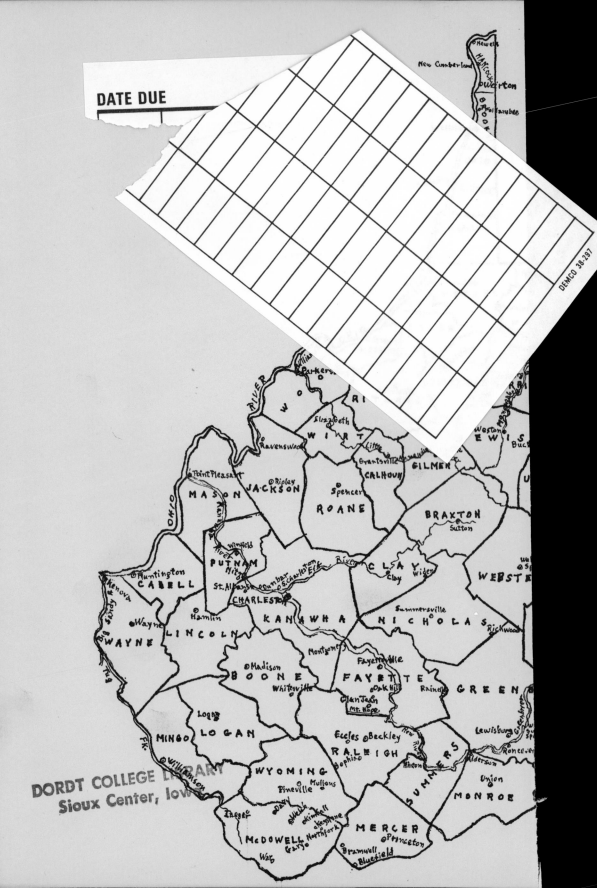